THE
UKRAINIAN
AMERICANS

Roots and Aspirations
1884–1954

Myron B. Kuropas

UNIVERSITY OF TORONTO PRESS

Toronto Buffalo London

© University of Toronto Press 1991
Toronto Buffalo London
Printed in Canada

ISBN 0-8020-2749-0

Canadian Cataloguing in Publication Data

Kuropas, Myron B.
　The Ukrainian Americans

　Includes bibliographical references.
　ISBN 0-8020-2749-0

　1. Ukrainians – United States – Social conditions.
　2. Ukrainian Americans – Social conditions.
　3. Ukrainian Americans – Ethnic identity.　I. Title.

E184.U5K87 1991　　305.891'791'073　　C90-095212-1

PHOTO CREDITS

Photographs courtesy of the Ukrainian Museum, New York, except for the
following:
The Rev. Ahapius Honcharenko and young Americans: courtesy of Johanna
Luciw, Minneapolis, MN.
Greek Catholic priests in Wilkes-Barre, PA; the Rev. Alexis Toth; and
Ruthenian/Uhro-Rusin ethnonational newspapers: reprinted with permission
from Paul Robert Magocsi, *Our People: Carpatho-Rusyns and Their Descendants
in the United States* (Multicultural History Society of Ontario, 1985).
Ukrainian ethnonational newspapers: courtesy of Dr. Wasyl Halich,
Superior, WI.

I dedicate this book to

my immigrant parents, Stephen and Antoinette Kuropas,

who instilled in me a love of Ukraine;

my Ukrainian-born wife Lesia, who nurtured that love;

and my sons Stephen and Michael, who inherited that love.

Contents

Illustrations

Foreword

In many ways the history of the Ukrainian Americans is similar to that of other hyphenated Americans, especially those of Slavic origin. Arriving in the late nineteenth to early twentieth centuries, they were part of the huge wave of immigrants from Eastern Europe whose assigned role was to provide cheap labor for America's burgeoning industries. Largely illiterate, confused, and undemanding, they were exploited mercilessly. For spiritual solace they clustered around their numerous churches; for mutual and material support they formed their fraternal associations. From these strongholds of ethnic culture they sallied forth on the long, wearisome, and stubborn climb into the American middle class. Entrance into the mainstream of American society usually meant the loss of ethnic community. Nonetheless, the imprint of ethnic background, even among ostensibly fully assimilated Americans, has been surprisingly persistent.

Within this general process, each ethnic group exhibited particularities which distinguished it, to a greater or lesser extent, from the others. Those of the Ukrainians were especially striking. Unlike other immigrants, Ukrainians have been for centuries, and until the 1980s, a stateless people. Lacking a state to mold and confirm their national identity, the first wave of immigrants had great difficulty in explaining to others – and to themselves – just who they were. It is, therefore, not surprising that a major theme in Myron Kuropas's work is their search for national identity, a task made all the more difficult because it occurred when the concept of the American "melting-pot" ruled supreme and the pressure to abandon one's ethnic heritage was pervasive. Disoriented by those who, for a variety of reasons, insisted that they were Austrian or Polish or Russian, many early immigrants became Americans without realizing that they had originally been Ukrainians.

Statelessness had an opposite yet equally powerful effect on the Ukrainians who arrived in the United States after World War I and especially after World War II. As a result of the intense but frustrated struggles to gain

Ukrainian independence between 1917 and 1945, they, in contrast to their predecessors, left Ukraine with a very distinct, even painfully acute, awareness of their nationality. Indeed, for many of the later arrivals their main political concern in their new American homeland was to continue the struggle for Ukraine's independence. This, too, is a major theme of the book. Indeed, this continuing commitment to "the cause" is a noteworthy phenomenon among American ethnic groups. Few have maintained a homeland-oriented crusading spirit with such vigor and consistency as have the Ukrainian Americans.

Organizations loom large in Myron Kuropas's book. Little wonder. It has often been noted that the Ukrainian community abounds in organizations (which does not necessarily mean that it is always effectively organized). To a certain extent this can be explained by the Ukrainian Americans' above-mentioned sense of "mission." Although many of them felt obliged to help their unfortunate homeland, they often disagreed on how best to do it. Hence the numerous organizations. They reflected the great – often fiercely competing – variety of means by which Ukrainians sought to attain a common, ardently desired end. The fact that a vast majority of the Ukrainian immigrants came from eastern Galicia, which had a strong tradition of community-based, nationally oriented organizations, is also an important consideration. Finally, the systematic Soviet attempts to eradicate Ukrainian national culture spurred Ukrainian-American efforts to sustain in America what was being destroyed in Ukraine. Today, as the lengthy isolation of the Ukrainian diaspora from the homeland is breaking down, visitors from Ukraine are often pleasantly surprised by how well their countrymen in North America managed to preserve their cultural heritage.

The time is right and the need is great for the book which Myron Kuropas has written. Since the appearance of Iuliian Bachynskyi's superb *Ukrainska Imigratsiia v Ziednanykh Derzhavakh Ameryky* in 1914 no major history of the Ukrainian Americans has appeared, largely because the attention of the community's scholars was focused on developments in Ukraine. However, the fast approaching centenary of such venerable Ukrainian-American institutions as the newspaper *Svoboda* and the Ukrainian National Association serves as a pressing reminder that this historiographical gap – especially disturbing when compared to the richness of the scholarly literature on Ukrainian Canadians – should be filled. Not only scholars want and need to know more about the Ukrainian-American experience. The descendants of the immigrants will benefit from insights which this book provides into the organizational and ideological world of their parents and grandparents. In Ukraine the desire to know more about the oft maligned by Soviet propagandists, yet barely known, Ukrainian diaspora has increased dramatically. And for Americans, who might soon have to deal with an important, sovereign Ukrainian state, the past and present aspirations of Ukrainian Americans may increase in relevance.

Orest Subtelny

Preface

The United States is a nation of nations.[1] This book is about one of those nations, its roots and its aspirations.

Americans are often perceived as a people of multiple loyalties with allegiances in the United States and sympathies to a non-American past which they perceive as essential to their quest for personal identity.[2] This is the story of one such quest: a study of the evolutionary development of Ukrainian consciousness in the United States, from its embryonic religio-cultural beginning in the late 1870s, through its ethnonational development in the 1930s, to its fruition in the 1950s.

The Ukrainian identity in America developed against a background of tremendous, often cataclysmic, change in both the United States and Europe. The growing political impact of socialism and nationalism, the urbanization and rapid industrialization of America, the growth of the American labor movement, World War I, the collapse of the Russian, German, and Austro-Hungarian empires, President Wilson's "14 Points," the triumph of bolshevism, the emergence of the modern states of Czechoslovakia, Poland, and Romania, the Great Depression, the Popular Front, the birth of fascism, the rise and fall of the Third Reich, the growth of Soviet-Russian imperialism, the fall of Czechoslovakia, and World War II are just some of the events that occurred over the hundred-year period during which Ukrainian national consciousness developed and matured. As a result of such rapid and epochal turbulence both here and abroad, every immigrant generation – and later almost every immigrant – left a histori-cally "different" Ukraine and arrived in a "different" America.

Once here, immigrants from Ukraine found themselves in a society in which their self-identities were questioned, affirmed, and reinforced by a process of intense religious, social, and political indoctrination. The "mak-ing" and "tempering" of the Ukrainian American took place in an atmo-sphere of passionate, often violent, ideological competition. The result was the emergence in the 1940s of a unique and peculiarly Ukrainian-American ethnonational hybrid, the product of a learning process which itself was a response to a recalled and learned collective European and American past, as well as to a perceived American and European present.

This book is a study of ethnic retentionism, defined by Joshua A. Fishman as "attempts by a minority group, either through the school or by any other means, to retain unique values and behavior, either in an altered form, or under maximal self-determining conditions which a given minority group has attained."[3]

In examining the aspirations of America's Ukrainians, I have focused my research on their organizational life. "It is the social organization under which men live," write Park and Miller, "that mainly determines the behavior inspired in them by their wishes."[4] Organizations, defined here as "social units constructed and reconstructed to seek specific goals,"[5] are reflections of the sentiments and values of their members. Analyzing their organizations enables us to determine *what* aspects of their emerging ethnic consciousness Ukrainians in America felt were worth preserving, and the *kinds* of institutions they created to help them achieve their goal. "Individuals may form communities," wrote Benjamin Disraeli, "but it is institutions alone that create the nation."

Although this is a book about Ukrainian Americans, some attention is also devoted to Ukrainian life in Europe. There are three reasons for this: (1) readers in the West are generally uninformed regarding East European history in general, and Ukrainian history in particular; (2) no meaningful understanding of Ukrainian-American life is possible without an appreciation of the symbiotic relationship that existed between historical and ideological developments in the homeland and aspirations in the United States; (3) an appreciation of national myths and symbols enhances one's understanding of the aspirations of ethnic groups.

Readers may also wonder why, if this is a study of Ukrainian Americans, so much attention is paid to Ruthenians. Why not follow a precedent set by other authors and call all immigrants from Ukraine "Ukrainians." I couldn't do this for two reasons: (1) it might be perceived as a tendentious historical deception; (2) it could diminish a major theme of the study, namely the Ukrainianization of immigrants in the United States.

I have wrestled with the problem of ethnonational identity from the beginning. It is a fact that prior to 1914 few immigrants from Ukraine called themselves "Ukrainian." Many had no sense of identity outside their religious beliefs and the village from which they came. Those whose identities extended beyond these parameters called themselves Rusyns in Ukrainian, and either Ruthenians or Russians in English. In order to present a more accurate account of the nationalization process, I decided to respect the appellations that Ukraine's early immigrants themselves adopted and to review chronologically, using these same appellations, the process by which one group of Ruthenians gradually evolved from Ruthenians to Ruthenian-Ukrainians to Ukrainians. It is for this reason that all immigrants from Ukraine are identified as Ruthenians – either Galician Ruthenians or Hungarian Ruthenians (Uhro-Rusyns) – in chapters 1 and 2. In chapter 3, a further distinction is made between Ruthenian-Ukrainians – i.e., those Ruthenians who were in the process of being Ukrainianized – and Carpatho-Ruthenians – i.e., those Uhro-Rusyns who were slowly rejecting their Hungarian ties and developing an identity that was different from, and often antagonistic towards, the Ukrainian ethnonational stream. It is not until chapter 4 that the term "Ukrainian American" begins to appear on a consistent basis. I realize that my solution to the identity question may not satisfy everyone, but I ask readers to be patient and remain alert to ethnonational nuances as they emerge in the text. They are not meant to confuse but to illuminate the complexities involved in studying peoples with a history of oppression and national submersion.

A word about what this study is not. It is *not* a review of Ukrainian contributions to American life and culture. Such information is available elsewhere[6] and is not germane to the major theme of this book.

I have purposely avoided certain problems of definition that have engaged historians and social scientists exploring similar themes. To assure clarity, however, some terms – culture, religiocultural group, ethnic group, nation, nation-state, nationalism, and ethnonational group – need to be defined.

Culture refers to the social heritage of a group, the ways of feeling, thinking, and acting that are passed down from generation to generation through formal and informal methods of teaching and demonstration.[7] Culture is *created* by "a group of people who live together with common bonds of customs, language and life style, who recognize among themselves a kind of unity which is the result of shared similar experiences and backgrounds."[8]

A religiocultural group is one whose sense of cultural kinship is based primarily on shared religious beliefs, traditions, and practices.

Without dwelling on the many difficulties inherent in a precise conceptual interpretation of ethnicity,[9] an ethnic group can be broadly defined as "a collection of people united by physical similarities, cultural traditions, or common visions of the past and future."[10] Ethnic groups precede the creation of a nation-state, are involuntary, and have an influence, in many cases substantial, on the lives of individual members of the nation-state. Membership in the group is influenced both by how members define themselves and by how they are defined by others.[11]

A nation is an aggregation of people of common origins and language. A nation-state is a nation organized as a sovereign political reality.

Nationalism has been variously defined as "a state of mind in which the supreme loyalty of the individual is felt to be due the nation-state";[12] as "whatever a given people, on the basis of their own historical experience, decide it to mean";[13] or as whatever "nationalists have made it."[14] Although I accept all these definitions, the one that is most appealing was articulated by Prof. Paul Robert Magocsi: "Nationalism is an ideology professing that humanity is divided into nationalities, that national self-government is the only form of government, and that political sovereignty or some form of independence is the primary goal."[15]

One final point regarding nationalism begs clarification. In the United States, nationalism was initiated by statesmen and political leaders. As a unifying mass movement, nationalism came into existence *after* the proclamation of the nation-state; loyalty was demanded to an ideal that was already a political fact of life. In other parts of the world, and this is especially true of ceratain eastern European peoples, nationalism began as a cultural movement, the hope and dream of poets, philogists, and historians.[16] Loyalty was initially demanded to a national goal or aspiration rather than to a functioning government. It is within the latter context that the evolution of Ukrainian nationalism can be best understood.

An ethnonational group is an aggregation of ethnic people with a common language and a nationalistic orientation.

Because the ethnic identity of Ukrainians in America developed in response to European and American influences, this study is chronologically organized in a manner that makes it possible to comprehend the nature of these pressures. It also indicates how, during different periods of Ukrainian-American history, such pressures evolved to produce progressively more sophisticated levels of ethnic and ethnonational reaction. Where appropriate, the text also addresses certain myths concerning the Ukrainian people, their interaction with other ethnic and national groups, and various historical experiences that provide clues regarding present-day Ukrainian-American likes, dislikes, prejudices, and hatreds.

Chapter 1 is devoted to the European roots of the Ukrainian ethnonational identity. Most of the chapter is devoted to historical developments in the three regions of Ukraine – Carpatho-Ukraine (Transcarpathia), eastern Galicia, and Bukovina – from which the vast majority of pre-1914 immigrants from Ukraine emigrated. The remainder of the chapter provides an overview of developments in Ukraine prior to the second and third mass immigrations. More extensive historical reviews of relevant events in Ukraine are provided at the beginning of chapters 4, 5, 6, and 7.

Chapter 2 discusses the American roots of the Ukrainian-American community, the relationship between immigrants from Carpatho-Ukraine and Galicia, the leadership role of the Ukrainian-oriented Catholic clergy, the struggle for an autonomous national church, and the circumstances that precipitated the adoption of three ethnic identities – Carpatho-Ruthenian, Russian, Ukrainian – among pioneer immigrants from Ukraine.

Chapter 3 is devoted to the role of various institutions in the "making" of the Ukrainian American, i.e., the process by which the religiocultural identity of some Ruthenians was transformed into a Ukrainian ethnonational identity.

Chapter 4 concentrates on the Ukrainian-American response to Ukrainian sovereignty and the subsequent "tempering" of the Ukrainian identity in America. Examined are the circumstances associated with the permanent split between Carpatho-Ruthenians and Ukrainians, the rise of an ethnonationally conscious lay leadership, and the struggle for ideological supremacy by the socialists.

The next three chapters examine the post–World War I political aspirations of the Ukrainian-American community from the perspective of the Communists, the Monarchists (Hetmanists), and the Nationalists as well as the various responses that some of their organizational activities elicited from the American government.

Ukrainian religious aspirations as manifested by the birth of the Ukrainian Orthodox church in America, the growing universalism of the Ukrainian Catholic church, and the vehement and bitter religious conflict that erupted within the Ukrainian-American community between the two world wars are the main topics of chapter 8.

Community efforts to nurture and preserve the Ukrainian-American cultural inheritance are discussed in chapter 9.

Chapter 10 is devoted to the concerns of older Ukrainian Americans regarding the ethnic character of their offspring, the formal endeavors of the former to involve the younger generation in Ukrainian-American affairs, and the organizational response of American-educated Ukrainian youth.

The epilogue reviews Ukrainian-American efforts to resettle Ukrainians in the United States after World War II.

As for technical matters, I have attempted to simplify a complex linguistic situation in the spelling of certain Ukrainian names and in the process of transliteration from Ukrainian into English. The spellings of proper names, place-names, and special terms generally accepted in English usage have been retained (e.g. Kiev, Lviv, Dnieper). Russian and Polish proper names were also retained where appropriate. The Library of Congress transliteration system was used for Ukrainian proper names. Where I was aware of a preferred English spelling by a person identified in the text, however, that spelling was used. I did this for two reasons: so that (1) progeny could readily recognize their forbears, and (2) English-language researchers would have an easier time locating names in non-Ukrainian sources.

Much of the research associated with this study was completed in preparation for my 1974 doctoral dissertation at the University of Chicago entitled "The Making of the Ukrainian American, 1884–1939: A Study in Ethnonational Education." I am grateful to the members of my inter-departmental dissertation committee – Professors Donald Erickson (education), Andrew Greeley (sociology), and Arthur Mann (history) – for their unceasing encouragement and erudite suggestions. Additional research was made possible by modest grants from the National Endowment for the Humanities, largely the result of technical assistance from Dr. John Kromkowski, president of the National Center for Urban Ethnic Affairs, and Prof. Ted Radzialowski of Southwestern State University in Minnesota, and the Olzhych Foundation, the result of a special interest in my work by the late Dr. Peter Stercho.

I greatly appreciate the cooperation and encouragement I received from the staffs of the Immigration History Research Center at the University of Minnesota, especially Prof. Rudolph Vecoli and Halyna Myroniuk; the American Jewish Committee, especially David Roth; *Svoboda*, especially Zenon Snylyk, the editor; the Ukrainian National Association, especially Ulana Diachuk, formerly the Supreme Treasurer and now the Supreme President; and the Ukrainian National Museum in Chicago. My special thanks to Volodymyr and Pauline Riznyk, Walter Sochan, and the late Antin Dragan whose comments following a review of the entire text were welcome. I was also fortunate to have several specialists who reviewed all or part of the text and provided conceptual and factual criticism. They are Michael Hanusiak, Alexander Lushnycky, Daria Markus, Fr. Andriy Partykevich, and Fr. Ivan Terlecky. Full responsibility for any errors that still remain, however, is mine alone.

Special thanks is owed Orest Subtelny, who was extremely supportive during an especially difficult period.

I also wish to acknowledge the work of two oustanding typists, Sue McMillan and Barbara Sherman. Their dedication to deadlines and their ability to type difficult Ukrainian transliterations are tributes to their professionalism.

Special thanks are also due to the editorial staff of the University of Toronto Press. Ron Schoeffel greatly expedited the book's publication with his encouragement and enthusiasm. The late Lydia Burton and Lorraine Ourom, the copy-editors, were masters of their profession with whom it was a pleasure to work.

I am grateful to my father, whose own activity as a Ukrainian-American pioneer inspired me throughout the writing of this book. He also corrected factual errors and provided invaluable insights regarding events and individuals.

Finally, deepest respect must be paid to my wife Lesia who read this work almost as often as I did, agonized over every setback, cheered every forward step, and with her grace under pressure, sustained me throughout the entire process.

Abbreviations and Acronyms

This study mentions a number of Ukrainian orgnizations and institutions with somewhat lengthy and complex names. To avoid confusing the reader by spelling out these names every time they are used, they are given either as abbreviations or as acronyms. The most frequently used abbreviations and acronyms (which usually follow the original Ukrainian spelling of the name) are listed below, some with transliterated titles.

CP(b)U   Communist Party (Bolshevik) of Ukraine

CPUSA   Communist Party of the United States of America

"Endeks" Nickname for members of the National Democratic Party of Poland

GCU   Greek Catholic Union, a Ruthenian (Rusyn) fraternal association in the United States

IWO   International Workers' Order

IWW   International Workers of the World; also referred to as "Wobblies"

LUC   League of Ukrainian Clubs, an Orthodox youth organization

LUN   Legion of Ukrainian Nationalists, a European-based organization

ODWU   Ukrainian acronym for the Organization for the Rebirth of Ukraine, a Nationalist organization in the United States

ORDEN   Ukrainian nickname for the Ukrainian section of the IWO; in English, the Ukrainian American Fraternal Union

OUN   Organization of Ukrainian Nationalists

RCP   Russian Communist Party

RNS   Ukrainian acronym for the Ruthenian National Union, later the Ukrainian National Association

SUNM   Union of Ukrainian Nationalist Youth, an early nationalist youth organization in Europe

SURO	Ukrainian acronym for the United Ukrainian Toilers Organization, a communist federation in the United States
UACC	Ukrainian American Coordinating Council
UCCA	Ukrainian Congress Committee of America
UCYL	Ukrainian Catholic Youth League
UFA	Ukrainian Fraternal Association, formerly the Ukrainian Workingman's Association
UFCPA	Ukrainian Federation of Communist Parties of America, communist successor to the UFSPA
UFSPA	Ukrainian Federation of Socialist Parties of America
UHO	United Hetman Organizations, a monarchist federation in North America
UkrSSR	Ukrainian Soviet Socialist Republic
UNA	Ukrainian National Association, the oldest and largest fraternal insurance organization in the United States
UNAA	Ukrainian National Aid Association, a fraternal insurance organization
UNDO	Ukrainian National Democratic Union, a powerful organization in Galicia after World War I
UNWLA	Ukrainian National Women's League of America, commonly referred to in Ukrainian as "Soyuz Ukrayinok"
USSR	Union of Soviet Socialist Republics
UUOA	United Ukrainian Organizations of America, commonly referred to in Ukrainian as "Obyednanya"
UVO	Ukrainian Military Organization, a veteran's organization
UWA	Ukrainian Workingman's Association, a fraternal insurance organization now known as the Ukrainian Fraternal Association
UYLNA	Ukrainian Youth League of North America
ZOUNR	Ukrainian acronym for the Western Province of the Ukrainian National Republic, formerly ZUNR
ZUNR	Ukrainian acronym for the Republic of Western Ukraine

POLAND

• Berestya   Pinsk •   *Pripet*

Chernihiv

Kholm •

Styr

Lutsk •   • Rivne

VOLHYNIA   Zhytomyr   Kiev •

Peremyshl •   Lviw •
GALICIA   Ternopil •   Khmelnytskyi •   UKRA

LEMKIVSHCHYNA   *Seret*   • Vinnytsia

CZECH.   CARPATHO-   Ivano -
Uzhorod •   UKRAINE   Frankivsk •   *Zbruch*

Mukachiv •   • Khust   Chernivtsi •   *Dniester*   *Boh*
HUNGARY   BUKOVINA

Prut

ROMANIA   • Odessa

—— Ukrainian S.S.R.

Ukrainian ethnic territory
outside present-day borders

0 _____ 100 **Miles**
0 _____ 100 **Kilometres**

BLACK

The Ukrainian Americans

1 European Roots

Basic to any understanding of Ukrainians in America is an appreciation of historical events in Europe that have molded the Ukrainian identity.[1] Like other American ethnic groups from Eastern Europe, Ukrainians immigrated to the United States during three separate time periods. The first and largest wave began during the 1870s and ended in 1914. The second and smallest contingent of Ukrainians arrived in America between the two world wars. The third mass immigration commenced after World War II and ended in 1954. Each wave of immigrants left a different Ukraine and arrived in a different America. Although most of this book is devoted to their life in the United States, this chapter reviews the European experience of the first Ukrainian immigration, emphasizing especially those events that had a direct impact on their organizational development in America.

In the Beginning

The roots of Ukrainian ethnonational identity date back to Kievan Rus', a vast Slavic state which once stretched from the Baltic Sea in the north to the Black Sea in the south.[2] Soon after Christianity was formally adopted as the state religion by Kievan Prince Volodymyr the Great in 988, a distinct Byzantine-Slavonic religiocultural community began to coalesce. When the Christian church split in 1054, the Ukrainian religiocultural tradition continued to be associated with its Greek Orthodox spiritual fount in Constantinople. However, religious contacts with the Roman Catholic West were never completely severed.[3]

Even before the adoption of Christianity, some inhabitants of Kievan Rus' migrated to Transcarpathia (hereafter referred to as Carpatho-Ukraine,[4] its present name), an area along the upper slopes and valleys of the Carpathian Mountains. In 1015, Carpatho-Ukraine was annexed by Hungary; it remained under Hungarian domination for the next nine hundred years. Because of their isolated location, however, the inhabitants of Carpatho-Ukraine preserved their ancient Rus' name and their religio-cultural traditions during the entire period.

As the Kievan state began to fragment and decline in the twelfth century, Galicia and Volhynia, two principalities in the southwest, united to form a separate state. From that moment on, the heritage of Kievan Rus' developed in a specific Ukrainian context, differentiating the Ruthenians of Ukraine from the other Slavic heirs of the ancient Kievan state, the "White Ruthenians" (Belorussians) and the Muscovites (Russians). By the beginning of the fourteenth century, a unique ethnonational tradition had emerged in what would later become known as Ukraine.[5]

Ukraine under Poland

During the fourteenth century, most of Ukraine fell under Lithuanian and later Polish rule. A Roman Catholic state, Poland attempted to convert the Ukrainian population from Orthodoxy to Catholicism. The Ukrainian people resisted the proselytizing efforts of the Poles, but with no political state of their own, and with the Greek Orthodox church in decline and Moscow claiming to be the third and final "Rome" of the Christian world, maintaining the religiocultural integrity of Ukrainian Orthodoxy became increasingly difficult.

Believing that ecclesiastical recognition by Rome could strengthen their hand against the Muscovites and give them respite from the Poles, a group of Ukrainian bishops traveled to the Holy See to present their case. It was a propitious moment. Over the years Rome had attempted, albeit unsuccessfully, to reunite the Christian church by offering concessions to the Greek Orthodox in return for the latter's recognition of the primacy of the bishop (pope) of Rome. From the Roman Catholic perspective, the Ukrainian appeal was a welcome opportunity to demonstrate good faith to the Orthodox world by recognizing the religiocultural integrity and autonomy of the Ukrainian church. Thus, on 23 December 1595, Pope Clement VIII issued *Magnus et laudabilis nimis,* a papal bull proclaiming the reception of the Ukrainian church and nation, and recognizing the ecclesiastical authority of all its bishops and priests as well as "all sacred rites and ceremonies which they use according to the institutions of the sacred Greek fathers, in the divine offices, the sacrifice of the Holy Mass, the administration of all sacraments and other sacred functions, as far as these are not in opposition to the truth and doctrine of the Catholic faith and do not exclude communion with the Roman Church." Included was the exemption of lower clergy from the Roman (Latin-rite) requirement of clerical celibacy.[6] Those who accepted this union with Catholicism became known as Uniates or Greek Catholics.

Union with Rome did not prevent the Polish Catholic hierarchy from continuing their proselytizing efforts despite admonitions from the Holy See to cease and desist. Polish actions and growing resistance from the masses as well as the Orthodox gentry convinced some Ukrainian bishops that union with Rome had not achieved the desired result and they decided to disavow their earlier support for the union and to remain Orthodox.[7] From that day forward until the emergence of Protestant movements in Ukraine during the eighteenth century, Ukrainians remained either Orthodox or Greek Catholic.

Ukraine under Russia

In eastern Ukraine, meanwhile, Ukrainian religiocultural traditions were kept alive by the Cossacks, a group of staunchly Orthodox warriors who built *siches* (forts) along the Dnieper River to protect their homeland from Turks and Crimean Tartars. Led by freely elected *hetmans* (supreme commanders), the Cossacks began to press for greater political autonomy as their numbers and power increased.

Hoping to rid Ukraine of Polish and Catholic domination, Hetman Bohdan Khmelnytskyi defeated Poland's combined armies in 1648 and proclaimed Ukraine's independence. Seeking allies in order to buy time to consolidate his government, Khmelnytskyi concluded a mutual assistance pact with the Muscovites at Pereiaslav in 1654, and began to build a nation-state. The Muscovite tsar, however, interpreted the treaty as an invitation to rule and before long the Muscovite army was in Ukraine, ostensibly to protect the fledgling state from the Poles.

Fearing further Muscovite encroachment, Hetman Ivan Vyhovskyi, Khmelnytskyi's successor, initiated negotiations with the Poles. The result was the 1658 Union of Hadiach, which provided for the reconstruction of the Polish state as a federation of three autonomous nations: Ukraine, Lithuania, and Poland. When the Muscovites protested, Vyhovskyi went to war, defeating the tsar's armies at the battle of Konotop in 1659. Vyhovskyi's victory was short-lived. Unable to accept union with a Catholic Poland, a group of Cossack officers deposed Vyhovskyi and proceeded to come to terms with the Orthodox Muscovites. In 1667, however, the Muscovites betrayed their Cossack partners and concluded a separate treaty with the Poles. Meeting at Andrusovo, the Poles and Muscovites agreed to partition Ukraine along the Dnieper River.

One final Cossack attempt to free Ukraine of Muscovite domination was made by Hetman Ivan Mazepa. Concluding a secret alliance with Charles XII of Sweden, Mazepa's Cossacks joined the Swedes in their military effort to check Muscovite expansionism. Ukrainian aspirations were crushed when the combined Swedish-Ukrainian forces were defeated at the historic battle of Poltava in 1709, sealing the fate of left-bank Ukraine for the next two hundred years. Significantly, it was only after their victory over Sweden that the Muscovites began to call their state the Russian Empire.[8]

Life for Ukrainians under the Russians proved to be as difficult as it had been under the Poles. The Ukrainian Orthodox church was officially absorbed by the Russian Orthodox church in 1686. In 1775, the Zaporozhian Sich, the last vestige of Cossack independence, was destroyed by the Russian armies of Catherine II. Six years later, eastern Ukraine was formally incorporated into the administrative structure of the Russian Empire.[9]

The Ukrainian national spirit lived on, however, and in time gave birth to a literary and national renaissance. The literary revival began in 1789 when Ivan Kotliarevskyi published *Eneida,* a Ukrainian vernacular adaptation of Virgil's *Aeneid,* in which the heroes are wandering Zaporozhian Cossacks who survived Catherine's destruction of their *sich.* The height of the Ukrainian literary renaissance was reached in the works of Taras Shevchenko, Ukraine's national bard. Born a serf, Shevchenko was a poet of the people, who was able to capture the true sentiment of the Ukrainian nation and to translate it into literary form. Condemning the Russian tsars for their treatment of his people, Shevchenko often thought of the freedom enjoyed by Americans as a result of their War of Independence. Reflecting on the events of 1776, Shevchenko wrote:

> When will we have a Washington
> With a new and righteous law?
> One day we shall have him.

Shevchenko's works became widely read, and fueled the Ukrainian literary revival. His call for freedom was repeated by many other writers in eastern Ukraine, most notably Mychailo Drahomanov and Lesia Ukrainka. Concerned with Ukrainian activism, the Russian minister of the interior denied the existence of a separate Ukrainian people, insisting that Ukrainians were really "Little Russians" who spoke a language that was actually a substandard Russian dialect. In 1876, Tsar Alexander II issued the Ems Ukaz, a proclamation prohibiting the publication of all books and materials in the Ukrainian language.[10]

While Ukrainians living in eastern Ukraine were forced to submerge their ethnonational identity by the repressive policies of the tsars, Ukrainians living in western Ukraine, especially in Galicia and Bukovina, were experiencing a national revival due, in large measure, to a shift in political fortune for Poland. What was unfortunate for Poles proved to be fortunate for Ukrainians.

Because most early Ukrainian immigrants to the United States emigrated from Galicia, Bukovina, and Carpatho-Ukraine, the unique and often conflicting history of these three regions deserves our attention.

Ukraine under Austria

Galicia

Late in the eighteenth century Poland was partitioned among Russia, Prussia, and Austria, placing predominantly Ukrainian eastern Galicia* under Austrian rule. In contrast to the Romanovs, the Habsburgs pursued a minority policy of divide and control. Realizing that many minorities in their empire harbored ancient animosities toward each other, Austria permitted and occasionally encouraged ethnonational diversity by favoring first one group and then another at various opportune times. National minorities that competed with each other, Vienna reasoned, could hardly be expected to unite in opposition to the regime.

Habsburg policy proved to be a blessing for the Ruthenian† Catholic church, which had struggled to maintain its religiocultural identity under the Poles. Thanks to the Austrian crown, Ruthenian seminaries were established in Vienna and in various Ukrainian provinces and it was in these seminaries that an articulate, literate, and ethnonationally conscious clergy was trained. The emergence of this new clerical elite in Galicia began the long and complex process that eventually led to the development of a conscious and mobilized Ukrainian nation. After establishing the historical and cultural uniqueness of the Ruthenians vis-à-vis the Poles, these individuals began to espouse different national orientations in competing for the allegiance of the Ruthenian people. Some intellectuals and clerics (the so-called Russophiles) maintained that the Galicians were really a branch of the larger Russian nation. The Ukrainophiles, hereafter referred to as Ruthenian-Ukrainians, argued that they were in fact a part of the Ukrainian nation, a people not only comprising the Greek Catholics of Galicia and Carpatho-Ukraine, but also including the millions of Orthodox Ukrainians

---

* Henceforth, the term "Galicia" is used to denote only the eastern part of the region having Lviv as its capital. Western Galicia, with Cracow as its capital, is Polish territory and remains outside the scope of this study.

† Ruthenian ("Rusyn" in Ukrainian) is the singular derivative of the term "Rus'." Prior to the "national awakening," many inhabitants of Galicia and Carpatho-Ukraine referred to themselves as "Ruthenians" while Ukrainians in eastern Ukraine were called "Little Ruthenians" (Malorossy). The Latin word for Rus' was "Ruthenos." The term was used almost exclusively by the Holy See and the West in references to Ukrainians.

in the Russian Empire. This orientation proved to be the most popular with the masses, and subsequent decades saw the development of an extremely vital and conscious Ukrainian community and culture in Galicia.[11]

Three students of the Lviv seminary – Markian Shashkevych, Ivan Vahylevych, and Jakiv Holovatskyi – became leaders of the literary revival in Galicia that blossomed during the nineteenth century. Known as the Ruthenian Triad, they promoted the use of the Ukrainian vernacular as well as a distinct Ukrainian orthography in their writings. Other Ruthenian-Ukrainian writers supported the adoption of either the Polish Latin script or Russian orthography, however, and the matter was not settled until the 1848 Congress of Ruthenian Scholars when the majority of delegates voted in favor of Ukrainian orthography. Influenced greatly by the pioneering efforts of eastern Ukrainian writers, Galicia soon produced its own literary tradition best exemplified by the writings of Ivan Franko.[12] In time, the Ukrainian revival in Galicia passed from a purely literary activity to a political, educational, and economic endeavor aimed at greater ethnonational autonomy.

In 1848, a Supreme Ruthenian Rada (council) was formed and proclaimed that Galician and Carpatho-Ukrainian Ruthenians were part of the great Ukrainian nation which had once been independent. Addressing the Austrian government, the Rada demanded that Galicia be divided into Ukrainian and Polish provinces and that Carpatho-Ukraine be united with Ukrainian Galicia. When the Poles opposed the demands, Ruthenian-Ukrainians organized their own political parties (most of which were socialist in orientation) and successfully promoted candidates for local and national office. It was not enough. Forced to respond to the wishes of the powerful Polish gentry after suffering a defeat at the hands of Prussia, Austria gradually (1868–73) turned the whole of Galicia over to Polish control. Polish quickly replaced German as the official language of Galicia, and the Poles returned to their centuries-old policy of Polonizing Galicia's Ukrainians.

Although politically weak, Ruthenian-Ukrainians were not without other resources, especially in educational and economic arenas. The Shevchenko Society was founded by a group of Ukrainian professors from Lviv University and Ukrainian cultural activists from the Russian Empire. Changing its name to the Shevchenko Scientific Society in 1892, the society managed to publish some 123 volumes of research on Ukraine-Rus' in fifteen separate scholarly series by 1918. A Ukrainian Pedagogical Society (Ridna Shkola) was created in 1881 and charged with the responsibility of establishing Ukrainian private schools. A year later, a Ukrainian-language Chair of East European History was established at Lviv University and occupied by Prof. Michael Hrushevsky, Ukraine's foremost historian of the undertakings ... The Magyar rulers attempted to keep the Rusins illiterate and ignorant as opposed to the Austrian policy of permitting a cultural awakening in Galicia and Bukovina."[32]

Especially affected by the Magyarization campaign were the Catholic clergy, who came to adopt an "Uhro-Rusyn" identity, that is, Ruthenian in religiocultural orientation and Hungarian in national feeling. "Unlike the Uniate priests of eastern Galicia who led the local Ukrainian movement," writes Macartney, "the Ruthene clergy eagerly absorbed Magyar culture for themselves, and from genteel heights thus attained, looked down on their flocks, too often with indifference or contempt. Far from leading any national movement, they were among the chief obstacles which prevented such a movement from arising."[33]

The advent of Austrian influence in Carpatho-Ukrainian affairs (Austrian annexation of Hungarian territory began in 1526) improved the religiocultural climate considerably. At the intercession of the Habsburgs, Pope Clement XIV raised the bishopric of Mukachevo to the level of an eparchy in 1771 and created a second eparchy in Preshov in 1816.[34] With Andrii Bachynskyi's ascension to the bishopric of Mukachevo in 1772, the eparchical seat was moved to Uzhhorod and the first phase of the Carpatho-Ukrainian culture awakening began.

An able administrator, Bachynskyi introduced instruction in the vernacular in all schools under his jurisdiction and persuaded many capable priests to pursue their theological studies in Vienna and Lviv. Soon after, a number of histories appeared, as well as dramas, poetry, and essays with Carpatho-Ukrainian themes. Significantly, most of these early works were by priests who had studied at the theological seminaries established by the Habsburgs.[35]

The dominant figure in the cultural awakening of Carpatho-Ukrainians during this period was Rev. Oleksandr Dukhnovych who, while sympathetic to closer ties with Ukrainians in Galicia ("the Carpathian Mountains cannot separate us forever," he wrote in 1860), was reluctant to support the literary development of either the Ukrainian or the Carpatho-Ruthenian vernacular. For Dukhnovych, the Great Russian language was the best literary medium for Carpatho-Ukraine's Ruthenians.[36]

Support for the Russian option by Carpatho-Ukrainians was greatly enhanced in 1849 when Russia, at the invitation of the Habsburgs, invaded Hungary to assist in putting down the Revolution of 1848–9. The Russian army entered Hungary via Carpathian mountain passes, and it was then that Carpatho-Ukrainians met Russians for the first time. Awestruck by the fact that they could communicate with Slavs who represented such a powerful nation, Carpatho-Ukrainians welcomed the invading army. "One thing really gave me joy in life," wrote Dukhnovych, "and that was in 1849 when I first saw the glorious Russian army ... I danced and cried with delight."[37] Having no military or political might with which to impress their kinsmen, Ukrainians in Galicia were forced to rely on cultural ties and the personal efforts of intellectuals such as Ivan Franko and others to convince their ethnic brethren that Ukraine was their common homeland.

Having put down the Hungarian uprising, Austria proceeded to divide the land into five administrative regions, one of which included the Carpa-tho-Ukrainian district of Uzhhorod. The creation of this distinct political entity helped to foster an identity that was neither Russian nor Ukrainian, but rather was based on the distinctness of the inhabitants of the area. It was during this period that the Carpatho-Ruthenian option began to assert itself as still another ethnic alternative for the Carpatho-Ukrainians.[38] The second phase of the cultural revival, therefore, ended with three groups competing for the ethnonational identity of the Carpatho-Ukrainians: the Ukrainophiles, the Russophiles, and the Carpatho-Ruthenians.[39]

The Magyars did not remain disenfranchised for long, however. Recovering from the defeat at the hands of Austria and Russia, Hungary was powerful enough by 1867 to be accepted as an equal partner in a dual monarchy by a considerably weakened Austria,[40] an event that signaled the beginning of the final phase of the cultural renaissance. Carpatho-Ukraine was back under Hungarian domination and the Magyars came to support, albeit briefly, the Carpatho-Ruthenian faction. Led by scholars such as Viktor Gebei, George Zsatkovich, and Antal Hodinka, a Carpatho-Ruthenian literary tradition that repudiated both Ukrainian and Russian influences was soon beginning to blossom.[41]

Hungary abandoned this support very quickly, however, and reinstituted a Magyarization program that all but obliterated Ruthenian consciousness among the intelligentsia.[42] The Hungarian administration demanded a voice in the nomination of Carpatho-Ukrainian bishops and after the ascension of Bishop S. Pankevych in 1866, only pro-Hungarian bishops served in Carpatho-Ukrainian eparchies. In 1902 and 1907, the so-called Apponyi laws introduced the Hungarian language into all Carpatho-Ukrainian parochial schools.[43] Those who entered these schools "emerged invariably as Hungarians."[44] By 1914, there was not a single Carpatho-Ukrainian school in which the vernacular was used.[45] In 1916, the Hungarian Ministry of Education ordered that all Carpatho-Ukrainian publications use Latin script and Hungarian spelling.[46]

Significantly, the Hungarian leadership continued to maintain an active interest in its Ruthenian emigrants long after their arrival in the United States. Alarmed by the number of émigrés leaving Hungary for the United States at the turn of the century, Budapest operated an "American Action" program from 1904 to 1914 in order to maintain immigrants' loyalty to

Hungary and to keep alive their resolve to return to their homeland. The program supplied funds to support priests and ministers in America, provided down payments on church buildings, subsidized newspapers, paid Hungarian heritage school teachers, and bought books for heritage classes.[47]

Bukovina

A part of the Kievan-Rus' since the tenth century, Bukovina* was later included in the Galician-Volhynian kingdom. During the second half of the fourteenth century, the region was annexed by Moldavia and later, in the sixteenth century, it came under Ottoman rule. Bukovina, therefore, was not a party to the Union of 1596 and its Ukrainian population retained an Orthodox religiocultural heritage. The province was occupied by the Austrian army in 1774, and remained under military rule until 1787 when it was incorporated into the Austrian Empire as a part of Galicia. In 1849, Bukovina became a separate crownland within the Austrian Empire.[48]

Greatly influenced by the Galician cultural revival, Bukovina soon developed its own Ukrainian literary tradition, of which Sydir Vorobkevych and Iurii Fedkovych are considered the leading lights.[49] In 1869, the Ruthenian Club (Ruska Besida) was founded, followed by the establishment of chairs of Ukrainian literature, language, theology, and homiletics at Chernivtsi University by 1875.[50] In time, many of the same organizations that played such an important role in the cultural revival in Galicia were flourishing in Bukovina, owing in large measure to the rather favorable political conditions prevailing in the crownland. On the eve of World War I, Bukovina, with only 300,000 Ukrainians, could boast of more Ukrainian schools and cultural-educational institutions per capita than any other Ukrainian land.[51]

The First Immigration

Ukrainian immigration to the United States began in the 1870s at a time when Ukrainian national consciousness was just beginning to take shape. Most immigrants who arrived prior to 1914 began their journey to the United States from the region of Carpatho-Ukraine and the provinces of Galicia and, later, Bukovina. Still calling themselves Ruthenians (a religiocultural appellation dating back to ancient Rus'), most planned to remain

---

* The term "Bukovina" refers to the northern part of that area with Chernivtsi as its capital. Southern Bukovina is a largely Romanian territory and is outside the scope of this study.

in the United States only long enough to save enough money for a better life in their homeland. Many Ruthenians, however, either elected to remain or were forced to do so by personal circumstances, and for them the United States became not a melting pot but a school for their ethnonational development.

Ukraine's occupation by Poland, Russia, Hungary, and Austria during the first ten centuries of its existence as a nation prevented the early emergence of a distinct national consciousness among Ukraine's masses. In the eighteenth and nineteenth centuries Ukrainians living in the Russian Empire were called Little Russians (Malorossy). Those in the Austrian Empire continued to call themselves Ruthenians (Rusyny). It was only after the national awakening of the nineteenth century that the designation "Ukrainian" was promoted by a nationally self-conscious Ukrainian intelligentsia to identify the inhabitants of Ukraine. Given the obstacles of foreign domination, widespread illiteracy, the lack of an adequate system of mass communication, and the natural resistance to change of most human beings, acceptance of this "new identity" was slow and often painful. As late as 1914, many Ukrainians in Carpatho-Ukraine, Galicia, and Bukovina still called themselves Rusyns.[52]

Most immigrants from Ukraine who arrived in America before 1900 began their journey in Carpatho-Ukraine, the least ethnonationally developed region of Ukraine. They arrived with a strong religiocultural identity, preserved by the Greek Catholic church for centuries. In the United States, they came to call themselves Uhro-Rusyns (Hungarian Ruthenians) in the beginning, Ruthenians or Russians later. Some eventually called themselves Ukrainians.

Most immigrants who came to the United States after 1900 were born in Galicia or Bukovina. They arrived with a strong religiocultural identity as well as a developing Ukrainian national orientation. In the United States they called themselves Rusyns (Ruthenians) first, Russians or Ukrainians later.

The major historical development during this early period in Ukrainian-American history was the struggle among the emerging Russian, Ruthenian, and Ukrainian leaders for the religious and political loyalties of pioneer immigrants.

The rise and fall of the Ukrainian National Republic between 1917 and 1920 had a profound effect on America's fledgling Ukrainian community. Among other things, the establishment of a Ukrainian nation-state clarified the hazy ethnonational and religiocultural lines dividing Russians, Ruthenians, and Ukrainians; established the political direction of Ukrainian community life for the next three decades; and played a role in the religious

conflict that emerged among and between Ukrainian Catholics and Orthodox during the 1920s and 1930s.

Ukraine's postwar partition among Poland, Czechoslovakia, Romania,
and Soviet Russia also affected the Ukrainian-American community, leading, in time, to the emergence of political parties supporting Leninism/
Stalinism, the monarchism of Hetman Pavlo Skoropadsky, and the nationalism of the Organization of Ukrainian Nationalists.

The Second Immigration

Having endured the trials and turmoil of nation-building, the second mass
immigration to the United States was significantly different from the first.
Far less numerous but somewhat better educated, most immigrants identified themselves as Ukrainians.[53] The question during this period of Ukrainian-American history was no longer *whether* one was a Ukrainian but,
rather, what kind of Ukrainian one was: Catholic, Orthodox, Communist,
Hetmanist, or Nationalist. All five groups claimed ethnonational superiority
over the others. As we shall see, all of America's Ukrainian factions reacted
to the major events in Ukraine during the next two decades – the Polish
pacification, Stalin's artificial famine, Carpatho-Ukraine's declaration of
independence, the rise of Adolf Hitler, and the advent of World War II –
albeit in different ways.

The Third Immigration

Ukraine's third mass immigration to the United States was largely a refugee
population fleeing Soviet domination over all of Ukraine after the war.
Having endured the mindless brutality of Nazi Germany and Soviet Russia,
the threat of forced repatriation to the USSR, and the loss of all material
possessions, Ukrainians were allowed to immigrate to America as a result
of the Displaced Persons Act of 1948.[54] Better educated than any previous
Ukrainian immigration, the third immigration was welcomed by a community that was well established, relatively affluent, and prepared to offer
organized assistance in the resettlement.

2 American Roots

The First "Ukrainians"

It is difficult if not impossible to determine the precise date of arrival of America's first "Ukrainian." If by Ukrainian is meant a person who consciously identified him- or herself as such, or who demonstrated an appreciation of certain distinct ideals or symbols common to the Ukrainian national revival, then that Ukrainian could not have come earlier than the latter half of the nineteenth century. If, however, by "Ukrainian" we mean anyone whose origins can be traced to Ukrainian ethnographic territories, then the first Ukrainian could have come to America at a much earlier time. Yaroslav Chyz, a noted student of Ukrainian-American history, believed it possible that Ukrainians of the latter category were on this continent prior to the American Revolution.

Examining a number of primary sources, Chyz discovered, for example, that in his account of the Virginia Colony, Captain John Smith wrote about a certain Lavrenty Bohun, whose name strongly suggested a Ukrainian origin. Captain Smith also mentioned coming to "America" with a man called "Malasco," a "Polian." Smith traveled across Ukraine following his Turkish captivity, and it is possible he met the man there or, as Chyz himself points out, in Belorussia.

Albert Saboriski, who arrived in America in 1662 and whose name appears under various spellings, including "Zaborisko" and "Zabbroisco," could have been of Ukrainian or Belorussian origin because of the typical "ko" ending to his name. Others who settled in Pennsylvania between 1726 and 1776 with names such as Nicholas Orich, Matheis Hora, Christian Hallitchke, and Anna Kunegunda Russ also probably had Ukrainian roots. The same could be true of Henry Dorich, Thomas Masney, and Peter Zawadowsky, whose names appear in revolutionary-war archives, and Julius Kryvoshinsky, Joseph Krynicki, John Zarewich, and Andrew Podolsky, who are listed among those who fought in the Civil War.[1] Many of the same individuals are also claimed by Polish Americans whose major documentation seems to be the Slavic structure and sound of the names. Because in most instances little information is available concerning the exact region of origin of these individuals, the "name game" is intriguing but hardly conclusive, barring further documented evidence.

A good deal of recent Ukrainian interest centers around a discovery by Orest Horodysky, who, in reading through a Chicago Polish newspaper, came across the name of Gen. John Basil Turchin,* a Civil War general in the northern army. According to *Dziennik Chicagoski,* General Turchin was a Rus-Ukrainian.[2] Born in the Don River region of the Russian Empire on 24 December 1822, Turchin graduated from the St. Petersburg Military Academy, and rose to the rank of colonel in the Russian Imperial Army during the Crimean War. His ability as a military engineer during that campaign came to the attention of Capt. George B. McClellan of the United States Army, then serving as a military observer in Russia. Later, after McClellan returned to the United States to become vice-president and chief engineer of the Illinois Central Railroad, we find Turchin serving as a "constructive" engineer for the same railroad in Mattoon, Illinois. With the outbreak of the Civil War, Turchin accepted a colonel's commission with the 19th Illinois Regiment of Infantry Volunteers. Promoted later to the rank of brigadier general, Turchin assumed command of a brigade consisting of five (four Ohio and one Kentucky) regiments. Known as "The Terrible Cossack," Turchin and his brigade won military laurels in numerous military encounters, the most famous of which was the battle of Chickamauga. After the war, Turchin returned to the Illinois Central as an immigration agent and, among other things, is reported to have "founded a colony of Polanders at Radom in Washington County, Illinois." He died on 18 June 1901 and is buried in Mound City, Illinois.[3]

Although Turchin identified himself as a Russian, ethnically he was of the Don Cossack people, a group described by D. Mirsky as closely related to "their cousins the Ukrainian Cossacks."[4] It is possible that Turchin himself might have been a direct descendant of those Cossacks who immigrated to the Don region after the destruction of the Zaporozhian Sich, but this has not been determined.

The ethnic roots of Rev. Ahapius Honcharenko (1832–1916), who arrived in the United States in 1865, are more certain. Born in the village of Kryvyn, Honcharenko was enrolled in the Kiev Theological Seminary at the age of eight and later, after completing his religious studies, served Metropolitan Filaret as liaison among the Orthodox monasteries under Filaret's juris-

---

* Turchin shortened his name in the United States. Originally he was known as Ivan Vasilevitch Turginoff.

diction. In 1857, Honcharenko was assigned to the Russian embassy in Athens as a chaplain and it was there that he became associated with the Russian revolutionary journal *Kolokol*, then edited and published in London by Alexander Herzen. Arrested by the tsar's police for publishing statements critical of the Russian regime, Honcharenko was taken to Constantinople en route to incarceration in Russia. With the help of Greek friends, he was able to free himself of his captors and make his way to London where he revived his association with Russia's intellectual exiles. Honcharenko remained in London for a year and a half and later spent time in Constantinople and Greece before embarking for the United States.

Arriving in Boston early in 1865, Honcharenko moved to New York City where he found employment as a Greek language teacher, a part-time Orthodox priest, and a typesetter and editor for a bible society then in the process of publishing Greco-Slavonic and Arabic bibles.

In 1867, Honcharenko moved to San Francisco where he planned to publish a Russian-language newspaper for the Russian and Ukrainian populations of California and Alaska. It was at this time that his talents came to the attention of U.S. authorities who, after the purchase of Alaska, were searching for a medium of communication with the inhabitants of the newly acquired territory. With the help of government subsidies, Honcharenko published *The Russian and English Phrase Book for Traders, Travellers and Teachers*. On 1 March 1868, he began to publish the *Alaska Herald*, a bilingual, semimonthly gazette, first with government subsidies and later as an independent publication.[5] Honcharenko eventually sold his interest in the newspaper and, in 1872, purchased a fifty-acre farm in Hayward, California, naming it "Ukraina"; he remained there until his death in 1916.[6]

Reading through the first volume of the *Alaska Herald*, one can hardly deny the strong ethnonational commitment of this Orthodox Ukrainian priest-intellectual. Of all the Slavic poets with whom Honcharenko was undoubtedly familiar, he chose to mention Taras Shevchenko in his first issue.[7] In the second issue, he wrote about the Cossack Hetmanate, praising Hetman Mazepa, whose struggle with Tsar Peter I he described as an attempt to regain Ukraine's "ancient independence" and to "reunite the whole of Little Russia and erect there a wholly independent kingdom."[8] Accused of "imposture" by the Russians, Honcharenko replied: "As for imposture, it amounts to this. Born in the country of the Cossacks, we have never pretended to be other than Cossack."[9] It is these clearly expressed and documented sentiments that best qualify Ahapius Honcharenko for the title of "America's first Ukrainian."

As a medium of communication with Alaska's Russian and Ukrainian inhabitants, Honcharenko's *Alaska Herald* served a worthwhile function. In addition to news items in the Russian language, the newspaper carried translations of the American constitution,[10] various military regulations,[11] and other items of immediate significance to the new Americans of Alaska. At the same time, the *Herald* felt a need to expose the "excesses" of certain "unprincipled" Americans, "brought suddenly into contact with a population totally ignorant of the language and the customs of the new rulers,"[12] who purposely "hide the resources of the country in hopes that secrecy will promote their own selfish interests."[13] Nor was Honcharenko able to ignore certain nefarious practices then being perpetrated by the Ku Klux Klan and other groups[14] against the blacks, described by Honcharenko as "native-born Americans who would lift themselves to knowledge and equality under the constitution of this country."[15] As for the Chinese in his midst, Honcharenko wrote: "The Chinese among us are treated worse than anything in the shape of man has ever been treated in any civilized country. Jews were as badly treated in Europe in the Middle Ages; and considering the pretensions of San Francisco to a high rank among cities of the 19th century, we beg pardon of the Middle Ages for the scurvy comparison."[16]

A willingness to address all aspects of American life, good as well as bad, probably accounts for the fact that on 2 May 1868 the *Alaska Herald,* by then called the *Free Press and Alaska Herald,* lost its government subsidy and declared itself an "independent" paper.[17] On 30 May, the *Free Press and Alaska Herald* separated, with the *Free Press* resuming publication as a weekly and the *Alaska Herald* becoming the *Alaska Herald-Svoboda* and continuing on a semimonthly basis under Honcharenko's sole ownership.[18]

While Honcharenko played an important role in the history of Alaska, another immigrant from Ukraine, Dr. Nikolai Konstantinovich Sudzilovsky, who later changed his name to Russel, participated in the political life of Hawaii. Arriving in San Francisco in the early 1880s, Dr. Russel, a physician from Kiev, practiced medicine there until 1895 when he moved to Hawaii. In 1896, he helped organize the Hawaiian Medical Society and later, after Hawaii came under U.S. jurisdiction, headed the native party that pushed for self-government. Dr. Russel was elected to the Hawaiian senate in 1901 and became president and presiding officer that same year. While in the senate, he was instrumental in the passage of a homestead law that helped numerous landless families, including some immigrants from Ukrainian Galicia, to obtain land. Dr. Russel eventually left politics, practiced medicine for a time in Hilo and Olaa, and in 1909 left for Nagasaki, Japan. He died in Tientsin, China, in 1931.[19] Although from Ukraine, Russel considered himself a Russian.

The activities and contributions of individual "Ukrainian" immigrants such as Gen. Basil Turchin, Rev. Ahapius Honcharenko, and Dr. Nikolai Sudzilovsky are of historical relevance inasmuch as they reflect both the degree of ethnonational identity and the sociopolitical orientation of three different intellectual contemporaries from areas in the Russian Empire that were either wholly or partially Ukrainian in ethnographic composition. Honcharenko is especially fascinating not only because his ethnonational consciousness was more fully developed, but because he felt a need to explain the unique political history of the land of his birth to the American reading public.

The First Mass Immigration from Ukraine

The Ukrainian mass immigration to the United States began in the early 1870s[20] from three regions of western Ukraine: Carpatho-Ukraine (Subcarpathian Rus'), Bukovina, and Galicia. Few immigrants during this early period were from eastern Ukraine.[21]

Among the first to leave Ukrainian lands were the so-called Lemkos who lived on both sides of the Carpathian Mountains in the southwesternmost region of Galicia. The Lemkos probably learned about the United States from the Poles,[22] who began their emigration at a much earlier date.[23] Next to emigrate were the Carpatho-Ukrainians who learned about the United States from the Hungarians, who preceded them to the United States by at least a decade. Although there were Ukrainians from Galicia and Bukovina in the United States earlier, the majority arrived after 1890.[24]

Ethnic Awareness

While it can be generally assumed that immigrants from Galicia and Bukovina were somewhat conscious of their ethnonational heritage, few of them actually called themselves "Ukrainian" upon their arrival in the United States. If they identified with any ethnic designation at all, it was usually "Rusyn" or "Rusniak."[25] The first English translation of Rusyn adopted by the early immigrants was "Russian," a choice that only added to the ethnonational confusion that became prevalent early in the history of the Ukrainian-American community. It was not until the early 1900s, some twenty years after the immigration began, that the term "Ruthenian," the more accurate English translation of Rusyn, became common. Because this and the following chapter are devoted to the U.S. experience of the first immigrants from Ukraine, they will be identified as Ruthenians.

The problem of early ethnic self-identification does not end there, however. It is further complicated by the fact that emigrants from Carpatho-Ukraine, then part of the Hungarian kingdom, adopted the appellation "Uhro-Rusyns" (Hungarian Rusyns). For reasons that will become obvious later, most Uhro-Rusyns in the United States began to identify themselves as Rusyn Ruthenians, Carpatho-Ruthenians, or Carpatho-Russians after World War I, leading to the eventual disappearance of the term "Uhro-Rusyn" from the lexicon of American ethnic groups.

Still another complication regarding the early ethnic identity of the first immigrants from Ukraine is that most Ruthenians who arrived in the United States prior to 1914 also identified themselves as Greek Catholic. In the minds of many Americans, this meant that they were really of "Greek" ancestry.

To avoid confusion, therefore, the reader should be aware that prior to World War I most immigrants from Ukrainian ethnographic territories came from three regions (Carpatho-Ukraine, Galicia, Bukovina), and one subregion (the Lemkian section of Galicia); most identified themselves as Uhro-Rusyns, Rusyns, or Lemkos in Ukrainian and as Russians (later Ruthenians) in English; they were not "Greeks" but Greek Catholics. As we shall learn later, some of them eventually came to call themselves Ukrainians.

One final point concerning ethnic awareness needs to be made for purposes of historical clarification and perspective. Ukrainians were by no means unique among America's ethnic groups in their initial incapacity to adopt a clearly defined ethnonational identity. The same was true of other groups. Most early immigrants, according to Oscar Handlin, came to the United States as Masurians, Corkonians, Apulians, Bohemians, and Bavarians rather than as Poles, Irishmen, Italians, Czechs, and Germans. The terms Ukraine, Poland, Ireland, Italy, Czechoslovakia, and Germany were identifications with which the immigrant was not familiar simply because, in the words of Handlin, they "referred to national states not yet in existence or just coming into being ... The immigrants defined themselves rather by the place of their birth, the village, or else by the provincial region that shared dialect and custom."[26]

Reasons for Emigrating

Seven major factors contributed to the Ukrainian emigration process:

1 The population explosion in all of Galicia resulting in an 80 percent population increase between 1880 and 1900.
2 The lack of a mature industrial complex to provide greater employment and to serve as an economic countercondition for the burgeoning population. Industrialization was slow in coming to Galicia, while in Carpatho-Ukraine what little industry did develop was hardly enough to affect significantly the life of the average peasant.
3 The progressive division of land from generation to generation. As each

father would divide his landholdings among his sons, there was less and less land left for each successive family. By 1870, the average Ruthenian peasant's farming land consisted of about four acres; in many instances the land was not contiguous but split into one-half-acre or one-acre strips interwoven with similar strips belonging to other families.

4 Growing peasant indebtedness that resulted in a feeling of hopelessness concerning the future. Excessive taxation, combined with the usury of moneylenders (who charged the then outrageous rates of 6–10 percent interest), contributed to a loss of status among Ruthenians, forcing many of them to sell their meager property in order to climb out of deepening debt. Prior to World War I, some 2,500 to 3,000 peasant holdings were auctioned off yearly.

5 The aggressive colonizing policy of more affluent Poles who aggravated an already dismal condition by immigrating to eastern Galicia and displacing the Ruthenian peasant. News of liberal homestead provisions in Brazil and Canada* and the promise of the "fast dollar" in the United States were viewed as honorable alternatives by the Ruthenian immigrant accustomed to land ownership of some kind, no matter how meager.

6 The stimulation of shipping-line agents and representatives of American corporate concerns in search of new labor pools for the expanding U.S. industrial complex.[28] Coal-mining representatives, beset with labor problems at home, were especially active in this regard. The promise of almost $1.20 per day for an unskilled peasant accustomed to earning twelve cents per fourteen-hour day was an attractive inducement.

7 Letters and money from immigrants to the United States underscored the economic opportunities in America and were significant in the immigration process. Each village was aware of those villagers who had moved to the United States so that every letter from the New World was eagerly awaited not only by the immigrant's relatives, but by the entire village as well. Some Austro-Hungarian government officials, concerned lest whole villages emigrate, often held back correspondence which praised the United States.[29] That letters and contacts in the United States

* In the 1880s, when land agents from Brazil and mining company agents from the United States were luring Ukrainian peasants with fantastic descriptions of the potential of their respective countries, Ukrainian leaders associated with *Prosvita* became concerned. In 1895, *Prosvita* published "About Free Lands," a pamphlet written by Dr. Joseph Oleskow in which the peasant was urged to forgo Brazil, where the climate was difficult for a temperate-zone individual, and the United States, where economic conditions were judged unstable, and to homestead, instead, in Canada. Later, Dr. Oleskow personally selected a number of Canadian homestead sites for Galician and Bukovinian émigrés and helped coordinate their trek to the New World with Canadian authorities and shipping agents.[27]

influenced many emigrants to come to America is borne out by the fact that of the 12,361 Ruthenians who immigrated to the United States in 1908, only 389 or 3.1 percent were *not* coming to join relatives or friends.[30]

Despite the economic hardships they suffered in Austro-Hungary, Ruthenians anxious to leave for the United States managed, somehow, to come by the necessary money. They either borrowed from relatives[31] or a lending establishment, or sold some of their livestock. Occasionally they leased land to a neighbor.[32] Because they almost invariably planned to return to their villages, Ruthenian immigrants to America rarely sold their land, preferring, if necessary, to mortgage it.

Social Statistics

The typical Ruthenian who immigrated to the United States prior to 1900 was, by the standards of an expanding industrial society, poor, illiterate, and unskilled. Moreover, despite the best efforts of the Galician intellectuals, he was, even as late as 1914, still too preoccupied with his day-to-day survival to have given much thought to his present and future political status.[33]

According to the 1890 Austrian census, the chief occupation for 77 percent of the Galician population was in agriculture or forestry,[34] and the average daily wage, with board, of an agricultural laborer in 1891 was twelve cents in Galicia and fifteen cents in Bukovina.[35]

In the 1890s, 65 percent of the males and 72 percent of the females over six years of age in Galicia could neither read nor write.[36] In 1900, 49 percent of the Ruthenian immigrants to the United States were illiterate.[37] By 1910, the illiteracy figures for Galicia had dropped considerably but the decrease was by no means uniform throughout the province. In certain areas of Carpathian Galicia, illiteracy was still around 61 percent.

Although the illiteracy rate remained relatively high in Carpatho-Ukraine (93 percent),[38] the average rate for *all* immigrants from Ukraine between 1910 and 1914 declined to 41 percent.[39]

Immigration Statistics

At no time has it been possible to determine with any degree of accuracy the exact number of Ruthenians who immigrated to the United States during this early period. Prior to 1899, immigrants were listed according to the country issuing the passport so that Ruthenians were listed as either Austrians or Russians.[40] After 1899, United States immigration authorities and the Census Bureau adopted the designation "Ruthenian," but many Ruthenians were still listed as Austrians, Russians, and even as Poles,

TABLE 1
Number of Ruthenian immigrants to the United States,
1899–1914

Year	Number
1899–1900	4,232
1901–1902	12,821
1903–1904	19,435
1905–1906	30,730
1907–1908	36,442
1909–1910	43,715
1911–1912	39,689
1913–1914	67,009

SOURCE: Wasyl Halich, *Ukrainians in the United States*
(Chicago: University of Chicago Press, 1937), pp. 150–3.

Hungarians, Slovaks, and Croatians by shipping agents in Europe as well
as by immigration authorities in the United States. Those with no sense of
ethnonational background and those who did not clearly specify "Ruthenian" were simply not categorized according to their true ethnic background. Even identifying oneself as a Ruthenian, however, was no guarantee of a proper ethnonational listing. Polish and other ethnic American
immigration officials, anxious to increase the official statistics for their own
ethnic group, would often arbitrarily list Ruthenians as members of their
own nationality.[41] In considering the official U.S. figures for the Ruthenian
immigration between 1899 and 1914 (see table 1) these factors as well as
the lack of accurate figures for Ruthenian immigration prior to 1899 should
be borne in mind. Officially, a total of 254,376 Ruthenian immigrants arrived
in the United States between 1899 and 1914. Of this number, 202,211 (87
percent) settled in the states of Pennsylvania, New York, and New Jersey
(see table 2).[42]

An attempt to determine the approximate number of Ukrainians living
in the United States in 1909 was made by Iuliian Bachynskyi, author of *The
Ukrainian Immigration in the United States of America,* a monumental study
published in Lviv, Galicia, in 1914.* Utilizing a number of official sources
such as U.S. immigration figures for Austro-Hungary and Russia, as well
as surveys conducted by *Svoboda* (a Ruthenian-American newspaper)[43]
prior to 1899, Bachynskyi estimated that 33,886 Ruthenians immigrated to
America between 1877 and 1887 and an additional 74,379 arrived between
1888 and 1898. Assuming that at least half the Polish immigration, two-
thirds of the Magyar and Slovak immigration, and three-fourths of the

* In his study, Bachynskyi identified all immigrants from Ukrainian ethnographic
  territories as "Ukrainian" rather than Ruthenian.

TABLE 2
Destination of Ukrainians at the time of their arrival in the United States (1899–1914)

Year	Penn.	NY	NJ	Ohio	Conn.	Mass.	Ill.	Mich.
1899	608	339	257	27	70	31	13	4
1900	1,332	560	359	54	111	125	66	22
1901	2,854	967	621	132	132	230	146	25
1902	4,133	1,594	746	328	195	176	111	16
1903	5,675	1,854	874	391	213	220	193	36
1904	5,336	1,653	1,094	405	255	156	199	40
1905	8,510	2,275	1,666	522	362	232	230	51
1906	8,243	3,626	1,692	552	426	353	407	53
1907	11,779	5,090	2,714	671	765	564	601	164
1908	5,229	3,318	1,182	396	218	342	374	101
1909	6,364	4,085	2,136	435	433	516	525	137
1910	13,386	5,946	3,274	1,071	824	660	922	208
1911	6,902	4,991	2,247	564	465	552	647	206
1912	7,909	5,982	2,889	848	741	627	823	298
1913	12,007	7,642	3,327	1,467	988	965	1,275	729
1914	12,937	9,961	4,046	1,526	1,079	1,336	1,871	1,009
Totals	113,204	59,883	29,124	9,389	7,277	7,085	8,403	3,099

SOURCE: Halich, *Ukrainians in the United States*, pp. 150–3.

Russian immigration for the representative year 1905 were, in actual fact, ethnically Ruthenian, Bachynskyi concluded that the *official* Ruthenian immigration figure for that year represented only four-sevenths of the *true* Ruthenian immigration. Assuming again that the same disproportion existed in other years, Bachynskyi calculated that a total of 284,400 Ruthenians immigrated to the United States between 1899 and 1909. Using the death statistics of the Ruskyi narodnyi soiuz* for the year 1908 as a base, Bachynskyi estimated that no more than 25,479 Ruthenians died between 1877 and 1909. Bachynskyi then calculated the probable number of U.S.-born on the basis of the 3 to 7, female to male, proportion of immigrants, subtracted the number of estimated returnees and second-round immigrants who might have been counted twice, and came up with a grand total of 468,930 or approximately 470,000 first- and second-generation Ruthenian Americans living in the United States in 1909.[44] If we accept Rev. Ivan Ardan's 1904 assessment that "even the most conservative estimate cannot place the number of Ruthenians in the United States much below 350,000,"[45] and if we add to that estimate the thousands of immigrants who came to America during the peak immigration years that followed, then it

* The Ruskyi narodnyi soiuz (Ruthenian National Union) is a fraternal insurance society founded in 1894. Today, it is called the Ukrainian National Association.

seems highly probable that there were at least 500,000 first- and second-generation Ruthenians in the United States in 1914, especially if we include the Ruthenians from Carpatho-Ukraine in our estimate.

Regardless of the "statistics" one is willing to accept, however, there can be little debate regarding the low level of education and marketable skills of America's first Ruthenians. Of the 14,473 Ruthenian immigrants listed by the United States Bureau of Immigration in 1905, for example, seven came with what might be considered a higher education (four priests, one lawyer, one musician, one teacher), 209 were skilled laborers (blacksmiths, bakers, cabinetmakers, and so forth), while 12,854 were unskilled laborers (mostly agricultural workers and servants). The remainder were either children under the age of fourteen or those who gave no occupation of any kind.[46]

Ruthenian Social Attitudes and Perceptions

Ruthenians who came to America prior to 1914 brought with them certain social attitudes, prejudices, and perceptions about class, work, and the significance of their emigration for family and friends in Ukraine.

In the mind of the Ruthenian peasant, the hierarchical order of the larger society was pyramidal and consisted of three classes of people – the *pan* (lord) who was Polish or Hungarian, the *kupets* (merchant) who was usually a Jew,[47] and the *muzhyk* (peasant) who was always a Ruthenian. In reality, economic class structure within the Ruthenian community, especially in Galicia, conformed more to the shape of an oval than a triangle. At the top were those few independent Ruthenians, the *hospodars*, who were fortunate enough to own relatively large tracts of land and who were able to hire servants to assist them in the management of their property. In the middle were the vast majority of Ruthenians, the small, semi-independent landowners who could not survive from their land alone and were forced to hire themselves or their children out to supplement their incomes. At the bottom were the beggars, usually blind or deformed individuals, who were dependent upon the generosity of others for their survival.

Among Ruthenians, great wealth, like complete destitution, was rare.[48] Furthermore, the relationship between *hospodar* and hired hand was not one of master and servant but rather one of foreman and laborer. The *hospodar* and his hired help worked, ate, and slept side by side, the latter being considered members of the family. It was not unusual for a hard-working farmhand to marry into the family with the grateful blessing of his *hospodar*.[49]

If proverbs and folksayings are any reflection of attitudes, then the Ruthenians who immigrated to the United States were certainly not averse to hard work. "Khto rano vstaie tomu Boh daie" (God gives to him who rises early), "Boha vzyvai a ruk prykladai" (Call on God but also use your hands), and "khto v liti kholodnyi toi v zymi holodnyi" (He who stays cool in the summer goes hungry in the winter) were typical maxims repeated by Ruthenian peasants throughout Galicia and Bukovina.[50]

The exodus of early immigrants to America usually had the blessing and support not only of the family but of the entire village as well. In a sense, the first emigrant was looked upon as a leader, a pioneer, a man headed for almost certain success. In the words of some early immigrants who recorded their impressions of the departure, emigration was indeed a momentous experience:

> I was still a young lad – not even ten years of age – when in 1878, word got out in my part of Lemkivshchyna* that Pavel Khyliak of the town of Luhy, of the parish Zhdynia in the province of Horlytsko had returned from the army and was preparing to leave for a distant land beyond the sea, America ... When the priest announced in church that Pavel Khyliak, the son of Semen Khyliak is preparing for America and that a divine liturgy will be celebrated on his behalf, a large group of people came to the church. On that day I didn't go to school because I wanted to see how a man prepared for America. A large group of people had gathered at the home of Semen Khyliak. A buffet was served at the home. The father rose to speak. He recited the Our Father and then blessed his son ... The people spoke about how Pavel Khyliak had learned about America from his Czech friends in the army.[51]

> It will be over 50 years now since our Lemkos began to leave Lemkivshchyna for America. It was a great occasion when they were escorting the first Lemko, Michailo Durkot of the village of Hanchova, on his first steps into the distant world. He was accompanied by a huge procession. The entire community came to say farewell, not only his mother and father, but his wife and children too. And everyone wept such tears that a stranger who didn't know what was taking place might have thought that someone was being led to the gallows or some equally horrible fate. But he was respected by the community and that is why he received such a grand farewell.[52]

* The Lemko subregion of Galicia.

Obviously, not all émigrés received such a dramatic bon voyage but for those who did, the desire to succeed in the New World, no matter how difficult the obstacles, must have been strong indeed.

Ruthenian Life in America

At the time of the first Ruthenian immigration, the United States was establishing itself as a world power overseas and experiencing a period of tremendous industrial and technological growth at home. The population increased during this period from about 40 million in 1870 to some 76 million in 1900, immigrants accounting for approximately 12 million of this increase. Most were from England, Scotland, Ireland, Scandinavia, and Germany, but almost 3 million – the so-called "new immigration" – were from southern and eastern Europe. It was also a period of social upheaval and ideological ferment during which women became more active in political and economic affairs, blacks established their own colleges and entered the political arena, the first labor unions were established, and the socioeconomic ideas of Karl Marx were discussed and debated.

With growth and industrial progress, however, came economic and social repression. In the south, the Ku Klux Klan was terrorizing blacks. In the west, the Chinese were exploited and brutalized while American Indians were systematically put on reservations, occasionally slaughtered, and finally subdued. It was the era of Rockefeller, Morgan, Vanderbilt, Carnegie, Harriman, Gould, and Frick, the so-called "robber barons," who amassed immense fortunes in oil, steel, railroads, lumber, meat packing, and mining. By today's standards, working conditions in the slaughterhouses, steel mills, coal mines, and other work sites were abominable, with labor exploitation the rule, and accidents and even death a common occurrence.[53]

One of the means by which America became an industrial power was cheap immigrant labor. By the 1870s, for example, the Carnegie Steel Company in Pittsburgh had begun to hire immigrants on a systematic basis. According to one social researcher who prepared a report for the Sage Foundation during this period:

> It is a common opinion in the district that some employers of labor give the Slavs and Italians preference because of their docility, their habit of silent submission ... and their willingness to work long hours and overtime without a murmur. Foreigners as a rule earn the lowest wages and work the full stint of hours.
>
> Many work in intense heat, amidst the din of machinery and the noise of escaping steam. The congested condition of most of

the plants in Pittsburgh adds to the physical discomforts ... while ignorance of the language and of modern machinery increases the risk. How many Slavs, Lithuanians, and Italians are injured in Pittsburgh in one year is unknown. No reliable statistics are compiled ... When I mentioned a plant that had a bad reputation to a priest, he said, "Oh, that is the 'slaughterhouse'; they kill them there every day."[54]

Living accommodations were hardly better than working conditions, with laborers often living in rundown tenements with cellar kitchens, dark and overcrowded sleeping quarters, no drinking water, and few sanitary facilities. Even when living arrangements were adequate, as in Pullman, Illinois, workers were often forced to become totally dependent on company-owned stores, apartments, and public utilities as well as company-organized recreational and religious facilities, all of which were there to realize a profit for the owner.[55]

Resistance to such exploitation was not long in coming. Between 1870 and 1900, America experienced the Haymarket Riot, the Homestead Strike, the Lattimer Mine Massacre, and the Pullman Strike, events which had a profound effect on America's working class. With the advent of the first serious economic depressions during the same period, socialism came to be viewed as a viable alternative to rapacious capitalism by certain labor leaders who intensified their organizational efforts and began to adopt an increasingly militant posture towards the industrial ruling class.[56]

It was against this background of turmoil and intense social, economic, and political change that America's first Ruthenians began to build their community.

Early Ruthenian Life in Pennsylvania

Ruthenian males who immigrated to the United States during the late 1870s and early 1880s generally came to work in the anthracite coal mining counties of Northumberland, Colombia, Luzerne, Lackawanna, Carbon, and Schuylkill in northeastern Pennsylvania. Many came as unwitting strikebreakers[57] at a time when Slavs were displacing the English, Welsh, Irish, and Germans as the dominant ethnic groups in the area. They settled in multiethnic towns such as Shenandoah, Shamokin (once considered the most Polish town in Pennsylvania, if not in the United States),[58] Mount Carmel, Hazleton, Freeland, Mahanoy City, Olyphant, Wilkes-Barre, and many towns in the surrounding area.

"Coal," writes journalist-historian Paul Beers in *Pennsylvania Sampler*, "brought employment to millions, death to thousands, riches to a few, poverty to many."[59] The average miner worked from dawn to dusk in dark, damp mines, often knee-deep in water, for ten to twelve dollars a week. Death was his constant companion. During one seven-year period, 566 miners were killed and 1,655 were injured in Schuylkill county alone.[60] "In the anthracite coal fields," writes Michael Novak, "three men died every two days on the average. Nearly every miner bore external signs of injuries: a missing finger, stitches, scars, limps. Bluish specks of coal dust were implanted under the skin of their faces and arms from each blow of the pick and from the blast of explosives."[61] For Ruthenians, accustomed to working outdoors in fields nestled in the lush greenery of the Carpathian Mountains, laboring in the mines was an incredibly difficult, dangerous, and ultimately dehumanizing experience.

Initially, the coal-mine owners were in complete control of the industry. Organized dissent was systematically crushed by the lowering of wages; union busting; the importing of cheap, docile, new immigrant labor; and vigilante terrorism. By the late 1870s, the coal barons of northeastern Pennsylvania had successfully resisted the first serious threat to their control – the so-called long strike of six weeks – reducing many miners and their families to a diet of water and bread in the process. Moreover, the "Molly Maguires," a clandestine group of Irish miners who had earlier attempted to fight terrorism with terrorism, had been disbanded and their leaders hanged.[62] It was hardly an auspicious time to begin work as an immigrant laborer in the mines of Pennsylvania.

Like other immigrants during this period, Ruthenians began their mining careers as coal-miners' helpers, subcontracted by individual miners who were paid on the basis of the amount of coal they extracted rather than the number of hours they worked. Helpers usually received a third of the miner's wage, despite the fact that they often worked longer hours. Assigned the task of loading coal after the actual mining was completed, miners' helpers remained in the mines long after sunset, completing their assignments and other cleanup chores left behind by the regular miners.[63]

The Ruthenian coal mine worker usually lived in one of the ubiquitous boardinghouses that abounded in the mining towns, often sharing a bed with another miner who worked another shift. His work day began with a long, shrill blast from the company horn. After a breakfast consisting of black coffee and bread, the worker started out on foot for the mines where he reported promptly at 7:00 a.m. Eight to ten hours later, he returned to his room, removed his shirt, filled his wash basin with water, and kneeling and stooping, began to wash out the coal dust, often with the help of his landlady. Later, he sat down to supper along with the other boarders.[64]

After supper, the mine worker's leisure-time activities depended on individual taste and inclination. Options included returning to one's room and sleeping; talking with one's roommates (as many as four to five men often shared a room) about "troubles in the old country" or about girls, the job, or religion (the latter discussion more often than not ended in a fistfight and soon became increasingly rare); singing; ordering a bucket of beer or a bottle of whiskey and singing; writing (or asking someone to write) a letter; reading (or asking someone to read) a newspaper; playing *durak* (dummy), a primitive form of poker; and going for a walk. Occasionally, when a more ethnically conscious group was found, serious discussions based on Ruthenian newspaper articles were organized. This routine was followed five days per week.

Weekends were different. On occasion, Saturday night "balls" were organized by churches or fraternal lodges; when no dance was scheduled, the alternatives were visiting friends, a pool hall, or a saloon. Often, an enterprising boardinghouse landlord would organize his own party with the adults sharing the liquor expenses. Everyone – the landlord, his wife, the boarders, and even the children – would participate in the festivities with the adults singing, dancing, shouting, and arguing far into the night. On Sunday, there were church services followed by visits to friends, pool halls, or saloons. During the summer, many Sundays were passed at all-day picnics organized by church societies and fraternal brotherhoods. Trains were boarded to the various picnic sites by young and old alike and there was food, drink (occasionally drunken revelry),[65] and dancing for the adults and games for the children. Both the balls and the picnics proved to be substantial money-makers for the churches and lodges that organized them.

In addition to the leisure-time activities already described, there were the traditional family gatherings – christenings, weddings, and funerals. Because of the differences that existed among Ruthenians from various parts of Ukraine and later as a result of the influence of other ethnic groups with which Ruthenians came in contact, no two families followed exactly the same tradition in observing these occasions.[66]

Despite occasional social excesses, probably initiated from the desire to brighten what was essentially a dehumanizing experience,[67] the typical Ruthenian immigrant rarely lost sight of his major goal in the United States: making money. He shunned luxuries and, like other Slavs, managed to survive on much less money than his non-Slav compatriots. He walked barefoot whenever possible to conserve shoe leather, rummaged for fuel in the culm piles, purchased secondhand clothes (after first buying one good American suit and watch), often raised his own vegetables on a small plot of land behind the house, and got by on a diet composed largely of cereals, potatoes, and other starchy foods.[68] According to Greene, in the year 1904, "one store in Schuylkill county showed the average expense for

Slavs to be $2.86 per capita per month while the Anglo-Saxons paid almost twice as much."[69] Other reports, probably exaggerated, indicated that Slavic mine workers in the area managed to save at least half their yearly salary.[70]

That some Ruthenians prospered in the coal-mining areas is clear because a few early immigrants were able to go into business for themselves. One of the more popular enterprises in the area was the boardinghouse. While young Ruthenian single women dreamed of getting married and raising a family,[71] young Ruthenian men who got married thought of opening a boardinghouse, to be run by their wives while they continued to work in the mines. And many a young man succeeded in doing just that. In describing the daily routine of such a boardinghouse wife, Bachynskyi wrote:

> From early morning until late in the evening, she is always on her feet, always working in miserable, perpetual, and monotonous boredom. She awakens in the morning and prepares breakfast for her boarders; then she washes the dishes and cleans the house; later, she cooks supper and again she washes the dishes and cleans the house; in her spare moments, she washes the boarders' clothes and in the anthracite region she heats wash water and washes the boarders' neck and back. And so it goes, day after day. All that and children too![72]

Not all women could stand the pace. Most aged rapidly. Some died at an early age. A few found other means to mitigate their dismal circumstances. Writes Bachynskyi:

> But in all that boring and depressing life, so fraught with health-killing forces, the wife-slave did look, often desperately, for some respite. And she found it – in whiskey. Opportunities for indulgence were all around – so many boarders. "How about it, landlady, let's have a short one" – today she drinks with one boarder, tomorrow another. Everyone offers. Slowly she becomes so accustomed to whiskey that soon she can't live without it. And with whiskey, all kinds of things happen – so many boarders – and all so young, so healthy ... And it happens. The husband returns from work one day and his wife is gone – left with a boarder.[73]

But wives were not the only ones guilty of desertion; husbands fled too, sometimes with younger women. "How often" wrote Bachynskyi, "does one read notices in the Ukrainian press asking whether anyone has seen my husband (wife)? His (her) name is _____ and he (she) ran away with _____. Whoever sees him (her) should write to _____."[74]

The most prosperous business enterprise for the first Ruthenian immigration was, of course, the saloon. "Saloonkeepers," wrote Bachynskyi, were the "bosses" of the immigration and they never complained that "business is bad."[75] The saloons, however, served an important social function in the life of the immigrant. The mainstays of the early Slavic-American communities, the church, the boardinghouse, and the saloon provided the newcomer with religiocultural continuity, inexpensive living accommodations, and social companionship.[76]

Other popular business ventures for Ruthenians were butcher shops and grocery stores. Less popular but still relatively successful enterprises were funeral parlors, real estate offices, printing establishments, and, later, bookstores and co-op banks.[77]

The Beginnings of American Prejudice

Like other ethnic groups that had preceded them into the anthracite coal mining regions of Pennsylvania, Ruthenians contributed their brawn and their sweat to America's industrial growth while receiving relatively little in return. Many Ruthenians, of course, were able to save enough money to return to the old country and buy land. Many more, however, were not. Death, crippling accidents, and the dreaded black lung disease cut short the plans of countless miners who died penniless and forgotten.

Another debilitating aspect of Ruthenian life in the mining towns of the region was the emergence of inaccurate and prejudicial perceptions among certain Americans who came to resent both the presence and what they chose to believe was the life-style of the expanding eastern-European population. This sentiment was best expressed by Henry Root in an 1892 article in *Forum* magazine:

> Already the stream of immigration from Southern Europe is
> sweeping toward the Northwest and the South; but it began to
> pour into the mining regions of Pennsylvania over a dozen years
> ago ... one of the richest regions of the earth overrun with a
> horde of Hungarians, Slavs, Polanders, Bohemians, Arabs, Italians,
> Sicilians, Russians, and Tyrolese of the lowest class; a section
> almost denationalized by the scum of the Continent, where
> women hesitate to drive about the country roads by day, where
> unarmed men are not safe after the sinking of the sun. There he
> will see prosperous little cities like Hazleton, Mahanoy, Ashland,

Shenandoah, with fine business houses and educated people
of fortune, and surrounding these towns great wastes of the
Commonwealth diseased by thousands and tens of thousands
of foreigners who have no desire to become Americans, who
emigrate to the United States for a few years to make money,
who have driven to the cities and to the West the great army
of English, Scottish, Irish, Welsh, Germans and Americans who
once gave stability to the coal regions.[78]

Apparently, Henry Root was not alone in his attitude concerning the new
immigration. In 1897, when jobs were becoming scarce, the Pennsylvania
legislature passed an alien tax of 3 percent to be regularly deducted from
the payrolls of miners, and further decreed that all future mine workers,
even miners' helpers, had to be naturalized Americans.[79] Given the bias
that existed against the new immigration, it was not long before various
pejorative epithets emerged. One such ethnic slur was "Bohunk," a derivative of Bohemian, once used to refer to all Slavs. A far more common ethnic
slur was "Hunkie," a derivative of "Hungarian," which was what all east
Europeans were once called in the anthracite coal region.[80]

Other Early Ruthenian Settlements

Prior to 1914, Ruthenians also could be found working in the coal mines
of West Virginia, where a community soon developed around Wheeling;
in the southeastern section of Ohio; in Illinois, around Zeigler; in Texas,
around Bremond; as well as in Wyoming and North Dakota. In addition,
Ruthenians were engaged in the diverse mining operations of New Jersey
and Colorado, where by 1905 over 500 families had settled in Denver and
Pueblo;[81] the zinc and lead mines of Missouri, near Desloge and St. Francois;
and the iron and copper mines of Minnesota and northern Michigan.[82]

Beginning in the late 1890s and early 1900s, many Ruthenians began to
leave the mines and, along with new Ruthenian arrivals from Galicia, to
settle in the industrial centers of Boston, Hartford, New York City, Jersey
City, Rochester, Newark, Philadelphia, Pittsburgh, Youngstown, Gary, Chicago, Detroit, Milwaukee, St. Louis, Minneapolis, and Omaha where they
found employment in the iron and steel, glass, rubber, textiles, furniture,
automobile, and rail-car industries and in flour mills and sugar refineries[83]
(see table 3 for comparative salaries).

A tragic incident occurred in Pullman in 1894 when Ruthenians were
brought to the Illinois town as unwitting strikebreakers. According to
Dr. Semen Kochy, an immigrant pioneer in Chicago, approximately one
hundred Ruthenians were involved in the riots and disturbances that

TABLE 3
Average wages for representative industries (male) in 1910

Industry	Daily pay	Hours
Coal		
Miner	$2.00–$5.00	9
Helper	$1.20–$1.75	10
Breaker		
Age 13–16	$0.75–$0.90	9
17–20	$1.00	9
Over 20	$1.25	9
Iron and Steel		
Qualified worker	$2.00–$5.00	10
Helper	$1.00–$1.70	10
Textile		
Qualified worker	$2.00–$2.50	9
Helper	$1.50–$1.75	9
Furniture	$1.50	10
Rail Car		
Qualified worker	$2.00–$3.00	10
Helper	$1.30–$1.90	10
Glass	$1.65–$2.00	11–12

SOURCE: Iuliian Bachynskyi, *Ukrainska Imigratsiia v Ziednanykh Derzhavakh Ameryky* [The Ukrainian Immigration in the United States of America] (Lviv: Iuliian Bachynskyi and Oleksander Harasevych, Publishers, 1914), pp. 148–62.

occurred during the strike period, and some perished during the melee. Those who survived changed their names and attempted to forget their past by remaining as ethnically anonymous as possible. Dr. Kochy once met with two of the survivors and tried to involve them in the Ukrainian-American community, but they asked to be left alone, remaining estranged from their compatriots for the rest of their lives.[84]

Single Ruthenian women also played a role in the pre–World War I immigration. Official immigration statistics for the years 1910 to 1915 indicate that in that five-year period alone a total of 26,749 Ruthenian women between the ages of fourteen and twenty-nine immigrated to the United States. "Most American women," wrote Grace Abbott in 1919, "have never heard of the Ruthenians, the representatives of the Ukrainians who come from eastern Galicia and Hungary, and yet there are 23,101 under 21 years of age coming to the United States – more than the number of Scandinavian girls who we know so well."[85] Although life for the married Ruthenian woman was no bed of roses, it was better than the life initially led in America by the single Ruthenian girl who was alone, bewildered, and

TABLE 4
Average wages for representative industries (women) in 1910

Industry	Pay	Hours
Domestic Help		
In Ukrainian, Polish, and Slovak homes	$3–$5 per month plus room and board	From morning till night
In Jewish homes	$4–$8 per month plus room and board	6:00 a.m. till 7:00 p.m.
In American homes	$10–$25 per month plus room and board	6:00 a.m. till 7:00 p.m.
Restaurant		
Waitress	$25–$30 per month	12
Laundry	$0.75–$1 per day	10–11
Shoe	$0.50–$0.85 per day	10
Soap	$0.65–$1.25 per day	10
Cigar	$0.75–$2 per day	10
Clothing	$0.50–$2 per day	10
Paper	$0.50–$0.85 per day	10

SOURCE: Bachynskyi, *Ukrainska Imigratsiia v Ziednanykh Derzhavakh Ameryky,* pp. 156–9.

almost always overworked. Accustomed to pasturing milk cows in Ukraine, she was hardly in a position to find rewarding and fulfilling work in the urban centers of America where she usually settled.[86] Her most common employment was as domestic help in private homes where wages varied according to the ethnicity of the employer (see table 4). Single girls also worked as waitresses; in shoe, soap, and cigar factories; in laundries and paper mills.[87]

Women who were able to find respectable, relatively steady work were fortunate compared to those who, for a variety of reasons, were forced to spend their working lives in America as unwed mothers and/or prostitutes.[88] Commenting on the problem, fairly common among immigrant girls living in American cities, Grace Abbott wrote:

> There are many explanations for the fact that the immigrant
> girls sometimes become unmarried mothers. There is the greater
> helplessness which is due to their ignorance of English; there is
> also the more dangerous environment in which they live for it
> is near an immigrant or colored neighborhood that disreputable
> dance halls and hotels are tolerated ... The demand for some sort

of excitement after a hard and uneventful week, has become too strong to be ignored. But the danger is that because of her physical and nervous exhaustion and her demand for acute sense stimulation, the girl will become an easy victim for the unscrupulous.[89]

Having once been "ruined" by a work foreman, the master of the house, the restaurant owner, or a "friend," prostitution often seemed to be the only viable option for many immigrant women.[90]

A final alternative for Ruthenian immigrants, especially those who planned to settle in America with their families, was farming. Among the first Ruthenian farmers in the United States were Teofan Zhytsia, who settled in Wisconsin in 1866, and Hryhorij Hordan, who immigrated to Illinois. In an article which appeared in *Ameryka*, the first Ruthenian-American newspaper, Hordan urged Ruthenians to leave their unhealthy and dangerous mining and factory jobs and to move to Illinois where, he wrote, "the air is fresh, the soil good, where farms are available at a reasonable price, and where prospects for establishing a Ruthenian village are excellent." Hordan's appeal met with little response. Those Ruthenians who were truly interested in becoming farmers in the New World usually immigrated to Canada or Brazil where homestead land was more readily available. At the same time, Ruthenians who were already in the United States had become too accustomed to the steady dollar to become overly enamored with what they considered to be risky agrarian ventures. Other proposals to purchase land in Mexico as well as other U.S. states were later discussed and supported by *Svoboda*, another Ruthenian-American newspaper. All were greeted with a similar lack of enthusiasm by Ukraine's early emigrants.[91]

Nevertheless, a number of Ruthenians did settle on U.S. farms, some as a matter of choice, others by accident. In 1892, a group of five families from eastern Ukraine, all Protestant Stundists (Evangelicals) fleeing Russian religious oppression, settled near Yale, Virginia.[92] More Stundists arrived in 1896 and 1897 and purchased land in the vicinity. In 1898, another group of Stundists, originally scheduled for Virginia, were persuaded by Peter Zeller, a German-Ukrainian coreligionist, to follow him to Trip, South Dakota, where they eventually settled. Some remained in the state but others decided to move to North Dakota where they filed homestead claims in McHenry and McLean counties.

In 1896 and 1897, a group of Ruthenians from Galicia immigrated to North Dakota (after first planning to live in Canada), settling around Belfield and Wilton. In 1906, they built a Catholic church, St. Demetrius, in what came to be called Ukraina, North Dakota. Joined by other immigrants from Galicia, Ruthenians soon dominated the area, numbering some 10,000 by 1933. Some of the early pioneers, however, decided to move again, settling in Scobey, Montana, where a community had already been established by Ruthenians from Canada.[93]

In 1896, nineteen Galician families, originally scheduled for Canada, found themselves in Georgia as the result of the unscrupulous machinations of one F. Missler, an agent for the German-based Lloyd Shipping Line. After complaining to the Austro-Hungarian consul, a number of them were allowed to continue to Canada at Missler's expense. Some, however, elected to remain in Georgia.

That same year Missler sent another Canada-bound contingent of Ruthenians to Texas. Some forty-five families settled near Bremond, twenty-five families elected to live near Anderson, ten families went to Marlin, eight families settled in Schulenberg, and three families ended up in Austin. In 1908, Albin Bala contracted 25,000 acres of land near Dundee in an attempt to establish a Ruthenian community in the area. Within a year, over 1,500 of these acres were being worked by Ruthenians. Later, some thirty-five Texas Ruthenian families moved to Oklahoma, settling near Harrah.

In 1897, the notorious Missler persuaded some thirty-four Canada-bound Ruthenians to sign English-language contracts for work on sugar plantations in Hawaii. Unknown to the hapless immigrants, they were practically signing their lives away. The contract stipulated that they would work for three years in return for their transportation fees, their lodgings, and eighteen dollars per month, most of which would be returned to the plantation owner for their food. After spending four months at sea on a sail clipper that took them around the continent of South America, the immigrants arrived in Papaikon, on the island of Hawaii, where they were soon laboring fourteen to sixteen hours a day. Forbidden to leave the plantations unless they were able to post a $120 deposit, the immigrants became virtual slaves of the plantation owners. Missler, meanwhile, continued to bring in fresh supplies of immigrant labor – Ruthenians (some 350 by the end of 1898), Poles, Lithuanians, and Jews – to work under similar conditions on the isles of Oahu, Maui, and Hawaii. In 1899, thirty-seven Ruthenians working in Waipahu, Oahu, appealed for help to the Austro-Hungarian consul and went on strike. The consul, Mr. F. Hakfeld, however, not only refused to intervene but ordered the strikers arrested. Within a year, a number of other workers also went on strike, only to be arrested by the authorities. Word of the plight of Ruthenians somehow reached the office of *Svoboda*, which inaugurated a letter-writing campaign to American congressional leaders demanding an investigation. At the same time, the

San Francisco Examiner learned of the situation and began to write on the subject, pointing out, among other things, that Hakfeld had invested personal funds in some of the sugar plantations. Finally, on 15 June 1900, Congress passed a bill nullifying all such Hawaiian immigrant contracts and ordering the plantation owners to free their workers. Most Ruthenians headed for the United States soon after their release, while those who remained on the plantations worked under improved conditions and a wage scale beginning at twenty-six dollars a month. Later, twenty-two Ruthenian families purchased farms at six to twelve dollars an acre near Mountain View, Hawaii.[94]

Fortunately, not all Ruthenians interested in agriculture were exposed to such shabby treatment. Beginning in the first decade of the 1900s, many immigrants were successful in establishing farms in New England, the middle Atlantic states, and the Middle West. Averaging 100 acres in size, most of the farms were small by American standards but quite large by old-country standards.

In New England, Ruthenian farms were scattered, but in New York state, where a sizable group of Ruthenians began to farm after 1910, farms were located in close proximity to each other, resulting in the establishment of Ruthenian communities in Galway, Broadalbin, Lee Center, Glenfield, Spring Valley, Hudson, and Durhamville.

The first Ruthenian farm community in New Jersey was established in 1908 around Great Meadows. In 1912, an enterprising Ruthenian real estate agent, W. Metolych, advertised the availability of farmland around Millville and was able to induce some 200 Ruthenian families, some from as far away as North Dakota, to purchase land in the area. The land, according to some disgruntled buyers, was not all that it was made out to be and Metolych was accused of misrepresentation. In time, however, the farms proved to be quite productive.[95]

In the late 1890s and early 1900s, Ruthenians also purchased land in Wisconsin, around Clayton, Lublin, and Thorp, and in Michigan, around Copemish, Fruitport, Pinconning, and Saline. Most of the land purchased in this part of the country was wooded and required great effort to make it agriculturally productive. As in New Jersey, however, the hard labor eventually paid off.[96]

Father Ivan Wolansky and America's First Ruthenian Community

While Ruthenians could be found in many states of the union during this early period of the immigration, it was in Pennsylvania, the state with the highest concentration of immigrants from Ukraine, that organized

Ruthenian community life first emerged. It began as a response to a grow-ing need for religiocultural sustenance in an environment that was grim, culturally barren, and devoid of emotional and spiritual fulfillment.

Finding no Ruthenian churches upon their arrival in the anthracite coal towns of eastern Pennsylvania, Ruthenians initially attended churches closest in ethnic character to their own – usually Polish and Slovak[97] – a not uncommon practice among early immigrants from eastern Europe.[98] In 1884, Ruthenians attending the Polish-Lithuanian Church of St. Casimir in Shenandoah began to object to the Polish pastor, a Fr. Joseph A. Lenarkie-wicz, for what they considered to be his attempt to suppress their heritage.[99] Receiving no satisfaction, they turned to Carl Rice, a respected and prosper-ous Lithuanian businessman, for assistance in obtaining a Ruthenian priest. A letter was subsequently sent to Galician Metropolitan (later Cardinal) Sylvester Sembratovych asking that a priest be sent because "something is lacking in us. Lacking to us is God, Whom we could adore in our own way." Along with the letter went fifty dollars to cover transportation costs[100] and a promise to pay the new priest a regular monthly salary.[101] In a letter dated 24 October 1884, Sembratovych replied that he was sending a married priest and concluded his remarks with a plea to the Shenandoah Ruthenians to "remain true to your Ruthenian rite" and "behave your-selves: morally, industriously, virtuously, soberly, as true Christians."[102]

Fr. Ivan Wolansky (1857–1926), America's first Ruthenian-Ukrainian Catholic priest, left Galicia late in November and arrived in New York in December 1884. From New York, he headed directly for Shenandoah to meet with his fellow countrymen. A few days later he journeyed to Phila-delphia to present himself to Roman Catholic Archbishop Patrick Ryan. Wolansky was met by Ryan's vicar-general who had learned of his arrival from Father Lenarkiewicz[103] and who, upon assuring himself that Wolan-sky was indeed a married priest – an unacceptable status in the Latin-rite Catholic church – suggested that the good father return to Europe immediately because, under the circumstances, Archbishop Ryan could hardly meet with him. Reasoning that only his metropolitan could rescind his mission in the United States, Wolansky ignored the suggestion and returned to Shenandoah.

Refused the use of St. Casimir by Father Lenarkiewicz, Father Wolansky rented a hall and, with a capacity crowd of Ruthenians, celebrated the first Ruthenian-Ukrainian divine liturgy on the evening of the feast day of St. Nicholas, Thursday, 19 December 1884. The official opening of a temporary chapel came on Sunday, 22 December, and, because that particular Sunday was also the Feast of the Immaculate Conception, the chapel came to be called by the same name.[104] According to an account which appeared in a January 1885 edition of *Dilo* (no. 6), in which an excerpt from a letter by a young Ruthenian American to his parents in Europe was cited, Ruthenians traveled from miles around to attend the service and "almost everyone wept with joy as we sang 'Hospody Pomylui' (Lord have mercy)." Archbishop Ryan, meanwhile, issued a letter, subsequently read from all Shenandoah Catholic churches, forbidding all Catholics, under pain of mortal sin, to attend any religious services at which Father Wolansky was the celebrant.[105]

Wolansky's arrival in Shenandoah and his treatment by Archbishop Ryan created a sensation in the coal-mining town. In a lengthy article that appeared in the *Shenandoah Herald* on 10 January 1885, Wolansky (interviewed with the help of an interpreter) was described as "about twenty-eight years of age, fully six feet in height, and somewhat sparsely built. His countenance is of the Greek cast, and beams with intelligence and good nature and his bright brown eyes fairly dance with joy when he meets an American who evinces a disposition to treat him cordially."

The reporter went to great lengths to trace the history of the Greek Catholic church, especially its union with Rome and the fact that the clergy were permitted to marry prior to ordination. Significantly, the reporter also mentioned that Wolansky was enjoined "to acknowledge no allegiance to local church authority in America or elsewhere, but to remain subject always to the Pope through the metropolitan and the representative of the Church at Rome who is Archbishop Joseph Sembratovych, a brother of the metropolitan of Lemberg."*

In describing Wolansky's feelings regarding the United States, the reporter wrote:

> He had met but few people, and didn't think he had been treated fairly by some of them. Americans, generally, he thought, were an active, intelligent and progressive race. Inhabiting a country of boundless resources the limit of the possibilities they may attain he thinks inconceivable. He is pleased with the country so far as he has seen it, and says it will be his consistent aim to make good Christians and good citizens of his congregation. He is happy and contented, and is constantly surrounded by members of his congregation, who come either to give advice or to seek spiritual consolation. He moves among them gracefully, and his easy, affable and affectionate manner has won him the esteem of all those over whom he has charge. He speaks four or five dialects, and has already begun the mastery of English in a manner that will enable him to speak it fluently in a few months.

* Lviv was called "Lemberg" by the Austrians.

Wolansky's wife was described as a brunette "with a Russian cast of countenance" who "appears happy and good natured, and endeavors as best she
can to entertain their visitors." Wolansky's sister, who came to America
with him, was described as about the same age as his wife and "refined
and dignified."

As for his rejection by the Roman Catholic hierarchy, Wolansky regarded
it as a "rank discourtesy" but told the reporter he was not concerned "since
it was only a matter of courtesy that he was directed to visit them."[106]

Ryan's behavior created a number of problems for Father Wolansky but
none was more immediately acute than the problem of proper burial for
the deceased. Roman Catholic priests not only refused him permission to
conduct graveside services in their cemeteries but soon began to balk at
burying Greek Catholic dead in ground consecrated for Roman Catholics.
Bodies often lay in the homes of relatives for days before Wolansky could
find a suitable place, usually in a Protestant cemetery, for burial. The
problem was finally resolved with the purchase of a cemetery lot for the
exclusive use of Ruthenians, months after Wolansky's arrival.[107]

In the spring of 1885, two lots were purchased (at $700) in Shenandoah,
and the first Ukrainian Catholic church in the United States, St. Nicholas,
was completed the next year.[108] In 1886, under Wolansky's guidance and
inspiration, church committees were organized in Jersey City, New Jersey,
in Kingston, Freeland, Olyphant, Shamokin, and Wilkes-Barre, Pennsylvania, and in Minneapolis, Minnesota.[109] Again, Father Wolansky met
opposition from the Roman Catholic clergy. In Shamokin, for example,
a Father Kalinowski, upon hearing of the proposed Ukrainian church,
requested his parishioners to pray for its failure.[110]

In March 1887, after repeated requests from Wolansky for more priests
to help organize additional parishes in the United States, Metropolitan
Sembratovych sent Fr. Zeno Lachovich to the United States to assist Wolansky in his mission. Leaving Lachovich in Shenandoah to act as assistant
pastor, to oversee the construction of a church in Kingston, Wolansky left
on an extended trip, visiting Ruthenian communities from New York to
Minneapolis. Along the way he performed marriages, baptized children,
and urged all larger communities to organize themselves and to begin
planning for a church edifice. Upon Wolansky's return to Shenandoah,
Lachovich went to Kingston as pastor of the new St. Mary's Church, built
in 1887. Father Wolansky was also instrumental in the building of St.
Mary's in Freeland (1887), Sts. Cyril and Methodius in Olyphant (1888), and
Transfiguration of Our Lord in Shamokin (1890) as well as churches in
Jersey City (Sts. Peter and Paul), Minneapolis (St. Mary the Protectoress),
and Wilkes-Barre.[111]

In January 1885, Wolansky organized the first Ruthenian mutual aid or burial society, the Brotherhood of St. Nicholas, in Shenandoah. By 1887, the brotherhood had branches in Shamokin, Hazleton, Freeland, Kingston, and Olyphant. That same year a convention of all branches was held in Olyphant and the Union of Ruthenian Brotherhoods (Spoluchennia bratstv ruskykh) was born. By 1889, the organization had fourteen branches.

St. Nicholas Church remained at the center of Ruthenian life until 1889. On 20 September 1886, the *Shenandoah Herald* wrote that Father Wolansky "probably has the largest parish in the United States" because "people from Baltimore, New York, and other areas come to Shenandoah to get married." St. Nicholas parish eventually became St. Michael's parish. A new church was built in 1908. Kingston shared the Ruthenian limelight with Shenandoah between 1887 and 1889. By 1893, Scranton, Mahanoy City, Shamokin, and Pittsburgh were important centers, and during the late 1890s, Olyphant, Mt. Carmel, and Philadelphia were gaining in prominence.[112]

When Father Lachovich arrived in the United States he was accompanied by Volodymyr Simenovych (1858–1932), a third-year law student at the University of Lviv, the son of a priest, a friend of Ivan Franko, and an energetic activist in ethnonational organizations in Galicia. Simenovych came to the United States at the request of a priest in Galicia who was responding to a plea from Father Wolansky "to send me an intelligent young man to assist me in my work in America."[113] Upon arriving in Shenandoah, Simenovych was put to work as the assistant editor of *Ameryka*, a monthly newspaper Father Wolansky had established on 15 August 1886. In June 1887, Simenovych became the editor.[114] That same year, with assistance from Wolansky, Simenovych organized the first reading room, where illiterates were taught to read,[115] and the first choir.[116] Later, again under Wolansky's direction, Simenovych became active in the organizing of cooperative stores, for a time managing the store in Olyphant.[117]

The establishment of co-ops was still another accomplishment of the indefatigable Father Wolansky. In October 1887, Wolansky called together Mychailo Kushwara and Stefan Yanovicz, both of whom had small grocery stores in Shenandoah, and convinced them to combine forces and to open a large "Cooperative General Store" in Shenandoah. It was decided that Kushwara should manage the store while Yanovicz, a much younger man, would go to Philadelphia to complete a course on the latest business techniques. The project was an immediate success. In 1888, two branches were opened, in Olyphant and Plymouth, and in 1889, three more branches were in operation in Hazelton, Shamokin, and Pleasant Hill.[118]

Nor was Wolansky oblivious to the economic exploitation suffered by Ruthenians and other immigrant groups during this period. He joined America's fledgling labor movement and, as head of a Knights of Labor assembly, he became a leading unionist in Shenandoah,[119] holding the distinction of being the only Catholic priest in the nation who belonged to a labor organization. In 1888, when a local strike erupted into violence and the Shenandoah clergy, most notably Father Lenarkiewicz, urged parishioners to return to work – and even national labor leaders were advising caution – it was Father Wolansky who rallied the strikers. On Monday, 6 February 1888, a meeting of strikers was called by Wolansky and, according to one account, "here in the jammed Opera House all the constituent nationalities had articulate representatives on stage: the editors Szlupas of the Lithuanian *Balsas* and Semenovich (*sic*) of the Ukrainian *Amerika* (*sic*), the Polish shoemaker Smoczyniski, and the Slovak merchant Wislosky. Charley Rice, 'headman of the foreigners for twenty years,' led the meeting and after a ninety-minute session pronounced the resolutions." Significantly, the strikers were upset that their English and Irish counterparts had not joined in the struggle.[120] The strike was not successful, but it was important in the sense that it "was the first time that the Slavic anthracite community participated as a whole in a labor dispute."[121] It was not to be the last. Nor was it to be the last time that Ruthenians were to play an important role in the labor movement in Pennsylvania.

Father Lachovich died in 1887 and Simenovych was dispatched to Lviv to plead with Metropolitan Sembratovych to send a replacement. The metropolitan was faced with a dilemma. Pressured by Rome to keep married priests away from American shores, Sembratovych was finding it difficult to find single priests willing to take on the exceptionally arduous conditions of parish life in the United States.[122] A replacement was finally found in the person of Fr. Constantine Andruchowicz, who, upon arriving in the United States, took up his pastoral duties in Kingston.[123]

In 1889, three more priests arrived from Europe: Fr. Alexander Dziubaj,[124] an Uhro-Rusyn, who settled in Wilkes-Barre; Fr. Havrylo Gulovich, another Uhro-Rusyn, who settled in Freeland; and Fr. Gregory Hrushka from Galicia, who took up his duties in Jersey City. That same year, Metropolitan S. Sembratovych, bowing to pressure from Rome and from Archbishop Patrick Ryan, recalled Father Wolansky.[125]

In his selection of Father Wolansky to pave the way for the organization of the Ruthenian-American community, Metropolitan Sembratovych could hardly have made a better choice. Wolansky was truly a "people's pastor," a man imbued with a desire to meet not only the spiritual needs of his flock but their cultural and economic needs as well. Considering the short time that he spent in the United States and the obstacles with which he had to contend, it can be safely stated that no other priest accomplished more. His recall proved to be the first significant turning point in the history of the community.

The Ruthenian Religious Response

At the time of its first mass immigration to the United States, Ukraine had been a stateless nation for over 200 years. The Ukrainian religious tradition, however, was very much alive. This was especially true in Galicia and Carpatho-Ukraine where, over the centuries, the national character of the Eastern church had been carefully preserved. Thus, even though the average Ruthenian may have come to America with little or no sense of his ethnonational heritage, he came with a religiocultural tradition that was truly national in orientation.[126]

Crucial to an understanding of the role of the Greek Catholic church in the initial organizational phases of Ukrainian-American life is an appreciation of the symbiotic relationship that existed between religion and Ukrainian national consciousness. In the words of one Russian scholar, "The church for the Ukrainian did not become an external and superior force whose sanction sanctified the nation (as it was in Muscovite Russia) but a natural function of the nation, an individual attribute important rather because it was national than because it was religious."[127]

Although officially both Greek and Roman Catholics were members in full communion of the same church, differences were all too obvious and, as far as Ruthenian peasants were concerned, they belonged to a different church. In terms of externals, of course, the differences were very real. Ruthenians saw that their church venerated different saints, followed the Julian (or "Ruthenian") calendar as opposed to the Gregorian (or "Polish") calendar, and celebrated the divine liturgy in a language different from the language of the Polish churches.[128] Like the Orthodox, Greek Catholics called the divine liturgy a "god's service" (Sluzhba Bozha) rather than a mass; they bowed rather than genuflected; they stood during the service; and they made the sign of the cross with the thumb and first two fingers from right to left. Greek Catholics used leavened bread for the altar (as had been done for centuries in the West), received communion under two species (observed in the West till the twelfth century), were baptized by immersion or partial immersion, and were confirmed immediately following the baptism. Organs and statues had no place in the Ruthenian church, only icons, wall paintings, and mosaics.[129]

The greatest external difference between Greek and Latin Catholics, especially in the United States, was that Greek Catholic priests were married. According to one Roman Catholic scholar, "The custom of a celibate clergy has become so firmly rooted in Western Catholic consciousness ... that we are prone to forget that it is not an evangelical precept and that it took a thousand years for it to become general in the West."[130] In the Greek Catholic church, celibacy was never the rule for lower clergy. A man could be ordained to the diaconate and priesthood and retain his wife but he could not marry after he was ordained. Bishops, in contrast, had to be single or widowers.[131] "All of this," wrote S. Smolka in *Die Russiche Welt*, "is taken to heart by the Ukrainian peasant and ties him so much closer to his national church," distinguishing it from the Roman Catholic church "which is put before him as an aggressive institution trying to permeate his *Tserkvas* [churches] with the dangerous Polonism."[132]

Not only did the Austrian government fully support the custom and tradition of the Greek Catholic church, Rome did also – at least initially. In 1624, when Ukrainian bishops complained to Rome about continued Jesuit efforts to convert Greek Catholics to the Latin rite, the Holy See ruled that "in the future it should not be lawful for any of the united Ruthenians, whether lay folk or ecclesiastics, secular or regular, and especially monks of the Order of St. Basil the Great,* to go over to the Latin rite, for any reason, however urgent, without the special permission of the Apostolic See." When Roman Catholics began to assert that Greek Catholic clergy were inferior, Rome published a decree (1643) which declared that the Greek Catholic clergy enjoyed the same privileges *fori, canonis, immunitas, liberatis* as the Latin-rite clergy. In a letter to Ukrainian bishops in 1751, Pope Benedict XIV wrote that "Our predecessors have detested and we detest these changes of rite since we very much desire the preservation and not the destruction of the Greek rite." In 1683, an agreement styled *Concordia* was reached by Latin- and Eastern-rite bishops declaring that all Greek Catholics, those living under Russian domination as well as those in western Ukraine, were prohibited from joining the Latin rite. Further good faith on the part of Rome was indicated by the establishment of a bishopric in Stanyslaviv in 1885 and a special Ruthenian college in Rome in 1897.[133]

Ruthenians had a profound affection for their church. This was true of both the peasant and the intellectual agnostic. For peasants, the church was the one institution that clarified their identity in this world and offered them salvation in the next. For intellectuals, the church was an important vehicle for enhancing ethnonational consciousness.[134] Because the church was such an integral part of Ruthenian existence, it was the first institution Ruthenian immigrants attempted to establish in the United States. As they

* The Order of St. Basil the Great was founded by St. Basil, Archbishop of Caesarea, Cappadocia, in Asia Minor, in the latter half of the fourth century A.D. The Basilian order was introduced into Ukraine after 988 but declined in influence in subsequent years. It was revived as a Greek Catholic order after the Union of 1596.

were soon to learn, however, conditions in the United States were quite different from those existing in Ukraine.

The American Catholic Church

In Europe, churches were supported either by state funds or by income derived from church property. In the United States, support was voluntary, which meant that if a particular group wanted its own church, it had to build and support it by itself. Reasoning that because they paid for their own churches they should have some voice in their administration, a number of early Roman Catholic parishes adopted the Protestant practice of electing a board of trustees to oversee all church property. This practice was later challenged by American Catholic bishops who demanded that all church property be signed over to them. Despite a period of turmoil that led to a number of defections and excommunications, the bishops were eventually victorious. In 1884, the third Plenary Session of the Catholic church, meeting in Baltimore, ruled in favor of central control.

By the 1890s, the Roman Catholic hierarchy in the United States was dominated by Irish Americans. Dismayed by what they considered to be Irish discrimination against German Catholics in Cincinnati, St. Louis, and Milwaukee, German Americans protested to Rome. In 1890, the St. Raphael Society, supported by a number of German, Italian, and Polish clerics, presented the so-called Lucerne Memorial to Rome. Largely the work of Peter Paul Cahensly, a German philanthropist, the document suggested that Catholic dioceses in the United States be organized according to nationality rather than geography. Rome, however, ruled in favor of the Irish-American opposition, declaring that the idea was essentially a denial of the catholicity of the church. Later controversies between Irish-American bishops and other nationality groups resulted in the establishment of an independent Polish National Catholic church, an independent Lithuanian church, and, for a time, an autonomous Italian church.

Final victory for the Irish-American clergy came in the latter half of the 1890s. Strongly conservative in their outlook, the Irish bishops opposed all attempts by more liberal elements in the American Catholic church to permit greater democratic flexibility and concern for social reform programs aimed at amelioration of the human condition. The Irish bishops argued for strict adherence to dogma and unquestioning obedience to the hierarchy. In their struggle against the liberals, the Irish were supported by Pope Leo XIII, who, in the 1899 bull *Testem Benevolentia*, formally condemned what he called the doctrine of "Americanism."[135] Thus, while the papal edict argued against democratization within the American Catholic church, it also, in effect, rejected cultural pluralism. Henceforth, the church was to serve as a vehicle of assimilation rather than as a means of ethnic preservation.

Given the kind of *realpolitik* that typified the thinking of the Irish-dominated American Roman Catholic church, the cool and unwarranted reception accorded Father Wolansky and the subsequent efforts of Archbishop Ryan to discredit the Greek Catholic cleric in the eyes of other Catholics were to be expected. Striving to consolidate control over the American Catholic church economically, nationally, and ideologically, the Irish Catholic hierarchy was in no mood to permit a potentially disruptive Ruthenian Catholic church to take root on U.S. soil, no matter how ecclesiastically legitimate such a church was in the eyes of Rome.

The Growth of the Greek Catholic Church

Despite opposition from the Catholic hierarchy as well as from the Polish-American community,[136] the Greek Catholic church in America continued to grow. By the end of 1889, two more Ruthenian priests arrived – Viktor Toth and Ivan Zapototsky. In 1890, Alexis Toth and Stefan Jackovich, both from Carpatho-Ukraine, and Teofan Obushkevych, from Galicia, made their appearance. Shortly thereafter, three more Ruthenian clerics found themselves in America – Nikifor Khanat, Cornelius and Augustin Lawryshyn. By 1891, there were nineteen Ruthenian priests in the United States, of whom sixteen were from Carpatho-Ukraine and three from Galicia. In 1893, Fr. Ivan Konstankevych (1859–1918) arrived from Galicia and settled in Shamokin where he remained for the next twenty-five years. By 1894, there were thirty Ruthenian priests, of whom only four were from Galicia.[137]

With the arrival of more priests, church building began in earnest. In 1891, a new and larger church was completed in Jersey City and churches were completed in Duquesne (St. Nicholas) and Scranton (St. Mary's). In the next three years so many churches were in the process of construction that *Svoboda* asked for a halt in the building program lest "before long there will be more churches in the United States than Ruthenian families." By 1898, there were fifty-one Ruthenian churches or chapels in America.[138]

On the surface, it would appear that the Greek Catholic church had at last overcome its environment and, despite financial and ecclesiastical restrictions, was well on the way to becoming an ongoing religiocultural enterprise in the United States. Such was not the case, however. Between 1889, the year Wolansky returned to Europe, and 1907, the year the first Ruthenian-American bishop was appointed by Rome, the Greek Catholic church in America was engaged in a life and death struggle with its own priests, with the Russian Orthodox Mission, and with the Holy See in Rome.

Clerical Discord

Much of what had been accomplished by Fr. Ivan Wolansky was subsequently undone by his successor, Father Andruchowicz. In 1889, when Simenovych left *Ameryka* to become manager of the Ruthenian co-op in Olyphant, Andruchowicz became the editor. That same year, over the protests of Simenovych and other lay leaders, all title to and assets of *Ameryka* were signed over to the Shenandoah parish. By the end of 1890, *Ameryka* was liquidated. A new newspaper, *Ruske Slovo,* published and edited by Andruchowicz, was introduced on 1 January 1891. The paper lasted one year.[139]

Having taken over the newspaper, Andruchowicz next attempted to assume management of the Cooperative General Store. Failing in that, he organized, in October 1889, the so-called Ruska Torhovlia (called "Greek Store" in English), promised to pay one-half of the profits to the Shenandoah parish, and, utilizing both *Ameryka* and the pulpit, urged all Ruthenians to boycott the Cooperative General Store, alleging, among other things, that it was being run by aristocrats. The ploy worked. In January 1890, the co-op was forced to liquidate and Andruchowicz took over the entire operation, renaming it "The Shenandoah Russian Store Co." The new enterprise folded a short time later.

Having failed in their first real cooperative economic venture in the United States, some of the involved lay leaders returned to Europe.[140] Simenovych, however, decided to try his hand at something else. Moving to Baltimore, he completed medical college and returned as a medical doctor first to Shenandoah and later to Shamokin. Later still, he moved to Chicago where, by the beginning of 1897, he had a well-established practice.[141]

Andruchowicz's strange behavior, especially his later endeavors to sign over all Ruthenian-owned church and public property to himself, came to the attention of Metropolitan Sembratovych. Father Wolansky was asked to return to Shenandoah to rectify the matter. Andruchowicz, however, refused to meet with Wolansky, locking him out of the church, and forcing Wolansky to file suit against the rebel priest in an effort to oust him and to retrieve the parish. Because everything was legally in Andruchowicz's name, Wolansky lost the suit and, in time, returned to Galicia.* Upon hearing of Andruchowicz's action, Metropolitan Sembratovych ordered his immediate recall. Again Andruchowicz refused to obey his superior. Finally, in 1892, after promising his parishioners he would leave in return

---

* Father Wolansky returned to Ukraine in 1890. In 1896, he was dispatched to Brazil to help organize Ukrainian parishes there. After the death of his wife that same year, he requested and was granted permission to return to Ukraine.

for $1,500 in cash (which they subsequently raised and presented to him), Andruchowicz sold everything for $5,000 to John Smith, one of the founders of the Greek Catholic Union, and left for Galicia. Smith later resold everything to the Ruthenian community at a profit.[142] As things turned out, the "Shenandoah Affair" was only the first of a number of scandals perpetrated by unscrupulous clergy upon the fledgling Ruthenian-American community.

With the arrival of new priests, and with no authority to regulate assignments, competition for the older, more affluent parishes or communities became quite fierce. Sometimes, a priest would arrive in an established parish and attempt to gain a following from among the church trustees and other parishioners in an effort to oust the resident pastor. If he succeeded in convincing the trustees of the church that he was the better man, he became the new pastor. If not, he either left for another town or rallied his following and began to create his own parish and to build his own church, often just a few blocks from the original church. On other occasions, two candidates would arrive in a particularly large Ruthenian community and attempt to organize a parish, each competing with the other. Because of such irregularities the little community of Hazleton had three Ruthenian churches by 1894, with each of the pastors regularly accusing the other two of all manner of improprieties.[143]

The emergence of priestly avarice and the lack of ecclesiastical discipline were an embarrassment to those priests – the majority – who truly desired to fulfill their spiritual and national mission in America. The more responsible segment of the religious community initiated a series of attempts to bring about certain controls and to institute a system of self-imposed centralized authority. It was at this juncture in the history of the community that the battle for the national soul of the Ruthenian American really began. At issue was control of the Ruthenian-American church, and the struggle initially involved two irreconcilable religiocultural factions, the Uhro-Rusyn priests from Carpatho-Ukraine, whose national sentiments were essentially Hungarian, and the Galician priests, whose ethnonational loyalties were increasingly Ukrainian. At first, the Uhro-Rusyns enjoyed a distinct advantage, both in total number of immigrants and, as we have seen, in terms of the number of priests. Official Hungarian statistics indicate that in the year 1902 there were a total of 262,815 Greek Catholic Ruthenians from Austro-Hungary living in the United States. Of this number, 70 percent (190,935) were from Carpatho-Ukraine, while only 30 percent (81,929) were from Galicia.[144] Although the numbers may be open to question,[145] the fact remains that during the early days of the emigration from Ukraine, Ruthenians from Carpatho-Ukraine outnumbered those from Galicia by more than two to one.

TABLE 5
Number of Ruthenian priests in the United States in 1909

Diocese of origin	Monks	Celibates	Married	Widowers	Total
Galicia					
Lviv	4	8	5	5	22
Peremyshl	0	6	12	2	20
Stanislaviv	0	2	2	1	5
Total	4	16	19	8	47
Carpatho-Ukraine					
Preshov	0	1	13	10	24
Mukachevo-Uzhhorod	2	1	30	5	38
Krentz	0	1	0	0	1
Total	2	3	43	15	63
United States	0	6	2	0	8
Total	6	25	64	23	118

SOURCE: Walter C. Warzeski, "Religion and National Consciousness in the History of the Rusins" (PhD dissertation, University of Pittsburgh, 1964), p. 145.

Greek Catholic priests from Ukraine came from three European eparchies: Mukachevo (Uzhhorod), Preshov in Carpatho-Ukraine, and Lviv in Galicia. Of the three, the Mukachevites were in the majority (table 5). The least "Ukrainian" of all, the Mukachevites had adopted the Latin alphabet and were totally loyal to the Hungarian crown. They called themselves Uhro-Rusyns. The Preshovite clergy, in contrast, were also from Carpatho-Ukraine, but tended to vacillate among the Hungarian, Slovak, and Galician-Ukrainian cultural influences that prevailed at the time. They had adopted the etymological Slavonic alphabet and usually sided with the Galician priests in matters of church order in the United States. The smallest group of priests in America were those from Galicia. The most "Ukrainian" of the three, it was they who, imbued with the spirit of the national revival in their homeland, eventually laid the foundation for the development of a distinct Ukrainian ethnonational identity among a segment of the Ruthenian-American population.*

Rome, meanwhile, concerned with the growing chaos in the Greek Catholic church in America, and the justifiable protests of Roman Catholic bishops regarding the opportunistic behavior of some clerics, appointed Nikifor Khanat, a Mukachevite, to bring order to the community, and to

---

* While many Catholic priests from Galicia came with a Ukrainian orientation, there were others who did not. As we shall discover later, some of the Galician clergy were Russophiles.

serve as intermediary between the priests and bishops. In August 1895, Khanat called a convention in Scranton where the Brotherhood of Greek Catholic Priests in America under the Patronage of St. Andrew Pervozvanyi came into being. Both the Preshovites and the Galicians boycotted the convention, however, and the brotherhood dissolved within two years. While the Mukachevites were meeting in Scranton, the Galicians and Preshovites attempted to form their own organization in Freeland, but failed. In June 1896, all three factions met in Shamokin but no agreement was reached. They met again in August in Olyphant but were still unable to accomplish anything. The three groups met for the last time on 18 July 1899 in Philadelphia and the Sts. Cyril and Methodius Society of Greek Catholic Priests was born. It lasted a year.[146]

The fortunes of the Galician faction improved considerably between 1893 and 1898 with the arrival of a group of eight ethnonationally conscious priests from Lviv who had come to the United States with a single mission in mind: to develop the Ruthenian community along lines clearly consistent with the Ruthenian-Ukrainian* national revival in Galicia. Christened the American Circle by Iuliian Bachynskyi, the group included Revs. Ivan Konstankevych (1859–1918), Nestor Dmytriw (1863–1925), Mykola Stefanovych (1870–1911), Ivan Ardan (1871–1940), Antin Bonezevsky (1871–1903), Stefan Makar (1870–1915), Mykola Pidhoretsky, and Pavlo Tymkevych.[147] Trained during the halcyon days of the Ukrainian national revival in Galicia, all were ethnonationally conscious and, even more important, unusually capable individuals. Representative of the "new breed" Ruthenian Catholic cleric in Western Ukraine, they soon assumed the leadership in both the religiocultural and ethnonational Ruthenian-Ukrainian arenas in America.† Under the leadership of the American Circle, a convention of Galician priests, some Preshovite priests, and a number of Ruthenian lay leaders was held in Shamokin on 30 May 1901. The major accomplishment of the group was the establishment of the Society of Ruthenian Church Communities in the United States and Canada, an organization headed by Father Konstankevych and an executive board of three priests and three laymen. Renamed the Ruthenian Church in America in 1902, the organization existed until 1907. For the first time since the departure of Father Wolansky some order was restored in the Ruthenian church, at least among the fifteen member communities.[148]

* The term 'Ruthenian-Ukrainian' refers to the nationalization process which transformed Ruthenians into Ukrainians. A Ruthenian-Ukrainian was someone who was still being "processed." He was no longer a Ruthenian, but not yet a Ukrainian.
† The American Circle and its role in the ethnonational arena will be discussed in greater detail in the next chapter.

The Struggle for Religiocultural Dominance

The next phase in the battle for the hearts and minds of Ruthenian Americans began with a fight for religiocultural dominance by the Russian, Uhro-Rusyn, and Galician-Ruthenian clergy. At stake initially was local religious authority but the struggle soon evolved into a fierce battle for the national loyalty of Ruthenians among supporters of the Russian, Hungarian, and Ukrainian orientations. Ultimately involved in the ensuing ideological combat were the institutional leadership of the Russian Orthodox and American Roman Catholic churches; the Ruthenian, Ukrainian, and Russian fraternal societies; the Holy See; and the governments of Russia and Hungary.

The Russian Orthodox Church

While Ruthenian priests from Carpatho-Ukraine and Galicia were competing for local religiocultural control, their efforts were being undermined by yet another religiocultural presence in the United States, the Russian Orthodox church. The Russian effort was relatively late in starting but once under way, it made tremendous gains in the Ruthenian community.

The Orthodox had decided advantages over their Catholic competitors. The Greek Catholic and Russian Orthodox churches were almost indistinguishable in their external manifestations. In terms of dogma and tradition, moreover, the only truly significant disparities between the two religious faiths lay in the Catholic doctrine of the *Filioque*[149] and in the prayer for the pope of Rome rather than for the tsar.[150] Because Ruthenian Americans were hardly aware of dogma, and often because they called themselves "Russians" in English, it was not difficult to convince them that their true identity was Russian Orthodox.

Another advantage enjoyed by the Russian Orthodox church in America was the financial support it regularly received from the tsarist government. For a Ruthenian parish struggling to find money to pay its pastor and to pay off a new church edifice, this was a major consideration. For a tsarist government aware of the fact that many Ruthenians planned to return to Carpatho-Ukraine – a region that St. Petersburg had already begun to covet – fiscal support for the Ruthenians was an investment in the future.

A final advantage on the side of the Russians was, ironically, the religiocultural insensitivity of Roman Catholic bishops in America. Forcing financially strapped Ruthenian parishes to sign their church deeds over to Roman Catholic dioceses, and treating Ruthenian priests as second-class clergy, America's Catholic hierarchy helped pave the way for the "return to Orthodoxy" movement that was soon to engulf the Ruthenian-American community and that would result, ultimately, in the conversion of some 20 percent of America's Ruthenian Greek Catholic parishes.

The history of the Russian Orthodox church in North America began in 1794 with the arrival in Alaska of ten Russian monks and the establishment of a Russian mission. Despite a variety of initial problems associated with the difficulty of life in the region, the mission eventually prospered and by 1840 a separate Orthodox diocesan seat was created in Sitka. When the United States purchased Alaska in 1867, about half the Russian population either remained in the territory or elected to move to California; five years later, the Russian Orthodox diocesan seat was moved to San Francisco.[151] It was not until the late 1890s, however, that the Russian Orthodox church in America began to demonstrate any substantial growth.

In 1886, soon after a visit by Father Wolansky, the Ruthenian community of Minneapolis – composed mainly of immigrants from Carpatho-Ukraine – established a church construction committee. Three years later, the new church, St. Mary the Protectoress, was completed and subsequently blessed by Father Wolansky. In 1890, the new parish received its first pastor, Fr. Alexis Toth, a former professor of canon law at the Preshov Seminary. Presenting himself to Roman Catholic Bishop John Ireland of St. Paul, Father Toth was informed by the Irish-American hierarch that his presence in the diocese was neither sanctioned nor desired. Toth was shocked by the bishop's remarks. The brief conversation between the two clerics was conducted in Latin and Toth later recalled the exchange as follows:

- Do you have a wife?
- No! I answered.
- But you did have?
- I am a widower ...
- When he heard my answer, he threw his papers on the table and loudly exclaimed:
- I already sent a protest to Rome not to send me such priests ...
- What kind do you mean?
- Such as you ...
- But I am a Catholic priest of the Greek Rite! I am a Uniate!
  I was ordained by a lawful Catholic bishop ...
- I do not consider you or that bishop a Catholic; furthermore,
  I have no need of Greek Catholic priests; it is sufficient that in Minneapolis there is a Polish priest; he can also be priest for the Greek Catholic ...
- But he is of the Latin rite; our people cannot understand him; they will not go to him for service; it is for this reason they have built themselves a separate church ...

> – I gave them no permission to build, and give you no jurisdiction to act in any capacity here.[152]

Like Father Wolansky before him, Father Toth decided to ignore the wishes of the local Roman Catholic bishop and to continue his mission. Before long, however, the parishioners of St. Mary found themselves in a financial crisis, a not uncommon phenomenon among the somewhat overambitious Ruthenian immigrants. Hoping to solve the problem with help from other communities, a number of parishioners traveled to other cities. One of them, John Mlinar, went to San Francisco where, purely by chance, he met with the Russian bishop. Upon learning of Mlinar's plight, the Russian hierarch not only offered financial support for the Minneapolis community but, as a token of goodwill, presented Mlinar with thirteen icons and a three-barred Orthodox cross for the new church. Delighted with the reception he had received, Mlinar returned to Minneapolis, convened a secret meeting of the parish board, and convinced them to accept the gifts and, significantly, to join the Russian Orthodox diocese. Father Toth, who had not been invited to the meeting, was subsequently informed of the board's decision. Still smarting from the rude reception he had received from Bishop Ireland, and realizing that without financial assistance his parish was in trouble, Toth made no effort to dissuade his board, deciding instead to accept its initiative completely. In February 1891, Father Toth was formally accepted into the Russian Orthodox church and on 25 March the 365 parishioners of St. Mary the Protectoress Church were formally accepted by Bishop Vladimir Sokolovsky into the Russian Orthodox diocese of Alaska and the Aleutian Islands.

With financial assistance from the Russian Orthodox Episcopal See, Minneapolis became, for a time, the center of Russian religiocultural life in America. A missionary school was founded in 1897 and reorganized into a seminary in 1905. Other Russian organizations established in the city during this period included the St. Mary's Russian Women's Society (1904), the Russian Brotherhood of St. John the Baptist (1907), the Russian Library Society (1908), and the Russian Theatrical Circle (1911).[153] According to Petro Zaichenko, a teacher sent to the parish from eastern Ukraine in 1892, however, "there was not a single man from Russia in the city of Minneapolis" when he arrived.[154]

The Russians could not have found a more dynamic and dedicated proselyte to promote the cause of Russian Orthodoxy in the United States than Father Toth. Considered by many to be the "Father of American Russia,"[155] he labored tirelessly on behalf of the Orthodox mission, arguing that Ruthenians had a patriotic duty to return to the faith of their ancient Rus' forefathers. "If we don't place ourselves under the protection of the

Holy Orthodox Church," he declared, "the Irish Catholic bishops will soon take our churches from us."[156] Toth's arguments did not fall on deaf ears. Unable to obtain a Greek Catholic priest on their own terms, parishioners in Wilkes-Barre, Pennsylvania, called on Father Toth for assistance and, on 9 July 1893, the parish joined the Russian Orthodox fold. Officiating at the rededication services were Bishop Nicholas of San Francisco and two chaplains from imperial Russian warships then docked in New York harbor. Significantly, choral responses to the Russian liturgy had to be provided by crewmen from the Russian vessels.[157]

Realizing that the Greek Catholic Ruthenian community offered a fertile field for conversion, the Russian church in America began to identify itself as the "Russian Orthodox Greek Catholic Church," and to proselytize in earnest. The results were nothing short of phenomenal. During the administration of Bishop Nicholas (1891–7), Ruthenian parishes in Chicago, Pittsburgh, New York, Streator (Illinois), Ansonia, and Scranton were converted to Orthodoxy. By 1900, there were thirteen Ruthenian parishes within the Orthodox fold with 6,898 faithful (4,450 Uhro-Rusyns and 2,448 Galician Ruthenians).[158] During the administration of Bishop Tikhon (1898–1907) – who later became patriarch of Moscow and all Russia – the number of conversions more than tripled, with the greatest growth occurring among the Galicians. By 1906, the Russian church had 19,111 members (11,794 Galician Ruthenians, 6,430 Uhro-Rusyns, and 887 Russians).

The vigorous growth of the Russian Orthodox church in America was due to three significant factors: the fiery devotion of Fr. Alexis Toth; the foresight and organizational ability of the Holy Synod in Russia to respond to the needs of the church in America with money as well as with spiritual support; and the capable and sensitive leadership of America's Russian bishops who were willing to extend themselves in order to gain Ruthenian converts. When Bishop Tikhon, for example, learned of the Ruthenian-Ukrainian desire to establish a separate Catholic eparchy in America, he did not discourage the Galician priests from also appealing to the Holy Synod for a separate Orthodox eparchy in America. Such a request was actually considered by the Holy Synod but rejected out of fear that such recognition would precipitate a similar request from Orthodox clergy in Ukraine.

Evidence of the high priority that the Holy Synod placed on the work of the Russian Orthodox mission in America is provided by the fact that Bishop Tikhon was elevated to the dignity of archbishop in 1906 and two suffragan bishops were added to assist him in his work.[159] During the previous year, the Russian diocesan seat was moved from San Francisco to New York where a beautiful new cathedral had just been completed.

Since there were few Russians in the east, the move could have had no other purpose than that of placing the episcopal seat of the Russian church closer to the center of the Ruthenian population.[160]

The Rise of Fraternal Benefit Societies

The fraternal benefit system in America grew out of a need to provide low-cost life insurance for workers unable to afford rates charged by commercial companies. Especially vulnerable were coal miners whose daily risk of life and limb prohibited reasonable insurance premiums. Great hardships were often visited upon the families of miners who were killed or disabled. Many were barely able to pay the funeral expenses, let alone survive after the death of a miner.

Beginning in 1868, various individuals in Pennsylvania began to organize local mutual aid clubs, initially called "burial societies," for the purpose of establishing a survivors' benefit fund. The plan was simple. Every member contributed a small amount, usually a dollar, to an insurance fund which the member's beneficiaries received upon his death. As the membership of such societies grew, they took on certain fraternal characteristics with rituals and ceremonies designed to dramatize the concepts of brotherhood and exemplary living.[161]

As noted earlier, Father Wolansky established the first Ruthenian burial society, the Brotherhood of St. Nicholas, in 1885. It passed out of existence soon after Wolansky returned to Ukraine.

The first fraternal insurance society to establish an ongoing presence in the Ruthenian-American community was the Soiedyneniie hreko-kato-lycheskykh russkykh brastv (Union of Greek Catholic Ruthenian Brother-hoods), hereafter referred to simply as the Greek Catholic Union or GCU. Founded in Wilkes-Barre in 1892, the GCU, which in the beginning enjoyed the tacit support of all segments of the Ruthenian community, began to publish a newspaper, *Amerikansky Russky Viestnik* (The American Ruthenian Messenger), hereafter referred to simply as *Viestnik*, that same year. Initially dominated by the Mukachevite clergy, it was the GCU and its house organ *Viestnik* that came to be identified with the Hungarian orientation in the minds of most Galician Ruthenians. As we shall discover, however, this perception was not entirely accurate.

The second fraternal society to attain permanent status within the Ruthenian community was the Ruskyi narodnyi soiuz (The Ruthenian National Union), referred to in this chapter as the RNS. Founded in Shamokin in 1894 by Ivan Konstankevych, a member of the American Circle of Galician priests, and Theodosius Talpash, the RNS adopted *Svoboda* (Liberty), a newspaper founded by Gregory Hrushka (1860–1913) in 1893, as its official organ.[162] Ostensibly established as a protest against alleged mismanagement of funds within the GCU – which, at its first convention in 1894, reported a deficit of $7,000[163] – the RNS eventually came under the ideological influence of the American Circle. Within a short time the RNS and *Svoboda* were in the forefront of the Ukrainian ethnonational movement in America.

Despite the bad blood that emerged between the two Ruthenian fraternals as a result of the circumstances that led to the establishment of the RNS, they were united on one issue: the need to create an autonomous, Ruthenian, Greek Catholic exarchy (diocese) free of Latin-rite Catholic control as a countermeasure to the growing tide of Russian Orthodoxy. As the RNS took on a more "Ukrainian" ethnonational posture, however, the Uhro-Rusyn camp (partially out of self-interest and partially, no doubt, in response to clandestine Hungarian prodding) began to assume a posture towards the RNS and its supporters that was vehemently anti-Ukrainian. Thus, long before Rome had ever decided to create a Greek Catholic exarchy for Ruthenians in America, the question of *who* would be the first bishop became the issue of paramount concern, not only in America, but in Europe as well.

Both the Uhro-Rusyn and Ruthenian-Ukrainian camps were keenly aware that the ethnonational sentiment of Rome's appointee could well determine the future ethnicity of the community. While both sides supported the establishment of a separate exarchy, each side labored to achieve it in a manner designed to serve its own interests.

Towards Religiocultural Autonomy

Serious efforts to establish a Ruthenian exarchy in the United States were precipitated by an 1890 papal decree mandating that all Ruthenian priests wishing to emigrate to the United States in the future would have to follow a complicated, multistep procedure involving: (1) a formal request to their bishop in Ukraine; (2) processing of the request by the Sacred Congregation for the Propagation of the Faith of the Eastern Church; and (3) forwarding of the request to the Latin-rite bishop of the American diocese in which the priest planned to work. In order to be accepted, priests had to be celibate. Upon their arrival in America, they were obliged to report directly to the Roman Catholic bishop, who would then present a series of guidelines that Ruthenian priests were required to follow while residents of the diocese. The 1890 decree also dictated that all married priests already in the United States were to be recalled to Ukraine immediately.[164]

Other decrees issued by Rome in 1892, 1895, 1897, and 1902 tended to discriminate even more against the Ruthenian-American church. The papal encyclical *Orientalum Dignitas,* for example, promulgated by Pope Leo XIII on 30 November 1895, declared that Greek Catholics should join the Latin church in those areas where no Greek Catholic church existed but forbade Roman Catholics from attending Greek Catholic services. These pronouncements, plus Rome's hesitancy in ameliorating practices by Roman Catholic bishops and priests by which Ruthenian priests were ignored or ostracized by their Latin-rite colleagues, the denial of Latin-rite churches for Greek Catholic services, the prohibition of Ruthenian priests from freely traveling to other dioceses in order to attend to the spiritual needs of other Ruthenian communities – even when those communities formally requested such visitations – and the awarding of parish tenure rights to Ruthenian priests for brief periods of time (usually no longer than six months),[165] only served to increase the resentment of the Ruthenian-American community, and to provide grist for the propaganda mill of the Russian Orthodox mission. In cases where a particular Ruthenian priest defied his American bishop, retribution was swift and unequivocal. Pavlo Tymkevych, for example, was excommunicated in 1899 for organizing a parish without the local bishop's sanction.[166]

These developments, as well as the growing numerical significance of the Ruthenian community, the multiplication of parishes, increasing conflicts among Ruthenian priests, the threat of Latinization, and the danger of Russification of more Ruthenians in America by the Russian Orthodox mission, strengthened the resolve of Ruthenian leaders to achieve their goal of religiocultural autonomy at all costs, even, some were later to argue, if it meant severing all ties with Rome.

Formal petitions for a Ruthenian bishop were made to Rome at the Wilkes-Barre convention of Ruthenian priests in 1890, at the 1897 GCU convention, and at a Philadelphia conclave of Ruthenian clergy in 1899.[167]

Viestnik began calling for a separate Ruthenian exarchy as early as 1894,[168] advancing the argument that only such a papal initiative could bring order to the community and end the "schismatic trend" to Orthodoxy.[169] The Uhro-Rusyn clergy, however, refused to cooperate with their Galician brethren in their efforts to achieve the same end. Accusing the Galicians of attempting to destroy the spiritual morality of the community,[170] *Viestnik* dismissed a Galician initiative to convene an all-Ruthenian conference to discuss the exarchy question in 1901 as "one humbug more."[171]

The Hungarian Intrusion

Ruthenians in America were not the only ones working on behalf of an autonomous exarchy in America during this period. Hungarian officials also endorsed the idea, but for different reasons. While most Ruthenians desired a bishop in order to protect their religiocultural heritage in America, Budapest supported the establishment of a separate Ruthenian-American exarchy in order to protect Hungarian national interests. Believing that many Ruthenian immigrants would eventually return to Carpatho-Ukraine, Hungary had adopted a paternalistic posture towards Ruthenian Americans soon after the immigration began. Since 1892, for example, Greek Catholic priests from Mukachevo and Preshov who were departing for the United States were instructed to remain "faithful Magyars" in America and to remember their Hungarian homeland.

Concern for the ideological direction of the Ruthenian-American community began to mount in Hungarian government circles when it was learned that a number of recently converted Orthodox Ruthenians had indeed returned to Carpatho-Ukraine and were actively encouraging their friends and neighbors to join the Russian Orthodox church. For the Hungarians, this discovery only increased their fear of what they perceived to be a rising tide of Russophilism in Carpatho-Ukraine. Rumors were already circulating among the Russophiles that, upon the death of Emperor Franz Josef, Carpatho-Ukraine would be annexed by Russia.

An official government investigation was launched and when it was discovered that a group of Ruthenian-American returnees from Father Toth's Minneapolis parish had succeeded in convincing at least one priest in their home town of Becheriv to reject the authority of the pope, Hungarian officials decided to nip this threat at its source. Utilizing its diplomatic channels with the Holy See, Budapest prevailed upon the Sacred Congregation for the Propagation of the Faith to appoint Andor Hodobai, a thoroughly Magyarized canon in Preshov, as an apostolic visitor to the United States. In 1902, Father Hodobai and his assistant, Fr. Janos Korotnoki, left for America. To assist them in their work, the Hungarian minister of religion addressed a communiqué to Roman Catholic bishops in America, stating, among other things, that Hungary was deeply concerned about the loyalty of future Slovak and Ruthenian returnees who were being subjected to "pan-Slavic temptations" in the United States.[172]

Hodobai was boycotted by the Galician priests from the beginning; the Mukachivites soon followed suit, and he was left with the Preshovites, who followed his leadership for only two years.[173] Suspecting his motives, *Viestnik* warned its readers that Hodobai wished to turn the Ruthenian church over "to the old country" and concluded that the church "was in danger."[174] Slovak priests in America, meanwhile, had somehow obtained a copy of the Hungarian memorandum, sent a copy to the United States State Department, and published a pamphlet entitled *Hungary Exposed: Secret State Document Reveals Plotting of That Government in the United States.* The exposé caught the attention of the *Washington Post* and the *New York Times,* which reported on the communiqué in 1903.[175] Commenting on the incident in the *New York Times* on the following day, Joseph Horvath, managing editor of *Szabadsag*, a Hungarian-American newspaper, confirmed Hungarian involvement in Slovak and Ruthenian-American affairs and made it clear that it was nothing new; that it was, after all, simply a matter of maintaining "surveillance and guidance" so that Ruthenians and Slovaks "would not be taught to be disloyal to their native land."[176] The biggest threat in this regard, Horvath concluded, came from the Russian Orthodox church.[177]

Hodobai continued his mission throughout his stay in America, energetically pursuing a course of action that he believed would best serve Hungarian national interests. When the GCU proved recalcitrant, he moved to discredit its leadership. Learning that *Viestnik* editor Pavel Zatkovich had left Hungary soon after being accused of misappropriating public funds, Hodobai tried to have him extradited. The attempt failed, serving no other purpose than to strengthen the editor's resolve against the apostolic visitor. When the Ruthenian community intensified its pressure on Rome to appoint a Greek Catholic bishop, Hodobai supported the movement but slanted his reports in a manner which suggested that only a bishop acceptable to Budapest could stem the growing tide of resentment against Rome. Hoping to abort any such appointment, the GCU insisted that only clerics who were citizens of the United States be eligible for the episcopal post. Hodobai was forced to agree and then proceeded to recommend Father Korotnoki, his assistant who would become eligible for citizenship in 1907, for the coveted position.[178]

Hodobai, apparently, was not the last cleric sent to the United States by the Hungarian government. Late in 1906, *Viestnik* reported that Rev. Andrii Tutkovych, described by the GCU as "one of the biggest renegades, outcasts, and traitors of the poor Uhro-Rusyn people," was coming to the United States.[179] Tutkovych's true purpose in America was revealed early in 1907 when he attempted to create an independent Hungarian Greek Catholic church.[180]

The Appointment of the First Ruthenian-American Bishop

Meanwhile, a conference of Uhro-Rusyn clergy was held in Scranton in 1903,[181] and demands for a separate Ruthenian bishop continued to appear in *Viestnik* throughout 1904.[182] A Greek Catholic congress was convened by the Uhro-Rusyns in Brooklyn in 1905[183] and another was scheduled for 13 March 1906, but was postponed at the request of the apostolic delegate in Washington.[184] It was at this latter conference that the Uhro-Rusyn clergy had planned to select three candidates for the position of bishop and to submit their names to Rome.[185]

Actions supporting an autonomous Ruthenian-American exarchy were also manifested by the Galician clergy, who adopted a decidedly more militant posture regarding Rome's seeming indifference to their plight. In a *Svoboda* article entitled "Skazhim sobi pravdu v ochi" (Let's Be Honest with Ourselves), Fr. Ivan Ardan strongly criticized the policies of the Holy See and the Roman Catholic bishops in America, concluding his censure of their actions with the call: "Proch z Rymom" (Away from Rome).[186] As pastor of the Ruthenian church in Olyphant, Ardan later sent a letter to Bishop Hoban of Scranton informing him that he no longer considered the bishop his ecclesiastic superior, and requesting Hoban to strike his name from the diocesan roster of subordinate priests. Hoban responded by excommunicating Ardan.[187]

Never one to be intimidated by a higher authority he considered to be in error, Ardan pushed for a convention of the recently organized Ruthenian Church Association so that the question of a Ruthenian-Ukrainian national church in America could be settled once and for all. On 26 March 1902, a conclave was held in Harrisburg, Pennsylvania, with nine Galician priests (Ardan, Bonezevsky, Dmytriw, Konstankevych, Makar, Nizhankovskyi, Pidhoretsky, Simialo, Tymkevych) and sixteen lay delegates representing eleven communities in attendance. In addition, a number of telegrams and letters were received from various community leaders praising the initiators of the conference and promising support for all decisions. A total of nine questions were discussed including the most crucial one: "Should we American Ruthenians recognize the Pope of Rome as the head of the Ruthenian Church or not?"[188] After much heated debate, the following conclusion was reached: "Those gathered here consider the matter of breaking with Rome to be absolutely essential for the future good of the Ruthenian Church and people in America. Nevertheless, due to the gravity of such a step, we think it necessary to carefully consider all of the nuances of such an action in an open discussion with the entire community before any further action is taken."[189]

Other resolutions adopted involved:

1 The formal acceptance of the name Ruska Cerkov (in English) for all Ruthenian churches. Names such as "Greek Catholic," "Hungarian Greek Catholic," and "United Greek Catholic" were ruled unacceptable.
2 The guarantee of Ruthenian Catholic church autonomy with complete independence from Roman Catholic bishops and priests.
3 The immediate nullification of all guidelines set down by the Congregation for the Propagation of the Faith which governed the Greek Catholic Church in America.
4 The appointment of a Ruthenian bishop in America who would be:

a elected by Ruthenian priests and representatives of church lay
   councils;
b directly responsible to the pope and not to the Congregation for the
   Propagation of the Faith.[190]

The resolutions passed at the Harrisburg meeting elicited an impassioned
discussion in *Svoboda* in the weeks and months following the conclave[191]
but no further steps were taken to disassociate the Ruthenian-American
church from Rome. The Ruthenian Church Association, however, continued to push for religiocultural autonomy in its publications, the most
significant of which was *Union in America* (issued on 12 October 1902), and
at subsequent conventions of the association.[192]

There is reason to believe that the Holy See had already made a tentative
decision to appoint a Ruthenian bishop by the summer of 1906 when it
requested the apostolic delegate in Washington to gather statistics from
American Catholic bishops indicating the number of Greek Catholics residing in their dioceses. Some bishops, either deliberately or out of ignorance,
provided figures that were somewhat on the low side. The bishop of
Pittsburgh, for example, reported that there were only 15,000 Greek Catholics in his diocese at a time when Hodobai was estimating the count to be
closer to 48,000. Although the latter figure was probably an exaggeration,[193]
it was closer to the real number, which could not have been fewer than
40,000, than to the approximation of the Pittsburg diocese.

In Europe, meanwhile, Count Szecsen, the Austro-Hungarian ambassador to the Holy See, met with Cardinal Gotti, prefect of the Congregation
for the Propagation of the Faith, and, sensing that a decision to appoint a
Greek Catholic bishop in America had already been reached, made one last
appeal to the cardinal to recommend only candidates from the eparchies
of Mukachevo and Preshov for the post. Uhro-Rusyns, the ambassador
correctly argued, outnumbered Galician Ruthenians by a substantial
margin.

Rome made its decision known in the spring of 1907. On 8 March,
Cardinal Gotti notified Reverend Hodobai that his tenure as apostolic
visitor to the Ruthenian rite in America had been terminated and that he
should return to Hungary.[194] On 26 March, Rome appointed Rev. Soter
Ortynsky, a Basilian monk from Galicia, the first bishop for Greek Catholics
in America. Consecrated at St. George's Ukrainian Catholic Church in Lviv,
Bishop Ortynsky arrived in America on 27 August.[195] Before his arrival,
however, the new bishop traveled to Carpatho-Ukraine where he met with
Hodobai and Bishop Valyi, prelate of Preshov, who, among other things,
suggested that Ortynsky consider an annual stipend from the Hungarian
government. Reporting on his conversation later, Valyi indicated that even

though Ortynsky refused the stipend, he had assured Valyi that he would not pursue "the politics of nationalities."[196]

Ortynsky also traveled to Budapest where he met with Prime Minister Albert Apponyi, the initiator of the Magyarization campaign in Carpatho-Ukraine. Upon learning of the visit, *Svoboda* commented on the fear that existed among certain "Hungarian patriots" within the Uhro-Rusyn camp that Ortynsky would interfere with their efforts to maintain the Hungarian orientation within their community.[197] Justified or not, the fear was real and proved to be a major barrier to the bishop's future efforts to unify the Ruthenian community.

From Ea Semper *to* Cum Episcopo

According to Rev. Isidore Sochocky, the Harrisburg convention of Galician priests was a "false step." Those attending, in Sochocky's opinion, "did more harm than good because they used illegal means to obtain their ends."[198] While it is probably true that, as Rev. Leo Sembratovych once pointed out, "to believe that the convention was crucial in the decision-making process which led to the establishment of a separate Ukrainian episcopate or diocese in America is naive thinking,"[199] it is difficult to simply dismiss the convention as a mistake. Given the commitment of the American Circle to ethnonational education and in view of the strength of Uhro-Rusyn and Hungarian competition as well as American Catholic opposition, the Harrisburg convention should be remembered not so much for its influence on Rome, which was probably negligible, but for its impact on the development of ethnic unity among Ruthenian Ukrainians in the United States.

Major credit for Rome's decision to appoint a Galician bishop for the Ruthenians of America belongs, in all probability, to Metropolitan Andrei Sheptytsky (1865–1944), archbishop of Lviv. Definitely a member of the pan-Ukrainian ethnonational school of thought, Sheptytsky lobbied for the appointment of a Greek Catholic bishop in America because he, like others, was convinced that recognition of the unique status of the Ruthenian church in America would effectively stem the tide of Russian Orthodox proselytization. Despite the fact that Uhro-Rusyns outnumbered Ruthenian Ukrainians, he was able to convince Rome that the task could be best accomplished by a bishop from Galicia.[200]

While the appointment of Bishop Ortynsky was initially greeted with great jubilation by most Ruthenian Americans, *Ea Semper*, the papal bull issued on 14 June 1907, defining the new bishop's prerogatives, was not.[201] The decree specified that the right of nomination of a Ruthenian-American bishop belonged to the Apostolic See, and that the bishop was directly responsible to the apostolic delegate in America. Still supporting local Roman Catholic control of the Ruthenian church in America, the bull also specified that: (1) the Ruthenian bishop was required to obtain permission from the local Latin-rite bishop before visiting a Ruthenian parish; (2) a full report of his visit had to be filed with the Latin-rite bishop; (3) Ruthenian priests were now required to obtain permission from both Ortynsky and the Latin-rite bishop in order to transfer to another parish; (4) Latin-rite bishops had the right to assign priests from their own diocese when vacancies in Ruthenian parishes occurred "with the understanding of" Ortynsky insofar as this was possible; (5) Ruthenian priests were denied their ancient privilege of administering the sacrament of confirmation; (6) Latin-rite Catholics still maintained their primary position in mixed marriages; (7) Greek Catholics were still permitted to join a Latin church in those areas where no Ruthenian church existed.

Despite the fact that Ortynsky was a bishop, his authority was hardly different from that of Khanat or Hodobai. The restrictions placed upon Ortynsky as well as other measures tending to place the Greek Catholic church in a secondary position were invaluable ammunition for the Russian Orthodox mission, which continued to maintain that Rome had no intention of fully honoring the agreement reached in Brest in 1596.[202]

Soon after learning of the decree, Bishop Ortynsky filed a formal complaint with Rome demanding the revocation of *Ea Semper* and asking permission to establish a Ruthenian exarchy which enjoyed full episcopal powers. A similar protest, *Rationes Graeco-Catholicorum Ruthenorum Missionarum Americe Septensionsalis Contra Bullam "Ea Semper" de die 14 Juni 1907*, was signed by seventy-three of the total eighty Galician and Uhro-Rusyn priests in America at the time and sent to Rome early in 1908. Rome, however, bided its time.[203]

For his part, Ortynsky ignored the dictates of the decree and proceeded to organize a Greek Catholic exarchy. He called a convention of priests for New York on 15–16 October 1907 and followed it with a similar conference for lay representatives on 17–18 October. Requesting that all churches deed their property to him, Ortynsky obtained title to forty-six parishes by 11 January 1908.[204] Fifty parishes continued to hold out for trustee ownership (some even went to court over the issue) while twenty-four parishes, almost all Mukachevite, remained in the hands of Latin bishops.[205] With reference to the 1890 celibacy decree, Ortynsky elected not to enforce it.

Bishop Ortynsky proved to be a worthy organizational heir to the Wolansky tradition. In 1908, a cathedral and the adjoining block were purchased in Philadelphia and a cemetery was acquired in suburban Fox Chase. Later, a 122-acre plot of ground was purchased in Yorkton, Virginia, for the purpose of erecting a seminary.* Both the cathedral and the cornerstone of the proposed seminary were blessed by Metropolitan Sheptytsky during his visit to the United States in 1910.[206] In 1911, after visiting a number of Ruthenian communities, Ortynsky established an orphanage which, by 1913, had 113 children. The following year, a 300-acre farm in Chesapeake, Maryland, was acquired to serve as a summer camp for the orphans. Talented, dedicated, and a capable administrator, Ortynsky had 206 churches and 159 priests under his jurisdiction by 1914.[207] His accomplishments did not come easily, however. At one time or another, Bishop Ortynsky was opposed by members of the Roman Catholic hierarchy, the Russian Orthodox mission, the GCU, the Uhro-Rusyn priests, and, finally, his strongest early ally, the RNS.

The attitude of the Latin-rite hierarchy varied. Some bishops, such as Hoban of Scranton and Canevin of Pittsburgh, cooperated with Ortynsky, granting him all of the ordinary and extraordinary faculties he required to conduct his work effectively. Other bishops forbade Ortynsky to visit Ruthenian churches not deeded to him, to bless cemeteries and churches not deeded to the church corporation, to purchase real estate of any kind, to take up collections in their dioceses, or to contract debts without their permission. In many cases, only the direct intervention of the apostolic delegate prevented a permanent impasse.[208]

The Russian Orthodox mission, meanwhile, continued its attacks on the Greek Catholic church, accusing Ortynsky of "Polish" sympathies and repeating the idea that Rome's reticence to grant full episcopal powers to Ortynsky was really part of a plot to keep the Ruthenian church subordinate to the Roman Catholic church in America. Significantly, some 90,000 Greek Catholics, primarily Uhro-Rusyns, joined the Russian Orthodox church after *Ea Semper*.[209]

Bishop Ortynsky's most vehement opposition came from the GCU, which by 1909 had grown to 28,000 members.[210] Never enthusiastic about the appointment of a Galician priest as their bishop, the GCU was initially reluctant to criticize the appointment and even expressed thanks that a bishop had been assigned. "Praise God we have our own Ruthenian bishop," declared *Viestnik* in 1907. Reflecting on the kind of bishop he would be, *Viestnik* was hopeful: "Some say he will be a big 'Latinik' and will support Roman Catholic hierarchical interests ... Others say he will make one big Ukrainian province out of our American Rus ... We hope we

---

* No seminary was ever constructed there. Candidates for the priesthood attended St. Mary's Seminary in Baltimore. The building constructed in Yorkton was later used for postgraduate studies in Ukrainian rite and tradition.

will receive an archpastor who will not play politics but will care about the church and the people ... and will work for the preservation of our Holy Greek Catholic Church."[211]

Ortynsky's honeymoon with the GCU was short-lived. Announcing that the bishop planned to change the GCU articles of incorporation so that administrative control of the organization would pass from the laity to the bishop's chancery[212] – a move that Ortynsky could not have legally accomplished without the consent of two-thirds of the delegates attending the next GCU convention – the GCU launched an attack on both his person and his actions. Before the year ended, *Viestnik* accused Ortynsky of being a man of "weak character"[213] and urged all Ruthenian parishes to resist his alleged "Ukrainianization" efforts by refusing the bishop title to their churches – a right which all Roman Catholic bishops enjoyed – and by ignoring the 5 percent exarchical assessment fee which had been levied by the chancery office.[214]

During the next few years, *Viestnik*'s criticism of Bishop Ortynsky became increasingly vitriolic. Unsubstantiated and flimsy evidence was often presented as "proof" of a Ukrainian conspiracy to undermine the Uhro-Rusyn community, while the bishop's every action was interpreted as an example of personal instability. Given Ortynsky's low-key approach to the Uhro-Rusyns, his tolerance of the diatribes of the Magyarized clergy, and the problems he himself was later to experience with a segment of the Ruthenian-Ukrainian camp, it is difficult to conclude that it was Ortynsky's behavior alone that elicited such heated opposition and the subsequent demand for a separate Uhro-Rusyn exarchy. If there was a conspiracy, it was more likely on the side of the Uhro-Rusyn clergy. Hungary, after all, had crushed the Russophile stream in Carpatho-Ukraine, and at the time of the Ruthenian emigration was involved in a Magyarization campaign in the region aimed at eliminating all vestiges of a Ruthenian ethnonational identity. Hungary had also demonstrated an inordinate interest in the development and direction of America's Ruthenian community and was rewarding loyal Uhro-Rusyn priests with financial subsidies. Finally, Hungary had opposed the appointment of a bishop from Galicia and stood to gain from a split in the Ruthenian-American community which an anti-Ukrainian campaign was certain to precipitate. Although the influence of the Hungarian government in the Uhro-Rusyn community tended to decrease in the years that followed, Hungarian intrigues were nonetheless an important factor, at least initially, in the irremediable conflict which developed between the two Ruthenian communities in America.[215]

In 1908, *Viestnik* alleged that Bishop Ortynsky was planning to have twenty-two Uhro-Rusyn priests recalled to Hungary and to replace them with priests from Galicia.[216] Continuing the attack on Ortynsky's personal character, *Viestnik* also questioned the bishop's mental health – citing alleged Galician court records as evidence of his instability[217] – and his "moral fitness" for the position he held.[218] That same year the Uhro-Rusyn clergy issued a communiqué outlining some of the reasons that the appointment of Bishop Ortynsky could not be tolerated. *Viestnik* contended that the conflict began prior to Ortynsky's appointment when, as a result of "different intrigues and hindrances," the Uhro-Rusyn community had not been permitted to hold a congress to nominate three acceptable candidates. For that reason, the communiqué argued, the appointment was not in accordance with the "requirements and needs of the Greek Catholic people." On the contrary, the communiqué concluded, Bishop Ortynsky's appointment had been engineered by Metropolitan Sheptytskyi to meet the needs of certain "Polish aristocrats."[219]

Still portraying Ortynsky as an agent of Ukrainian national interests, *Viestnik* urged its readers to reject the bishop "because we represent 80 percent of the Ruthenian community ... and we don't want a Ukrainian bishop."[220] Ukrainophobia in the Uhro-Rusyn community reached a new pitch in 1909 when *Viestnik* wrote: "The Uhro-Rusyn people have labored for twenty years to strengthen their community ... They gave us Soter Ortynsky for a bishop, a product of the Basilians who is pensive, forgetful, very nervous, given to holding grudges, vengeance oriented, and a fanatic promoter of the cult of Ukrainianism."[221]

Early in 1910, a congress of Uhro-Rusyn parishes was held in Johnstown, Pennsylvania, and an executive committee, headed by GCU president John Uhrin and *Viestnik* editor Pavel Zatkovich, was formed for the purpose of recalling and replacing Bishop Ortynsky. "The Executive Committee of Johnstown," wrote *Viestnik*, "is asking Ruthenians to stand fast with their spiritual leaders, the Church and the people. And if they do, we will have our own Uhro-Rusyn bishop and the victory will be theirs."[222] Concerned with the growing discord between Ortynsky and the Uhro-Rusyns, Metropolitan Sheptytskyi, on a visit to the United States that same year, met with a delegation of Uhro-Rusyn priests on 30 November. After voicing their grievances, the priests presented a petition, signed by forty-six of their clerical colleagues, demanding Ortynsky's recall.[223] *Viestnik*, meanwhile, continued to fan the flames of discord with articles describing Uhro-Rusyn discontent[224] in emotionally charged detail and the many legal battles instituted to prevent transfer of church deeds to the bishop.[225]

On 30 August 1911, another meeting of Uhro-Rusyn priests was held to consider future action against the bishop. Led by Revs. Cornelius Lawryshyn and Gabriel Martyak, the clergy decided to intensify the anti-Ortynsky campaign. Finally losing his patience with the recalcitrant clerics, Ortynsky suspended all forty-four participants.[226]

Relations between Bishop Ortynsky and the Uhro-Rusyn clergy continued to deteriorate until 28 May 1913, when the Holy See granted the bishop "full and ordinary jurisdiction over all Greek Catholics coming from Galicia and Podcarpathia," an action which, in effect, officially created a Greek Catholic exarchy* in America. Forced to acknowledge Ortynsky's substantially enhanced jurisdictional powers, the Uhro-Rusyn clergy were still not prepared to give in totally. Meeting with the bishop, they demanded that all Uhro-Rusyn property be deeded to a newly formed corporation, the so-called Greek Catholic Congregation of Hungarian Rusyns; that only Uhro-Rusyn priests be permitted to serve in Uhro-Rusyn parishes; that Uhro-Rusyn schools be permitted to use their own, non-Ukrainian texts; and that Ortynsky promise to work on behalf of the appointment of a Uhro-Rusyn bishop and, until such time as one was appointed, to accept an Uhro-Rusyn as his vicar-general. The bishop agreed to all of the demands on the condition that they be approved and accepted by the Uhro-Rusyn laity. The following month, a congress of Uhro-Rusyn church representatives was held in Johnstown and, as Ortynsky had hoped, the original demands were modified. On 13 December, Ortynsky received a proposal for the creation of a new church corporation which would effectively unite all Ruthenian churches, both Galician and Uhro-Rusyn, under his jurisdiction. Pleased with the apparent gesture of conciliation demonstrated by the Johnstown congress, Ortynsky agreed to use the influence of his office to obtain a separate Uhro-Rusyn bishop and to permit Uhro-Rusyns to use the etymological alphabet in all of their publications. On 13 December, he appointed Rev. Alexander Dziubaj, an Uhro-Rusyn, as his vicar-general.

On 17 October 1914, an additional decree, *Cum Episcopo Graeco Rutheno*, was promulgated by the Holy See, further enhancing Ortynsky's stature as a bishop. The decree contained provisions that: (1) granted greater powers to Ortynsky to visit parishes, to maintain the purity of the rite, to discipline the clergy, and to perform all the necessary duties of his episcopal office; (2) nullified the more offensive canons of *Ea Semper*, including those which forbid Ruthenian Catholic priests to administer the sacrament of confirmation, permitted changes of rite without permission from the Apostolic See, and accepted mere attendance at Latin-rite churches as a change in rite.

---

* Before 1958, the Ukrainian Catholic church in the United States existed canonically as an "exarchy," i.e., a diocese whose permanent status had not been validated by the Holy See. Today, the Ukrainian Catholic church in the United States is headed by a metropolitan archbishop and three suffragan bishops each of whom heads an eparchy. Together, they constitute an ecclesiastical province.

For Ortynsky, Rome's actions in 1913 and 1914 were a godsend. They placed him on an equal footing with Latin-rite bishops, they were useful in countering Russian Orthodox attacks, and they led to the eventual apology from and reinstatement of the dissident Uhro-Rusyn clergy.[227] Thus, after seven years of turmoil, Bishop Ortynsky was finally able to assume full and unquestioned ecclesiastical authority over a legitimate exarchy composed of Ruthenians from both Galicia and Carpatho-Ukraine. Few people believed, however, that the tranquillity which seemed to prevail in the Ruthenian-American community was a permanent phenomenon.

The Beginnings of Ukrainian-American Protestantism

While the Galician Catholics, Uhro-Rusyn Catholics, and Russian Orthodox were warring with each other over religiocultural control of the Ruthenian community, a fourth group, the Protestants, were quietly and without much fanfare converting Ruthenians to the Baptist and Presbyterian faiths. Their accomplishments, although relatively modest, are still another aspect of the religious response of the Ruthenian American.

The first Ukrainian Protestants to arrive in the United States were Stundists, members of a Baptist sect that settled first in Virginia and later in North Dakota, where their spiritual needs were met by Rev. Oleksa Mykolaiv (1862–1914). A second Baptist community was organized in Scranton by Rev. Ivan Kolesnykiv (1860–1918) in 1904. Later, Baptist congregations were organized in Chicago (1915)[228] and Chester, Pennsylvania (1915). Of the four prewar Baptist congregations, only two, Chicago and Chester, used the Ukrainian language in their services. In North Dakota and Scranton, the language of worship was Russian.[229]

Although Baptist congregations in the United States were organized by religious leaders who were already Baptists when they arrived, this was not the case with the first Ukrainian Presbyterian church. In 1909, in a dispute with Bishop Ortynsky over his refusal to permit Ivan Bodrug to serve as pastor of a Catholic church, eighty-eight members of the Newark, New Jersey, Ukrainian parish left the church and approached the Presbyterian Extension Committee to accept them into the Evangelical church. The request was originally denied but, after two more appeals, the congregation was accepted by the Newark Presbytery on 20 June 1909. During the first few years an unusual relationship developed between the Ukrainians and the presbytery. Under the patient guidance of Rev. Davis W. Lusk, superintendent of the local mission work, who decided "to make no radical changes in their form of worship at once," the first Ukrainian Presbyterian congregation was permitted to worship in its own traditional Ukrainian manner with its own ministers. A sensational account of the unusual Protestant church appeared in a local newspaper and caused a good deal of controversy, especially among Presbyterians. Dr. Lusk, however, defended his action on the ground that a long period of education was necessary before "all the customs and superstitions of the Greek Church" could be eliminated. In a report on his Ukrainian work he later wrote:

> Religious prejudices are strong and deep-seated. The customs of generations are not easily given up. We must make haste slowly, and not too rapidly cut people off from things that have meant everything to them ... I never told them not to cross themselves; I never told them not to bow before the crucifix; I only let in the light and gave them a chance to learn and now everything has fallen into harmonious relation, and these people feel and see and know as we do. It took nearly seven years, but what are seven years for such a result?[230]

In 1911, with the help of the Newark Presbytery, St. Peter and Paul, a Byzantine-style church complete with a three-cornered Byzantine cross, was constructed in Newark. Under the leadership of Rev. Kusiw, a Ukrainian, who served as pastor from 1912 to 1918, the church continued to prosper, retaining its unique Ukrainian flavor. Sunday schools and evening adult classes emphasized the work of Shevchenko, Franko, and Drahomanov as well as the ideas of Luther, Calvin, and Hus. The choir, organized in 1911, performed in both English and Ukrainian.[231]

The first immigrants to the United States from Ukrainian ethnographic territories called themselves Ruthenians and came at a time when America was experiencing a period of industrial expansion and ideological ferment. Mostly illiterate and lacking in marketable skills, they found themselves at the bottom of the socioeconomic ladder, where they were easily exploited by those who stood to gain by their ignorance.

Having established an economic foothold in this country, America's Ruthenians turned to their church, the only institution which, at the time, could give a spiritual significance to their lives and provide them with an ethnic identity. Given the peculiar nature of the Ruthenian church – which was administratively Catholic but culturally Orthodox – its permanent establishment on American soil was no easy task. The Roman Catholic church hierarchy was anxious to Americanize the Ruthenian church while the Russian Orthodox hierarchy was determined to bring it within the

Orthodox fold. The establishment, after many years of turmoil, of a legitimate, autonomous Greek Catholic exarchy in America was a victory of
tremendous significance for those who wished to preserve the unique
religiocultural character of Ukraine's immigrants.

The same ethnocultural heritage, however, did not inevitably lead to the
same ethnonational loyalties. As in Europe, different learning experiences
and outside influences resulted in divergent national sentiments. Thus,
while all Ukraine's early émigrés called themselves Ruthenians, their experience in the United States provided them with a new ethnic identity. A
few became Hungarians, Poles, or Slovaks. The vast majority, however,
eventually became members of one of three ethnonational communities:
Ukrainian, Carpatho-Ruthenian, or Russian. It is to this latter historical
phenomenon that we now turn our attention.

3 The Making of the Ukrainian American

The development of an ethnonational identity is essentially a process of education and socialization. Different historic experiences, combined with divergent interpretations of those experiences by various socializing institutions, result in different perceptions of significant events, produce different responses to these events, and have different effects on the identity of the group. The role of nationally oriented institutions is to serve as a kind of consistent "filter," first for the creation and later for the maintenance of certain ethnonational sentiments and symbols within a context of group uniformity. As the institutional credibility of nationalizing agencies increases, a sense of group solidarity is enhanced. In time, the group comes to exhibit certain uniquely national characteristics which are then reinforced by the very same national institutions that helped create them.

While almost all Ruthenians in the United States shared the same religio-cultural heritage, their ethnonational development was influenced by different national streams. A few Ruthenians became "Hungarians" in America. Others became "Slovaks"[1] or "Poles." Most became "Ukrainians," "Carpatho-Ruthenians," or "Russians."

The purpose of this chapter is to identify those institutions in the latter three groups that played a major role in the nationalization of Ruthenian Americans and to assess their impact on Ruthenian group solidarity. Because this is a study of the making of the *Ukrainian* American, more attention will be devoted to the Ukrainian orientation than to the Carpatho-Ruthenian or the Russian. The latter two will be examined largely from the perspective of their reaction to and interaction with the Ukrainian ethnonational stream.

In addition to the Greek Catholic and Russian Orthodox churches in the United States, four fraternal insurance societies were in the forefront of the battle for the ethnonational loyalty of Ruthenian Americans. In what was to become the Ukrainian camp, it was the Ruskyi narodnyi soiuz (hereafter referred to by its current name, the Ukrainian National Association or UNA). Within what was to become the Carpatho-Ruthenian stream, it was the Greek Catholic Union or GCU. In the Russian camp, there were two fraternal groups that played a significant role: The Russkoe pravoslavnoe obshchestvo vzaimopomoshchi (The Russian Orthodox Mutual Aid Society or POV) and the Obshchestvo russkikh bratstv (now called the Russian Brotherhood Organization or RBO). The major focus of this chapter will be on the programs, activities, and community impact of these four organizations.

From Ruthenian to Ukrainian

The making of the Ukrainian in America, that is, the metamorphosis of the immigrant from Ukrainian lands from a Ruthenian religiocultural identity to a Ukrainian ethnonational identity, took place during a span of some thirty years. Name changes of the Ukrainian National Association between 1894 and 1915 reflect the chronology of this transformation. The original English name of the UNA was the Russian National Union, and Father Hrushka, the first editor of *Svoboda*, the UNA organ, advised all of his readers not to be ashamed to say "I ie ruskyi," which he translated as "I am Russian."[2] For the first six years of its existence, *Svoboda* advertised itself as a "Russian" newspaper. In 1899, it became a "Little Russian" publication.[3] In 1904, it was billed as "Ruthenian (Little Russian),"[4] remaining so until 1906 when it began to identify itself simply as "Ruthenian."[5] The UNA, meanwhile, officially changed its name to Little Russian Union in 1900.[6] It was not until the thirteenth UNA convention in 1914 that the name was officially changed to Ukrainskyi narodnyi soiuz in Ukrainian and the Ukrainian National Association in English.[7]

The Origins of the Ukrainian National Association

Following the demise of the Brotherhood of St. Nicholas, established by Father Wolansky in 1885, Ruthenian membership in other benevolent societies increased. Especially popular was Jednota (Unity), a Slovak fraternal society. Concerned lest their people adopt a Slovak ethnic orientation, a group of Ruthenian priests gathered at Wilkes-Barre in February 1892 and gave birth to the Greek Catholic Union (GCU). The GCU organ, the *Amerikansky Russky Viestnik*, made its debut that same year. Differences between Greek Catholic priests from Carpatho-Ukraine (Subcarpathia) and Galicia concerning the ethnic orientation of the GCU emerged at the 1893 GCU convention. Four priests from Galicia, Revs. Konstankevych, Obush-kevych, Poliansky, and Hrushka, met in Jersey City to discuss the formation of another Ruthenian fraternal group and to promulgate the idea in *Svo-boda*, a Ruthenian periodical founded by Father Hrushka on 15 September 1893.[8] On 1 November 1893, an article entitled "We Need a National Organization" appeared in *Svoboda*:

> Just as the fish needs water, as the bird must have wings, as the thirsty need to drink and the hungry need bread, just as every one of us needs air, so do we Ruthenians scattered across this land need a national union that will embrace each and every Ruthenian no matter where he lives ...
>
> It is clear then that in unity there is strength, and it is not easily defeated. Therefore, let us unite brothers, voluntary exiles from our native land, our fatherland, let us come closer together and get to know each other better, and take a closer look at our poverty, our want, our shortcomings, our needs ...
>
> Nowadays, it is only with extreme difficulty that we manage to build a Ruthenian church here and there, and we really must beg for the money. Wouldn't it be better if we had our own national fund and helped those churches? A new Ruthenian generation is rapidly growing up here in America, but who is to provide a good future for the youth? What will happen if this youth grows up without knowledge of the Ruthenian language, history, and religion? ...
>
> Come what may, we are bravely calling on the people: Have faith in our idea! ... Wake up and see who is your brother and who wishes you well. You have eyes, look at what is happening around you, how you are being abused and ignored, and how only your work, bathed in sweat and blood, is appreciated by those who care solely for their own pockets. They get rich on your ignorance, stupidity, and helplessness while you, poor man, rot deep in the mine, or like an ox, pull trucks in the factory, slaving for everybody but yourself: for the lawyers, for the Jews, and for the debts that you left behind in the old country. But when you become ill and die in pain, your friends must beg for money among your own people so that your sinful body is not thrown to the dogs but buried in a Christian way with a cross on your grave humbly awaiting the day of resurrection ...
>
> If your fellow Ruthenians fail to respond to our call and if they neglect this important and burning matter, they will have given a sad account of their spiritual maturity and determination. But we do not believe that ... Our people will raise their mighty voice

and Ruthenians everywhere will say: We need the Ruskyi narodnyi soiuz, we must get to know each other better, we must unite,
we must work together to improve our lot in this new land.[9]

A constituent assembly of the proposed new organization was held early
the following year. In a subsequent article entitled "It Has Come to Be,"
Svoboda wrote: "On February 22 1894, on the day when all America cele-
brates the birthday anniversary of the great Washington, fearless fighter for
liberty and the rights of man, Ruthenian priests, delegates of the Ruthenian
brotherhoods, and Ruthenian patriots from many areas assembled at 9:00
a.m. in the Ruthenian Church in Shamokin, Pennsylvania, to ask God's
help in launching this all-important project—the founding of the Ruskyi
narodnyi soiuz."[10]

The first executive included Theodosius Talpash of Shamokin, president;
Michael Yevchak of Wilkes-Barre, vice-president; Rev. Ivan Konstanke-
vych, secretary; and Ivan Glova of Excelsior, Pennsylvania, treasurer. In
addition, ten advisers, all laymen, were elected, as well as four auditors,
all of whom were clergymen.[11] Significantly, the latter included Rev. Alexis
Toth, who was already associated with the Russian Orthodox mission;
Father Gregory Hrushka, who was to adopt Orthodoxy in 1896; Father
Havrylo Gulovich, who was to join the Uhro-Rusyn camp; and Father
Teofan Obushkevych, a Russophile.

In 1894, the UNA had 439 members and assets of $220.35. By 1912, there
were 14,917 UNA members and the organization could boast of assets of
$140,530.64.[12] The GCU, in contrast, had approximately 32,000 members
and some $400,000 in assets in 1912.[13]

The American Circle

With Uhro-Rusyn priests outnumbering Galician priests in 1894 by a margin of almost eight to one, the future of a separate Ruthenian-Ukrainian
fraternal society was hardly auspicious. The arrival in the mid 1890s of the
so-called American Circle, a group of ethnonational enlightened Galician
priests, changed the odds, however. From that moment on, the fortunes
and the future of the Ruthenian-Ukrainian stream improved dramatically.

The circle was established in 1890 by seven Lviv seminarians, all close
personal friends, who vowed to (1) take up their pastoral duties in the
United States; (2) remain celibate in order to be free of family obligations
and to avoid friction with the Irish-American Roman Catholic hierarchy;
and (3) organize the Ruthenian community in America along Ukrainian
ethnonational lines.[14] Politically active in Galicia, circle members were

sympathetic to the ideals of the Ukrainian Radical party, a socialist group that included, among others, the venerable Ukrainian poet Ivan Franko.[15]

The first member of the American Circle to leave Galicia was Fr. Nestor Dmytriw who arrived in the United States in 1895 and settled in Mount Carmel, Pennsylvania, where he became pastor of Sts. Peter and Paul Church. That same year another member of the circle arrived: Fr. Mykola Stefanovych who, after a few months in Buffalo, became pastor of St. John the Baptist Church in Pittsburgh. Fr. Ivan Ardan arrived in 1896 and eventually settled in Jersey City. In 1898, three more circle members made their appearance – Fr. Antin Bonezevsky, who took up his duties at Sts. Peter and Paul Church in Ansonia, Connecticut; Fr. Stefan Makar, who took Father Dmytriw's place in Mount Carmel while the latter visited Ukrainian communities in Canada; and Fr. Mykola Pidhoretsky, who took Father Ardan's place in Jersey City when the latter went to Olyphant. The last member of the circle to immigrate to America was Fr. Pavlo Tymkevych, who came in 1898 and settled, after a time, in Yonkers, New York, where he was pastor of St. Michael the Archangel Church. The circle was later enlarged when Fr. Ivan Konstankevych, who had been in the United States since 1893, joined the group.[16]

If a single group of individuals can be credited with the making of the Ukrainian in the United States, it is the American Circle. Composed of unusually competent, highly motivated, and militant individuals, it was the American Circle that led the Ruthenian-Ukrainian fight against Latinization, Russification, and Magyarization. American Circle members were in the forefront of the struggle to establish an autonomous Ruthenian exarchy in the United States. They helped establish the Ukrainian National Association, took over its leadership, and moved that organization away from its initial Russophile orientation. Under American Circle leadership, the UNA became involved in the establishment of Ukrainian reading rooms, enlightenment societies, cultural enterprises, youth organizations, and ethnic heritage schools. Most significantly, members of the American Circle edited *Svoboda* for a period of twelve years (1895–1907), establishing the UNA gazette as the primary vehicle of Americanization, Ukrainianization, and political action in the Ukrainian ethnonational camp.

Svoboda *as a Vehicle of Americanization*

"My people," Father Tymkevych once told an American writer, "do not live in America; they live underneath her ... What my people need most is leaders, leaders to form themselves upon, leaders to give them a standard of ambition."[17] Both the leadership and the standard were provided by

Svoboda, especially during that period when Fr. Nestor Dmytriw (1895), Fr. Stefan Makar (1897–1900), and Fr. Ivan Ardan (1900–7) were editors.

Almost from its inception, *Svoboda* was aware of the dearth of intellectual leadership in the Ruthenian-American community and the fact that the only educated Ruthenians were priests. In an 1894 article entitled "The Future of the Ruthenians in America," *Svoboda* commented: "The future of the Ruthenian people in America and their national existence depends upon the priests ... Uhro-Rusyn priests are interested only in making money and in returning to the old country ... There are only four priests from Galicia and they are working as hard as they can ... If there were at least 10 such priests, the future of the Ruthenian immigration would be far brighter."[18]

A major community problem that had to be solved was adult illiteracy, a handicap that *Svoboda* addressed early in its existence. In reply to the question "Can an Older Person Learn to Read?" *Svoboda* responded with an emphatic "yes" and stated: "Of all places, a man here in America without the ability to read cannot advance ... Instead of playing billiards in saloons, buy yourself a Ruthenian alphabet book from *Svoboda* and find someone to teach you the letters ... Within a month you'll do it yourself ... Let's go, Ruthenians, try it."[19]

Subsequently, *Svoboda,* in cooperation with the UNA, published a *Self-Teacher and Dictionary for American Ruthenians*[20] and in 1900 began to print a Ruthenian-English dictionary and fact sheet in its pages.[21]

Initially, *Svoboda* projected an optimistic view regarding life in the United States. Describing America as a land where "everyone has the freedom to learn and to write and to become enlightened through books,"[22] *Svoboda* was critical of the apathetic attitude of some Ruthenian Americans. "Let's remember that in America the motto is 'Pomahai sobi sam' – Help Yourself," *Svoboda* declared on a number of occasions.[23] Pointing to Ruthenian indifference as the main cause of their backwardness in the United States,[24] *Svoboda* would often appeal to Ruthenian pride: "Negroes have 7 colleges, 17 academies and 50 high schools in America. And what do Ruthenians have? Seven layers of lazy skin."[25]

Comparing Ruthenians to Slovaks in America, *Svoboda* declared: "Hey Brother Ruthenians! Our brother Slovaks already have a national home, schools, a hospital and a printing press ... and we don't even have enough to send a student for a higher education ... whose people are we?"[26]

Drunkenness, a common problem among Ruthenian coal-miners, was also condemned: "Some may ask, 'Is *Svoboda* forbidding us to drink or what?' Hold on! We don't say that a man not drink for his health, for his own money; but to get drunk and lie on the road like a pig in the mud, against that we take our stand."[27]

"Don't waste money,"[28] *Svoboda* urged the Ruthenian worker, "read, read and read ... it is very important."[29] "Some people say that if Ruthenians had their liberty," wrote *Svoboda*, "how nice life would be ... we take the opposite view ... Our people don't need liberty. First they must have enlightenment and schooling."[30] Ruthenians "need schools."[31]

Critical of Ruthenian reluctance to become active in American life, *Svoboda* declared that "American life and the life of the American Ruthenian are two separate worlds ... It is clear that we are Americans because we live on American soil, we eat American bread ... We are Americans for the purpose of sending that dollar to the old country ... We are Americans also in order to buy a keg of beer and a quart of whiskey for that dollar."[32]

"Let's Americanize" through self-improvement, urged the UNA gazette. "Let's be critical of that which is bad in America but by all means let's take advantage of that which is good."[33]

Tensions resulting from generational differences were also considered by the UNA organ. In the U.S. milieu, *Svoboda* advised, the admonition "it must be so because I command it" was an improper educational technique to use with American-born children, who had come to expect a more reasoned approach from their authority figures.[34] But *Svoboda* was also aware of the other extreme, the son or daughter who justified disobedience on the basis of "American freedom." Rev. Stefan Makar wrote a two-part article entitled "American Boy," which condemned a young man who informed his parents that he was aware of the rights guaranteed by the American constitution, that "this is not the old country," and that he was now of age, he was no longer obligated to pay heed to parental advice. Such boys, concluded Father Makar, more often than not begin to associate with bad company and many "end up in jail."[35] In an effort to reach the younger element in the Ukrainian population, especially those in the elementary grades, *Svoboda* inaugurated a series of children's stories in the English language that appeared regularly beginning 22 August 1900.[36]

Finally, there was the problem of family desertion, an issue *Svoboda* once addressed as follows:

> A trial was held involving Vanko Koralia, accused of polygamy. Vanko left his wife in Galicia, came to America and got married in Jersey City a second time and later, in ... Michigan, a third time. He was arrested because Wife #2 accidentally discovered the existence of Wife #3 ...
>
> Later, after serving his sentence, Vanko returned to his fatherland, found his house, his fields, his trees, his Mary, and his children, which, unfortunately, instead of two, now numbered four.[37]

Svoboda as a Vehicle of Ukrainianization

"The revival of national consciousness in the subject peoples," wrote Robert E. Park, "has invariably been connected with the struggle to maintain a press in the native language."[38] Although *Svoboda* cared about the social problems of the Ruthenian immigrant, it was equally, if not more, concerned with the development of a unique sense of ethnonational consciousness based on a clearly defined platform of ethnic unity. The "Ten National Commandments," published in *Svoboda* on 20 April 1894, illustrate the spirit of the UNA and its official organ:

> I am *Svoboda* that wishes to lead Ruthenian Americans out of the darkness of ignorance and spiritual slavery.
> 1 You will not read any newspapers printed in Ruthenian but devoid of the Ruthenian spirit.
> 2 Do not call yourself Ruthenian if you are indifferent to the Ruthenian cause in America.
> 3 Do not forget to become a member of the Ruskyi narodnyi soiuz and belong to a reading club and make sure that you subscribe to *Svoboda*.
> 4 Honor, respect, and support sincere Ruthenians and you will lead a long and happy life in America.
> 5 Do not kill your body and spirit by leading a life of drunkenness and debauchery.
> 6 Do not engage in friendly relations with the Magyarophile clique, hostile to the Ruthenian cause.
> 7 Do not seek to obtain *Svoboda* free of charge. First pay for it, then read it.
> 8 Do not testify falsely against the Ruskyi narodnyi soiuz or *Svoboda* but make sure you know where the truth lies.
> 9 Do not seek to become a traveling agent of *Viestnik* or you will suffer for it.
> 10 Do not seek the purse of the haughty Magyarophiles because it is empty; the people are wise and do not throw away "quarters"; neither seek their bigotry nor their fox-like shrewdness – they belong to them.[39]

Ruthenian leaders who adopted other national cultures or who were not contributing what *Svoboda* felt they could were rebuked by the UNA periodical. Lamenting the fact that throughout Ruthenian history there were those who "betrayed their people" and spent their entire lives working "against the interests of their people," *Svoboda* complained: "Within recent times, our spiritual leaders seem to be following the same path ... Among our priests, unfortunately, there are Hungarian poets, Hungarian writers and journalists. Hungarian literature does not need their service because it is rich without it ... Our peasants will not develop a command of our literary language when our lay leaders and even our priests are abandoning it."[40]

According to the UNA periodical, the priest in the community had a dual responsibility. "The Ruthenian priest," declared *Svoboda* in 1895, "not only has a spiritual role to fulfill, he must also be active in the arena of the national revival."[41]

But priests were not the only ones who had a national obligation to fulfill. Others who were blessed with an education were also expected to contribute. When it was discovered that Dr. Volodymyr Simenovych, the Shenandoah pioneer, was living in Chicago and associating with Polish intellectuals, *Svoboda* commented:

> One must know that in Chicago the Poles have great strength ... so it is not surprising to find in the Polish dailies the name of Dr. Simenovych. Fate has decreed that he should find himself among the Polish community and being an energetic, intelligent and responsive individual, he did not refuse to aid those with whom he lives ... It is self-understood that Dr. Simenovych did not cease being a sincere Ruthenian and is still interested in Ruthenian matters. He is the author of many interesting articles in Galician-Rus' publications, especially *Dilo* concerning the life of Ruthenians in America ... We only wish to add this ... without detracting in any way from his wonderful work ... it would be heart-warming if Dr. Simenovych would just send us his valuable talks and we would gladly publish them in *Svoboda*.[42]

Three weeks later, an article by Dr. Simenovych entitled "Education Concerning Health" appeared in *Svoboda*.[43]

In the early years, before the conflict between the Russian Orthodox church and the Ukrainian Catholic church developed into an ethnic rather than a religious issue, the editor of *Svoboda* urged tolerance between Catholics and Orthodox: "Dear brothers, don't argue among yourselves over who is Uniate and who is Orthodox. One mother, Rus', gave birth to both of you, and you were both baptized in the same Ruthenian Church."[44]

The call for ethnonational unity was echoed again in a plea to all "patriotic Ruthenians" to leave Jednota and to join the UNA: "In Slovak newspapers we have discovered that many Ruthenians in Pennsylvania belong to the Catholic Jednota. We call attention to all patriotic Ruthenians to find these lost people and ask them to join Soiuz."[45] A week later, in an article entitled "A Lack of Patriotism," *Svoboda* commented that it was "very sad" to find Ruthenians in Jednota because "it shows that such a Ruthenian has lost his national consciousness."[46]

In the eyes of *Svoboda*, a similar denationalizing threat was posed by the GCU, so much so that when a Ruthenian left that organization and joined the UNA, his name was glorified. "Mr. Olexa Shlianta, a Ruthenian patriot from Mayfield," wrote *Svoboda* in 1894, "left the Soedinenie [GCU] and joined the Soiuz [UNA]. Honor and Glory to him."[47] Attacking *Viestnik* for "barking against any and all,"[48] *Svoboda* described the GCU as a "rotten log," an organization of eight thousand members who, "even though they speak Ruthenian and Slovak, are all good Hungarian patriots."[49] *Svoboda* mocked the "Greek Catholic" appellation of the Uhro-Rusyn society and stated: "We don't say only 'Greek Romans' or 'Roman Greeks' can belong to Soiuz, but all Ruthenian people, from both sides of the Carpathians."[50]

As for the nature of the Ruthenian identity, by the onset of the twentieth century *Svoboda* had become unequivocal: "We are not Poles, nor Muscovites, nor Hungarians, but Ruthenians, a part of the 30 million strong Ruthenian-Ukrainian nation."[51] The same national approach was reflected in *Svoboda*'s appeals to the Bukovinians[52] and to the Carpatho-Ruthenians: "Hey, fellow Carpatho-Ruthenians! Awake from your sleep both here and in Carpatho-Rus'. Let's join hands in a sincere effort for the good of our people and our common struggle for our national and civil rights. If we do this, no force can beat us – not the Hungarians, not the Russians, not the Poles, not anyone."[53]

Our "national question," declared the UNA gazette in 1906, "will not be solved in Galicia, but in Rus'."[54] First, however, "unity must be achieved here, in America, the land of the free."[55]

In developing the Ukrainian consciousness of Ruthenian immigrants and urging them to accept the Ukrainian nomenclature as part of their ethnonational identity, *Svoboda*'s approach was, of necessity, one of caution. The terms "Ukraine" and "Ukrainian" were introduced unobtrusively, almost casually, to the Ruthenian community.

Svoboda's first reference to Ukraine occurred as early as 1893,[56] and almost a year later the reader was informed that "Sche ne vmerla Ukraina" ("Ukraine Has Not Died") was sung for the first time on American soil at the UNA convention in 1894.[57] The term "Rus'-Ukraine" was used repeatedly and with increasing frequency in the years that followed. The concept was fully examined in 1902 in a series of articles by Fr. Mykola Strutynsky entitled "Understand, Ruthenian, Which Road Is Yours":

Most people in the old country belong to the so-called Ukrainian-

Rus' party. Almost all of the young priests, the majority of the older priests, almost all lawyers, professors, doctors, and students, in short, all the intelligentsia and the enlightened masses call themselves Rus'-Ukrainians ... They call themselves this name because they realize that even though they are in Galicia, their ancestors came from Ukraine ... Galicia, our country, is the child of Ukraine. Just as we came to America, the Ruthenian-Ukrainians came to Galicia.[58]

Calling attention to the upcoming 1910 census, *Svoboda* urged its readers to indicate that they spoke the "Ruthenian language" so that "we Ruthenians will not be counted as Poles, Muscovites, or Hungarians."[59] In response to the article, a *Svoboda* correspondent urged his fellow Ruthenians to identify themselves as "Ruthenians, not Russians or Little Russians."[60] "There are no 'Russians' in Subcarpathia or Galicia," proclaimed *Svoboda*, "only Ruthenians."[61] Despite a decided trend toward the acceptance of the Ukrainian ethnic appellation, however, at no time prior to 1914 did *Svoboda* appear to force the use of the nomenclature upon its readers. Those who preferred to call themselves Ruthenians continued to do so, while others, more and more each year, adopted the more nationalistic identity. An example of the *Svoboda* approach can be ascertained from an examination of various issues in which, as late as 1912, ads announcing planned local events employed either "Attention Ruthenians" or "Attention Ukrainians" as headlines to catch the eye of the reader.[62]

National symbol-building was another significant component of *Svoboda*'s Ukrainianization campaign. One such symbol was Taras Shevchenko, Ukraine's national bard who, in 1895, on the thirty-third anniversary of his death, was introduced to the Ruthenian-Ukrainian community as follows: "It is true that few of our people here know about Taras Shevchenko and the kind of glory he earned for himself." After describing Shevchenko's monumental efforts on behalf of the Ukrainian national revival, *Svoboda* exclaimed: "We will follow in the footsteps of Taras ... we have established a newspaper which will serve the national politics of all of Austrian Rus' and, in fact, all of Rus'-Ukraine. We are for that and we will support it in memory of Shevchenko."

Father Hrushka, the editor, concluded the article with an original poem:

Spiritually, Taras
    We are at your grave.
and for you we pray to God
    Grateful for that strength
Which we find in our words.

> The dead will be resurrected
> On the ruins of Ukraine
> For liberty we will fight.[63]

The full acceptance of the phonetic alphabet was still another aspect of the ethnonational educational process. In an 1897 *Svoboda* article entitled "What Shall We Keep?" we read: "People! Do not be afraid of the phonetics but read any book, no matter how it is written ... It is good if someone knows Ruthenian but if he doesn't, let him not be ashamed to write phonetically using Ruthenian letters because if he writes in Polish letters, he will be Polonized and soon forget Ruthenian."[64]

As time went on, articles written in phonetic Ukrainian became increasingly frequent. In the beginning, they were usually introduced by an editorial comment to the effect that "people in Rus'-Ukraine are beginning to write this way now."[65] In reply to *Viestnik*'s criticism of *Svoboda* for using the phonetic alphabet, *Svoboda* defended itself on the grounds that while it was still utilizing the Ruthenian alphabet, *Viestnik* had adopted "Latin letters and the Slovak language."[66]* The use of the phonetic alphabet for all UNA publications was formally sanctioned by delegates attending the 1906 UNA convention.[67]

Another important contribution of *Svoboda* to the development of a distinct Ukrainian identity among Ruthenian Americans was its publication of yearly "kalendars" or almanacs issued in cooperation with the Ukrainian National Association. A total of fifteen such kalendars (1897 and 1901 through 1914) were published before the war, averaging 225 pages in length. Each kalendar contained historical articles on Ukraine and the Ruthenian-American community, poems and other literary pieces by such well-known Ukrainian writers as Taras Shevchenko and Ivan Franko, articles on the development of the Ukrainian church and the Ukrainian language, facts concerning life in America (laws, population statistics, educational opportunities), translations of foreign and American stories, creative works by Ukrainian-American writers, and the usual monthly calendars listing holy days, saints' days, and other ethnoculturally significant historic events.[68] Of special interest were the many exhortative articles urging Ruthenians to preserve their heritage in the United States. In 1911, for example, an article entitled "Let's Respect Our Native Language" stated:

> In Galicia, it is enough for any common bum to speak to our man

---

* In reality, *Viestnik* was published in both Cyrillic and Latin editions for many years. Latin letters were not used exclusively by *Viestnik* until the 1930s.

in a foreign language and already our Ruthenian is reversing his course; already he has forgotten his national pride which demands that he, always and everywhere, speak his native language; he has forgotten that he is the host in his native land and that all others are guests who should use his language and not he theirs. And here on foreign soil? Barely had the Ruthenian grasped 20 words, barely has he learned to pronounce them ... and already, when he meets another Ruthenian, he speaks English, ashamed to speak his native language ...

We should not miss one opportunity, be it in church, in school, at a meeting, or in private life, to remind ourselves that it is our national obligation to respect and to gain literary command of our native language and only then to begin to learn another language ...

Don't forget that people all over the world are beginning to talk about the Ruthenian people — they are beginning to realize that the Ruthenian people have not died, that they have not disappeared as the Poles were saying a little while back and as the tsarist regime is saying now. Let's show that we are truly proud of our glorious past, that we no longer want to trample on our language by using words of another, that we are sincerely proud of our glorious name ...

Ruthenian people! If you want to be free, strong, and powerful, if you desire to become masters in your native land, then add to God's Ten Commandments an eleventh and teach it to your children: *Remember your native language and respect it always!*[69]

By the end of 1914, after the term "Ukrainian" became the official ethnic designation of the UNA, *Svoboda*'s parent organization,[70] the newspaper did indeed promulgate eleven national commandments:

1 The Ukrainian child should associate exclusively with Ukrainian children and speak only in Ukrainian when in their company.
2 Parents or older members of the family should teach children to read and write Ukrainian during the child's preschool years.
3 Homes should be beautified with Ukrainian religious and historical paintings and pictures.
4 The Ukrainian child should learn Ukrainian sayings, as well as Ukrainian verses, songs, and games.
5 Let Ukrainian tradition live in the Ukrainian family. The father or older members of the family should always remember the important national dates from our history.

6 The family should read Ukrainian books in unison during the long winter evenings.

7 Every Ukrainian home should have *Svoboda*, the truly Ukrainian national newspaper.

8 The treasure of each family should be its library containing the best Ukrainian books.

9 The Ukrainian family should take advantage of every opportunity to attend a Ukrainian play, concert, or a commemoration of a national holiday.

10 Every father, mother, and older member of the family should belong to the Ukrainian National Association and they should enroll their children in the juvenile division. They should never refuse to contribute to worthwhile public and national causes.

11 Every family should try to bring back those members who have fallen away from Ukrainian traditions.[71]

Although the role of *Svoboda* in the making of Ukrainian Americans was certainly significant, Ruthenians did not become Ukrainians in America simply by reading *Svoboda*. To be maintained, ethnic identities need to be constantly reinforced and nurtured through active communion with individuals of similar conviction. To be preserved, an ethnic identity in America requires successful transmission to the next generation. These roles were assumed by other agencies within the Ukrainian community, most of which worked in concert with the UNA and *Svoboda*.

The Significance of Reading Rooms

An important contribution to the development of Ukrainian consciousness in America was made by the so-called *chytalni* or reading rooms organized by priests, local UNA chapters, and other organizations endeavoring to expand the intellectual and cultural horizons of the educationally disadvantaged Ruthenian immigrant. The task of establishing such reading rooms was not an easy one. Little in the European experience of the early Ruthenian immigrant left him with a burning desire for self-improvement, while much of his American experience was such that his natural inclination in pursuing leisure-time activities was toward pleasures that left him little time to think. Ethnic group progress, however, was dependent upon the enlightenment of the peasant turned laborer and it was upon him that the national work of the American Circle and others was concentrated.

The first phase of the reading-room movement was initiated in 1887 with the establishment of a reading room in Shenandoah by Volodymyr Simenovych. By the end of 1888, reading rooms were in existence in

Olyphant, Plymouth, and Hazleton, largely as the result of financial support from the Cooperative General Store. With the demise of this first Ruthenian-American co-op, the movement came to a temporary halt.

The second phase of the reading-room movement was initiated in 1894 when *Svoboda* began to push for establishment of such rooms by every UNA chapter. That same year rooms were organized in Shamokin, Mount Carmel, Jersey City, Mayfield, and Minneapolis. By 1907, they existed in Ansonia, Shenandoah,[72] Carnegie, Pittsburgh, Philadelphia, New York City, Baltimore, and Balfour, North Dakota.[73] Reading rooms were later established in Wilkes-Barre, Ramey, Monessen, McKeesport, and McKees Rocks in Pennsylvania; in Newark, New Jersey; in Holyoke, Massachusetts; and in San Francisco, California.[74]

Most reading rooms were located either in a church hall or in the home of one of the dues-paying members and most followed a regular program during meetings held, as a general rule, on Sunday. The common procedure was to have some literate member read a passage from either a book or a newspaper, usually *Svoboda*, and then to lead the discussion that followed. Following this introductory exercise, literate members settled in one corner of the room with reading materials while those who were still unable to read were given instruction in the Ukrainian language. Because most early immigrants planned to return to Ukraine, it was not difficult to convince those who had a desire to read to learn Ukrainian before they learned English. Later, as more and more of the arriving immigrants came with a reading knowledge of Ukrainian, English-language courses were introduced in cooperation with local American boards of education. With literacy on the rise, the reading room was soon functioning as a lending library.[75] Through the years, many such self-education enterprises were able to build substantial collections. As early as 1907, for example, the Carnegie reading room boasted a total of 419 volumes and eleven periodicals.[76]

The Role of Enlightenment Societies

In 1896, *Svoboda* began to call for the formation of an enlightenment association patterned after the highly effective Prosvita (Enlightenment) society in Ukraine. The issue was raised again by Fr. Stefan Makar in *Svoboda* in 1898 and an attempt was made by Father Bonezevsky to gain popular support for such an endeavor in the years that followed. Father Bonezevsky continued to crusade on behalf of an enlightenment society until his untimely death in 1903.

Father Bonezevsky's pioneering efforts were recognized in 1904 when three other members of the American Circle, Revs. Ardan, Dmytriw, and

Makar, established "The Bonezevsky Press, *Slovo*" using $500 Fr. Bonezev-sky left in his will for that purpose. Like Prosvita, the newly formed organization published monthly booklets on a variety of ethnonational and scientific themes, but the lack of a ready market forced its dissolution in 1906. Father Ardan, however, at his own expense and with some financial risk, was able to keep the operation alive until 1907 under a new name, "The Bonezevsky Press, Reading Room." Between 1896 and 1907, the American Circle led the way in the publication of fifty-five booklets published by *Svoboda* (30), *Slovo* (16), and "Reading Room" (9).

The next attempt to establish a permanent Prosvita in the United States was made in Philadelphia at the "Enlightenment Conference" called by Bishop Ortynsky in 1909.[77] Under Ortynsky's direction, the project had an auspicious beginning. Adopting the same name as its European counter-part, the American Prosvita promulgated the following aims: (1) to establish reading rooms in every Ruthenian community; (2) to organize a course for illiterates in every reading room; (3) to establish a Ruthenian school in every parish; (4) to organize a Ruthenian teachers' seminary; (5) to implement an ethnic education course for Ruthenian-American high-school students; (6) to build a theological seminary.[78] Unfortunately, these goals were never achieved. Despite strong financial support from the bishop and an impres-sive headquarters housed in a $6,000 building donated by Ortynsky, the tripartite division which was to split the Ruthenian-Ukrainian community in 1910 proved to be too much for the fledgling society. Within a few years it was no longer in existence.[79] The goals, however, remained, to be partially achieved by other organizations at another time.

The third attempt to establish a viable nationwide enlightenment society was made by the Ukrainian National Association. At the 1912 Wilkes-Barre convention, the UNA gave birth to the so-called Enlightenment Committee and charged it with the task of providing for the educational needs of the Ruthenian-Ukrainian immigrant. Selected to lead the UNA Prosvita were Dr. Volodymyr Simenovych, president; Mrs. Emily Strutynsky, secretary; and Dmytro Andreiko, Rev. M. Balogh, A. Horbal, Iuliian Pavchak, Dr. I. Kopystianskyi, and Mrs. Olena Kysilevskyi, members. With a convention-approved educational fund which assessed every member three cents a month, the UNA Prosvita enjoyed a sound financial base from its inception. Within three years, the committee had (1) sent three representatives to all sections of the United States to determine the educational needs of each Ruthenian-Ukrainian community; (2) organized new reading rooms in Chicago, New York, Pittsburgh, Scranton, and Olyphant; (3) enrolled 2,000 new members; (4) provided the bulk of the publication costs for Iuliian Bachynskyi's monumental study of the Ukrainian-American immigration;

(5) published a collection of Taras Shevchenko's poems in commemoration of the one hundredth anniversary of the poet's birth; (6) published a total of forty-five booklets on a variety of economic, social, scientific, historical, and cultural topics; (7) given birth to *Tsvitka* (Floweret), an illustrated children's journal; (8) organized a speaker's bureau, which by 1917 had presented some seventy-four popular lectures throughout the United States; (9) provided both moral and financial support for a newly organized Ukrainian Teachers' Society; (10) established close contacts and a cooperative forum with the Ukrainian Information Committee in Lviv.[80]

The Role of Women's Organizations

Despite an almost total lack of leisure time, Ukrainian-American women began their organizational activity with the establishment of the Sisterhood of St. Olga, a mutual benefit society, in Jersey City in 1897. Led by Jersey City's example, branches of the St. Olga Society were soon in existence in New York City, Brooklyn, Yonkers, Bloomfield, Elizabeth, Elizabeth-Port, Hackensack, Newark, and Passaic. A convention of all branches was held in December 1905 and a constitution uniting all of them into the national Sisterhood of St. Olga was formally approved. According to the bylaws, the purposes of the newly constituted association were to (1) organize reading rooms for its members; (2) organize courses for illiterates; (3) work toward a greater cooperative effort with American women; (4) work toward the strengthening of "the Ruthenian patriotic spirit in the United States"; and (5) provide financial assistance to the families of members who died or were seriously disabled.

Elected to the first national executive were Fr. Mykola Pidhoretsky, president; Anna Medvid, vice-president; Emily Strutynsky, secretary; Ievheniia Kalakura, treasurer.

The Sisterhood of St. Olga survived as a national enterprise until 1907 when internal dissension, due in large part to the emergence of pro-Russian sentiments among certain local members, resulted in its dissolution. The demise of the Sisterhood of St. Olga ended, for a time, organized national and regional activity among Ruthenian-Ukrainian women. Local sisterhoods, however, continued to exist.[81]

Four women deserve mention for their pioneering efforts on behalf of Ukrainian enlightenment in the United States during this period. The first is the indefatigable Emily Strutynsky, who, in addition to her work with UNA's Prosvita and the Sisterhood of St. Olga, later helped organize a women's mutual benefit society in the Midwest. A frequent contributor to *Svoboda*, where she constantly exhorted Ruthenian women to improve their lot in life through self-education, Mrs. Strutynsky, the wife of Fr. Mykola Strutynsky, was greatly influenced by the social work of her acquaintance Jane Addams of Chicago's Hull House.

Another female pioneer was Maria Cheremshak, elected the first vice-president of the UNA in 1908. Also a *Svoboda* contributor, Maria Cheremshak was keenly aware of the significant mediating role that women could play in the ethnonational revival, especially with reference to cross-generational preservation. Soon after being elected to her UNA post she wrote:

> If we want Ruthenian children to be good, industrious, tough, patriotic and progressive, then we must strive to make their mothers that way.
>
> Until now, few people have considered this aspect of our life. Ruthenian women and girls sleep blissfully. Their husbands argue about religion, about the priests ... while their children grow, unsupervised, like weeds.
>
> Those few sisterhoods that we now have are too few to meet all the needs of our Ruthenian women ...
>
> Let us remember ... if we continue to be indifferent ... then future generations will curse us and write that it was our apathy that led to the downfall of the Ruthenian American community.[82]

While Emily Strutynsky and Maria Cheremshak were active in the social and political arena, two other dynamic women were busying themselves with enterprises aimed at cultural enhancement. In the New York area, Olena Krykivsky's work in the establishment of choirs and the subsequent production of numerous Ukrainian musicals and dramas was, for a time, unequaled. In Chicago, a similar contribution was made by Mrs. Natalie Hrynevetsky who was also involved in the direction of a choir and musical productions.[83]

The Role of Cultural Enterprises

Among the most popular vehicles for ethnic development and preservation were the numerous societies which arose out of a desire to sing and produce plays. A choir was easiest to organize, especially when a church was already in existence and in need of musical assistance at the divine liturgy. Finding enthusiasts to participate was one thing, but achieving unity of interpretation and rendering was another matter. Subtle but significant local differences in liturgical music had developed over the centuries in the various regions of Ukraine and most of them, it seems, were brought to America by the first immigration. Each immigrant, of course, insisted that his version was the "correct" one and that all other interpretations were obviously false. With no immediately available authorities to whom they could turn, choir directors were hard pressed to keep their musical ensembles together. As might be expected, the greatest differences in the musical rendering of liturgical music existed between the Galicians and Uhro-Rusyns.[84]

The first Ruthenian choir was organized by Volodymyr Simenovych in Shenandoah in 1887. Two years later, a second choir was established in Shamokin by Ivan Hapii. Later, choirs were organized in Olyphant and Mayfield by Father Obushkevych. All three individuals were competent musicians. In the years that followed, however, the rapid growth of Ruthenian churches far surpassed the availability of knowledgeable choir directors and for a few years some churches were forced to do without church choirs. The arrival in the early 1900s of a number of cantor-teachers schooled in Lviv and Peremyshl helped to fill the void.[85]

From an ethnic perspective, the emigration of ever-increasing numbers of individuals and cantor-teachers familiar with the latest patriotic Ukrainian songs in Europe provided much-needed emotional reinforcement for the development of a pan-Ukrainian identity. Melodic and martial music such as "My Haidamaky" (We Are Haidamaks), "Za pravdu, voliu, svobodu" (For Truth, Self-Determination, and Liberty), and "Sokoly, sokoly" (Falcons, Falcons) did much to translate the ethnonational aspirations of the Ukrainian people into expressive forms which could be easily understood and felt by even the most unenlightened Ruthenian immigrant.[86]

Most early choirs were organized as singing societies, which, in addition to participating at various religious services, also performed at concerts, picnics, and ethnonational festivals sponsored by UNA branches, reading rooms, and church societies. Although many of the early choirs left much to be desired in terms of musical accomplishment, they were generally well supported and appreciated by a community willing to overlook flaws in return for a modicum of cultural sustenance. Where there was musical talent to lead the way, however, excellent choirs existed. Prior to the war, the choirs of Philadelphia, Pittsburgh (under the direction of Father Stefanovych), Chicago (under the direction of Mrs. Hrynevetsky), Newark, New York, Jersey City, and Perth Amboy were identified as outstanding choral ensembles.[87]

Orchestras and marching bands were another popular means for meeting the cultural needs of Ruthenian immigrants. The first band was organized in Shamokin by Father Obushkevych in 1891 and was led by Joseph Valyish, a Czech. Instruments were purchased by Shamokin's Brotherhood of Sts. Cyril and Methodius, but the driving force behind the operation was Obushkevych, who discovered Valyish, recruited promising and talented youth, and provided space for instruction and rehearsals, as well as the necessary moral and financial support. After leaving Shamokin, Obushkevych helped form similar bands in Olyphant and Mayfield. Prior to 1914, bands also existed in Shenandoah, Pittsburgh, Braddock, and Cleveland.[88]

Interest in the establishment of drama groups was also high among Ukraine's first immigrants. The first drama societies were organized in Shenandoah in 1887 and Shamokin and Olyphant in 1900; they were soon followed by similar groups in Mayfield, Mount Carmel, Passaic, New York, and Syracuse. In 1909, the New York drama troupe, under the direction of Vasyl Martyniuk, attempted to organize a Ruthenian-Ukrainian national theater that could serve the entire community, an idea first proposed by members of UNA Branch #117. On 16 January 1910, the group performed the well-known Ukrainian operetta "Zaporozhets za Dunaiem" (Cossack beyond the Danube) for the first time in the United States. Later the troupe appeared in Newark, Perth Amboy, and Elizabeth. The road tour proved to be financially disastrous, however, and the first attempt to establish a permanent Ruthenian-Ukrainian theater on a national scale ended in failure.[89]

Early difficulties notwithstanding, choirs, bands, and drama societies contributed immeasurably to the growing number of so-called musical-declamation concerts which, beginning in the mid 1890s, came to play an increasingly significant role in the making of the Ukrainian American. The first such concert was held in Shamokin on 30 May 1894, in conjunction with the first convention of the UNA. The program consisted of fourteen items and was highlighted by the appearance of a well-schooled choral ensemble consisting of fifty members of the Shamokin and Olyphant choirs under the direction of Simenovych and Obushkevych. It was at this concert that "Shche ne vmerla Ukraina" (Ukraine Has Not Died) was sung for the first time on American soil. A number of non-Ukrainians were present at the affair and to enlighten them, Father Konstankevych presented a short English-language talk on the importance of the UNA in the development of the Ruthenian-Ukrainian community in the United States.

At the 1895 UNA convention concert in Olyphant, the first Ruthenian-Ukrainian band made its national debut and the amateur drama *Znimchenyi Iurko* (Germanized George) was performed. In the years that followed, concerts became more frequent and were soon held in almost every Ruthenian-Ukrainian community in the United States.

America's first original Ruthenian-Ukrainian drama, *Amerykanskyi shliakhtych* (American Aristocrat), was performed in Olyphant in 1900.[90] Written by Fr. Stefan Makar, *Shliakhtych* was a comedy depicting a Ruthenian immigrant eager to become part of the American mainstream who is bilked by conmen ready to take advantage of his ignorance and naïveté.[91]

Still another communal cultural event was the *sviato*, a commemorative concert usually held in honor of a revered Ukrainian of the past. The first such *sviato* took place in Shamokin on 30 May 1900, on the occasion of the thirty-ninth anniversary of the death of Ukraine's Taras Shevchenko. In 1901, Shevchenko *sviata* were held in Shamokin and Mount Carmel, and within a short time they became an annual part of the social calendar of almost every Ruthenian-Ukrainian community. In the years immediately preceding 1914, similar *sviata* were produced commemorating Mychailo Drahomanov, Markian Shashkevych, and Ivan Franko.[92]

The Role of Youth Organizations

The rapid growth and popularity in Galicia of the Sokol and Sich organizations, two groups with special appeal to younger Ukrainians, precipitated their establishment in the United States. The first Sokol branch in the United States was organized in Yonkers by Father Tymkevych in 1902 and that same year Rev. Strutynsky established the first Sich branch in Olyphant. A Zaporozhian Sich was organized by Father Makar in McKeesport in 1905. Later, Sokol and Sich branches were established in Pittsburgh, New York, Philadelphia, and a number of other locales.

Ostensibly gymnastic societies, both Sokol and Sich, were athletic associations in name only because neither facilities nor instructors for gymnastic exercises were usually available. Attired in colorful uniforms, members of both organizations generally limited their prewar activities to parades and honor-guard participation at ethnic functions, religious ceremonies, and funerals.

In 1913, Dr. Simenovych prevailed upon the UNA to reorganize all Ukrainian gymnastic societies into one national Sich organization with local branches. With an eye toward the future, Dr. Simenovych's dream was to provide Ukrainian-American youth with military training so that, in the event of a war, they could form the first cadres of a Ukrainian liberation army. Sich branches were subsequently established as separate UNA branches, and a press organ for the exclusive use of Sich was promised by the UNA.[93]

The Role of Heritage Schools

One of the more tragic aspects of the first Ukrainian immigration was the abominably poor environment to which children of immigrants were exposed, especially in the anthracite coal regions of Pennsylvania, where youngsters were occasionally found working as "breaker-boys" as early as the age of ten. Some parents, concerned more with financial security than with the physical and mental well-being of their offspring, used every available subterfuge to circumvent the legal requirement that children attend public school until the age of fourteen. Such flagrant flouting of the local law was not uncommon in the Pennsylvania coal-mining areas and was practiced not only by Ukrainians but by other ethnic groups and even nonethnic Americans as well.[94] Because the education of these children was neglected, the "street," according to Bachynskyi, "became their teacher" and the only "real value" for them, as for their parents, became the "almighty dollar." Still, Bachynskyi was not unduly pessimistic over the long-term effects of this kind of environment.[95] There was, he wrote, a hidden blessing:

> Ukrainian youth in the United States is already an entirely different kind of Ukrainian youth – it is not the old country youth we find in the isolated villages of Galicia or Hungary which is often crushed, frightened, and poverty-stricken – this youth is clever, bold, proud, and self-confident — occasionally friendly, occasionally boorish. But from this type of youth, America prospers and grows; that America which so often leaves the European amazed and bewildered.[96]

Peripheral psychosocial benefits notwithstanding, the Ruthenian child was culturally deprived and efforts to relieve this condition were initiated soon after the Ruthenian-American community was organized. Following the establishment of churches and benevolent societies that carried the burden of Ukrainianization among adults, the next priority to be broached was the emerging problem of cross-generational ethnic preservation. That this was not a major concern prior to the 1890s can be explained by the fact that most early immigrants were young, single men who planned to return to their native villages within a short time. Initially, therefore, the Ruthenian immigrant had no need to be concerned with the cultural development of the next generation.

Credit for the first Ruthenian "school" belongs to Father Wolansky, who organized heritage classes in Shenandoah in 1888.[97] Directed by Simenovych, the school lasted for only a short time and never had more than three children enrolled.[98]

The first successful heritage school was established in Shamokin by Father Konstankevych in 1893.[99] Within a year, similar schools were functioning in Shenandoah, Mount Carmel, Olyphant, Wilkes-Barre, and Minneapolis.[100]

The history of the Ruthenian-Ukrainian heritage school movement in the United States prior to 1914 can be divided into two phases, the first beginning soon after *Svoboda* identified and articulated the need. As early as 1894, *Svoboda* argued:

> It is not he who is unfortunate whose parents left him an orphan without any visible means of support but he who is forced to grow old without any education or enlightenment, he who must be forever content to pull his ignorant soul with him throughout his miserable life ... Parents! Don't worry about leaving your children a rich inheritance. Leave them a far more valuable treasure — an education. Work towards the organization of Ruthenian schools by donating a few cents for this worthy cause. Your children, your grandchildren and your great-grandchildren will always remember you for it and will pray for your souls.[101]

Svoboda promoted the heritage school movement throughout 1894, offering free assistance from Father Konstankevych for those who requested it[102] and praising each newly established school as an outstanding community achievement.[103] In terms of ethnonational development, the UNA viewed the creation of a heritage school system as a national responsibility to be shared by all Ruthenian families:

> It is the obligation of parents to teach their children Ruthenian in order that children, in the family circle, can speak the language of their mothers and fathers and in order that they may know that they are of Ruthenian ancestry. Be sure, Ruthenian parents, to kindle a fire of love for their native land in the hearts of your sons ... The future of our people depends upon the education of our youth. If it were possible to educate our new generation in Galicia today in true patriotic fashion, then a Pole would not be a parliamentary representative from the Ruthenian section of Lviv. He would be sweeping the streets with a number on his cap.[104]

Initially housing their ethnic schools in church basements, some communities such as Leisenring (1896), Mayfield (1899), Passaic (1899), Mount Carmel (1904), and Mahanoy City (1904) were eventually able to provide separate buildings for heritage classes.[105] Thanks largely to the efforts of three members of the American Circle — Konstankevych, Tymkevych, and Makar, who, in addition to authoring exhortative articles in *Svoboda*, also traveled to various communities to generate local support — there was hardly a sizable Ruthenian-Ukrainian community in America which did not eventually have some form of heritage school for its youth by 1913.[106]

In addition to heritage schools, an attempt to establish a *bursa* or prep school was also made during this period. A pet project of Fr. Pavlo Tymkevych, who began to lobby on its behalf soon after his arrival in the United States, the enterprise became a reality when a *bursa* in Yonkers, New York, opened its doors to fourteen young men in the fall of 1904. The avowed purpose of the school was to prepare young men to be "enlightened leaders" who would dedicate themselves to work "on behalf of God and their people."[107] Tuition was ten dollars per month and the initial plan was to have the enrollees, all of whom received room and board, attend a local public school during the day and then, during their "free time," receive religious instruction (including literature and song) as well as Ukrainian reading, writing, history, geography, and literature. Unfortunately, the project proved to be too ambitious. Unable to muster support from parents who reasoned that the purpose of the *bursa* could just as easily be fulfilled by the public school and local heritage classes, Father Tymkevych was forced to abandon his project the following year.[108]

Organizing Ruthenian-Ukrainian heritage schools and *bursas* was one matter, but attaining the desired educational objectives through quality education was quite another. On the surface, the establishment of ethnic schools committed to cross-generational heritage preservation in most Ruthenian-Ukrainian communities appeared to be a tremendous accomplishment. Beneath these impressive statistics, however, was the appraisal that in far too many instances these schools represented what Bachynskyi quite candidly called a "pedagogical absurdity."[109]

The most serious shortcoming of the early Ruthenian-Ukrainian schools was the lack of qualified teaching personnel. Most of the teaching was conducted by the so-called *diak-uchytel* or cantor-teacher who, in addition to his duties as church cantor, often doubled as teacher, choir director, and drama coach. In Ukraine, the cantor-teacher was a full-time professional who attended a special school to prepare himself for his calling. Many of these professionals found their way to the United States and were able, in the more affluent parishes, to employ their skills on a full-time basis.[110] Most early Ruthenian-American cantor-teachers, however, had little or no professional preparation, worked on a part-time basis, and were frequently hired only because no one else was available. Lacking in education and pedagogical expertise, it was the latter type of individual who often did more harm than good in the Ruthenian ethnic school. Some, according to *Svoboda*, "were barely literate themselves."[111] Nevertheless, many of these "teachers" demanded to be called "Pan Professor" (Mr. Professor), behaved as "autocrats and dictators" in their classrooms, used any textbook they desired, and taught as they pleased.[112] Things got so bad that in 1905 *Svoboda*, complaining that for far too many cantor-teachers "the only pedagogical tool was the stick," concluded: "One would probably not be too far wrong if one said that of all the Ruthenian teachers in the United States, the number who truly deserve to be called teachers can be counted on the fingers of one hand."[113]

Another negative aspect of the early heritage school movement was the poor physical environment provided for the children. While some facilities were adequate, most classes were conducted in crowded, dark, and damp church basements or halls without benefit of even the most primitive teaching aids.

Finally, classes were generally held between 5 and 7 p.m., a most inopportune time if one considers the physical and educational readiness of a child. Tired from a full day in the public schools, yearning to be with their non-Ruthenian friends enjoying noneducational pursuits, it is small wonder that the Ruthenian-American child showed little enthusiasm for heritage school studies. "Are we not hurting our children by forcing them to sit in such schools?" asked *Svoboda*.[114] "What kind of teaching can take place in these schools?" echoed Bachynskyi a few years later.[115]

The second phase of the Ruthenian-Ukrainian ethnic school movement began with the realization that the best of intentions and the greatest desire to provide vehicles of cross-generational ethnic maintenance were no substitutes for professional skill and leadership. In 1903, Father Dmytriw urged employing American-trained teachers in Ruthenian ethnic schools, arguing that unless this were done, Ruthenian ethnonational education would always remain inferior.[116] Two years later, Father Makar proposed the establishment of a nationwide teachers' organization, arguing that all Ruthenian churches, institutions, and organizations were of little value unless an American-born generation with "a Ruthenian upbringing" was developed to take over the leadership. The newly formed organization, wrote Makar, would form a council, the purpose of which would be to (1) gain support for its objectives; (2) organize or cause to be organized schools in those locales where no ethnic school existed; (3) establish a uniform curriculum for both lower and upper grades; (4) approve uniform texts and teaching guides; (5) initiate the publication of texts and a youth gazette; (6) devise ancillary teaching aids such as children's games and plays; (7) establish a teachers' college for the training of cantor-teachers; (8) recruit teacher-cantors, either from Galicia or from among those already here, for those communities requesting them; (9) administer teaching examinations and award teaching certificates; (10) raise money from among the wider Ruthenian-Ukrainian community to subsidize those teachers working in communities unable to afford the services of a qualified teacher; and (11) institute a school visitation program under the direction of a competent staff of supervisors.[117]

Little was done to implement these progressive suggestions until the arrival of Bishop Ortynsky. At the New York conference of priests and laymen in 1907, an educational board of examiners, consisting of three priests and two laymen, was appointed and given the responsibilities of certifying new teachers and coordinating new assignments and transfers. At the same time, a committee of nine priests, with power to co-opt additional personnel, was formed to oversee the publication of a Ruthenian-American reader and a catechism using the etymological alphabet. All educational decisions reached at the New York conference were subsequently approved at the convention of Ruthenian cantor-teachers held in Pittsburgh on 10 and 11 December 1907.[118]

The UNA, meanwhile, dissatisfied with the majority Uhro-Rusyn- and Russophile-engineered decision to adopt the etymological alphabet, sponsored a contest for the writing of an alphabet book, a reader, and a catechism in the Ukrainian phonetic script. Contest rules specified that the winning catechism must receive the imprimatur of Bishop Ortynsky and that the alphabet book and reader should: (1) be relevant to the experience of Ruthenian-American children; (2) include some Ukrainian history and geography; and (3) be modeled after the best American readers. An award of fifty dollars was offered for each of the three books accepted.[119]

On 15 September 1909, Bishop Ortynsky sponsored an Enlightenment Conference in Philadelphia which brought together 113 delegates representing forty-seven communities. Three Ruthenian-Ukrainian teachers read papers at the conference. E. Hvodyk discussed the nature of education and the role of heritage schools; Joseph Stetkewicz discussed ways and means to preserve the Ruthenian heritage in the United States; and Dmytro Andreiko reiterated the need for immediate reform in the Ruthenian heritage school system. Among other things, Andreiko stressed a more functional and coordinated curriculum, improved texts, more educational conferences, greater emphasis on demonstration lessons, in-service training for employed teachers, a journal for youth, and the establishment of a curriculum and instruction center where the latest American educational innovations could be assessed for possible use in Ruthenian heritage schools.[120]

A 1910 fraternal society split in the Ruthenian-Ukrainian camp precipitated the demise of Ortynsky's Prosvita (an organization that might have implemented the many creative programs proposed by Ruthenian-Ukrainian educators) and produced a hiatus of constructive endeavor on the educational frontier. In 1909, *Svoboda*, sensing the widening gap between word and deed among educators, wrote: "Much, very much, has been written about the organization of quality schools. Pleas have been addressed to our intelligentsia and we have exhorted the masses. All the furor has now died down. All that remains are black marks impressed on paper in printer's ink, and nothing more."[121]

Community division and criticism notwithstanding, a number of Ruthenian-Ukrainian educators continued to press for greater profession-alization and ethnonational clarity within their ranks, an effort that led, finally, to the establishment of America's first Ukrainian teachers' society.

In 1912, twelve Galician teachers, irreconcilably estranged from Uhro-Rusyn and Russophile educators, met in Ansonia and formed an organiza-tional committee to undertake the task of organizing a society of educators. Led by Fr. Nestor Dmytriw, two organizational meetings were held in Newark and, on 12 August 1913, the first convention of Ruthenian-Ukrai-nian teachers was convened in Philadelphia. A constitution, prepared by Rev. Peter Poniatyshyn (1876–1960), was subsequently approved by the twenty-one teachers in attendance. Bishop Ortynsky was elected president of the newly formed Ruthenian Greek Catholic Teachers' Association and Theodosius Kaskiw and Andrii Gela were elected secretary and treasurer, respectively. In the years that followed, it was this organization that was to have the greatest initial influence on Ukrainian heritage education in the United States.

Mention should also be made of the role played by the Sisters of St. Basil the Great (OSBM) in maintaining the Ruthenian orphanage established by Bishop Ortynsky in 1911. The first nuns to immigrate to the United States were Mother Helen (Lanhevych) and Sisters Euphemia and Paphnutia who arrived in New York City on 2 December 1911. They were from the convent in Yavoriv in Galicia. A year later, Sisters Apolinaria and Mytrodora from Yavoriv, and sister Makryna from the Galician convent in Slovitsky, came to work at the orphanage. With six sisters and several candidates for the sisterhood, the orphanage was able to accommodate some 121 children by 1915.[122]

Svoboda *as a Vehicle of Political Action*

Efforts by the UNA newspaper Svoboda and various educational, enlighten-ment, cultural, and youth organizations to instill ethnic pride in the Ruthenian-Ukrainian were paralleled by an equally intense drive to trans-late this newly acquired consciousness into ethnonational political action. Two arenas were involved, one American, the other Ruthenian.

The first Ruthenian political response to the American environment came in the form of joint union activity which began in Shenandoah in the mid-1880s. Father Wolansky, Father Lachovych, and Volodymyr Simenovych were all active members of the Knights of Labor and all three were successful in their efforts to involve more Ruthenians in the strengthening of the union movement in the anthracite coal areas of eastern Pennsylvania.

What had been initiated by these pioneer leaders was continued by their successors. In 1894, *Svoboda* wrote:

> A number of English-American newspapers, servants of capital-ism, are bleating that the owners of coal mines should not raise the pay of striking coal miners but rather, they should hire Negroes who are willing to work for lower wages. What terrible speculation over human sweat and blood!
>
> Once Irishmen and Englishmen were making $5.00 a day as miners but today a poor Hungarian or Slav – Pole, Ruthenian, Slovak – is expected to work for 75¢ a day.[123]

In 1897, after citing a speech by Eugene V. Debs in which the noted American socialist and union organizer declared that strikes were protests against tyranny in the tradition of Patrick Henry, George Washington, and John Hancock,[124] *Svoboda* suggested that attempts to better one's economic life were an American manifestation worthy of emulation by Ruthenians. When all else failed, *Svoboda* argued, strikes were the only protection workers had against exploitation by unscrupulous industrialists.[125] That same year *Svoboda* branded the infamous Lattimer massacre in which nine-teen miners were killed and thirty-nine wounded while leading a march on the Pardee Company's mine in Lattimer, Pennsylvania, an episode of "murder," and an example of "bestiality" on the part of the American deputies sent to restore order.[126] Even though no Ruthenians had lost their lives, *Svoboda* established a special Lattimer fund, headed by Father Stefanovych, for the purpose of raising money for the widows and orphans of those who had died.[127] A similar fund drive was initiated in 1909 when a number of Ruthenians were hurt during strike disturbances in McKees Rock.[128]

Scabs, of course, were condemned by *Svoboda* for their "greed, lack of dignity, and inability to look to the future."[129] At the same time, leaders like Father Konstankevych, who, during a 1900 strike in Shamokin, offered to mortgage the church in order to provide funds for financially hard-pressed Ruthenian strikers, were praised for their courage, determination, and foresight. "How good it is," declared *Svoboda* in 1900, "that the church is not deeded to the bishop but to the people."[130]

Supporting union organization and legitimate strike activity was not the only role played by *Svoboda* in its efforts to improve the lives of Ruthenian workingmen. Soon after its creation, *Svoboda* inaugurated a labor situation column in which job opportunities in various parts of the United States were reviewed on a regular basis.[131] Later, a column entitled "Worker's Forum" was established in which topics such as the growing threat of automation, laborers as an economic class, and the value of trade unions were discussed.[132]

Political power was another objective of the UNA and its organ, *Svoboda*, during this early period. Urging its readers to become active in American political affairs, *Svoboda* promoted the establishment of political clubs which could someday organize themselves into a national federation. "Having few opportunities to organize in the old country," observed *Svoboda*, "we were poor politicians. But here we have no excuse."[133]

The federation idea was never realized and the few clubs that were established were ineffectual. An exception was the Ukrainian-American Citizen's Club of Philadelphia, organized in 1909 with the help of Bishop Ortynsky and Ivan Bereshkevych, who had been active in a similar club in Ansonia. Beginning with 35 members, the club grew to 104 members within a year, promulgating the following aims:

1 To promote greater community participation among people from our native land;
2 To convince immigrants to obtain their citizenship and to assist them in this process;
3 To preserve Ukrainian customs and traditions ...
4 To become active in American politics;
5 To promote mutual assistance and aid.[134]

Despite the fact that in some locales Ruthenians were in a position to elect fellow Ruthenians to public office, interest in American political affairs remained low. "Most immigrants," concluded Bachynskyi in 1912, "are foreigners until they die."[135] As for political clubs, few, wrote *Svoboda*, were worthy of respect:

> We have, praise be to God, Ruthenian political clubs but unfortunately, some of them not only bring no benefit but actually bring harm and shame to the Ruthenians because their chairmen or other executives take money for the votes of their membership. Small wonder that Americans call such clubs "boodle clubs" (sell-out, piggish clubs) and their members "voting cattle."[136]

Of the major American political parties and ideologies available to American Ruthenians during this period, the one that eventually had the most appeal to the editors of *Svoboda* was socialism.[137] In 1894, *Svoboda* observed that "people have come to realize that life is better during Republican times,"[138] but by 1900, *Svoboda* had changed its perspective. In an editorial entitled "Who Should Ruthenians Vote For," *Svoboda* argued that there was little real difference between Republicans and Democrats because both are controlled by rich men and both make "many promises" before the election. They compete with each other, *Svoboda* explained, "because the Republican party is the party of very rich men while the Democratic party is the party of fairly rich men who are not permitted to become richer." The Socialist party, in contrast,

> wants everyone to be treated fairly, regardless of race, creed, or sex; it wants to abolish the army; it wants people to stop fighting like animals and to settle their differences peacefully – and what is more – it wants all natural resources such as land, forests, mines as well as factories, trains, telegraphs ... to be the property of all the people in order that the benefits of all these riches could go to all the people rather than to just a few. If all of this could come to be, life would be very different on this earth.[139]

The editorial was, in all probability, the work of Fr. Ivan Ardan, by far the most radical member of the American Circle. In 1901, when all of America recoiled in horror at the death of President McKinley at the hands of an anarchist, Rev. Ardan was hardly moved by the tragedy. There is no end to the righteous indignation of the bourgeois press when a representative of American capitalism meets an untimely death, wrote Ardan in *Svoboda*, but when capitalism kills thousands of workers, the American press pays little attention.[140]

As for *Svoboda*'s political aspirations for Ukraine, the UNA gazette's initial posture was one of caution, accommodation with Russia, and the recognition of certain cultural rights. In 1894, *Svoboda* was conciliatory.

> We sincerely respect Russia, we appreciate Russian literature which gave the world Turgenev, Tolstoy, Dostoyevsky ... We are saddened, however, when we learn that 20 million Ruthenians in Russia do not have the right to write in their own language ... An idiot is he who thinks of an independent Ukraine: she is so closely tied to Russia, both spiritually and materially, that this tie cannot be broken. But gentlemen, permit us to have a free spirit.[141]

Later in the year, *Svoboda* addressed another appeal to the Russians: "That God may grant that the present tsar would ... permit Little Russia freedom to speak its native language and to develop that language in schools, in government offices, and in the theater. Rus'-Ukraine wants only that and nothing more."[142]

In 1895, when it was evident that the Russification campaign in Ukraine would continue, *Svoboda* began to cautiously consider other alternatives. The Ruthenian people are seeking greater freedom, *Svoboda* concluded, but they "cannot move forward too quickly in their desire for political independence."[143]

By 1900, *Svoboda*, now firmly in the hands of the American Circle, had changed its political platform completely. Appeals were replaced by demands and when demands failed, political action became the logical next step:

> As everyone knows, the life of our people in the old country is extremely difficult in every respect. In the three countries in which they live, the Ruthenian people are oppressed as much by the governments as by their "good neighbors." Our leaders are doing everything in their power to improve the lot of the Ruthenian people but at last they have arrived at the conclusion that half-hearted means will bring no results and that the only possible way out of their misery is for the Ruthenian people to unite into one sovereign, independent state with a democratic system of government. This idea has been gradually gaining support among the Ruthenian people and recently some of the most prominent leaders of the Ruthenian youth (500 persons) assembled in Lviv and not only endorsed this idea wholeheartedly but adopted it as the guiding principle and supreme objective of their life. What is our reaction to this as Americans? Are we to remain indifferent? The answer is no!

Svoboda then proposed the establishment of a national fund in America "which would serve to support our people's struggle for independence," pointing out that such funds had already been established by the Slovaks, Poles, and other nationalities.

> We can, we should, we must have an independent state where neither the German, nor the Russian, nor the Pole, nor the Hungarian, but the Ruthenian will be master in his own house. And once we have built a free Ruthenian state we won't have to wander about the world like homeless orphans. We shall return to our own Ruthenian country, to our Ruthenian home, for only in one's own home is there truth and strength and freedom! To action brothers![144]

Having proclaimed a political platform in 1900 that called for the creation of an independent Ukrainian state, *Svoboda* rarely wavered in its determination to popularize the separatist ideal among Ruthenians and to gain moral and financial support for its realization. Once again the appeal was to ethnic pride and to the revolutionary example of others. In 1901, *Svoboda* wrote:

> Let the accomplishments of the Irish, attained through bloody sweat, be our example and our motivation in the fight for the freedom of the old country. Abominable conditions, oppression, and slavery left their mark on our peasant as much as they did on the Irish. Ignorance, an indifference towards education, inferiority, lack of character, and a penchant for drunkenness are also characteristics of the Ruthenian but there is hope that Ruthenians, like the Irish, will rid themselves of these ills once they reside on free soil.[145]

"We must be revolutionaries and agitators of the caliber of George Washington ... who mobilized the American people to overthrow the English yoke" exclaimed *Svoboda* in 1903.[146]

Becoming increasingly nationalistic in its approach to the Ukrainian question, *Svoboda* questioned the wisdom of those Galician Ruthenians who advocated continued fidelity to the Habsburgs as the only realistic means by which to achieve ethnonational autonomy: "That too is a lie since it was precisely because Ruthenians were loyal to the king that everyone considered us fools while the Poles and Magyars who agitated against the dictates of the king today enjoy significance and strength ... those who lick the hands and feet of aristocrats will be rewarded with spittle in their soup and a kick in the shins by the same aristocrats they venerate."[147]

Nor was the UNA periodical swayed by the arguments of other Galician Ruthenians who, enamored with the idealistic dreams of the pan-Slavic movement, flirted with the idea of Slavic federation under the aegis of Moscow: "Chains, whether they be of gold or steel, still bind. It doesn't make sense to rid ourselves of one set of chains and then to turn around and push our hands into another set. We don't want to change masters. We want to be our own masters. We want freedom, not another surrender. We want independence, not new 'protectors.'"[148] "Russia," concluded *Svoboda* in 1908, represents "national slavery, hell for peasants and workers, darkness and decay, and the end of our people."[149]

In Galicia, meanwhile, the Poles had gained control of the provincial diet and, in an effort to reduce the influence of Ruthenians of a Ukrainian orientation, were actively supporting Ruthenian candidates with a Russophile orientation and engaging in illegal activities designed to prevent

Ukrainians from voting. During the 1908 election, clashes broke out between Poles and Ukrainians resulting in the death of a number of Ukrainian peasants. In retaliation for their death, Miroslaw Sichynsky, a Ukrainian university student, assassinated Count Potocki, the Polish governor of Galicia. Sichynsky became an instant hero to Galician Ruthenians in America and when, in 1909, he was condemned to death, *Svoboda* launched a press campaign urging its readers to organize national protest rallies. This time, the response was encouraging. *Svoboda* happily reported on the demonstrations, mentioning those in Pittsburgh, where some 1,000 demonstrators reportedly participated, and Chicago, where 400 were involved. Singled out for lavish praise were those speakers who, like I. Kostiuk, a cantor-teacher in Chicago, addressed themselves "to the independence of the Ruthenian-Ukrainian people."[150] To the relief of the Ukrainian community, Sichynsky's sentence was later commuted to life imprisonment.

For *Svoboda*, the outbreak of hostilities in Europe in 1914 offered a golden opportunity for the Ukrainian people to finally exercise their national will. "The war may bring a new order to Europe ... An independent Ukrainian state, that is the dream of every enlightened Ukrainian."[151]

The Russophile Threat

Svoboda's exhortations and the appeals of the UNA to unite all Ruthenians into a strong Ukrainian ethnonational organization remained tenuous so long as a Russophile contingent remained a viable force within the organization. Although many Russian-oriented Ruthenians had left the UNA earlier to join the Russian stream, there was still a small but active Russophile minority in the UNA that continued to interfere with the UNA's Ukrainianization program. A showdown was reached at the seventh UNA convention in 1902. Warning that the Russophiles had organized many delegates and were planning either to "wrest control" of the UNA or to force its dissolution, *Svoboda* sounded the alarm two weeks before the convention, urging "all honest delegates to show that there is no room for traitors" in the UNA. The convention began with the Russophile contingent lobbying on behalf of the rejection of the phonetic script and the adoption of Slavonic orthography as well as the resurrection of the designation "Russian" in the association's name. "Hold counsel for the good of the Russian people," they cried, "not the priest-radicals who abandoned their father's faith and nationality, nor for their stupid Ukraine." Hopelessly outnumbered, the Russophiles were quickly disfranchised. Early during the conclave, V. Hladyk, editor of *Pravda*, a periodical published by the Russian Brotherhood Organization, was voted out of the hall and all subsequent Russophile resolutions were overwhelmingly defeated.[152] The convention was a decisive victory for the Ukrainian stream and it signaled the end of Russophile influence within the UNA. As for the Russian orientation itself, *Svoboda* expressed Ukrainian sentiments quite succinctly in 1912 on the three hundredth anniversary of the Romanov dynasty: "We curse today the moment when the famous Cossack Hetman Bohdan Khmelnytskyi, weakened after long battles with the cursed Jesuit-aristocratic Poland, losing faith in his own strength ... joined Moscow. The 300th anniversary of the Romanovs is for us Ukrainians a black jubilee."[153]

The Demise of Ruthenian-Ukrainian Unity

As long as members of the American Circle, especially Revs. Konstankevych, Dmytriw, Bonezevsky, Ardan, Stefanovych, and Makar, were leading the fledgling but progressively conscious Ruthenian-Ukrainian community, unity was assured. The Catholic church and the UNA, the two largest and most influential institutions in the Ukrainian stream, were, for all practical purposes, one in their desire to preserve the religiocultural heritage and to develop a Ukrainian ethnonational identity among the Ruthenians. "Our church in America," wrote Father Peter Poniatyshyn, one of the pioneer leaders, "not only served God and offered spiritual sustenance, it also enlightened our immigrants nationally ... In this way, our church in America became, one could say, a school for Ukrainianization."[154]

The UNA, however, remained a secular organization. Despite the fact that until 1910 five of the first seven national secretaries, four of the first six *Svoboda* editors, and two of the first seven national presidents had been Catholic priests,* the UNA, in contrast to the GCU, was never an exclusively Catholic society. Membership was open to all Ruthenians, Catholic and Orthodox alike, and the general tenor of the organization, again in contrast to the GCU, was in the best liberal, progressive tradition of the time.

By the middle of the first decade of the 1900s, however, the perspective of Ukrainian priests in the United States had changed. Reflecting a shift in political climate in Galician Ukraine – and increasingly sensitive to charges of spiritual bankruptcy from the Uhro-Rusyn and Russian opposition – the newest contingent of clerical émigrés gradually adopted a more conservative approach to their ministry in the United States. Spiritual conformity

---

* UNA presidents included Fr. Antin Bonezevsky (1900–2) and Fr. Mykola Stefanovych (1902–4); secretaries included Fr. Ivan Konstankevych (1894–5), Fr. Nestor Dmytriw (1895–6), Fr. Mykola Stefanovych (1896–7), Fr. Ivan Ardan (1897–8), and Fr. Antin Bonezevsky (1898–1900). Four priests served as editors of *Svoboda*: Fr. Gregory Hrushka (1893–5), Fr. Nestor Dmytriw (1895–7), Fr. Stefan Makar (1897–1900), and Fr. Ivan Ardan (1900–7).

eventually replaced temporal progress as the major emphasis of Ukrainian priests, and, in the process, the leadership role of the laity was eroded.

The first significant shift toward more stringent Catholic control of the community occurred at the 1906 UNA convention, when, at the insistence of a number of recently arrived priests, the delegates agreed to create the office of spiritual adviser, an executive position that was eventually awarded to Fr. Mykhailo Balogh. Unlike his counterpart in the Russian Brotherhood, Father Balogh was not content to play a secondary role. By 1909, he was pressuring *Svoboda* to cease publication of various articles on the natural sciences lest they undermine the faith and morals of the uneducated masses.[155]

Another step toward Catholic control of the UNA was made at the 1908 convention. Jubilant over the arrival of a Greek Catholic bishop, convention delegates first made Ortynsky an honorary UNA member and then, pledging their loyalty and support for all his projects and endeavors, proceeded to proclaim him "patron" of the UNA. Ortynsky accepted the honor, placing himself in an incongruous position. "It is obvious," Father Poniatyshyn later reflected, "that a Catholic bishop, as a natural consequence of his office, cannot serve as patron of an organization which accepted non-Catholics." Especially critical of Ortynsky's "unCatholic" behavior was the GCU, an organization which at the time Ortynsky was still attempting to woo to his side.[156]

A turning point in the history of the Ukrainian-American community occurred at the 1910 UNA convention in Cleveland. Deciding to clarify his status within the UNA, Bishop Ortynsky accepted the chairmanship of the bylaws committee and, despite strong lay opposition, was able to push through a series of resolutions which (1) changed the name of the Ruskyi narodnyi soiuz to the Greek Catholic Ruthenian Association; (2) effectively subordinated the newly named fraternal society to the bishop's office; (3) restricted the election of future convention delegates to Catholics exclusively; (4) obligated all members to attend confession at least once a year during Easter.[157]

The bishop's action and its subsequent approval by majority vote of the convention were devastating to the UNA. Led by Ivan Ardan and the Brotherhood of St. John the Baptist of Olyphant, fourteen branches walked out of the convention. These same branches later joined forces with other newly established local brotherhoods, called a convention, and, in 1911, gave birth to the "new" Ruskyi narodnyi soiuz.[158] Elected to the executive of the fraternal society (hereafter referred to as the Ukrainian Workingmen's Association [UWA], a name adopted in 1918) were Ivan Ardan, president; Matvii Semeniuk, vice-president; Mykhailo Bielia, secretary; Ivan Fedan, treasurer.[159] The first UWA house organ, *Szerszen* (Hornet), made its debut soon after the ill-fated 1910 UNA convention. On 15 July 1911, the UWA began publishing *Narodna Volya* (People's Will),[160] a gazette that was soon to challenge the preeminent position of *Svoboda* and the "old" Soiuz in the Ruthenian-Ukrainian community.

Faced with a crisis that cost the association 1,016 members out of a total 1910 convention membership of 14,430,[161] the UNA leadership attempted to pacify the dissidents with appeals to national unity. "From time immemorial," *Svoboda* declared, "our national life has been plagued by internal strife and conflict. What will the Ruthenian American and the Ruthenian people as a whole gain if the UNA breaks up into three or four small and insignificant groups? We know that we are weak separated from our native mainstream, surrounded by a sea of foreigners ... only in unity can we hope to preserve our heritage and our faith."[162] *Svoboda*'s appeals fell on deaf ears. Neither the bishop, who was urged to negotiate a settlement by some of his priests,[163] nor the UWA was amenable to reconciliation. The UWA remained separate and by 1912 had a membership of 4,683.[164] That same year, the UNA had 14,917 members.

Ironically, the changes proposed by Bishop Ortynsky were never put into effect. Soon after the convention concluded, the UNA executive was informed by legal counsel that according to laws governing such matters, changes adopted at the convention were, in reality, changes in the charter of the UNA and therefore required a prescribed set of procedures. Because these procedures were not followed by the convention, the resolutions were, in effect, null and void. Legally, the UNA was forced to revert to its preconvention organizational and administrative status.[165]

Bishop Ortynsky was disappointed by the ruling but his determination to control a Ruthenian fraternal benevolent society in America did not diminish. Ignoring protests by the UNA, he helped establish the Association of Ruthenian Greek Catholic Brotherhoods, Christian Love in 1911. The following year the name of the new fraternal was changed to the Providence Association of Ruthenian Catholics of America and Rev. Ieronim Barysh of Pittsburgh was elected president. Incorporated into the Providence constitution was the provision that no decision of the executive board was valid without the approval of the bishop or his successor. By the end of the year, Providence gave birth to its own newspaper, *America*,[166] and *Svoboda* was forced to retreat even farther from its previously unchallenged position as the national conscience of the Ruthenian-Ukrainian community.

Bishop Ortynsky and the UNA were never able to reconcile their differences. In 1914, after an increasingly acrimonious polemic battle with *America*, *Svoboda* reviewed Bishop Ortynsky's record since the 1910 imbroglio and accused him of being responsible for "the acceptance of Orthodoxy by many of our people." Bishop Ortynsky, concluded *Svoboda*, is "the enemy of the Ruskyi Soiuz ... the enemy of progress and enlightenment ... and the enemy of our church."[167] For the Ruthenian-Ukrainian community in America, the *Svoboda* editorial marked the end of an era.

On the surface, the tripartite fraternal division within the Ruthenian-Ukrainian community appeared to be a serious setback for the Ukrainian-ization movement. It cannot be denied that the schism resulted in a lack of unity, much duplication of effort, and the weakening of many worthwhile projects, but, in retrospect, the split was probably unavoidable. In a very real sense, it heralded the attainment of a higher developmental stage of the Ukrainian national movement.

As long as the crucial question in the Ruthenian-American community was "What ethnic identity should we adopt?" unity of effort among competing ethnonational streams was essential. Once a degree of consensus regarding the acceptance of the Ukrainian identity had been reached by a segment of the Ruthenian community, however, conflict within that segment was inevitable. A new set of questions, all emanating from the broader issue of means to be adopted in the realization of the recently articulated national will, began to be heard. It was at this juncture in the making of the Ukrainian American that diversity of opinion concerning ethnonational priorities, lay versus clerical control, socioeconomic models, and the nature of the future Ukrainian nation-state came to occupy the attention of Ukrainian Americans. It was a preoccupation that was to remain an integral part of Ukrainian community life in America until the present time.

The Rise of Ideology

"Revolutions," wrote a *Svoboda* contributor in 1904, require "ideological preparation; there must be organization; one must know for what to fight and how to fight and among those who emigrated neither one nor the other existed."[168] Once the Ukrainianization process had begun to take hold, however, political naïveté fell by the wayside along with outdated ethnic identities. In the United States, Ukrainians were able to think, to organize, and to accept ideologies that were soon to provide the political underpinning for the next phase in the nationalization process.

The first political ideology to influence the thinking of the Ruthenian community was, as we have noted, socialism. Under the leadership of the American Circle, the posture of the community was essentially a reflection of the ideology of the Radical party of Galicia. After the Radicals split in 1899 into National Democrats and Social Democrats, the UNA leadership – with the exception of Father Ardan – came to lean toward the more moderate National Democratic position. By 1911, the UNA still represented the middle road among socialist ideologies while the more radical Social Democrats were associated with the UWA. There was also the Social Christian element of Ukrainian-American society gravitating, for the most part, toward the Providence Association.[169]

Despite the leftist leanings of all three Ukrainian fraternals during this period, none of them, not even the UWA, could be considered a political party. Nor, apparently, was there much interest among the established leadership of the three competing societies to create a Ukrainian political organization. By 1900, however, the ideological groundwork for such an eventuality had been laid by *Svoboda*. Interest in the establishment of a separate socialist party heightened during the remainder of the decade largely as a result of three new historical developments: (1) the increased circulation within the community of socialist periodicals from Ukraine; (2) the arrival in America of more politically sophisticated émigrés, many of whom had been exposed to the Marxist ideology of the Social Democrats while working in Germany before emigrating;[170] (3) growing sympathy with the ideals of the American Social Democratic party of Eugene V. Debs (founded in 1897) and later the American Socialist party (founded in 1901) among the Ruthenian-American working man. Ruthenians were hardly alone in their sympathy. In 1912, the Socialists were able to capture some 900,000 votes during the American presidential campaign, a number representing 6 percent of the voters.[171]

The first socialist party to make its appearance in the Ruthenian-Ukrainian community was an organization which called itself Haidamaky, an appellation applied to eighteenth-century Ukrainian peasants who organized themselves into bands and attacked Polish landowners. Organized as a Sich branch in 1907, the new organization began to publish its own periodical – also called *Haidamaky* – in 1908. During the following year, the society was reorganized as a fraternal insurance association and renamed the Ukrainian Progressive Workers' Organization, Haidamaky. Every effort was made by the socialist organization during its early years to work with the American Socialist party in the promulgation of common objectives as well as to reflect conscientiously the ideology of the Social Democrats in Galicia.[172]

Other radical socialist groups also emerged during this period. In 1908, one such group in Salem, Massachusetts, started to publish *Khlopskyi Paragraf* (Peasant's Paragraph), a Marxist periodical that was forced to go out of existence a short time later. A longer press life was enjoyed by *Proletar* (Proletarian), which began its existence in Detroit in 1911, and by *Robitnyk* (Worker), which made its debut in Cleveland in 1912. By 12 April 1917, *Robitnyk* was a daily. A number of American urban centers had Ukrainian socialist societies in 1912, with Philadelphia, Detroit, and Cleveland leading in terms of organizational size and activity. Following the example of the Russians and the Poles, who had organized socialist federations earlier, the Haidamaky attempted to form a similar federation among Ukrainian socialists. The attempt failed because of a lack of coordination among several organizations, and the press war which erupted between *Robitnyk* and *Proletar* over which of the two newspapers would become the official organ of the Ruthenian-Ukrainian socialist movement in America. This latter fight was so divisive that, by the end of 1913, only the Detroit socialist club was still in active existence. Recovery took two years.[173]

The First National Committee

On 1 January 1900, the Ruthenian-Ukrainian community convened its first national congress in Jersey City, New Jersey. Chaired by Fr. Nestor Dmytriw, the congress was devoted to a discussion of such community issues as church organization, education, and assistance for newly arrived immigrants. A decision was reached to establish a Ruthenian immigrant's home.

A second congress was held on 20 December 1903, in Yonkers, New York. A highlight of the congress was a discussion of the Ruthenian-Ukrainian political posture and the subsequent establishment of a National Committee to coordinate all community activities. Elected to head the new organization was Fr. Mykola Stefanovych. A national fund was also created of which 25 percent was earmarked for combating Russian Orthodox propaganda, 25 percent for the support of Ruthenian-Ukrainian schools in America, 25 percent for the establishment and maintenance of a national home, 15 percent for assistance to organizations in Ukraine, and 10 percent for miscellaneous needs in the United States. Subsequent conventions of the Ruthenian National Committee were held in Olyphant in 1904 and in McKeesport in 1905. It was at the latter congress that Fr. Mykola Strutynsky succeeded Father Stefanovych as head of the organization. At the same time, a decision was reached to adopt the name Society of Ruthenian Patriots to identify all local branches of the committee.

Internal disagreements eventually led to the demise of the Ukrainian National Committee and the awarding of national fund monies – less than $600 had been collected – to Father Tymkevych's *bursa* in Yonkers, New York.

The UNA, meanwhile, established its own national fund and collected a total of $10,173.74 by September 1913. A similar fund was created by the UWA and by October 1913, a total of $3,148.12 had been donated.[174]

The Rise of Fund-Raising Campaigns

A final aspect of the prewar phase of Ruthenian political activity in the United States was the growing involvement of Ruthenian-Ukrainians with a variety of causes, all of which, in one way or another, promoted Ukrainian separatism. As early as 1897, for example, the UNA collected $260 for the families of Ruthenians who had lost their lives during election disturbances in Galicia. That same year the UNA created the so-called Political Agitation Fund for the expressed purpose of supporting Ruthenian autonomy in Galicia. The fund, however, never exceeded a total of $61.40, simply because it was easier to collect for a specific purpose than for such a vaguely articulated and nebulous objective.

Once begun, fund-raising campaigns within the Ruthenian-Ukrainian community never seemed to end. During the next few years a number of special funds were inaugurated, the more successful of which were:

1. *The Student Fund*   In 1902, a total of $1,165.14 (5,800 Austrian crowns) was collected for students who boycotted the University of Lviv in protest over its Polonization policies. In 1903, $2,000 (10,000 crowns) was collected as stipend money for university students in Galicia. In 1907, $917.20 (4,900 crowns) was collected for the support of demonstrating Ukrainian students at the University of Lviv.

2. *Election Reform Fund*   In 1906, $1,862.82 (9,300 crowns) was gathered for election reform agitation in Austria.

3. *The Miroslaw Sichynsky Fund*   Initiated in Pittsburgh on 23 May 1909, the Sichynsky Fund was used for a number of purposes. A total of $2,000 (10,000 crowns) was sent to the Association of Ukrainian Teachers for the support of Ridna Shkola (school) in Galicia, while another $840 (4,200 crowns) was earmarked for agitation on behalf of the release of Sichynsky following his arrest for the assassination of Count Potocki. Additional money was collected by Iryna Sichynsky, Miroslaw's sister, who visited Ruthenian-Ukrainian communities throughout the United States in an effort to obtain money for legal assistance for her brother in Austria.

4. *The Adam Kotsko Fund*   A total of $600 was collected in 1910 in memory of the Ukrainian student slain in the Ukrainian and Polish student disturbances at the Lviv University. The money was sent to the Sichynsky School Fund in Galicia.

5. *The Father Mykola Stefanovych Fund*   In 1911, a special fund was organized in memory of Father Stefanovych, the second member of the American Circle to die on American soil. The Association of Ukrainian Pedagogues received $2,000 from this fund.

6. *The Ridna Shkola Fund*   Financial support for the Ridna Shkola in Galicia was initiated in 1910 with a $500 donation from the UNA. A similar

UNA donation was made in 1911, and in 1912 Dr. Semen Demydchuk, a representative of Ridna Shkola, collected an additional $9,400.87 during a fund-raising tour of Ukrainian communities in the United States.[175]

By 1914, *Svoboda* reported that the UNA was involved in a total of thirteen separate fund-raising drives including, in addition to the Ridna Shkola and Sichynsky funds, campaigns for a Ukrainian garden in Lviv, a private Ukrainian gymnasium in Zbarazh, Prosvita in Lviv, a jubilee gift for Ivan Franko, a Ukrainian *bursa* in Horlychakh, a private Ukrainian gymnasium in Rohatyn, a Ukrainian *bursa* in Nadrivneie, political activists in Galicia, and a Ukrainian *bursa* in Sianochi. Significantly, only two funds had been established for Ukrainian projects in the United States: Ridna Shkola in America and the School Enlightenment Fund.[176]

From Uhro-Rusyn to Carpatho-Ruthenian

While Ukrainian-leaning Ruthenians were gradually shedding their Ruthenian identity, developing and nurturing a new ethnonational awareness, wrestling with political ideologies, and raising monies for separatist causes in Ukraine, Uhro-Rusyns were traveling along a different road.

Initially, *Viestnik,* the Uhro-Rusyn periodical, and *Svoboda,* the Ruthenian-Ukrainian organ, viewed the Ruthenians and their American environment from a similar perspective. Both regularly condemned drunkenness, parental indifference, sloth, and other social shortcomings of their early Ruthenian immigrants. Both stressed the importance of education,[177] the heritage school movement,[178] and the need to preserve one's European heritage.[179] Respect for one's roots, observed *Viestnik* in 1895, comes about only when one is familiar with the history of one's own people.[180] He who does not love his nationality "sins against God."[181]

Viestnik was also united with *Svoboda* in its condemnation of the Roman Catholic hierarchy's clumsy endeavors to Latinize the Ruthenian church,[182] the weak character of Ruthenians who joined other faiths,[183] and Fr. Alexis Toth's tsarist-financed proselytization campaign.[184] Analyzing the latter phenomenon, *Viestnik* warned: "Ruthenians are corpses of the Ruthenian nation ... We will not remain silent as various speculators take advantage of the weak spirits of Ruthenians but will identify and support the interest of the Ruthenian people."[185]

Unlike the UNA and *Svoboda,* however, the GCU and *Viestnik* began their existence in America with a political orientation that was essentially Hungarian. In 1896, *Viestnik* urged Ruthenians who were being tempted by Father Toth's followers to join the Russian Orthodox church to remember their "Magyar patriotism."[186] Three years later, the GCU leadership became indignant when *Szabadzag,* a Hungarian-American gazette, accused the GCU of falling prey to "pan-Slavic influences." Replying in *Amerikai Nemzetor*, another Hungarian periodical published in the United States, an Uhro-Rusyn correspondent (believed to be Fr. Cornelius Lawryshyn) argued that most members of the GCU were loyal Hungarian patriots, reminding *Szabadzag* that the GCU sponsored stipends for children proficient in the Hungarian language and that the GCU secretary could not speak a single Slavic tongue. The only reason *Viestnik* was not published in Hungarian, concluded the writer, was that many GCU members could not read the language.[187]

The Hungarian ethnonational orientation promoted by Magyarized priests, however, had little real chance of being successfully adopted by Ruthenians in the United States. The major obstacle was language. The vast majority of GCU members spoke Slavic dialects that are more closely related to Ukrainian than to any other language. Hungarian, in contrast, is a non-Slavic language remotely related to Finnish. To expect Ruthenian Americans to master Hungarian while learning English was unrealistic. The language problem was further complicated by the fact that in order to accommodate its readers, *Viestnik* had to be printed in two scripts, Cyrillic for the Carpatho-Ruthenians and Latin for the Lemkos.[188] But even if the language problem could have been resolved, the future of the Hungarian alternative was considerably diminished by the 1902 discovery of the Komlossy Memorandum, which documented direct Hungarian involvement in the affairs of Ruthenian Americans. It was probably as a result of both the language hurdle and the Hungarian intrusion that delegates attending the 1902 GCU convention voted to ban the Hungarian language from all deliberations.[189]

Once the Hungarian option was discredited, three ethnonational alternatives presented themselves: the Ukrainian, the dream of the Galician leadership; a non-Ukrainian Ruthenian (Carpatho-Ruthenian); and the Russian.

Almost from its inception, the Carpatho-Ruthenian ethnonational stream was predicated on a broad and massive program of anti-Ukrainian reaction rather than on the cultivation and nurturing of what was still an underdeveloped ethnonational foundation. "Under the impact of Ukrainophile propaganda which refused to consider the peculiar tradition of the Ruthenian people," the Carpatho-Ruthenian leader Rev. Stephen Gulovich later wrote, "it was inevitable that a countermovement should make its weight felt and become, as it were, a standard by which all persons, activities, and organizations were to be judged."[190]

Animosities between the two Ruthenian communities really began the moment four Galician priests left the GCU and proceeded to establish the UNA as a competing fraternal insurance organization. Responding to the

Svoboda platform of 1894, *Viestnik* described it as "fooling the people"[191] and as being "boastful and aggressive."[192] During the remainder of the year *Viestnik* was filled with increasingly negative articles aimed at discrediting the UNA and *Svoboda*.[193] In 1895, the goals of *Svoboda* were described by *Viestnik* as an "unheard of myopia"[194] and in 1896, the UNA periodical was accused of participating in "diabolical intrigues."[195]

By 1901, when the statements and actions of the American Circle suggested a more progressive ethnonational direction within the Ukrainian stream, *Viestnik* warned its readers to be wary of the "dangerous epidemic of radical socialism among American Ruthenians."[196] Labeling circle members *popike radicale* (radical priests),[197] *Viestnik* censured them for "attempting to destroy" the "spiritual morality" of the Ruthenians.[198]

Criticism of the American Circle continued unabated throughout 1902. One lengthy *Viestnik* article, for example, was headlined: "The Latest Attempt of the Popike-Radicale to Cause Trouble among Ruthenian Americans."[199] That same year, in an obvious effort to underscore circle members' alleged lack of spiritual grace, *Viestnik* devoted a number of articles to the excommunication of Father Ardan, an outspoken member.[200]

The early attacks on the Ruthenian-Ukrainian camp laid the foundation for the Ukrainophobia that was soon to infect the entire Uhro-Rusyn community. Ostensibly, the pro-Hungarian clergy was no longer setting the pace for the growing surge of anti-Ukrainian sentiment. The tone, however, had been established. It was maintained, relentlessly and incessantly, for the next twelve years.

The arrival of Bishop Ortynsky from Galicia in 1907 provided the Uhro-Rusyn leadership with a convenient whipping boy against whom to rally their community. "Bishop Ortynsky was guilty of an unpardonable crime," wrote Gulovich, "he came of Ukrainian stock."[201]

By 1908, the battle lines between Uhro-Rusyns and Ruthenian-Ukrainians were clearly drawn. In an especially scathing article, *Viestnik* declared:

> Ukrainian priests are pushing the lying *Svoboda* into the hands of peasants instead of the lives of the saints which they themselves haven't read. Ukrainian priests are leading the way to Ukrainian slavery, one in which our national ideals will be lost. "Ukrainchiks" are confusing our meetings. We have reached a time when our "Ukrainchiks" offer division, robbery and thievery ... A priest is supposed to spread the Kingdom of God and not the Kingdom of Ukraine ... Ukrainians are ripping our Christian faith from our hearts. The Pole is stealing our rite. The Ukrainian is stealing our very faith ... Ukraine is separating children from parents, brothers, sisters, priests from parishes ... evil and diabolical hatred burns in

the hearts of Ukrainians ... Our tattered, hungry sons of Ruthenian soil run to America but even here they are caught by the
Ukrainians.[202]

The anti-Ukrainian diatribe was continued later in the year with Ortynsky as the target. *Viestnik* editorialized:

Upon the arrival of the bishop ... Ukrainian leaders and their little
Soiuz and *Svoboda* lifted their heads. They knew that the bishop
is a flaming Ukrainian ... Galician priests lie, confuse, gypsify ...
the Uhro-Rusyn people and all with the approval of the bishop
whose heels they lick. They wanted to make Uhro-Rusyns into
Ukrainians. They thought if Uhro-Rusyn saw the bishop's staff
and received his blessing, they would fall on their stomachs and
listen to him. Poorly and with great difficulty is Ukraine being
built here in America.[203]

Simply opposing Bishop Ortynsky and the Ruthenian-Ukrainians, of
course, was hardly enough of a foundation upon which to build a distinct
ethnonational identity. A more definitive perspective was needed, and this
was provided in 1908. Meeting in Braddock and Scranton, the Uhro-Rusyn
clergy drafted a communiqué outlining their ethnonational posture and
their perception of the relationship which then existed between the two
Ruthenian communities. The historic document was later published by
Viestnik – in the two Slavic scripts as well as in English. The substance of
the English version read as follows:

TO ALL GREEK CATHOLIC PARISHES, GREEK CATHOLIC SOCIETIES AND
ESPECIALLY TO ALL GREEK CATHOLIC PEOPLE LIVING IN THE UNITED
STATES OF AMERICA – WITH THE EXCEPTION OF THE UKRAINISTS AND
RADICALS IMPORTED FROM GALICIA – AND TO ALL WHOM IT MAY
CONCERN

*The Affairs of the Greek Catholics of the United States of America and
Their Bishop*

There are in the United States of America more than 400,000
United Greek Catholics (*Graeciritus Catholici Cum Sacra Sede
Romana Uniti*) with over 100 churches and about the same number
of priests ...
     All of them are emigrants from the Austro-Hungarian Empire,
that is, to be more precise, from Hungary and Galicia.

Regarding their nationality, a very small part of them are Hungarians (Magyars). The rest are the so-called Sub-Carpathian Russians (Ruthenians). The Russians speak three dialects. Most speak the Slavonic-Russian dialect, which in America has been incorrectly called Slovak by many. The remainder are Russians from Hungary and Galicia, and each has a dialect of its own.

The Greek Catholics of Hungary comprise four-fifths of the entire population while those from Galicia represent only one-fifth. The consequence is that the Russians of Hungary are an absolute majority.

All of these people are peaceful and religious, especially the Greek Catholics of Hungary who are in no way interested in the harmful politics of their former country. A great number of them have become American citizens and have made the United States their permanent residence.

It is a characteristic fact that while the Russians of Hungary give more attention to their churches and institutions and less income to their pastors, the Russians of Galicia donate more to their priests than to their churches and institutions.

The Greek Catholics of Hungary are inclined towards refinement and exhibit an honest, sincere, open-hearted, and active nature. This cannot be said of those from Galicia. The reason for this is that the Russians of Hungary were not as politically and religiously oppressed as were those of Galicia. The Russians of Hungary enjoyed quite enough liberty while those of Galicia for many hundreds of years were almost slaves under the power of the Poles. For this reason, the Greek Catholics of Galicia are more responsive to political and social campaigns than either the Magyars or Russians of Hungary.

The Russians of Hungary and those of Galicia never had anything in common until they came to America. It was here that an attempt was made to bring them together and to make them one in religious and national matters. These attempts were not only unsuccessful but in some ways served to widen the breach between them ...

The reasons for the present separation are:

1. In their native country, they were never united. The Galicians were under the yoke of the Poles for 500 years and for the past 137 years they have been under the rule of Austria. The Russians of Hungary, on the other hand, have been under the rule of Hungary for at least 1,000 years. The two groups shall never be united, regardless of the political or social standard. In their

customs, thought and purposes, they are separate. They are totally different regarding their nature, character and manners.

2. Although the language of both is Russian, the dialects are very different.

3. Even though they are both of the Greek Catholic rite, even here there are great and significant differences between them. The Russians of Galicia have brought into their ritual many alien new customs and the Russians of Hungary, being of a conservative nature, want to know nothing of these alien creations, customs, and rituals. The greatest differences exist in the "church hymns." The hymns of the Galician Greek Catholics differ greatly from those of the Greek Catholics of Hungary.

4. The Russians of Hungary are very devout Catholics, are loyal to the Holy Apostolic See, and have always been so. This cannot be said of the Russians of Galicia; politics decides whether they are good Catholics or not. This fact has been demonstrated by the so-called "ukrainists," not only in Galicia but in America.[204]

Having moved the Uhro-Rusyn community closer to a Russian ethnonational identity, the communiqué concluded by once again condemning the "ukrainist party," the "spirit of socialism, radicalism and even anarchy which it spreads," and its endeavors "to establish a powerful state under the name 'ukraina' upon the territories which are inhabited by the so-called 'Little Russians' of Galicia, Hungary and Russia whom the ukrainist politics have entirely separated from the 'Great Russian' people and that on a 'ultra social-radical' basis and with an entirely separate literature and an extra phonetic orthography."[205]

Significantly, the lower case "u" in identifying the Ukrainians was used consistently in the original text. Despite a number of other grammatical errors, this could hardly have been unintentional, especially since "Russian," "Hungarian," and "Little Russian" were properly capitalized. Also significant, not only in the communiqué but in other *Viestnik* articles as well, was the consistent association of the designation "Ukrainian" with terms such as "slavery," "radical," and "anarchist."

In 1903, the Preshovite clergy established their own fraternal insurance society, Sobranie Greko-Katolicheskich Bratstv (United Societies of the Greek Catholic Religion), which in 1910 began to publish a periodical entitled *Rusin*. Supportive of Ortynsky, *Rusin* suggested that the alleged Ukrainian threat was a red herring. Accusing the *Rusin* editorial staff of being "pharisees,"[206] *Viestnik* continued to debate the Preshovite gazette, consistently condemning it for its many "falsehoods."[207]

The polemic war with the Ruthenian-Ukrainian community became increasingly bitter in the years that followed and the archvillain continued to be Bishop Ortynsky. In the eyes of the GCU, Ortynsky was responsible for literally all of the problems in the Ruthenian-American community. Complaining of the "brutality" of the "Ukrainian Hetmanate" which the bishop had "established in America," *Viestnik* even went as far as to suggest in 1911 that "Galicians and Hungarians lived together in harmony and no one thought to separate until the arrival of Ortynsky."[208] If *Viestnik* was interested in restoring peace to the community, however, its articles hardly reflected that sentiment. Throughout the entire conflict, the GCU periodical seemed to go out of its way to fan the flames of discord by publishing emotionally charged commentaries on the sundry conflicts which erupted between Uhro-Rusyns and Ruthenian-Ukrainians in communities such as South Chicago,[209] Cleveland,[210] Northampton,[211] Peekskill,[212] Barnsboro,[213] McKeesport,[214] Whiting,[215] and Perryopolis,[216] to mention but a few. Typical of the rhetoric employed to describe the "polemics" involved were head-lines such as "Action of the Ukrainian Radicals and Bootlickers,"[217] "The Foulest Chameleon Activities,"[218] "The End of Violations and Cruelties Draws Near,"[219] "Brutal Actions of Bishop Ortynsky,"[220] "Latest Example of the Undermining Work of the Ukrainians,"[221] and "Terrible Injustices and Still Worse Brutality of Bishop Ortynsky."[222] Most of the articles bore the nom de plume N.N. or "Z" (probably Zatkovich).

Despite the Ukrainophobia of *Viestnik* and the GCU, there were Carpatho-Ruthenians during this period who endeavored to create a separate Carpatho-Ruthenian consciousness not on an "anti-identity" basis but rather on the cultural foundations that had been developed by Oleksandr Dukhnovych and others between 1848 and 1868 in Carpatho-Ukraine. Such an approach was suggested at the 1910 Carpatho-Ruthenian congress in Johnstown by the associate editor of *Viestnik:*

> Dear Brothers! It is about time to know more about ourselves ... Why are you so afraid of the Ukrainians? People say there are twice as many of us as there are of them so what is there to be frightened of? ... Ukrainians ... have a national ideal and they work on its behalf. That is why they seem so frightening to us. It's about time that we too, brothers, began to do this kind of national work.[223]

With the Ruthenian national movement all but obliterated by the Hungarians in Carpatho-Ukraine, however, hopes for its resurrection in the United States appeared dim.

The GCU never did reconcile itself to the Ortynsky episcopacy, even when the bishop agreed to many of the Uhro-Rusyn demands. To the very end of Ortynsky's life *Viestnik* seemed to search for any pretext – and perceived every slight – as "proof," once again, that the bishop was the leader of a Ukrainian conspiracy. In 1914, for example, long after Ortynsky had broken with the UNA, the leading organization in the Ukrainian camp, *Viestnik* published an article entitled "Protest against Ukrainian Slyness":

> The bishop made peace with the Uhro-Rusyns and promised them in writing that their desire not to have anything to do with Ukrainians, outside of church, will be honored by him. At the same time, the bishop's chancery writes letters to Uhro-Rusyn priests in phonetics. In addition, the bishop is calling to Philadelphia a Ukrainian Congress where he wants to bring together all of the Ruthenian people who have lived in Hungary for 1,000 years ... Some Uhro-Rusyn parishes supported the so-called People's Convention but when they learned that Ukrainians want to build an independent state, they protested because they don't want to betray their homeland ... We Uhro-Rusyns have our own state and we don't need any Ukrainian state.[224]

In retrospect, it is difficult to justify the behavior of the GCU and *Viestnik* toward Bishop Ortynsky and the Ukrainian community. It is true that the American Circle, the UNA, and *Svoboda* were anxious to Ukrainianize all Ruthenians. It is also true that some "converts" were overly zealous in their efforts to bring more Ruthenians within the Ukrainian fold. But the rhetoric of *Viestnik* was far too inflammatory to have been precipitated by occasional Ukrainian excesses. What danger did Ukrainians really pose when, as *Viestnik* never tired of reminding its readers, Galician Ruthenians represented no more than 20 percent of the total Ruthenian-American community? The GCU, moreover, was surely aware of the controversy that had been precipitated by Bishop Ortynsky in 1910 and the subsequent dissolution of Ukrainian unity. Under such circumstances, there was little justification for describing the bishop as a Ukrainian "hetman."

From Ruthenian to Russian

The first phase of the Russification process in the Ruthenian-American community was initiated by the charismatic Fr. Alexis Toth, a former Greek Catholic priest from Carpatho-Ukraine. His work was continued by capable Russian bishops of the so-called Russian Orthodox Greek Catholic church in America and by priests trained in Russia. While Greek Catholics always seemed short of priests and money, the Russian Orthodox lacked for neither. By 1916, the Russian diocese in North America consisted of one archbishop, two coadjutor bishops, three bishops, three archimandrites, five archpriests, 243 priests, forty-three hieromonks, three archdeacons, and two deacons. There were also 164 churches, most of which were former Greek Catholic parishes in America; 126 parochial heritage schools (with 6,903 children); and 135 youth societies claiming a membership of 8,284.[225]

Such phenomenal growth could not have been achieved without the direct involvement of the Russian imperial government. Russian support began when Father Toth's Minneapolis parish started receiving an annual stipend soon after converting to Orthodoxy.[226] When Bishop Nicholas described Father Toth's missionary success among a group the Russian bishop identified as "Carpatho-Russian Uniates," Count Witte, the Russian minister of finance, and other high government officials were surprised by the number of "Russians" from Austro-Hungary then living in the United States. As it became evident that many Ruthenians were returning to their homeland and that their conversion in America could strengthen the Russophile contingent in Carpatho-Ukraine, Russian imperial interest in America's Ruthenians increased dramatically. By 1897, the Holy Synod was reporting that Ruthenians in the United States were "of Russian spiritual heritage."[227] In 1899, Tsar Nicholas II was made aware of the Ruthenian conversions and pledged his support "for this great Christian work." Later the tsar made substantial personal donations for the rebuilding of the church in Minneapolis, the construction of the cathedral in New York City, and church building projects in Chicago[228] and Pittsburgh.[229] Before long, the Russian church in North America was being subsidized by the Russian state – working through the Holy Synod – by as much as $77,850 annually. This was in addition to the regular contributions of the Missionary Society of Russia.[230]

Prior to 1907, the year Bishop Ortynsky arrived in the United States, most of the Ruthenian parishes that converted to Russian Orthodoxy were from the Ruthenian-Ukrainian camp.[231] It was during this period that Fr. Gregory Hrushka, first editor of *Svoboda* and one of the founders of the UNA, converted to Russian Orthodoxy. Assigned to a parish in Old Forge, Pennsylvania, Hrushka eventually denounced the Ukrainianization campaign of the American Circle and worked within the Russian national stream until his return to Ukraine in 1901.[232] The powerful influence of Hrushka, the disillusionment with the Roman Catholic church brought about by Rome's discriminatory actions (exacerbated by the militancy of the American Circle), and the shortage of priests from Galicia were all factors contributing to Russian successes among Galician Ruthenians during this period.

After 1907, most of the parishes that converted to Orthodoxy were from the Uhro-Rusyn community.[233] The GCU- and *Viestnik*-orchestrated anti-

Ukrainian campaign, the ready availability of Orthodox priests, the relative affluence of Russian parishes, and a growing sympathy for the Russophile, Carpatho-Russian ethnonational orientation among some Uhro-Rusyn clergy, all contributed to the progress enjoyed by the Russian Orthodox among Uhro-Rusyns.

The Role of Fraternal Benefit Societies

The second phase of the Russification process began with the creation of Russian fraternal benefit societies. In 1895, the Russian Orthodox mission called a meeting of its supporters to the same Wilkes-Barre church in which the GCU was founded and gave birth to the Russian Orthodox Mutual Aid Association (POV).

The founders of the POV were Bishop Nicholas, Fr. Alexis Toth, and Alexis E. Olarovsky, the Russian consul general in New York who, from 1895 to 1897, also served as the first president of the new fraternal society. The POV was the only American organization authorized by the Holy Synod and in its founding statement, the leadership declared that there was but one, undivided, Russian people. Despite financial assistance from the Holy Synod, the POV grew slowly. In 1912, there were only 12,000 members. That same year, the GCU, founded in 1892, just three years earlier, had 32,000 members while the UNA, founded in 1894, had 15,000 members.

In 1897, the POV began publishing *Svet* (the Light), a newspaper edited by Fr. Gregory Hrushka until 1900. From its inception, *Svet* adopted the position that the union with Rome in 1595 had been a mistake and that salvation for the Ruthenian people would come only when they reunited with the Holy Russian Orthodox church.[234] In 1899, the Holy Synod contributed $600 to *Svet* because, in the words of the synod, "it was of significant interest to the Little Russian Uniates who have converted to Orthodoxy."[235]

Every president of the POV from 1897 to 1910 immigrated to the United States from the Russian Empire. All POV presidents, even those—both immigrants and American born – who headed the society after 1910, were totally loyal not only to Russian Orthodoxy but also to the political objectives of the Russian Empire in Eastern Europe.[236] In 1915, for example, Fr. Peter Kohanik, the second president of Ruthenian background to head the society,* committed the POV to full support of the Russophiles in Austria, declaring: "The society is dedicated to fight for Orthodoxy wherever it is threatened ... Therefore we have already sent $600 to Austria with the aim of liberating Orthodoxy from tyranny."[237] For the POV as for the Holy

* Kohanik was also the editor of *Svet* for many years.

Synod, the religiocultural identity "Orthodox" and the ethnonational identity "Russian" were synonymous. In a history of the organization published in commemoration of its tenth anniversary, President B. Turkevich wrote that all POV members "must be completely Orthodox, without any other nationality" (*bez drugikh narodnostei*).[238]

Another pro-Russian fraternal association came into existence in 1900 soon after Ivan Zhynchak-Smith, an Uhro-Rusyn businessman, was defeated for the presidency of the GCU by Fr. Cornelius Lawryshyn. Taking umbrage over what he considered to be clerical encroachment into lay affairs, Smith helped establish the Russian Brotherhood Organization (or RBO), a fraternal insurance society that initially banned all priests from membership. By 1914, RBO had some 14,000 members.

In 1902, RBO began publishing its own periodical, *Pravda* (Truth), which, like *Viestnik*, was soon attacking the *popike radicale* associated with the UNA and *Svoboda* for their "anarchism, socialism and atheism."[239] *Pravda* also published annual almanacs containing articles, poems, and other information of interest to its readers. In 1911, a poem written by Mikhail Baland, the RBO general controller, appeared in the annual almanac. Entitled "Do russkikh molodtsov" (To Russian Youth), the poem declared:

> You are the sons of the holy Rus'! ...
> May this land of your mother remain dear to your heart ...
> The Poles and Jews would subvert you with the idea of "Ukraine"
> An ideal land in which there are no Polish landlords and no Jews.
> That is double talk
> No such land exists.
> Study the history and writings of Rus'.
> And thereby strengthen your resistance to the Ukrainians.
> And you will grow to be proud sons of Mother Rus'.[240]

In its 1919 almanac, *Pravda* reaffirmed its allegiance to Russian imperial aims in Eastern Europe – despite "intrigues" from the "so-called Ukrainians" – and to the principle of one united and indivisible Russian state.[241]

The Role of Reading Rooms

Still another important vehicle of the nationalization process in the Russian community – as in the Ruthenian community – was the reading room. Supported by the Russian Orthodox mission and the Russian fraternals, the typical reading room contained various books as well as newspapers such as *Novoe Vremia* (New Times) from Russia, *Russkoe Slovo* (Russian Word) from Galicia, *Nedelia* (Sunday) from Hungary, *Svet, Pravda,* and even *Viestnik*.[242] "*Svoboda*," wrote one immigrant pioneer from Mayfield, Pennsylvania, "was read until it became an organ of the treacherous followers of Mazepa rather than the true followers of St. Vladimir."[243] Describing an evening in one of the Russian reading rooms in 1911, Father Fekula of Coldale, Pennsylvania, reminisced about the kinds of discussions held in the Russian community during this period: "People meet in the reading room and read newspapers and books from both America and the old country. The leaders discuss the burning issues of the day, especially the plight of all Russian people in Galicia who are persecuted by the Poles and their followers – the Ukrainians who are lackeys of the Poles."[244]

Ruthenians who joined the Russian Orthodox church in America rarely returned to the Ruthenian fold. They were absorbed by the Russian ethnonational stream and became, in both religious belief and national orientation, thoroughly and irrevocably Russian.

☙

After some thirty years in the United States, the Ruthenians of America had adopted three ethnonational identities – Ukrainian, Carpatho-Ruthenian, and Russian. Of the three, the Russian camp could claim some 20 percent of the Ruthenians while the remainder were about equally divided between the Ukrainian and Carpatho-Ruthenian streams.

The making of the Ukrainian American, that is, the ethnonational metamorphosis of the Ruthenian immigrant by the Ukrainian stream, was largely the accomplishment of eight Galician priests, the so-called American Circle, working through two major institutions – the Ukrainian Greek Catholic church and the Ukrainian National Association – as well as other vehicles of the Ukrainianization process such as *Svoboda*, and various reading rooms, enlightenment societies, women's organizations, cultural enterprises, youth organizations, and heritage schools.

Ruthenians from Carpatho-Ukraine who wished to retain their original identity found themselves in a quandary. With the Ruthenian revival all but dead in the homeland, a Carpatho-Ruthenian stream did not enjoy the benefit of new and unique ethnonational currents to invigorate its development. Unable to live comfortably with a Hungarian national identity – the hope of the Magyarized clergy – the Ruthenians from Carpatho-Ukraine were initially propelled into adopting an ethnic consciousness predicated on anti-Ukrainian sentiments and perceptions. Realizing that a more stable national base upon which to build an ethnic identity was necessary, the leadership of the Ruthenians from Carpatho-Ukraine eventually turned to a quasi-Russian alternative and began drifting towards a "Carpatho-Ruthenian" orientation.

On the eve of World War I, the Ukrainian community was seething with anticipation. The religious and ethnic battles for the soul of the Ruthenian American had been fought and partially won and a new, heretofore unknown Ukrainian ethnonational identity was being forged on American soil. As events in Europe began to unfold, the tempering of that identity was about to take place.

4 The Tempering of the Ukrainian American

Ukrainian immigration to the United States ceased during World War I and did not resume until the 1920s. The second mass immigration was different from the first both in size and in terms of ethnonational sophistication. In Europe, Ukraine had attained statehood, an achievement which forever changed Ukrainian-American aspirations.

The Rise and Fall of the Ukrainian National Republic

With the exception of a brief period during the early 1900s when censorship was temporarily lifted and the Russian Academy of Sciences officially recognized Ukrainian as a distinct and separate Slavic language, Russian scholars and government officials consistently referred to Ukraine as a Russian land and to the Ukrainian language as a Russian dialect. The revival in eastern Ukraine could not be stopped, however. As in Galicia, the literary renaissance led to a national awakening and the emergence of Ukrainian political parties, most of which supported autonomy in one form or another. In contrast to Galicia, however, their activities were of necessity largely clandestine.

After the Russian Empire collapsed in 1917, Ukrainian political and organizational leaders went to Kiev, formed a Central Rada (council), and established the Ukrainian National Republic. Plans to federate with a democratic Russian republic faded when the Bolsheviks overthrew the Kerensky government in October 1917. On 22 January 1918, the Rada declared that from that day forward, the newly created Ukrainian republic would be the "independent, free, and sovereign state of the Ukrainian people."

Under the leadership of Michael Hrushevsky, Ukraine's first president, and the Central Rada, the Ukrainian people established a socialist government that abolished capital punishment, offered land to peasants, and guaranteed the rights of the major minorities by creating subcabinet level posts for Jewish, Polish, and Russian affairs. Ukrainian periodicals and publications multiplied, Ukrainian cultural activities thrived, schools in the Ukrainian language were organized, and Ukrainian Orthodoxy was revived with the birth of the Ukrainian Autocephalous Orthodox church.

There were problems, however. Ukrainian independence was not fully recognized by any of the Western Allies who hoped for a reunited Russia fighting to defeat the Germans and Austrians. With no support from the democratic nations of the West and under pressure from Bolshevik forces, the Rada was forced to sign a peace treaty with Germany and her allies in return for diplomatic recognition and military support. Included in the treaty was a Ukrainian promise to supply grain and other agricultural products for Germany and Austria-Hungary. When Ukraine's new peasant farmers resisted the requisitions for the required foodstuffs, the German army command in Kiev dissolved the Rada.

On 29 April 1918, a congress called by the Alliance of Landowners, a conservative coalition of political leaders opposed to the land reform measures of the Rada, proclaimed General Pavlo Skoropadsky hetman of Ukraine. Despite his lack of popular support, Skoropadsky proved to be an efficient administrator who increased the treasury, curbed inflation, upgraded the Ukrainian school system, and strengthened the Ukrainian diplomatic corps.

With the Austro-Hungarian Empire on the verge of collapse, Ukrainian leaders from Galicia and Bukovina came together in Lviv and, on 1 November 1918, established the Republic of Western Ukraine (ZUNR). In Carpatho-Ukraine, the Council of Khust, then the most representative of the Ruthenian-Ukrainian councils, met on 21 January 1919, and voted to unite with the Ukrainian National Republic.

The German army withdrew from Ukraine soon after the armistice. The Sich Riflemen (Sichovi Striltsi), a ZUNR military brigade under the command of Colonel Ievhen Konovalets, helped defeat the remnants of Skoropadsky's forces (Skoropadsky himself fled to Germany) and on 19 November 1918, the Ukrainian republic was reestablished under the leadership of a five-man Directory headed by Symon Petliura and Volodymyr Vynnychenko. In an imposing ceremony in Kiev on 22 January 1919, the ZUNR formally joined the Ukrainian National Republic as the Western Region (*oblast*) of the UNR (or ZOUNR) and the Ukrainian nation was united for the first time in almost seven hundred years.

By then, however, the Ukrainian republic was being besieged by enemies from all sides. Determined to establish a Ukrainian soviet republic, the Red Russian army invaded from the east. Planning to include Ukraine in a new, nonsocialist Russian state, the Allied-supported White Russian army headed by General A.I. Denikin invaded from the south. Eager to incorporate all of Galicia in their newly established republic, the Poles invaded from the west.

Unfortunately, the two leading members of the Directory parted ways, adding to the political fragmentation that plagued the Ukrainian movement throughout. Even in 1918, the left wing of the Ukrainian Socialist Revolutionaries, the largest Ukrainian political party, split off and formed a new grouping, the Borotbists, which gravitated toward the Bolsheviks and were ultimately merged into the Communist Party (Bolshevik) of Ukraine in 1920. The second largest Ukrainian party, the Social Democrats, also splintered, with its left wing evolving into the pro-Soviet Ukrainian Communist party (known as the Ukapists), the remnants of which were also merged into the Bolshevik party in 1925. Against this background, Vynnychenko hoped for some type of accommodation with the Bolsheviks, while Petliura saw any such accommodation as impossible. As a result, Vynnychenko broke with Petliura, went into exile, and founded an émigré group associated with the Ukapists. In the summer of 1920, Vynnychenko even traveled to Moscow and Kharkiv and was briefly named a member of Ukraine's Soviet government. Quickly disillusioned with the Bolsheviks' hostility toward anything Ukrainian, Vynnychenko went back into exile after only a few weeks and broke with pro-Soviet elements in the Ukrainian movement. But the damage already done was immense.

Compounding Petliura's problems were the actions of various independent *otamans* (guerrilla commanders), whose political loyalties were always in doubt, and various self-appointed bandit chieftains who roamed the Ukrainian countryside in search of booty. Capitalizing on Ukrainian peasant frustration in the wake of five years of unrelenting strife, and pointing to the inordinate number of Jewish Bolshevik leaders, Denikin and a group of Ukrainian *otamans* instigated pogroms resulting in the death of thousands of innocent Ukrainian Jews. Petliura immediately issued an executive order (#131) ordering Ukrainian military personnel "to drive away with your arms all who incite you to pogroms" and to "bring them before the courts as enemies of the state." In addition, Petliura's government provided financial relief for pogrom victims (administered by the Ukrainian minister of Jewish affairs, M. Pinkos Krasnyi, himself a Jew) and publicly invited a number of internationally prominent Jewish leaders to form an Extraordinary Commission of Inquiry to investigate the matter. Despite these measures and the fact that the pogroms occurred in the fall and winter of 1918 and the spring of 1919 in areas where the Ukrainian national government no longer exercised effective control, it was Petliura and the Ukrainians rather than Denikin and the Russians who came to be perceived as perpetrators of these anti-Semitic crimes.

Realizing that Ukraine could not win against all her enemies, a Western Ukrainian delegation approached Denikin to seek an armistice. When Denikin refused to include Petliura in the negotiations, ZOUNR president Ievhen Petrusevych reestablished the Republic of Western Ukraine (ZUNR) and agreed to a separate peace treaty in the hope that such an act would win favor with the peacemakers in Paris. Signed in Odessa on 17 November 1919, the treaty effectively divorced the future of Western Ukraine from that of the Ukrainian National Republic.

Bitter over what he considered a betrayal by Petrusevych, Petliura approached the Poles for an armistice and, on 20 April 1920, signed a peace treaty relinquishing all claims to eastern Galicia in return for Polish recognition of the Directory as the legitimate government of Ukraine. While the Bolsheviks were busy routing Denikin's forces in the south, a combined Ukrainian-Polish army invaded from the west, arriving in Kiev on 7 May. Rallying their forces, the Bolsheviks quickly recaptured Kiev and drove the Ukrainians and Poles back across the Zbruch River. By August the Red Army was deep inside Polish territory and the Poles were suing for peace. On 18 March 1921, Warsaw signed a treaty with the Bolsheviks recognizing the legitimacy of the recently established Ukrainian Soviet Socialist Republic (UkrSSR) and the Zbruch River frontier.[1]

A Ukrainian delegation was in Paris soon after the peace conference that would determine the future of Europe began. There was reason for optimism, especially when President Woodrow Wilson committed the United States to the principle of national self-determination. By the time the conference ended, the Austro-Hungarian Empire was no more, the Russian Empire had been reduced, and seven newly independent states had been recognized: Finland, Estonia, Latvia, Lithuania (all formerly occupied by tsarist Russia); and Poland, Czechoslovakia, and Yugoslavia.

For Ukrainians, however, the Paris Peace Conference was a disaster. From the beginning, when the conference refused to accord official recognition to the Ukrainian delegation, to the end, when the conference all but denied the existence of a separate Ukrainian nation, Ukrainian ethnonational aspirations were ignored.

The British and French delegations argued that (1) Ukraine was really "Little Russia," an integral part of Great Russia; (2) Ukrainian nationalism was a German invention; (3) Petliura was a Russian traitor; (4) the Directory was "practically Bolshevik."

Woefully unfamiliar with the nationality question in the Russian Empire, the American delegation supported the future unification of Russia, comparing the Ukrainian-Russian conflict to the disagreement which existed between northern and southern states during the American Civil War. In recalling some of the questions put to him by an American delegate, Arnold Margolin, a Jewish member of the Ukrainian delegation, was later to write that his interrogator "had no prejudice or bias against any nation in the world. He did not, however, have enough information about the situation in Eastern Europe, especially about the psychology and aspirations of the numerous non-Russian racial, national, and linguistic groups which formed more than half of the population of the Russian Empire. He was ignorant of the central fact that the Ukrainians and the peoples of the Caucasus and Turkestan had lived in their respective territories long before the appearance of Moscow as a city, or of the greater Russian nation itself."[2]

An equally serious obstacle to the recognition of Ukrainian independence was the lack of unity between delegates from the UNR and those from the ZOUNR (later, the ZUNR).* Differences were based on administrative prerogative and political ideology. UNR delegates claimed higher authority because they represented an all-Ukrainian government. The ZOUNR government was better organized, more efficient, and provided a stronger army. The UNR consisted of political parties that were almost exclusively leftist; the ZOUNR enjoyed the support of liberal parties with conservative leanings. The differences, however, became moot once Petrusevich concluded an agreement with Denikin and Petliura renounced all claim to eastern Galicia in return for Pilsudski's support. Both sides felt betrayed by the other. "In the final analysis," writes Professor Subtelny, "it was clear that the vast cultural, psychological, and political differences that accumulated between East and West Ukrainians during the centuries of living in very dissimilar environments were now coming to the fore."[2]

When the Paris Peace Conference ended, Ukraine was once again a partitioned nation.

Carpatho-Ukraine, ancestral homeland of America's Carpatho-Ruthenians and Uhro-Rusyns, united with the new state of Czecho-Slovakia (the hyphen was later dropped after the Prague government informed the Slovaks that they did not constitute a separate nation). Despite considerable division of opinion in Carpatho-Ukraine between those favoring union with Czechoslovakia and those favoring union with Ukraine, the area was occupied by Czech military forces in January 1919 and its annexation was legalized by the Treaty of St. Germaine-en-Laye on 10 September 1919.[3] Promises of autonomy, made to both the Slovaks and Ruthenians by Prague, were never observed.

Northern Bukovina was annexed by Romania, an act sanctioned by the

* The ZUNR was reestablished in November 1919.

Treaty of St. Germaine and the Treaty of Sevres concluded on 10 August 1920.

Eastern Galicia came under Polish control after the Treaty of Riga between Poland and the new Russian Soviet Republic. Still hopeful that the Republic of Western Ukraine could survive on eastern Galician territory, ZUNR representatives established diplomatic missions in Western Europe as well as in the United States and Canada to lobby on behalf of international recognition. On 23 March 1923, however, the Council of Ambassadors formally awarded eastern Galicia to Poland, thus sanctioning Polish rule of Western Ukraine.

Eastern Ukraine remained the Ukrainian Soviet Socialist Republic and, on 29 December 1922, was incorporated into the Union of Soviet Socialist Republics.[4]

Ruthenian-American Division and the Second Immigration

With the Russification of Ruthenians in the Russian Orthodox camp all but complete, America's Ruthenian community was left with two increasingly estranged ethnonational streams: the Ukrainian and the Carpatho-Ruthenian.

The advent of World War I, the collapse of the Russian tsarist regime, the Bolshevik takeover of Russia, America's entry into the war, President Wilson's Fourteen Points underscoring the right of national self-determination, the demise of the Austro-Hungarian Empire, the rise and fall of the Ukrainian National Republic, the Paris Peace Conference, and the final partition of Ukraine were events that had a profound effect upon the national consciousness and political aspirations of Ukrainians and Carpatho-Ruthenians in America. Each ethnonational stream developed a separate set of political objectives and as each attempted to achieve its own aims, the two camps drifted further, and in time permanently, apart. It was during this period of revolutionary change in Europe that the ethnonational identity of the Ukrainian American was tempered.

Most Ukrainians who immigrated to the United States after World War I had participated in Ukraine's liberation struggles and many came as political exiles unwilling to live in a homeland partitioned by foreign powers. Better educated than their prewar immigrant predecessors, they were more conscious of their ethnonational heritage and dedicated to the restoration of Ukrainian statehood. Because of United States immigration policy, however, their numbers were small. A series of restrictive immigration laws passed during and after the war discriminated against Southern and Eastern Europeans by establishing quotas in proportion to the national origins of the United States population in 1890. Ukrainians were doubly discriminated against, first because there was no official count of "Ukrainians" in 1890 and second because quotas were not awarded according to nationality, but rather to nation-states in existence after World War I. Those few Ukrainians who did immigrate to the United States between the two world wars were admitted within the quotas allocated to Poland, Czechoslovakia, Romania, and other nations where they resided.

The Ukrainian Stream

When the war began, *Svoboda* was ecstatic. The long-awaited opportunity for national emancipation from Russia had finally come. "Let all Slavic people live full, sovereign, and independent lives and among them the Ukrainians," the UNA periodical declared. "And that's how all Slavic people should think. Everyone for himself. Enough is enough!"[5]

A few days later, the UNA established an organizational committee and charged it with the responsibility of creating an all-Ukrainian political action committee. "At this time we have no news from our native land," observed *Svoboda*, "but soon the curtain which separates us will be lifted and we will hear from our brothers. It is of paramount importance that they have someone to speak to, that there be a single organization of Ukrainian Americans."[6]

The need for a national coordinating council that could define Ukrainian-American aspirations was reaffirmed just before the 1914 UNA convention. A *Svoboda* editorial entitled "Let's Be Ready" predicted that a peace conference would be convened at the end of the war and that "Poland and Ukraine will have their chance." But, warned the UNA organ, the Ukrainian agenda could be ignored. "The Poles will no doubt want to attach Galicia and Kholm to their Poland ... or Austria may want to have all Ukrainian lands ... or all Ukrainian lands may be awarded to Russia." Ukrainians must play a role in the negotiation process, *Svoboda* argued, and, to do that, "we must be prepared."[7]

The proposed council was established at the thirteenth UNA convention in Buffalo and, on 10 September, issued its first formal statement regarding the war. Observing that while "Ukrainians have no reason to be friends of either Austria or her ally Germany," nevertheless it said,

> We hope Russia is defeated in war and the Russian empire is broken up into its constituent parts. And we have good reason to feel as we do: for the Treaty of Pereiaslav, violated and trampled upon by the Tsar; for Poltava, for our hetmans, shamefully disgraced; for the destruction of the Zaporozhian Sich; for the Kozak bones on which St. Petersburg was built; for the spirit

that was kept in chains; for the language that was mutilated; for the many prisons and for Siberia; for the blood and tears of Ukrainian women and children; for centuries of torture, cruelty, and oppression.[8]

The council established itself in the UNA offices in Jersey City along with two newly created affiliates – the Ukrainian Information Bureau and the Fund for the Liberation of Ukraine – and began what it considered to be its major task: the dissemination of information about Ukraine. In 1915, the council distributed two English-language pamphlets published in London in 1914: *Ukraine* by Bedwin Sands and *The Memorandum on the Ukrainian Question in Its National Aspect* by Yaroslav Fedortchouk. Two additional pamphlets – *Russia, Poland and the Ukraine* by Gustaf Steffen[9] and *The Russian Plot to Seize Galicia (Austrian Ruthenia)* by Vladimir Stepankovsky[10] – were published by the UNA council in 1915. The following year, it published *The Russians in Galicia*, a monograph describing Russian army behavior in Galicia, reiterating the Ukrainian contention that Russia's major goal in the war was to expand its empire and to Russify Ukrainians in eastern Galicia.[11] The council also reported that as of September 1915, the Fund for the Liberation of Ukraine had collected a total of $21,661.44 from Ukrainians in America.[12]

Despite its success, the council remained a UNA institution and, as such, could hardly claim to speak on behalf of the entire Ukrainian-American community. Anxious that a more representative body be formed in America, the Ukrainian General Council of Lviv dispatched Dr. Semen Demydchuk, who had been to the United States in 1912 on behalf of Ridna Shkola and was well known to most Ukrainian-American leaders, to assist in its creation. On 8 October 1914, representatives of the UNA, the UWA, the Providence Association, and the Haidamaky met with Dr. Demydchuk, formed an organizational committee headed by Dr. Volodymyr Simenovych, and began to prepare for the convocation of a "Ukrainian Diet" in America.

In keeping with the new spirit of cooperation precipitated by events in Europe, the UNA and UWA (which at the time still called itself the Ruthenian National Union) joined forces and convinced American authorities to grant political asylum to Miroslaw Sichynsky, the 1908 assassin of Polish Count Potocki.[13] With monies supplied by Ukrainian Americans, Sichynsky had bribed his way out of his Austrian prison in 1911 and was living in Sweden. The United States agreed and on 21 October 1914, Sichynsky arrived to a hero's welcome in the Ukrainian community.[14]

Another joint UNA-UWA project was the publication of *Ukraine's Claim to Freedom* in the English language. After reviewing the history of the

Ukrainian national movement, the publication declared that "the ultimate goal" of the Ukrainian people "is the establishment of an independent Ukrainian state." Realizing, however, that complete independence might not be achieved in the near future, the publication concluded: Ukrainians "demand that in Austro-Hungary, Ukrainian territory be organized into a self-governed province on federal lines where the Ukrainian population, not dominated by the Poles or their aristocracy, shall solve its own national and economic problems." A similar plea for autonomy was made on behalf of Ukrainians in "Russian Ukraine."[15]

For the moment, at least, it appeared as if the entire Ukrainian-American community, seriously divided since 1910, would unite around a common cause. The Demydchuk mission was well received and the cooperation of the UNA and UWA, unthinkable two years earlier, augured well for the future.

The first break in what appeared to be a united Ukrainian front came late in 1914. Asserting his authority as leader of both the Carpatho-Ruthenians and the Ukrainians, Bishop Ortynsky unexpectedly announced the convocation of his own political action conclave. Before anyone could effectively protest – let alone dissuade the bishop – a joint Carpatho-Ruthenian–Ukrainian congress was held and, on 8 December 1914, the Ruthenian National Council came into being.* Caught by surprise, the nonsectarian fraternal leaders attempted to cooperate with Ortynsky's initial efforts. By 1915, however, relegated to a secondary role by Ortynsky's initiative, they decided to proceed with their original plans[16] without the participation of the Providence Association. Reflecting on the unfortunate turn of events, a *Svoboda* editorial asked, "What is the Biggest Fault of Our People?" The "answer to that question is very short," was the reply. It is "their lack of unity. A lack of unity was the reason for the fall of the Ukrainian nation. It was a problem during the Kievan era and then again during hetman times." Now, concluded the UNA gazette, "while our history is again being written in Ukrainian blood, we need to take a long, hard look at ourselves."[17]

Svoboda continued to push for the creation of an all-Ukrainian political action committee, exhorting all Ukrainians in America to realize their "national obligation" and to contribute to the Fund for Ukrainian Liberation.[18] At the same time, news from Ukraine was carried in huge banner headlines such as: HRUSHEVSKY ARRESTED IN KIEV,[19] RUSSIANS KILLING WOUNDED SOLDIERS,[20] HUGE MUSCOVITE POGROM IN GALICIA,[21] MUSCOVITE

---

* The Ruthenian National Council passed out of existence with the death of Bishop Ortynsky and is not to be confused with the Uhro-Rusin National Council formed later by the GCU and other Carpatho-Ruthenian organizations.

POGROM NEAR PEREMYSHL,[22] and MUSCOVITE BEHAVIOR IN UKRAINE.[23] Commenting on the war in an editorial entitled "Why Ukrainians Are on the Side of Austria," the UNA periodical argued that if Austria won, Ukraine would at last be "free of the Russian yoke."[24] The United States had nothing to gain from the conflict, *Svoboda* concluded, and should therefore remain neutral.[25]

The Federation of Ukrainians in the United States

The first "diet" of Ukrainians in America was convened in New York City on 30 and 31 October 1915,[26] with 295 delegates (holding mandates from 457 local, nonsectarian organizations) in attendance.[27] During two days of deliberation, a new central Ukrainian organization, the Federation of Ukrainians in the United States, headed by Dr. Volodymyr Simenovych and an executive board of twenty-one persons,[28] was created and charged with the dual task of representing the Ukrainian people in the United States and establishing local branches throughout the country. Four major resolutions were passed reflecting the political aspirations of the Ukrainian community:

1 The Ukrainian Congress and that organization which it has established represents the will of Ukrainians organized in 457 nonsectarian Ukrainian organizations in the United States.
2 Ukrainians, citizens and future citizens of the United States, appeal to the President to empower the future American delegation to the peace conference to proclaim, in the name of the United States, the principle that every nationality is the rightful ruler of its own country and no nationality is subject to the rule of another.
3 Our program with reference to the Ukrainian question is based on the establishment of a Ukrainian republic formulated on the most far-reaching democratic principles and on radical agrarian reform.
4 We support the fight for autonomy of Russian and Austrian Ukraine if, after the war, Ukrainian lands have not been incorporated in a Ukrainian republic.[29]

The federation also resolved to aid the homeland "in its struggle for self-determination based upon democratic principles," to provide financial assistance to victims of the war, and to promote the ethnonational development of Ukrainian Americans with more study courses for illiterates, night schools, libraries, lecture series, drama clubs, choirs, sports clubs, and youth organizations.[30]

Svoboda, meanwhile, continued its criticism of Bishop Ortynsky's behavior. Responding to articles in *Rusin*, which accused it of being against the Greek Catholic church, *Svoboda* defended itself by pointing to the bishop's apparent silence "when Muscovy was destroying the Greek Catholic church a year or so ago" and "when Metropolitan Sheptytsky and other priests were taken to Russia as prisoners of war."[31] *Svoboda* blamed Ortynsky for precipitating turmoil within the community and urged Ukrainians to take their example from Galicia, "where there is unity, agreement and love," and not from Philadelphia, "where among much goodness there exists a nest of division."[32]

Seeking to familiarize Americans with Ukraine and her people, *Svoboda* devoted its entire 29 February 1916 issue to an English-language review of Ukrainian national aspirations. While the people of Eastern Europe "prefer the ways of the British to the ways of the Prussian Junker," wrote Bedwin Sands in an article entitled "Ukrainians to the Anglo-Saxon World," Ukrainians perceive the war as "a conflict between Austria and Russia as to who should dominate the Slav-world outside of the Russian empire." As far as Ukrainians are concerned, "there can be no comparison between the treatment they received at the hands of Austria and the treatment they received from Russia." Ukrainians in Galicia, concluded Sands, "are considerably happier than their brothers across the border in Russia" and since Germany is an ally of Austria, "the wonder is that Ukrainians are not more emphatically pro-German."[33]

In addition, there were articles on Ukrainians in America (which author Emil Revyuk estimated at 600,000), Ukrainians in Canada, the Treaty of Pereiaslav (which, the article argued, had been nullified by Moscow when Ukraine was denied autonomy), Russian army behavior in Ukraine, Ukraine's rich natural resources, and her unique literary tradition. An ethnographic map of Ukrainian territories was also provided, along with translations of Ukrainian poems and copies of letters from American organizational leaders to Miroslaw Sichynsky, federation secretary.

Of special significance was an article entitled "The Ukrainians Hope to Obtain Liberation after the War," which reiterated Ukrainian-American willingness to settle for cultural autonomy after the war. "The demands of Ukrainians are not difficult to follow," the article began. "In Russian Ukraine, they suffer from oppression, persecution, and the stifling of their national life due to a desire to Russianize them. In Hungarian Ukraine, they are not even admitted to exist." Arguing that in Bukovina, Ukrainians "have at least the possibility of securing their liberties" – and accusing the Polish aristocracy of denying Ukrainians these same liberties in Galicia – the article concluded with a suggestion that if at the end of the war Ukrainians were not in a position "to decide alone the future of the territory in which they form the majority," then a number of other options might be acceptable. In the event of an Austrian victory, Ukrainians would agree to partnership in an Austro-Hungarian federation in which the Ukrainian nation "may develop its own national and economic salvation independent of Polish Western Galicia and of the Rumanians, Magyars, and Austro-Germans of Bukovina and Hungary." If eastern Ukraine also became part of Austria, the peace congress should guarantee the existence of an autonomous Ukrainian state "to be made up from as much of the original Ukrainian territory as will secure common consent." Should Russia win the war, the *Svoboda* article argued, the peace congress must mandate Russia's recognition of a separate Ukrainian nationality, guarantee Ukraine "at least the same measure of autonomy as Finland before 1900," and provide Ukrainians in Galicia and Bukovina with "the same small amount of self-government they possessed under Austria."[34]

Seemingly doomed from its inception, the federation never succeeded in its efforts to unite the Ukrainian community. Surprised by Bishop Ortynsky's sudden retreat from the original Demydchuk committee, federation organizers were faced with a dilemma – join the predominantly Catholic Ruthenian National Council and negate the influential socialist camp or ignore Ortynsky and incur the wrath of the powerful Catholics. In the end, both alternatives were tried. When cooperation with Ortynsky proved untenable, Ukrainian lay leaders proceeded to organize the federation and, predictably, the Ukrainian Catholic press began its attack, beginning with the fact that the congress had not opened with a prayer and had not sent a greeting to the pope.

A more serious problem, however, was faced by the federation within its own ranks. As the war in Europe progressed, the overriding issue became the question of continued support for Austria's war effort. The right-wing view was represented by Demydchuk who, as a representative of the pro-Austrian Ukrainian General Council in Lviv, urged continued moral support, a position that, if overemphasized, could alienate American political leaders who were mostly pro-British. The left wing, led primarily by Sichynsky, favored an anti-Austrian stance that, if widely promulgated, could conceivably help the Russian war effort. In time, the dilemma split the federation into two camps with executives from the same member organization taking different sides on the issue. The conflict was never resolved within the federation. In 1916, anticipating rapprochement with the Catholic church following the untimely death of Bishop Ortynsky, the right wing withdrew to form another all-Ukrainian organization, the Ukrainian Alliance of America.[35] The defection was led by the UNA, leaving the socialists as the federation's main base of support.

The Ukrainian Federation of Socialist Parties of America (UFSPA)

Of the separate political groups that emerged to compete for the political allegiance of the Ukrainian American during World War I, the Socialists were first to establish a functioning political apparatus. Local socialist clubs were in existence before the war and, despite some temporary reverses, they had managed to survive and to multiply. By 1915, Ukrainian socialists were prepared to form a new national organization, the Ukrainian Federation of Socialist Parties of America (UFSPA).

The first convention of Ukrainian socialist organizations was held on 28–30 November 1915. It was not an auspicious beginning. Present were twelve delegates representing twenty organizations, four members of the organizing committee, a few Haidamaky members, and three distinguished guests – Miroslaw Sichynsky, Andrii Dmytryshyn, a Ukrainian Marxist from Canada; and Charles Ruthenberg, a representative of the Socialist party of America. After agreeing that there were two principal causes for war – "the struggle between nations for colonial domination" and the desire of some nations "to rule over people who have no nation" – the newly established UFSPA resolved to support "the movement for the emancipation of Ukraine and all captive peoples along with the revolution- ary proletariat of all nations." Not surprisingly, the UFSPA also decided to "support first that segment of the Ukrainian freedom movement which is purely socialist."

Despite its organizational head start within the Ukrainian-American community, the UFSPA was stymied by internal dissension as a result of events in Europe. A crucial split in thinking emerged early in the history of the organization between those who gave first priority to national reform, the so-called Social Patriots led by Miroslaw Sichynsky, and the Bolsheviks or, as they initially preferred to be called, the "internationalists" who supported a broad-based program of social reform. The influence of the Social Patriots within the UFSPA started to wane soon after the convention, owing largely to the organizational activities of A. Dmytryshyn and George Tkatchuk, another Bolshevik who had moved to the United States from Canada. Internal strife, however, did not stifle growth. By 1916, the UFSPA had forty branches and was the sponsoring organization for *Robitnyk,* a Cleveland-based gazette initially edited by Sichynsky.[36]

The Decline of the Federation of Ukrainians

Following the UNA-led exodus of the right wing, the Federation of Ukraini- ans was forced to rely on the UWA, which maintained a decidedly socialist orientation, and the UFSPA for the bulk of its support.

At a federation convention in 1917, Dr. Kyrylo Bilyk, a member of the UWA board of directors, succeeded his good friend and mentor Dr. Simenovych as president of the organization.[37] While Bilyk provided administrative leadership, Miroslaw Sichynsky and Nicholas Ceglinsky served as federation ideologues. Both were UFSPA activists committed to the Social Patriot perspective and both served brief tenures as editors of *Narod* (The People), a federation periodical which folded a few months after its inception.

Early in 1918, the federation began publishing a second newspaper, *Ukrainska Hazeta* (Ukrainian Gazette) under the editorship of Emil Revyuk. After six weeks, Sichynsky replaced Revyuk as editor, remaining with the publication until 1919 when it too went out of existence.[38] Ceglinsky, meanwhile, became editor of *Robitnyk*, the UFSPA newspaper.

In addition to its own two periodicals, the federation enjoyed the full support of *Narodna Volya*, the UWA organ, and *Ukraina*, a Chicago-based gazette which billed itself as "an independent, national, patriotic, and progressive newspaper."[39] Edited by Simenovych, *Ukraina* received most of its financial backing from its editor and from Dr. Stepan Hrynevetsky, another Chicago physician.

Much of the early criticism of the federation was found on the pages of *Svoboda* which, by its own later admission, launched an all-out campaign aimed at discrediting Sichynsky and Ceglinsky in the eyes of the Ukrainian-American community. In the beginning, the attacks were relatively mild. An article entitled "How the Federation Is 'Liberating' Ukraine" accused *Narodna Volya* of having Russophile tendencies and suggested that the federation had lost all its credibility within the community.[40] A few weeks later, *Svoboda* published an article entitled "Is That the Way to Do It, Mr. Sichynsky," alleging that Sichynsky had insisted the first all-Ukrainian coalition be called a federation because his secret plan was to have the UFSPA absorb it. "Through the Federation of Ukrainians," the writer concluded, "Sichynsky and the socialists planned to pull our people into the socialist federation."[41] *Svoboda*'s attacks on the two socialist leaders later became so personally abusive and malicious that they were forced to institute legal action against the UNA gazette, a process which ended in their vindication.[42]

Still another problem faced by Sichynsky and Ceglinsky during this period was the erosion of Social Patriot influence within the UFSPA. Better organized and far more dedicated to their goals than their opposition, the Bolsheviks managed to gradually infiltrate the UFSPA executive and to set the ideological pace for the entire organization. Eventually, they took over completely and in 1917 engineered the withdrawal of the UFSPA from the federation. For all practical purposes, the federation was now left with no meaningful support within the Ukrainian-American community other than that provided by the UWA and socialists in the anti-Bolshevik camp.

Despite the loss of most of its original membership and strong opposition from the alliance, the UNA, *Svoboda,* and later, the UFSPA, the federation somehow survived its right- and left-wing crises and managed to make a tangible contribution to the Ukrainian cause.

The most significant legacy left by the federation was its role in the campaign to have President Wilson proclaim a nationwide "Ukrainian Day," as he had done for Jews, Lithuanians, and Armenians in 1916, so that Ukrainians could legally solicit war-relief funds on street corners throughout America. Both the federation and the alliance supported the idea and both claimed credit for its genesis and realization. As for the role of the federation, this much is certain: (1) on 4 January 1917, a federation delegation consisting of Dr. Simenovych, UWA president Osyp Zaplatyn-skyi, Dr. Kyrylo Bilyk, and Emily Strutynsky met with President Wilson to speak on behalf of the proclamation; and (2) organizations associated with the federation collected a total of $32,217.35 for the Ukrainian people during the Ukrainian Day collection.[43]

Once the United States entered the war, federation leaders joined in the formation of the Central European Union, an alliance masterminded by Thomas Masaryk* designed to dramatize the plight of "oppressed national-ities" within the Austro-Hungarian Empire. With the blessing of the White House, the newly established coalition issued a "Declaration of Common Aims" proclaiming full support of the Allies and the principles of national self-determination. Ceglinsky signed the manifesto on behalf of the federa-tion along with the Uhro-Rusyns (represented by Gregory Zatkovich) and representatives from ten other nationalities present at the Philadelphia convention that gave birth to the union.[44]

Still striving to regain its lost momentum, the federation convened a second diet of Ukrainian Americans in Washington, DC, on 16 December 1918. A national fund was created and a new call for Ukrainian-American unity under the federation banner was promulgated. Later a Washington office was established, headed, for a time, by Mykola Repen, former mem-ber of the Radical party in Galicia and a frequent contributor to *Ukrainska Hazeta.*[45]

When the war ended, federation members, like most Ukrainian Ameri-cans, believed the United States would not forget Ukraine at the peace

---

* Like Ignace Paderewski who had come earlier to lobby on behalf of an independent Polish republic, Masaryk was in the United States to gain support for the creation of a Czech and Slovak state following the dissolution of the Austro-Hungarian Empire.

table and Ukrainian aspirations would finally be realized. Even Sichynsky, opposed as he was to the capitalistic system, expressed his faith that President Wilson's many assertions regarding national self-determination would be implemented in Ukraine. Although "America is a capitalistic state," he wrote in 1919, it should not be assumed that "the same capitalists who manage American industrial and financial concerns also have a deciding voice ... in the formulation of foreign policy. They do not ... There can be no doubt that America will represent the principle of national self-determination for all peoples at the peace conference."[46]

Meanwhile, in a last-ditch effort to generate U.S. support for Ukrainian aspirations, the Petliura government, now in full retreat from its enemies, dispatched a diplomatic mission to Washington. Headed by Iuliian Bachynskyi, a socialist, the Ukrainian delegation arrived on 2 August 1919. Federation leaders initially viewed the mission as a godsend. Always more in sympathy with the socialist programs of the Rada and the Directory than its Ukrainian-American rival, the alliance, the federation had high hopes that a close association with a mission from Ukraine would bolster its sagging prestige in the United States. "We send them greetings," declared *Ukrainska Hazeta* soon after Bachynskyi's arrival, "and sincerely wish them every success in their difficult task."[47]

Bachynskyi had spent time in the United States before the war, however, and had no intention of becoming embroiled in local power plays. Analyzing the Ukrainian-American situation, he called a meeting of representatives of the federation, the alliance (which had changed its name to the Ukrainian National Committee in 1918), the UNA, the UWA, the Providence Association, and the Ukrainian National Aid Association (UNAA) – a new fraternal benefit society founded in Pittsburgh in 1914 – and pleaded for unity of effort in the important task which lay ahead. When it became clear that a united front was impossible, Bachynskyi was forced to side with the Ukrainian National Committee and the Catholic church, that segment of the divided community that offered the greatest potential for sustained support. Disappointed by what they considered to be a betrayal of their common socialist cause, federation leaders began attacking Bachynskyi and his mission.[48] This only served to alienate more Ukrainian Americans and, by the middle of 1920, the federation was no longer a viable factor in the Ukrainian political arena.

The Ukrainian Alliance of America

The untimely death of Bishop Ortynsky on 24 March 1916 prompted Rome to propose that two interim administrators, one for the Ukrainians and one for the Ruthenians, be selected by their respective clergies to serve until such time as a successor could be nominated. Ukrainian Catholic priests in America elected Rev. Peter Poniatyshyn, who assumed his new administrative duties on 11 April 1916.[49] Soon after Poniatyshyn took office, relations between the Ukrainian Catholic church and the UNA improved dramatically.

On 1 November 1916, the UNA announced its withdrawal from the federation, accusing it of not having fulfilled the mandates outlined by the all-Ukrainian diet which brought it into existence. "Some members of the Federation's executive board," wrote *Svoboda,* "took advantage of their high position in the Federation to pursue the objectives of their political party."[50]

On 5 December 1916, representatives of the UNA, the Providence Association, the Union of Brotherhoods, and the Ukrainian Catholic diocese in America met and formed the Ukrainian Alliance of America. Elected to the executive were Fr. Volodymyr Dovhovych, chairman, Dmytro Kapitula and Petro Kyryliuk, vice-chairmen, Hryhorii Zaiachikivskyi, secretary, and Konstantyn Kyrchiv, treasurer. This executive remained in office until 15 July 1918, when a second meeting of the alliance was convened and another Ukrainian organization, the Ukrainian National Aid Association (UNAA), joined its ranks. A new executive board, consisting of Semen Yadlovsky, chairman, Fr. Volodymyr Spolitakevych and Petro Kuzmych, vice-chairmen, Fr. Ievhen Bartysh, secretary, and Konstantyn Kyrchiv, treasurer, was elected.[51] Almost from its inception, however, the major spokesman for the alliance was Father Poniatyshyn.

One of the first projects undertaken by the alliance was the proclamation of a nationwide "Ukrainian Day" by President Wilson. Upon the advice of William Kerns, the diocesan lawyer, Father Poniatyshyn traveled to Washington to meet with Congressman James A. Hamill (D., NJ),[52] a close friend of Kerns, for information on how best to proceed. Hamill recommended a meeting with Joseph Tumulty, President Wilson's secretary, who advised Father Poniatyshyn that the president could not issue such a proclamation without a unanimously approved joint congressional resolution that had the prior blessings of both the Foreign Affairs Committee of the House and the Foreign Relations Committee of the Senate.

A resolution was subsequently drafted by the alliance and another meeting was arranged with Congressman Hamill. Traveling to Washington this time were Father Poniatyshyn, Kerns, Volodymyr Lototsky of the UNA, and Father Dovhovych of the Providence Association. Congressman Hamill suggested that because so few American congressmen were familiar with the term "Ukrainian," it would be wise to also include the term "Ruthenian" in the text of the resolution. This was done and, on 24 January

1917, Hamill turned the resolutions over to the two congressional foreign affairs committees.

With the legislative assistance of Senators Henry Cabot Lodge and William Hughes, the resolution had little difficulty passing the Senate Foreign Relations Committee and, later, the Senate. In the House, however, the measure lost by one vote the first time it was considered. A second vote was taken on 22 February and this time it passed unanimously.[53] Signed by President Wilson on 2 March and proclaimed two weeks later, the resolution called attention to the "wretchedness, misery and privation" of the "Ruthenian (Ukrainian) people" in war-torn Europe and established 21 April 1917 "as a day upon which the people of the United States may make such contributions as they feel disposed for the aid of stricken Ruthenians (Ukrainians) in the belligerent countries."[54]

As a direct result of Wilson's proclamation, Ukrainians associated with the alliance collected a total of $53,189.32, of which $22,000 was immediately sent to the Rada in Kiev.[55] In addition to the financial benefits, the proclamation served to promulgate the name "Ukrainian" in the American press.[56]

America's entry into the war forced the alliance and *Svoboda* to abandon its pro-Austrian posture. In an editorial entitled "Let's Stand under the American Flag," *Svoboda* argued that America's somewhat belated support of the Entente was a reflection of the will of the American people and to resist would be unwise at best and at worst could be construed as disloyalty. "America," *Svoboda* reminded its readers, "is our adopted homeland. Some came here for money, some came as temporary immigrants, both found a good life in this country ... we owe America our loyalty."[57]

Ukrainian aspirations, however, were not to be forgotten. Explaining that "this was a time of nationalism" – a concept defined as "love for our own and respect for others" – *Svoboda* warned of the dangers of internationalism. "We Ukrainians still need to proclaim our national 'I,' to exercise our national will. Internationalism creates national indifference and this is detrimental to our aspirations."[58] Later, *Svoboda* urged its readers to forget their religious and political differences and "become extreme nationalists."[59]

Responding to Ukraine's Revolution

The establishment of Rada rule in Ukraine electrified the Ukrainian-American community, significantly raising nationalistic expectations. The euphoria of the moment, however, was quickly replaced by a realization of the difficulties that had to be overcome. During the uncertainty that followed, a new round of debates was inaugurated regarding the future political alignment of the Ukrainian nation.

In May 1917, *Svoboda* again reviewed Ukraine's tragic past and, reflecting on its own recent advocacy of independence, reluctantly observed:

> To argue now in favor of independence is very nice, in words, but we must be aware of the present situation in Ukraine, the present strength as well as the political maneuvering of her nearest neighbors. We are not saying that Ukrainians should not have national aspirations. God forbid! We would love to have an independent Ukraine today but looking at things realistically, we are afraid that the struggle might have an unfortunate ending ... we believe we should seek an autonomous Ukraine united with Russia on the basis of an equal with an equal ... That means we believe Khmelnytskyi's plan to be a better plan than that of Mazepa ... Selecting union with Russia as the most realistic plan for the formation of our national life in keeping with Khmelnytskyi's ideal does not mean, however, that we are rejecting the future realization of the Mazepa ideal.[60]

Soon after the Rada began to dissociate Ukrainian aspirations from those of a federated Russia, however, the UNA press organ wrote:

> Until very recently, the ideal prevailed among Ukrainian revolutionaries ... of a federated, cooperative life between Ukraine and Moscow on the basis of a partnership between equals; when, however, Moscow is demonstrating its desire to continue to rule and to direct all Russian peoples, including Ukrainian, then for the Ukrainians there is only one road and that is the mobilization of all of their strength towards freeing themselves from the hands of the Muscovite occupants and the establishment of their own nation.[61]

The Bolshevik takeover of the Russian revolutionary government and the subsequent promulgation by the Communists of freedom for all nationalities were initially welcomed.[62] Federal union was still possible, wrote the UNA gazette, if Russians were willing to accept "separation for all non-Muscovite peoples from the Muscovite nation."[63] When Bolshevik deeds failed to match Bolshevik pronouncements and relations between the Rada and the Bolsheviks deteriorated, however, *Svoboda* changed its mind again. Accusing Lenin of desiring a Rada which was exclusively Bolshevik, *Svoboda* declared: "Ukraine does not need one party in command."[64] Why, *Svoboda* later wondered, was a Russian Social Democratic party necessary in Ukraine when a Ukrainian Social Democratic party already existed?[65] The answer was provided in an editorial entitled "Why Ukrainians Can't Agree with Lenin." "As even the most neutral observer must admit," it concluded, "within Lenin's program there exists a wide streak of Russophilism."[66]

By the end of January 1918, *Svoboda* was once again supporting the Mazepa ideal of Ukrainian independence. Observing that the Rada had supported the proclamation of the Fourth Universal (Ukraine's declaration of independence) by a vote of 508 to 4, *Svoboda* editorialized:

> This change in posture did not come about as the result of
> the Rada's own initiative. This change was precipitated by
> Muscovy's traditional posture toward Ukraine.
> Ukraine has had enough of Muscovite brotherhood. Ukraine
> united with Tsarist Muscovy as a free and autonomous nation –
> Muscovy trampled this freedom and subjected the Ukrainian
> people to a yoke of oppression.
> Ukrainians fought alongside Muscovites to rid themselves of
> tsarist oppression. They toppled the tsar and his bureaucracy;
> it appeared as if the two brotherly peoples could now enjoy their
> freedom and independently decide their destinies.
> But no. The regime of Prince Lvov "permitted" Ukrainian
> students to learn in their own language and there the matter
> ended ...
> The socialist Kerensky came into power but he too hesitated in
> permitting full autonomy to Ukraine ...
> The Bolsheviks took over. *In principle*, they not only recognize
> Ukraine's right to autonomy but to independence as well; *in
> practice*, however, they support the Muscovite-Bolshevik front in
> Ukraine ... *with rifles and cannons*.
> To all of these provocations of the new Muscovy, from Lvov to
> Lenin, the Rada only now, in unequivocal terms — *has answered
> with the proclamation of the independent Ukrainian republic* ...
> If a regime were established in Muscovy which was similar to
> that of Ukraine and her neighbors – then it is not inconceivable
> that Ukrainians and Muscovites could unite once again ...
> Today it is not possible to talk of this. Life itself will determine
> the future developmental path of the two largest Slavic peoples.[67]

The alliance, meanwhile, established a Ukrainian information bureau in the Capitol office suite of Congressman Hamill and intensified its efforts to influence U.S. foreign policy. In his reflections on the events which transpired during this critical period in Ukrainian-American history, Father Poniatyshyn related how, with the assistance of Congressman Hamill, alliance executives met with members of the Senate Foreign Relations Committee, East European specialists in the State Department, and even Secretary of State Lansing. The response was always the same: it is in the best interests of the United States to have Ukraine remain an integral part of Russia.[68]

The Ukrainian National Committee

Soon after the armistice in Europe was announced, alliance leaders decided to free themselves of their antifederation image and to try again to unite the Ukrainian-American community, this time under a new banner. On 18 November 1918, the alliance changed its name to the Ukrainian National Committee, realigned its leadership, and, with renewed dedication, embarked on a new phase of international lobbying. Heading the newly constituted coalition was an interim board consisting of Fr. Peter Poniatyshyn, chairman, Volodymyr Lototsky, secretary, and Fr. Mykola Pidhoretsky, treasurer.[69] It was at about this time that Dr. Simenovych and Dr. Bilyk, both former leaders within the federation, decided to join forces with the committee.

Still maintaining a Ukrainian information bureau in the office of Congressman Hamill, the committee issued a memorandum to President Wilson on 29 November. Declaring that Ukrainians in the United States desire to have "introduced and established in their motherland, the Ukraine and adjacent Russian territory, American ideals of government and the American system of education in order to perpetuate sound democratic principles among their people, and to avert future conflict between races in Eastern Europe which were formerly antagonistic to each other," the memorandum requested that:

1 Ukrainian ethnographic territory be recognized as one and indivisible.
2 The ethnographic contents of the Ukraine include the larger part of the former Austrian province of Galicia ... the northern half of the former province of Bukovina, the Hungarian Ruthenia, and the province of Kholm ...
3 The inhabitants of this ethnographic Ukraine, as above outlined, be accorded their natural right and opportunity to self-determination through their constituent Assembly to be elected by free popular vote.
4 If the eventualities of the peace conference, soon to be held in

Paris, should result in the recommendation of a free federation of the peoples comprising the territory of former Russia, then that Ukraine be accorded its right and opportunity ... to enter into a free union with the peoples of former Russia on a federalistic basis similar to that which obtains in the United States under the American federal complex.[70]

Congressman Hamill tried to gain an audience for the committee's leadership with Wilson prior to the president's departure for Europe. When this failed, he attempted to influence Wilson with a congressional mandate. On 13 December 1918, Hamill introduced a joint resolution (H.J. Res. 368) calling upon the U.S. delegation in Paris to recognize "the right to freedom, independence, and self-determination of all Ukrainian territories, both in Austro-Hungary and Russia." To the consternation – but not the surprise – of the committee, the measure was defeated.

On 16 and 17 January 1919, 570 delegates representing organizations associated with the committee met in New York City and approved both the name change and the new executive board. Despite the commitment of Petliura's government to total independence for Ukraine, the idea of an autonomous Ukrainian nation within a federative Russian state was still not a dead issue among some leading members of the committee. According to *Svoboda*, a discussion of the idea was held during the convention, with Lototsky defending it and Simenovych in opposition.

The two-day session ended with a political manifestation at Cooper Union Hall led by Dr. Bilyk. Included among those who addressed the 4,000 delegates and guests were Father Strutynsky, Congressman Hamill, and William Kerns.[71] Resolutions passed at the conclave supported "the American peace process," reiterated past demands for Ukrainian self-determination, and condemned the Polish invasion of eastern Galicia. The convention ended with appeals to President Wilson – "to allow representatives from both the Ukrainian republic and western Ukrainian province (ZOUNR) to participate in the peace conference" – and to Ukrainian Americans of all political persuasions "to unite within the Committee."[72]

The Bachynskyi Mission to America

By the time Iuliian Bachynskyi and his delegation arrived in Washington (2 August) as representatives of the Ukrainian National Republic, the Big Four had already agreed to permit the Polish army to advance to the Zbruch River (25 June); General Denikin had captured Kharkiv (25 June) and was advancing on Odessa; news of the Jewish pogroms in Ukraine had reached the United States, alarming the Jewish-American community;

the United States was preparing to formally declare its support of a united Russia following the defeat of the Bolsheviks (29 October); and the western Ukraine province (ZOUNR) was three months away from concluding a unilateral treaty with Denikin (17 November). Unlike Ignace Paderewski, the Polish leader who had come to the United States in 1914 to lobby on behalf of a Polish state, and Thomas Masaryk, who came in support of a Czech-Slovak state, Bachynskyi (who could count on assistance from only a segment of the Ukrainian-American community) was faced with the additional handicap of having to begin his mission on the defensive.

Realizing that American Jews were opposed to Petliura (whom they blamed for the pogroms), Bachynskyi issued an open letter to the American press documenting the fact that the massacre of Jews in Ukraine was in no way the result of official Ukrainian policy. The Ukrainian government, Bachynskyi pointed out, had invited Jewish leaders from Western countries to form a special committee and come to Ukraine to investigate the matter for themselves. Bachynskyi's letter was published by the *New York Globe,* the *New York Evening Post,* the *Brooklyn Eagle,* and the *Philadelphia Eagle,* as well as by Jewish newspapers in New York, Boston, Fort Worth, New Orleans, and St. Louis in October and November 1919. The message was later reprinted in pamphlet form[73] by Friends of Ukraine, the mission's publishing arm.

Hoping to convince the American public of the validity of the Ukrainian cause, "Friends" also published the complete text of a memorandum Bachynskyi sent to the American secretary of state concerning the Ukrainian question. After providing evidence substantiating the ethnonational exclusiveness of the Ukrainian people, Bachynskyi concluded that American recognition of the Ukrainian National Republic would end, once and for all, "the historic struggle between Poland and Russia to control the natural resources of Ukraine." As for the argument that the Treaty of Brest-Litovsk "proved" that Ukraine had been an ally of Germany, Bachynskyi pointed to Romania's separate treaty with Germany and the fact that this did not deter her from being "considered an ally of Germany's opponents." Everyone seems to recognize, continued Bachynskyi, that given the circumstances, Romania had had little choice. "Ukraine was in far worse condition than Rumania when she concluded her peace with Germany," Bachynskyi observed. "Ukraine had to choose between submitting entirely to the Bolsheviki [*sic*], in which case the country would be overrun by Germany anyway, or making any kind of outright peace with Germany and hoping for the best."[74]

In the end, Ukraine's only diplomatic mission in America failed. Bachynskyi never did meet with President Wilson or even with Secretary Lansing. The most that he ever received from a highly placed U.S. government official was a memorandum from Lansing repeating the official American position that Ukraine was an integral part of Russia.

The final blow for Bachynskyi, a staunch supporter of a united western and eastern Ukraine, came when Petliura negotiated a separate treaty with Pilsudski at the expense of Galicia. A short time after the pact was signed, Bachynskyi left Washington and returned to Ukraine.[75]

The Bilyk Mission to Paris

Frustrated by their inability to gain acceptance of Ukraine's aspirations from the Wilson White House, leaders of the Ukrainian National Committee turned their attention to the peacemakers in Paris. In March 1919, Congressman Hamill (who spoke fluent French) and Dr. Bilyk left for Europe as official representatives of the Ukrainian National Committee of America. Hamill returned after a few months but Bilyk remained for over a year, returning on 27 May 1920. Before his departure, Bilyk was instructed to assist the Directory and ZOUNR delegations in their efforts to gain recognition for a united Ukraine but to refrain from developing any political initiatives of his own. "Defend Galicia in every possible way," he was informed, "not one part of Ukrainian Galicia must ever belong to Poland."[76]

Upon arriving in Paris, Bilyk joined the fifteen-person Ukrainian delegation already functioning there and was assigned liaison responsibilities with American and other English-speaking delegations. Working with him were Ivan Petrusevych from Canada and Dr. S. Zarkhii, a Ukrainian Jew from the Ukrainian liaison office in London.

Meeting with members of various delegations proved to be a relatively easy matter. Convincing them of the righteousness of the Ukrainian cause, however, was not. Colonel House, Wilson's aide, seemed sympathetic but Secretary Lansing refused to consider a Ukrainian state free of Russia. Aware, no doubt, of the loss of administrative control in Ukraine by the Petliura government, Lansing stated quite categorically: "We cannot recognize the independence of Ukraine. If we did, then anybody who wanted to, could go there and do as he pleased." Professor Robert H. Lord of Harvard, another member of the American delegation, also rejected the possibility of Ukrainian sovereignty. "Smart politics," he advised the Ukrainians, "requires you to come to terms with Russia."

Bilyk's contacts with the British were equally discouraging. One member of England's delegation advised Bilyk and ZOUNR representatives not to associate too closely with the Directory because of its "Bolshevik tendencies." Lloyd George, in contrast, wanted to know with which nation, Russia or Poland, Ukrainians would be willing to unite if it came to a forced choice. The answer, of course, was neither.[77]

As it became evident that the "all or nothing" position of the Ukrainian delegation was making little progress in Paris, Bilyk attempted to find compromise solutions. Convinced that the United States would never agree to an ethnographically united and independent Ukrainian state, he suggested that Directory representatives settle for an autonomous Ukraine within a federated, democratic Russian state. Even Secretary Lansing, who, like other world leaders, still believed the collapse of the Bolshevik regime was imminent, appeared amenable to such a solution to the Ukrainian question. Bilyk's suggestion, however, was promptly rejected by Petliura's delegation. Still hopeful, Bilyk approached representatives from the newly reestablished ZUNR.* Believing that Wilson's commitment to Poland was such that any proposal for a western Ukrainian republic that included Lviv and its environs would be unacceptable, Bilyk counseled the ZUNR delegates to settle for a republic minus their beloved capital. This too was rebuffed.[78]

All hope of a settlement in Paris for a united Ukraine finally evaporated when it was learned that Petliura had come to terms with Poland renouncing all claim to eastern Galicia. Enraged, the ZUNR representatives formally withdrew from the Ukrainian peace delegation, charging that the remaining Ukrainians "do not have a mandate from the Ukrainian people because the Ukrainian people want unification and liberation from Poland."

Thoroughly disillusioned, Dr. Bilyk also resigned from the delegation and returned to the United States. In a report to the Ukrainian National Committee subsequently published in *Svoboda*, Bilyk enumerated the loss of Hungarian Rus' (Carpatho-Ukraine), Bukovina, and the Kholm region and suggested that even though Galicia was under Polish military occupation, there was still room for an acceptable settlement. Bilyk was especially critical of Petliura. He is a leader with no national administration, no army, no authority, and no popular support, reported Bilyk.[79]

The Decline of the National Committee

With Bilyk in Paris, the Ukrainian National Committee continued its efforts to influence American foreign policy in Washington. Protests over Polish actions in Galicia were sent to President Wilson;[80] another Ukrainian information bureau, headed by Milton Wright, was established in New York City; two English-language books, *Ukraine on the Road to Freedom*[81] and *Polish Atrocities in East Galicia*, were published;[82] and, in July 1919, a delegation consisting of Poniatyshyn, Lototsky, Kerns, Hamill, and Alexander Granovsky met with Secretary Lansing in Washington.[83]

---

* The Republic of Western Ukraine (ZUNR) was reestablished in November 1919.

When news of the Polish invasion of western Ukraine reached the United States, the committee, assisted by some 150 local branches, organized two nationwide protest days – 15 and 22 June 1919 – and coordinated a barrage of over 400 telegrams to the White House.[84] Other protest days were arranged early in 1920 along with more telegrams.[85]

During the fall of 1919, the committee joined forces with the Lithuanians, Latvians, and Estonians in the United States to create the League of Four Nations.[86] The league sent a delegation to meet with the Senate Foreign Relations Committee,[87] and was instrumental in having Congressman Fiorello La Guardia (R., NY) introduce a resolution calling for the establishment of U.S. consuls in the four nations represented by the league.[88] The league later published a book entitled *The Case of the New Republics.*

With the decline of the federation, the committee also became involved with the revitalization of the Central European Union, which, now minus the Poles, was still under the nominal leadership of Thomas Masaryk.[89]

The second convention of the Ukrainian National Committee was held in New York on 15 and 16 January 1920 and the future of Ukraine, still in doubt, was discussed once again. Much time was spent considering Professor Hrushevsky's proposal for a new Eastern European federation composed of ten nations formerly under Russian rule. Hrushevsky had explored such a possibility while in Paris and had become convinced the plan had merit. Commenting on Hrushevsky's idea, a committee spokesperson suggested that because the United States "is itself a federal union," American leaders would be committed to this principle and would therefore support a similar arrangement for Ukraine if agreement could be reached among the nations involved.[90]

Despite all their frenzied activity and optimistic rhetoric, however, it was becoming painfully clear to the committee's executive that time was running out. All hope for a united Ukrainian nation-state had long since faded. Ukrainian national idealism had been tarnished by Petliura's treaty with Pilsudski. Many Ukrainian Americans, most of whom traced their roots to Galicia, felt Petliura's action was a betrayal of Ukrainian aspirations, but they conveniently forgot the ZOUNR's earlier agreement with General Denikin at the expense of eastern Ukraine. Ukrainian Bolsheviks in the United States were trumpeting the existence of an "independent" Ukrainian Soviet republic. Carpatho-Ruthenians in America had managed to create an autonomous Ruthenian republic with relatively little effort and at practically no cost to the community. Finally, Dr. Bilyk had stripped away all the political rhetoric associated with Wilson's concept of national self-determination and laid bare a reality which Ukrainian Americans had secretly suspected but were reluctant to accept: the United States did not and would not recognize Ukraine's national aspirations. In describing the impact of these events upon the morale of Ukrainians in the United States, Father Poniatyshyn was later to write: "The Ukrainian defeat at the peace conference at Versailles, that is, the negation by that conference of Ukrainian requests, left the Ukrainian-American community thoroughly disillusioned and in a deep state of depression. In the main, that depression was utilized by 'our' Bolsheviks and the Ukrainian National Committee began to lose ground."[91]

Unlike the nationalists who had little to show for all of their efforts, the Bolsheviks controlled Ukraine and that reality was devastating to their opposition.

The ZUNR Mission and the Galician Alternative

The Ukrainian National Committee was in desperate need of a catalyst to revitalize its leadership and reignite America's Ukrainian nationalist community. The arrival of the ZUNR mission in 1920 provided just such a spark.

Headed by Dr. Longin Cehelsky, the mission arrived in Washington and made immediate contact with the committee. "Don't despair," declared Dr. Cehelsky, "all is not lost. Galicia can still be ours."

A special convention of the committee was called within a short time and the Ukrainian Defense Committee, headed by Cehelsky, Roman Slobodian, Dmytro Andreiko, Andrii Savka, and Teodor Hrytsei, was established. Rising to the occasion, the UNA donated $2,000 to get the newly formed Ukrainian nationalist organization started.[92] Dr. Cehelsky eventually returned to Europe and was succeeded by Dr. Luka Myshuha as head of the mission.

Svoboda, meanwhile, continued the difficult task of keeping Ukrainian-American hopes alive. An editorial entitled "The Mistaken Foreign Policy of the American Government" drew a distinction between the views of the White House and those of the American people. After reminding the reader of America's own struggle for freedom, *Svoboda* argued that under President Wilson, "neither the principles of America's Declaration of Independence nor the ideals articulated by President Wilson himself have any meaning today." But the American people are different, concluded *Svoboda.* They "will never forsake their traditional principles and values ... they will never agree to the reestablishment of the Russian Empire."[93]

Bitterly disappointed with President Wilson's actions, Ukrainians in the United States could take solace from the fact that they were not the only ethnic group to be disillusioned with American foreign policy. In the words of Louis Gerson:

By 1920, millions of ethnic Americans saw the various promises and pledges made during the war neglected, refused, or compromised at the conference tables. With the notable exception of the Polish-Americans all were ready to vent their bitterness and disappointment on Wilson and the Democratic Party. Wilson, once the champion of self-determination, spokesman for the oppressed and downtrodden, became the betrayer of the nationalistic hopes of those peoples who, because of Wilson, had seen their native lands emerge from centuries of bondage.[94]

Of the many variables that contributed to Wilson's defeat, the ethnic factor was one of the most significant despite the achievements of the Poles.[95] While American isolationists voted "a plague on Europe," millions of ethnics voted "a plague on Wilson."[96]

The Ukrainian Committee made one final effort to interest American political circles in the Ukrainian plight early in 1921. Soon after President Harding's inauguration, members of the committee met with Secretary of State Charles Hughes to discuss the future of the Ukrainian question. They pointed out that General Haller's Allied-equipped Polish army had not been employed against the Bolsheviks but against the Ukrainians in Galicia and that the Galician problem would never be resolved unless Ukrainians were permitted to exercise the same right of self-determination as the Poles. Writing many years after the meeting took place, Father Poniatyshyn still remembered the exact words used by Secretary Hughes in reply to these statements. "Everybody wants independence now," answered Secretary Hughes, "even the town of Fiume. But what will happen to Europe when it is divided into small pieces? What will become of law and order?" The meeting with Hughes was the last time members of the committee met with highly placed United States officials to discuss the Ukrainian question.[97]

The Ukrainian Committee, however, was still not willing to give up. A Ukrainian Defense Fund rally was held in Philadelphia on 20 April 1921[98] and this was followed by numerous appeals for money including one entitled "Listen Ukrainian Immigrant, Your Native Land Calls" in which *Svoboda* reminded its readers that "only that people will attain nationhood which is willing to sacrifice, to give more than it receives."[99] Similar rallies were held in other cities during the next two years, all for the purpose of raising money to save Galicia. Toward the end, *Svoboda* kept interest alive by providing a daily countdown of progress in bold, two-inch, front-page headlines.[100] By 1923, a total of $138,500 had been collected.[101]

The most forceful opposition to committee efforts to rally the Ukrainian nationalist community around the Galician alternative came from the Bolsheviks, who argued that they and they alone would liberate the Ukrainian province. "We'll take care of Galicia next," announced *Robitnyk*. "Under the red worker's flag, all of Ukraine will be united."[102] "LONG LIVE FREE AND INDEPENDENT SOVIET, SOCIALIST UKRAINE."[103]

Given the grim reality of the Bolshevik triumph, *Svoboda* was hard pressed to counter the increasingly persuasive Bolshevik platform. In an article entitled "Ukraine and the Russian Bolsheviks," Professor Michael Hrushevsky pointed to the intensive centralization efforts of the Russians, observing that "in Ukraine itself Ukrainian Communists reject the new principle of the Russian Bolsheviks and, in order not to compromise themselves in the eyes of the Ukrainian people, are fighting them at every turn."[104] The Ukrainian Soviet Socialist Republic is only "independent in theory," *Svoboda* declared.[105] "Russia's Communists don't want Communists in Ukraine if they are Ukrainian Communists."[106]

Although some Ukrainian Americans were swayed by Bolshevik appeals, most remained steadfast. During the entire two-year period from 1921 to 1923, their hearts remained with Galicia and the ZUNR. As Ukrainian anti-Polish sentiment began to mount, protest marches were organized in front of the Polish embassy in Washington and the consulate in New York. *Svoboda* continued the pressure with stories such as "Polish Bombs being planted under Ukrainian Institutions"[107] and "New Knives for the Polish Republic."[108] Long appeals for assistance from ZUNR President Ievhen Petrusevych appeared in both English and Ukrainian.[109]

In the end, the Galician alternative was rejected. On 16 March 1923, *Svoboda* informed its readers that the Council of Ambassadors had awarded Galicia to Poland.[110] Outraged, the nationalists organized another series of protests[111] but to no avail. All of Galicia was now in the hands of the Poles.

In the end, Ukrainian Americans accomplished little of any lasting significance during their long, exhausting, and costly crusade to wrest their homeland from foreign occupation. Ukraine was partitioned by the peacemakers and the Ukrainian-American community was forced to come to grips with a political reality which would ultimately render Ukraine far worse off than it had ever been before.

The nine-year period was not totally devoid of benefits, however. Two changes took place within the psyche of the Ukrainian Americans which were irrevocable. First, they no longer called themselves Ruthenians. All lingering doubts concerning their ethnonational identity vanished when Galicia united with the Ukrainian National Republic. Second, they saw that national uncertainty and lack of preparation lead to disaster, a lesson of great significance for the Ukrainian-American community in the interwar period.

There was a negative side, however, to the tempering of the Ukrainian Americans. The bitter disappointment with the failure of democracy in Ukraine and the disillusionment with what was perceived as the hypocrisy of American foreign policy left them open to ideologies of national liberation which were dogmatic, uncompromising, and authoritarian.

The Carpatho-Ruthenian Stream

The events of World War I forced Carpatho-Ruthenians to come to grips with their political identity: Carpatho-Ukraine was suffering the ravages of war; Hungary was more determined than ever to keep the province within its borders; Russia was claiming that the region was really "Russian"; and the Carpatho-Ruthenian's Ukrainian brethren – both in Europe and in America – were preparing for a united Ukrainian republic that would include Carpatho-Ukraine. Under such influences, it was difficult to remain politically indifferent.

The first public expression of what might be considered a Carpatho-Ruthenian political position occurred during a Russian Congress in New York City on 13 July 1917. Organized by Petro Hatalak, a Galician Russophile, the congress included representatives of the Russian Orthodox hierarchy, the GCU, *Viestnik,* an organization called American Russian National Defense, and delegates from various pro-Russian Carpatho-Ruthenian organizations. A memorandum was issued by the congress calling for "the broadest autonomy" for Carpathian Ruthenia and its unification "with its older sister ... a great democratic Russia."[112]

In January 1918, *Viestnik* suggested that it was time for Carpatho-Ruthenians to think about their political future and to consider union with four alternative states: Hungary, Czecho-Slovakia, Ukraine, or Russia.[113] Within two months a group of Uhro-Rusyn priests met in McKeesport, Pennsylvania, and unanimously declared their loyalty to Hungary. As late as May, however, most Carpatho-Ruthenians remained disinterested in the future of their homeland, preferring to defer in such matters to the opinions of their clergy.[114]

By summer, the Greek Catholic lay establishment started to stir and to organize its forces. A political-action committee was formed at the fifteenth GCU convention in June and in July, soon after Secretary Lansing announced that "all branches of the Slav race should be completely freed from German and Austrian rule" (28 June), lobbying on behalf of the homeland began in earnest. Coming together in Homestead, Pennsylvania, representatives of the GCU and the Sobranie Greko-katolicheskich bratsv (United Societies of the Greek Catholic Religion) established the National Council of Uhro-Rusyns and, declaring themselves the legal representatives of the Uhro-Rusyn community,[115] passed the following resolution:

> If the pre-war boundaries remain, Rusyns, as the most loyal *gens fidelissima*, deserve that Hungary provide her with autonomy.
>
> If new boundaries are made, they should be made according to nationality; thus, Uhro-Rusyns can belong nowhere else than to their nearest brothers by blood, language and faith, to the Galician and Bukovinian Rusyns.
>
> But if we are divided by foreign aspirations from Ukrainians and Old Russians (Galician Russophiles), the national Council demands in this case autonomy for Uhro-Rusyns so that they can preserve their national character.[116]

The Homestead resolution did not mention union with Czecho-Slovakia and the Carpatho-Ruthenian press was not favorably disposed toward such an option, especially after the Slovak-American press began discussing certain nationally mixed counties as if they were part of Slovakia. Addressing the Slovaks on 22 August 1918, *Viestnik* warned:

> Hold your horses, brethren, and be satisfied with your boundaries made a year or two ago when you thought that the Uhro-Rusyns were dead ... We want liberty and independence ... and as Ruthenians we are trying to achieve unity with other Ruthenians, excluded from Russia and Ukraine ... in Galicia and Bukovina, and to create for our fathers and brethren a free Carpathian republic, instead of being the gain of anybody.[117]

Between August and November, the Galician-Bukovinian option received much favorable attention from *Viestnik*, while union with Hungary faded rapidly as a viable national alternative. One plan called for the creation of a federated Carpathian Republic – "after the example of Switzerland" – with three separate ethnic groups: Carpatho-Ruthenians, Ukrainians, and the Lemkos.[118] The major argument against such a federation, however, and in favor of closer association with Slovaks was the ever-present Carpatho-Ruthenian fear of amalgamation by the Ukrainian ethnonational stream. According to one *Viestnik* commentator, Ukrainians had a distinct language and literary tradition while the Slovaks had no literature. The danger of "losing our miserable but dear to us Uhro-Rusyn language" was therefore greater with Ukrainians than with Slovaks.[119]

If a union of Carpatho-Ukraine with Galicia and Bukovina had any future at all at this point, it was considerably weakened by the presence in

America of Thomas G. Masaryk, architect of the Czecho-Slovak republic. Arriving early in 1918, Masaryk was able to gain access to the Wilson administration and to win the support of Congress – largely through the efforts of Rep. Adolph J. Sabath, a Bohemian-born Democrat from Illinois – for the creation of a "Bohemian-Slovak" state after the war. Enjoying a favorable response from important government officials, Masaryk toured America's Czech and Slovak communities to promote his idea. The warm reception he received served to increase his stature in Washington. His mission was partially fulfilled on 30 May 1918, when leaders of America's Czech and Slovak communities met in Pittsburgh and signed an agreement creating a federated Czecho-Slovak state.[120]

Hoping to enhance the size of the new republic with the inclusion of Carpatho-Ruthenia – a possibility he first proposed in 1915 – Masaryk now turned his attention to the Carpatho-Ruthenian community in America.[121]

Masaryk first approached Nicholas Pachuta, recently elected secretary of the Russian Orthodox Brotherhood and a former assistant editor of *Viestnik*. After engineering the removal of Pavel Zatkovich as editor of *Viestnik*,[122] Pachuta converted to Orthodoxy and began to support union with Russia. The Bolshevik coup d'état forced him to reluctantly abandon that option. Pachuta then turned to the Slovak community and, after meeting with its leadership, he developed a memorandum proposing union with Czecho-Slovakia, shared it with Secretary Lansing, and, on 30 May 1918, presented it to Masaryk. The Czech leader chose to wait, however, pending a meeting with the far more influential Uhro-Rusyn Greek Catholic leadership.

In October, the Uhro-Rusyn National Council approached Gregory Zatkovich, the American-educated son of the former *Viestnik* editor, requesting that he prepare a memorandum on the Carpatho-Ruthenian question for presentation to President Wilson. Brought to the United States at the age of four, Gregory Zatkovich had a law degree and no enemies in the community because of an early reluctance to become involved in Uhro-Rusyn affairs. These factors, combined with his knowledge of American ways and the stature of the family name, made him the ideal spokesman for the Uhro-Rusyn community. Zatkovich prepared a text listing three alternatives: full independence; autonomy within Hungary; autonomy within a yet unspecified Slavic state. Not only was the memorandum different from the Homestead resolution, it made no mention of either Czecho-Slovakia or Galicia-Bukovina.

Zatkovich presented the Uhro-Rusyn memorandum to President Wilson on 21 October. Two days later he was in New York City as the duly recognized Uhro-Rusyn representative to the first convention of the Central European Union. Masaryk visited with Zatkovich during his New York stay and broached the subject of Carpatho-Ruthenian autonomy within a federated Czecho-Slovak republic. Borders with Slovakia were discussed but never resolved. A Czecho-Slovak republic was proclaimed on 29 October 1918.

On 29 October, Zatkovich met with the National Council executive and reported on his meeting with Wilson and Masaryk. A second meeting of the council was held in Scranton on 12 November and Zatkovich suggested that a plebiscite be conducted among Uhro-Rusyns in the United States to determine "where Uhro-Rusyns in the old country belong, as an autonomous state or in a Czechoslovak or Ukrainian federation." The council adopted a resolution supporting unification with Czecho-Slovakia "with the broadest autonomous rights as a state, on a federative basis." A proviso was included listing all of the "original Uhro-Rusyn counties" which "must belong" to the Carpatho-Ruthenian state. Meeting with Zatkovich the following day, Masaryk emphasized the need for a plebiscite, lest the Scranton resolution be rejected by the Paris Peace Conference as "only a decision of members of the national council." Zatkovich reviewed his progress in a telegram to President Wilson the following morning and received a highly favorable response.

The historic plebiscite took place in December 1918 among GCU lodges, *Sobranie* chapters, and Uhro-Rusyn parishes. Each location was allowed one vote for every fifty members on a winner-take-all basis.* Because only 372 of the 874 existing GCU lodges and 46 of the 158 *Sobranie* chapters returned their ballots, the total validated vote count was a low 1,110. If each of the votes represented fifty Uhro-Rusyns, then a total of 55,500 people – approximately 20 percent of the estimated 250,000 members of the Uhro-Rusyn half of the Greek Catholic church in America – participated in the plebiscite.[123] Results were reported as follows:[124]

Union with Czecho-Slovakia	735
Union with Ukraine	310
Total independence	27
Union with Galicia-Bukovina	13
Union with Russia	10
Union with Hungary	9
Union with Galicia	1

Significantly, some 28 percent of those Uhro-Rusyns who voted chose unity with their Ukrainian brethren. Given the history of anti-Ukrainian sentiment among Uhro-Rusyn leaders, the lack of any real opportunity for an impartial hearing of the Ukrainian alternative within the Ruthenian

* This meant that if in a given location one parish or fraternal branch had twenty-five ballots for Ukraine and twenty-six ballots for Czecho-Slovakia, the allotted single vote would be cast for Czecho-Slovakia.

community, the absence of Ukrainian poll watchers during the vote tally, and the winner-take-all approach of the plebiscite, the relatively favorable response to Ukrainian aspirations by Uhro-Rusyns during this period is surprising. In retrospect, the plebiscite proved to be the closest the two ethnonational streams would ever come to unification in America.

Zatkovich was delighted with the outcome and, after cabling the results to Czech representatives at the peace conference, prepared to leave for Europe as head of an official three-person delegation from the National Council of Uhro-Rusyns. Assured by the Council of Five in Paris that the Uhro-Rusyn/American proposal was acceptable to the peacemakers, Zatkovich quickly left for Carpatho-Ruthenia, where he arrived on 10 March 1919.

The most difficult hurdle facing Zatkovich upon his arrival was the amount of local support that still existed for union with either Russia, Hungary, or Ukraine. Because none of the three existing Carpatho-Ruthenian councils initially favored Czecho-Slovakia, Zatkovich helped create another political body – the Central Ruthenian National Council – in Uzhhorod and proceeded to lobby for the Uhro-Rusyn/American plan. With Hungary, Russia, and Ukraine in the throes of Communist revolution, the Uhro-Rusyn/American proposal soon emerged as the only viable option. On 8 May 1919, the Central Council declared that "in the name of the whole nation it completely endorses the decision of the American Uhro-Rusyn Council to unite with the Czech-Slovak nation on the basis of full national autonomy."

A second hurdle for Zatkovich was the potential threat to the autonomous integrity of the region posed by Russophile and Ukrainophile Ruthenians in Galicia. This was overcome when Zatkovich convinced the Central Council to reject all attempts to unite with Galicia.[125]

On 7 August 1919, Thomas Masaryk, now president of the newly constituted Czecho-Slovak republic, appointed Zatkovich chairman of a five-member Directorate charged with the task of organizing the Carpatho-Ruthenian territory. Incorporation of the region was officially sanctioned by the Treaty of St. Germaine-en-Laye on 10 September 1919, and, on 26 April 1920, Gregory Zatkovich, still retaining his American citizenship, became the first governor of the Carpatho-Ruthenian state, now officially called Podkarpatska Rus' or Subcarpathian Ruthenia.[126]

Efforts to form a single, unified, and representative organization to speak on behalf of the entire Ukrainian-American community got under way shortly after the start of World War I under the leadership of the Ukrainian National Association. Later, in response to pressure from the Ukrainian leadership of Western Ukraine, the four existing Ukrainian fraternal organizations – the UNA, the UWA, the Providence Association, and the Haidamaky – agreed to convene an "All-Ukrainian Diet" for the purpose of establishing a coalition that was more representative of the community. This endeavor was only partially successful. A Federation of Ukrainians was formed, but without the Providence Association or Bishop Ortynsky's approval. Ortynsky had decided to form an "All-Ruthenian" council himself, an action which other Ukrainian organizations found unacceptable.

Rapprochement between the UNA and the Providence Association was reached after the death of Bishop Ortynsky and the nomination of Father Poniatyshyn as interim head of the Ukrainian church. Unhappy with the increasingly socialistic tenor of the federation, the UNA withdrew and, in cooperation with the Providence Association, established a rival coalition group, the Ukrainian National Alliance. Politically, there were now two ideological wings within the Ukrainian ethnonational camp: the left, represented by the federation, the UWA, and the Ukrainian Federation of Socialist Parties of America (UFSPA); and the right, represented by the Ukrainian Catholic church, the UNA, and the National Alliance. Despite President Wilson's avowed support of the principle of national self-determination, neither the Ukrainian nationalist left nor the right was ever able to convince the White House to support Ukrainian national aspirations.

When the war ended, the influence of the federation within the Ukrainian nationalist community began to fade. Meanwhile, the alliance changed its name to the Ukrainian National Committee and continued to lobby on behalf of Ukraine in both Washington and Paris. When it became clear that the Allies were opposed to a united Ukrainian republic independent of Russia, the committee devoted its energies to saving ZUNR for the Ukrainians. Again the peacemakers ruled in favor of Ukraine's enemies and awarded all of Galicia to Poland. After nine years of feverish effort, Ukrainians in the United States were left with nothing. Neither in the United States nor in Ukraine were Ukrainians ever provided with the opportunity to exercise their right of self-determination in an internationally sanctioned manner.

Their ethnonational identity tempered during the effort to gain freedom for their homeland, Ruthenian-Ukrainians became and remained irrevocably Ukrainian.

In contrast to Ukrainian Americans, Uhro-Rusyns in the United States were more successful. Realizing that the imminent collapse of the Austro-Hungarian Empire offered new national opportunities for their homeland, they established the National Council of Uhro-Rusyns in 1918 and began to question the necessity and even the desirability of continued allegiance to Hungary. Uhro-Rusyn priests remained loyal to Budapest but the Uhro-

Rusyn/American lay leadership focused its attention on three other options: independence, union with Bukovina and Galicia, and autonomy within a yet unspecified federated Slavic state.

Autonomy within a newly established Czecho-Slovakia became a viable option once Thomas Masaryk voiced an eagerness to incorporate sub-Carpathian Ruthenia into the republic. Supported by President Wilson, Masaryk was able to convince America's Uhro-Rusyn leaders that Czecho-Slovakia was a safer alternative than Ukraine, a nation beset by internal problems and still lacking recognition by the Allies. A plebiscite among Uhro-Rusyn Americans was subsequently organized to decide the issue and union with Czecho-Slovakia over Ukraine was preferred by a two-to-one margin. The plebiscite, combined with Rome's earlier decision to appoint separate church administrators for Carpatho-Ruthenians and Ukrainians, eventually led to a separation between the two Ruthenian groups that exists to the present day.

5 Communist Aspirations

Ukraine's partition was a severe blow to Ukrainian nationalists who found it difficult to comprehend what had gone so terribly wrong. Why, they agonized, had they failed to maintain their independence after the collapse of the Austro-Hungarian and Russian empires when so many other submerged nations had succeeded? Many theories to explain the debacle were developed along with political programs for the future. The three ideologies which had the greatest impact on the Ukrainian-American community between the two world wars were Communism, monarchism, and Nationalism.*

Ukrainian Communists in America argued that the Ukrainian people had rejected the bourgeois Ukrainian National Republic and established the Ukrainian Soviet Socialists Republic (UkrSSR) in its place. Irrevocably united with the Russians and other so-called "fraternal peoples" within the Union of Soviet Socialist Republics, Ukrainians in the UkrSSR, they proclaimed, were building a democratic paradise for the working class. The reality, of course, was quite different.

Ukraine under the Soviets

To the dismay of Ukrainian Bolsheviks, Russian behavior in Ukraine during the first years of the occupation was predicated on terror and intimidation. Ukrainian cultural and scientific institutions were closed, treasury funds were confiscated, and armed bands sanctioned by the Cheka, the Soviet secret police, roamed the countryside commandeering food and supplies

---

* The capital N is used throughout this study to designate those nationalists who were affiliated with the Organization of Ukrainian Nationalists (OUN). Those Ukrainians who favored a Ukrainian nation-state free of foreign rule (socialists, monarchists, etc.) were nationalists in the broadest sense of the term and are identified with a lower case n.

to sustain the new regime. It was, in Lenin's own words, a period of "militant communism" during which "we actually took from the peasant all the surplus grain and sometimes part of the grain the peasant required for food, for the purpose of meeting the requirements of the army and of sustaining the workers." A final blow was dealt by nature when a severe drought hit Ukraine in 1920. Combined with Bolshevik raiding parties, the ravages of war, and the disruption of transport facilities, lack of grain proved to be the precipitating cause of a famine which added countless thousands to Ukraine's already high death toll.

Eventually, the Bolsheviks reversed themselves and introduced a series of reforms which came to be called the New Economic Policy (NEP). Forced requisitions were replaced with a tax in kind, a policy which permitted peasants to keep or sell all they produced over a fixed production quota that the state requisitioned. Other NEP concessions included incentives for development of small industries, either private or co-op, and the leasing of nationalized small businesses to their former owners for a fixed rental fee. In Ukraine, the NEP significantly improved living conditions and helped ameliorate dissatisfaction with the Bolsheviks.

On 20 December 1920, the Ukrainian Soviet Socialist Republic signed a treaty with the Russian Soviet Federated Socialist Republic (RSFSR), relinquishing control of the commissariats of the Army, Navy, Foreign Trade, Finance, Labor, Communications, Post and Telegraph, and the Higher Economic Council to the RSFSR in return for the RSFSR's recognition of the UkrSSR as an "independent and sovereign state." In practice, however, even this latter concession was an illusion. Despite repeated protests by the UkrSSR leadership, Ukraine was treated as an intrinsic part of the RSFSR. The same held true for the theoretically independent Communist Party of Ukraine, the CP(b)U. In reality, the CP(b)U was forced to function as a subunit of the Russian Communist party (RCP). The independence of the UkrSSR was further diminished in 1922 when its leaders elected to become part of the Union of Soviet Socialist Republics (USSR) along with the RSFSR, the Belorussian SSR, and the Transcaucasian Federation.

From Ukrainianization to Russification

In 1923, continued resistance to Soviet rule in Ukraine and other non-Russian areas led the Communists to proclaim a radically different nationality policy designed to give Soviet regimes outside Russia a veneer of national legitimacy and thereby to enable them to "take root" in local soil. Known as "indigenization" (*korenizatsiia*) on the all-union level, its Ukrainian variant was known as Ukrainization and included programs to develop Ukrainian culture, switch state and party work to the Ukrainian language, and recruit Ukrainians to work for the regime. In the years of Ukrainization (1923–33), the number of books published in Ukrainian rose dramatically, a Ukrainian-language education system extended from primary school to university and beyond, the largely non-Communist All-Ukrainian Academy of Sciences received generous state subsidies for scholarship, and Ukrainian literary and cultural activities flourished. Indeed, Ukrainians remember the cultural attainments of the period as the *rozstriliyane vidrodzhenniya*, literally "the executed rebirth," both for its tremendous promise and for its abrupt and violent suppression by Stalin.

In the late 1920s, Ukrainian fortunes took a decided turn for the worse. Determined to consolidate the Kremlin's control over the Bolshevik empire, Joseph Stalin instituted a terrorization campaign in the UkrSSR aimed at obliterating all vestiges of Ukrainian autonomy. Ukrainian "nationalist deviations" were soon discovered in a variety of cultural and economic institutions and their proponents were forced to recant. To assure loyalty to the Kremlin, Stalin purged tens of thousands of Ukrainian Bolshevik leaders, scholars, and others considered to be "unreliable."

But Stalin was not satisfied. The marketing of agricultural production still had not reached prewar levels, the peasants were becoming increasingly independent (many even refused to sell their surplus to the state until the price was right), and, most disconcerting of all, industrialization of the Soviet state, dependent as it was on monies garnered through agricultural exports, was proceeding at a slow pace.

Stalin had one solution to *all* these problems: agricultural collectivization. By establishing large state-owned farm cooperatives, he could at one and the same time eliminate the so-called *kurkuls* (in Russian, *kulaks* or independent farmers), who represented a strong obstacle to centralization; increase the state's share of the agricultural surplus; enable Moscow to increase its export sales; and, with the newly gained monies, speed up his sagging industrial programs. As we shall learn shortly, forced collectivization resulted in the death of millions of Ukrainian men, women, and children from starvation.

Stalin eventually eliminated all his Ukrainian opposition and proceeded to institute a program of "Sovietization" which was little more than Russification in socialist form. Purged CP(b)U leaders were replaced by ethnic Russians, the principle of the supremacy of local languages in the republics was denounced, and the Russian working class was extolled for its role in "liberating from national, political and economic oppression the whole family of peoples inhabiting former tsarist Russia." Summarizing the new rationale at the fourteenth CP(b)U Congress in 1938, First Party Secretary Nikita Khrushchev condemned the "bourgeois nationalists" for driving the Russian language from the schools of Ukraine, concluding that all people in Ukraine were now eagerly studying the Russian language because Russian workers represented the vanguard of the revolution.

Thus, in a little over twenty years after the establishment of the Ukrainian National Republic, the Ukrainian people had come full circle.[1]

The Great Famine

But Russification was a relatively mild vehicle of de-nationalization compared to others employed by Stalin during the 1930s. The most catastrophic was genocide through starvation, a willful form of mass murder which came about in Ukraine in the wake of the collectivization campaign.

With only 1.7 percent of the peasant households collectivized in 1928, implementation of Stalin's new agricultural policy proved to be no simple undertaking.* Peasant resistance included outright refusal to comply with the new dictates and, once forced requisitions became commonplace, the mass destruction of crops, machinery, and farm animals scheduled for collectivization. Despite such violent contravention, the Bolsheviks never relented in following their objective. Laws authorizing the death penalty for theft or destruction of "state property" were strictly enforced and villages that continued to resist were simply surrounded by police and army units and forced to surrender. In the end, what had begun as a war against the *kurkuls* turned out to be a broad offensive against all peasant farmers. Thousands were killed and millions more either perished in the subsequent famine of 1932–3 or were deported to Siberia to be replaced by more trustworthy workers. By 1933, 65.6 percent of the peasant households were collectivized. Five years later, the Soviet Union boasted of having some 242,000 collective farms representing 93.5 percent of the rural population.

Hardest hit by collectivization was the UkrSSR, where opposition to the new order was strongest.† Rising to the challenge was CP(b)U secretary

---

* Just prior to the reintroduction of the collectivization program, the USSR had 25,550,000 private holdings in the hands of peasant farmers. Of this number, between 5,000,000 and 7,000,000 were classified as *bidniaks* or poor peasants, some 18,000,000 were *seredniaks*, or middle peasants, and some 800,000 were *kurkuls*, or, by Soviet standards, prosperous peasants. Since the *kurkuls* had the most to lose by both centralization and collectivization, they resisted it most. Communist strategy involved pitting the *bidniaks* against the *kurkuls* in a calculated effort to eliminate the latter completely.

† Ukrainians, who had known private ownership of land for centuries, were violently opposed to collectivization. In Russia, in contrast, where communal land tenure had a long tradition behind it, resistance to the new order was relatively mild.

Pavel Postyshev, who, within a few months after his arrival from Russia, announced that with the help of some 10,000 party faithful, he had organized a total of 843 political brigades and dispatched them to supervise work in the countryside. Brigade members trusted no one and left no stone unturned in their desire to uncover "enemies of the state." In his book *Ukraine under the Soviets,* Prof. Clarence Manning describes how the brigades operated:

> They entered the villages and made the most thorough searches of the houses and barns of every peasant. They dug up the earth, broke into the walls of buildings and stoves in which the peasants tried to hide their last handfuls of food. They even in places took specimens of fecal matter from the toilets in an effort to learn by analysis whether the peasants had stolen government property and were eating grain. Wherever they found any, the peasants were severely punished while the detachments carried off not only the grain but everything edible.

The final result of Stalin's agricultural policy in Ukraine was hunger the magnitude of which staggers the imagination. In his classic study *The Harvest of Sorrow: Soviet Collectivization and Terror Famine,* Sovietologist Robert Conquest concludes that "the cause of the famine was the setting of highly excessive grain requisition targets by Stalin and his associates; Ukrainian party leaders made it clear at the start to Stalin and his associates that these targets were highly excessive; the targets were nevertheless enforced until starvation began; Ukrainian leaders pointed this out to Stalin and his associates and the truth was also made known to him and them and others."

Stalin's genocide was investigated by the Commission on the Ukraine Famine. Funded by the U.S. government, the Commission submitted its report to the U.S. Congress on 22 April 1988. Sixteen findings were presented, the most significant of which are: "The victims of the Ukrainian Famine numbered in the millions"; "Stalin knew that people were starving to death in Ukraine by late 1932"; "Attempts were made to prevent the starving from traveling to areas where food was more available"; "Joseph Stalin and those around him committed genocide against Ukrainians in 1932–1933."[2]

The American Response

The first Marxist socialists in America were German immigrants who emigrated following the abortive German revolution of 1848 and began organizing socialist societies during the late 1860s. A branch of the International Workingmen's Association – the so-called First International organized in London with the help of Karl Marx in 1864 – was formed in the United States in 1869. The Workingmen's Party of the United States was born in 1876 and changed its name to the Socialist Labor Party of America (SLP) in 1877.

Eugene V. Debs became a socialist in 1897 but, instead of joining the SLP, founded a rival organization, the Social Democratic party (SDP), a year later. In 1901, a splinter SLP group joined Debs to give birth to the Socialist Party of America (SPA) bringing together Christian socialists, Marxists, immigrant workers, intellectuals, trade union officials, and millionaire social reformers.

From its inception, the SPA was split between a right wing, which supported improvement of working-class life through economic action and trade unionism, and a left wing, which favored a fundamental change in the social order. Accusing their rivals of "class collaboration," the left wing rejected the gradual-reform model and came out in support of class struggle and the need for developing America's revolutionary proletariat.

The SPA, especially the left wing, had a natural appeal for Eastern European immigrants who were either neglected by the major political parties or exploited by them to keep corrupt political machines in power. Given the largely American-born leadership of the SPA, however, the foreign-born never really felt at home within its ranks. Beginning in 1904 – when Finnish socialists created their own autonomous federation within the SPA – the trend among ethnic Americans was toward the formation of affiliated organizations closer in ideological spirit to socialists in the homeland than to their U.S. counterparts. By 1915, there were fourteen separate foreign-language federations within the SPA. Out of a total party membership of 80,126 in 1917, some 32,894 (40 percent) belonged to ethnic affiliates.[3]

SPA membership declined during World War I because of disagreements regarding U.S. military involvement. The Russian Revolution, however, rekindled interest in the SPA and dues-paying members increased to 108,000.[4] Especially jubilant with events in Russia were immigrant Jews, Russians, Ukrainians, Lithuanians, Estonians, and Latvians, who joined the Socialists in droves. The subsequent Bolshevik revolution provided the left wing with the program it was seeking, increased its allure, and firmly established the Russian Federation as the preeminent group within Socialist-party ranks. By 1918, the SPA had 70,000 members in its ethnic federations.[5]

The Ukrainian Federation of Socialist Parties of America

As we have seen, Ukrainians in America followed the general immigrant pattern. Imbued with both the nationalist and social-reform ideals of the

Radical party in Galicia, Catholic priests associated with the American Circle took over the major Ukrainian institutions in America and proceeded to raise the national and social consciousness level of the community. In 1900, *Svoboda* rejected the political platforms of the Republican and Democratic parties and urged Ruthenians to vote for Socialists as the only candidates truly interested in the problems of the working class. A number of socialist clubs were eventually established and in 1915 the Ukrainian Federation of Socialist Parties (UFSPA) was organized with the encouragement of Charles Ruthenberg, a left-wing member of the SPA who was later to become known as "America's Lenin." The major focus within the UFSPA, however, was on Ukraine. A split soon occurred in party ranks between the Social Patriots, whose first priority was national reform, and the internationalists (Bolsheviks), who emphasized class warfare and world revolution.

A unique aspect of early socialist activity in the Ukrainian-American community was the apparent harmony that prevailed between Ukrainian and Russian socialists. In Chicago, for example, a mass meeting was held on 3 June 1917 to welcome the advent of the Russian revolution and to send the following statement to the Russian Duma:

> Taking into consideration the successfully achieved Russian revolution, we, Russian and Ukrainian peasants and workers, unanimously resolve: (1) The expression of thanks to all fighters for Russian liberty and the wish of a successful restoration of peace and order in a free country; (2) The expression of full confidence in the provisional government insisting on a victorious outcome of the war in order, once and for all, to put an end to militarism; (3) To give to all nationalities inhabiting Russia freedom on the basis of autonomy; (4) The confiscation in favor of the people of all the natural riches and a just distribution of such; (5) The return to parishioners of all Russian church property appropriated by the bishops; (6) Dismissal of all former tsarist officials, consuls, and representatives in America and their replacement by representatives of free Russia; (7) The taking of measures against the Russian clergy who agitate against the new people's government and for the restoration of monarchy in Russia; (8) The confiscation in favor of the people of all property received as a reward for service to the former tsars; (9) Prohibition of the sale of liquors; (10) The establishment of a democratic Russian republic; (11) The introduction of obligatory general education for the people; (12) The expression of deep thanks to the American republic which

has taken under its protection all Russians who suffered from the former tsarist regime.[6]

The second convention of the Ukrainian Federation of Socialist Parties of America (UFSPA) was held on 26, 27, 28 May 1917, with delegates representing forty-six branches and almost 1,000 members in attendance. This time, the internationalists were in firm control. The convention resolved that: (1) As long as capitalistic rule exists, there will be slavery, nation will go against nation, and class will fight class. Imperialism, the capture of colonies and their subsequent annexation and incorporation into large nations, is a necessary by-product of capitalism. (2) Capitalism can be destroyed only through class warfare. The day capitalism is destroyed, all other slavery will be destroyed. (3) Whoever follows a different path is not striving for national freedom for his people. He has only painted the yoke a different color while the form remains the same.

In keeping with their new ideological direction, the UFSPA also decided to sever all ties with the Federation of Ukrainians and to find a new editor for *Robitnyk*. Elected to the new executive were A. Dmytryshyn, D. Moisa, M. Korzh, I. Bychek, N. Kobrynsky, and T. Pochynok. All were associated with the internationalist camp except Pochynok.[7] With the change in editors, *Robitnyk* assumed a more strident posture towards the nationalists, attacking both the Ukrainian Alliance of America and the Federation of Ukrainians. This, in turn, intensified criticism of UFSPA activities by *Svoboda, America, Narodne Slovo* (National Word, the press organ of the Ukrainian National Aid Association), and *Narodna Volya*.[8]

Ceglinsky's successor at *Robitnyk* was E. Kruk, a dedicated Social Democrat. As long as Vynnychenko, nominal head of Ukraine's Social Democrats, played a significant role in Rada affairs, Kruk maintained a policy of tacit support of its activities. Between the March and November 1917 revolutions in Russia, *Robitnyk* consistently praised the efforts of not only Vynnychenko but other members of the Rada as well. So strong were Kruk's convictions concerning the Rada that when I. Kulyk, a *Robitnyk* correspondent who wrote under the pen name "Rolinato," visited Ukraine and began to send dispatches criticizing its policies, Kruk inaugurated a long series of polemic discussions. While Kulyk stressed the common struggle of all nationalities in the coming social revolution, Kruk continued to defend the nationalism of the Rada.[9] Replying to accusations that he was insensitive to the class struggle in Ukraine, Kruk wrote:

Blood is being spilt in Ukraine. There is a mad and crazy war over there. Our workers find themselves in circumstances that are historically unique. They must fight the class war against those who would usurp their civil rights and at the same time they must fight those who would override their national rights ... They are fighting two wars and therefore, they are in double jeopardy. To spend all of their energies fighting for their national dignity would mean they would of necessity neglect the class war. Not to defend their national dignity, on the other hand, is out of the question. Still, they can't very well operate on the principle that the national war unites all classes ... therein lies the tragedy of our situation.[10]

In explaining the presence of German and Austrian troops in Ukraine as a result of the Treaty of Brest-Litovsk (an occupation denounced by other internationalists) Kruk argued that the armies of these two nations were under Ukrainian control. "For the time being, it is simply impossible to determine the real reasons for the present state of affairs and who is responsible for them," wrote *Robitnyk*.[11] By April 1918, however, Kruk was beginning to hint as to where the blame might be placed. "The Council of People's Commissars," he wrote, "didn't know how or didn't want ... to answer the voice of Ukrainian revolutionary democracy and to accept its relevant and legitimate demands and needs in a spirit that should exist between equal and free brothers."[12]

To suggest that the Bolsheviks and not the Rada were to blame for the breakdown in relations between Russia and Ukraine was too much for the internationalists. A special UFSPA council was convened and, on 16 May 1918, *Robitnyk* announced that "in keeping with a decision reached by the Party Council of the UFSPA of May 13, 14, and 15, in Cleveland, Ohio, the full responsibility for the editorial policy of *Robitnyk* lies with an editorial committee of four comrades and not Comrade Kruk who was editor until now."[13] Replacing Kruk were H. Lehun, P. Ladan, D. Moisa, and I. Svitenky. A short time later, the internationalists, anxious to repair any damage caused by the Kruk heresy, sent their top organizers – A. Dmytryshyn, H. Tkachuk, and S. Soroka – into the field to strengthen local cadres of the organization.[14]

The growing influence of the internationalists – who were rapidly evolving into full-fledged Bolsheviks – in the UFSPA was a reflection of a phenomenon then affecting the entire socialist movement in America. "For the harassed Left in America," writes Sidney Lens, "Bolshevism was a cool rain after a long dry spell ... There was hardly a radical meeting, whether Socialist, anarchist, or IWW, where the mere mention of Soviet Russia did not bring deafening applause."[15] Capitalizing on their wide popularity, the

Bolsheviks were, by the spring of 1919, *the* party for a number of American Socialist party branches as well as for seven of the semi-autonomous ethnic federations within the American Socialist party.[16]

At an emergency convention of the SPA in St. Louis in April 1917, the left wing successfully pushed through a resolution opposing "war and militarism." Once the Espionage Act was passed in June, the St. Louis resolution provided the United States government with its chief legal weapon for prosecuting a number of socialist leaders (including Debs and Ruthenberg) and for suppressing the socialist press.[17] During the summer of 1918, federal authorities raided *Robitnyk* offices in Cleveland, confiscated literature, and arrested all who were present. That same day, George Tkach, perhaps the most talented of the early Ukrainian-American Bolsheviks, was arrested in Detroit and interned for the duration of the war. Fined and released after a few weeks in jail, the *Robitnyk* staff elected to move its headquarters to New York City where, on 12 December 1918, a month after the armistice, the newspaper resumed publication.[18]

Robitnyk adopted the Bolshevik line from the moment of its resurrection. In an article entitled "Do We Want a Free Ukraine?" the Bolshevik position regarding Ukraine's future was clearly and unequivocally enunciated:

> We want a free Ukraine but as long as Ukraine has one capitalist within its borders, it will not be free. We won't save our house from fire until we are sure who's going to live there. We will let the house burn if it cannot be ours. In its place we will build another and we won't let anyone near it ...
>
> We do not want hooligans to rule. We will throw out all robbers, be they Russian, Polish, Jewish, or Ukrainian. Only then will Ukraine be able to call itself free. That is the kind of Ukraine that the peasant and worker needs.
>
> Every Ukrainian worker is fooled by the many beautiful words devoted to the blue and yellow flag, our famous past, the beauty of Ukrainian culture and so on ...
>
> Why can't the worker see that all of this is a cover-up? The people who talk about such things want to get their nails into the body of Ukraine. The Ukrainian bourgeoisie – Ukrainian professors, doctors, writers, priests, church cantors – are trying to embrace the Ukrainian peasant as they send him out to free Ukraine.
>
> Bourgeois Ukrainians will not achieve a free Ukraine. Ukraine will be free when it rids itself of capitalism and the bourgeoisie.
>
> Workers cannot go hand in hand with the bourgeoisie even to

protect the homeland. Workers and peasants must first rid themselves of the bourgeoisie ... then all the proletariat will be one and
will stand in defense of a free, socialist Ukraine.[19]

"Liberty," wrote *Robitnyk* in February 1919, "will be achieved by proletarian
Ukraine through the dictatorship of the proletariat and that will come just
as soon as victory is achieved over the parasites."[20]

When the Red Army was expelled from Ukraine later in the month,
Robitnyk cautioned "the Ukrainian yellow press" not to celebrate yet.
"French bandits won't be around to support Petliura just as the German
bandits weren't always around."[21] The politics of the Ukrainian Committee
and the Federation of Ukrainians "are going bankrupt," declared *Robitnyk*,
because they support "a politics against the working masses – on both
sides of the ocean."[22] Don't trust *Svoboda*, "a yellow rag which supports
those gentlemen who suck the blood of the Ukrainian working masses,"
admonished *Robitnyk*.[23]

The most powerful arguments in the Bolshevik arsenal were those that
directly addressed the growing frustration of Ukrainian nationalists over
Allied indifference to their aspirations. When Ukraine was under their
control, the Bolsheviks were quick to exploit their advantage. "Almost all
Ukrainian territories," wrote *Robitnyk* in March 1919, "are in the hands of
the Bolsheviks ... The Ukrainian revolutionary proletariat does not beg for
anything. HE TAKES WHAT BELONGS TO HIM. Ukraine belongs to him. He
takes it. We are proud of our comrades in the old country."[24] Repeating
the same theme, *Robitnyk* later asked Ukrainian-American nationalists:
"How long are you going to walk on the skin of the Ukrainian working
man? You begged the allies to let you join their club but the allies refused
and now you are ready to sell your soul to anyone."[25]

Rejecting the nationalist argument that Russian Bolsheviks created the
UkrSSR, *Robitnyk* replied:

> They believe that since the Skoropadsky regime was created by
> the Germans, and the Petliura regime by the French, then Soviet
> Ukraine had to be created by someone ... The Ukrainian Soviet
> Socialist Republic is firmly constituted on the will of the Ukrai-
> nian people ... And if the Ukrainian yellow press contradicts this,
> then there is only one reason, and that is, it doesn't want Ukraine
> to be ruled by the working and peasant masses ... for them Ukraine
> does not exist.[26]

As for UkrSSR ties with Moscow, *Robitnyk* argued: "Ukraine loses nothing
in its union with Russia, not its autonomy, not its independence. The

Ukrainian Socialist Republic ... is always independent because in reality, her status is dependent upon her will ... Ukraine can freely enter into any kind of union and just as freely break that union. That is a sign of her independence."[27] For the Ukrainian workingman, finally, *Robitnyk* saw only two choices: "either join the bourgeoisie and live in chains" or "join the revolutionary proletariat and fight for bread and liberty."[28]

The Communist International (Comintern)

The world, meanwhile, was still in a state of turmoil. Although the war had officially ended in 1918, peace had not been achieved.* The collapse of the old order brought in its wake new wars many of which were being fought in and around Soviet Russia. Convinced that the popularity of his revolution was a signal to commence a worldwide proletarian revolution – an event he also believed would guarantee the survival of his still fragile state against capitalist encroachment – Lenin issued a clarion call to all socialist parties in January 1919.

> WORKERS OF THE WORLD! In the struggle against imperialist barba-
> rism, against monarchy, against the privileged estates, against
> the bourgeois state and bourgeois property, against all kinds and
> forms of class or national oppression – UNITE! Under the banner
> of the worker's Soviets, under the banner of revolutionary strug-
> gle for power and the dictatorship of the proletariat, under the
> banner of the Communist International – WORKERS OF THE WORLD!
> UNITE!

Announcing that the Communist International – also known by its acronym, the Comintern or Third International† – would meet in Moscow, Lenin later laid down its fundamental purpose as that of "a Communist

---

* In 1919, Ukrainians were fighting Poles and Russians; Poles were fighting Czechs; the Irish were fighting the British; Turkey invaded Russia and Britain invaded Turkey; France invaded Syria and Russia and Britain invaded Persia; Japan seized parts of Asiatic Russia; the Greeks were preparing to fight the Turks; the British army had mutinied in France; the French army had mutinied in France and Russia; Panama was about to attack Costa Rica; Haiti was preparing to go to war with the United States; an influenza epidemic was killing millions and in many parts of the world there was famine as well as inflation, recession, and depression. Red revolutions, moreover, were brewing in Hungary, Saxony, Thuringia, and the Ruhr. "Palpably," write Brown and MacDonald, "the world was no tranquil place; plainly, the preconditions for a successful world revolution of the proletariat existed."[29]

† The Second International of socialist parties was formed in Paris in 1889.

underground," funded by the Soviet government but subservient to its own Executive Committee. On 2 March, fifty-two men and women (only five of whom were delegates from foreign countries) formally established the Comintern and confirmed Gregory Zinoviev as its head. From the beginning it was clear that although the Comintern was ostensibly autonomous – Soviet leaders often denied any knowledge of its activities – its purpose was to serve Soviet foreign policy interests, to facilitate the expansion of Soviet secret police influence in the international arena, and to maintain ideological unity and discipline among the world's Communist parties.[30] It was also clear that the first phase of Comintern activity was to be the immediate realization of the "universal dictatorship of the proletariat in view of the present dissolution of the capitalist regime of the whole world." All this was to be accomplished by "the seizure of government power, the disarmament of the bourgeoisie, the general arming of the proletariat, and the suppression of private property."[31]

From Socialism to Communism

Responding to Lenin's call, the SPA left wing met in New York on 16 February 1919 and adopted a "Manifesto and Program" urging American workers to follow the example set by their Russian brothers. The SPA New York Executive promptly expelled its left wing for supporting the manifesto, sparking a party purge that eventually led to the expulsion of two-thirds of the membership. Within six months the Socialist party declined from a high of 110,000 members to less than 40,000.[32]

Despite their disfranchised status within the SPA, the leadership of the left wing was still not prepared to form a separate Communist party in America. Its hope was to take over the SPA and to revolutionize it from within. The ethnic contingent (representing some 90 percent of the total left-wing membership), however, rejected any further association with the SPA and began to push for the immediate formation of a separate revolutionary party. Led by the Russian Federation, representatives of the Ukrainian, Latvian, Estonian, Lithuanian, and Polish federations met with American left-wing leaders and convinced most of them – including Ruthenberg, Louis Fraina, and Bertram Wolfe – that only a separate Communist party could develop a revolutionary proletariat in America. Opposed to such a move were Benjamin Gitlow and John Reed, who decided to attend the SPA convention scheduled for 20 August at Machinist's Hall in Chicago in hopes of taking over the leadership. The main body of the left wing moved to hold a separate Chicago convention at the Russian Federation headquarters (renamed Smolny Hall in honor of the

Bolshevik headquarters in St. Petersburg) at 1221 Blue Island Avenue beginning on 1 September.

Gitlow and Reed never succeeded in taking over the Socialist party. Ejected from the convention hall by Chicago police after refusing to leave, they and some eighty-two followers retreated to the billiard room of Machinist's Hall and proceeded to organize the Communist Labor Party of America (CLP). At the time, CLP founders enjoyed the support of some 69,000 former SPA members.

At Smolny Hall, meanwhile, about 128 delegates, led by Fraina and Ruthenberg but clearly dominated by the Russian Federation, gave birth to the Communist Party of America (CPA). Fraina was elected international secretary and Comintern delegate and Ruthenberg became general secretary.

At the moment of its inception, the CPA had 26,680 members, the vast majority of whom belonged to Eastern European ethnic groups. With 7,000 and 4,000 members respectively, Russians and Ukrainians alone accounted for 40 percent of the membership.* Only 1,100 party members were native Americans and even this figure was reduced when the 800-member Michigan organization left the CPA in January to form the Proletarian party.[33] Given this lopsided representation, it was inevitable that conflict between the ethnic groups (who were initially content to allow the English-speaking members to assume leadership roles within the party as long as they continued to enjoy autonomy within their federations) and the American-born members (who came to resent the privileged status of "foreigners" in an American institution) would erupt. Of all the ethnic federations, it was the Russian that set the pace for the new party. Reflecting on the birth of the CPA many years later, Gitlow, whose CLP later merged with the CPA but who himself was purged from the party in 1929, wrote:

> The determination of the Russian Federation to control the movement out of Russian nationalist considerations certainly characterized its early phases. When better contact was established with Soviet Russia and the Communist International, the Russian heritage was not cast off, the Party did not become American, but instead more Russian. The Russians still rule, although the dominance of the Russian Federation has been done away with and their leaders have been replaced by American leaders. For the Russians now rule from Moscow. Their decisions and orders must

* Other large groups included Lithuanians (4,400), South Slavs (2,200), Poles (1,750), Latvians (1,200), Hungarians (1,000), and Jews (1,000).

be obeyed. The American Communist Party is only a tool in their hands, its leaders their puppets.'[34]

The Ukrainian Federation of Communist Parties of America (UFCPA)

The third convention of the UFSPA was held on 14–19 April 1919, with ninety-four delegates representing 5,711 members (5,199 men and 512 women) in attendance. Pressing their delegate majority, the Bolsheviks pushed through a resolution recognizing the Third Communist International, an act tantamout to full recognition of Russian Bolshevik dominance of the world's socialist movement. Within days, the Socialist Party of America expelled the UFSPA from its ranks.[35] Joining the other expelled ethnic federations at Chicago's Smolny Hall in September, UFSPA delegates officially changed the name of their organization to the Ukrainian Federation of Communist Parties of America (UFCPA) on 1 September 1919 and proceeded to found the Communist Party of America. The transition from a Socialist to a Communist organization eventually cost the newly created federation almost half the UFSPA membership. By the end of September, only 3,133 members were eligible to cast ballots for the new executive.[36]

Robitnyk became the official UFCPA organ on 11 September.[37] It wasted little time in renewing its attacks on Ukrainian priests ("who employ all manner of Jesuit trickery to retain control of the unenlightened masses"), the UNA ("which fools its dues-paying members into believing the Ukrainian Committee is really working on behalf of Ukraine"[38]), the Bachynskyi mission ("which bluffs and lies to the Ukrainian American community"[39]), *Narodna Volya* ("which falsely accuses the UFCPA of fomenting revolution in America"[40]), and the Social Democrats of Ukraine ("who work hand in glove with Ukrainian reactionaries and have become the enemies of the workers and peasants"[41]).

So sweeping was the enthusiasm of Ukrainian-American Communists during this period and so convinced were they that the victory of the proletariat in America was just around the corner – "a few more days, weeks, months, and not a trace of the old order will be found," wrote one correspondent in *Robitnyk* – that all other Ukrainian and American institutions were viewed as anachronistic. In the words of *Robitnyk*: "The time when Socialism was a divided hope, a dream, an ideal, has gone. Socialism exists. The idea of Socialism has been realized. But – not everywhere. Our harvest is not full. The big part of the earth is not yet ripe. But she is getting ripe in our eyes. With every day, every hour, every minute, we are nearer and nearer our full harvest ... On the ruins of capitalist civilization we will build our civilization," concluded *Robitnyk*. "That will be our harvest."[42]

Elections to the executive bodies of the UFCP were held on 25 September. K. Pytlar was elected secretary and A. Dmytryshyn the organizer. P. Ladan was later reelected secretary-translator.[43]

The Palmer Raids

The revolutionary fervor of American Communists and other extremist groups did not go unnoticed by the United States government. Plagued by a wave of bombings (eight cities were hit), strikes (some 4 million workers were out at one time or another), riots, and other disturbances either organized or encouraged by anarchists, the IWW* syndicalists, or other extremist groups, thirty-five states passed antiseditionist laws. Alarmed by a war department general staff estimate of some 1,142,000 leftist extremists in the United States and the discovery of a Comintern directive to American Communist leaders to form "a military commission" and to carry out Comintern instructions "in the strictest secrecy," the Justice Department began to enforce a law making it possible to immediately deport aliens for advocating the overthrow "by force or violence" of the American government.[44] While the legislation was aimed at extremists – some 556 aliens with radical backgrounds, including 249 Russians, were deported – it precipitated a wave of mass hysteria which reverberated among school boards, college presidents, religious pulpits, and self-appointed vigilante groups. The worst acts, however, were perpetrated by the Justice Department itself. On the authority of Attorney General A. Mitchell Palmer, federal agents directed by J. Edgar Hoover rounded up thousands of Americans, making little distinction among socialists, communists, labor organizers, anarchists, pacifists, aliens, and suspected aliens. On 2 January and again on 5 January 1920, Palmer raids were conducted in thirty-three cities across the United States, resulting in some 5,000 arrests. Led by Dean Roscoe Pound and Felix Frankfurter of the Harvard Law School, a group of distinguished American law professors reviewed the activities of Palmer's Justice Department and accused it of engaging in "continual illegal acts."

Legal or not, the raids were effective. The Russian Federation lost about 3,000 members, while UFCPA membership dropped to 2,000.[45] Those who remained in the party went underground.

United States government suppression of radical activities came at a most inopportune time for Ukrainian Communists. Their organizational potential had never been so promising. The postwar recession, the brutal

---

* The initials IWW stand for the Industrial Workers of the World, a revolutionary syndicalist labor union founded in Chicago in 1905.

treatment of striking workers, the somewhat xenophobic American reaction to "foreigners," and the loss of prestige suffered by the Ukrainian nationalist camp at Versailles were variables that augured well for the Ukrainian Communist movement. Even *Svoboda*, for a brief moment in its history, seemed prepared to take another look at the Bolshevik platform. In September 1920, before the failure of Vynnychenko's attempts to create a more Ukrainian Soviet government was known, the UNA organ wrote:

> Our newspaper always has been and is now in favor of the principle that the Ukrainian people will win by means of revolution – while counterrevolution will result in a defeat – and for that reason we have always supported revolutionary politics in Ukraine. When today the only true defenders of revolution – defenders with weapons in their hands – remain the Bolsheviks (and those parties which support them) then our newspaper says that Ukrainians should join the one revolutionary front of the Bolsheviks.[46]

With such a fertile field before them, Ukrainian Communists in America were faced with a dilemma: remain underground and enhance their revolutionary character or adopt a new structure, become legally acceptable, and broaden their base.

While debates over future direction within Communist party ranks continued, the Ukrainian Communist press grew and prospered. In 1920, *Ukrainski Shchodenni Visti* (The Ukrainian Daily News) made its debut followed by *Molot* (Hammer), a humoristic journal, and *Komunistychnyi Svit* (The Communist World). At the same time, the Ukrainian Marxists faithful to Vynnychenko attempted a journalistic comeback with *Nash Shliakh* (Our Path) in 1920, *Chervona Zoria* (Red Star) in 1921, and *Robitnycha Pravda* (Worker's Truth) in 1922. The latter publications, all of which were edited by E. Kruk, offered only token opposition to the powerful UFCPA, and all disappeared after a brief existence.[47]

The Birth of Oborona Ukrainy (Defense of Ukraine)

Stunned by the Bolshevik coup, Social Patriots within the UFSPA attempted a comeback. Arguing that expulsion of the UFSPA from the SPA meant the organization was defunct, they tried to establish another federation prior to the August 1919 convention of the SPA. Under the leadership of a New York City group led by Ivan Mateiko, Hryhorij Cherkas, and Mykola Repen, the dissidents appealed to other disenchanted socialists within the Ukrainian community for support. "Only by means of an organization, only by means of a unified struggle and the assistance of the progressive element of our socialist proletariat will we be able to achieve a free Ukraine," read their plea. "Lies are being spread by those who claim that the socialist program is against national liberty. Those who are against national liberty are not socialists but those who pretend to be socialists." Their entreaties, however, accomplished little.

A second, more successful endeavor to establish a national, anti-Bolshevik socialist coalition was made by Sichynsky, Ceglinsky, Repen, and other Social Patriots in 1922 when *Oborona Ukrainy* (Defense of Ukraine Association) came into being. By 1923 the new socialist society was publishing its own newspaper, *Ukrainska Hromada* (The Ukrainian Community), and by the late 1920s, branches were active in Scranton, New York City, Boston, Detroit, and Chicago, as well as in smaller communities such as Rochester, New York, and Lansing and Grand Rapids, Michigan.

With the election of Sichynsky to the presidency of the Ukrainian Workingmen's Association in 1933, Ukrainian socialists in America finally had a power base. For the next eight years the center of socialist vigor was located in Scranton, headquarters city of the UWA.[48]

The "Americanization" of American Communism

With CPA ranks decimated by the Justice Department, Ruthenberg approached the CLP leadership to discuss rapprochement. The CLP agreed, provided the ethnic federations were willing to relinquish their privileged semiautonomous status and consent to total amalgamation within a reorganized party structure. When Ruthenberg brought the CLP proposal to the CPA Central Executive, it was voted down 9 to 4. Angered by the rejection and the undiminished revolutionary fervor of the ethnic majority, Ruthenberg and two other executive members left the CPA in April 1920 and organized a second Communist Party of America.

By now the Comintern had begun to weary of the strife among U.S. Communists and sent over a "representative" to bring them into line. Heartened by the apparent staying power of the Soviet state and chastened by the disastrous outcome of Communist revolts in Hungary and Germany, the Comintern had abandoned its "revolution now" approach and was easing into a second phase of international activity based on the slogan "boring from within." A secret unity conference was held in Bridgeman, Michigan, and the result was the creation of the United Communist party (UCP). Because the UCP acknowledged the value of ethnic federations as "propaganda committees," but not their autonomous status, the original CPA refused to join.[49]

The Comintern, of course, was angered by its failure to bring the American-born and immigrant factions together and presented the CPA and UCP delegates to its Second Congress with an ultimatum: unite or face expulsion from the Comintern. Determined to reorganize the Communist party in America "without regard to the existing parties," the Comintern dispatched three representatives, all Americans, to the United States and, in May 1921, a second unity convention was held in Woodstock, New York. After much heated debate, still another Communist Party of America was established and duly recognized by the Comintern at its Third Congress in 1921. The Comintern now urged the American delegation to come in from the cold, adopt the new party line, and proceed to establish a legal, open party conducive to American laborers.[50]

For the old-line revolutionaries associated with the ethnic federations, the Comintern directive was difficult to accept. Still, the Comintern was not to be disobeyed and in July 1921 the Ukrainian Worker's Club and nine other Communist auxiliary organizations dutifully came together in New York to form the American Labor Alliance. Aware that the alliance was merely a reshuffling of old Bolsheviks, the Comintern rejected it as inadequate. A second attempt by the CPA in December led to the formation of the Workers' Party of America.[51] To maintain its underground network, however, the Comintern retained the CPA clandestine apparatus, designating it as *number one* among party faithful and the newly created party as *number two*. The relationship was explained in a Comintern directive: "It must always be remembered that the real revolutionary party – the American section of the Third International – is the Communist Party of America and that the legal party (Workers' party) is but an instrument which it uses to carry on its work among the masses."

The ethnic federations were not fooled. Angered by their loss of power and status in the new party structure, and eager to retain the revolutionary purity of their organizations, they formed a left opposition and called an emergency convention in January 1922. "The so-called Workers' party is a menace to the proletariat of America," their manifesto declared. "It is a party of dangerous compromisers, opportunists, and centrists masking themselves as Communists. The (new) Communist Party of America calls upon all workers and workers' organizations to refuse to support or to join this prototype of the decadent Socialist party ... this party of Mensheviks called the Workers' Party of America." Mindful of the Comintern command for party legality, however, the left opposition organized the United Toilers of America (composed almost entirely of Russians, Ukrainians, Latvians, and Lithuanians) as its legal apparatus and, confident that it still represented the majority among Communists in the United States, presented its case to the Comintern.

Again the Comintern was unequivocal. Majorities don't matter, the left opposition representative was informed. "Whose comrades are you?" he was asked. If you belong to Lenin "you must obey ... discipline." Rationalizing that their position had been misrepresented, the left opposition decided to make a final appeal to the Comintern Congress in November 1922.[52]

Sending over another representative, a European Communist this time, the Comintern called for another unity conclave in Bridgeman, Michigan, in August 1922. A major topic of discussion, of course, was the future of the ethnic federations and their relationship to *number one*. Describing the work of the foreign-born, one party stalwart complained that the foreign-born were out of touch with America. Ethnic federations, he argued, were more "European" than "American" and were of little value in recruiting American laborers into the Communist fold.

In November, the Comintern Congress came down on the side of the Americanizers. While immigrants "play an important part in the American labor movement," the Congress declared, "their greatest weakness lies in the fact that they desire to apply experiences they have acquired in the various countries of Europe mechanically to American conditions." The "most important task," the Comintern emphasized, "is to arouse the American-born workers out of their lethargy" and to allow them "to play a leading part in the movement." The left opposition was ordered back into the American Communist fold and the CPA was warned not to delay in its efforts to legalize its operations and to broaden its base. Those who cannot follow these simple directives, the Comintern concluded ominously, should "leave the Party."

Thus ended the three-year struggle between native Americans and Slavic immigrants for supremacy within the fledgling Communist movement of America. The name Communist party was temporarily rejected in favor of the Workers' Party of America until 1925 when it was changed to the Workers' (Communist) Party of America. In 1929, it became the Communist Party, U.S.A. (CPUSA).[53] The American contingent had won, but their victory gave them nothing. All Communist power resided with the Comintern in Moscow, and with Stalin rising rapidly to the pinnacle, even that subterfuge was soon to be abandoned.

Ukrainian Communists lost nothing by the Comintern decision. They never did feel comfortable in the American milieu and with the major responsibility for Communist party growth resting squarely on the shoulders of native Americans, they returned to their communities and began to organize new, albeit legal, coalitions. They were still revolutionary Communists and they could still devote their energies to that which they enjoyed most and did best: proselytizing the masses and fighting Ukrainian nationalists directly and through front organizations approved and encouraged by the Comintern in Moscow.

The United Ukrainian Toilers Organization (UUTO)

In 1923, the debate within the Ukrainian Federation of Communist Parties of America over organizational direction came to an end with a decision to convene an All-Ukrainian "Toilers Congress." The future looked bright. The Ukrainian-American nationalist camp was still reeling from the Galician debacle and morale was lower than ever. Militant communism had ended in the UkrSSR and the Ukrainization campaign was just getting under way. Suppression of radicals in America appeared to be over and the United States was becoming increasingly disinterested in European affairs. It was time to forget about a revolutionary underground – the United States was not about to collapse – and to build party support around broadly based cadres within the Ukrainian-American community.

Adding to the strength of the Communists was their press. *Robitnyk* had been succeeded by *Ukrainski Shchodenni Visti* (Ukrainian Daily News, hereafter referred to simply as *Visti*) and unrelenting attacks on the nationalist community were having an effect. "The Ukrainian bourgeoisie lost and are therefore yelling at the top of their lungs," declared *Visti* in 1921. Ukraine's "liberty and independence has been decided by the working masses ... that's why the bourgeoisie are crying."[54] Still holding to the Leninist belief that the elimination of class struggle would result in the eradication of national antagonisms, *Visti* observed:

> The Ukrainian bourgeoisie with their various "doctors,"
> "professors," "lawyers," "editors" of various yellow rags, former
> Austrian corporals ... accuse the class conscious Ukrainian worker
> and his newspaper of being Moscowphiles of the Red variety ...
> The Ukrainian *panky* from *Narodna Volya, Svoboda, America,* and
> *Ukrainian Voice* accuse us of not having enough of a national
> emphasis ... We say too much national emphasis is wrong for
> the worker ... In a capitalist country, the worker really has no
> nation ... when the proletariat wins over the bourgeoisie, there
> will only be one fatherland, the world.[55]

A similar note was struck in notices inviting Ukrainian Americans to the upcoming Toilers Congress.

> The Ukrainian Toilers Congress does not pretend to know "high
> politics." It is not interested in the building of national homes
> or in the collection of hundreds of thousands of dollars for projects
> of a similar nature.
> It presents for itself a humble, straight and clear task: to analyze

all of the shortcomings of our present reality, to determine all of our most dire needs, cultureducational as well as econopolitical, and to find a way to satisfy them ...

Here we are being exploited not only by the American *pan*,* but by our own kind, in the role of priests and so-called "intellectuals ..."

We came here seeking a better life and the truth and they have followed us in order to keep us in ignorance, to live off of our bloody labor, and to make us faithful servants of the American *pan*, just as in the past they kept us faithful servants of the Austrian and Russian pans ...

"Give," "give," "give," that's all we've heard from our pans during the last few years ...

Let's say enough to all of this, enough of being cared for by people without a conscience ...

We must take our destiny into our own calloused hands ...

The notice ran for many pages, attempting to convince the Ukrainian workingman that all of his financial and moral sacrifices during the war years were a waste of time, a hoax perpetrated by the clergy and the nationalist leadership to keep him in bondage. For many Ukrainians, the notice, coming as it did on the heels of the Council of Ambassadors' decision to award all of Galicia to Poland, made sense. Even Dr. Simenovych voiced approval of the aims of the congress. In the end, congress conveners were able to boast of having delegates from church brotherhoods as well as Sich and Prosvita branches, organizations usually included on the nationalist side of the community's ideological ledger.[56]

The congress was held in New York City on 13–14 April 1924, with 191 delegates in attendance. Despite a heavy dose of Communist rhetoric, one of the main emphases of the first congress was on the sociocultural education of the Ukrainian workingman. "In a capitalist society," began one of the resolutions, "the school does not enlighten the working mass nor does it educate its youth. Children must leave school and go to work at an early age because the wages of the father are not enough to sustain the family." The resolution ended with a promise to establish courses for illiterates, special classes for school children and laboring youth, a publishing house, teacher preparatory courses, choirs, drama troupes, and

---

* The word "pan" has two meanings in the Ukrainian language. It can simply mean "Mr." or it can be a reference to a member of the aristocracy. Communists adopted the latter meaning and always addressed themselves as "Comrade" to underscore the difference.

dance ensembles. Other resolutions passed by the congress pledged full support of the UkrSSR, the "true" government of Ukraine; called for unification of all Ukrainian lands under the Red Soviet Ukrainian flag; and pledged full support of the American laboring class in its fight against "capitalist exploitation."

Congress delegates also voted to establish a new coalition, the Soiuz ukrainskykh robitnychykh orhanizatsii (The United Ukrainian Toilers Organizations, henceforth referred to as UUTO), headed by a twenty-five-member national committee and a seven-member executive board subsequently elected from among committee members. Membership in the new organization was open to all established central and local Ukrainian organizations in America.

Within a few months after the congress, local coordinating committees – consisting of representatives of member organizations – were created in Boston, Buffalo, Chicago, Cleveland, Detroit, Grand Rapids (MI), Newark, New Haven, New York, Pittsburgh, Rochester, Scranton, and Wilkes-Barre. During the next year and a half, however, the progress of the new organization – then under the nominal leadership of Damian Borysko, its secretary – was slow, largely because of the loose organizational structure dictated by the congress. To strengthen the network, the full national committee, meeting for the first time on 7 October 1925, agreed to permit the creation of local UUTO branches which could also become part of the national body as member organizations. By the middle of 1926, at about the time M. Tkach became the national secretary, some fifty branches had already been formed. In October 1926, the national committee elected Tkach to head the organization, while M. Kniazevych became the secretary. The two remained in their respective posts until 1939.

The second UUTO convention was held in New York City on 26–28 December 1926. Reporting on the progress of the organization, M. Kniazevych declared that UUTO had fifty-five branches with about 1,300 members and approximately thirty other affiliated local organizations, with an additional membership of some 1,500. At the same time, reported Kniazevych, UUTO had recently published a third- and fourth-grade reader to be used in the thirty-three cultural schools (serving some 1,200 children) that the organization sponsored. "The Ukrainian nationalist camp," he concluded, "is dying. It is forever dead in the old country while among Ukrainian immigrants, sympathy for the UkrSSR is increasing."

During the next few years, UUTO member organizations established local reading rooms, classes for illiterates, cultural classes for children, and preparatory courses for Ukrainian teachers. In addition, UUTO organized protest demonstrations against Poland's occupation of western Ukraine and managed to raise approximately $12,000 for Ukrainian Communists then active in Poland. A number of "labor temples" were either built or purchased and Ukrainian cultural activities – choirs, dance troupes, orchestras, drama groups – flourished.[57]

The success of Ukrainian Communists in America was based on their ability to fulfill two important needs of Ukrainian working people: a better education and ethnonational self-respect in a strange and foreign land. "Great emphasis," writes John Kolasky, a former Ukrainian Communist in Canada, "was placed on educational, cultural, and social activities as a means of disseminating the Communist ideology."[58] At the same time, concludes Kolasky, it was easier for Ukrainians than for others to fall under the influence of Communist propaganda:

> They were attracted by reports of the renaissance of the Ukrainian language and culture, which had been repressed under the tsars, and were convinced that the national problem in Ukraine had been solved. Their impoverished peasant background, lack of education, and centuries-long foreign domination bred in them a deep sense of personal and national inferiority. To them, the USSR, in which Ukraine was supposedly a willing and equal member, appeared as a great Slav power destined to a leading role in humanity's march to a new social order. Identification with the Soviet Union and its ideology gave them a sense of strength and personal worth.[59]

Meanwhile, the second phase of Comintern activity had matured. The emphasis now was on the cultivation of fellow travelers and the formation of front groups, described by a 1926 Comintern resolution as "sympathizing mass organizations" which were ostensibly self-governing and independent but were "in reality under Communist leadership."[60] Responding to the newest Moscow directive, the UUTO leadership went to work and by the fifth convention of 1932 was able to count 112 branches (with some 2,750 members) and an additional 3,400 members in various affiliated front organizations. The entire UUTO apparatus at this time included twelve Young Pioneer branches (with about 300 children), thirty-six heritage schools, sixty-four reading rooms, thirty-five drama groups, seventeen choirs, and twelve mandolin orchestras, most of which were housed in twenty-three separate "labor temples" or homes owned or rented by the Communists.[61]

The Roosevelt-Litvinov Accord

At the height of the Great Famine in Ukraine – and only a few months after assuming office – President Franklin D. Roosevelt wrote a letter to

USSR President Kalinin expressing his desire "to end the present abnormal relationship" between the two countries and requesting the arrival in Washington of a high-level envoy to discuss future ties. From the White House perspective, improving relations between the United States and the USSR could lead to two highly desirable outcomes: increased trade to help America out of the Great Depression and the cessation of Soviet espionage activities within United States borders. Stalin, of course, was delighted with the American initiative and sent his foreign minister, Maxim Litvinov, to meet with Roosevelt.[62]

Signed on 16 November 1933, the Roosevelt-Litvinov Accord consisted of eleven letters, one memorandum, and a "gentlemen's agreement." In return for diplomatic recognition, the Soviets promised to respect the religious and civil rights of American citizens living in the USSR, to consider payment of some $100 million of American claims against the Soviet government, and to negotiate a trade agreement.[63] Both governments also agreed "not to permit the formation or residence on its territory of any organization or group ... which has as its aim the overthrow ... or the bringing about by force of a change in the political or social order."[64] Commenting on the United States–Soviet agreement, the Ukrainian Weekly, an English-language supplement to Svoboda, reported that some 8,000 people had participated in a New York City march protesting Soviet policies in Ukraine and added that while the protest was "not intended to hinder the policies and movements of the United States government – we Ukrainians are anxious as anyone else to cooperate with our beloved president," nevertheless, "we look dubiously upon the value of any benefits which America may obtain from having official relations with a government whose rule is based on direct force alone," a government that is unable "to provide for its subjects even the most ordinary necessities of life, and which has shown itself capable of the most barbaric cruelty, as evidenced by its reign of terror and the present Bolshevik fostered famine in Ukraine."[65]

The Soviets never lived up to their promises. Debts were not paid, the trade agreement proved disappointing, and the Comintern continued its clandestine existence in America. Denying that the accord had in any way mentioned the Comintern,[66] Litvinov met with the Secretariat of the American Communist party and assured its members that they had little to fear. "After all, comrades," he said, "You should know by this time how to handle the fiction of the tie-up between the Comintern and the Soviet Union. Don't worry about the letter. It is a scrap of paper which will soon be forgotten in the realities of Soviet American relations."[67]

The Red Decade

For America's Communists, Roosevelt's recognition of the USSR was a propitious event which increased the aura of respectability their party needed to finally divest itself of its 1920s' image of revolutionary illegality. Exploiting the economic turmoil and uncertainty which plagued the United States during the 1930s, the radical left was able to transform that unfortunate period in American history into what Eugene Lyons has labeled "the red decade."

> It was not Red in the sense that councils of workers and peasants took over the government, or that, as rightists argued after 1933, a socialist upstart was ensconced in the White House. But it was Red in the sense that the center of political gravity swung sharply to the Left, and millions of jobless war veterans took to the streets in demonstrations or "seized" factories in sit-down strikes. It was Red in tone, mood, flavor as thousands of artists, intellectuals, movie stars and literary figures found an emotional haven with various radical parties.[68]

Two major historical developments contributed to the rebirth of leftist sentiment in America. The first was the Great Depression – which some interpreted as the inevitable by-product of capitalism – and the second was the rise of fascism and Hitler's Germany – which was explained as capitalism *in extremis*.[69] In the minds of many Americans during this period, capitalism – which had wrought the depression, war, and fascism – had failed. They concluded, according to Professor Schlesinger, that "civilization could endure only by a transfusion of moral energy from some new faith, austere in its severity, uncompromising in its dedication ... The Bolshevik was the man of the future; and the worker-hero of the Soviet Union became the model for his American counterpart."[70] In the forefront of the campaign to popularize the "Soviet Way" were American intellectuals, correspondents, and even government officials who grossly exaggerated Communist accomplishments, ignored or rationalized a myriad of failures, and, when necessary, conspired to cover up Bolshevik crimes. Especially impressed were those who traveled to the USSR during the 1930s, almost all of whom, it seems, found something to admire.

Some found a Judeo-Christian spirit. Sherwood Eddy, an American churchman and YMCA leader, wrote that "the Communist philosophy seeks a new order, a classless society of unbroken brotherhood, what the Hebrew prophets would have called a reign of righteousness on earth." A similar theme was struck by the American Quaker Henry Hodgkin. "As we look at Russia's great experiment in brotherhood," he wrote, "it may seem to us that some dim perception of Jesus' way, all unbeknown, is inspiring it."[71]

Others discovered a sense of purpose and cohesive values. Corliss and Margaret Lamont concluded that the Soviet people were happy because they were making *"constructive* sacrifices with a splendid purpose held consciously and continuously in mind," despite some "stresses and strains" in the Soviet system.[72]

Still others found humane prisons. "Soviet justice," wrote Anna Louise Strong, "aims to give the criminal a new environment in which he will begin to act in a normal way as a responsible Soviet citizen. The less confinement the better; the less he feels himself in prison the better ... the labor camps have won high reputation throughout the Soviet Union as places where tens of thousands of men have been reclaimed."[73]

American intellectuals were not alone in their praise of the USSR. A collection of writings about the Soviet Union by Western intellectuals published in 1932 contained tributes from such prominent authors as Thomas Mann, Johannes Becher, Gerhart Hauptmann, Ernest Toller, Anatole France, Romain Rolland, André Maurois, George Bernard Shaw, H.G. Weils, Theodore Dreiser, Stuart Chase, John Dos Passos, George Lukacs, Floyd Dell, and Henri Barbusse.[74]

The Soviet Union had something for everyone. Intellectuals found social justice and equality, wise and caring leaders, reconstructed institutions, and intellectual stimulation.[75] Rebels found support for their causes: birth control, sexual equality, progressive education, futuristic dancing, Esperanto. Even "hard boiled capitalists," wrote Eugene Lyons, a reporter in Moscow during the 1930s, "found the spectacle to their taste: no strikes, no lip, hard work."[76]

Contributing to the liberal chorus of solicitous praise for Stalin's new society were American diplomats such as U.S. Ambassador Joseph E. Davies who argued that Stalin was "a stubborn democrat" who resisted autocracy and insisted on a liberal constitution "even though it hazarded his power and party control."[77] Like most liberals, Davies never accepted the notion that Stalin's purge trials were staged. "To assume that," he wrote, "... would be to presuppose the creative genius of Shakespeare and the genius of Belasco in stage production."[78] Nor did he believe Stalin – who he described as "clean-living, modest, retiring" – was personally involved in the elimination of his former colleagues.[79] Even though he had personally met and dined with many of the purge victims, Davies later concluded that their execution was justified because it eliminated Russia's Fifth Column which, in keeping with "Hitler's designs upon the Ukraine,"[80] had conspired to "dismember the Union."[81] In 1941, Davies had his papers, letters, and diary notations published in a collection entitled *Mission to Moscow*, which Warner Brothers later made into a movie.[82] A wealthy Washington lawyer who contributed $17,500 to Roosevelt's reelection campaign in 1936, Davies was appointed in 1937. Soon after he left for Moscow, unidentified pressures from the White House led to the abolishment of the State Department's Russian section and the dispersion or destruction of many of its documents.[83]

The most adamant apologists for the Stalinist cult, however, were found among certain Moscow-based correspondents for America's liberal press, especially the *New York Times*'s Pulitzer Prize winning foreign correspondent Walter Duranty – a cynical careerist who excused Bolshevik excesses with the oft-repeated assertion "you can't make an omelet without breaking eggs" – and the *Nation*'s Louis Fischer who once seriously described the dreaded GPU (the predecessor of the KGB) as "a big educational institution."[84] At no time were their Sovietophile tendencies more pronounced than during the Great Famine in Ukraine.

The first reliable report of the catastrophe to reach the outside world was presented by Gareth Jones, an English journalist who visited Ukraine secretly early in 1933 and then left the USSR to write about what he had seen. When his story broke, members of the American press corps – most of whom had seen pictures of the horror taken by German consular officers in Ukraine – were besieged by their home offices for more information. Angered as much by the Jones scoop as by his unflattering picture of Soviet life, a number of American correspondents met with Comrade Konstantin Umanskii, the Soviet press censor, to determine how best to deal with the famine story. According to Eugene Lyons, who at the time was a Moscow correspondent for both the United Press and Tass, a statement was drafted after which vodka and *zakusky* were ordered and everyone sat down to celebrate with a smiling Umanskii.

The agreed-upon format was followed faithfully by Duranty. "There is no actual starvation," reported the *New York Times* on 30 March 1933, "but there is widespread mortality from diseases due to malnutrition." When the famine reports persisted over the next few months, the *Times* admitted "food shortages" but insisted that any report of famine "is today an exaggeration or malignant propaganda." "You have done a good job in your reporting of the USSR," Stalin told Duranty.[85]

Extensive coverage of the famine in the American press was provided by the Hearst newspaper chain, which attempted to "update" its reports of the famine by placing it in 1934 rather than 1932–3. Writing in the *Nation* (13 March 1935), Louis Fischer "exposed" the series indignantly, pointing out that he had visited Ukraine in 1934 and had witnessed no famine! In a book entitled *Soviet Journey* published in 1935, however, Fischer finally admitted a "problem" in Ukraine explaining it in very neat and simple terms: "The peasants accordingly sabotaged – and had nothing to eat. It was a terrible lesson at terrific cost. History can be cruel ... The peasants wanted to destroy collectivization. The government wanted to retain collectivization. The peasants used the best means at their disposal. The government used the best means at their disposal. The government won."[86]

At no time during this period did either Fischer or Duranty – who devoted only thirty pages to the 1928–34 Soviet period in *I Write As I Please*, his 300-page defense of the Soviet Union – publicly speculate about the number of Ukrainians who perished during Stalin's man-made famine.

But even when millions of famine dead could no longer be denied, there were still many who stood ready to defend the sanctity of the Bolshevik revolution. In a 1933 publication entitled *The Great Offensive*, Maurice Hindus wrote that if the growing "food shortage" brought "distress and privation" to certain parts of the Soviet Union, "the fault is not of Russia but of the Russians."[87] Recalling a conversation he once had with an American businessman, Hindus wrote:

> "And supposing there is a famine in Russia," continued my interlocutor ... "what will happen?"
> "People will die, of course," I answered.
> "And supposing three or four million people die."
> "The revolution will go on."[88]

If a famine was necessary to preserve the revolution, so be it. "Maybe it cost a million lives," wrote Upton Sinclair, Pulitzer Prize novelist and another of America's growing army of Soviet apologists, "maybe it cost five million – but you cannot think intelligently about it unless you ask yourself how many millions it might have cost if the changes had not been made ... Some people will say that this looks like condoning wholesale murder. That is not true; it is merely trying to evaluate a revolution. There has never been a great social change in history without killing."[89]

In the end, the Bolsheviks succeeded in sufficiently muddling the issues surrounding Ukraine's Great Famine to keep it from the eyes of the world. Concealing the barbarism until it was ended, they generated doubt, confusion, and disbelief. "Years after the event," wrote Lyons in 1937, "when no Russian Communist in his senses any longer concealed the magnitude of the famine – the question whether there had been a famine at all was still being disputed in the outside world!"[90]

The Popular Front

By the mid 1930s, America's perception of the USSR had been dulcified and the left was riding a new crest of popularity.[91] It was precisely at this moment in history that Moscow – fearful now of the rising power of Nazi Germany – took another turn in its ideological road and began urging reconciliation with powerful capitalist states and the creation of a "Popular Front" against fascism. The shift in party line, articulated at the seventh Comintern Congress in 1935, now defined the major world struggle as not that of capitalism vs. communism but rather democracy vs. fascism. In the words of Prof. Frederick L. Schuman, an outspoken defender of the Soviet Union:

> The great cleavage between contemporary societies is not between "capitalism" (democratic or fascist) and "communism," but between those (whether in Manchester, Moscow, Marseilles, or Minneapolis) who believe in the mind and in the government of, by, and for the people, and those (whether in Munich, Milan or Mukden) who believe in might and in government of, by, and for a self-appointed oligarchy of property and privilege.[92]

Basic to the new approach was the promulgation of the notion that whatever was "antifascist" was automatically "democratic."

> Hence evolved the practice of never identifying Communists as anything but "anti-fascists" unless forced to do so. The corollary of this was the parallel thesis posed to noncommunists to accept, that Communism and Fascism represented the really fundamental choices which had to be made ultimately, drawn up as images of Light and Dark. Once these two approaches had become internalized, everything that followed was self-explanatory. "Anti-Fascism" without its complement of full devotion to Communism would have meant little to liberal and radical opinion-makers.[93]

Intellectual apologists for the Soviet regime, many of whom began to call themselves "progressives," responded to the clarion call of the Popular Front with vigor and dedication. Writing in *Soviet Russia Today*, a monthly journal, Upton Sinclair, Max Lerner, and Robert M. Lovett praised Russia's important role in defending democracy.[94] For Louis Fischer, Russia was the first true democracy and anyone who didn't believe it was "either malicious or ignorant."[95] Writing in the *New Republic*, Lewis Mumford argued that communism was a "false bogey" while fascism was the real enemy."[96] Later the *New Republic* editorialized: "the Communists today are not acting as a revolutionary group; they are so committed to the policy of cooperation with all democratic forces that one can hardly tell them from the New Deal Democrats."[97]

The CPUSA, which in 1935 had no more than 30,000 members, had finally arrived. Gone were such slogans of the past as "Workers of the World Unite." Rash talk about gaining power by violence was, in the words of Stalin, "a comic misunderstanding." The party, it was soon proclaimed, "opposes with all its power, and will help to crush with democratic means any clique, group, faction, circle, or party, from within or without, which acts to undermine, overthrow and subvert any democratic institution of the American people." Pointing to Thomas Paine, Thomas Jefferson, Andrew Jackson, and Abraham Lincoln as glorious forerunners, party leaders promulgated a new slogan: "Communism Is the Americanism of the Twentieth Century." By "continuing the traditions of 1776 and 1861 the Communist party is really the only party entitled by its program and work to designate itself as 'sons and daughters of the American Revolution,'" explained Earl Browder, the general secretary. Members with Anglo-Saxon names were soon favored for top party posts while those with foreign-sounding surnames were urged to adopt anglicized pseudonyms. "We are an American party composed of American citizens," Browder exclaimed. "We view all our problems in the light of the national interests of the United States."[98]

Joining the Popular Front movement were literally hundreds of Communist-controlled organizations – with such high-sounding names as the American League against War and Fascism (later known as the American League for Peace and Democracy), the Hollywood Anti-Nazi League, the Workers' Alliance, the Civil Liberties Union, the National Negro Congress, the League of American Writers, the Theater Arts Committee, and the American Youth Congress – that sprang into existence to join in the struggle "to preserve democracy."[99]

By 1939, the Popular Front was at the height of its power. When a group of 140 American intellectuals associated with the Committee for Cultural Freedom included the USSR in their list of nations that denied civil liberties and cultural independence, the Popular Front was able to mobilize some 400 Americans – including university presidents and professors and such prominent names as Langston Hughes, Richard Wright, Max Weber, Granville Hicks, Louis Untermeyer, Clifford Odets, and James Thurber – to sign and to agree to have published an open letter branding as "Fascists" all those who dared suggest "the fantastic falsehood that the USSR and the totalitarian states are basically alike." An all-out attack on the Committee for Cultural Freedom was subsequently launched by the *Daily Worker*, the Communist party organ, and, of course, by the *Nation* and the *New Republic*, albeit with somewhat less bravado.[100]

For the Communists, the Popular Front was a resounding success which helped whitewash the horrors of Soviet life and significantly crippled those who were struggling to expose the realities behind Moscow's smiling face. In the words of Earl Browder:

> For the American Communist party in 1930 the USSR began as something to be "defended" against a world *hostile to it*; by 1936 the USSR was being increasingly transformed into a potential *ally* of America as part of the concerted defense of both countries against rising fascist powers *hostile to both*. Then for the first time the agitation of the American Communist party began to get a *response in depth* when it spoke of the USSR; the special relationship of Communists to the USSR for the first time became a political asset to the party instead of a net liability.[101]

By 1938, Communists could count on at least a million American friends in various front groups, exclusive of any trade union support the party enjoyed.[102]

The International Workers' Order (ORDEN)

The dramatic shift in America's political climate during the 1930s emboldened Ukrainian Communists to challenge their most powerful opposition, the nationalist-oriented Ukrainian fraternal insurance societies, head on. Encouraged by the International Workers' Order (IWO), a Communist-controlled fraternal insurance organization whose president was a member of the Communist party executive,[103] Communists in Chicago organized the first Ukrainian IWO branch in January 1932. Within a short time additional branches were organized in Buffalo, Philadelphia, Cleveland, Youngstown, Rochester (New York), and Syracuse, growing, by 1 April, to a total of seventeen branches* and 275 members. On 1 October 1932, the IWO national executive approved the creation of a Ukrainian section which came to be called Ukrainska sektsiia mizhnarodnoho ordenu in Ukrainian (hereafter referred to simply as ORDEN) and the Ukrainian American Fraternal Union in English.

The growth of ORDEN was phenomenal. At the first convention, held

---

* Branches were granted charters when they enrolled a minimum of fifteen members.

in Chicago in 1932, the organization had about 1,200 members. At the second convention, held in New York in 1935, ORDEN had a total membership of 5,600. By the third convention, in Pittsburgh in 1938, the organization had grown to a membership of 15,000, of which one-fifth were children. Like its counterparts in the nationalist camp, ORDEN began to publish its own "kalendars" (which, oddly enough, contained the dates of both Roman Catholic and Ukrainian Catholic religious holidays) and a journal called "The New Order," and to develop various youth activities including Young Pioneer branches and softball teams.[104]

Funds for political causes were also mobilized. When the Popular Front began organizing the so-called Abraham Lincoln Brigade to fight on the Loyalist side during the Spanish Civil War, ORDEN and UUTO joined forces to raise $1,000 for the cause.[105] A number of Ukrainian Americans later joined the brigade and at least two of them, Michael Zayats of Brooklyn and Dmytro Semeniuk of Philadelphia, were killed in action.*[106]

In keeping with the Popular Front movement, UUTO and ORDEN helped establish the so-called Ukrainian National Front beginning with a congress convened in New York City on 5–6 September 1936. A total of 353 delegates, representing some 20,000 Ukrainians, participated in the congress, including some UNA, UWA,† and GCU members. The congress turned out to be a political demonstration under a broad preamble that declared: "Let there be unity everywhere under the motto – Away with Fascism, Fascism is our enemy! ... Away with war, it only hurts the poor ... Away with the chains of nationalism ... We want liberty, bread and peace!"[107]

The congress signaled the beginning of an intense effort by Ukrainian Communists to associate the equally fast-developing Ukrainian Nationalist Front in America with the fascist label. In the forefront of the drive to paint all Ukrainian nationalists fascist black and everything Soviet white was *Visti*, the Ukrainian Communist daily.[108] For the editors of *Visti*, all criticisms of the USSR were part of a fascist conspiracy, especially stories about the famine. "There is no famine in Ukraine," *Visti* declared in 1934, "gone is the perpetual fear of hunger."[109]

Committed to their holy cause and convinced that the enemy was lying, Ukrainian Communists followed the dictates of the party, right or wrong. The party's logic was simple. Fascism is antidemocratic. Communists are

---

* Zayats was born in Lychburg, Pennsylvania. Semeniuk was born in western Ukraine and came to America in 1927 at the age of sixteen.

† *Narodna Volya* was incensed with the Bolshevik suggestion that the UWA had taken part in the Congress. "Out of 284 branches and some ten thousand members," declared the UWA organ, "only four branches ... representing no more than 156 members" had participated.[110]

prodemocratic and anti-fascist. Ukrainian nationalists are anti-Communist. Ukrainian nationalists are therefore antidemocratic and pro-fascist.

ORDEN "helps the Ukrainian working man in many ways," observed a promotional pamphlet in 1937. It supports labor strikes, struggles for labor benefits, and fights fascism. "Fascism and reaction are a menace to the worker, a danger to progress, a threat to democracy ... No worker's organization – in fact no organization which calls itself democratic – can ignore this great danger."[111] "Fascists are planning to take over the UNA," alleged *Visti* that same year. Commenting on an alleged "secret caucus" held during the UNA convention in May, *Visti* quoted one participant as openly admitting: "We are fascists."[112]

Labeling a Ukrainian nationalist rally in New York "a fascist manifestation," *Visti* described an emotional hand-raised tribute to Ukraine during which the speaker shouted "Slava Ukraine" (Glory to Ukraine) as a "Hitlerite salute."[113] A rally "for democracy and peace" was organized by the Ukrainian Communists in Cooper Union a few weeks later. Resolutions were passed condemning Germany, Japan, and Italy, "the oppression of the Ukrainian people in Western Ukraine by the Polish government," and "the agents of Hitler among Ukrainians ... who claim for themselves the right to register the Ukrainian people without their consent on the side of fascism and in their name to approve the aggressive policy of fascism." Condemning the arrival in America of leaders of the Organization of Ukrainian Nationalists (OUN), a resolution was passed protesting the ease with which "Hitler's agents" were coming to America "from Berlin with instructions from German fascism for arousing the Ukrainian people against Democracy, organizing among them fascist groups, and merging them in this country with similar organizations among the German population."[114]

For many Ukrainians in America, communism had a special appeal. During the Great Depression, the party presented a simple and believable solution to America's economic problems. Ukrainians were also mesmerized by the Soviet Union. "Ukraine and the USSR became the holy land" writes John Kolasky, "and Moscow the Mecca to which they looked for inspiration and guidance."[115] The rank and file really believed that workers and peasants had seized control, abolished unemployment, and were joyously building a paradise on earth.[116] They became true believers, people for whom faith is more important than understanding.[117] Nothing was allowed to interfere with their dream of a universal utopia, not slave labor camps, not purges, not famines.[118] Never for a moment did the dedicated Ukrainian Communist believe all the "lies" being preached by the nationalists. Always willing to parrot the latest party line from Moscow, whether it was condemnations of "fascist" Poland's denationalization campaigns against Ukrainians[119] or the "Hitlerite regime" in the Republic of Carpatho-Ukraine (1938),[120] both UUTO and ORDEN consistently praised the UkrSSR and steadfastly maintained that it was truly a sovereign state. As late as 1939, at a time when Khrushchev was heralding the abolition of the last vestiges of Ukrainian autonomy in the UkrSSR, one Ukrainian Communist in the United States wrote:

> In our readings of late, we often come across the word "sovereign." Not every reader, however, understands that word the way it should be understood. What does it really mean?
> One can explain sovereignty as follows: (1) the highest right of state authority; (2) the full independence of a state with reference to decisions related to internal problems. A sovereign state is an independent state. National sovereignty connotes national independence.
> The Stalinist Constitution has mandated the sovereignty of the Union of Soviet Socialist Republics which are strongly united in a federated and socialistic state of workers and peasants. But at the same time, in keeping with the constitution, every republic of the Union of Soviet Socialist Republics is an independent republic and is able to deal with its state functions in an independent way. Every Soviet republic has its own constitution which takes into account specific matters concerning the republic; every republic has the full right to freely secede from the USSR; the territory of any one of the republics cannot change without the republic's sanction ... The strength of the USSR lies in the fact that the Soviet republics, of their own free will, are members of the brotherly family of soviet nationalities which exists on the basis of full equality and mutual faith.[121]

With the rise of ORDEN, UUTO's membership began to decline. By the seventh convention in 1938 – when the name of the organization was changed to the Soiuz ukrainskykh robitnykiv (Union of Ukrainian Toilers) – there were approximately 1,500 members active in only sixty-six branches. By the eighth convention in 1940 – when the name was changed to Liga amerykanskykh ukraintsiv (League of American Ukrainians) – the organization was down to fifty branches and some 1,200 members.[122] The decline was also due, no doubt, to the Stalin-Hitler pact, which temporarily devastated the entire Communist network.

The Nationality Revival

In many ways, the success of ORDEN and other nationality-based organizations within the IWO network was a victory for the language federations that were once the foundation of the CPUSA. Like many other Americans during the early 1930s, the CPUSA leadership believed that nationality groups were fast disappearing as significant factors in American political life. Neglected and often accused of white chauvinism by CPUSA central committee members, the nationalities found a receptive home in IWO. Although the single largest IWO component in 1935 was Jewish, two-thirds of the membership came from Hungarian, Slovak, Ukrainian, Italian, and Serbo-Croatian units. "For many foreign-born Americans too timid or frightened to join the Communist party," writes Harvey Klehr, "membership in the IWO enabled them to participate in the 'progressive' movement without suffering any serious consequences."[123] As Professor Klehr points out, only 7.3 percent of the 116,407 IWO members in 1936 were Communists. It really didn't matter. The IWO contributed to the CPUSA by advertising heavily in party newspapers, providing employment for loyal Communists, and issuing appeals for contributions for party work.

Realizing that the nationalities had not disappeared, the CPUSA addressed the issue at its 10th convention in 1938. A "Report on National Groups" pointed out that only the Jewish Bureau (with some 4,000) had more than 1,000 members. Trailing far behind with between 500 and 800 members each were the German, Italian, Hungarian, Ukrainian, Lithuanian, Russian, Finnish, and Greek bureaus. Inspired by Comintern chairman Georgi Dimitroff's proclamation that he was proud to be a Bulgarian, the CPSUA convention did a policy about-face by acknowledging the importance of nationality feelings in party work. "It is necessary that our comrades be not only *good Communists* but *good Germans, good Jews, good Irishmen*," declared Israel Amter, a CPUSA officer.[124]

One Step Back, Two Steps Forward

Stalin's unexpected alliance with Hitler caught America's Communists by surprise and put an ignominious end to the Popular Front charade. "The masquerade is over," wrote *New Republic* columnist Heywood Broun, a staunch Soviet defender. Shocked by Stalin's duplicity, thousands turned their backs on the Popular Front. They included Louis Fischer, who vigorously attacked the USSR in his 1941 book *Men and Politics* but carefully avoided episodes he himself had helped blur, such as Ukraine's Great Famine.[125]

Left to defend the USSR were the true believers who quickly recovered to promulgate the new party line: the USSR was promoting peace; the United States was pushing war. Lend-lease, military production, and the draft should be stopped immediately; the "imperialist war" between the Allies and Germany must end with a negotiated peace.[126] Typical of the new rhetoric was an editorial that appeared in the monthly English-language section of *Visti* in March 1941:

ALREADY THE U.S. ARMY HAS ORDERED 4½ MILLION KIA TAGS (KILLED IN ACTION)

Mothers – these tags are for your sons! If they do not expect to have the men of America sacrificed for the profits of the millionaires, WHY SHOULD THE GOVERNMENT GO TO THE EXPENSE OF PREPARING THESE TAGS?

The agony and suffering of humanity in this war torn world ... has brought joy and added riches to the bankers of Rome and Berlin, London and Wall Street. THIS IS A RICH MAN'S WAR ...

We, the people, are asked to sacrifice our sons, sacrifice our future, our liberties, our living standards – so that Wall Street and the British Empire can continue to grow richer through the DESTRUCTION of the people.[127]

Supporting the new Communist approach was a myriad of *new* front organizations such as the New York Peace Council, the American Committee for the Protection of the Foreign Born, the Miami League for Peace and Human Welfare, the Needle Workers' Council for Peace and Civil Rights, and, the most popular of all, the Yanks-Are-Not-Coming Committee.[128]

No sooner had Hitler invaded the USSR than it was back to a collective security posture against fascism and nazism. All the old Popular Front bromides were resurrected and by the time the United States entered the war, the USSR – whose leader was affectionately referred to as "Uncle Joe" – was once again her partner in the struggle to save democracy. By 1944, Communist party membership soared to 80,000, a new high.[129]

Exploiting their newly restored luster in American life, Communists floated the notion that because the USSR was America's partner in "the great democratic war against fascism," any American who criticized the Soviets was unpatriotic at best and at worst an obvious "fascist," bent on sabotaging the war effort. Keeping a watchful "democratic" eye out for such saboteurs was the Communist press in America as well as a number of Stalinist-oriented American periodicals, three of which eventually took on the Ukrainian nationalist community.

The first was *New York PM*, an afternoon newspaper launched in 1940 with financial backing from such capitalist luminaries as Marshall Field III, Philip A. Wrigley, and John Hay Whitney. Edited by Ralph Ingersoll – who prior to the Stalin-Hitler pact had hoped to make *PM* an organ of the Popular Front – the tabloid recruited 151 staff people, many of whom turned out to be either members of the Communist party or pro-Stalin sympathizers. The second Soviet-oriented publication to make its debut during this period was *Friday*. Also established in 1940 and edited in time by Michael Sayers, a confirmed Stalinist, *Friday*'s editorials generally followed the official party line.[130] The third and, as we shall soon discover, the most virulent in its attacks on the Ukrainian-American nationalist community was *The Hour*, a newsletter headed by Albert E. Kahn, another active Stalinist, and an editorial staff which included Frederick L. Schuman and Leland Stowe, two Popular Front fellow travelers, who remained loyal to the Popular Front line long after their intellectual associates had left the fold.[131]

During World War I, socialist dominance of Ukrainian political life quickly evaporated. It was replaced for a time by Ukrainian Bolsheviks who usurped the socialist initiative, created a Ukrainian Communist federation, and, along with other disfranchised ethnic federations in the Socialist Party of America, went on to establish America's first Communist party. Hounded by the Justice Department for their seditious ardor, Ukrainian Communists went underground and lost more than half their members in the process. During the next few years Ukrainians and other ethnic communists struggled for control of the party, eventually losing to the American minority by Comintern fiat. Forced to subdue their revolutionary zeal, Ukrainian Communists followed Comintern dictates and began to establish new, broadly based, legitimate coalitions within the Ukrainian-American community.

Two organizations emerged to dominate the Ukrainian communist movement. During the 1920s, it was the United Toilers Organization (UUTO). In the 1930s, it was the Ukrainian section of the communist-dominated International Workers' Order (ORDEN). Within the framework of these two organizations, Ukrainian Communists offered their members two very important benefits: enlightenment and Ukrainian pride. Unlike their cohorts in the UkrSSR, America's Ukrainian Communists were successful because they enhanced the ethnonational identity of Ukrainians with schools, books, youth organizations, choirs, drama troupes, and a variety of other cultural products and activities geared to perpetuate the Ukrainian heritage. With ethnic development, however, came communist indoctrination. At no time did the Ukrainian Communist leadership in America deviate from the official party line developed in Moscow.

The rapid growth of communism in the Ukrainian-American community in the 1930s was a result of a number of factors, the most significant of which was economic turmoil and uncertainty. Being communist in America during the "red decade" was a unique and consuming experience. A dogmatic and uncompromising ideology offered structure and predictability for those seeking purpose and direction. For the demoralized, the party provided visions of a better world, identity, and a cause for which they could struggle. The left pointed to the future, the right to the past. Aided and abetted by thousands of intellectuals, government officials, foreign correspondents, writers, poets, movie stars, reporters, and other molders of public opinion, the Communist-dominated Popular Front was able to create a mood and climate in America that was red in both tone and substance. Thanks largely to their efforts, many innocent Americans came to honestly believe that the USSR was a democratic state which had successfully solved the problem of interethnic strife, that no famine had occurred in Ukraine, that Ukrainians were happy with their lives in the Soviet Union, and that nationalism was really a form of fascism.

The U.S. alliance with Moscow against the Axis powers significantly improved the status of America's Communists and permitted them to settle accounts freely with some of their ideological opponents. As we shall soon discover, it was the Ukrainians, of all of America's ethnic communities, who were to suffer most for their anti-Communist militancy.

The Rev. Ahapius Honcharenko, a Ukrainian Orthodox priest, hosts a group of young Americans who frequently visited his homestead in Hayward, California. Editor of the *Alaska Herald* and its supplement *Svoboda*, Honcharenko is believed to be the first ethnonationally conscious Ukrainian to arrive in the United States.

European immigrants arrive in New York on the ss *Patricia*, December 1910.

OPPOSITE

St. Michael's, the first Ruthenian Catholic church in the United States, founded in 1884 in Shenandoah, Pennsylvania, by Fr. Ivan Wolansky.

The Rev. Ivan Wolansky, America's first Ukrainian Catholic priest.

One of the earliest group photographs in the United States of Greek Catholic priests, Wilkes-Barre, Pennsylvania, 1890. Seated left to right: Gabriel Vislocky, Ivan Zaptocky, Alexis Toth, Teofan Obushkevych; standing left to right: Eugene Volkay, Alexander Dziubaj, Stefan Jackovich, Gregory Hrushka.

A group of "Stundists" from Ukraine. Fleeing religious persecution in Ukraine, they emigrated from eastern Ukraine, finding a haven in the prairies of North Dakota. Late 1890s.

Breaker Boys picking slate in 1885 at Eagle Hill Colliery, P & R C & I Co., New Philadelphia, Pennsylvania. The slate picker boss always carried a stick and knew how to use it.

The so-called "American Circle," a group of eight priests from Galicia (Western Ukraine) who came to the United States for the purpose of establishing the Ukrainian-American community. Clockwise: the Reverends Ivan Konstankevych, Nestor Dmytriw, Mykola Stefanovych, Ivan Ardan, Antin Bonezevsky, Stefan Makar, Pavlo Tymkevych, and Mykola Pidhoretsky.

Members of the Sts. Cyril and Methodius Society seen with Fr. Ivan Konstankevych, Shamokin, Pennsylvania, 1908.

OPPOSITE

top The Most Rev. Soter Ortynsky, osbm, consecrated the first Ukrainian Catholic bishop in the United States in 1907.

bottom The Rev. Alexis Toth, the "father" of Russian Orthodoxy in the United States.

Metropolitan Andrei Sheptytsky at the blessing of the Ukrainian Catholic Cathedral of the Immaculate Conception in Philadelphia, 1910.

The "Zaporoska Sich" branch of the Ukrainian National Association in Minneapolis, 1914.

ABOVE *left*

Dr. Volodymyr Simenovych, Ukrainian-American pioneer and first president of the Federation of Ukrainians in the United States.

ABOVE *right*

The Rev. Peter Poniatyshyn, appointed Apostolic Administrator of the Ukrainian Catholic Exarchy of Philadelphia in 1916 and head of the Ukrainian National Committee of the United States.

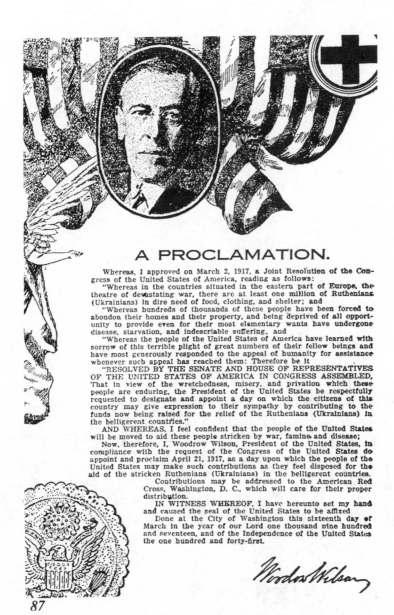

A PROCLAMATION.

Whereas, I approved on March 2, 1917, a Joint Resolution of the Congress of the United States of America, reading as follows:

"Whereas in the countries situated in the eastern part of Europe, the theatre of devastating war, there are at least one million of Ruthenians (Ukrainians) in dire need of food, clothing, and shelter; and

"Whereas hundreds of thousands of these people have been forced to abondon their homes and their property, and being deprived of all opportunity to provide even for their most elementary wants have undergone disease, starvation, and indescriable suffering, and

"Whereas the people of the United States of America have learned with sorrow of this terrible plight of great numbers of their fellow beings and have most generously responded to the appeal of humanity for assistance whenever such appeal has reached them: Therefore be it

"RESOLVED BY THE SENATE AND HOUSE OF REPRESENTATIVES OF THE UNITED STATES OF AMERICA IN CONGRESS ASSEMBLED, That in view of the wretchedness, misery, and privation which these people are enduring, the President of the United States be respectfully requested to designate and appoint a day on which the citizens of this country may give expression to their sympathy by contributing to the funds now being raised for the relief of the Ruthenians (Ukrainians) in the belligerent countries."

AND WHEREAS, I feel confident that the people of the United States will be moved to aid these people stricken by war, famine and disease;

Now, therefore, I, Woodrow Wilson, President of the United States, in compliance with the request of the Congress of the United States do appoint and proclaim April 21, 1917, as a day upon which the people of the United States may make such contributions as they feel disposed for the aid of the stricken Ruthenians (Ukrainians) in the belligerent countries.

Contributions may be addressed to the American Red Cross, Washington, D. C., which will care for their proper distribution.

IN WITNESS WHEREOF, I have hereunto set my hand and caused the seal of the United States to be affixed

Done at the City of Washington this sixteenth day of March in the year of our Lord one thousand nine hundred and seventeen, and of the Independence of the United States the one hundred and forty-first.

Woodrow Wilson

Text of the proclamation issued by President Woodrow Wilson designating 21 April 1917 "Ukrainian Day" in the United States.

Ukrainian women picket the White House, protesting Polish rule in Western Ukraine, January 1922.

Ukrainian-American children in Newark, protesting the awarding of Western Ukraine to Poland by the Allies, March 1923.

The first Synod of the Ukrainian Autocephalous Orthodox Church of the United States convoked on 13 March 1924, by Bishop John Theodorovich.

The Most Rev. Constantine Bohachevsky, STD, was appointed bishop of the Ukrainian Catholic exarchy in May 1924.

The children of the School of Ukrainian Studies in Bronx, during a visitation by the Rev. Peter Poniatyshyn, 1926.

Newspapers associated with the Ruthenian/Uhro-Rusin ethnonational stream, 1892–1928.

Newspapers associated with the Ukrainian ethnonational stream, 1893–1939.

Members of the Hartford, Connecticut, branch of the Ukrainian Federation of
Communist Parties of America (UFCPA), 1922.

FAMINE

IN

UKRAINE

A

73rd CONGRESS
2nd SESSION **H. RES. 399**

IN THE HOUSE OF REPRESENTATIVES
May 28, 1934

Mr. FISH submitted the following resolution; which was referred to the Committee on Foreign Affairs and ordered to be printed.

RESOLUTION

Whereas several millions of the population of the Ukrainian Soviet Socialist Republic, the constituent part of the Union of Soviet Socialist Republics, died of starvation during the years of 1932 and 1933; and

Whereas the Government of the Union of Soviet Socialist Republics, although being fully aware of the famine in Ukraine and although having full and complete control of the entire food supplies within its borders, nevertheless failed to take relief measure designed to check the famine or to alleviate the terrible conditions arising from it, but on the contrary used the famine as a means of reducing the Ukrainian population and destroying the Ukrainian political, cultural, and national rights; and

Whereas intercessions have been made at various times by the United States during the course of its history on behalf of citizens of states other than the United States, oppressed or persecuted by their own governments, indicating that it has been the traditional policy of the United States to take cognizance of such invasions of human rights and liberties: Therefore be it

NEW YORK CITY
1934

UNITED UKRAINIAN ORGANIZATIONS
OF THE UNITED STATES

The House of Representatives resolution condemning the Great Famine in Ukraine introduced by Rep. Hamilton Fish, Sr. (R-NY) on 28 May 1934.

ПОЗІР!   ПОЗІР!

СОЮЗ ГЕТЬМАНЦІВ ДЕРЖАВНИКІВ В АМЕРИЦІ І-ИЙ ОКРУГ ФИЛАДЕЛФІЯ, ПА.

уладжує

ПРИ УЧАСТИ ПЕРШОГО УКРАЇНСЬКОГО ЛІТАКА "УКРАЇНА"

СВЯТО УКРАЇНСЬКОГО ЛЕТУНСТВА

в Неділю, дня 21 Жовтня 1934 року

У ФИЛАДЕЛФІЇ, ПА. В ШІЦЕНПАРКУ

НА СЕ СВЯТО ПРИЛЕТИТЬ ЛІТАК "УКРАЇНА" З ДІТРОЙТУ ТА ЛІТАК "ЛЬВІВ" З ШІКАГА.

В часі свята відбудуться маневри воздушної фльотилі українських і американських літаків.

Програма Свята:

1. Молебен і водосвяття в Шіценпарку, о годині 1-шій пополудни.
2. Святочні промови.
3. Похід на летниче поле, де осядуть літаки.
4. Ріжні ігри, танці, забави і несподіванки.

Всі матимуть змогу оглянути літаки "УКРАЇНА" і "ЛЬВІВ"

Просимо все Українське Громадянство Филаделфії і околиці взяти найчисленнішу участь в цім першім святі Українського Летунства на Сході

Парк буде отворений о годині 9.30 рано.

ЧИСТИЙ ДОХІД НА УКРАЇНСЬКУ ЛЕТУНСЬКУ ШКОЛУ В ДЕТРОЙТІ, МИЦ.

Проситься всіх українських патріотів (-ок) зголошуватися в Добродії (-ійки) українського летунства.

Імена Добродіїв (-ійок) будуть надруковані.

A flyer announcing a "Ukrainian Aviation Day" to be held 21 October 1934 in Philadelphia. Highlighting the day's events was the arrival of the airplanes *Ukraina* and *Lviv* from Detroit and Chicago respectively. The event was organized by the local branch of the Ukrainian Hetman Organization (UHO).

Members of the officers' corps of Branch 4 of the United Hetman Organization (UHO) who organized the welcoming of Hetmanych Danylo Skoropadsky to Detroit during his tour of the United States and Canada in 1937.

Colonel Ievhen Konovalets, leader of the Organization of Ukrainian Nationalists (OUN), with members of Branch 6 of the Ukrainian Veterans' Organization (UVO) in Chicago in 1929. Most of those pictured later founded Branch 2 of the Organization for the Rebirth of Ukraine (ODWU).

Members of the New York branch of the Organization for the Rebirth of Ukraine (ODWU) in 1935.

1732 1932

UKRAINIAN BICENTENNIAL COMMITTEE
— in —
TRIBUTE
— to —
WASHINGTON
presents
ALEXANDER KOSHETZ
and his
UKRAINIAN CHORUS
"—most amazing and beautiful singing heard in the memory
of a middle aged man." (New York Evening Sun.)
also
VASILE AVRAMENKO
and his
UKRAINIAN FOLK BALLET
"—a most inspired pageant of historical and festive dances."
(Pittsburgh Sun-Telegraph.)
CARNEGIE HALL
7th AVE. & 57th STREET, NEW YORK CITY.
SUNDAY, MAY 8th, 1932
MATINEE, at 3 P. M. and EVENING at 8.15 P. M.
Tickets: $1.00 to $3.00.
Regular sale opens at Carnegie Hall, Monday, May 2nd.

Program from a concert held
in New York's Carnegie Hall
in 1932 on the occasion of
the bicentennial celebration of
the birth of George
Washington.

The Ukrainian Pavilion at the Chicago World's Fair, June 1933.

OPPOSITE

The Ukrainian National Association's Supreme Assembly and editorial staffs of *Svoboda* and the *Ukrainian Weekly* in 1937.

Ukrainian servicemen and nurses representing various branches of the United States armed forces take part in a flag-blessing ceremony at St. George's Ukrainian Catholic Church in New York City in 1943.

A Ukrainian chorus takes part in a Victory Bond rally in New York City in 1943.

Representatives of the United Ukrainian American Relief Committee (UUARC) welcome a newly arrived Ukrainian family who immigrated to the United States under the Displaced Persons Act, March 1949.

6 Monarchist Aspirations

Between 1914 and 1923, Ukrainian nationalists in the United States struggled to gain recognition for an unknown nation from an indifferent world. They organized. They published books, pamphlets, and newspaper articles proclaiming and explaining their cause. They raised thousands of dollars in support of the Ukrainian nation-state. They lobbied the White House and Congress. They demonstrated. They argued their cause at the Paris peace talks. In the end, they lost. No one, it seemed, was interested in the Ukrainian people and their aspirations.

Unable to accept the Ukrainian Bolshevik argument that Ukraine was really independent, and unwilling to reconcile themselves to Ukraine's partition, America's Ukrainians were desperate to understand what had gone wrong. They yearned for political ideologies which could both explain the past and offer hope for the future. The program which captured the imagination of a segment of the Ukrainian-American nationalist community during the 1920s was that of the monarchists.

The Monarchist Ideology

The principal ideologue for the monarchist movement was Viacheslav Lypynskyi, whose major premise was that the Russian Revolution had come too soon for the Ukrainian people. Ukrainians, he believed, were ethnonationally unprepared for statehood. Ukraine's leadership never realized this fact and as a consequence failed to concentrate its nationalization campaign on the agrarian-peasant class, that segment of the Ukrainian nation that offered the greatest potential for the creation of a permanent nation-state.

Lypynskyi's vision of a future Ukrainian state was based on what he called a "classocratic" society wherein all productive classes – laboring, technical, academic – would have a role to play under the benevolent guidance of a hereditary *hetman* who would be above party and class interests. Rejecting republican forms of government and characterizing socialist democracies as "mobocracies" ruled by "nomadic barbarians united by some kind of primitive fanatical faith and a primitive morality" based on "the rule of the fist" and "the authority of fear," Lypynskyi pointed to Great Britain as an example of what was best for the Ukrainian people. The British model, wrote Lypynskyi, is not an "oligarchical class-less military bureaucracy which constantly stands guard over the nation"; nor is it a "magical democracy" that does not recognize classes. England, he argued, enjoys class cooperation because the right of the productive classes to participate in the economic life of the nation is recognized along with the moral authority which resides with the aristocracy within each class.

Initially a supporter of Hetman Pavlo Skoropadsky's claim to hereditary leadership of the monarchist movement, Lypynskyi broke with Skoropadsky in 1930, alleging that he had behaved in an autocratic manner and had agreed to renounce all future claims to Carpatho-Ukraine in return for a yearly stipend from the Hungarian government.

Lypynskyi died in 1931, and his ideological place in the pro-Skoropadsky political stream was taken by Dmytro Doroshenko. The fundamental monarchist posture, however, changed little during the 1930s. The church was to remain independent but allied with the hetman. Ukraine was to be a classocratic society based on the orders of the "plow," the "workbench," and the "word," with everyone guaranteed employment according to his calling. The benevolent, hereditary hetman was to protect class rights by assuring due process of law. Finally, and this was the only major shift from Lypynskyi's ideals, the Ukrainian nation was declared to be an organized collective belonging to the "Aryan" race. The last point, in all probability, was included as a concession to Nazi doctrine. Skoropadsky had once been close to Kaiser Wilhelm and after Hitler came to power, he had begun to cultivate ties with the Nazis.[1]

Although the monarchists (Hetmantsi in Ukrainian) had relatively few followers in Europe, in the United States they came to enjoy wide support among immigrants eager to develop a Ukrainian liberation strategy based on the traditional principles of authority, cohesion, and purpose.

The American Response

The political organization that enjoyed the greatest vigor in the Ukrainian-American nationalist camp all through the late 1920s and much of the 1930s was the Hetman Sich. Originally established as the Ukrainian Athletic Association, Sich, it evolved into a paramilitary society that recognized Hetman Pavlo Skoropadsky as the legitimate head of the Ukrainian government in exile and the leader of the Ukrainian liberation movement. As the only Ukrainian political organization with tacit support from the Ukrainian Catholic church, Sich – later renamed the United Hetman Organization (UHO) – was initially the nationalist community's only viable ideological alternative to Ukrainian communism.

Transforming Ukrainian nationalists in America into monarchists was no easy task. While most Ukrainians could relate to the Cossack era and the glories of the Zaporozhian Sich, their sentiment was based on romanticized nostalgia rather than on a specific political orientation. The Cossacks, moreover, had developed a democratic tradition. They elected and deposed their *hetmans* at will and it was this aspect of Cossack life that appealed most to nationalists. Hetman Skoropadskyi had not followed that tradition and was generally perceived as a usurper.

The defeat of a democratic regime in Ukraine, however, moved some nationalists to reassess the Ukrainian approach. On the one hand, the world's democracies had ignored Ukraine's democratic aspirations. On the other hand, her authoritarian enemies were victorious. Perhaps, Ukrainians reasoned, it was time to postpone democracy and to organize a liberation front based on the winning principles of unity, authority, power, and will.

The Ukrainian Athletic Association, Sich

The first Sich organization in the United States was established by Fr. Mykola Strutynsky in Olyphant in 1902. Patterned after Kyrylo Trylovskyi's athletic Sich in Galicia, this prewar effort never included more than a few local branches.

World War I and the birth of the famed Sichovi Striltsi in Ukraine rekindled Ukrainian-American enthusiasm for Sich, resulting in the creation of new branches in New York, Pennsylvania, and New Jersey. Encouraged by the socialists, who demonstrated an early interest in its development, Sich was strong enough by 16 November 1916 to hold its first national convention. Elected to the new executive were Mykhailo Rybak, Supreme Otaman; Vasyl Serbai, Supreme Koshovyi; Petro Zadoretsky, Supreme Osaul; Oleksa Mereshchak, Supreme Treasurer; Emil Revyuk, Supreme Teacher; Ivan Ardan, Supreme Arbitrator; and Miroslaw Sichynsky, honorary member of the executive.* On 15 July 1917, and again on 14 July 1918, two mass gymnastic rallies were held by the newly formed

---

* As in Europe, the Sich organization adopted those military ranks and titles that had been used by the Ukrainian Cossacks during the fifteenth and sixteenth centuries. The reader is reminded that the term "Sich" itself is the Ukrainian name for a Cossack fort.

national organization to popularize the Sich ideal among Ukrainian-American youth. By July 1918, Sich had a total of fourteen branches in New York, New Jersey, Pennsylvania, Connecticut, and Massachusetts, and could afford to support its own press organ, *Sichovi Visti*,[2] which made its debut on 13 July 1918.[3] The objectives of the organization were later outlined by J. Sharowskyi:

> When we look more closely at the life of the immigrant, we notice that all nationality groups have their own organizations in order to get together now and then. The so-called athletic organizations draw our attention particularly. There is hardly a national group in this country that doesn't recognize the value of physical drills and athletics. Take the Czechs, for example. They take particular care in the training of their youth ... Why? Because they know that physical drills build a healthy body, beautify it, build perseverance, and add years to one's life. If the children are healthy so will be the nation ...
>
> Let us turn our attention to ourselves ... It has been over thirty years since our immigration started to come to this country and nobody has ever mentioned anything serious about athletics yet. All of us seemed to look at it indifferently ... Meanwhile our youth, feeling the necessity of physical drill, joined organizations hostile to us, for the sake of gymnastics. This is why today we find a number of Ukrainians in the ranks of the Polish Eagle organizations. They speak Polish as fluently as if they didn't know their native language.
>
> To counteract this situation, we have established the Sich organization which has as its purpose the training of Ukrainian youth, both physically and spiritually ... The Sich organization answers all of the requirements of the Ukrainian nation.[4]

The second convention of Sich was held on 25 August 1918. Electing Petro Zadoretsky Supreme Otaman, delegates passed resolutions regarding its press organ which made it clear that their organization was still essentially apolitical.

1 *Sichovi Visti* will continue to be published once a month.
2 *Sichovi Visti* shall not infringe upon any Ukrainian political party nor upon any fraternal society.
3 *Sichovi Visti* must always maintain an impartial stand.
4 The purpose of the Sich press organ is to propagate physical and spiritual culture among the Ukrainian people in America.

5 The Sich newspaper has no right to insert or publish any propaganda which might mislead the Ukrainian people.[5]

As the only Ukrainian-American organization catering almost exclusively to the younger generation, Sich became immensely popular, growing to twenty-nine branches by 1919.

Meanwhile, news of the formation of a Polish-American Legion to fight in Europe reached the Ukrainian-American community. Immediately, the most important question became: "If the Poles can form their own army here, why not the Ukrainians?" Through the efforts of Dr. Simenovych, Dr. Stepan Hrynevetsky, Father Strutynsky, and others associated with Sich, the United States Congress authorized the inclusion of Ukrainians in a proposed Slavic Legion to be composed of "5,000 Jugo-Slavs," "12,000 Czecho-Slovaks," and "8,000 Ruthenians." The War Department's plan was that "these forces should ... be organized in units no larger than a regiment and should form component parts of our Army"; that the legion should exclude "citizens of the United States and persons subject to the draft"; and that there should be no recruiting "in coal mining districts, as the services of men of these races, employed in coal mining, are more valuable to the government in that capacity than in the army."[6] A special memorandum concerning Ukrainian participation in the legion was issued by the military intelligence division of the War Department on 11 September 1918, in the following form:

MEMORANDUM FOR COLONEL CONRAD:
Subject: Eligibility of Ukrainians for Slavic Legion

1 The bill authorizing the Slavic Legion contains the following clause – "Slavic Legion ... to be composed of Jugo-Slavs, Czecho-Slovaks, and Ruthenians (Ukrainians) belonging to the oppressed races of the Austro-Hungarian or German Empire," etc.
2 The Ukrainians inhabit the southwest portion of Russia as well as a considerable portion of the Austrian province of Galicia, and a small portion of Hungary. However, these Ukrainians of Austria and Hungary are usually called Ruthenians.
3 The bill therefore admits to the Slavic Legion only those Ukrainians who form part of the people of Austria-Hungary, viz: the Ruthenians. It does *not* admit to the Slavic Legion the Ukrainians from Ukraine, i.e., the territory formerly part of Russia and now autonomous.
4 (Though the Ukraine is now very largely under German control, it is of course diplomatically wholly out of the question that it could

be admitted to be part of the *German* Empire in order to bring the
Ukrainians of Ukraine technically within the scope of the bill.
In the wording of the bill, the word "Ukrainians" must be taken
merely as explanatory of the Ruthenians and as emphasizing
their racial kinship with people of the Ukraine.)
    (Signed) John M. Dunn
    Colonel, General Staff[7]

Plans to mobilize a Ukrainian-American force for the Slavic Legion on
the basis of the federal guidelines never materialized. Rallies called for this
purpose by Supreme Otaman Zadoretsky and Dr. Simenovych resulted in
only a handful of volunteers offering their services.[8] Sich participation in
the Slavic Legion, moreover, was opposed by the Federation of Ukrainians
in the United States and by the Bolsheviks in the UFSPA who were beginning to infiltrate the Sich organization. So popular were the Bolsheviks at
this time that two Sich branches, one in Chicago and another in New York,
elected to call themselves "Soviet Sich."[9]

Some Sich members, nevertheless, remained determined to transform
the organization into a training vehicle for Ukrainian fighting units that
could someday fight for Ukraine's liberation. At a meeting of the Sich
supreme executive held in May 1919, Supreme Otaman Zadoretsky proposed a constitutional change in keeping with this ideal. His plan was
rejected, however, and he was later replaced by I. Boiko as Supreme
Otaman.[10]

The third national convention of Sich was held on 31 August and 1
September 1919. Led by Boiko,[11] most members of the newly elected
supreme executive board favored maintaining the purely gymnastic character of the organization.

Among certain members of the Chicago Sich, however, hopes of a future
paramilitary organization persisted and the debate over future direction
was soon renewed. In an article entitled "A Call to Arms," Chicagoan Petro
Didyk addressed an emotional appeal to readers of *Sichovi Visti.* "Our
countrymen call upon us for help," Didyk wrote. "We must unite into
one fighting body, one Sich army unit ... My Sich colleagues, children of
Cossacks, the mother weeps for the father who was killed by Polish
Jesuits ... to arms for Ukraine and her people ... Join the Sich rank and file!
Become disciplined sons of Ukraine!"[12]

A few months later, the struggle between the promilitary faction, led by
Hrynevetsky, Didyk, and other members of the Chicago Sich, and the
opposition, led by Supreme Otaman Boiko, was out in the open. In April
an article entitled "To All Sich Branches in the United States" appeared
in *Ukraina,* a Chicago periodical. Accusing Boiko of poor administration,

mismanagement of funds, and insensitivity to the needs of the Ukrainian people, the appeal urged the calling of a special Sich convention to settle what had developed into a bitter internal struggle in the organization.[13]

A special convention was held in Pittsburgh on 1–2 May 1920, and the militarists prevailed. The bylaws were amended and it was agreed that the new executive, headed by Supreme Otaman P. Novodvorsky, and the Sich press should be moved from Philadelphia to Chicago; a resolution was also passed declaring that the main purpose of Sich was to strive for the establishment of an independent and sovereign Ukrainian state.[14]

By the time of the Pittsburgh convention, Bolshevik influence had all but vanished, and Sich was firmly in the hands of the nationalists. Reflecting the intensity of political frustration many Ukrainian Americans felt during this period, Supreme Otaman Novodvorsky, a veteran of the United States Army, wrote:

> During the war we honorably and honestly fulfilled our duties toward our American government ...
>
> We gave the American government everything we could to help America win the war ...
>
> We spent large sums of money, which we earned by the sweat of our brows, in purchasing American Liberty bonds ...
>
> At the call to the colors by the American government thousands of Ukrainians joined the United States army and shoulder-to-shoulder we fought and shed our blood, helping America to gain victory, glory, and power ...
>
> The ex-president, Mr. Woodrow Wilson, in the name of the Allies and the American government, solemnly declared that we should go beyond the sea to destroy the aggressive robbers and imperialistic militarists and win independence for all subjugated nations ...
>
> Ex-president Wilson, in the name of the American Government, in the name of the American people, solemnly declared before the whole world that we would fight for justice and that all subjugated nations would get their freedom and independence ...
>
> We sincerely believed ex-president Wilson meant what he said and would show himself to be a great and just man. We believed that when he spoke in the name of all of the American people, he would fulfill all promises to the letter.
>
> But President Wilson shamelessly did not keep his promise to us. For our sincere loyalty and our great sacrifices ... he paid us back with a terrible injustice ...
>
> Although President Wilson and the Allies promised justice and

independence for all subjugated nations, Mr. Wilson was the
first one who ruthlessly stepped upon us and permitted the savage Polish bandits to murder the Ukrainian people and to pillage
and plunder our Ukrainian land ...

We cannot keep silent! We can no longer plead!

We American Ukrainians have a full right not to ask but to
demand that the American government right this wrong!

The article, which appeared in *Sichovi Visti* in the spring of 1921, ended
with a plea to Sich members to send letters to President Harding and to
Congress protesting Polish occupation of Ukrainian Galicia.[15]

As Bolshevik oppression in eastern Ukraine intensified, *Sichovi Visti* condemned the Soviets – "a pack of rabid, savage ... robbers and bandits ...
who pillage and plunder, castigate and burn ..." – and reminded its readers
that the Ukrainian people were not defeated. "We rid ourselves of the tsar;
we have driven out the pro-German hetman; we have annihilated the
bandit Denikin and God will also help us do away with hideous
Communism."[16]

After a year and a half as Supreme Otaman, Novodvorsky resigned from
his post for personal reasons. On 1 March 1922, following a poll of Sich
branches, the Chicago-based Supreme Executive elected Dr. Stepan
Hrynevetsky* Supreme Otaman of some forty Sich branches then in
existence.[17] Asserting firm control of the organization from the onset, Hrynevetsky informed all Sich branches that according to the revised bylaws,
"the decisions of the Supreme Otaman, with his assistants, in all things
pertaining to the business of the organization, have full legitimacy and can
be changed only by a general convention." Criticizing what he believed
was a general lack of organizational discipline, he also issued his first
set of elaborate "general orders." Included was a decree which made it
mandatory for all branches to hold regular "discussions of questions dealing with the popular sciences in order to help the membership broaden its
horizon of general knowledge."[19]

---

* Born in Ukraine in 1877, Dr. Hrynevetsky completed his medical studies in Vienna
  where, according to Dr. Osyp Nazaruk who knew him as a student, he was an
  atheist and flirted with the anarchist ideology of Nikolai Bukharin. After practicing
  in Vienna for eight years, he emigrated to America, settling in Chicago a few
  years before the war. A wealthy man before the Great Depression, Hrynevetsky
  was married to a former Viennese opera singer, the famed Natalie Pidliashetko,
  who later made Ukrainian-American musical history as the director of the Ukrainian choir in Chicago.[18]

The fourth Sich convention was held in Cleveland on 28–30 May 1922. Hrynevetsky was confirmed as Supreme Otaman and resolutions were passed to change the title of each Sich branch to that of *sotnia* (company) and to endow each branch head with the military rank of *sotnyk* (captain).[20] It was also decided that military uniforms should be worn more frequently by Sich members.

Although Sich was becoming more militaristic during this period, politically it remained relatively neutral. It was nationalistic to the degree that Sich members were opposed to communism and supported the establishment of an independent Ukrainian nation; concern for the nature of that future state or its ideological foundation, however, was still not part of the Sich agenda.

The Ukrainian Hetman Organization, Sich

Sich began to change in 1923, soon after Dr. Osyp Nazaruk arrived in Chicago to become editor of *Sichovi Visti*. A former member of the ZUNR mission in Canada, as well as a one-time supporter of Petliura, Nazaruk adopted the monarchist ideology of Viacheslav Lypynskyi and became a staunch advocate of Skoropadsky following Petliura's alliance with Poland's Pilsudski. Hrynevetsky, who had known Nazaruk in Vienna, welcomed him to the Sich fold and as their organizational contacts became more frequent, the two became close personal friends. Reviewing the Sich structure and program, Nazaruk convinced Hrynevetsky that the organization was in need of greater centralization. Both later agreed to resign from Sich if the powers of the otaman were not broadened at the next convention. Elaborating his ideas further, Nazaruk also persuaded Hrynevetsky that the next logical step in the evolution of the organization was to adopt a liberation philosophy which would provide Sich with unity and purpose and serve as an alternative to the increasingly popular Bolsheviks. The only meaningful option, Nazaruk convincingly argued, was Skoropadsky's monarchism. As Nazaruk later admitted, however, both gentlemen were keenly aware of the fact that in view of the poor reputation of Skoropadsky in America, the political metamorphosis would be difficult, perhaps impossible.[21]

To lay the groundwork for their ambitious aspirations, Nazaruk initiated a series of articles in *Sichovi Visti* on the political development of the Ukrainian people in which the relative merits of a monarchy and a republic were discussed.[22] Hrynevetsky, meanwhile, continued to strengthen his control of the organization with "orders" ranging from the procedure to be followed in the educational portion of all Sich meetings – the major topic of conversation was to be a discussion of articles appearing in *Sichovi Visti*[23] – to the manner in which Sich delegates were to gain permission for addressing the next convention.[24]

If Hrynevetsky and Nazaruk hoped to have the next Sich conclave declare its allegiance to Hetman Skoropadsky, they must have been sorely disappointed. At the fifth Sich convention held in Philadelphia on 30 May 1924, it became painfully obvious, from the lack of attention of the delegates and their frequent moving about the convention hall during a long political speech by Nazaruk, that they were not ready to accept the monarchist ideal.[25] Hrynevetsky, however, was prepared to bide his time and to engineer the ideological transformation in another manner and at another place. Fearing that too drastic a change would turn the delegates against him, he pushed for his other objective, greater consolidation of power in the office of the Supreme Otaman. In this he was successful. The convention passed a series of resolutions giving Hrynevetsky the power to appoint all company commanders and extending his term of office to three years. In addition, it was resolved that:

1 The Sich organization considers only those people enlightened who are regular members of one or more Ukrainian organizations and who regularly carry some burden for the sake of their Ukrainian nation ... All others are merely ethnographic material – Little Russians or Little Poles – who, through their inactivity are undependable when the chips are down ... Therefore, the convention calls upon all Ukrainians to join the Ukrainian national organizations, to fulfill their obligations to these organizations, and to train their children to do the same.

2 The convention considers Sich as the only organization which can unite all Ukrainians, regardless of creed or political party on the whole earth – Europe, the United States, Canada, Brazil, and other parts of South America as well as in Asia and elsewhere. Therefore, the convention appeals to all Ukrainians, in whatever part of the world they may be, to form clubs and groups within the Sich organization.

Delegates also passed resolutions that (1) condemned the religious strife between Catholics and Orthodox as harmful to the Ukrainian nation; (2) supported the establishment of a united Ukrainian liberation front in America; (3) made it an obligation for all Sich members to contribute regularly to the Ukrainian National Fund and to subscribe to the Sich newspaper; and (4) annulled all decrees previous to the acceptance of the new bylaws by the convention.[26] "Thus reorganized," *Sichovi Visti* later declared, "Sich will flourish and grow ... The officer who demonstrates subordination and discipline to his superiors will surely command subordination from his subordinates and general respect from the people."[27]

Having consolidated their control, Hrynevetsky and Nazaruk were now ready to take the next step. Reasoning that a direct appeal to the eight Chicago Sich branches to accept the idea of a hetman might backfire and result in the loss of all the branches, Nazaruk decided to test the waters in Detroit where only one Sich branch existed at the time. To his surprise, the Detroit Sich supported his suggestion that the Supreme Executive declare its loyalty to Hetman Pavlo Skoropadsky.[28] Delighted with his apparent success, Nazaruk returned to Chicago and advised Hrynevetsky that the time for change had come.

On 24 November 1924, at an impressive ceremony in Chicago commemorating the ZUNR's Declaration of Independence, Hrynevetsky – scheduled to receive a *bulava* (staff of office used by Cossack otamans) at the affair – made his move. Accepting his *bulava*, Hrynevetsky expressed deep gratitude and then, in the presence of the eight company commanders sharing the stage with him, he declared that it really belonged to the legitimate hetman of Ukraine, Pavlo Skoropadsky. Before anyone could protest, Hrynevetsky took the oath of allegiance to the hetman and then proceeded to administer the same oath to the assembled Sich officers.[29]

Hrynevetsky's unexpected acceptance of Ukrainian monarchism, an ideology which was still poorly regarded in the Ukrainian-American community, and the increasingly authoritarian manner in which he presided over the organization, resulted in the loss of a substantial number of Sich members. In his letter of resignation, Supreme Vice Otaman Vasyl Tytanych observed that in Philadelphia alone, Sich membership declined from 800 to 100 members.[30] Other former Sich members such as Petro Zadoretsky, Stepan Musiychuk, and Philip Wasylowsky contended that many Sich members were unhappy with the change but remained until an organization alternative was offered by Col. Ievhen Konovalets and the newly created Organization for the Rebirth of Ukraine (ODWU).[31]

Although the organization suffered an initial reduction in membership, the new Hetman Sich was able to survive and eventually to flourish among the segment of the Ukrainian nationalist community that was weary of political bickering, yearned for an authority figure to point the way, and still believed it was possible to train a Ukrainian liberation army in America. So potent was the Sich call for order and discipline that even Dr. Simenovych succumbed. Agreeing to serve as interim editor of *Sich*,* he wrote:

* On 20 July 1924, *Sichovi Visti* was renamed *Sich*.

Almost from my youngest years, I have been active in national
work ... I have recognized many reasons why we have not
moved forward with other peoples. One of the most important
is the lack of a program ... the lack of authority.

A lack of direction is chaos, a lack of goals brings circular
striving. An articulate program is order, it is the gathering of
many scattered efforts into one force ...

In order to emerge from chaos, we must accept a clear idea.
In my opinion, there is absolutely nothing left but to support
the Hetman idea ...

It makes little difference if this program is accepted immediately
or not among our people ...

To trouble the people with "democracy" and self-rule will lead
us nowhere ... First we must get our liberty and then the people
will decide what will come next ... We will not attain our liberty
until we base it on something positive and stable. And that ... is
today the idea of the Hetmanate.[32]

In the years that followed, Dr. Simenovych's sentiments were echoed time
and again by the Sich organ. A few months after the above statement appeared,
Sich praised the Poles, Lithuanians, Czechs, and other Eastern European
groups for their ability to forget some of their individual liberties for the sake
of a united effort. But, concluded *Sich*, "Ukrainians understood 'liberty' in a
different way from other peoples." "Even today, they don't want to acknowledge an authority who is descended from their own people or who comes
from their own milieu. We are individualists at all times and under all circumstances of life. A Ukrainian is his own authority."[33] Later, in an article entitled
"The Basis of the Sich Organization," the monarchist periodical observed:

An organization is created when the people know *what they want* –
that means, when they have one *idea*. We did not have strength
or a nation until now because we did not have *one* idea. There
was only a cry: "We want Ukraine." But each person who made
that cry wanted a different Ukraine. Every editor and every newspaper, every meeting, wanted something different but no one
knew what they wanted ...

In order to eliminate once and for all the fighting among our
"leaders" where each believes that only he is capable of being
the "head" of the people – condemning and defaming all others –
Sich in America ... has said: "Over all parties and leaders there
must be one – the Hetman."

"There is nothing to discuss concerning this matter," the article concluded, "because we have discussed enough ... for America, a republic is good ... America is not surrounded by enemies as is Ukraine."[34] As for the so-called Democratic Sich that was formed in opposition to the monarchists, *Sich* wrote:

> We cannot fool ourselves that we are this or that. We must take a good look at ourselves and admit the truth, i.e., that we are an unorganized, little-educated mass which needs long years before it can understand itself and its position. Not understanding ourselves, we cannot begin self-rule, we cannot begin something that could ruin us ...
>
> To convince the people that they have matured to self-rule is empty phraseology which tempts and spoils the uneducated mass. It is similar ... to the indulgent parent who, out of love for his offspring, tells him that he is big, wise, strong ...
>
> Democratic Siches are based on demagoguery ... and will not help our people because they don't teach the value of work, obedience, and respect for leadership ... Looking at the Democratic Sich we immediately see that this is a straw fire.[35]

For many Ukrainian Catholic priests, then under attack from Communists, Socialists, Ukrainian Orthodox, and a growing number of nationally concerned Catholics, the emergence of Hetman Sich was a welcome development. In the words of F. Filimon Tarnawsky, pastor of St. Nicholas Ukrainian Catholic Church in Chicago: "Only Sich is in a position to bring order into our community life ... Because Sich is founded on the premise of respect for authority and obedience and all other organizations were and are infected with socialism. And a nation can only be built with people who respect their nation and their leaders."[36]

Increasingly authoritarian in its approach, the Hetman Sich soon developed an elaborate series of educational directives and instructional aids for the teaching of Ukrainian history, political economics, Ukrainian culture, and, of course, obedience and respect for authority. For the loyal Sich member, the only important institutions were *the church* ("the national ectoderm, the mind and nerves of the Ukrainian nation"), *the Sich* ("the national mesoderm," the fount of the "people's national consciousness"), and *the School* ("the Ukrainian endoderm ... that institution which supplies bricks for the building of the Ukrainian nation").[37]

According to *Sich*, a member of the Hetman Sich was to be:

In Everyday Life and Behavior
A sincere citizen and conscientious worker on the job upon which his future depends.

He is forbidden to lie or to spread other lies like a flying crow.

He doesn't take part in intrigues nor does he stand for the intrigues and all manner of plotting by others.

In the community in which he lives and actively participates, he talks less and does more good work and with this action offers the best example to other members of the community as to how one should work for the common good ...

He controls his thoughts and controls his words even more and does not allow his tongue to grind out foolishness ...

He behaves in a mild manner with other people and does not look down his nose at others ...

He tries to teach others the same truth he has recognized, doing this, however, in the manner of a good teacher ...

In order to become a teacher and leader among his people he is always learning himself – he learns in schools, he learns from good and worthwhile books, journals, and he learns from the lives of other cultured and organized peoples ...

He comes out everywhere in favor of law and order as well as national-social discipline ...

In Family Life

He is to be an exemplary father (mother) or son (daughter). He must always remember that his family is a small monarchical nation and it is on the degree of order, love, fairness, and mutual respect which he demonstrates there that his test of social maturity as a member of the Hetman organization and the Ukrainian national patriotic community will depend.

If a Hetman member is a poor family member he will be even worse as a member of the Hetman organization ... The Ukrainian family is the beginning of the Ukrainian nation.

In His Church Community

The Hetman member is the most desired member of his parish. His obligation to his church is his most holy obligation. Respect for his spiritual authority is his demonstration of a deep love for God.[38]

During the late 1920s, the Hetman Sich also realized its dream of a Ukrainian army, at least in part. Soon after the monarchist takeover, efforts were made to completely militarize the organization even to the point of having uniforms, patterned after those of the Sichovi Striltsi, mandatory for all male members. In addition, separate female Sich companies were organized as Red Cross units and taught first aid techniques. At first, only military drills and gymnastics were practiced but later, as Sich membership grew, field maneuvers were held in various forest preserves, wooded areas, and farm fields. Speaking at one of the early field maneuvers in Chicago, Dr. Hrynevetsky remarked:

> It would be a sin not to mention America, this beautiful land of the many starred flag which waves so proudly among us, this, our adopted fatherland in which we are permitted to cultivate our national spirit and to even have army exercises with our uniformed Sich soldiers without a special police permit, without phony old country swaggering ... America my beloved! This is the only country in the world where the national government permits all peoples to organize as they please. Here the Lithuanians organized and now they have their own nation. Here the Czechs organized and now they have their own nation. Here the Poles organized and now they have their own nation. Here we are organizing and we are certain we will have our own nation.[39]

Sich maneuvers soon became one of the more exciting aspects of Sich membership, especially for the youth. In time, military exercises were held throughout the Midwest and later still, joint maneuvers, involving companies from two or three cities, became a regular part of the Sich summer program.[40] Every able Sich member participated, the men as "combatants," the women as field nurses. A full Sunday's program usually consisted of a field divine liturgy in the morning, the maneuvers in the afternoon, and a gala outdoor dance and social in the evening.[41]

The caliber of Sich maneuvers was enhanced in 1930 when it was learned that the United States militia (National Guard), eager to bolster its sagging ranks in a postwar and antimilitary era, would permit Ukrainians to form their own military units under the command of American officers. Among the first to enlist were Chicago Sich members who formed Company B (commanded by Captain F.W. Rice) of the 33rd division of the 132nd Infantry.[42] In explaining the value of such enlistment, *Sich* observed:

> Joining the American army by a Ukrainian in no way detracts from his patriotism just as his patriotism was not hurt when he became a citizen of the United States. On the contrary, as a citizen of this country, he is obligated to protect the borders of this nation against enemies ...
> The United States is the only country in the world where when

one becomes a citizen one does not betray his own nation ... and
that is because the American nation is composed of many nations
which have joined together to form a common state ... There is
no other country in the world where when one becomes a citizen
one can continue to be a son of his European Fatherland and
actively help and fight for it. As an example we have the Irish
who, after a few hundred years of Americanization and material
growth, fought England for their independence ... Another example are the Poles ... The Czechs accomplished the same thing
being Americans and Czech warriors and patriots at the same
time. The same was done by the Slovaks and the Lithuanians.

Americans love liberty and have permitted many immigrant
groups to form legions to win their freedom ...

We, the members of the Hetman Sich must reach our goal
because we are Americans! We must prove to America and the
rest of the world that we are a nationally conscious people and
by doing so, we shall gain the confidence of American's upper
echelons. By joining the American militia, we shall realize the
main aim, i.e., to be the base and the beginning of the new
Ukrainian army. If we don't realize our objectives and aspirations
in this way, we will only play at being soldiers ...

The Hetman Sich member now has an opportunity to pay
America back for his good life here ...

The Hetman Sich member in the militia stops being a dumb
foreigner and becomes a real American in the eyes of true and
sincere Americans.[43]

Eventually, Ukrainians joined the militia in Cleveland, where they
became part of the 112th Engineers, and in Detroit, where they joined a
medical support battalion.[44] With specialized training, United States Army
uniforms and equipment, and the professional supervision of United States
military personnel, Sich maneuvers took on a new significance. Later issues
of *Sich* carried military critiques of the maneuvers,[45] regular militia news
pertaining to Ukrainians such as promotion sheets,[46] excerpts from U.S.
military manuals,[47] and news of Sich participation in United States Army–
sponsored expositions.[48]

The final step in the development of a Ukrainian fighting force was the
creation of a Ukrainian "air corps." During the 1930s, the Hetman Sich
obtained three airplanes – two biplanes and a four-passenger, single-wing
model – naming them, in order of purchase, *Ukraina, Lviv,* and *Kiev.*[49]
Owning aircraft enabled Sich to establish air corps companies and aviation
schools in Chicago, Cleveland, and Detroit where the Hetman movement

had its largest membership.[50] At the same time, the Hetman press organ – renamed *Nash Stiah* (Our Banner) in 1934 – began publishing articles on aviation such as "Who Can Fly"[51] and "Night Flying,"[52] as well as general news items concerning the development of the Hetman "air corps."

In the meantime, a number of changes occurred in the upper echelons of the Ukrainian monarchist movement. Dr. Nicholas Bodrug, who eventually succeeded Dr. Nazaruk as the permanent editor of *Sich*, resigned on 2 December 1929[53] and, on 13 October 1930, was formally replaced by Alexander Shapoval, a former officer in the Ukrainian army[54] and a Skoropadky loyalist.

Far more significant, however, was the organizational crisis precipitated by Lypynskyi's denunciation of Skoropadsky in 1930. Soon after reading Lypynskyi's "Communiqué," Dr. Hrynevetsky called an emergency meeting of the Supreme Executive and suggested that the Hetman Sich follow Lypynskyi's lead and sever all relations with Hetman Skoropadsky. After a long and acrimonious debate that lasted into the early hours of the morning, the Supreme Executive decided that such a move would result in irreparable damage to the organization's unity and refused to concur. Hrynevetsky promptly resigned[55] and on 12 November 1930, Skoropadsky sent a telegram from his headquarters in Berlin promoting Shapoval to the rank of colonel in the Ukrainian army and appointing him the Supreme Otaman of the Hetman Sich in North America.[56]

The United Hetman Organizations (UHO)

With the departure of Hrynevetsky, the Hetman Sich changed its name to the United Hetman Organizations (UHO) and eventually came under the helm of four different Supreme Otamans – Shapoval, Dr. Omelian Tarnawsky, Nicholas Hull,[57] and Dr. Myroslaw Siemens (Simenovych), a nephew of Dr. Volodymyr Simenovych. The real leader of the organization during most of this period, however, was Skoropadsky's personal emissary Colonel Shapoval, who, as editor of *Nash Stiah*, was directly responsible for defining and implementing the ideological and organizational direction of the Hetman movement in North America. The defection of the dynamic Hrynevetsky, combined with the subsequent rise of OUN Nationalism, cost the monarchists their momentum and the attraction of UHO, for many years the single most viable anticommunist organization in the Ukrainian-American community, started to fade.[58]

Following Lypynskyi's death in 1931, his political theories began to suffer interpretations that followed current ideological fashion but which were largely inaccurate. In 1932, for example, during the depths of the Great Depression, one contributor to *Sich* identified Lypynskyi's ideology as a form of fascism, a label which Lypynskyi himself had rejected. Condemning the democratic system for bringing "cultural, political, and commercial life to a disastrous stage," the author defined fascism as "all that is against international communism and international capitalism and its agent, democracy" and concluded that Ukrainians have their own fascism. It was formulated by Lypynskyi and it is "superior to Italian or German fascism ... The fascism of Lypynskyi rejects all dictatorships." It is a "new sociopolitical idea based on Christian teachings and faith ... this Ukrainian fascism can be called classocraticism or the rule of the classes."[59]

The unfortunate labeling of Lypynskyi's ideology was no accident. Fascism, especially the Italian variety, was in vogue among many Americans seeking alternatives to the shortcomings of capitalism and the rise of communism. For many, the messianic diatribes of people like Fr. Francis Coughlin, the highly popular American radio commentator who opposed both communism and capitalism – and who praised Mussolini – had a special appeal.*

The emergence of Adolf Hitler later induced some Ukrainians associated with the monarchist camp to become increasingly enamored with the branch of nationalism represented by the Third Reich. For them and for a number of prominent Americans as well,† Hitler's anticommunism, his emphasis upon national pride, and his obvious charismatic ability to unite

---

* Father Couglin, who received part of his higher education at St. Michael's Basilian College in Toronto, Canada, inaugurated his "Golden Hour of the Little Flower" in 1926. "Christian parents," he would ask, "do you want your daughter to be the breeder of some lustful person's desires and, when the rose of her youth has withered, to be thrown upon the highways of Socialism? ... Choose today! It is either Christ or the Red Flag of Communism." During the depths of the depression, Coughlin declared: "Modern capitalism is not worth saving. In fact, it is a detriment to civilization. During the height of his popularity he employed a staff of 150 and would receive 80,000 letters a week.[60]

† Ezra Pound, for example, was convinced that "usury had spoiled the Republic" and that "only the surgeon's knife of Fascism can cut it out." William Randolph Hearst visited Germany in 1934 and wrote: "Hitler is certainly an extraordinary man ... We estimate him too lightly in America." Hearst was impressed with Hitler's anticommunism, which he believed saved Germany from disaster. "This is the great policy, the great achievement which makes the Hitler regime popular with the German people," wrote Hearst upon returning to America, "and which enables it to survive very obvious and very serious mistakes." Avery Brundage, who championed the cause of America's participation in the 1936 Olympics in Germany against strong opposition from America's "anti-Fascist" camp, told a wildly cheering German Day gathering in Madison Square Garden that the United States had much to learn from Nazi Germany if it desired to preserve its institutions. Similar sentiments concerning Nazi Germany were later expressed by Charles Lindbergh, Jr.[61]

the German people during difficult times were viewed as worthy of emulation. Ukrainian monarchists had not forgotten that it was Germany that
had enabled Skoropadsky to come to power, and now it was Germany
again that represented all that the Hetman movement maintained the
Ukrainian people lacked – national will, authority, order, and discipline.
With the rise of the German Bund in America,* certain Hetman leaders
took it upon themselves to cultivate personal ties with Bund leaders, a
move apparently not discouraged by Hetman Skoropadsky.[63]

The Visit of "Hetmanych" Skoropadsky

Hoping to bolster their sagging appeal, UHO invited Danylo Skoropadsky,
the son and heir ("hetmanych") of the hetman, for a visit to the United
States and Canada.† His official tour lasted four months (11 September 1937
to 10 January 1938) and began in Chicago, where, on 19 September, he
spoke at a Ukrainian Day rally organized to raise funds for St. Basil's
Ukrainian Catholic Preparatory School in Stamford, Connecticut. Also fea-
tured were remarks by Bishop Constantine Bohachevsky of Philadelphia
and a parade of uniformed local units of UHO.

On 22 September, the young Skoropadsky was a guest of Chicago's
German Bund, whose members he addressed in German. Reviewing the
history of Ukrainian national aspirations, Skoropadsky explained that the
Ukrainian nation was defeated as a result of the people's attraction for
"internationalistic ideas, to the detriment of their nationalistic aims and
ideals." But, he concluded, today our struggle "has a more organized
character ... Ukrainian patriots have learned much from the struggles of
nationalist Germany" and "how it is possible for a nation, utilizing its own
forces, to be reborn and to strengthen its own people and state." The
hetmanych's stay in Chicago ended with a banquet in his honor during
which Bund leader M. Balderman delighted the audience with the observa-

---

* The Deutschamerikanisch Volksbund, more simply called Bund, was the successor
  to an organization called New Friends of Germany. Led by Fritz Kuhn, the Bund
  was a nationwide association of German Americans with Nazi-style uniforms and,
  according to the Dies Committee investigation of its activities, part of a German
  espionage network created in America by Berlin. One of the more sensational
  displays of the American Nazi power occurred at a George Washington commemoration sponsored by the Bund on 20 February 1939. Speaking before about 22,000
  participants, Kuhn declared: "If you ask what we are fighting for under our
  charter, I will repeat here the declaration I made public some time ago: A socially
  just, white-Gentile-ruled America."[62]
† The UHO had active branches in Montreal, Hamilton, Toronto, Sudbury, Edmonton, and other, smaller towns in western Canada. The Canadian UHO published
  its own newspaper, *Ukrainski Robitnyk* (Ukrainian Worker).

tion that he had been a witness to the construction of the Ukrainian state during Hetman Skoropadsky's reign. Praising the statesmanship and devotion of the hetman to Ukrainian national aspirations, Balderman concluded his remarks with a ringing cry in the Ukrainian language: "Long live the free and independent Ukrainian state of the Hetmans!" In his remarks to the gathering, Skoropadsky's son thanked Balderman and reaffirmed the basic Hetmanite tenet that "only control from the top ... can create a strong organizational skeleton around which healthy Ukrainian elements, hitherto dispersed, can unite."

The hetmanych remained in Chicago until 9 October when he was flown in the newly acquired UHO airplane, *Kiev,* to Michigan where, on 22 October, he was the guest of Henry Ford at Greenfield Village, Dearborn. After visiting with UHO members in Detroit, Skoropadsky traveled to Cleveland, Philadelphia, and New York City, where his U.S. tour ended. A young, articulate, Hollywood-handsome electrical engineer who had taken up residence in England, he received a royal welcome everywhere he traveled, not only from UHO members, but from the top echelons of the Ukrainian Catholic church as well.[64] Given his reception by Ukrainian Americans, UHO leaders had every reason to believe that their organizational decline would be reversed by young Skoropadsky's visit.

The First FBI Probe

Concerned that the anti-Soviet militancy of the Hetman Sich was in violation of the Roosevelt-Litvinov Accord that pledged the United States to *"reciprocally adhere"* to a provision forbidding "the formation or residence ... of any organization or group ... which has as its aim the overthrow ... or the bringing about by force of a change in the polical order of the whole or any part of the United States," the U.S. State Department asked the Department of Justice to investigate. On 11 February 1936, U.S. Attorney General Brien McMahon requested the FBI to probe "the activities of the so-called 'Hetman of Ukraine Aeronatical School' at Detroit, Michigan, and in particular the Rev. Stiutytynsky [sic] who, it appears ... is interested in preparing the younger members of his church to be ready to render assistance to the Ukraine in any movement that may develop against the Moscow government; and it is for this purpose that instruction in flying is being imparted." McMahon's memorandum to FBI director J. Edgar Hoover made it clear that the original request had come from the State Department. Attached was the complete text of the Roosevelt-Litvinov Accord.[65]

Interviewed by an FBI agent in April, Father Strutynsky recalled Ukraine's tortured history and repeatedly made known his feeling that "all Ukrainian people are friends of Russia's enemy and would fight with them or for them against Russia." Strutynsky further observed, however, "that the Hetman clubs in this country owe their first allegiance to the United States" and that "although it is possible that some of the Ukrainians in this country may go to Ukraine and offer assistance ... against Russia," the UHO did not have as its major purpose the preparation of young men and women "to go against the Union of Soviet Socialist Republics." The FBI report made special mention of the willingness of Father Strutynsky and Philip Demian, president of the Detroit UHO branch, to provide more information and to have that information forwarded "in order that the Government might be in a position to understand the Ukrainian side of the question."[66] The report recommended no further action and FBI concern with UHO ended – at least for the time being.

The Dies Committee Probe

Increasingly alarmed by the growth in America of Communist, fascist, and other potentially subversive organizations, the United States Congress decided to act. On 10 May 1938, Congressman Martin Dies of Texas submitted a report on House Resolution 282 from the Committee on Rules calling for the creation of a special committee to investigate un-American activities. As set forth in the first section of the resolution, the committee was authorized to conduct an investigation of: "(1) the extent, character, and objectives of un-American propaganda activities in the United States; (2) the diffusion within the United States of subversive and un-American propaganda that is instigated from foreign countries or of a domestic origin that attacks the principle of the form of government as guaranteed by our constitution; and (3) all other questions in relation thereto that would aid Congress in any necessary remedial legislation"[67]

Debate on the resolution began in the House on 26 May and concluded with a vote in favor of its acceptance. On 6 June, seven congressmen were appointed to the committee: Martin Dies, who became chairman, Arthur D. Healy (Massachusetts), John J. Dempsey (New Mexico), Joe Starnes (Alabama), Harold G. Mosier (Ohio), Noah M. Mason (Illinois), and J. Parnell Thomas (New Jersey).[68] Chief investigator for the committee was J.B. Matthews, a former member of the American League for Peace and Democracy.[69]

Procedural techniques employed by the Dies Committee came under attack soon after its work began. When the House Rules Committee met to consider its continued existence, a petition was presented condemning the Dies probe for its alleged lack of fairness and its use by other individuals to publicize charges unsubstantiated by objective proof. The petition had little effect. All but one of the members of the Rules Committee voted to have it continue and on 3 February 1939, the future of the investigative group was assured on the House floor by a vote of 344 to 35.[70]

On 28 September 1939, Emil Revyuk, then president of the United Ukrainian Organizations of America (UUOA) – a coalition of Ukrainian nationalist organizations established after the demise of the Ukrainian National Committee – and an associate editor of *Svoboda,* appeared before the Dies Committee to testify on the activities of UHO, the UNA, and the Organization for the Rebirth of Ukraine (ODWU). In his responses to questions regarding UHO,* Revyuk testified that:

1 UHO supported a future hereditary, monarchistic regime in Ukraine under the aegis of the Skoropadsky family.
2 UHO had its headquarters in Berlin and had branches in other parts of the world.[71]
3 A Hetman press release issued in Berlin had the following caption: "Hitler Sympathizes with the Slovaks, Poles, Magyars, and Ukrainians."[72]
4 UHO left the UUOA when the coalition refused to become a monarchist organization.[73]
5 UHO had "sympathetic feelings for the Nazis."[74]
6 The monarchists in America were headed by Dr. Siemens, a reserve officer in the United States army.[75]
7 UHO members occasionally wore uniforms and had rifles.[76]

Neither Revuyk's revelations regarding well-publicized UHO activities nor his statement regarding UHO's "sympathetic feeling for the Nazis" were ever demonstrated to be in any way related to espionage or even conspiratorial. His testimony, moreover, was based on hearsay – most responses began with "People told me that" or "I believe that" or "He told me" – and no UHO member was ever subpoenaed to present a rebuttal. None of this, however, troubled Congressman Dies. One man's testimony during the day's hearings was enough to indict three leading societies in the Ukrainian nationalist community. "Here are organizations that have been shown to be nothing in the world but agencies of foreign powers," concluded Dies at the end of the day. "That is all they are by their admission."[77] The *Chicago Daily News* headline for that day's Dies probe report read: "Nazi Groups Woo U.S. Ukrainians – King Chosen Already."[78]

On 14 June 1940, Congressman Jerry Voorhis – who replaced Congressman Healy on the Dies Committee early in 1939[79] – introduced the antici-

---

* Revyuk's testimony regarding the UUOA, the UNA, and ODWU is discussed in chapter 7.

pated "remedial legislation" in the form of a bill requiring registration with the attorney general of all United States organizations that (1) carried on political activities the purpose of which was the control or overthrow of the American government; (2) engaged in civilian military activities – including maneuvers and military drills – in preparation for military action; (3) were subject to foreign control.[80] Passed in the House on 1 July[81] and in the Senate on 4 October,[82] it was signed by President Roosevelt on 17 October 1940.[83] Commonly referred to as the Voorhis Act, the new law provided the Justice Department with full authority to expand its investigation of subversion in America.

The Second FBI Probe

The FBI, meanwhile, reopened its probe of UHO on 15 May 1940, in response to allegations by an unidentified informant of the Jewish Anti-Defamation League of B'nai B'rith in Chicago who reported that the UHO was pro-German, used military titles such as "colonel," had three airplanes, and was once refused permission to perform "Nazi drills" at the airfield where their planes were housed.[84] The FBI investigated and discovered that the planes were no longer being used and were up for sale, that an aviation school had existed in Chicago but that no trainees ever qualified for a pilot's license, and that the owner of the airfield was angry with UHO because he was still owed rental money.[85]

The FBI continued its probe under the Voorhis Act, however, and during the next four years compiled four volumes (sections) of anonymous letters, interviews with informants (both pro and con), translations of UHO newspaper articles, correspondence, and other publications, as well as UHO membership lists. Although the names of confidential informants who condemned the UHO are still protected by the Department of Justice, their organizational affiliations are known. Most were associated with the Anti-Defamation League (ADL); the Stalinist Popular Front; *Visti,* the Ukrainian Communist press organ; and the Ukrainian Workingmen's Association, then dominated by its president, Miroslaw Sichynsky, and his socialist followers. Given the similarity that existed in statements made by detractors, it is difficult not to conclude that revelations volunteered to the Department of Justice were orchestrated. Much of the information regarding UHO found in the FBI files consists of reprints from two Stalinist periodicals: *The Hour,* edited by Albert E. Kahn, and *Friday,* edited for a time by Michael Sayers.

A major theme of the detractors was that UHO, a monarchist organization, and ODWU, a Nationalist organization at loggerheads with UHO, were part of the same Nazi-controlled espionage network. Offered as evidence were two pieces of purely circumstantial evidence. Early in August 1940, a confidential informant from the ADL provided the FBI with a translated copy of "The Chicago Chronicle," a column which appeared in the 1 June 1940 issue of *Svoboda*. The author was Stephen Kuropas, an officer of ODWU, who, in his capacity as *Svoboda's* Chicago reporter, attended the opening of the new UHO home. Despite his association with ODWU, Kuropas was warmly received and heard speeches calling for greater understanding and less friction between the two organizations. "Perhaps," mused Kuropas in his column, "what is happening in the old country and in America will put an end to brotherly bickering."* The informant cited the article as evidence that "pressure from the German War office had made itself felt in the United States and Canada and that in effect the Hetman Organization and ODWU were joining hands."[86] To corroborate the charge, the informant offered a second article entitled "Ukrainian Fascists in Midwestern Drive," which appeared in *The Hour* on 10 August 1940. Outlining the elaborate preparations being made by UHO and ODWU to welcome Monsignor Buchko – described as having "Nazi connections" – *The Hour* concluded that the German War Office had ordered the two organizations to end their "impractical rivalry" and join forces. The two organizations have much in common, observed *The Hour* – "anti-semitism, fascism, sabotage, terrorism, anti-Sovietism."[87] Not mentioned, of course, was the fact that Metropolitan Sheptytsky had appointed Buchko auxiliary bishop of the Ukrainian Catholic exarchy in the United States and that the entire Ukrainian nationalist community was preparing to welcome him with all the pomp and ceremony due his office. The Communist newspaper *Visti* quickly adopted the UHO-ODWU unity theme on 25 February 1941, describing the "fascist merger" as "the unification of the Hetman boil with the Nationalist sore into one ulcer."[88]

The charge that a UHO-Nazi connection existed was pursued by *The Hour* even when it was learned that UHO was planning to disband. The dissolution, argued *The Hour*, was ordered by the German War Office after so much publicity "made it impossible to successfully carry on under-cover operations." The FBI, however, was not deceived by *The Hour's* charges regarding UHO. Noting that "previous issues of this publication have made

---

* On 15 May 1982, Kuropas informed the author that he was invited to attend the UHO affair as a *Svoboda* reporter by UHO Supreme Otaman Alexander Shapoval, a protagonist he had come to admire and who later became a close personal friend. "We occasionally met in private," recalls Kuropas, "and we agreed that our bickering was counterproductive. Neither of us could do much about it, however, because our respective members had been taught to dislike each other ... My column was a reflection of my personal wishes rather than of the reality which existed."

reference to the alleged Nazi domination of this organization," the FBI concluded that "investigation has failed to substantiate these claims."[89]

Another consistent theme introduced by the ADL informant was the allegation that the UHO was *directly* connected with Alfred Rosenberg's Aussenpolitisches Amt* in Berlin.[90] This idea was repeated by *The Hour* on 10 August 1940[91] and on 22 March 1941.[92] Again, the FBI was not deceived. Reviewing all the data supplied by confidential informants on 1 October 1941, FBI Director J. Edgar Hoover informed Lawrence M.C. Smith, chief of the Department of Justice's Special Defense Unit, that there was reason to believe that *The Hour* "is definitely affiliated with the Communist Party although this fact is carefully concealed from the public." Furthermore, wrote Hoover, "the campaign carried on by *The Hour* against Ukrainian organizations seems vastly exaggerated." Observing that *The Hour* is "completely financed by the Anti-Defamation League," Hoover concluded that this "may explain the similarity between information furnished this Bureau by the Anti-Defamation League, Chicago, Illinois, and information appearing in various issues of *The Hour*."[93] None of this information, however, was ever made public by the FBI.

The Dissolution of UHO

Already weakened by earlier defections to the Nationalist camp as well as by the resignation of other members who were upset with Skoropadsky's apparent ties with the Nazis, the end came swiftly for UHO. The adverse publicity generated by the Dies Committee and *The Hour* stunned and confused the loyal UHO rank and file who knew they had never dreamed of engaging in espionage activities against the United States. When their cries of a Communist conspiracy fell on deaf ears, however, and when the FBI intensified its probe once America entered the war, most became convinced that the FBI knew more about UHO activities than they did. Fearing deportation, they left the organization in droves.[94]

On 7 March 1942, exactly three months after the Japanese attack on Pearl Harbor, UHO's Supreme Executive adopted the following resolution:

> Whereas, the Central Committee of the United Hetman Organiza-
> tions, a corporation of Illinois, is of the opinion that the desire

---

* An ethnic German, born in Estonia while it was still part of the Russian Empire, Alfred Rosenberg moved to Munich after the war and joined the Nazi party. In 1921, Rosenberg became editor of *Volkischer Beobachter*, the party organ. After Hitler's ascension to power, Rosenberg was appointed head of Aussenpolitisches Amt, the party's foreign policy office. Of all the leading Nazis, Rosenberg was the most sympathetic to Ukrainian independence aspirations.

of the members of the United Hetman Organizations as well as
of all persons of Ukrainian descent for a free and independent
Ukraine should be subordinated to the undivided effort of all
Americans to win the war; and

Whereas, members of the United Hetman Organizations as
loyal citizens of the United States, in these times of emergency,
should merge their efforts into the common unity of action
towards the end that America's enemies may be defeated:

BE IT THEREFORE RESOLVED that United Hetman Organizations
be dissolved and its assets liquidated in accordance with the
law ...

The last issue of *Nash Stiah* appeared on 28 March 1942, and the UHO
home was eventually sold to the UNA district committee in Chicago.[95]
The defamation campaign against UHO, however, continued throughout 1942 and the FBI was obliged to prolong its investigation. On 9 November, *The Hour* alleged that General Skoropadsky "was selected by Hitler to
head a Nazi regime in the Ukraine"; that his organization was maintaining
contacts with "Fascist Ukrainian spies and saboteurs in the United States";
that Danylo Skoropadsky's visit to America had been financed by the
Aussenpolitisches Amt in Berlin; and that the younger Skoropadsky maintained "a secret headquarters" in London.[96] Interviewed by the FBI in 1943,
The Hour's editor could provide no evidence that his charges regarding
Hetman Skoropadsky's ties with Ukrainian-American spies and saboteurs
were factual, nor could he recall his source. As for the younger Skoropadsky, editor Kahn believed he learned about him from people associated
with the Anti-Defamation League in Chicago. During the interview, Kahn
informed FBI agent Tracy Osborne "that it was *not* always possible for him
to prove statements that were contained in *The Hour* and that proof need
not be as positive for his publication as it was for prosecution."[97]

Ukrainian socialists associated with Oborona Ukrainy (Defense of
Ukraine Association) and the UWA were also willing to provide information to the FBI. *Narodna Volya,* the UWA organ, mentioned the alleged
Rosenberg plan to coordinate the work of the UHO and ODWU in America
in 1941.[98] In 1943, Miroslaw Sichynsky, former UWA president and chairman of Defense of Ukraine, ventured the opinion that both organizations
"adhered to the Nazi party" and that both had been consolidated under
the leadership of Hetman Skoropadsky. He denied any knowledge of
espionage, however.[99] Volodymyr Levytsky, former editor of *Narodna Volya*
and editor of *Hromadsky Holos* (Voice of the Community), press organ of
Defense of Ukraine, informed the FBI that Adolf Hitler had appointed

Skoropadsky head of all Ukrainian immigrants in America. When questioned by special agent Wesley C. Carter, he could provide no substantial evidence to support his allegation.[100] By the time Levitsky was interviewed, however, J. Edgar Hoover had been informed by Assistant Attorney General Tom C. Clark that, based on the evidence, prosecution of any UHO member is "not warranted" and that "no further specific investigation is at this time requested."[101] Unfortunately for UHO, this decision also remained classified information and was never released to the press.

Lack of evidence regarding UHO subversion – as well as the absence of United States prosecution of UHO members under the Voorhis Act – did not prevent Albert E. Kahn, editor of *The Hour*, and Michael Sayers, a frequent contributor to *Friday*, from continuing their defamation campaign against the Ukrainian-American nationalist community. In 1942, they authored *Sabotage! The Secret War against America*, a book described as an "exposé" of the subversion network which existed among America's German, Japanese, and Ukrainian communities. In a chapter entitled "Bombers and Killers" – devoted exclusively to Ukrainian nationalists – Kahn and Sayers described UHO and ODWU as "two of the most dangerous espionage-sabotage organizations in the world ... It is remarkable that in all the literature dealing with the world-wide machinations of the Axis," they wrote, "practically no mention has been made of the most important auxiliary of the international Nazi espionage and sabotage machine: the Fascist Ukrainian fifth column ... Just how Hitler got hold of these terrorists among the Ukrainians and converted a section of them into the Ukrainian-American fifth column makes a story of international treachery unparalleled in all the weird annals of the underworld of political crime."[102] Heartily endorsed by Walter Winchell, America's leading radio news commentator, *Sabotage!* was condensed by the *Reader's Digest* in October 1942. Describing *The Hour* as "a confidential newsletter published for the use of editors, columnists and radio commentators which has won a nationwide reputation for its exclusive news scoops on Axis plots in the United States," and Sayers as a person who "studied first hand the work of the Axis fifth column in Europe before the war," America's widely read periodical concluded that the author's "facts have been carefully authenticated."[103] Given such enthusiastic endorsements, *Sabotage!* became a national best-seller, providing one more nail for the UHO coffin.

Soon after the war ended, Sayers and Kahn coauthored *The Great Conspiracy: The Secret War against Russia*, an "exposé" of the anti-Soviet conspiracy. "The Soviet forces were driven from Kiev and Kharkov," they wrote in describing the birth of the Ukrainian National Republic, "and a puppet 'Independent Ukraine,' controlled by the German Army of Occupation, was formed with General Petliura as its head. Declaring his aim to be the establishment of 'National Socialism,'* Petliura instigated a series of bloody, anti-Semitic pogroms throughout Ukraine."[104] Sayers and Kahn followed the standard Stalinist line in their newest publication, praising the Soviet dictator for his "great wisdom" in destroying the Nazi-inspired "Trotsky-ite-Zinoviete Terrorist Center" and his vision in purging old Bolsheviks and army generals who were cooperating with the Nazis. They concluded their sanctimonious defense of Stalin with a quotation from Col. Raymond Robins, described as a witness to the Bolshevik revolution and an American "with passionate concern for the welfare of the common man" who was "impatient with prejudice and greed": "Soviet Russia has always wanted international peace ... Soviet Russia exploits no colonies, seeks none to exploit ... Stalin's policies have wiped out racial, religious, national, and class antagonisms within the Soviet territories. The unity and harmony of the Soviet peoples point to international peace."[105]

Not mentioned, of course, was the fact that Robins, the former representative of the American Red Cross in Petrograd, was a known Bolshevik fellow traveler who met clandestinely with Comintern agents in the United States.[106] Significantly, Sabotage! and The Great Conspiracy were required reading for American prisoners of war captured by the Chinese Communists during the Korean War.

In 1955, Albert E. Kahn collaborated with Angus Cameron in the publication of False Witness, a book written by Harvey Matusow in an attempt to discredit the U.S. government investigation of Communist subversion. Kahn was called before the U.S. Senate Internal Security Subcommittee and asked if he was then or had ever been a member of the Communist party or "met in a session of the Communist Party," or "ever lectured in a closed meeting of the Communist Party." Claiming his constitutional privileges under the fifth amendment, Kahn refused to answer. On 11 July 1958, the subcommittee issued a report which argued that False Witness was "a confection of falsehoods" which had as its immediate goal new trials for convicted Communist leaders. "Its broader and long-range goals," the subcommittee concluded, were "to immobilize the prosecution and investigation of the Communist conspiracy." The subcommittee reviewed Kahn's background, noting that he had met with Soviet intelligence officers and with members of the Comintern, and had, at one time or another, belonged to some twenty-five Communist-front organizations. The report

---

* Had Petliura indeed proclaimed a Ukrainian republic based on the principles of "National Socialism," he would have been the world's first "Nazi," predating the formation of Hitler's own National Socialist German Workers' party by two years.

also noted that Kahn had "cooperated in the effort of the Soviet Government to discredit anti-Soviet Russians abroad through his magazine *The
Hour* and through his book *The Great Conspiracy.*"[107]

Beginning as an apolitical gymnastic society dedicated to the principle of
a sound mind in a sound body, Sich was taken over by a small group of
zealots eager to train a future Ukrainian liberation army in the United
States. Pointing to the precedent set by other ethnic groups during Wilson's
administration, they encouraged Ukrainian youth to obtain their military
training in the United States militia – which agreed to the formation of
separate Ukrainian companies – and dreamed of that glorious day when,
in keeping with the Wilsonian principle of national self-determination,
Ukrainian Americans would contribute to Ukraine's resurrection.

To provide the kind of unity of purpose that a liberation struggle
required and to overcome what they believed was an innate Ukrainian
penchant for individualism and anarchy, the Sich leadership recognized
Hetman Pavlo Skoropadsky as their political and ideological authority,
changed the name of their society to reflect their new political commitment,
and proceeded to develop a national liberation program based on personal
dignity, respect for the family, the church, enlightenment, the UHO cause,
discipline, obedience, and community dedication. For Ukrainian Americans
in search of individual purpose and social cohesion – as well as an ideological alternative to Communism – the monarchist program was ideal. It
provided them with a meaningful identity during difficult economic times
in America and offered an opportunity to work for Ukraine with the
blessings of the American government whose military leaders appeared
willing to provide military expertise for the fledgling Ukrainian "army."

But the United States was changing. Roosevelt became president and
the emphasis during the 1930s was on domestic survival and foreign coexis-
tence. When the Soviets questioned the existence of a handful of anti-
Communist Ukrainian Americans armed with obsolete rifles and three
vintage airplanes, the State Department felt compelled to investigate.

Europe had also changed. Hitler was transforming Germany from a
bankrupt democracy into an ostensibly stable, united world power determined to undo the humiliation of Versailles and to destroy Communism.
It was this Germany that appealed most to Ukrainian monarchists as well
as to some Americans. Increasingly enamored of Germany, UHO leaders
began to flirt with the German-American Bund, a pro-Nazi organization.

As much as they desired a free Ukraine, at no time did the monarchists
in America oppose the American government. Most of them loved the

United States and respected her laws, traditions, and customs. But Ukraine and America were different, they argued. What was the best and most productive form of government for one was not necessarily good for the other.

In the end, UHO actions and rhetoric, combined with allegations of Skoropadsky's association with Rosenberg's Aussenpolitisches Amt, proved to be the monarchists' undoing. Responding to charges of a UHO-Nazi connection, the Dies Committee investigated and, on the basis of one man's testimony during one day's hearing, concluded that UHO was indeed part of a foreign-controlled espionage network. A four-year FBI investigation failed to uncover any evidence linking the monarchists with subversion and, despite a barrage of allegations, no UHO member was ever arrested, prosecuted, or deported for crimes against America. There was only circumstantial evidence linking some UHO members with the German Bund and Skoropadsky with Rosenberg; the rest was pure fabrication orchestrated, FBI files strongly suggest, in Moscow and promulgated by the Comintern and its American agents. Fabrication or not, it was enough to immobilize a once active anticommunist organization in America and to leave a segment of the Ukrainian-American community more pessimistic than ever regarding the future of their homeland.

7 Nationalist Aspirations

The last major political ideology to have a significant impact on Ukrainian-American thinking was that of Nationalism, specifically, the Nationalism developed and practiced by the Organization of Ukrainian Nationalists (OUN).

Nationalist Foundations

The ideological foundation for the Ukrainian Nationalist movement was laid by Dmytro Dontsov, who believed that Ukraine's loss of statehood was precipitated by a lack of clear purpose and will among Ukraine's former leaders. Rejecting the pluralistic nationalism of Shevchenko, Franko, and Hrushevsky (which, Dontsov argued, promoted unrealistic ideals based on the intellect), he developed an ideology of organic nationalism predicated on national purity, faith, irrationality, and will. The masses, wrote Dontsov, need to be enlightened by a small, sophisticated elite through a process of "creative coercion." He insisted that Ukraine's ruling elite be ethnonationally pure, chosen rather than elected, and clearly distinguishable from the masses. Ukrainians should rid themselves of slogans, Dontsov declared, and replace them with national egoism. He believed that a nation that wished to be in command of its own destiny had to have the self-confidence common to people who were accustomed to rule. The attainment of such self-confidence required the development of a nationalism that was anti-communist, antidemocratic, and anti-internationalist, and which represented a rebellion in the name of work, discipline, ancestral culture (our own blood, our own land, the church), and organization in opposition to disorganization. Dontsov urged his followers to reject traditional morality in order to achieve victory. "The morality I am discussing," he concluded, "rejects concepts and principles such as 'humanity,' not hurting others, the sanctity of life above all else ... ; good is that which strengthens the nation; evil is that which undermines it ... good behavior is that which is beneficial to the nation; bad behavior that which is detrimental." When the Organization of Ukrainian Nationalists was created in 1929, many of Dontsov's ideas were incorporated into the OUN political platform. Originally a Western Ukrainian manifestation, most early Ukrainian Nationalist activity was concentrated in the Ukrainian regions of Czechoslovakia, Romania, and Poland. Treatment of national minorities by the governments in these three countries varied greatly.[1]

Ukraine under Czechoslovakia and Romania

The Ukrainian minority faced difficulties in all regions of their divided homeland. Although life for Ukrainians in Czechoslovakia was relatively good – the Czech government permitted Ukrainian institutions to flourish and even subsidized the education of Ukrainian university students – Prague's policy towards the 500,000 Ukrainians in Ruthenia was one of tolerance and benign neglect. Germany's invasion of Czechoslovakia in 1938 provided an opportunity for Ukrainian nationalists in Ruthenia to proclaim an independent Republic of Carpatho-Ukraine under the presidency of Monsignor Augustyn Voloshyn. Given Hitler's many speeches supporting national self-determination, Ukrainian nationalists believed Germany would recognize their new government. The Nazis, however, awarded Carpatho-Ukraine to Hungary, an ally. When World War II ended, Carpatho-Ukraine was annexed by the Soviet Union and formally incorporated into the UkrSSR on 29 June 1945.[2]

Bucharest attempted to Romanianize its 792,000 Ukrainians by officially classifying them as "Romanians who have forgotten their mother tongue." With the exception of a democratic interlude that lasted from 1928 to 1934, Romanian policy in Bukovina was one of repression and denationalization. When King Carol II ascended the throne, Romania became an authoritarian monarchy predicated on neofascist principles. After the annexation of Bessarabia and Bukovina by the Soviet Union in 1940, Carol II abdicated his throne. He was succeeded by Gen. Ion Antonescu who continued the authoritarian, neofascist tradition.[3]

Ukraine under Poland

Poland's 4 million Ukrainians represented fully 15 percent of the new country's population. They were concentrated in relatively backward Volhynia (formerly ruled by Russia) and the far more nationally conscious territory of eastern Galicia (formerly ruled by Austria). In order to prevent the spread of Ukrainian nationalism from Galicia to Volhynia, Poland maintained the old Austro-Russian border, confident that it could assimilate the Volhynians with little effort. Because of the cordon, Volhynians and Galicians were largely cut off from each other in the interbellum period, unable to cross the border or even to subscribe to periodicals published on the other side of it.

Although Volhynia became a hotbed of procommunist and pro-Soviet sentiment, eastern Galicia was clearly the Polish government's main worry. In the beginning, Polish minority policy wavered between repression and accommodation. By the mid-1920s, however, Warsaw adopted a policy of Polonization in eastern Galicia which was implemented in a variety of ways. The region was renamed Malapolska Wschodnia (Eastern Little Poland), Ukrainian inscriptions were removed from all official buildings, and a number of Ukrainian institutions were closed. Laws passed in 1920 and 1925 permitted the division of a number of large Polish estates in Western Ukraine among Polish war veterans, resulting in the migration of approximately 300,000 Poles into the region.[4]

Hardest hit by the Polonization policy was the Ukrainian school system. Ukrainian-language elementary schools declined from a prewar high of over 2,000 to 452 in 1937. Most were forced to accept bilingual instruction in Polish and Ukrainian. In an area that had twice as many Ukrainians as Poles, the Polish government provided 58 Polish-language *gymnasiums* and only 6 Ukrainian-language *gymnasiums*. The Lviv University systematically discriminated against Ukrainians by matriculating Polish army veterans exclusively. A free university founded by Ukrainians in 1921 (by 1923, the school had an enrollment of 1,500 students) was closed by the Polish government in 1925 along with the Ukrainian Higher School of Polytechnics.[5]

Ukrainian religious institutions also suffered from Warsaw's discriminatory policies. On 1 February 1925, Poland and the Vatican concluded a concordat which established Latin-rite Catholicism as the state religion of Poland, recognized the autonomy of the Ukrainian Catholic church, and provided for the financial support of all Catholic churches, including Ukrainian, by the Polish government. At the same time, however, the concordat stipulated that: (1) only three Ukrainian dioceses could exist; Ukrainians living outside these dioceses had to attend Latin-rite churches; (2) no Ukrainian bishop could be appointed nor could any priest be assigned to a parish without prior approval of the Polish government; (3) Ukrainian bishops take an oath of allegiance to Poland in the presence of the president of the republic and that they endeavor to gain similar loyalty from their priests and faithful; (4) married and celibate clergy be taxed equally and that married priests hold no more property than celibates; (5) all Ukrainian churches hold special services on 3 May, the Polish national holiday, to pray for the prosperity of Poland. Finally, the concordat made provisions

for the financial compensation of former Ukrainian Catholic properties in
Volhynia seized by Poland from the Russian Orthodox church. All such
payments were to be made to the Holy See, however, and not to the
Ukrainian Catholic church.[6] In accordance with the agreement, Poland
made payments to Rome in 1929 and again in 1938.

Despite the discriminatory nature of these dictates, the concordat did
recognize the existence of a separate Ukrainian Catholic church and provided some measure of legal latitude in the development of religiocultural
consciousness. The Ukrainian Catholic church, however, was at no time
treated as the political equal of the Latin-rite Catholic church. Ukrainians
were aware, for example, that if they desired work within Polish governmental institutions it would help if they became Latin-rite Catholic,[7] and
Ukrainian priests knew that the use of the Ukrainian transliteration
in baptismal and other vital records (for example, recording a surname
"Vytvytskyi" instead of "Witwicki") could result in their being charged
with the "falsification" of official documents.[8]

While the Rome-Warsaw Concordat protected the Ukrainian Catholic
church from open discrimination, the Ukrainian Orthodox church enjoyed
no such advantage. Numerous attempts were made by Poles to induce the
Ukrainian Orthodox to accept Catholicism. When these endeavors proved
unsuccessful, an effort was made to introduce the Polish language and the
Gregorian calendar into Orthodox practices and observances. Ukrainian
Orthodox later came under the jurisdiction of the Autocephalous Orthodox
church of Poland, a religious institution controlled by the Polish government. When Orthodox resistance increased, a number of churches were
simply closed. Of the over 300 Ukrainian Orthodox churches in existence
in 1914, only 51 survived until 1939.[9]

Following the 1923 Council of Ambassadors' decree, most Ukrainians in
eastern Galicia reconciled themselves to Polish rule, believing that accommodation through political and economic action was the only reasonable
course of action. A number of political parties were created, the largest of
which was the Ukrainian National Democratic Union (UNDO). In the 1928
election, some seventy Ukrainians were elected to the Polish National
Assembly, twenty-three of whom were members of UNDO.[10]

In the educational arena, Ukrainians created Ridna Shkola (Native
School), a private alternative school system that established forty-one elementary schools by 1937 and twenty-two gymnasiums and sixteen lyceums
by 1939. During the same period Ridna Shkola published its own biweekly
educational journal and a variety of children's books which were placed
in some seventy children's libraries established by the organization
throughout Western Ukraine. A number of youth organizations were reac-
tivated during this period, including the gymnastic organizations Sich and

Sokol, and the Ukrainian scouting organization, Plast. A new organization, the Union of Ukrainian Nationalist Youth (SUNM), was founded after the war.[11]

Another prewar activity successfully continued between the two world wars was the co-op movement. Beginning with the enactment of the Polish Cooperative Law of 1920 and the creation of Kraiovyi komitet orhanizatsii kooperativ (Land Committee for the Organization of Cooperatives) by Ukrainians in 1922, the cooperative revival developed faster and at a more consistent pace than any other Ukrainian enterprise. By 1938, there were a total of 3,300 Ukrainian cooperatives in existence in Polish Ukraine, with some 600,000 members.[12]

Efforts to preserve and to further develop the Ukrainian ethnonational tradition in Polish-occupied Ukraine during the interwar period were not restricted to the peaceful, legal ones adopted by Ukrainian parliamentarians, youth organizations, Ridna Shkola, and the cooperative movement, however. There was another aspect, a far more militant one, to the total Ukrainian response to the Polish presence in Western Ukraine. In the forefront of this revolutionary component, at least initially, was a group of Ukrainian war veterans who could not bring themselves to accept Polish suzerainty over their homeland under any circumstances and who were willing to adopt terrorism as a means of expressing their sentiments.

Organized resistance to Polish rule began in 1921 with the creation of the Ukrainian Military Organization (Ukrainska viiskova orhanizatsiia – UVO) by former Sichovi Striltsi commander Ievhen Konovalets and his compatriots (Andrew Melnyk, Roman Sushko, Yaroslaw Chyz, Omelian Senyk, and others).[13] UVO's militant posture was articulated that same year by Captain V. Kuchabsky in an article entitled "The Immediate Task Facing the Ukrainian People." "For the healthy development of a nation," wrote Kuchabsky, "that is, for the protection of the freedom of development of the individuals who comprise the nation, it is absolutely essential to have a nation-state." Achieving the nation-state, concluded the UVO ideologist, requires mass action in an armed struggle; "the question of life is a question of force and force alone."[14]

An assassination attempt against General Pilsudski was made by UVO in 1921. The following year, Sydir Tverdokhlib, a Ukrainian political leader who advocated Ukrainian participation in the Polish election (interpreted by UVO as tacit recognition of the Polish regime), was killed for promulgating his views. An assassination attempt was made against S. Wojciechowski, the Polish president, in 1924, and in 1926, S. Sobinski, a Polish school official, was killed for his overly zealous efforts on behalf of school centralization. Other UVO-initiated terrorist acts during the 1920s included the bombing of Polish government installations (postal, railroad, and telegraph stations), the burning of Polish estates, and physical attacks on Polish officials. To help finance its operations, UVO devised a system of "expropriations" which were "levied" against the Polish government and "collected" by means of attacks on Polish banks and postal trucks carrying federal payrolls. All such acts were met with severe reprisals (mass arrests, the banning of certain organizations, and the torture of suspected UVO members and sympathizers) by the Polish government.[15]

By the mid-1920s, however, a kind of malaise had settled over the Ukrainians in Poland. Weary of years of strife and struggle, most had come to accept Polish domination of Western Ukraine and were learning to cope with the bitter reality. Their view of UVO, therefore, was either one of indifference or hostility. Two things, the UVO leadership reasoned, were necessary to overcome this national languor. The first was an ideology that would remind the Ukrainian people of their lost statehood and inspire them to regain it. The second was a broadened organizational network that could entice the younger generation, the future cadres of Ukraine's liberation struggle, into active membership.

The ideological foundation for the new UVO-inspired Ukrainian organization was provided by Dmytro Dontsov,[16] whose books were widely read throughout Western Ukraine. The organizational groundwork for the establishment of a permanent Ukrainian Nationalist organization was laid by UVO, the Ukrainian National Youth Group (UNM), the Legion of Ukrainian Nationalists (LUN), and the Union of Ukrainian Nationalist Youth (SUNM). UNM was organized in Prague in 1922 by a small group of Ukrainian veterans from Galicia to serve as an ideological wing of the Ukrainian Academic Society. As its membership increased, UNM began to publish its own organ – Natsionalna Dumka (National Thought) – and to create branches in Western Ukraine.[17] LUN, one of the first Ukrainian organizations to use the appellation "nationalist" in its title, was founded by veterans from eastern Ukraine in Prague in 1925 as an amalgam of three other Ukrainian organizations created earlier: the Ukrainian National Federation, the Association of Ukrainian Fascists, and the Association for the Liberation of Ukraine. Under the leadership of Mykola Sciborsky, LUN was founded on two major ideological principles: (1) the development of a Ukrainian nationalism that was based on Ukrainian ethnonational tradition and spirit and (2) the creation of an ethnonational program which incorporated the experience of other peoples, especially the Italian Fascists. LUN was headquartered in Podebrady, Czechoslovakia, and published its own organ, Derzhavna Natsiia (The Nation-State).[18] All four organizations had come under the ideological influence of Dontsov, who had a profound impact upon the younger generation (many of whom were still flirting with the utopian idealism of Ukrainian Communism) and upon the development of Ukrainian Nationalist ideals.

Dmytro Andrievsky summarized the essence of the emerging Nationalist political philosophy in an article that appeared in *Natsionalna Dumka*, a UNM publication, in 1927. Within a ten-year period, he wrote, the Ukrainian nation has undergone an ethnonational evolutionary process that has taken other nations a hundred years to complete. What was once an amorphous ethnic mass is now a nationally conscious people which, because of the political frustration of its national will, is lacking in self-esteem and confidence. What is needed, suggested Andrievsky, is an organization that can help overcome this national inferiority complex – an organization that can stabilize the ethnonational readiness of the Ukrainian people, enable them to develop their national instincts, cultivate their spiritual and physical strengths, and provide them with the opportunity to take their rightful place among other nations. In anticipation of this final objective, concluded Andrievsky, a hierarchy of national priorities must be established, the most important of which is ethnonational unity and solidarity. Achievement of the latter end requires a centralized organization that can implement the national will and can subordinate individual and particularistic interests to its own program of iron discipline and obedience.[19]

Developing Andrievsky's views further, Mykola Sciborsky called for:

> the cultivation and stabilization of powerful leadership which is uncompromising, iron-strong, willful, and imbued with a noble and ideal spirit which has as its first premise and final objective, the nation, the nation and once more the nation.
>
> The nation – rather than international and cosmopolitan delusion.
>
> The nation – instead of "eternal and universal human rights and brotherhood."
>
> The nation – with a will to self-government and a leadership which is not given to hysterical prostration and spiritual servility in the name of "humanity."
>
> The nation – as the conclusive and culminating objective of all political striving.[20]

In 1927, LUN and UNM joined forces, created the Association of Ukrainian Nationalist Organizations (SOUN), and began to press for an All-Ukrainian Nationalist congress. "Our strength lies in ourselves alone" became the Nationalist motto.[21]

As recruits grew in number, a definitive Nationalist educational program began to emerge. Great stress was placed on maintaining the "purity" of the Ukrainian language and culture. Moderation was rejected. The Ukrainian ethnonational struggle was glorified and romanticized. Finally, terrorism and other forms of illegality were rationalized as legitimate forms of resistance in light of the illegitimacy of the Polish occupation.[22]

Thirty delegates attended the first Congress of Ukrainian Nationalists held in Vienna from 28 January to 3 February 1929. The congress formally established the Organization of Ukrainian Nationalists (OUN) and appointed a new Provid (leadership) to oversee its operation. Headed by Col. Ievhen Konovalets, the Provid included M. Sciborsky, V. Martynets, D. Andrievsky, Iu. Vassiyan, Gen. M. Kapustiansky, D. Demchuk, L. Kostariv, and P. Kozhevnykiv. In addition to promulgating a series of resolutions related to the socioeconomic, cultural, military, educational, and religious nature of the future Ukrainian state, the congress made it clear that the attainment of an independent Ukraine required, during the course of the "liberation struggle" and subsequent "revolution," the creation of a "national dictatorship" which will "insure the internal strength and external resistance of the Ukrainian nation."[23] The Nationalists, stated the newly adopted OUN bylaws, will be guided by the principles of "active idealism, moral self-legitimacy,* individual initiative," and the concepts of "pan-Ukrainianism, nonpartisanship, and monocracy."[25] No other Ukrainian political party can realize Ukrainian statehood, the congress declared, because all of them are either under the control of provincial and class interests or remain divided by internal strife.[26] A movement which was above party politics was needed to lead the struggle for an independent Ukraine.

The congress also ruled that all UVO members would automatically become members of OUN. Thus, in one administrative decision, the new Nationalist organization inherited not only the revolutionary tradition of UVO but its trained and tested cadres as well.[27] The sacrifice and militant fervor expected of the OUN members were underscored in the "Ten Commandments of the Ukrainian Nationalist," adopted by the Provid in June 1929. Included were such directives as "You shall win a Ukrainian Nation-state or you shall perish in the struggle for Her"; "You shall not allow anyone to sully the glory and honor of your nation"; "You shall avenge the death of the Great Heroes"; "You shall not hesitate to carry out the most dangerous act, if required to do so for the good of the Cause."[28]

To regain statehood in the future, Nationalists believed, the Ukrainian

---

* The principle of moral autonomy adopted by OUN was, in effect, a rejection of the Judeo-Christian moral code.[24]

nation had to function as a whole. The primary role of Ukrainian Nationalism, therefore, was to bring about the kind of national "wholeness" (not
just in Galicia but in all regions of Ukraine and the immigration as well)
that could generate statehood. To accomplish this goal, OUN ideologues
argued, one had to understand that the nation is not merely the sum
of equivalent and equal individuals; the nation is a living organism, a
hierarchical whole, which consists of the coordinated interconnection of
individual persons who are different, both in terms of social class and in
collective character. Nations, like all living organisms, have to struggle to
exist. As Darwin – and World War I – demonstrated, OUN argued, only
the strong survive.

To become strong, a nation has to have a "wholeness" oriented, goal-
directed leadership which is both democratic (because it guarantees the
involvement of all members of the nation in the process) and dictatorial
(because it alone determines the means and ends of this process). Because
every nation is different (the manifestations of a nation's physical and
spiritual vitality are peculiar to it alone), the national leadership must be
intimately familiar with the nation's soul and astute enough to develop an
ideology that grows out of the needs and aspirations of that nation alone.
The highest good, first, last, and always, is the nation. Only the conscious
Ukrainian with a Nationalist orientation can adequately participate in the
liberation struggle.[29]

There were, of course, many similarities between Ukrainian nationalism
and fascism. Both glorified the nation and the state, exalted faith, will, and
power, believed in the "iron logic of nature" (the strong always prevail),
stressed activism organized by an authoritarian leadership and elite,
repudiated peace and harmony, rejected Marxism and Communism, and
subordinated class conflict to national unity. Both were also committed
to state-regulated capitalism and a hierarchical state in which the principal
economic functions (banking, industry, labor) are organized as corporate
unities.[30]

Ukrainian Nationalists and fascists differed, however, on one crucial
point. Fascists believed that all good resided in the state; there were no
spiritual or human values outside the state. The state *creates* the nation and
fascism is a way of *organizing* the state. OUN, in contrast, argued that the
nation *generates* the state, which, in turn, is the *condition* that guarantees
the nation a place in the international arena. Ukrainian Nationalism, therefore, was a way of *attaining* the state – in short, a movement for national
liberation.[31] Viewed from this revivalist perspective, Ukrainian Nationalism
was similar to the revisionist Zionism of Vladimir Jabotinsky.[32]

While Nationalists advocated a "national dictatorship" which "would
guarantee the internal strength of the Ukrainian nation" during the libera-

tion struggle, they also saw the need for the "creation of legislative organs based on the representation of all organized social strata with consideration for the differences of the individual lands that will enter into the Ukrainian state." The nation-state, they concluded, will be developed in response to the observable needs of life within the framework of certain ethnonational limits. The "cultural process," for example, though predicated on "freedom of cultural expression," would have to be in line with "the spiritual nature of the Ukrainian people." In the meantime, OUN's foreign policy would revolve around alliances with "peoples hostile to the occupiers of Ukraine."[33]

Although many Ukrainian youth welcomed the birth of OUN as a milestone in Ukrainian ethnonational development, older and more moderate elements in Western Ukrainian society expressed their misgivings about the nature and purpose of the new Nationalist organization. "If the Nationalists are against political parties," wrote *Dilo,* the UNDO organ, "then one must surely come to realize that in their reorganized state they are nothing else but a new Ukrainian party themselves – a party with Fascist leanings."[34]

The endeavors of more circumspect Ukrainian leaders to dissociate the Ukrainian public from UVO and OUN activities notwithstanding, the Polish government decided to settle the Ukrainian question once and for all. Frustrated by the recalcitrance of the terrorists, Warsaw inaugurated a "pacification" campaign in the fall of 1930 ostensibly aimed at UVO and OUN, but which was really an attempt to teach all Poland's Ukrainians an ethnonational "lesson."[35] In the words of Hugh Seton-Watson:

> In 1930, "pacifying expeditions" were sent to the Ukrainian provinces. Whole villages were burnt down, numbers of innocent peasants were killed, and abominable tortures and outrages were committed on men, women and children. The official justification for this bestial performance, that some peasants had harbored terrorists and that a "demonstration" was necessary, was entirely unconvincing.[36]

It is beyond the scope of the present work to provide a lengthy and detailed account of the brutality exercised by the Polish government against Ukrainians during the pacification.[37] Selected excerpts from the English-language press reporting on the incidents, however, should serve to indicate both its scope and its impact. A *New York Times* reporter, for example, wrote the following account:

> Ruthlessly police and cavalry detachments marched from town to town and from village to village to break up the secret terrorist

organization. Neither priest nor deputy were spared – indeed, seventeen former deputies and eleven parish priests are in jail now.

Charitable institutions, co-operatives, and sporting and educational associations were dissolved. Two high schools ... were closed. The number of those arrested, mostly young students, is not yet known but it is believed to total about five hundred.[38]

A correspondent for the *Manchester Guardian* described the pacification as a "Polish terror in the Ukraine" and concluded that it was "not directed against individuals but against its co-operative creameries and institutes – its whole civilization, in fact."[39] Polish sources indicate that only 117 villages were severely affected by the pacification, but Ukrainian sources argue that the true figure is well over 250.[40] Suffering most during the pacification (which lasted from 16 September to 30 November 1930) were those Ukrainians who lived in the remote rural areas.

If the primary goal of the pacification campaign was to crush OUN, the effort failed. The Polish actions only resulted in greater mass sympathy and new recruits for OUN. Especially responsive were rural youths. Bitter over what they had witnessed in their villages, and frustrated by the prospects of an increasingly grim future under Poland, they joined the Nationalists. Within OUN, their political naïveté and relative lack of sophistication made them ideal subjects for the well-disciplined, romantically chauvinistic, and "all or nothing" ethnonational indoctrination they received.[41] Under the direction of such energetic local or *krai* leaders as Stepan Bandera, Osyp Boidunyk, Stepan Lenkavsky, and Mykola Lebed, new, fiercely loyal OUN zealots were quickly mobilized for action against the Polish government.[42]

Its membership expanding,[43] OUN continued its terrorist activities in spite of Polish reprisals and condemnations from the Ukrainian Catholic church, various co-op leaders, and UNDO. The arrest and subsequent execution of OUN members only served to produce martyrs for the cause and greater sympathy for OUN.[44] Heading an OUN call for an economic boycott of state-controlled monopolies in 1932, thousands of Ukrainians gave up buying tobacco and alcoholic beverages at state-run stores.[45] In retaliation for the 1932–3 famine in the UkrSSR (extensively covered in Poland's Ukrainian-language press), an attempt was made on the life of the Soviet vice-consul in Lviv in 1933.[46] A year later, Bronislaw Pieracki, the Polish minister of internal affairs, was assassinated in Warsaw for his role in the pacification campaign. In the early 1930s, OUN members staged over 60 actual or attempted assassinations in addition to hundreds of acts of sabotage and dozens of "expropriations."[47]

Terrorism and economic boycotts were not the only activities in which OUN and its supporters were engaged, however. Considerable energy was expended in influencing Ukrainian popular opinion by the OUN-controlled press, which by 1939 numbered ten separate publications in Western Ukraine, four in Carpatho-Ukraine, three in Bukovina, two in France, and one in Czechoslovakia.[48] In addition, the OUN Provid spent a good deal of time overseas developing ties with newly established Nationalist organizations in the United States, Canada, and Argentina.[49]

Alarmed by the economic devastation that the pacification campaign left in its wake, UNDO and other moderate Ukrainian leaders attempted to normalize Ukrainian-Polish relations during most of the remaining prewar years. The Warsaw government eventually responded to the Ukrainian gesture by releasing a few political prisoners and by extending credits to faltering Ukrainian economic institutions. But Polonization continued unabated. In 1931, Poland's court system was reorganized and 80 percent of the Ukrainian judges were either removed from their posts or transferred to Poland proper. In 1933, rural districts were reorganized into larger administrative units and Polish was formally established as the official language. In the Kholm region, Ukrainian reading rooms were banned, Ukrainian cooperatives were subordinated to Polish cooperative unions, and all Ukrainian reading material, even newspapers, was prohibited.

Attempts to improve relations between Ukrainians and Poles never succeeded. The average Ukrainian grew increasingly resentful of Polish behavior in his homeland and expressed that feeling through participation in mass demonstrations and rallies designed to bear witness to Ukrainian ethnonational solidarity. Ukrainian national holidays such as Western Ukrainian Independence Day (1 November) and Ukrainian Independence Day (22 January), as well as the birthdays of Shevchenko, Franko, and Shashkevych, were commemorated by large numbers of Ukrainians all through the 1930s. Other occasions that brought out thousands of Ukrainians in a demonstrative fashion were the Thirtieth Anniversary Celebration of the Audit Union of Cooperatives, the Ukrainian Youth for Christ Congress (during which some 50,000 young people gathered in Lviv), the National Sokil Congress (8,000 participants), and the funeral of Gen. Myron Tarnavskyi in 1938, which became an occasion for mass national mourning.[50] Still believing Hitler's bogus proclamations of national self-determination for Eastern European minorities, few Ukrainians wept when the Germans invaded Poland.

Ukraine under the Nazis

Convinced that a showdown between Hitler and Stalin was inevitable, OUN leaders embarked on a course of tactical collaboration[51] with Hitler, believing he represented the lesser of two evils. Hitler was fiercely anticommunist, his movement possessed a purpose and will which the Nationalists admired, and, most important, German officials were giving signals suggesting support for the establishment of a Ukrainian nation-state.

During the winter of 1937–8, Adolf Hitler shifted from a foreign policy aimed at removing restrictions placed upon Germany by the Treaty of Versailles[52] to a policy which had as its primary objective the attainment of *Lebensraum* (living space) for the German people. This had always been Hitler's goal but until the late 1930s he was too busy consolidating his power and building his military machine to actively pursue it. Aware that Poland, Romania, and the Baltic nations were not an effective barrier against the Soviet Union should Moscow decide to invade Europe, England and France were apparently content to permit Hitler to rearm and to create a strong, militantly anticommunist state as a counterpoise to a militantly anticapitalist USSR.[53]

Hitler's initial success during the next few years can be attributed to two major factors: (1) the reluctance of major European powers to challenge him militarily until it was too late and (2) his understanding of the potential which the frustrated aspirations of national minorities within the Central and Eastern European complex of nation-states offered his foreign policy. In an obvious attempt to undermine the national cohesion of Czechoslovakia, Poland, and the Soviet Union, Hitler borrowed a political page from Woodrow Wilson and began to fulminate about the oppressed people of Europe and their inherent right to national self-determination.[54] It was this rhetoric that Ukrainians initially found so appealing. Hitler, of course, never had any intention of allowing the submerged peoples of Eastern Europe to enjoy national sovereignty, especially the Slavs, a people he described in *Mein Kampf* as biologically inferior and incapable of self-rule. Like most other people of the world at the time, Ukrainians knew very little about Hitler's true plans, and their faith in Hitler's sincerity eventually led to their subjugation by the Nazis.

In 1938, Ievhen Konovalets, the charismatic and revered supreme OUN leader (*vozhd* in Ukrainian), was assassinated in Holland by a Bolshevik agent who had infiltrated his organization. A second OUN congress was hastily convened in Rome in 1939 and Col. Andrew Melnyk was elected to succeed his former chief. Andrievsky, Kapustiansky, and Sciborsky were retained in the Provid while Gen. Viktor Kurmanovych, Col. Roman Sushko, Omelian Senyk, Riko Iari, and Iaroslav Baranovsky were added. Before the new Provid could consolidate its leadership, however, Germany concluded a surprise alliance with the Soviets and invaded Poland.[55]

Germany's invasion of Poland was welcomed by most Ukrainians but especially by the OUN, whose ranks were increased with the release of Ukrainian political prisoners from Polish prisons. A Ukrainian National

Committee was quickly organized in Cracow and subsequently recognized by the newly created German General Gouvernement of occupied Poland.

At the same time, however, the German invasion precipitated an organizational split between the Provid and a younger leadership element within the *krai* contingent headed by Stepan Bandera. Unlike their leaders, most *krai* dissidents had spent time in Polish prisons and upon their release were highly critical of the Provid for what they believed was its somewhat lethargic response to the political realities of the times. Failing in their efforts to replace certain members of the Provid, *krai* dissidents held their own congress in Cracow, electing Bandera as their head. By February 1940, the Nationalists were permanently divided[56] between the supporters of Melnyk – OUN(M) – and the supporters of Bandera – OUN(B).[57]

Hitler, meanwhile, vacillated between two different Nazi party views regarding Ukraine. One group, headed by Alfred Rosenberg, argued that only an independent Ukrainian state under Berlin's protection could serve as a bulwark against Polish and Russian expansionism and assure German control over Eastern Europe. Opposed were Erich Koch, his mentor Martin Bormann, Herman Goering, and Gestapo Chief Heinrich Himmler, who favored a *Lebensraum* policy based on the principle that all Eastern Europeans were inferior people (*Untermenschen*) unfit to rule. The sole purpose of Slavs, they argued, was to serve the German *Herrenvolk*, their biologically superior masters.[58]

Despite the duality of Nazi policy, Berlin established and maintained contact with Ukrainian émigré political leaders, dangling the prospect of an independent Ukrainian state. Rosenberg's Aussenpolitisches Amt worked with Hetman Skoropadsky's monarchists while Admiral Canaris's military intelligence unit Abwehr cultivated both OUN factions. As plans for an attack on the USSR began to materialize, it was OUN(B) that provided most of the manpower for Roland and Nachtigall, the two Ukrainian battalions organized by the Germans to assist in the invasion.[59]

Germany invaded the UkrSSR on 22 June 1941 and, by November, practically all of the Ukrainian republic was in German hands.[60] A total of 3,806,000 Soviet soldiers surrendered to the Wehrmacht during its sweep across the USSR, while in the Baltic states and Ukraine the Germans were welcomed with open arms.

The Wehrmacht reached Lviv on 30 June 1941 along with Nachtigall, the OUN(B) battalion. That same night, OUN(B) leader Iaroslav Stetsko stood before a hastily organized "national assembly" gathered at Prosvita Hall and, speaking in the name of the Ukrainian people and "the Organization of Ukrainian Nationalists under the direction of Stepan Bandera," boldly proclaimed the "renewal of the Ukrainian state." Later, the proclamation (or *akt* as it has come to be called in Ukrainian parlance) was broadcast over Radio Lviv. Unaware of the split within OUN, most Ukrainians, including Metropolitan Sheptytsky, welcomed the proclamation, believing it signaled the beginning of a new era in Ukrainian national life.[61] Such was not to be. None of OUN(B)'s actions had been sanctioned by the Germans. Viewing Stetsko's activities as a direct challenge to German supremacy, the Nazis installed a German city commandant on 4 July and dispersed the newly proclaimed Ukrainian government the next day. Stetsko was arrested on 12 July. Bandera was taken to Berlin and, though treated with deference, was imprisoned.[62]

Hitler, meanwhile, decided to go ahead with plans to transform the newly conquered territories into a German "Garden of Eden" free of foreign elements, and on 16 July informed Rosenberg that an autonomous and united Ukrainian state was out of the question.[63] Romania was awarded Bukovina and the Ukrainian territory between the Buh and Dniester rivers (called "Transnistria" by the Romanians) in July and on 1 August Galicia was formally incorporated into the previously created "General Gouvernement for occupied Polish Territories." The remaining Ukrainian territories under German occupation became part of the "Reichskommissariat Ukraine" on 20 August with Erich Koch, Rosenberg's arch rival, as Reichskommissar.[64]

Hitler's strategy for creating a German Garden of Eden in Ukraine was based on a three-step program: (1) eradication of the Jews; (2) reduction of the Ukrainian population to servile status through denationalization, terror, and deportation; and (3) colonization.[65]

First to be eliminated were Ukrainian Jews. No fewer than 900,000 were annihilated by the Einsatzgruppen, a specially trained task force of SS and special police units, before Hitler's forces were pushed out of Ukraine by the Red Army.[66]

Ukrainian leaders and institutions were next. During the winter of 1941–2, Ukrainian intellectuals in Kiev, Kharkiv, Zhytomyr, and other major Ukrainian cities were executed.[67] Ukrainian libraries, museums, and scientific centers were plundered and burned. Educational enterprises were closed for months at a time.[68] Eventually, only elementary schools through the fourth grade were permitted to function.[69]

Nazi terror consisted of indiscriminate mass murder, planned starvation,[70] and internment in concentration camps.[71]

Mass deportations of Ukrainians began late in 1941. Classified as *Ostarbeiter* (Eastern workers), Ukrainians were shipped to Germany to work as slave laborers in factories and mines and on farms.[72] By August 1943, one of every forty Ukrainians had been deported; when the German occupation ended, there were 1,500,000 Ukrainians working in Germany.[73]

Unlike Gypsies and Jews, Ukrainians were never slated for total annihilation by Hitler. They were *Untermenschen*, nevertheless, and as such, they suffered grievously at the hands of the Nazis. While there is no consensus concerning the exact number of Ukrainians who died during the German-Soviet conflict, Soviet figures, traditionally on the conservative side, indicate that a minimum of 5.5 million people perished. Of this number, no fewer than 3.9 million Ukrainians (including 0.9 million Jews) were civilian victims of the Nazi Holocaust.[74]

Caught between the Nazi hammer and the Soviet anvil, Ukrainians began to join the partisans in ever increasing numbers, determined to fight both.[75]

The Ukrainian guerrilla force – which came to be called the Ukrainska povstanska armia (Ukrainian Insurgent Army) or UPA – was originally composed of three separate armed partisan units. The first was organized by Otaman "Taras Bulba" Borovets as early as 1940. The other two were created by OUN(B) and OUN(M) in 1942. Bulba-Borovets's partisans joined OUN(M) in 1943 and during the next few months the two remaining UPA factions fought Soviet partisans, Nazi SS units, and, occasionally, each other.

Gradually, the UPA came to be dominated by OUN(B), which was better organized, enjoyed more competent leadership, appealed more to youth, and was far more vigorous and Machiavellian in pursuit of its goals. Almost all of the clashes between the Bandera and Melnyk forces were initiated by the former. OUN(B) had two aims: (1) to totally dominate the Ukrainian resistance movement; and (2) to gain recruits from among the defeated OUN(M) units on a join-or-die basis.

As Soviet guerrillas and the Gestapo intensified their terrorism in Ukraine, UPA ranks swelled with additional Ukrainian recruits from among disenchanted Red partisans and the German-controlled Ukrainian auxiliary police. Escapees from Nazi labor camps and Soviet army deserters (among them Georgians, Tartars, Cossacks, and Azerbaijanis) also found a place in the Ukrainian underground army.

Before the end of 1943, the UPA had created a resistance apparatus that consisted of military training camps, hospitals, and schools. Ukrainians claimed a UPA force of about 100,000 during this period while German sources place the number closer to 40,000. Regardless of its true strength, however, the Ukrainian Insurgent Army represented a resistance movement on a par with any partisan group then operating in Nazi-occupied Europe.[76]

By the fall of 1943, the UPA controlled much of rural Volhynia and Polissia and had engaged the forces of SS General Bachynskyi-Zalewsky throughout the summer. The Gestapo lost 3,000 men to the Ukrainians during these encounters and retaliated with mass executions of thousands of innocent villagers and the obliteration of the towns of Remel and Malyn.

The UPA was also responsible for political assassinations (Victor Lutze, chief of the German SA, was killed in 1943) as well as attacks on military trains, railroad centers, concentration camps, and various military installations. As the Wehrmacht was retreating, the UPA's main objective became the securing of arms and supplies for the war, which, for the Nationalists, was far from over.

In January 1944, the UPA extended its activities to Western Ukraine and during the summer, just weeks before the Red Army recaptured all of Ukraine, Bandera's followers held a conference in Galicia. Reaffirming their undying commitment to the establishment of "one independent and sovereign Ukrainian state," they created the Ukrainska holovna vyzvolna rada (Ukrainian Supreme Liberation Council) proclaiming it as "the supreme and only guiding organ of the Ukrainian people for the period of its revolutionary struggle until the formation of an independent Ukrainian state embracing all Ukrainian lands."[77]

When the war ended, Moscow retained the "liberated" Ukrainian territories of Galicia and Bukovina. Only Carpatho-Ukraine remained outside the Ukrainian orbit. This was taken care of on 26 November 1944, when delegates from various "people's committees" in Carpatho-Ukraine – "encouraged" as they were by the presence of the Red Army – drafted a Manifesto of Union with the UkrSSR and presented it to the Kremlin. Stalin, of course, granted the request and, on 29 June 1945, agreed to the transfer.[78]

Thus, after centuries of separation, the Ukrainian people living in four, often divided, ethnographic territories were finally united. Few Ukrainian nationalists, however, celebrated. Ukraine was one but she was neither independent nor sovereign.

The American Response

A third political coalition forged by Ukrainians in the United States between the two world wars was dominated by the Organization for the Rebirth of Ukraine (ODWU, ODVU in Ukrainian). Established under the inspirational guidance of the Organization of Ukrainian Nationalists (OUN) in the early 1930s, ODWU became the most powerful political force in the anticommunist camp by 1938, effectively controlling both the United Ukrainian Organizations of America (UUOA) – successor to the Ukrainian National Committee – and the UNA.

The United Ukrainian Organizations of America (UUOA)

The dissolution of the Federation of Ukrainians in 1919[79] and the subsequent decline of the Ukrainian National Committee in the early 1920s left the Ukrainian-American community with no effective central organization to act on behalf of all nationalist Ukrainians. The need for a new umbrella organization was obvious and was addressed even before the Council of Ambassadors awarded Galicia to Poland.

Meeting at the June 1922 convention of the League of Americans of Ukrainian Descent in Washington, DC, a group of civic, religious, and fraternal leaders called upon the league to take the initiative in forming a new coalition. The community, they argued, is demoralized and in need of rejuvenation. Famine rages in eastern Ukraine. Western Ukraine is left with homeless orphans, invalids, and institutions in need of moral and financial assistance. We cannot abandon our overseas brethren in their hour of greatest need.[80]

On 30 June, representatives of the UNA, the Providence Association, the Ukrainian National Aid Association, the Union of Brotherhoods, Sich, the League of American Citizens of Ukrainian Descent, and the Ukrainian League of American Veterans met in Philadelphia and unanimously agreed to establish the United Ukrainian Organizations of America (UUOA) or, in Ukrainian, Obiednannia ukrayinskykh organizatsii amerytsi.

The first congress of the UUOA was held in Philadelphia on 26 and 27 October 1922, with 130 delegates representing 176 Ukrainian organizations in attendance. Commenting on the great "national catastrophe" of the Ukrainian people, Dr. Luka Myshuha, head of the ZUNR mission in Washington, stressed the need for action. "It is in times such as these," he stated, "that those in whose hands the leadership of the people has been left must exercise political wisdom" in order to turn the tide. "It is time for us to realize," concluded Dr. Osyp Nazaruk, then head of the ZUNR mission in Canada, "that the Ukrainian people cannot be vanquished and once they have said 'we will have our own state,' they will have it."[81]

A twenty-four member executive and board of directors was created consisting of three members from each of the seven national organizations plus three representatives of local organizations. Elected to the executive were Father Lev Levytsky, chairman; Teodor Hrytsai, Dr. Stepan Hrynevet-sky, V. Kryshko, and M. Kotsiuk, vice-chairmen; I. Borysevych, treasurer; Dr. Volodymyr Koval and Michael Darmopray, secretaries. Included among the board members were Dr. Simenovych and Father Spolitake-vych, former chairmen, respectively, of the Federation of Ukrainians and the Ukrainian National Committee.

The congress established a national tax of twenty-five cents a month from every UUOA member and designated that all funds collected from Christmas caroling,[82] Easter egg making, Flower Days (June), and Autumn Leaf Days (November) be allocated to Ridna Shkola in Europe. Also discussed was the creation of a Ukrainian People's University and a Ukrainian bank – two projects that never materialized – and the establishment of a Ukrainian Press Bureau.[83]

Unlike its predecessors, UUOA survived for eighteen years. Congresses were held in 1923, 1924, 1927, 1930, 1933, 1936, and 1939. The organization was headed by four chairmen – Father Levytsky (1923–4), Father Spolitakevych (1924–6), Emil Revyuk (1927–39), and Nicholas Muraszko (1939–40). Dr. Myshuha was elected secretary in 1924 and remained at that post until 1940.

The membership of the UUOA changed considerably during the course of its history. Some of the original founding organizations eventually became inactive and disappeared. Other societies left the UUOA for political or religious reasons.

The first political defection was that of the Hetman Sich, which left the coalition after the 1924 congress when delegates refused to change the UUOA democratic structure and to recognize Hetman Pavlo Skoropadsky as the head of the Ukrainian liberation movement.

Another serious defection from the UUOA occurred in 1926 when, under the leadership of Bishop Constantine Bohachevsky, the Providence Association exited over the issue of leadership within the Ukrainian-American community.* That same year, the UUOA called for a nationwide commemoration honoring Ivan Franko on the tenth anniversary of his death.[84] This action was severely criticized by Dr. Nazaruk in *America*, the Providence press organ. Franko, Nazaruk claimed, had been an atheist and attempts by the UUOA to create a "cult" in his memory were therefore inappropriate. A long series of polemic articles were subsequently published by *Svoboda* defending the UUOA decision.[85]

While some organizations left the UUOA between 1922 and 1940, others, most notably the Chornomorska (Black Sea) Sich, a number of Ukrainian Orthodox organizations, ODWU, and the Ukrainian Youth League of North America (UYLNA), joined. By the mid-1930s, the UUOA was firmly in the hands of the nationalist camp with two organizations – the UNA and ODWU – exerting the greatest influence over its activities.[86]

During the course of its eighteen-year history, the UUOA was involved in three major kinds of activities – humanitarian, cultural, and political. With the help of *Svoboda*, which supported appeals for a variety of different Ukrainian causes,[87] the UUOA collected a total of $367,753.83, which was used to help such cultural and humanitarian organizations in Europe as the Disabled Veterans,[88] Prosvita,[89] and Ridna Shkola, as well as for cultural and political activities in America such as the publication of English-lan-

---

* See chapter 8 for a complete description of the controversy which erupted around Bohachevsky's leadership during this period.

guage books and pamphlets. These included *Taras Shevchenko* by Stephen Shumeyko, *Moses* by Ivan Franko (translated by V. Semenyna), *Polish Atrocities in Ukraine* (edited by Emil Revyuk), *Ukraine and American Democracy* by Luka Myshuha, *The Ukrainian National Movement* by Stephen Shumeyko, and *Famine in Ukraine.*[90]

Throughout its existence, the UUOA endeavored to reflect and to respond to the needs of the Ukrainian-American community as well as to the needs of Ukrainians in Europe. Topics of discussion at the 1930 congress, for example, included the organization of financial resources in the Ukrainian-American community; the strengthening of Ukrainian cultural activities such as choirs, drama troupes, and dance ensembles; and the future of Ukrainian youth in the United States. For the first time, two young professionals, Dr. Neonilya Pelechowicz and Volodymyr Semenyna, addressed the congress in the English language, emphasizing the need for a nationwide organization for Ukrainian-American youth.[91] In responding to the needs of the younger generation, the UUOA helped establish the Ukrainian Youth League of North America (UYLNA) in 1933[92] and, in 1935, published *Spirit of Ukraine,* a monograph designed to provide young Ukrainian Americans with a better understanding of their ethnonational heritage.[93]

Political protests, rallies, and manifestations were also part of the UUOA agenda. In 1930, November was declared a month of "national mourning" for Ukrainians suffering under the yoke of the Polish pacification and Sunday, 16 November, a day of "National Prayer" for Ukrainians in Galicia.[94] Some 160 mass meetings were held in ninety-four American cities and towns during the month, bringing out an estimated attendance of 104,000.[95] In Philadelphia alone, thousands of Ukrainians marched in silent protest on 30 November, eventually overflowing both the Metropolitan Opera House and the Ukrainian Hall. According to the *Philadelphia Inquirer,* a resolution was adopted by the gathering which "vigorously protested before the civilized world against the reign of terror instituted by the Polish dictatorial Government against the Ukrainian population of Poland." Commenting on the demonstration, the *Philadelphia Record* wrote: "There are in Philadelphia some 20,000 persons of Ukrainian birth or antecedence. Last Sunday, 15,000 of them took part in an impressive demonstration against "terrorism" in the Ukraine ... The Ukrainians who made that orderly demonstration in this city on Sunday have an attentive audience for their protest, their stories of persecution."

Memoranda were sent to President Hoover and Secretary of State Stimson but, as the *Record* pointed out, "we have also, as Americans, to bear in mind that our population includes hosts of persons who were born in Poland or are descended from Polish ancestors ... The Government can't do anything immediately and directly. The utmost it could do would be to address an inquiry and possibly a remonstrance to the Polish Government."[96]

Similar demonstrations were organized by the UUOA and other Ukrainian organizations in 1933 around the theme "Save Ukraine from Death by Starvation." November was designated as a month of protest against the Soviet regime while 19 November was to be a day of "National Mourning."[97] This time, however, counterdemonstrations were staged by the Communists resulting in bloody clashes between the two groups in Boston, New York, Chicago, Bridgeport, and Detroit.[98] In Chicago, the encounter was especially brutal: "100 Hurt in W. Side Riot" read the *Chicago Tribune's* banner headline, "Attack Parade in Protest against Soviet." According to the *Tribune* account, several hundred Communists showered "bricks, clubs, eggs and other missiles" from an elevated train platform above the parade route of about 3,000 Ukrainian men, women, and children, and then proceeded to attack the marchers with blackjacks, brass knuckles, and lead pipes. The Ukrainians (among whom were a contingent of Sich members with unloaded rifles) fought back with fists, rocks, and rifle butts, sending a number of the attacking party to the hospital. After the clash, the parade continued to its destination for a mass rally.

The UUOA was also instrumental in calling congressional attention to Stalin's man-made famine in Soviet Ukraine. On 28 May 1934, Congressman Hamilton Fish, Jr. (R., NY) introduced House Resolution 399 urging the USSR to "place no obstacles in the way of American citizens seeking to send aid in the form of money, foodstuffs, and necessities to the famine-stricken regions of Ukraine." Not only did the Soviet Union fail "to take any relief measures designed to check the famine or to alleviate the terrible conditions arising from it," the legislation read, but it "used the famine as a means of reducing the Ukrainian population and destroying Ukraine political, cultural, and national rights." A 31-page UUOA brochure entitled "Famine in Ukraine" was published later that same year containing the full text of the house famine bill as well as excerpts from the *Christian Science Monitor*, the *Boston Post*, the *Manchester Guardian*, the *Montreal Daily Herald*, and other Western newspapers, all of which reported on the famine. The UUOA publication also contained the full texts of letters from Soviet Foreign Minister M. Litvinov and B. Svirski, counsellor of the Soviet embassy in Washington, DC, branding all stories about the Ukrainian famine "lies." Claiming that the population in Soviet Ukraine actually increased during the period in question, Svirski labeled Ukrainian-American accusations as "wholly grotesque."[99]

The last nationwide political manifestations organized by the UUOA were rallies in support of the Republic of Carpatho-Ukraine in 1938. Cooperating fully with the UNA, ODWU, and the Nationalist Front, the UUOA issued an appeal to the Ukrainian-American community on 3 October 1938, calling for demonstrations and telegrams demanding the right of Carpatho-Ukrainians "to express their will and determine their future course." One of the most active members on behalf of the UUOA during the Carpatho-Ukraine crisis was Dr. Luka Myshuha who became editor of *Svoboda* in 1933. Representing both the UNA and the UUOA, Dr. Myshuha traveled to London, Paris, and finally Vienna where, on 14 October, he delivered a brief radio message to the people of Carpatho-Ukraine.[100] Emphasizing that Carpatho-Ukraine had been a "natural part of Ukraine" since "time immemorial," Dr. Myshuha briefly reviewed the life of Ukrainians under Czech rule and concluded his remarks as follows:

> I am speaking officially in the name of the Ukrainian National Association, a 44-year-old organization which embraces tens of thousands of Ukrainian Americans. I am also addressing you on behalf of the United Ukrainian Organizations in America, a polit-ical-humanitarian organization which has supported the Ukrai-nian people in their struggle for liberation for the past seventeen years. I say "officially" because, among millions of Ukrainian immigrants on the North and South American continents, there is no Ukrainian political party, secular or religious organization, that has not already declared publicly what I will state now.
>
> Carpatho-Ukraine belongs to the 45-million Ukrainian nation which has been its neighbor for thousands of years. The entire Ukrainian nation feels bound by duty and right to help this land secure such rights as will once and forever make the Ukrainian people sole masters in their own home with a culture, language, and name that is also their own.
>
> The American-Ukrainian immigration, as well as the whole Ukrainian nation, have never felt or shown any enmity to the Czech or Slovak nations, and do not intend to show it now – in their hour of trial. They simply insist that the people of Carpa-tho-Ukraine must receive the status of a state and cease to be the object of national and cultural oppression and material exploitation ...
>
> In concluding the message which I have been authorized to deliver, I wish to congratulate our brothers and sisters in Carpa-tho-Ukraine upon their achievements and call upon them to stand firmly as masters of their Transcarpathia, our ancestral Ukrainian land. All of us, wherever we may be, are constantly with you and

ready to help you. Remember that your success is the success of all Ukrainian people and a victory for truth![101]

Dr. Myshuha's radio address from Vienna – then under Nazi control – was later to become the basis of a personal defamation campaign organized by American Communists and their fellow travelers.

The Organization for the Rebirth of Ukraine (ODWU)

The political group experiencing the greatest growth during the late 1930s was the Ukrainian Nationalists. Despite a relatively late organizational start, by 1939 Nationalists were the largest Ukrainian political faction in the anti-Communist camp and in firm control of the largest Ukrainian fraternal organization, the UNA.

The rise of Ukrainian Nationalism in America began in 1928 with the arrival of Col. Ievhen Konovalets, former commander of the Sichovi Striltsi and head of the Ukrainian Military Organization (UVO). His trip, arranged largely through the efforts of Dr. Luka Myshuha, had a twofold purpose: to acquaint Konovalets with the Ukrainian-American community and to create a fund-raising vehicle for UVO activities in Western Ukraine. Konovalets succeeded on both counts. He traveled throughout Ukrainian America and before his departure UVO branches were established in New York State – Astoria, Amsterdam, Troy, Cohoes – as well as in Chicago, Hamtramck (Detroit), and Hartford.

In 1929, soon after UVO had been transformed into the Organization of Ukrainian Nationalists (OUN), Konovalets returned to the United States for the purpose of creating a Ukrainian Nationalist organization with a broader community appeal than the UVO branches he had helped establish earlier. It was during his second visit that the idea for the formation of a new Nationalist association, the Organization for the Rebirth of Ukraine (ODWU), was born.[102] According to its New York State Certificate of Incorporation, the purpose of the organization was to:

- Associate Ukrainians for the purpose of instilling in them principles of racial solidarity, discipline, loyalty, and the love of national ideals;
- Cultivate self-respect, self-reliance and independence of thought and action;
- Encourage thrift and industry among members;
- School Ukrainians in the principles of American democracy and

its institutions and to compel observance of its laws and
constitution;

• Hold real and personal property necessary for the furtherance of
the above objectives and to maintain its branches in any state of
the United States and in any foreign country.[103]

A popular and charismatic leader, Konovalets was able to win the confidence of a number of Ukrainian community leaders as well as many former Sich members who had become disillusioned with the political direction of the Hetman organization.[104] Despised by the monarchists for his role in the overthrow of Skoropadsky, Konovalets was promptly labeled a "perpetual revolutionary" by the UHO press.[105]

The growth of ODWU on a national scale began in 1930 with the arrival of Omelian Senyk (a.k.a. Omelian Grabauskas [Hribiwsky in Ukrainian]), an OUN member who remained in the United States until 1932. An excellent organizer,[106] Senyk-Hribiwsky spent time in a number of Ukrainian communities, helped establish thirty-five ODWU branches, and, in retrospect, proved to be the man most responsible for the highly successful organizational beginning of the Ukrainian Nationalist movement in America.[107]

The first convention of ODWU[108] was held on 26–27 June 1931 in New York City, with delegates representing fourteen ODWU branches in attendance.[109] Accepting the UVO reorganization – OUN in Europe and ODWU in America – the convention also adopted the revolutionary ideology of OUN and elected Gregory Herman the first national president.

The second ODWU convention was held in New York City on 25 and 26 June 1932. In response to requests from other organizations in the nationalist camp, a decision was reached to consolidate those elements of the Ukrainian-American community sympathetic to OUN into one Nationalist Front. Present at the convention was E. Draginda, Supreme Otaman of the nonmonarchist Chornomorska Sich, who officially declared his organization's willingness to cooperate with ODWU in the consolidation effort. A similar declaration was made on behalf of the Ukrainian Veteran's Organization by Dr. Walter Gallan at the third ODWU convention in 1933.[110]

Two other Nationalist organizations came into being in the early 1930s – the Ukrainian Red Cross in 1931 (its name was later changed to the Ukrainian Gold Cross)[111] and the Young Ukrainian Nationalists (in Ukrainian, Molodi ukrainski natsionalisty or MUN), established in 1933.[112] Created under ODWU's initiative, both eventually became autonomous affiliates within the ODWU organizational structure.*

---

* The historical development of MUN, Gold Cross, and the Sich youth and women's companies is discussed in chapters 9 and 10.

By the fourth convention in 1934, there were fifty branches of ODWU in existence.[113] Still lacking, however, was a truly effective Nationalist press. While *Svoboda* gladly printed ODWU news releases, the organization's only official publication until 1935 was *Vistnyk ODVU* (ODWU News), an intraorganizational newsletter that began its existence in a mimeographed format and only later, after being published in letterpress print form, began to assume the character of a party organ.[114]

The first All-American Congress of Ukrainian Nationalists took place on 31 August–1 September 1935 in New York City, with 223 delegates representing ODWU, MUN, the Ukrainian Red Cross, the Chornomorska Sich, the Ukrainian Veteran's Organization, and a number of UNA branches in attendance. Greeting the congress on behalf of OUN was Gen. Mykola Kapustiansky, who urged the delegates to set aside any organizational differences that might exist and to consolidate their strength into one mighty, revolutionary Ukrainian Nationalist Front.[115] Reflecting the militant stance of OUN in Europe, the delegates resolved that:

1 The Ukrainian Nation, on its own native soil, is presently experiencing horrible terror at the hands of its occupiers and is denied the right to freely and openly present its true national-political objectives and ideals before international political leaders of the world.

2 For that reason, this congress of representatives of the Ukrainian immigration and the Ukrainian Nationalist movement in general, raises its voice before the entire world for the purpose of expressing the unfalsified will and the true national-political posture of the Ukrainian Nation on its native soil as well as in the immigration.

3 The Congress, therefore, wishes to announce to the entire political world that:

a) On the basis of its historical right and in complete agreement with the principles of President Wilson concerning the right of all peoples to self-determination, the Ukrainian Nation proclaimed and is still proclaiming its active will for the realization of an independent and sovereign state on its own ethnographic territory.

b) In opposition to the above-mentioned rights and principles, the territory of the Ukrainian people and their state, renewed in the years 1917–1920, was forcibly partitioned by various international treaties concluded by the Russian state, now known as the USSR, Poland, Romania, and Czechoslovakia.

c) The Ukrainian Nation considers all these international treaties acts of illegal force, does not recognize them as obligating in any way, and will use all avenues available to it to render them void, while, at the same time, striving to rid Ukraine of all foreign occupation in order to establish an Independent, Sovereign, Ukrainian State.

d) Only that Sovereign Ukrainian state of the Ukrainian People will be competent to conclude legitimate treaties with other states of the world and to accept the responsibility for their approval by the Ukrainian People.

e) As long as the Ukrainian Nation, consisting of forty-five million people, exists in a condition of foreign slavery, there can be no talk of a permanent peace in Europe, and the responsibility for all possible interference with peace in that area falls on those political forces which, in opposition to the will of the Ukrainian People, quartered their land in the past, and which today do not protest this state of affairs.

f) The Congress calls upon the people and the leadership of American and European countries for their objective opinion and their support of the Ukrainian Nation and its struggle for the realization of its national rights and with that, to come closer to the complete and total settlement of the Ukrainian question in a way that will improve the present international, political atmosphere.

After appealing to the political leaders of the world, the congress turned its attention to the Ukrainian people, articulating resolutions that addressed the need for a united Nationalist Front, the manner in which this Front was to be organized, and, significantly, the relationship between Nationalism and Christianity:

> The principles and dogma of the Christian Churches do not in any way interfere with the principles and thrust of active nationalism ... Ukrainian Nationalism stands on the principles of Christianity. Furthermore, the Congress emphasizes that every Ukrainian Church has a national and a moral obligation to support the Ukrainian Nation in its struggle for life, just as it has traditionally been in our history and is now the case for all Christian nations. Having stressed its support of religious education and the great significance of a National Church ... Nationalism does not approve of those representatives of the Church who take advantage of their position to promote ideas and organizations which have nothing to do with the church and religion and,

> with their influence and activity, are leading the Ukrainian people
> to national suicide.

The latter resolution was obvious reference to those religious leaders,
mostly Catholics, who, while not openly supporting the monarchists,
tended to lean in their direction. Recognizing OUN as "the only true
beacon in Ukraine's struggle for independence,"[116] the congress concluded
its deliberations with a political rally in Carnegie Hall, where, in the presence of some 2,500 delegates and guests, prominent OUN, ODWU, UNA,
and other organizational leaders pledged their support of the newly
created Nationalist Front.[117]

Encouraged by the success of the first Nationalist Congress and the
periodic visits of such leading OUN members as Konovalets, Senyk-Hribiwsky, Kapustiansky, Gen. Viktor Kurmanovych, Col. Roman Sushko, Iaroslav Baranovsky, and Oleksandr Kandyba, ODWU continued to increase
its organizational influence and prestige in the Ukrainian-American community. On 20 June 1935, ODWU began to publish *Natsionalist* (Nationalist),
a weekly newspaper edited for most of its existence by Walter Dushnyck.[118]

Approximately 200 delegates attended the sixth ODWU convention in
1936. Dr. Alexander Granovsky, a professor at the University of Minnesota,[119] was elected president, replacing Gregory Herman who remained
on the board as honorary president. By then, however, the rapid rise of
ODWU had come to the attention of the Ukrainian Communists who, in
keeping with ideals promulgated by the pro-Soviet Ukrainian National
Front, began labeling the nationalists "fascists." Responding to the charge,
the convention passed a resolution condemning the "unconscionable identification" of Ukrainian nationalists "under the rubric of fascism."[120]

ODWU's growing community influence soon extended beyond the
Nationalist organizational framework. At the nineteenth convention of the
Ukrainian National Association in 1937, delegates representing more than
30,000 UNA members elected eleven ODWU and Red Cross members to
the twenty-two-seat UNA Supreme Assembly. Those elected included the
president (Nicholas Muraszko), two vice-presidents (Gregory Herman and
Maria Malievych), two auditors (Stephen Kuropas and Roman Smook),
and six advisers (Taras Shpikula, Nicholas Davyskyba, Illia Hussar, Stephen
Slobodian, Onufrii Zapotochny, and Volodymyr Didyk).[121] By 1938, the
ODWU organizational network – which, according to Volodymyr Riznyk,
ODWU national secretary at the time, included seventy ODWU branches,
seventy Red Cross branches, and forty-one branches of MUN – had a total
American membership in excess of 10,000.[122]

As a vehicle of Ukrainian ethnonational and sociopolitical education,

ODWU, like its Communist and Hetman counterparts, was concerned with influencing the thinking of the broad Ukrainian-American community. Although few formal classes were created for this purpose, ODWU organizers did travel to various communities and presented ideological lectures at ODWU meetings and ODWU-sponsored rallies to which the local Ukrainian community was invited. During the summer, ODWU and its affiliates sponsored "Nationalist Day" picnics in larger Ukrainian-American communities where patriotic speeches were delivered and where a variety of social activities – dances, baseball games, airplane rides – were provided for the general public. Communities in close proximity to each other generally hired buses or trucks and attended each others' picnics.

Not to be outdone by the Hetman Sich, ODWU also made a serious attempt to organize an "army" and an "air corps," ODWU uniforms – patterned after the famed Sichovi Striltsi – were designed and purchased, and army surplus rifles were obtained for the fledgling force. From 1934 through 1938, maneuvers were held on an annual basis in Cleveland, Ohio, under the leadership of Theodore Swystun, a United States army veteran, and Ivan Popovych, a veteran of the Ukrainian army. ODWU members from the East and the Midwest traveled to the centrally located city to take part in the military exercises.[123]

An ODWU Aviation School was established by Mykola Novak and Eugene Skotsko in May 1934, to teach gliding and flying to the younger generation. "There has been much discussion about the preparation of a liberation army in America," wrote *Vistnyk ODVU*. "If we're serious, we must have aviators."[124] Later, ODWU purchased a biplane – appropriately named *Natsionalist* – and expanded the flying program to other cities.[125]

Finally, ODWU organized its own Ukrainian press service in New York City. Administered by Eugene Skotsko, the office provided releases for the American and Ukrainian press and served as a clearing house for Ukrainian bulletins from abroad.[126]

The major educational vehicle, however, was the ODWU press, which published *Vistnyk ODVU* from October 1932 to 20 May 1935, the *Natsionalist* from 20 June 1935 to 5 July 1939, *Ukraine* from 12 June 1939 to 15 January 1941, and *The Trident*, an English-language journal initially published by MUN. With the exception of *Vistnyk ODVU*, which contained only occasional English-language articles and announcements, all ODWU publications had a regular English-language supplement beginning in 1935.

Despite its allegiance to the authoritarian Provid of OUN, ODWU maintained a democratic organizational character. Local and national officers were elected and all meetings were conducted according to parliamentary procedures. In polemic arguments with their rivals, the Hetmantsi, ODWU members consistently emphasized this aspect of their organizational frame-

work as well as their support of a republican form of government in
Ukraine.[127]

The ODWU Ideology

Ideologically, however, ODWU was wedded to the OUN platform of revolutionary action and ethnonational transformation. "Nationalism," wrote
Eugene Lachowitch in a 1932 issue of *Vistnyk ODVU,* "is that spiritual
attitude and inner will, desire, and readiness to do battle in every place, at
any time, with every means at our disposal, with the occupants of our
lands for as long as it takes for us to establish our sovereign, independent
Ukrainian state." Once the state is established, argued Lachowitch, "circumstances" will dictate its future structure. Perhaps it "will be a democratic state or perhaps it will be necessary to temporarily institute a
dictatorship," but "all social reforms will be determined by the needs of
the people and the moment."

OUN's role, Lachowitch explained, was to fight for Ukraine construc-
tively "by strengthening our social institutions so that they continue to
maintain their separate national character and resist assimilation," and
"destructively" with "revolutionary work which reinforces the militancy
of the masses and encourages them to oppose the regime"; and with
"terrorism which on one hand reminds the world that Ukraine is not
reconciled to bondage, and on the other, undermines the authority of the
occupants so that our people's faith in their eventual victory is
sustained."[128]

Concerned that the Ukrainian-American community was languishing in
the throes of self-doubt, Nationalists tackled the problem head-on. "We
must stop behaving like serfs," wrote Eugene Skotsko in 1933. "We
approach others not like people who want a nation but like people who
have lost a nation." Skotsko wrote that Ukrainians often complained of a
lack of respect as a result of not having a nation. "But the Jews don't have
a nation and they are respected," Skotsko pointed out. Believing that the
Ukrainians' main problem was within themselves, Skotsko reminded his
readers "that just as a man who loses his house doesn't stop being a man
so a people who have lost their state don't stop being a people."[129] We
needed something to shake us out of national lethargy, wrote *Vistnyk
ODVU* in 1934, and this "national stimulus," this "shock," is being provided
by Ukrainian Nationalism.[130]

The inability of Ukrainians to unite among themselves could also be
solved by Nationalism. Differences among Ukrainians, argued *Vistnyk
ODVU* in 1935, are the result of centuries of regional division. Had Ukrainians succeeded in establishing a permanent nation-state, "the spiritual and

intellectual change required" to establish ethnonational unity would have occurred through "a process of natural evolution." Today, Ukrainians can no longer depend upon evolution, however, especially when their nation is divided again and "the process has been slowed by mass persecution and national oppression ... It is the task of Nationalism to rid the Ukrainian people of their fraternal prejudice and petty differences ... natural evolution must be revolutionized."[131]

Rejecting the criticism that Nationalism had a foreign origin, *Vistnyk ODVU* claimed its ideology was "Ukrainian by origin and characteristics" because:

> Nationalism accepts the value of material elements in the universe but does not recognize materialism as the basic criterion for the individual's existence ...
>
> Nationalism argues that the individual is not as important as the nation ...
>
> Nationalism believes in building industry but does not advocate technocracy ...
>
> Nationalism advocates cooperation between capital and labor, but is opposed to one or the other if they work independently of each other or cause discord ...
>
> Nationalism works towards the economic betterment of the entire nation and is against fabulous wealth for particular groups of people ...
>
> Nationalism does not interfere with any phase of tradition ... it also accepts all that is new and constructive ...
>
> Nationalism has as its aim the development of character within the individual ... Only that person who is able to faithfully perform his duties towards his nation will be recognized as Ukrainian ...
>
> Nationalism is the only idea which can save the Ukrainian nation from the suppression and disgrace which it is now suffering.

Ukraine's tragic past and her present circumstances make it "imperative that we gain our freedom with a strong, influential, unifying power which no force under the sun can impede." The Ukrainian people "have been kicked around" for too long.[132]

Like the monarchists, Nationalists believed Ukraine was overrun because the Ukrainian people had been too individualistic and had established a "democracy" which bordered on anarchy. Democracy, they argued, fostered national indifference, something Ukrainians could ill afford. Addressing Ukrainians in America in 1933, Eugene Onatsky described the "individualism" of democracy, which views society as "a purely mechanical or atomistic aggregate" rather than a whole greater than the sum of its parts. "The country of the most merciless individualism," he wrote, "(that is, of both liberalism and so-called democracy) has of late decades become the United States of America where the dominant idea has become the vulgar slogan 'mind your own business.'" Everyone in America is restricted to a specific area of expertise, concluded Onatsky. "Proper people engage in commerce ... that is their 'business' and politics is left to the politicians whose 'business' it is to get votes in return for favors rendered." The same is true of "capitalists who exploit the masses and tell them to 'mind their own business.'"[133]

The ODWU Approach

The close organizational ties which existed between ODWU and OUN were underscored in the ODWU membership pledge, which every new member was initially required to sign. "I promise to do my duty," the pledge began, "towards Ukraine according to the principles of the Organization of Ukrainian Nationalists and to obey orders from the Organization for the Rebirth of Ukraine which represents OUN in America."[134] It is up to us, wrote the ODWU executive in 1934, "to support our maternal organization OUN" with "action, enthusiasm, energy, and a sincere Ukrainian heart ... Then we will be certain that our brother revolutionaries will not bend before the enemy, will not lose their will, and will not cease for a moment the revolutionary struggle until we achieve our ideal – A FREE AND SOVEREIGN UKRAINIAN STATE!"[135] On the eve of the fourth ODWU convention in 1934, President Gregory Herman reminded the membership of their obligation to:

> Cultivate love for our people and faith in our struggle against our enemies ...
> Promulgate the idea that the one vehicle ... of the Ukrainian liberation struggle is OUN ...
> Develop active members who will be able to survive the darkest moments and frustrations and who will not break under attacks from national opponents here, and foreign enemies abroad ...
> Organize youth sections of MUN ...
> Work among Ukrainians so that all members of our scattered and fractured community in America can unite around one cause — the liberation of Ukraine ...
> Begin a new revitalization campaign within ODWU to raise funds for the liberation struggle in Europe.[136]

To instill pride in OUN, ODWU publications placed great emphasis on the leadership of Ievhen Konovalets[137] ("our beloved Ukrainian *Vozhd*"), the martyrdom of Bilas and Danylyshyn ("they were killed because they honestly, faithfully, and fairly fought for the holy ideal of the Ukrainian people"),[138] and Olha Bassarab ("her legacy is written in blood")[139] as well as the exploits of individual heroes of the resistance. Long articles on the lives[140] and arrest and trial[141] of Stepan Bandera, Mykola Lebed, and the other OUN members implicated in the assassination of Polish Interior Minister Bronislaw Pieracki for his role in the pacification were carried by *Natsionalist* in 1935 and 1936. The leadership of OUN, wrote *Natsionalist* in 1936, "does not instigate the Ukrainian masses against the respective oppressive regimes ... because the revolutionary spirit is developing within the masses themselves." OUN is creating a new type of Ukrainian and ameliorating the "heavy scars" that the environment and influences of four different invaders have made "upon our national character" and our ability to "unite into a homogeneous, cohesive nation."[142] To insure allegiance to the ideology of OUN, other Ukrainian political platforms were critically described and dismissed in a series of polemic articles by Mykola Sciborsky,[143] Eugene Lachowitch,[144] and Roman Sushko.[145] Hetman Skoropadsky was consistently portrayed as a Russophile[146] who favored federation with Russia.[147]

For ODWU, as for OUN, the motto was: *the nation above all else.* "The liberation of Ukraine," Sciborsky reminded ODWU members in 1934, "will never be accomplished by anyone except Ukrainians."[148] Establishing a Ukrainian state will require the creation of a disciplined cadre of Ukrainian Americans willing to follow orders. In order to make ODWU the "kind of organization of which we can all be proud" and "to which it will be an honor to belong," an ODWU membership circular (*obizhnyk*) urged the introduction "of *absolute discipline* in ODWU branches ... We realize we cannot expect military discipline from Ukrainian immigrants ... but surely we can achieve more discipline than exists in other immigrant organizations."[149] OUN "has grafted the idea of Ukrainian nationalism in America," wrote *Vistnyk ODVU* in 1934, "so that our present immigration can be revitalized with new life in order that it may assist in the revolutionary process which will lead to the rebirth of the Ukrainian nation and the rebuilding of the Ukrainian state ... we are not looking for just anybody to join ODWU. We need disciplined members who are committed, free souls of Ukraine, not serfs."[150] Ukrainians are too "individualistic," wrote Skotsko a few months later. "Every Ukrainian wants to be an 'otaman' and have everything done the way *he* says." Everyone wants to be "wise" and to give orders; no one wants to be the "dumb doer." We in America must remember that in the fulfillment of our revolutionary obligations, there must be order and discipline."[151] ODWU "is not a fraternal benefit society," concluded *Natsionalist* in 1936. "A Nationalist must be active ... prepared for great sacrifices ... and his organization must maintain moral discipline."[152]

Given their ideological fervor, members of ODWU were disparaging of those who could not immediately appreciate the value of Nationalism as a vehicle of ethnonational revival. Other nations, they argued, had been humiliated by the war and other nations had once been dominated by socialists. Nationalism had given their people new hope. Ukrainians who cannot support Nationalism "are stubborn as donkeys," wrote one ODWU member in 1934. They like "to bow before their enemies, to cringe and to plead for amnesty and autonomy and in their serfdom are incapable of taking a courageous stand ... even at a time when in other races their nationalism – as for instance fascism and Hitlerism – is crowned with success."[153] "Italian and German Fascism have destroyed socialism," wrote another ODWU member that same year, and have enabled "spiritually depressed peoples to feel good about themselves again[154] ... Socialists were not able to rescue their nations from economic ruination and were forced to leave the European stage as failures."[155]

While the power of nationalism in achieving ethnonational cohesion and rehabilitation in Italy and Germany was to be lauded, ODWU members argued, future cooperation with the leadership of these nations was still dependent upon what was best for Ukraine. "Conflict between Russia and Germany or Japan and Russia is desirable," wrote Lachowitch in 1936, "because it will force consideration of the Ukrainian question ... Our aim is to play power against power."[156] An editorial entitled "A New Enemy" in the same issue of *Natsionalist*, however, reminded its readers that the last time Germany helped Ukraine, a dictatorship was established. "How far will Germany go if Ukrainian Nationalists make another bid for freedom and call in Hitler's troops? Will they merely replace Stalin with Hitler, Communism with fascism, Russian oppression with German oppression?"[157] Arguing that there is "a contest among three imperialisms – Polish, German, Russian" – for the Ukrainian nation, *Natsionalist* concluded that "only a strong Ukraine can play any part in this contest, retaining, at the same time, her independence."[158] Hitler's outspoken designs on Ukraine's fertile soil has put Ukraine in the news again, *Natsionalist* wrote in the fall of 1936. "Ukrainians must not have any illusions," warned the ODWU gazette, "as to Hitler's objective having any connection with Ukraine's aspirations to sovereignty."[159]

Like the monarchists, Ukrainian Nationalists in America saw no conflict between love of Ukraine and loyalty to America. "We must remember," *Natsionalist* wrote in 1936, "that no country surpasses America's achievements or her place of honor in the world ... we must look upon the constitution as a sacred legacy." America threw out the British "so we American citizens should throw off the strangling hold of Communism."[160] "Nationalism is love of country and a willingness to sacrifice for her ... A person brought up in Ukrainian Nationalism will make a 100 percent better American citizen than one who was not taught any nationalism at all." ODWU has an obligation to protect America "from subversive elements."[161]

The Socialist Revival

Ukrainian socialists, meanwhile, were experiencing an organizational renaissance of their own. In the forefront of the revival were two organizations: Oborona Ukrainy (Defense of Ukraine) and the Ukrainian Workingmen's Association (UWA) which operated out of a national office located in Scranton, Pennsylvania. Ideologically, the two organizations were aligned with the Ukrainian Socialist Radical Party (USRP) in Galicia, and were opposed to both the Communists and the Nationalists. Despite their commitment to an independent Ukrainian state, however, both organizations preferred to work outside of the UUOA nationalistic framework.

Headquartered in Scranton from 1931 to 1941 and in Rochester, New York, thereafter, Defense of Ukraine had a national network of sixteen chapters and some 500 members by 1942. It published *Ukrainska Hromada* (Ukrainian Commonwealth), a weekly periodical, from 1923 to 1932, and a monthly, *Hromadsky Holos* (Voice of the Community), from 1936 to 1941. In 1939, Defense joined with other socialist organizations to form the Ukrainska natsionalna rada (Ukrainian National Council), a coalition that described itself as "progressive and democratic." The secretariat included N. Hryhoriv, V. Levytsky, and of course, Miroslaw Sichynsky.

A far more powerful organization in the socialist camp was the UWA, headed by Sichynsky from 1933 to 1941. Its organ, *Narodna Volya*, was edited by Yaroslav Chyz, an extraordinarily capable former member of the Sichovi Striltsi and UVO, who later became an avowed socialist. He was assisted by Volodymyr Levytsky,[162] who was also UWA vice-president.

For Ukrainian socialists, OUN and ODWU were anathema. As early as 1934, Andrij Hrivnak, a Ukrainian socialist member of the Polish Seim, visited Ukrainian communities in the United States and suggested that OUN was working in Germany's interests. In response, he was physically attacked by a group of Nationalists in Passaic, New Jersey.[163] The charge was later repeated by other socialists – primarily Volodymyr Kedrovsky, Arnold Margolin, and Yaroslav Chyz[164] – as well as in the pages of *Narodna Volya*. Accusing the Nationalists of borrowing their ideas "from current dictatorships,"[165] *Narodna Volya* condemned the OUN Provid for its willingness "to find allies anywhere, even in Hitler's Germany."[166] When *Svoboda* disagreed with the UWA organ, it was accused of engaging in "fascist agitation."[167] *Narodna Volya* advised Ukrainians not to take any sides in the event of war, "either for or against Russia but to look out for their own interests as working people.[168] Exchanging Moscow for Berlin would hardly be a fair exchange."[169] Despite its antipathy toward the Nationalists, however, the socialist stream was committed to the unification of Ukrainian lands in an independent Ukrainian state.

The Ukrainian Communist camp, of course, was even more pointed in its assault on the Nationalists. In 1935, *Visti,* the Ukrainian Communist daily, labeled ODWU "a Ukrainian fascist organization" and accused it of raising money "not for national liberation" but for "a terrorist campaign against the working movement in America."[170]

ODWU Prevails (1937–9)

Harassed by attacks from the Ukrainian-American left, ODWU responded quickly and unequivocally. "We have stated many times that we are not fascists nor do we support any kind of dictatorships," replied *Natsionalist* in 1937. American nationalism was responsible for the War of Independence, the war of 1812, and for sustaining Abraham Lincoln in America's loneliest hour, argued the ODWU periodical. "Was it 'naziism' or 'fascism' that guided Washington, Lincoln," and other American statesmen "who made the United States a world power? Or was it – American nationalism?"[171]

Responding to a *Narodna Volya* article by a young Ukrainian-American activist in which it was suggested that ODWU's fascination with fascism placed the organization outside the American democratic mainstream, MUN member Walter Bukata wrote:

> This writer conceives of a Ukrainian Nationalist as one comparable to those "rebels" in America who fought against oppression by a mother country. Our Nationalists rebel against oppression not of a mother country but of the traditional enemies of Ukraine. They do not wait for Hitler or Mussolini to guide them ...
>
> The Ukrainian Nationalist is intolerant of a quasi-intellectual, sentimental, pseudo-idealistic abhorrence of force when such is proven in fact to be the last resort, where all other means have been exhausted ... He is intolerant of those who would solve the problems of subjugated Ukraine by the radically different standards of life in free, rich and powerful America ... Above all, the Ukrainian Nationalist believes that to become free, Ukraine must be ready for freedom – her people must be bound with a com-

mon purpose and dedicated to a holy mission ... those furthering
dissension at a time like the present are virtual traitors to the
Ukrainian cause."[172]

Hitler's bogus rhetoric regarding Ukrainian self-determination –
"Ukraine was robbed of its recovered statehood," the Nazi party organ
Volkischer Beobachter announced in 1937, "and divided among four peoples" – soon came to the attention of the *New York Times* and other American periodicals, which suggested that the Ukrainian question was a
German provocation.[173] Commenting on the renewed interest in Ukraine,
Natsionalist rejected the assumption of the American press that Hitler's
invasion would inevitably succeed. "Everyone seems to be concerned about
it here," observed the ODWU organ, but "how do Ukrainians react to such
a proposal? Will Hitler be welcome? Will oppressed peasants side with
Stalin? Or will they rise, unite and rebel against both Hitler and Stalin
and demonstrate to the world that Ukraine is for Ukrainians!"[174] Treating
Ukraine as "a German problem," concluded *Natsionalist*, "is an insult to
the Ukrainian people."[175]

The Russian-American community was also apprehensive about Hitler's
plans for Ukraine. In 1938, the Russian periodical *Novoe Russkoe Slovo* cited
an article from *Nash Stiah* in which the Hetmanite organ condemned an
article by Dr. K. Haushofer in *Geopolitik,* a German journal, which argued
that Hetman Skoropadsky had little support in the United States and that
ODWU was the more powerful organization. "*Geopolitik* wrote the truth
about Ukrainians in the United States," responded *Natsionalist,* adding that
the Russians were angry because they believed the UHO allegation that
"ODWU is closely related to German and Italian fascism."[176]

Despite growing charges of fascist affiliation from the Russian and Ukrainian communist, socialist, and monarchist press, ODWU persisted in its
mission to maintain a united Nationalist Front in the United States. Speaking at an ODWU-sponsored meeting in New York City, president Granovsky reminded his audience that the laws of nature were irrevocable. That
which has been imposed by force over something "natural" cannot long
endure. Sooner or later, that which is natural will overcome that which is
"artificial" and "unnatural." The same laws can be applied to people and
their nations, declared Granovsky in describing the Versailles treaties. "We
see with our eyes how the spirit of the people has conquered in Germany.
The victors artificially create new nations and artificially destroy the natural
ones, but all the efforts of the enemies fail." Faith in the Ukrainian's
natural strength must be maintained, Granovsky concluded. "Don't believe
defeatists who say we are divided and have nothing. We are strong. One-
third of the Polish army is Ukrainian and the best military units in Russia

are also Ukrainian. People over there are just waiting for that big day ...
Force must be met by force ... nothing will stop the march of the Ukrainian
Nationalist movement ... We must at every step give aid and confidence to
the Provid of OUN and to Colonel Konovalets who has labored unselfishly
for over twenty years."[177]

On 4 September 1938, an estimated 5,000 participants and guests attending the second Nationalist Congress jammed the Hippodrome in New York
City for a manifestation of mass solidarity. Standing before a huge portrait
of the recently martyred Konovalets,[178] General Kurmanovych declared,
"Ukrainians believe in their own strength and must rely on their own
resources." "Ukraine is being reborn," cried Iaroslav Baranovsky. "It is
waging a battle against great odds and under constant threat ..." Roman
Sushko exhorted the crowd to remember their fallen heroes – "Petliura,
Bassarab, Bilas, Danylyshyn, Konovalets." "The Ukrainian people," concluded Granovsky, enunciating every word, "will *never* rest until THEY
HAVE OBTAINED THEIR INDEPENDENCE." At that he raised his right hand and
exclaimed "SLAVA UKRAINI" (Glory to Ukraine).[179] "Remember this, you
Ukrainian youth who are thrown into doubt by the tremendous out-
pouring of propaganda on all sides," wrote *Natsionalist* following the congress: "We Nationalists are American citizens; we believe in Americanism
and those great traditions which were achieved by constant struggle
against unbelievable odds just as our people are now struggling; we are
spreading no foreign dogma in the United States; rather we are promoting
love for American ideals in constant agitation for the rebirth of the land of
our fathers."[180]

Resolutions passed by the congress reaffirmed support for the Nationalist
platform, declaring that "the highest ethical value which determines a
person is his national identity ... The nation is the highest spiritual
organism ... Religion is the basis of individual and family morals which in
turn are the foundation of national strength ... Ukrainian culture must
cultivate Nationalistic heroism ... The strongest force of a nation is an
ideologically indoctrinated national army of ethnonationally educated
citizens ... The only proper method to construct the political system of the
Ukrainian nation is upon the principles of authoritarianism and leadership
which rest upon the principles of creativity, character, will, and the responsibility of the individual."

Condemning the "opportunism" of Skoropadsky and UNDO as well as
the imperialism of the USSR, Poland, and Romania, the congress resolved
to work on behalf of Carpatho-Ukrainian independence and declared:
"Only Ukrainians can liberate Ukraine but Ukrainians will work with
anyone who wishes to destroy Russian imperialism, White or Red."[181]
Significantly, the congress also honored a request from *Natsionalist* editor

Walter Dushnyck to pass a resolution affirming its commitment to a Ukrainian state "for Ukrainians alone instead of a rich territory exploited by and benefiting only foreign nations."[182]

As might be expected, the Ukrainian Communist press branded the congress a "fascist manifestation." "Kurmanovych, Baranovsky, Shushko. Who are they?" asked *Visti*. "Who sent them here? Who paid their way? ... For what purpose? ... And what was the most characteristic feature of this fascist gathering? ... the Hitlerite salute!"[183] The Nazi salute allegation was repeated by *Narodna Volya* the following year.[184] For enemies of ODWU, Dr. Granovsky's exuberant hand-raising during his salute to Ukraine was a clear demonstration of Nazi ties.

The Carpatho-Ukraine Debacle

A high point for delegates and guests attending the second Nationalist Congress was their euphoria regarding developments in Carpatho-Ukraine. Resolutions were adopted welcoming "the idea to create a Ukrainian nation in Subcarpathian Ruthenia which will, at the proper time, unite with the Ukrainian state" and warning that "any effort to unite Subcarpathian Ruthenia with any of her neighbors will meet with fierce opposition from all Ukrainians." In keeping with these ambitious ideals, the congress sent telegrams to the governments of England, France, Italy, and Germany, accusing Czechoslovakia of "crushing Ukrainian cultural life."[185] Explaining the temporary nature of the proposed mini-state, *Natsionalist* wrote: "In place of today's Czechoslovakia, there will be created three independent states – Czechia, Slovakia, and Carpatho-Ukraine. This is not a fantastic idea – if Luxembourg, Andora, and Liechtenstein can exist, and for a substantial period of time, then why can't there be a Carpatho-Ukrainian state – for a short time, at least, until it is united with Kiev!"[186]

Soon after its convention ended, ODWU began organizing political rallies throughout the United States in an effort to gain Carpatho-Ruthenian support and to mobilize popular American opinion in favor of Carpatho-Ukrainian independence. In October 1938, ODWU helped establish the Committee for the Defense of Carpatho-Ukraine. Headed by Father Omelian Nevitsky, the bipartisan committee was to be composed only of Americans who could trace their ethnographic roots to Carpatho-Ukraine. The committee sponsored a New York rally on 9 October repeating the desire of Nationalists for an independent state in Carpatho-Ukraine.[187]

The Munich Pact concluded by Germany, Italy, France, and England on 29 September 1938 gave Nationalists renewed hope that a Carpatho-Ukrainian state would soon be realized. In the words of one Ukrainian-American Nationalist writing in 1939: "To Ukrainians, the Munich Pact was indirectly the first act of international justice which they had obtained since the World War. It destroyed one of the four oppressors, forced the creation of a government friendly toward Ukrainian aspirations, and paved the way for the rise of Carpatho-Ukraine."[188]

In the months that followed, political developments in Carpatho-Ukraine moved at a pace that made it increasingly difficult for the Ukrainian-American Nationalist community to respond. Hardly had the new government established itself when, on 2 November, the Vienna Arbitration Committee awarded the cities of Uzhhorod and Mukachevo to Hungary, forcing the transfer of the Ukrainian capital to Khust. All that ODWU and the Defense Committee could do in the wake of these reversals was to send telegrams of protest to Washington, London, Berlin, and Rome. Carpatho-Ukrainian President Augustin Voloshyn, meanwhile, still determined to save the young republic at all costs, appealed to the Ukrainian-American community in a cablegram sent to ODWU, the UNA, and other Ukrainian organizations in the Nationalist camp:

> We, the government of Carpatho-Ukraine, are calling upon you, our brothers across the ocean, to show your solidarity with us in this crucial hour. The loss of Uzhhorod and Mukachevo, while inflicting a deep wound in the flesh of our Fatherland, will not sway us from our firm resolve to carry out this great historic mission. Your assistance to the government of Carpatho-Ukraine will show that you understand the gravity of the hour.

ODWU and its affiliate organizations responded to this request and to the pleas of Dr. Luka Myshuha, who on 19 November – soon after his return from Europe – addressed some 15,000 Ukrainians at a political rally in New York, by initiating a campaign to provide material and financial assistance to Carpatho-Ukraine.[189] The Ukrainian Gold Cross, an ODWU affiliate, gathered, packed, and shipped 63,000 pounds of clothing directly to Father Voloshyn in Khust.[190]

As events in Carpatho-Ukraine rapidly deteriorated, ODWU's executive sent telegrams to Czech President Hacha protesting his appointment of General Prchala, a Czech, to Voloshyn's cabinet,[191] and other telegrams to the governments of Great Britain, France, and the United States vociferously condemning the final Hungarian invasion.[192] *Natsionalist*, meanwhile, kept its readership abreast of developments with news stories and headlines such as HUNGARIANS ATTACK UKRAINE,[193] VOLOSHYN WINS WITH 98.5% OF VOTE TO DIET [SEJM],[194] SICH FIGHTS ON,[195] UKRAINIAN LEADERS EXECUTED BY HUNGARIANS,[196] and HITLER APPROVES HUNGARIAN INVASION.[197] Finally, on 19 April 1939 – a few days after Easter – the ODWU chronicle printed this terse and poignant message from Father Voloshyn: "CHRIST IS RISEN! It was God's will to give the Ukrainian people more experience ... Once again we have lost our freedom ... The Golgotha of the Ukrainian people has not ended."[198]

"If Ukrainians learned anything from the Great Betrayal," *Natsionalist* bitterly complained, "it should be that they can depend on no one, not even self-appointed supporters of their historic fight for independence. Ukrainians now and always must fight for themselves. If in the past there may have been some Ukrainians who were putting their hopes in Germany, from purely politico-opportunistic motives, they are at present undergoing a radical change of mind ... it is only logical to suspect that the ideal of self-determination ... is beginning to have little value for Germany ... it is merely being used by Chancellor Hitler for the promotion of German imperialism."[199] If Germany wins in the future, *Natsionalist* later predicted, the world will not be free, but if Russia wins, "the eventual spread of Communism and chaos could cause the downfall" of the democracies. Ukraine needs the support of the world's democratic nations, but are they interested in Ukrainian aspirations? "Will the democracies fail Ukraine again?"[200]

While ODWU, the UNA, and the UUOA were solidly behind the Nationalist defense of Carpatho-Ukraine, some Scranton-based socialists were not. "Those who are acquainted with the true situation in Carpathian Ukraine," wrote Paul Stachiw in *Narodna Volya*, "know that its inhabitants, isolated from civilization by the Carpathian Mountains, were and are probably the most backward component of the Ukrainian race."[201] Czechoslovakia cannot be blamed for "often working to the disadvantage" of the Carpatho-Ukrainians because "Ukrainians ... constituted a negligible quantity in the Czecho-Slovak republic" and Prague had to do what was best for the majority. That is how democracies function, Stachiw explained, but "though our American-Ukrainian Nazis and their playmates live in a democracy, they are so imbued with the one-party doctrine that to acclimate themselves to the idea of a democracy would be something akin to treason." Carpatho-Ukrainians were getting organized and their voice was being heard in Prague but they were betrayed by the Nationalists who pushed for independence – under German protection – long before the masses were prepared for such a move. In two subsequent issues, Stachiw repeated the socialist allegation that OUN was working for the Nazis.[202]

It is not the Nationalists who have betrayed Carpatho-Ukraine, responded *Natsionalist*. Rather, it is *Narodna Volya* that betrayed all of Ukraine.[203] It appears, wrote the *Ukrainian Weekly*, a UNA periodical, "that it is not enough that enemies of Ukraine attempt to link the Ukrainian Cause and those connected with it with the Nazis. An anonymous Ukrainian, 'Paul Stachiw' has to appear and do likewise, and in the English language too so that non-Ukrainians may read it also."[204] Stachiw replied by accusing the *Weekly* editor of being too closely tied to *Svoboda*, a "sister organ" of *Natsionalist*. "We would not go as far as to say their editors are fascists," observed Stachiw, "though we do have a distinct impression that many of their writings have looked that way." Still, if the *Weekly*, a *Svoboda* "supplement," is "not held captive by those who radiate such ideas," then "why has it been so significantly silent about fascism?" he asked.[205]

The Carpatho-Ruthenian community in America also opposed a Carpatho-Ukrainian republic under Ukrainian domination. *Viestnik* was especially critical of Father Voloshyn and endeavored to show that between October 1938 and March 1939 Ukrainians had conducted a reign of terror in the region.[206]

Far more damaging to nationalist aspirations was the attitude of the American press. "The Nazi's Ukrainian blueprint," wrote *Time* magazine early in 1939, "nominated" Carpatho-Ukraine "as the generating center for a movement to 'liberate' all Ukrainian lands from their present Polish, Rumanian and Russian masters and bring them under the benevolent protection of Fuehrer Hitler." "Ukrainian separatism of the 19th century," *Time* further informed its readers, "was little more than a dream fostered by a few Galician intellectuals ... During the war, it became a German imported article." At Brest-Litovsk, "a Russian delegation signed a humiliating treaty which detached from all the Russias not only Finland and the White Russian provinces of Estonia, Lithuania and Latvia but also the valued Ukraine." Today, concluded *Time*, "few discernible signs of separatist feelings have come from Soviet Ukraine."[207] There may have been problems in the UkrSSR during the early 1930s, wrote the *American Observer*, but now "conditions in Eastern Ukraine are better" and "there is little dissatisfaction."[208] *Look* magazine was even more misinformed, claiming that: "The 33 million Ukrainians in the USSR are neither oppressed nor a minority. They make up 80 percent of the population of the Ukrainian republic and except for matters of broad policy, enjoy self government ... thus far, Berlin's demands for an independent Ukrainian nation have been traced only to White Russian emigres or to Polish and Rumanian Nazis."[209]

Why, *Natsionalist* wondered, was the American press so anxious to constantly remind the world of Hitler's desires for Ukraine? "Such aimless repetitions," the ODWU organ observed, "serve no other purpose whatsoever unless they are deliberately calculated for one thing: to place upon the Ukrainian question the stigma of German inspiration." Such reports only benefit Germany, *Natsionalist* argued. "They are preparing the world for the eventual acceptance of a German Ukraine."[210]

Ukrainian enthusiasm for the Carpatho-Ukrainian Republic has been dampened, complained the *Ukrainian Weekly*, "by the rather cool reception accorded these auspicious developments by a good portion of American public opinion." The reason is not hard to find. It "is based on the wholly erroneous assumption that Germany alone is responsible for these developments; and since her Nazi form of government and her Nazi persecution of Jews have become unpopular here, anything that savors of her handiwork is regarded with distaste." Americans need to be educated about Ukrainian history, concluded the *Weekly*, and to understand "that for the past twenty years the Ukrainian people have been appealing for succor not to Germany but to the leading democracies of the world, especially America."[211]

ODWU Responds

Convinced that American public opinion could be turned around, ODWU took over publication of *The Trident*, an English-language periodical first published by Chicago MUN branches in 1936, and turned over the editorship to Walter Dushnyck, the talented and prolific bilingual editor of *Ukraine*. "How senseless," wrote Dushnyck, "are the attempts of Russia, Poland, and their supporters in Europe and America to attack the Ukrainian liberation movement as an inspiration of Germany." Hitler may be interested in the Ukrainian independence movement because "a free Ukraine would result in economic and commercial gains for Germany ... but is that the fault of the Ukrainian people? Does this give anyone the right to call the Ukrainian independence movement 'a creation of Hitler'?" Rejecting German inspiration as a factor in Ukraine's freedom crusade, Dushnyck concluded his editorial by explaining the reasons behind the overpowering sense of disillusionment, frustration, and anger Ukrainian Americans felt toward the world's democracies:

> Since the Ukrainian Republic fell in 1920, Ukrainians struggled
> ceaselessly to regain their freedom. They knocked at the doors
> of the great democracies, Britain, France, and the United States.
> They appealed to the League of Nations, the International Red
> Cross and to every institution which might be of help in aiding
> the Ukrainians against Russian, Polish and Rumanian tyranny.
> No help was forthcoming ...
> Likewise the United States responded to the appeals of starving
> Ukrainian peasants in Eastern Ukraine under Russia in 1933 by
> recognizing the greatest tyrant of modern times, the Soviet Union.
> This recognition in effect not only rejected the Ukrainian appeals
> for justice but seemed to lend United States sanction to the actions

of Stalin. More than 5,000,000 Ukrainians starved to death in 1932–33. Why didn't the United States, based on equality and justice for all, at least continue its policy of not recognizing Russia if it did not wish to go to the extreme of protesting as it began to do against Japanese and German actions a few years later?

Thus, how can the Ukrainian people feel toward Democracy as represented by the three great powers, Britain, United States and France, which so far have not only failed to aid the Ukrainian independence struggle in any manner whatever, but inadvertently or otherwise have hampered it as much as possible, condemning the nearly 50,000,000 Ukrainians in East Europe to more years of oppression?

... Ukraine wants to be free. In her unequal struggle with several occupants, she looks on all sides for aid. She speaks not only to Berlin and Rome but also to Paris, London and Washington. It is for these last three to decide whether they will aid justice by supporting the demand of Ukrainians for an independent state, or whether they will support the enemies of democracy, the occupants of Ukraine. This is the most dynamic question of our epoch.[212]

The pressures precipitated by the rising chorus of popular antinationalist sentiment in America – consistently reinforced by the unceasing barrage of Popular Front rhetoric that coupled nationalism with fascism – had an adverse effect upon attendees at the ninth ODWU convention in Newark in July 1939. Clearly on the defensive, delegates changed the name of their biweekly periodical from *Natsionalist* to *Ukraina* (Ukraine) and, lest there be any lingering doubt as to their intentions regarding the United States, they passed a series of resolutions under the heading "Our Situation in America":

1 As American citizens of Ukrainian descent, we value the blessings of American freedom and liberty, and we are ready to defend them against any danger. Therefore, because we are educated in the spirit of such great men of America as Washington and Lincoln, we all the more desire those blessings for our brothers, who are suffering the oppressive domination of Soviet Russia, Poland, Rumania and Hungary. Our activities on behalf of oppressed Ukraine in no way contradict the ideal of the American constitution and tradition, but on the contrary, strengthen

them. By closing our eyes to the suffering of our brother Ukrainians, we would prove that we were unworthy of those great American ideals.

2 Therefore, all incrimination on the part of our enemies, often of
Ukrainian descent, that we, the great majority of the Ukrainian
immigration in the United States, devote ourselves to "un-American activities and ideas" is baseless and unfounded and proves
that those who denounce us are themselves unworthy of this
American liberty because they seek to destroy the noble Ukrainian Independence Movement in the name of "Americanism."

Denouncing the monarchists, the "Social Radicals," the "Russian Socialists," and "Stalinist expositors" as groups that "have recorded themselves
in the history of the Ukrainian immigration in the United States as enemies
of the Ukrainian Liberation Movement,' " delegates turned their attention
to foreign affairs, approving resolutions under the broad heading "The
International Situation and Ukraine." Included was the following
statement:

Rapid realignments are now taking place in Europe, and it is
probable that the final struggle will occur on or near Ukrainian
soil. Because Ukrainians will be affected directly or indirectly, and
because they have no state, they try to find assistance in all countries. But the Ukrainian Independence movement is based on no
foreign ideologies or international blocks, and it especially has
nothing in common with the ideologies which now predominate
in Germany and Italy. On the contrary, the Ukrainian Independence movement is a century older than those ideologies and is
based on the vital necessity of the Ukrainian people themselves
for an independent state![213]

Having once again reaffirmed their loyalty to the United States and
clarified their aspirations for Ukraine, the delegates listened quietly as Dr.
Myshuha addressed the convention. "Did Hitler teach us to love Ukraine?"
he asked. "Stand tall," he urged, "Ukrainians have nothing of which to be
ashamed."[214]

For *Narodna Volya*, ODWU's "reaffirmation" was too little too late. Accusing the Nationalists of beating "the drum of Americanism and democracy"
because it was "fashionable," Stachiw labeled ODWU's resolutions a "Magnificent Hoax." When "one peers into nationalist ideology," he wrote,
"whatever there is of it, he will find that it is nothing more than an imitation
of the Fascist and Nazi political, social, and economic conceptions with all
of its antidemocratic venom, and that Nationalists themselves admit that

their movement, supposedly 'original' and 'independent' of other influences, is identified with the Hitler-Mussolini phenomenon." In all his later references to the Nationalists, Stachiw consistently identified them as "Nazionalists."[215]

In June 1939, *The Trident* conjectured about a second world war and the possibility of a German victory, a "solution," noted the ODWU publication, that "would hardly satisfy Ukrainian desires. The entire eastern policy of Hitler (*Mein Kampf*) is based on the conquest of new territories ... we would witness the rise of a series of new 'protectorates' and of a new German empire." A far better solution, as far as *The Trident* was concerned, would be a German victory over Russia followed by a British-French victory over a weakened Germany.[216]

In September, *The Trident* again reviewed Germany's attitude toward Ukraine and concluded that the Vienna Arbitration, German approval of Hungary's occupation of Carpatho-Ukraine, and the recently concluded German-Russian Non-Aggression pact were ample proof that the Ukrainian independence movement was not German-inspired. As for future American participation in the war, *The Trident* editorialized: "So far as the American attitude is concerned, there is no doubt that all Ukrainians are against American intervention for two reasons: (1) they remember what America got out of the last war; (2) no one can persuade them that Poland is a democracy." Ukrainians appeal, *The Trident* concluded, "to every democracy, especially their adopted land, to remember that so long as there is no free Ukrainian state, there can be no peace in Europe."[217]

Commenting on the war between Finland and Russia, *The Trident* argued: "Those who believe that by helping Stalin they may destroy Hitler, or vice-versa, are deluding themselves. Not one or the other, but both must go!"[218] For the United States, soon to become a wartime ally of Stalin, however, *The Trident* was a voice in the wilderness.

The Dies Committee and Its Aftermath

In his testimony before the House Un-American Activities Committee on 27 September 1939, Emil Revyuk revealed little of ODWU's true sentiment regarding Hitler's Germany.[219] Questioned by J.B. Matthews, Revyuk testified that:

1 ODWU was an organization established in 1930 as an American association which supported a revolutionary movement for a reconstructed Ukrainian state.
2 ODWU was associated with OUN.
3 ODWU used the term "Providnyk" (Leader) in referring to the head of the Provid. (At Matthews's urging, Revyuk adopted the term "fuehrer.")

4 The ODWU national executive had received letters from OUN post-marked in Berlin and Vienna.

5 ODWU occasionally sent money to OUN.

6 The editor of *The Trident* and *Ukraine* claimed to have been arrested in Belgium as a German agent.

7 ODWU and the Hetman Sich were "at daggers drawn."

8 The head of the Provid was Colonel Andrew Melnyk who succeeded Colonel Konovalets in 1938.

9 Baranovsky was a member of the Provid and was probably in Germany.

10 Baranovsky was probably a member of the nominating committee at the 1938 ODWU convention.

11 Dr. Alexander Granovsky was the President of ODWU and Volodymyr Riznyk was secretary.

12 ODWU seemed to be leaning toward the reconstruction of the Ukrainian state "on the basis of authoritarianism."

13 Levitsky, an editor of *Narodna Volya*, had warned Revyuk about dealing with OUN "because the organization is in close contact with the War Ministry of Germany."[220]

14 ODWU helped support the Ukrainian Press Bureau in Washington, D.C.

15 A number of Provid members – Konovalets, Kurmanovych, Senyk-Hrybiwsky, Sushko, Kandyba – had come to America from Germany.

16 Senyk-Hrybiwsky had allegedly helped organize a press bureau in New York City over the protest of ODWU. Roman Lapica, the bureau chief, had allegedly issued press releases favorable to Hitler.

17 Dr. Granovsky had attempted to register ODWU as "an agent of a foreign principle" but his request had been denied by the State Department.

18 Revyuk had heard that the "Nazi salute" was used at the Hippodrome rally.[221]

19 OUN had urged ODWU and other Ukrainian organizations to organize demonstrations in favor of an independent Carpatho-Ukraine.[222]

20 Dr. Granovsky had traveled to Czechoslovakia during the Carpatho-Ukrainian crisis.[223]

No mention was made of the fact that the "Nazi salute" allegation first appeared in a Communist newspaper, that Levitsky was the editor of a socialist periodical that openly and regularly criticized the UUOA, ODWU, and the UNA, and that OUN members "came" from Germany because they usually traveled on German ships. Nor was any attempt made to challenge Matthews when he consistently endeavored to have Revyuk translate "authoritarianism" as "totalitarianism" during the testimony. By midmorning, Chairman Dies had made up his mind, however. Summing up Revyuk's testimony, he declared:

> In other words, here are some 50 branches of ODWU in the United States, and they are affiliated with an international organization and the head of it is the *Provid* in Berlin, and they are exchanging information between the groups at different times, reporting as to what is going on in other countries of the world as well as leaders going from the United States. All of this has its fountainhead in Berlin, in Germany, where the *Provid* headquarters are and, naturally, Germany would be getting any information that would come through this source ... That is another way of saying that this whole thing is linked to Nazi Germany. The German Government would not tolerate the existence of this Ukrainian headquarters, however it is, unless the Nazi Government wanted to. In other words, they have complete control over the matter so that there is a strong link there – we do not know how strong – between the Nazi Government and this organization.[224]

Revyuk continued his testimony during the remainder of the morning, adding that:

21 It was possible that some ODWU members worked in airplane factories and munitions plants.
22 Eugene Onatsky, identified by Revyuk as both a member of Provid and a *Svoboda* correspondent residing in Rome, had submitted "letters" to Mussolini with copies to Count Ciano. (The contents of these "letters" were never revealed.)[225]
23 ODWU had its own airplane.
24 ODWU members occasionally wore uniforms.
25 Gregory Herman, former ODWU president, was an officer in the United States Army Reserve.[226]

Also entered into the record were outdated and tendentious quotations from ODWU publications, all of which were taken out of context.* Included were:

* Excerpts appear exactly as they were cited in the Dies Committee report. All were cited in their original context earlier in this chapter.

26 The Onatsky article in the September 1933 issue of *Vistnyk ODVU*
which was presented as follows:

... For democratic individualism the human society is purely a
mechanical or atomistic aggregate; every separate individual is
an atom equal to every other individual, which weighs on the
scales of life and power exactly as much as any other. And that
is why in every democratic-liberal regime they evaluate not the
quality of this or other person, not the value of his psychic traits,
which ought to be universally cultivated and developed ...

The country of the most merciless individualism (that is both
liberalism and the so-called democracy) has of late decades
become the United States of America where the dominant slogan
has become the vulgar slogan "Mind your own business."

Nationalism, which places at the foundation of its activities the
welfare of the entire race, remembers that the condition of the
whole depends upon the conditions of the individuals ... And that
is why, for instance, in Italy with the obtaining of control of the
Italian nationalists (known under the name Fascism), the Italian
nation assumed the name of ethical state, that is, of a nation
which is indifferent to the life of the nation and of the individuals
composing it, but has toward them its ethical duties, takes care of
their education (not only of their enlightenment), of the many-
sided development of their individualistic values.[227]

27 An article in *Vistnyk ODVU* (April–May 1934) written by Stephen
Kuropas in which the author describes Nationalism as an ideology which came "across the sea to America and it was grafted
here by the very same soldiers who in the time of the Ukrainian
uprising stood in the most dangerous posts at the front."

The same issue carried an article welcoming Senyk-Hribiwsky
back to America on behalf of MUN.[228]

28 An article in *Vistnyk ODVU* (January 1934) which declared:

The Ukrainian nationalists "have grafted, or inoculated, the
idea of the Ukrainian Nationalists in America" in order to make
them accomplish a part of the task in the rebuilding of the Ukrainian State.[229]

29 An article in *Vistnyk ODVU* (March 1934) in which the author
criticized those Ukrainians who had not accepted Ukrainian
Nationalism as those "who like to bow before their enemies, to
cringe and to plead for amnesty and autonomy and who in their
serfdom are incapable of taking a courageous stand, nay even to
demand openly what is justly ours – this section of our people

considers nationalism to be a prank of anarchistic young generation and a most destructive and dangerous phenomenon for
Ukrainians. To this opinion the said group adheres with the stub-
bornness of donkeys, even at the time when in other races their
nationalism – as for instance fascism and hitlerism – is crowned
with great successes.[230]

30 A report in *Nationalist* (20 September 1935) on the First Congress
of Nationalists in which the Congress resolved to intensify bonds
with the OUN Provid.[231]

31 Excerpts from a speech of Dr. Granovsky (cited in *Nationalist*, 13
May 1939) in which the ODWU President declared:
We see with our own eyes how the spirit of the people conquered in Germany. The victors (Allies) artificially create new
nations and artificially destroy the natural ones, but all the efforts
of the enemies will fail.
Over there (in Ukraine) the people are only waiting for "Der
Tag" ... Force must be met by force, and nothing will stop the
march of the Nationalist movement ... We must at every step give
aid and confidence to the Provid of OUN and to Colonel Konovalets.[232]

32 An article in *Nationalist* (17 August 1938):
The monthly *Geopolitik*, published in Germany by a former
German general and a professor, Dr. K. Haushofer, has said the
truth about the Ukrainians in America.
The League for the Rebirth of the Ukraine in America (ODWU)
is closely related to the German nazi-ism and Italian fascism.[233]

33 A statement in *Nationalist* (14 September 1938) which declared:
The only proper method to construct the political system of the
Ukrainian nation is upon the principles of authoritarianism and
fuehrership [the correct translation is "leadership," not "fuehrership"], which rests upon the principle of creativeness, character,
will, and responsibility of the individual.[234]

As his final exhibit, Matthews cited a passage from the December 1932
issue of *Vistnyk ODVU* in which OUN is described as follows: "We have
the organization of Ukrainian Nationalists, which strives to win back our
nationhood by two methods: constructive and destructive ... in destructive
method by destroying the occupants by means of revolutionary work, by
keeping alive the militant spirit among our wide masses, and calls them to
oppose the government and carries out various terroristic acts."[235] No other
articles from the Nationalist press were offered for the record.

Of particular interest to the Dies Committee were the activities of Dr. Luka Myshuha, editor-in-chief of *Svoboda*. Revyuk's testimony revealed that:

1 During his last visit to Europe, Myshuha had remained for a period of three months and had visited France, Germany, Czechoslovakia, Italy, and England. His trip was probably financed by the UNA.[236]

2 During his stay in Europe, Myshuha corresponded with Revyuk on a number of matters. Myshuha's correspondence, introduced into the Dies Committee record, revealed that:

a) Myshuha had had conferences with British editors and had protested Hungary's and Poland's aspirations for Carpatho-Ukraine.

b) The *Svoboda* editor had broadcast a message to Carpatho-Ukrainians via Vienna radio. (The text of the message was not included.)

c) Myshuha's second visa to England had been refused.

d) Myshuha had urged Revyuk to inaugurate a fund for Carpatho-Ukraine and to provide extensive press coverage to the Ukrainian Council in Uzhhorod billing it as the "only representative of the Sub-Carpathian Ukrainians."

e) Myshuha had asked Revyuk to send him money via American Express in Paris and to send him credentials authorizing him to represent the UUOA.[237]

f) Myshuha had written Revyuk concerning an article which had appeared in the *Voelkischer Beobachter*, a German publication, which commented on Carpatho-Ukraine's desire to become independent. Revyuk was then urged to raise at least $410,000 for Carpatho-Ukraine.

g) Myshuha had written that the OUN Provid strongly supported the Ukrainian mass demonstration in support of Carpatho-Ukrainian independence.

h) Myshuha was asked by a British consulate official in Paris if his efforts on behalf of Carpatho-Ukraine were not counter to American policy and replied: "... the U.S.A. is for self-determination of nationalities and justice and they don't interfere in anyone's efforts in such directions, but quite the contrary, they help."

i) Myshuha had met with a Dr. Enrico Ensabato [never identified in the testimony] and had proposed a union of Czechs, Slovaks, and Ukrainians in a confederation of independent nations.[238]

j) Myshuha had criticized ODWU for passing a resolution favoring an independent Carpatho-Ukraine and wrote: "The resolution about the independence passed at the Congress of ODWU has not helped the matter. It was, at any rate, premature and for this reason could even hurt the cause ... I wrote to Hrybiwsky [Senyk] a letter to give by telegram a command to ODWU to carry on no political activities without an understanding with the United Ukrainian organizations. Improper conduct of the matter is killing it, since it reveals us as having connections with the German intrigue."[239]

k) Myshuha wrote Revyuk that he had learned in Berlin that General Kurmanovych was on his way to America.

l) Myshuha had written Revyuk urging him not to "re-publish" an earlier communiqué concerning Melnyk's elevation to the post of *"fuehrer"* of OUN.

m) Myshuha had sent Revyuk the full text of his Vienna radio address for publication in Svoboda.[240]

All during his testimony, Revyuk was led by Matthews, his interrogator. Among other things, Matthews attempted to substitute the term "totalitarian" for "authoritarian," place the Provid headquarters in Berlin, and suggest that Myshuha was not able to obtain a second visa to England because he was a "political agitator."[241] Matthews also made an effort to substitute German words for Ukrainian words – "fuehrer" for "Vozhd," "der Tag" for "the day," and "Heil" for "Slava" (Glory) – in his references to translations of Ukrainian-language statements and articles.[242]

Much of Revyuk's testimony was contradictory. Early in his testimony, for example, Revyuk stated that ODWU and the UUOA were "in competition." Later he declared that the UUOA paid for the maintenance of a Ukrainian press bureau in Washington "on the recommendation of ODWU." Many of Revyuk's conclusions were based on hearsay as evidenced by responses that began with "People told me that" ... or "He told me that." Other comments began with "I believe that ..." and were never challenged by Matthews.[243]

At the end of Revyuk's inconclusive testimony, Congressman Dies exclaimed:

Here are organizations that have been shown to be nothing in the world but agencies of foreign powers. That is all they are under their own admission. They provide an elaborate espionage system in this country ...

As soon as the Committee returns I am going to submit the recommendation that all of these organizations be subpoenaed forthwith, be served with a subpoena duces tecum, to bring before

this committee a complete and accurate membership list ...
Because until we find out who they are and where they are
working, which ones are in the Government, which ones are in
the navy, which ones are in the trade-union movement, those
who are in the aircraft and munitions plants and other vital key
industries in this country; until we know that, we are dealing in
the dark.[244]

That same day a United Press dispatch read:

Emil Revyuk, associate editor of *Svoboda*, Ukrainian language daily
in Jersey City, told the Dies Committee today that efforts have
been made to organize 800,000 Ukrainians in an international
group under a fuehrer ... Odwu [*sic*], he said, is connected with
headquarters in Germany, and is dedicated to establishing a
Ukrainian monarchy under a ruler from the family of General
Paul Skoropadsky.

The *Chicago Daily News* ran the above dispatch under the headline "Nazi
Groups Woo U.S. Ukrainians, Dies Quiz Hear – Minnesota Professor at
Head of Group: King Chosen Already."[245] The Associated Press account
was equally distorted:

... From Emil Revyuk, Jersey City, N.J., assistant editor of *Svoboda*
in New York City, the committee received testimony today that
an organization called Odwu [sic], affiliated with an international
organization of Ukrainian nationalists, was seeking to establish a
"fuehrership" for the Ukraine.
      After he related numerous instances of persons in Berlin sug-
gesting Ukrainian mass meetings and other demonstrations in
this country, Dies remarked that "this is very clearly a Nazi organization with a close tie-up with Germany."
      Attorney General Frank Murphy said today the justice depart-
ment was prepared to act at the appropriate time against certain
"conspicuous foreign agents who have been a nuisance."[246]

Never questioning Revyuk's background as a socialist, a detractor of
OUN and ODWU, and the person who was demoted when Myshuha was
appointed editor of *Svoboda* (all of which would have cast doubt on his
reliability as a credible witness),[247] the validity of the blatantly biased documentation, which never mentioned the preponderance of positive commentaries about the United States,[248] or the objectionable manner in which

Matthews led his witness to elicit evidence, Congressman Dies suspended his own set of ten criteria to determine Nazi sympathies – none of which applied to any Ukrainian organization – and concluded that the UHO and ODWU were "obviously" Nazi.[249] Given the times and pressures he had to face – the Popular Front had attacked his committee for focusing on Communists while ignoring Nazis – one can perhaps understand Dies's pressing need to "expose Nazis," especially when such "exposures" brought no discernible political fallout. Ukrainians, after all, were a small minority in the United States. Based solely on the evidence, however, there was absolutely no justification for Dies to conclude that ODWU and the UHO provided "an elaborate espionage system in this country" or that there was a "strong link" between Nazi Germany and the two Ukrainian nationalist organizations. Nor, for that matter, was any testimony provided proving that either organization was "un-American" according to criteria established by the House Un-American Activities Committee itself: "By un-American activities we mean organizations or groups existing in the United States which are directed, controlled or subsidized by foreign governments or agencies which seek to change the policies and form of government of the United States in accordance with the wishes of such foreign governments."[250]

Although outraged by Revyuk's testimony, ODWU, convinced that the Nationalists would have their day on Capitol Hill, welcomed the Dies investigation. "Too many unfounded charges," wrote the ODWU press organ, "have been made during the past few years to poison the minds of the people. Now they can be aired fully in public before men who are interested in finding the facts, who are not prejudiced by nationality, and who have repeatedly stressed that they do not want merely to condemn."[251] In preparation for the anticipated hearing, Dushnyck and Roman Lapica compiled a 132-page affidavit which rebutted Revyuk's allegations and documented ODWU's loyalty to the United States and its principles.[252]

The Dies Committee, however, decided not to call any witnesses associated with ODWU and the UNA. Instead, on 1 November, they heard from two socialists, Volodymyr Kedrovsky[253] and Yaroslav Chyz,[254] both of whom, of course, corroborated Revyuk's allegations about OUN, ODWU, and Dr. Myshuha. There is no evidence that anyone from the Nationalist camp was ever called to testify before the committee.

In the meantime, John C. Metcalfe, the Dies committee investigator who had compiled the data related to the Ukrainian community, traveled around the country speaking to various groups about the Nazi menace in America. Learning that he would be addressing the Minneapolis Junior Chamber of Commerce on 10 January 1940, ODWU President Granovsky asked for a meeting. Metcalfe agreed. Granovsky arrived with a reporter and what was to have been a private get-together turned out to be an opportunity for Granovsky to publicly challenge the Dies Committee conclusion regarding ODWU.[255] It was the last time the Nationalists had a chance to present their side to the American press.

Still believing there was nothing "un-American" in any of their activities, the Nationalist rank and file went about their business. They were convinced that the entire affair had somehow been engineered by the Communists and that once the truth was known, they would be vindicated. Intensified criticism by *Visti* and *Narodna Volya* following Revyuk's testimony only reinforced the conspiratorial belief. "We thought the whole thing was a big misunderstanding," states Stephen Kuropas. "We knew the United States supported national self-determination and that most Americans hated the Communists. We just couldn't bring ourselves to believe that the American people would be opposed to a free Ukraine once they knew the facts."[256]

Their ideological differences notwithstanding, both the Nationalists and the socialists organized rallies protesting the Soviet invasion of Western Ukraine. Some 1,000 participants met in New York City early in November 1939 to hear a former member of the Central Rada, socialist Nykyfor Hryhoriv, declare: "The Ukrainian people ... have a right to rule themselves. So out with Russian troops from all Ukrainian lands!" They also heard Kedrovsky and Sichynsky condemn "self-made dictators" who "spread fascist ideas" and "orient themselves on Hitler."[257] A few weeks later, an estimated 3,000 people attended a UUOA-sponsored manifestation in Cooper Union and also heard various speakers, among them Dushnyck, who declared: "Neither Stalin nor Hitler created Ukraine and they will not bury her. On the contrary, Ukraine will be the beginning of the end of their imperialisms."[258]

The Birth of the Ukrainian Congress Committee

The eighth UUOA convention was held on 8 December 1939 with 110 delegates representing about 200 local organizations in attendance. When UUOA president Revyuk refused to answer questions regarding his testimony and threatened, instead, to sue any person or institution that dared impugn his integrity, he was neither reelected nor nominated to the forty-person governing board.[259] Convinced that the UUOA had been permanently damaged by the Dies probe, the delegates elected an interim executive headed by UNA president Nicholas Muraszko and resolved to call a congress in order to form a more broadly based Ukrainian-American political coalition.

The new all-Ukrainian body was to consist of a core executive composed of representatives from the four fraternal benefit societies – the UNA, the

UWA, the Providence Association, and the UNAA – and an advisory board of representatives from all other national organizations. Both the UWA and the Providence Association initially insisted that two organizations – UHO and ODWU – be banned from membership until the conclusion of the Dies investigation. When the UNA and UNAA objected, the UWA threatened to hold its own congress.[260] The UNA and UNAA refused to budge, however, and for a time it appeared as if the congress would proceed without the participation of all the fraternal societies.[261] A compromise was finally reached in April around ten points, the last of which mandated unanimous approval by the four fraternal associations for all organizational decisions.[262]

On 24 May 1940, 805 delegates from 168 different communities met in Washington, DC, and established the Ukrainian Congress Committee of America (UCCA). Elected to the executive were Nicholas Muraszko (UNA), president; Anthony Curkowsky (Providence Association), secretary; Stephen Korpan (UWA), treasurer; and Wasyl Shabatura (UNAA), controller.[263] Elected to the national advisory board were representatives from thirteen other national organizations.[264] Resolutions were passed appealing, once again, for American support of Ukrainian aspirations and denouncing Soviet and Nazi aggression in Europe. President Roosevelt's foreign policy was also upheld by special resolution.[265]

That same month, ODWU president Granovsky sent an appeal directly to the White House suggesting that the United States champion the cause of Ukrainian liberation, assist Americans of Ukrainian descent in their promotion of Ukrainian independence, bring the Ukrainian question to the attention of the free world's leaders, and provide both direct and indirect aid for Ukrainians in Europe. There are "two malevolent forces" in Europe, Granovsky cautioned President Roosevelt – German and Russian imperialism.[266]

A special UCCA delegation later appeared before the Senate Foreign Relations Committee with a memorandum outlining the brutality the Ukrainian people had suffered at the hands of their Russian and Polish oppressors and suggesting that only a free Ukraine could serve as a deterrent to German, Polish, and Russian imperialism.[267]

Neither the Granovsky appeal nor the UCCA memorandum had any impact on American foreign policy. The United States was soon to enter into an alliance with the USSR and a new era of Ukrainian-American life was about to begin.

The Defamation Campaign

For the Communists in America, such militantly anti-Bolshevik organizations as UHO, ODWU, and the UNA were "fascist" organizations that had to be discredited. When Stalin became one of Hitler's allies, the Bolsheviks tended to mute their criticism. Once the alliance began to get a little shaky, however, a new Soviet defense team sprang into action. Resurrecting the "findings" of the Dies Committee, they launched a coordinated defamation campaign against the Ukrainian-American Nationalist community that lasted three years. Even the UCCA was not immune.[268]

The campaign got under way in 1940 with the appearance of *The Fifth Column Is Here,* a book written by George Britt, feature writer for the *World Telegram.* Alleging direct Abwehr financing of ODWU's operations, Britt wrote:

> The drive has been made successfully by ODWU to gain control
> of the key positions of Ukrainian organizations and activities.
> Numbers have not been important but positions from which num-
> bers could be influenced have been vital. Through the churches
> and the clubs for young people, a wide social structure has
> been captured. One of the most important groups has been the
> Ukrainian National Association with 40,000 members and over
> $5,000,000 in capital. The present officers are members of ODWU.
>   Years of infiltration of Nazi ideas have borne fruit in thousands
> of converts. A crowd of 7,000 Ukrainians turned out in 1938 to
> greet a delegation of visiting officers from Germany at the New
> York Hippodrome and gave the Nazi salute ...

But that wasn't all, observed Britt:

> The extension has been accomplished also, into the heart of Ameri-
> can industry. The Ukrainians are good workers, represented in
> all great manufacturing plants. Through its privately fostered
> ODWU, the German intelligence office now has ready access to
> these plants and under the slogan of "Liberation" and "Rebirth"
> it can lay its hands on the layout of a factory, navy yard, or
> airplane factory.[269]

Angered by the allegations, ODWU demanded an immediate retraction from the publisher, Wilfred Funk, Inc., and the recall of all unsold copies.[270] Meanwhile, another attack on ODWU was launched by *The Hour,* a news-letter with Communist ties, accusing the Nationalists of engaging in anti-democratic propaganda, anti-Semitism, and espionage. Again ODWU demanded a retraction.[271]

On 1 September, a report entitled "Ukrainians Help Nazi Plots Here – Secret Revolutionary Society Tied in with Hitler's War on U.S.A." appeared in *PM.* Alleging direct ties with "Berlin" and the drilling of "uniformed storm troopers," the article concluded that ODWU was "pro-fascist and pro-nazi." Once again ODWU demanded a retraction.[272]

Last to join the anti-Nationalist campaign was *Friday.* Identifying both ODWU and UHO as "fascist" organizations, the periodical described the Nationalists as being associated with a "subsidiary organ of a body connected with the Intelligence Department of the War Office in Berlin, Germany."[273]

On 27 July 1940, *The Hour* gave full coverage to the efforts of the UWA and the Providence Association to exclude ODWU and UHO from the Ukrainian Congress Committee as well as UWA demands that the UNA cleanse itself of "Nazi elements."[274] The following month the periodical reported on the "Nazi conspiratorial network" consisting of ODWU and Bishop Buchko.[275] Bishop Buchko was a special target of the Stalinist front because of his unabashed support of OUN.[276] One month later *PM* reported on "a secret camp of Ukrainian terrorists, stooges of Hitler" living in the neighborhood of an explosion in New Jersey.[277]

All attacks and demands for retractions were widely publicized in the Ukrainian press, including *Ukraine,* the Nationalist press organ. While ODWU never received a full retraction from any of the publications, on 15 November *PM* did print a long article entitled "Ukrainians Move to Fight against Nazism," which reported on the formation of the ODWU-initiated "Ukrainian American Committee to Aid the Allies."[278] Perceiving the article as a retraction, *The Hour* condemned *PM* for being taken in by ODWU's "false claims to 'democracy' " and vowed to continue its "disclosures" of "saboteurs and spies."[279]

Unable to obtain relief through ordinary channels, ODWU announced the formation of a "Fund for the Defense of the Ukrainian Immigration" to "end, once and for all, this anti-Ukrainian campaign, to exonerate ... the good name of the Ukrainian immigration in America, and to present in a factual and accurate manner, the true purpose of the Ukrainian liberation movement." Monies, explained the ODWU executive, would be used for brochures, press releases, and "most important of all, for instituting law suits which will not only expose the source of the clandestine movement to destroy the organized Ukrainian-American community but will defend every Ukrainian who is today being unjustly accused of being associated with Nazism and Fascism."[280]

Meanwhile, the defamation campaign intensified. Early in 1941, *Svoboda* published an article entitled "Explosive Substances."[281] Written by Dmytro Horbach, it had originally appeared in *Zhyttia i Znannia* (Knowledge and Life), a Ukrainian journal published in Poland, meaning, significantly, that it had been cleared for public consumption by Polish censors.[282] *The Hour,* however, alleged that the article was inserted in order to teach Ukrainians "how to make bombs" and was an example of how *Svoboda* was training subversives in the United States.[283]

When a Cleveland to Pittsburgh train was derailed in March, *The Hour* ran a story under the headline "Ukrainian Fascists and Pennsylvania Train Wreck" demanding "an immediate investigation by the federal authorities of the Ukrainian terrorist groups active in and about Pittsburgh."[284]

Soon after Hitler invaded the USSR, *The Hour* went after Dr. Myshuha, who, *The Hour* alleged, spoke under the auspices of Dr. Joseph Goebbels over the Third Reich radio station, as well as the ODWU periodical *Ukraine*, which "continues to circulate throughout this country ... agitating its readers to take steps to further the aims of the Third Reich." Ardent readers of the periodical, the pro-Communist newsletter ominously concluded, "many of whom work in defense industries ... may hamper the national defense effort ... and give aid to the Nazi cause." When *Ukraine* published an appeal from Provid chief Melnyk asking Bandera's dissidents to return to the original OUN fold, *The Hour* described it as a manifesto "urging Ukrainians to rally to the support of the pro-Hitlerite Ukrainian Fifth Column."[285] This article was published a few months after *Time* magazine had written that Hitler had "discovered puppet Skoropadsky" and had "set him up as organizer of the Ukrainian nationalists." "Ukrainians were trained," concluded *Time*, "in espionage and sabotage."[286]

Even Ukrainian academicians were not immune from attack. When Yale University Press published *A History of Ukraine*, a one-volume condensation of Prof. Michael Hrushevsky's monumental history of the Ukrainian people, *The Hour* denounced the university for publishing a book "praising the pro-German Ukrainian Fifth Column" and "presenting Nazi racist myths about the Ukrainian people as a whole." Hrushevsky, the former president of Ukraine who had returned to his homeland during the Ukrainianization campaign only to disappear during Stalin's reign of terror, was a distinguished historian in his own right. He was dismissed by *The Hour* as one "who achieved more fame as a political intriguer than as a scholar."[287]

With Roosevelt proclaiming the United States as "the arsenal of democracy" ready to assist England and the USSR in their war against Hitler, Ukrainians were urged to mute their anti-Bolshevik diatribes for the sake of the war effort. Reflecting Ukrainian-American nationalist opinion during the early stages of the defamation campaign, the *Ukrainian Weekly* replied:

> Some people seem to think that the British alliance with the Soviets has placed us, Americans of Ukrainian descent, in a dilemma. They say our irreconcilable opposition to the Reds may be regarded with disfavor here, and even construed by some as

pro-Nazi. They counsel us, therefore, to become less intransigent on this issue, or at least, to soft-pedal it.

We fail to see the point. The fact that Stalin is fighting Hitler does not change our opinion of him in the least. We still think he is Freedom and Democracy's Public Enemy No. 1 – with Hitler, of course, a close second. We gave Pal Joey precedence here because his Reds have been far longer in power than the Nazis, their brutalities have been more cruel and on a far greater scale, their persecution of the Church much worse, and, finally, because their predecessor was the rapacious imperialist Tsarist regime which for centuries stood for autocracy in its most anti-democratic forms.

Aside from this traditional anti-democratic character of Moscow, however, we also have to consider in this connection the fact that the Reds are fighting the Nazis not for the sake of any principles of freedom and democracy but simply and only because of self-preservation – to preserve Communism with Moscow as its center.

If freedom and democracy had ever meant anything to the Reds, they would have joined forces with the Allies back in the summer of 1939 ...

So the best we can do is to hope that both these predatory powers, Nazi Germany and Soviet Russia, exhaust themselves in their war, to the extent that neither they nor their anti-democratic systems will menace world progress and civilization ...

So long as Moscow continues to thus brutally enslave and despoil our kinsmen in their native land, Ukraine, so long as it blocks their centuries-old movement to establish a free and independent and democratic Ukraine, so long will we and all other true friends of freedom and democracy keep up our fight against it.[288]

The above editorial, condensed somewhat here, was cited in its entirety in *Two Way Passage*, a book written by Louis Adamic and published in 1941. Repeating earlier allegations concerning the Nazi character of ODWU, UHO, and the UNA found in *The Hour*, Adamic, a respected liberal writer who had established credentials as being opposed to both fascism and Communism,[289] found the above passage a "tragedy," a statement he believed was issued "not from a balanced heart and mind, but from the compulsion of outer events upon an inner confusion rife among people, wherever they may be, who feel insecure."[290] Offering no further documentation, Adamic wrote:

From a reliable anti-Nazi source within the group,* I learn that there are about five thousand "Ukrainians in America" who are active in the Ukrainian cause in a pro-Nazi way. One-fourth to one-third of these are native Americans of Ukrainian parentage. Not a large number relatively. But it may be that their propaganda, directed by Hitler's agents for the last half-dozen years, has touched a quarter of a million people who in consequence are not anti-U.S.A. but are certainly anti-British and anti-Russian and to that extent, pro-Hitler – although most of them will deny this. In addition to being anti-Semitic, most are anti-Negro, some even refusing to work on the same jobs with colored men.[292]

Nor was Adamic reticent to outline the Ukrainian "Nazis'" purposes, which he observed "one Saturday night late in '38" when he attended "a banquet in Newark, New Jersey." Adamic saw Nazis at "every second or third table"[293] and, according to him, their task was threefold:

One: to strengthen the Ukrainian movement wherever it could be strengthened for possible use in Hitler's plan to disrupt Russia.
Two: to pick out people of Ukrainian nationality or background who through fanaticism or corruption might serve as saboteurs in American industries when and if necessary.
And three: to encourage anti-Semitism and other forms of antagonism against people in the United States who stemmed from countries holding Ukrainian territories.[294]

The Weekly was dismayed. "We have long had a warm spot in our heart for Mr. Louis Adamic," the UNA organ editorialized, especially for "his manifest sincerity and honesty ... his keen insight into immigrant problems, his painstaking research and labors, and his power of expression." Observing sadly that in his treatment of Ukrainian Americans Adamic was "singularly lacking in all of these qualities," the Weekly proceeded to rebut his allegations point by point.[295]

The height of the defamation campaign was reached in 1942 with the publication of Sabotage! The Secret War against America by Michael Sayers, associated with Friday, and Albert E. Kahn, editor of The Hour. In a chapter entitled "Bombers and Killers," Sayers and Kahn repeated all of the old Dies Committee "findings" and added a few defamatory flourishes of their own. Konovalets was depicted as "a tall blondish man with gray watery

---

* Revyuk admitted to the FBI that it was he who supplied Adamic with information concerning the Ukrainian-American community.[291]

eyes, a military bearing and a passion for jewels. He had earned himself considerable notoriety in the Ukraine," wrote Sayers and Kahn, "as a rapist and a killer."[296] Dr. Myshuha was called the "Big Mouse" and was described as "a tall, thin, fifty-five-year-old Ukrainian-born American with sharp, birdlike features, a narrow forehead, and a tight mouth that habitually twists in a caustic smile." Myshuha's trip to Europe was mentioned and cast in an unfavorable light with such "evidence" as: "From London, on October 28, 1938, he [Myshuha] mailed home a dispatch to his associates in the United States which informed them that he had 'just sent off two long telegrams to Ribbentrop and Ciano' ..." and "When Myshuha showed up in Vienna, he was welcomed by high Nazi officials, and the Nazi Propaganda Ministry invited him to deliver a special propaganda address over the controlled German radio." Myshuha spoke for the Nazis as "requested," concluded the authors.[297]

Careful not to paint all Ukrainian Americans as "fascists," Sayers and Kahn wrote:

> There are close to one million Ukrainian-Americans in the United States. The overwhelming majority of them are prodemocratic; but a Naziphile minority make up the ODWU and the Hetman, two of the most dangerous espionage-sabotage organizations in the world.
>
> The ODWU operates under the supervision of Colonel Nicholai's Section IIIB, German military intelligence.
>
> The Hetman operates under the supervision of Alfred Rosenberg's *Aussenpolitisches Amt*, Foreign Office of the Nazi party.
>
> The ODWU is more powerful than the Hetman and, if possible, more violent. Both organizations have built their cells in American industrial centers. Their agents work in munitions plants, mines, steel foundries, aircraft factories, shipyards, freightyards, and docks. A number of them have gained access to the United States Army.
>
> Both the ODWU and the Hetman are international organizations with branches throughout Europe, Asia and North and South America. Their activities include spying, sabotaging, spreading pro-Axis propaganda and, not infrequently, committing assassinations. The United States leaders of ODWU have been in regular communication with German, Japanese and Italian agents, and with spies in South and Central America. In the spring of 1941, one of the confidential ODWU bulletins emanating from Berlin triumphantly described the sinking of several British ships sabotaged by ODWU members in Argentina and Brazil.[298]

The activities of OUN members, allegedly trained in the arts of espionage, sabotage, and assassination in a German school that opened in Danzig in 1928, were also mentioned, including their assassinations of "a number of prominent Polish politicians."[299] The early organizational work of Senyk-Hribiwsky, described as "the most talented saboteur and ruthless killer in the OUN," was depicted as a German-financed operation involving the formation of various "front" organizations engaged with "Ukrainian Red Cross" work, "insurance companies," "sports clubs," and "film companies." According to the authors, Senyk-Hribiwsky founded the "Ukrainian Aviation School," which was described as "an ideal front for the training of spies and saboteurs."[300]

Using an envelope addressed to *Svoboda* as the only piece of photographic "evidence,"[301] Sayers and Kahn described the UNA organ as follows:

> With Myshuha as its head, *Svoboda* was converted into an organ of Axis propaganda and a medium for conveying instructions to ODWU spies. The *Svoboda* offices at 83 Grand Street, Jersey City, became a clearing house for espionage directives coming in from Berlin, Tokyo, and Rome. For many years, these directives have been regularly reaching the *Svoboda* offices by mail from Spanish and South American "drops"; or through the special "couriers" of the Axis spy systems. Liaison officers from Germany and Japan made their headquarters at 83 Grand Street when they visited the United States.[302]

Svoboda threatened to sue the authors and the publishers for libel and was able to obtain a letter in which the publishers wrote:

> We are writing with the authority and approval of the authors with respect to the references to Mr. Luke Myshuha and *Svoboda* in the book *Sabotage*. A careful examination of the facts indicates that there is no justification for including Mr. Myshuha and *Svoboda* in the chapter entitled "Bombers and Killers." You may be sure that any such reference will be deleted from the said chapter in any subsequent editions.[303]

The publishers were true to their word. In the 1944 edition of the book, Myshuha was not included in the chapter entitled "Bombers and Killers." The authors admitted in a footnote that they had "no evidence that Luke Myshuha is either a bomber or killer" and then proceeded to introduce a new chapter heading – "The Big Mouse" – containing the same information.[304]

In a wartime America fighting to save the world from fascism, the disinformation contained in *Sabotage!* was accepted as a patriotic contribution to the war effort.[305] Walter Winchell, America's popular news commentator, publicized the book over the radio calling it "one of the most exciting and important books of the war ... It names names from the small fry to the biggest of Quislings."[306]

The FBI, meanwhile, still had not arrested one Ukrainian American or disbanded any Ukrainian organization. *The Hour* tried again. "FASCIST UKRAINIAN ESPIONAGE-SABOTAGE RING STILL OPERATING IN THE UNITED STATES," ran its headline on 5 September 1942:

> Many ODWU members have been painstakingly trained in
> espionage and sabotage techniques at special schools established
> in the Third Reich and even in the United States by the German
> Military Intelligence. ODWU members learned how to steal
> military secrets, how to photograph factories and transportation
> facilities, how to disrupt trade unions, how to make bombs,
> explosive devices, etc.[307]

"Our fair-minded fellow Americans may not be aware of it," wrote the *Ukrainian Weekly* in October, "but we of Ukrainian extraction are being persecuted. Those who ... would break up our unity and strength, our institutions and our common ideals, are doing their utmost to blacken our good name and bring disrepute upon us ... they are usually careful enough when attacking us ... to add an inconspicuous footnote, to the effect ... 'the great majority of Ukrainian Americans are loyal and patriotic' ... But the average person rarely notices these weasel words and leaves his radio or book or paper with the general impression that those 'U-ka-rai-nians' are a bad pro-Nazi lot, and wonders why in heaven's name does not the F.B.I. do something about them." Observing that "if even a bare fraction of what he hears or reads about us in this connection were true then surely the F.B.I. would have apprehended all the 'culprits' and closed down all the 'guilty' institutions long ago," the *Weekly* concluded that the entire affair was a "smear campaign" conducted by "well-known Ukrainian Americans who because of their fanatically blind partisanship and their desire to discredit their political opponents do not hesitate to stoop to unscrupulous name-calling ... individuals of miserable character ... without visible means of support ... ," and the Communists "who have always had it in for us" and who now, "basking in the reflected glory of the valiant struggle the

Soviet Russian and Ukrainian people ... are waging against the brutal
hordes of Hitler," are receiving "the attention which ordinarily they would
not merit. So when they say we Ukrainians are pro-Nazi, some gullible
souls are found to give credence to such rot and to pass it on."[308] For the
Weekly, the most outrageous effrontery of the Ukrainian Communists was
their posing as "1000% Americans" when, during the duration of the
Nazi-Soviet pact, they vociferously "opposed various steps taken by our
president and Congress preparing and strengthening our country for the
conflict."[309]

The FBI Investigation

The FBI began its investigation of ODWU on 7 December 1939, following
a visit from John C. Metcalfe, Dies Committee investigator.[310] The Luka
Myshuha probe commenced on 9 January 1941, when a confidential informant notified the FBI that "Luke Mushugh ... is a sponsor and member of
the United Hetman organization of Chicago, a Ukrainian body under Nazi
control," and "an active German propagandist."[311] Various FBI agents
consistently misspelled Myshuha's name. Rather than correct the error –
perhaps because it was begun by J. Edgar Hoover himself – they listed
variations as aliases. By December, Luka Myshuha had the following aliases
after his name: Lucas Myschuga, Luke Mishugh, Luke Myshuka, and Lukas
Myshugh. The UNA came under surveillance on 16 May 1942.[312] There
were other investigations, principally of Gregory Herman[313] and Alexander
Granovsky[314] but their files are sparse and provide no significant data.
The bulk of the material regarding the Ukrainian-American Nationalist
community, much of which is repetitive and replicated in all the files, can
be found in the four sections (volumes) on the UHO, the first ten sections
on ODWU, the seven sections on the UNA, and a single section on Luka
Myshuha.

On 4 April 1941, the attorney general requested the FBI to determine if
the UNA, ODWU, and all related Ukrainian organizations "were in violation of the Voorhis Act." To determine whether they were or not, the FBI
was instructed to identify all leaders, members, and people reached by the
organizations; determine assets and liabilities; obtain copies of constitu-
tions, charters, bylaws, and other related documents; peruse all publications produced by the organizations; and evaluate oral statements, both
public and private, made by members.[315]

According to available FBI files, the most thoroughly investigated Ukrainian organization in the nationalist camp was ODWU. Major branch officers were interviewed; charters, minutes of meetings, and correspondence
were reviewed; subscription lists were obtained; periodicals were read;

and informants, both pro and con, were heard. The most significant facts established by the investigation were that ODWU was never involved in espionage or subversion and that it was not a Nazi organization.

The FBI also concluded that ODWU's role in the OUN network was one of ancillary support. When America's Ukrainian Nationalists were first being organized in 1929, Colonel Konovalets sent a draft constitution which clearly demonstrated that OUN visualized a Nationalist organization whose major purpose would be – and this is the most militant phrase in the entire text – to "acquaint as much of the Ukrainian population as possible with the present situation in Ukraine and to strengthen the idea that only by an armed struggle is it possible to bring about a united, independent Ukrainian state." In outlining the duties of officers, branches, and members, the proposed constitution made clear the fact that OUN viewed the Ukrainian Nationalist role in America as limited to education, promotion, and fund raising.[316]

The FBI files, however, do contain information from detractors, most of whom fall into one of four categories. In the first group were the confidential or anonymous informants who offered patently false, misleading, and often bizarre information, such as: "Ukrainian terrorists are planning the assassination of the President";[317] "Basilian monks in Chicago are passionately pro-Hitler";[318] Metropolitan Sheptytsky lives in Germany and is sending German orders to Bishop Bohachevsky "which in turn are turned over to priests in an attempt to influence the Ukrainian people in favor of the German government";[319] Ukrainian Orthodox priests are "storm troopers" whose "admiration for Hitler is boundless";[320] "A Nazi Ukrainian group is watching river traffic in Pittsburgh";[321] ODWU claims credit for sinking British ships.[322]

In the second group were known informants who had political scores to settle. Leading this group were Communists and their fellow travelers, persons such as Albert Kahn[323] who offered only verbal testimony – without any evidence – and made sure the FBI received all issues of *The Hour*.[324] Then there were the Ukrainian socialists, people like Sichynsky – who alleged that ODWU publications had "spread the Nazi propaganda line"[325] – and Kedrovsky and Revyuk.[326] Especially active in this regard was Revyuk, who continued to work at *Svoboda* until the end of the war.[327] Kahn admitted to receiving "considerable information" from Revyuk. A confidential informant who supplied news about Ukrainian activities to the B'nai B'rith Anti-Defamation League also identified Revyuk as the source of much of his "inside dope." According to UNA president Muraszko, Revyuk became very upset in 1942 when, during Myshuha's absence, Muraszko learned that Revyuk was planning to insert another article on explosives into *Svoboda* and forbade him to do so.[328]

A third group consisted of people who were apparently unscrupulous opportunists. Included in this cluster were Volodymyr Stepankiwsky and Stephen Mostowy. Both had helped establish the so-called Ukrainian Committee to Combat Nazism, an organization which Mostowy ran out of his home in New York City. Stepankiwsky, the FBI discovered, lived in a cheap rooming house and admitted to supplying information on the Ukrainian-American community to *The Hour*.[329] Mostowy also admitted working for *The Hour* as well as the UWA, the Anti-Nazi League, and the Anti-Defamation League. "During the conversation Agent Griffin had with Mostowy," reads the FBI report, "Mostowy made some very definite statements regarding alleged pro-Nazi activities on the part of Ukrainians. When the agent asked him for proof of these allegations, he replied that the parties about whom he had furnished information had never denied the accusations so, therefore, they must be true. This was the only proof offered by Mostowy," concluded Agent Griffin.[330]

The most credible detractors, however, were respected Ukrainian Americans who had once been associated with the Nationalists. According to a confidential informant, former ODWU president Gregory Herman indicated during an interview in the fall of 1941 that while he did not know to what extent the Provid controlled ODWU, he felt certain Hitler controlled the Provid.[331] In January 1942, Eugene Lachowitch, another ODWU activist, told an FBI agent that ODWU had "reached a pro-Nazi attitude in 1937 and 1938 and for that reason he had resigned" and gone to work for *Svoboda*. Walter Dushnyck told the same agent that he too left ODWU "in 1940 due to the extreme pro-Nazi attitude of the organization." When Luka Myshuha was interviewed, he indicated that "at one time he felt sure the ODWU was a pro-Nazi organization, but he felt sure the reason for this was ... the intense hatred of all Ukrainians for the Poles and Russians ... He stated he had realized at the time that it would be merely the trading of one harsh master for another, but had been unable to convince the leaders of ODWU." Myshuha also informed the FBI that ODWU's leaders had "finally reached this same conclusion and will no longer be in support of the present German government."[332]

Also revealing was Myshuha's interview with an FBI agent in May 1942 regarding his 1938 trip to Europe. According to Myshuha, the sojourn had the following aims:

1 To convince Ukrainians in Europe to side with the democracies in any future conflict.
2 To determine whom OUN was planning to send to the upcoming Nationalist Manifestation – which Myshuha opposed – and to dissuade them from coming directly from Germany because their arrival would have a negative impact on the Ukrainian cause.

3 To ascertain the sentiments of Ukrainian émigré communities in Europe regarding the upcoming conflict and to determine what they expected of their kinsmen in America.

4 To deal with *Svoboda*'s European correspondents who, in Myshuha's words, were unable

> to understand the true situation among us Ukrainian Americans, especially the fact that we were no longer Ukrainian emigrants ... but Americans of Ukrainian extraction ... who have grown up children and even grandchildren of American birth, and who are far more interested in what happens in America than what happens over in Ukraine ... All this our correspondents did not seem to realize. They continued to address us just like they would address Ukrainians in the old country. We did our best to set them right ... by editorials and articles in our paper but to no avail ... Some ... regarded our explanation ... as a subterfuge to rid ourselves of our moral obligation ... Another trouble was that sometimes some of these correspondents criticized democracy, yet left fascism and nazism alone ... it was my purpose ... to discover why this was so, whether because of the censor who would not allow them to write freely about these "isms" or because of some other reason.

5 To assist Carpatho-Ukraine in its efforts to gain autonomy.

6 To learn what the true situation was in Poland, whether a compromise had been reached between Ukrainians and Poles through UNDO, and whether monies being sent from Ukrainians in America were being used properly.

While in Vienna, Myshuha met with Provid members Riko Iari, Omelian Senyk-Hribiwsky, and Iaroslav Baranovsky and learned that OUN's decision to send a delegation to America from Germany was irrevocable and that travel plans had already been completed. When Myshuha tried to explain the American situation, Iari lectured him on "how to love Ukraine above all else" and urged him to argue in London for complete independence for Carpatho-Ukraine because Germany would "guarantee" it. Later that day, Myshuha had dinner with Senyk-Hribiwsky, who indicated that he was constantly followed by the Gestapo and that the OUN situation was still uncertain. In future meetings with Myshuha, all arranged through an intermediary and held in different places, Senyk-Hribiwsky admitted it was a mistake to send a OUN contingent to the United States from Germany. When Myshuha pointedly asked about OUN's relationship with the Nazis, Senyk-Hribiwsky replied that although there was no firm commitment from Hitler, he believed Rosenberg's ideas – which were yet to be spelled out – would prevail. Still, Senyk-Hribiwsky demurred; he didn't trust the Nazis and asked Myshuha to "help us through America and England." "We will," Myshuha replied, "provided your actions do not make our work difficult or impossible."[333]

The FBI concluded its investigation of Luka Myshuha in March 1943 with the following statement:

> In view of the fact that investigation has revealed the unreliable character of the original informants in this matter, and the fact that very extensive investigation in Ukrainian matters generally has failed to indicate any violation of the Registration Act and further since it appears that MYSHUHA is pro-democratic, pro-British, and pro-American, the outstanding leads in this case are being canceled, and this case is being considered closed.[334]

The FBI completed its investigation of ODWU in November 1943[335] and of the UNA in May 1944.[336] Both files were kept open, however, until the conclusion of the war. Significantly, the FBI found no substance to any of the allegations of subversion and Nazi ties for either organization.

The Aftermath

The defamation campaign and the concurrent FBI investigation seriously debilitated the Ukrainian nationalist community in America. The activities of OUN in Europe, especially the widely publicized OUN(B) proclamation of Ukrainian independence on the heels of Hitler's invasion of the USSR,[337] exacerbated the problem because they gave credence to detractors who insisted Nazis and Ukrainian Nationalists were working hand in glove to establish a new world order.[338] The FBI fully investigated the extent of OUN cooperation with Nazis in Europe[339] but, as with all of their findings regarding the "Ukrainian conspiracy," kept it a closely guarded secret.*

Hardest hit, of course, was UHO. Its leadership decided to formally dissolve the organization three months after the United States entered the war.

ODWU survived but lost most of its members. In November 1941, only thirty-nine of the original seventy-eight branches were still active.[340] By 1942, this number had been reduced to twenty-seven. The Gold Cross and

---

* The author received the FBI files under the Freedom of Information Act in June 1981. It took the Department of Justice eighteen months from the date of the author's application to review and declassify the information.

MUN also suffered membership losses, dropping from eighteen to eleven and from eighteen to four branches respectively.[341] "Our people were scared," comments Stephen Kuropas, still an active ODWU member in 1990. "Once America entered the war, we had no way of knowing what OUN was up to. When the FBI began to investigate, many of our members simply assumed there had to be a Nazi tie in Europe. Why else would the FBI be checking up on us?"[342]

The UNA was also affected. At the twentieth UNA convention in 1941, a pamphlet was distributed attacking Supreme Executives Muraszko, Herman, Halychyn, and other ODWU members for bringing shame on the organization. Citing excerpts from *The Fifth Column Is Here,* the pamphlet asked: "If none of this is true, then why hasn't the UNA taken these people to court?"[343] Unimpressed, the delegates proceeded to reelect or elect eleven ODWU members to the twenty-one-member Supreme Assembly including: Nicholas Muraszko, president; Gregory Herman, vice-president; Dmytro Halychyn, secretary; Roman Smook and Stephen Kuropas, auditors; and Stephen Slobodian, Taras Shpikula, Volodymyr Didyk, Nicholas Davyskyba, Eugene Lachowitch, and Dmytro Szmagala, advisers.[344]

The defamation campaign was the main topic of discussion at the first annual meeting of the Supreme Assembly on 23–28 February 1942. A law suit against the detractors was considered but the idea was shelved when Muraszko informed the assembly that he had been advised by legal counsel that a law suit would cost between $25,000 and $50,000 and that the libels had been phrased so carefully that it would be difficult to obtain a proper verdict, let alone a financial consideration. Of more immediate concern, however, was the fact that the UWA, the UNA's powerful competitor for new members, was reaping the benefits of the defamation by presenting itself as the largest "democratic fraternal" in the community. It was at this point that Muraszko suggested that, for the good of the organization, all Supreme Assembly members who still belonged to ODWU should resign immediately.[345] All but Lachowitch and Kuropas agreed.[346]

Even the UCCA, established in an effort to provide a united, "democratic" image for the Ukrainian-American community, suffered. Reeling from the steady barrage of anti-Ukrainian vindictiveness especially by radio news commentator Walter Winchell who regularly railed about the "U-ka-rai-ni-an terrorists in our midst," the UNA, UWA, and the Providence Association withdrew from the UCCA leaving only the UNAA and most of the other organizations to carry on. Without the three largest fraternal organizations, however, the UCCA remained inactive for almost two years. The need for a political action federation remained, nonetheless, and on 4 July 1943, a group calling itself the "Committee of the Council of Ukrainian Americans" convened in Detroit to plan the rejuvenation of the UCCA.[347]

On 14 September, committee members met with the UNAA, and a new UCCA structure based on full and equal membership for all Ukrainian organizations – rather than domination by the Big Four fraternals – was agreed upon. Finally, on 22 January 1944, the second convention of the UCCA was held in Philadelphia. Elected president was Stephen Shumeyko,[348] editor of the *Ukrainian Weekly*.[349]

Reviewing the deleterious results of the defamation campaign in his presidential address to UCCA delegates, Shumeyko declared: "Simply because we want our kinsmen in their native land to enjoy after this war the freedom and democracy that we are so fortunate in having here as Americans, we have become the object of ruthless vilification by those who regard with hatred the idea of a free and democratic Ukraine. Chief among them ... are the Communists in this country ... But what has made matters worse are those certain radio commentators who ... ignore the truth, and concentrate upon venom and cheap sensationalism ... When this war is over ... and when excited war feelings have died down, then this un-American, anti-Ukrainian calumny and vilification will be exposed in all of its dirty colors."[350]

The third and ultimately the most influential political force to emerge in the Ukrainian community during the interwar period was led by the Organization for the Rebirth of Ukraine (ODWU), the American affiliate of the Organization of Ukrainian Nationalists (OUN) in Europe.

Ideologically, ODWU was wedded to the principles of integral nationalism promoted by its European founder. Viewing themselves as ancillary supporters of OUN's revolutionary struggle, ODWU leaders preached personal redemption through ethnonational pride, dedication, loyalty, and obedience; and national restoration through adherence to the OUN principles of mass unity, will, and Nationalist rejuvenation. Only OUN, they argued, can liberate Ukraine and restore the honor Ukraine lost following her humiliating defeat. Only those who are willing to place "the nation above all else" are worthy to become OUN's partners in the sacred struggle. Impressed by Hitler's early accomplishments, some Nationalists in America began to point to Germany as an example of how to unite a nation and overcome the failures of the past. At the time, many other Americans were of a similar mind.

For the American Communists and their fellow travelers, UHO, UUOA, the UNA, ODWU, and the UCCA were threats not only because they were anti-Bolshevik organizations but because they were guilty of the Communist world's cardinal sin: advocacy of the dismemberment of the

Soviet Union. As soon as Stalin's embarrassing romance with Hitler began to fade, Soviet supporters in America initiated a defamation campaign which eventually helped destroy UHO and the UUOA, crippled ODWU and the UCCA, and damaged the UNA.

Some of Nationalism's wounds, of course, were self-inflicted. OUN(B)'s declaration of Ukrainian independence immediately after the German invasion of the USSR provided fuel for the anti-Ukrainian fire as did earlier OUN(M) cooperation with Nazi intelligence. Although ODWU was not directly involved – the FBI could never document any direct ties with Nazi Germany – the organization's open support of OUN proved damaging once Abwehr-OUN ties were revealed during the defamation campaign. In view of evidence suggesting that certain Provid members did at one time offer the services of their overseas affiliates to Abwehr – which Myshuha might have either sensed or learned about during his visit to Vienna in 1938 – it is possible that someone in the upper echelons of ODWU either suspected or knew about it also. Given the exit of Herman, Dushnyck, and Lachowitch, and Myshuha's own later condemnation of ODWU, it is at least plausible that this may have been the case. But even if a suggestion to cooperate with Abwehr had been made by someone who was unaware, to use Myshuha's own words, "that we were no longer Ukrainian emigrants ... but Americans of Ukrainian extraction," it most certainly was dismissed as insane. As the ODWU and UNA press and the four-year FBI investigation clearly bear out, no one associated with either of these organizations ever did or said anything that could be construed as disloyal to the United States. Like other loyal Americans during the Depression, ODWU members criticized capitalists and certain aspects of American life. But no ODWU, UHO, or UNA member was ever involved with sedition or subversion. On the contrary, as their publications consistently emphasize, ODWU members loved America and modeled their nationalism on the nationalistic patriotism they perceived in George Washington and Abraham Lincoln.

From the perspective of hindsight it would be easy to denounce those Ukrainian Americans who pointed to the unity and strength of Italy and Germany as examples of what nationalism could achieve, or who consorted with the German-American Bund. To do so, however, would be to forget that during the 1930s: (1) Bolshevism was making considerable inroads in American public life; (2) the United States and the other powerful democracies had recognized Lenin's illegal seizure of power and were condoning, in both word and deed, Stalin's hegemony over all his captive nations; (3) the Great Famine of 1932–43, artificially created by Stalin, had devastated Ukraine; (4) few Americans had read *Mein Kampf* and, of those who had, fewer still believed Hitler would do what he promised to do.

When Ukrainian Americans flirted with Germany, the final solution – with its execution squads, ovens, and record mass annihilation of Jews and other *Untermenschen* – was still in the future.

While some Ukrainian-American Nationalists were wrong about Hitler, none were wrong about Stalin. The UNA and ODWU never wavered, even under the most intense public pressure, in their efforts to warn Roosevelt and other influential Americans about the dangers of Soviet Russian imperialism. As in World War I, however, so again in World War II, Ukrainian-American aspirations were unnoticed, unheeded, and unrequited. Labeled a "German invention," Ukraine's legitimate freedom was defamed while the Soviets were depicted as idealists fighting to make "the world safe for democracy."

8 Religious Aspirations

Political ideology was not the only source of divisiveness among Ukrainian Americans during the interwar period. An equally significant concern was the church. It was not the spiritual aspects of Ukrainian religion that presented a problem but its national dimension. For many increasingly nationally conscious Ukrainian Americans during this era, the church had come to represent a national institution and when its historic ethnocultural integrity appeared threatened, the response was predictable.

The Poniatyshyn Era

With the appointment of a Greek Catholic bishop in 1907 and the subsequent creation of a separate Ruthenian exarchy in the United States, Ukrainian-American conflicts with the Holy See subsided. The nomination of a prelate from Galicia, however, greatly exacerbated the smoldering resentments which had emerged between Ruthenians from Hungary and from Galicia. Caught between the antagonism to the Ukrainian national movement of the Uhro-Rusyns and the unyielding Ukrainian national orientation of the Galician Ukrainians, Bishop Ortynsky was never able to reconcile the two groups, precipitating, no doubt, Rome's decision to appoint two interim administrators for the exarchy upon the bishop's death.[1]

Relations between the Ukrainian clergy and the more nationalistically oriented Ukrainian laity improved considerably during Fr. Peter Poniatyshyn's tenure as coadministrator. A soft-spoken, urbane, and revered leader, Poniatyshyn was not only successful in bringing the church and the UNA closer together; he was also able to reestablish Catholic initiative in all aspects of Ukrainian-American community life.

In addition to his national work, Father Poniatyshyn played a crucial role in church affairs, especially in the continuing struggle against the proselytizing efforts of the Russian Orthodox Mission. The battle intensified after the death of Ortynsky when the Russians began to circulate a rumor that Rome was reticent to appoint a successor because Russia would soon annex Western Ukraine and all Catholics would "automatically" become Orthodox.[2] The Orthodox thrust was weakened substantially after the Russian Revolution, however, and after 1920 Poniatyshyn was able to concentrate more of his energies on the internal consolidation of the church.

During his eight and a half years as coadministrator of the exarchy, Father Poniatyshyn enjoyed a relatively amiable relationship with Father Martyak, his Carpatho-Ruthenian counterpart, and with the nine exclusively Hungarian Eastern-rite churches assigned to his jurisdiction by the apostolic delegate.[3] During this period Poniatyshyn was also able to create twenty-four new Ukrainian parishes, an effort which was aided by Metropolitan Andrei Sheptytsky, who visited the United States for a second time in 1921–2.

Metropolitan Sheptytsky came to the United States in November 1921 with two goals in mind: (1) financial assistance for war orphans in war-torn Galicia; (2) informing high-ranking U.S. government officials of the plight of Ukrainians in Galicia. Although he achieved both of his goals, the results were disappointing. No more than $15,000 from all sources was collected for war orphans and talks with American leaders accomplished little of substance.

Thanks largely to the efforts of Senator Frelinghuysen of New Jersey (a political ally Father Poniatyshyn had cultivated earlier), Metropolitan Sheptytsky, Poniatyshyn, and exarchial attorney Kerns met briefly with President Warren G. Harding and informed him of the harsh realities of Poland's military occupation of Galicia. Later, again with the help of Senator Frelinghuysen, the three met with Secretary of Commerce Herbert Hoover to thank him for his assistance to Ukrainians while he was the U.S. war relief administrator. Late in October 1922, Metropolitan Sheptytsky, barely recovered from a convalescence in Chicago, met with Secretary of State Charles Hughes. Also present were Luka Myshuha, then the representative of the Republic of Western Ukraine (ZUNR) and author of an extensive memorandum on the Polish occupation in Ukraine, and Chicago attorney Bohdan Pelechowicz. Metropolitan Sheptytsky asked for U.S. intervention in Galicia on the side of the Ukrainian church and clergy. Hughes promised to study the problem.

Before sailing for Europe in November 1922, Sheptytsky visited a number of Ukrainian parishes and Latin bishops and directed a retreat for clergy in New Jersey. Fifty-three Ukrainian and twenty-two Carpatho-Ruthenian priests attended the retreat, after which both groups convened to discuss the future of the exarchy. Upon his return to Europe, the metropolitan met with Pope Pius XI to report his observations and to lobby, no doubt, on behalf of the timely appointment of a Ukrainian bishop in the United States.[4]

On 8 May 1924, Pope Pius XI named Rev. Constantine Bohachevsky, vicar-general of the Peremyshl diocese, the new Ukrainian-American bishop with Philadelphia as his episcopal seat.[5] At the same time, Rev. Basil Takach, rector and spiritual director of the Uzhhorod seminary, was named Carpatho-Ruthenian American bishop with an episcopal seat to be located in New York City. Both candidates were consecrated in Rome on 15 June and two months later the two bishops arrived in the United States. On 1 September, the two new church leaders formally assumed the administration of their respective exarchies with Bishop Bohachevsky receiving 144 churches, 102 priests, and 237,495 faithful, and Bishop Takach taking over a newly created exarchy of 155 churches, 129 priests, and 288,390 faithful.[6]

Bohachevsky's Early Years

Bishop Bohachevsky's episcopacy had an auspicious beginning. An ethno-nationally recognized and highly respected Catholic leader in Galicia,[7] Bohachevsky, in his first pastoral letter to his priests and faithful in October 1924, stressed how difficult it was for him to leave his beloved fatherland even though it was a "ruined" country and a "martyred" nation. "I wish to convey to you, my dear fathers and faithful," the bishop continued, "the sincere greetings of your native land, your families, your brothers and sisters, your countrymen, and all Galician Ukrainians. I wish to convey to you the tears of the widows and orphans, the victims of the war for freedom for our people."

Having begun on an ethnonational note, Bohachevsky then proceeded to stress a theme that was to become the hallmark of his episcopacy – Catholic unity.

> My dear Reverend Fathers and beloved faithful! I hope that the relationships which shall be established between us by the will of God will grow progressively closer, and that you will progressively feel the need to gather around the episcopal throne, so that with our united efforts we may achieve our common goal, the salvation of souls.
>
> It is my responsibility to serve God, to be concerned for the glory of God and for the good of our Catholic Church, to be anxious for the salvation of the souls of the flocks entrusted to me. I wish to be a "Good Shepherd" but a good shepherd must constantly have before his eyes the best interests of his people

who have moved to a new fatherland, there to love the Lord
their God and to serve Him as they did in the old country, because
only then will they become a great and glorious people.

Pledging not to be "indifferent to the fortunes of our nation" and to
be concerned with the need "to hurry to the aid of our native land,"[8]
Bohachevsky began his episcopal tenure.

As dynamic and productive as Father Poniatyshyn had been in the
political arena, the fact that he was not a bishop diminished his authority
in the ecclesiastical and spiritual spheres. Priests often disregarded his
directives, while the laity, increasingly accustomed to "democratic" latitude
in church affairs, came to perceive Father Poniatyshyn more as a politician
than as their spiritual director. Bishop Bohachevsky perceived this diminu-
tion of church dominion and began to restructure his organization, neglecting almost entirely the kind of political presence the Ukrainian-American
community had come to expect from the leader of the Catholic church.
The major focus of the new bishop's early years was on order, discipline,
uniformity, and centralization of power. Within months he issued a series
of directives dealing with all phases of Ukrainian church life. Among other
things, he demanded prompt payment of the *catedracticum*, the chancery
office's annual parish assessment; he prohibited the construction of church
buildings without prior approval of the chancery; and he defined chancery
taxes for dispensations, permissions, and assignments. Priests were made
more accountable. Failure to account for funds often led to suspension.
Instituting a practice prevalent in Galicia since the 1891 Council of Lviv,
Bishop Bohachevsky informed the clergy that beginning in January 1925
competitive examinations in theology would be instituted and the results
would determine pastoral assignments. Priests were subsequently reas-
signed, some to smaller parishes. The changes, combined with the growing
perception that Bohachevsky was indifferent to the future of Ukraine and
that he believed that he, and he alone, was responsible for the church,
began to trouble some lay leaders. As early as 1925 articles began to appear
urging Bohachevsky "to remain close" to his people.[9]

Bohachevsky stressed the fundamental doctrines of Catholic faith in his
pastoral letters, placing special emphasis on the dogma of papal primacy.
Later he approved the installation of confessionals in Ukrainian Catholic
churches, a move viewed with disfavor by many Ukrainian Catholics. Still
later the new bishop ordered May devotions in honor of the blessed Mother
and June devotions in honor of the Sacred Heart of Jesus, both of which
were observances peculiar to the Latin rite. By the time he approved the
introduction of the Gregorian calendar in parishes under his jurisdiction,
suspicion of his motives had turned into resentment of his episcopacy by
certain lay leaders.[10]

Adding to the growing discontent was Bohachevsky's decision to abide by the clerical celibacy provision mandated by *Ea Semper* despite the fact that Bishop Ortynsky had continued to ordain married seminarians after the decree was promulgated and that the later *Cum Episcopo* decree – which many Ukrainians believed had voided *Ea Semper* – did not even mention celibacy.[11] Another source of discontent for the more nationalistic laity was Bohachevsky's perceived failure to respond to certain discriminatory provisions contained in the Rome-Warsaw Concordat of 1925.

The bishop's response to UUOA plans in commemoration of the memory of Ivan Franko on the tenth anniversary of his death was still another source of friction. The bishop acknowledged Franko's contribution to the Ukrainian national movement but argued that since the poet had proclaimed himself an atheist and had attacked the church, requesting that same church to honor his memory was inappropriate. Despite the bishop's admonition, some priests did participate in memorial services, suffering no consequences. To his dismay, however, Bohachevsky soon discovered that even *America* was siding with his detractors. Two editors were removed and replaced by Dr. Osyp Nazaruk, editor of *Sich,* in March 1926.[12]

The Committee for the Defense of the Ukrainian Catholic Church in America

Incensed by what they came to believe was a planned conspiracy between Rome and Warsaw to denationalize the Ukrainian church, a number of Ukrainians, especially those associated with the leadership element in the UUOA and *Svoboda,* became openly critical of Bishop Bohachevsky. As attacks in *Svoboda* and by the UUOA leadership grew in intensity, the Providence Association withdrew from UUOA while *America* and *Sich* rose to the defense of the bishop and his policies.

Late in 1926, soon after the departure of the Providence Association from its ranks, the UUOA called for a Ukrainian church congress in America to decide the future of Ukrainian Catholicism.[13] *Svoboda* praised the move as the only available course of action,[14] *Sich* labeled the proposed conclave a "congress of dimwits,"[15] and *America* dismissed it as a manifestation of "sick nationalism."[16]

The congress opened on 29 December 1926, with *Svoboda* reporting 130 delegates representing eighty-four Ukrainian Catholic parishes in attendance. After hearing a series of impassioned speeches about the celibacy issue,[17] the church calendar, the Rome-Warsaw Concordat, and the general decline of the Ukrainian Catholic church in America under Bohachevsky's leadership, the congress passed resolutions which called for:

1 The recall of Bishop Bohachevsky by the apostolic delegate.
2 The appointment of future Ukrainian bishops from among candidates recommended by the clergy and laity.

3 The right of local parishes to hire and fire priests and to maintain control over all church finances.

4 A refusal to pay exarchial dues until Bohachevsky's removal with all due monies to be placed in escrow by a newly formed church committee.

5 An official church name change by Rome from "Ruthenian" to "Ukrainian," with the retention of the appellation "Greek Catholic" to distinguish it from the Latin-rite Catholic church.

Especially galling to Bohachevsky was the call to boycott all seminary fund collections and parish school construction.

The congress, which was held in the Ukrainian Citizen's Hall in Philadelphia, also gave birth to the Committee for the Defense of the Greek Catholic Church in America. Elected to the new executive were Theodore Hrycaj, chairman; Michael Darmopray, secretary; Ivan Vaverchak, treasurer; and Michael Kociuk, Ivan Ivanyshyn, Gregory Pipiuk, and Michael Biyan, members of the board.[18] In commenting on the congress and its results, *Svoboda* wrote:

> The Congress gave notice that American Ukrainians are an enlightened people who understand their responsibilities and obligations but who also understand their rights. Not only do they understand them but they are willing to stand up for them against anybody, no matter who. Ukrainian Catholics demonstrated that they have learned much from the democratic principles they have seen in operation in this country, a land in which they found not only a piece of bread but knowledge and a new outlook on life and the world as well. The congress demonstrated that no longer can an autocratic Church, which recognizes only blind obedience, count on the Ukrainian "serf."[19]

The conclave was a severe blow to Bishop Bohachevsky, who, on 6 January 1927, excommunicated nine of the principal organizers. On 23 January, the bishop responded to the charges against him during his sermon in the Cathedral, defending the Concordat as a significant protection for the Ukrainian Catholic church in Poland, and condemning those who opposed him, especially their campaign to sabotage his ambitious school building program. He reiterated his belief that providing leadership for the church is the sole responsibility of the local ordinary and promised that those who "were willing to listen to the word of the Holy Catholic Church will be blessed by God." On 12 February, Bishop Bohachevsky quietly left for Rome.[20] At about the same time, Dr. Nazaruk resigned from the editorship of *America* and also took leave of the country. Noting the dual departure, *Svoboda* declared: "We won't grieve over them ..."[21]

"The New York 26"

Opposition to Bohachevsky was not restricted to the laity nor did it end with his departure. During his absence, and despite a formal prohibition from the bishop's chancellor, a group of "old guard" Ukrainian priests, including the Revs. Strutynsky, L. Levytsky, Pelechowich, and the popular Joseph Zhuk, decided to hold a conference of their own. Calling themselves "priest-patriots," they met in New York City on 23 February 1927, and passed resolutions – subsequently signed by twenty-six of them – which:

1 Called upon the apostolic delegate to remove Bishop Bohachevsky. "His continued unpopular presence in America," the resolution read, "will bring about a great exodus from the Ukrainian Greek Catholic church."
2 Protested Polish interference in Ukrainian church affairs in Western Ukraine.
3 Urged Ukrainian Catholics to remain loyal to the church because "the matter will be settled soon."[22]

The Holy See, meanwhile, approved of Bohachevsky's actions and ordered him back to his exarchy; shortly after Bohachevsky's return the apostolic delegate demanded a public retraction from the New York 26.[23] The dissidents were provided with the exact form of the retraction and were given fifteen days to sign and publish it in the Ukrainian press or "suffer the full measure of canonical law." Angered by the ultimatum, *Svoboda* urged the dissidents to resist in the interests of maintaining a solid front.[24]

Caught between loyalty to their convictions and ecclesiastical obedience, most of the priests opted for the latter, a decision that won the sympathy but not the respect of the Committee for the Defense of the Ukrainian Greek Catholic Church in America. Commenting on the fact that all but a few of the dissidents had signed a retraction, the committee declared that such action "is not in agreement with the honor of priests as conscientious and patriotic Ukrainian community members." The fight, the committee pledged, would continue.[25]

Cum Data Fuerit

Despite the committee's pledge to continue the struggle within the church, the resistance was broken. The more intransigent clergy and laity simply joined the Ukrainian Orthodox church and the committee's influence began to decline.

Bohachevsky's stature, meanwhile, was strengthened in 1929 with the promulgation of *Cum Data Fuerit*, a papal decree that clarified any remaining doubt concerning the Holy See's position on celibacy of East-

ern-rite priests in America (Article 12) and the dissolution of the local
trustee system of ownership of church property (Article 6). That same year,
fifty-three Ukrainian Catholic priests, gathered in convention in Philadelphia, signed "a special document in which they underscored their full
obedience and loyalty to their Bishop and asked him to accept this public
proclamation as satisfaction for the previous injustices heaped upon him."
Those who were not present "sent letters of agreement with this avowal
and their personal loyalty."[26] By this time, however, such a gesture was
largely anticlimactic. The resistance had been quelled, and dissidence
within the Ukrainian church had begun to dissipate. Bad feelings continued, however. As late as 1931 at a concert honoring UVO members
who had passed away, a leaflet was distributed which called Bishop
Bohachevsky "the biggest enemy of the Ukrainian people in the United
States."[27]

The Bohachevsky Legacy

Changes within the Ukrainian Catholic church continued all through the
1930s. The Gregorian calendar was adopted by a number of parishes; the
use of Latin-rite rosaries and scapulars increased; the Stations of the Cross
were introduced into some churches; frequent confession and communion,
then a Latin-rite manifestation, were encouraged; altar boys replaced *diaks*
(cantors) in many churches; and congregational singing during the Divine
Liturgy was discouraged in favor of choral singing.[28]

Unable to obtain priests from Ukraine, Bishop Bohachevsky approached
the Order of St. Basil the Great in Europe for priests and nuns. One of the
first Basilian priests was the Rev. Epephanius Theodorovich, who arrived
in 1927 and became editor of *Katolytsky Provid* (Catholic Leadership) that
same year. Printed by Sich Press, the UHO publishing house, the periodical
defended Bohachevsky. In the first issue, the lead article blamed the "godless, non-believing leadership for the difficult moments and terrible pain"
which the community had to endure.

> They are to blame. Yes. Not a disease, not a terrible illness, not
> the last war has brought us as much pain as this leadership. Not
> even the Turks and Tartars, not the Muscovites and Poles ever
> put us into such captivity as that godless, non-believing leader-
> ship. Because of that leadership, our people are not defending the
> Catholic church, they're not helping her, they're running away
> from her. That leadership has fooled the dark masses into belie-
> ving that Rome serves Warsaw, that the Holy Father is a Pole,

that the Catholic church is the enemy of our nation, that our bishops sold out to the enemy.[29]

On 1 October 1932, Father Theodorovich became the Basilian superior at St. Nicholas Church in Chicago, then the largest Ukrainian church in the United States; Fr. Sylvester Zhuravetsky became the pastor. Two more Basilians, the Revs. Ambrose Senyshyn and Maxim Markiw, arrived in 1933.

In 1935, the Sisters Servants of Mary Immaculate were invited into the exarchy from Canada to assist the Basilian Sisters in staffing Ukrainian day schools. During the 1940s, Bohachevsky invited Ukrainian Redemptorists, Franciscans, the Sisters of the Mother of God, and the Sisters of the Sacred Heart into the exarchy.[30]

Politically, Bohachevsky tried to remain as uninvolved as possible. Since the United Hetman Organization and *Sich* supported the Catholic church – and urged obedience to the clergy – Bohachevsky was sympathetic to that organization but not to ODWU which, in the bishop's mind, stressed nationalism over religion. In keeping with Bohachevsky's apolitical approach to Ukrainian Catholicism, priests were forbidden to participate in Ukrainian political organizations while the laity was discouraged from active involvement if non-Catholics – especially Ukrainian Orthodox – were present.[31]

Contrary to assertions by his detractors, however, Bohachevsky was not indifferent to developments in Ukraine. Reminding the people, as Sochocky put it, "that the greatness of a nation does not depend upon its numbers or wealth but upon its spiritual strength," Bohachevsky called for "a special day of prayer and good deeds to help the starving" during the 1933 famine in the UkrSSR. Prayers were offered again for the people of the Lemko region in 1934 and a Sunday of prayer was set aside "for the well-being of the Ukrainian people" in 1938.[32]

Meanwhile, the older clergy and the European-born laity quietly resisted Bohachevsky's policies as unobtrusively as possible. Ukrainian after-school classes to preserve the Ukrainian heritage were continued, priests did announce meetings of non-Catholic organizations from the pulpit – actions frowned upon by Bohachevsky[33] – and Ukrainian Catholics did join with their Orthodox brethren in Ukrainian organizational activities, especially those initiated by the UNA, the UUOA, and ODWU.[34]

The weakest link in efforts to preserve the national character of the Ukrainian Catholic church in America – that is, those who seemed to be least concerned with this aspect of their church and therefore most supportive of Bohachevsky – was the American-born clergy. Reconciled to celibacy as a necessary component of their religious leadership, and anxious to maintain status with their Latin-rite counterparts – who all too often adopted a somewhat condescending posture towards other rites – younger priests appeared to have little sympathy for Ukrainian nationalism. In terms of priorities, Catholicism was the most significant aspect of their community lives.[35]

The sentiments of the younger clergy had an effect on American-born youth. In a much better position to relate to the second generation than European-born priests, younger priests had a golden opportunity to influence the young and to excite them about the beauty, originality, and significance of their rite. That too little of this type of education took place is evidenced by the fact that appeals for changes within the rite from among the younger generation during the late 1930s grew in both number and intensity.[36] For some Ukrainian leaders this phenomenon did not come as a surprise. As early as 1927, during the heat of the religious crisis, Dr. Simenovych wrote that the "second generation is not interested in preserving the rite" and warned that unless they see its value, "they will change to another."[37]

In the end, the Ukrainian Catholic church suffered. As changes were introduced, more and more European-born Ukrainians either joined the Orthodox or became indifferent to the practice of their faith, remaining Catholic in name only. At the same time, the younger generation, while welcoming the changes, believed they were too few and too infrequent. As long as the first-generation laity remained in the majority and continued to resist change, and as long as the second generation was growing up and too weak to effect change, the Ukrainian Catholic church still had a future as a vehicle of ethnonational preservation.[38] By 1939, however, this future appeared dim. Noting the declining number of Ukrainian immigrants, the death rate, the low birth rate of the second generation, and the Catholic secessions which continued all through the 1930s, Stephen Mamchur, then a student at Yale University completing his doctoral dissertation on nationalism and the Ukrainian church, predicted: "By 1965, the number of Ukrainian Catholics will be negligible and the Ukrainian dioceses by that time will, therefore, have probably disappeared."[39]

As unpopular as Bishop Bohachevsky had become – at one point he could count on the support of no more than one-third of his priests[40] – he was not the arch-villain his enemies argued he was. Nor was he a Latinizer working for Rome and Warsaw to diminish the Ukrainian Greek Catholic church. He was, first of all, a deeply spiritual man who grew up in an environment of discipline and obedience. He began his priesthood in 1909, at a time when many of the Latin-rite practices instituted by the 1891 Ukrainian Catholic Church Synod in Lviv were already in place. In Peremyshl, for example, priestly celibacy was the rule since the war. In the words of Fr. John Terlecky: "Whatever changes he [Bishop Bohachevsky] implemented were not the result of a personal policy of Latinization but rather a reflection of what the Church in Galicia in the 1920's looked like."[41]

Bohachevsky's willingness to deal with inherited administrative problems led to more loss of support. One of the first issues demanding his attention was the matter of parish corporations, of which there were a variety owing to the different circumstances prevailing at the time of incorporation. In 1924, there were only two states, New York and New Jersey, which had provisions regarding ownership titles of Ukrainian churches. Both Bishop Ortynsky and Father Poniatyshyn had made some progress but there were still some church councils which refused to turn their deeds over to the bishop's "Ruthenian Corporation." There were other problems as well. One parish, for example, had a Latin-rite bishop as one of its trustees. Another parish was a functioning Orthodox parish but its parishioners, most of whom were Ukrainian Catholic, wanted to be included in Bohachevsky's exarchy. Complex legal issues were always involved and the litigation which ensued did little to endear the bishop to the Ukrainian community, especially among those who lost.[42]

Another source of friction between Bishop Bohachevsky and many community leaders was the result of different priorities. Although he agreed that helping Ukrainians in Europe was important, Bohachevsky's major focus was on the spiritual growth of Ukrainians in America. He promoted the establishment of seminaries and parochial schools and urged Ukrainian Americans to concentrate on their needs in America. For a community accustomed to the kind of visible political leadership provided by Father Poniatyshyn, Bishop Bohachevsky's relative lack of interest in European affairs was difficult to accept. When the bishop insisted that all monies collected during church services for orphans and invalids be forwarded directly to bishops or relevant organizations in Europe – bypassing, thereby, UUOA channels – it was perceived as one more affront by some community leaders.[43]

In the end, it was probably Bishop Bohachevsky's administrative style that cost him the most support, especially among his priests. Ostap Prestai, a priest who remained loyal to Bohachevsky despite certain reservations, writes:

> Learned in church dogma, canon law, ecumenical and synodal proclamations, and the dictates of various popes, the new bishop, lacking in experience or special gifts, with no desire to learn more about human nature, began to feverishly reform the Church with the zeal of St. Peter in the Garden of Gethsemane. He relied on the power of episcopal authority, canon law, and

the discipline of the eastern Church. The bishop initiated the reformation process – so dangerous, especially in America – by himself, on his own authority, without anyone's counsel. On the contrary, he ignored the warnings of older, experienced priests and missionaries ... Somehow he got rid of older, experienced, and more practical consultors and replaced them with young, pliable former students of his or former school buddies ... He didn't want to meet with his priests, 52 of whom waited for him following religious recollections in Orange [NJ] in 1926 to discuss how best to combat the enemies of the Church. He said "I alone am the one who can defend the Church."[44]

The entire episode was a painful learning experience for the young bishop and led, according to Prystai, to a change in approach in his later years.

In some ways, the *Cum Data Fuerit* decree of 1929 strengthened Bishop Bohachevsky's hand against his detractors because it provided Ukrainian Greek Catholics with certain canonical protections from amalgamation by the Latin-rite church. Among other things, the decree stipulated that attendance of Ukrainians at Latin-rite churches, "even if it be continuous, does not effect a change of Rite." Only a petition approved by the apostolic delegate, preferably through the office of the Ukrainian bishop, made that possible. Another article declared that "persons born in the United States of North America of parents of different rites are to be baptized in the rite of the father."[45] These and other provisions should have calmed the fears of those who believed the Holy See was determined to Latinize Ukrainian Greek Catholics.

Bishop Bohachevsky survived his early years and went on to enjoy productive and relatively uneventful tenures, first as bishop and later as metropolitan. As we shall learn in chapter 10, his major contribution to the community was in education. How he perceived education was revealed early in 1933 when he wrote: "In the last nine years our community has lived through a great spiritual and intellectual crisis. It has become clear to us that the periodic outbreaks of conflicts, of everybody against everybody among our immigrants, arise from the fact that we lack our own schools that would spread our culture."[46] When the minor seminary was finally opened that same year in Stamford, *America* declared: "Perhaps for once it will be possible for us to develop from within ourselves a sense of authority. Perhaps we will realize that it is not for all of us to lead and stand at the head, but everyone must find for himself an appropriate place in the work of the people."[47] At the time, there were seventeen seminarians from the exarchy, twelve studying in Rome and five in Stanislaviv, Galicia.

In 1940, Bishop John Buchko, auxiliary to Metropolitan Sheptytsky, was unexpectedly appointed auxiliary to Bishop Bohachevsky. Visiting Ukrainian colonies in South America when World War II broke out, Bishop Buchko was unable to return to Europe until 1942 when he was appointed apostolic visitor to Ukrainian refugees in Western Europe. That same year, Ambrose Senyshyn, OSMB, was appointed auxiliary bishop in Buchko's place, assuring an orderly transition in the event of the untimely death of the ordinary. Official church membership reached 303,069 by 1945, of which some 28,000 had served in the American armed forces. In 1946, the Ukrainian Redemptorist Fathers (CSSR) established their permanent center at St. John the Baptist Church in Newark (NJ), increasing the number of priests that would be available in the United States when the third immigration arrived a few years later. In 1948, the Home of Divine Providence in Philadelphia was purchased and opened to senior citizens by the Sisters Servants of Mary Immaculate. By 1957, Bohachevsky, now an archbishop, could boast that his jurisdiction included 172 parishes, 11 missions, and 300 priests under the leadership of an archbishop and two bishops; 223 churches and chapels; three religious orders for men and four religious orders and communities for women; two orphanages, three homes for the aged, a summer camp for youth, major and minor seminaries, two colleges, four high schools, thirty all-day parochial schools, a national Ukrainian Catholic youth organization, a student's society, "Obnova," the Providence Association, and a vigorous Ukrainian Catholic press. "Our Ukrainian Catholic Church," concluded Bohachevsky, "stands with a firm foot upon this land."[48]

The Rise of Ukrainian Orthodoxy

The acceptance of Orthodoxy by Western Ukrainians in America passed through a number of historical phases. The initial phase, discussed previously, was led by Father Alexis Toth and involved the acceptance of Russian Orthodoxy by various Ukrainian and Uhro-Rusyn parishes. This era came to an end after 1917 when the Bolsheviks overthrew the Provisional government, thereby putting an end to Russian governmental support for Russian Orthodoxy in America, and the Russian church here split into a number of factions. Most Ukrainians who had joined the Russian Orthodox church during this period, however, remained there and became "Russian" in both religiocultural and ethnonational orientation.

The first phase of what was a distinctly *Ukrainian* Orthodox movement in America began in Chicago in 1915 when a group of parishioners belonging to the St. Nicholas Ukrainian Catholic Church became disenchanted with the pastorship of Fr. Mykola Strutynsky. Led by Jurij Masley, Joseph Kotsovsky, and Luka Riza – respectively, vice-chairman, treasurer, and curator of the St. Nicholas Church Council in 1914[49] – they left the church[50] and, with the support of Dr. and Mrs. Stepan Hrynevetsky,[51] established the so-called "Ukrainian National church."

The first pastor of the church was Fr. Hryhorii Khomitsky, ordained by Bishop Karfora of the "Old Catholic" church, established in Germany and Italy in the nineteenth century in opposition to assertions of papal infallibility. Under Khomitsky's direction, the Ukrainian National church in America expanded to six priests and six parishes by 1917. Formally under the jurisdiction of the Old Catholic church, these churches were essentially Orthodox in practice and Ukrainian in religiocultural orientation.[52]

The second phase of Ukrainian Orthodoxy in America was initiated in 1916 when Rev. Stepan Dziubaj, vicar-general for the Carpatho-Ruthenians under Bishop Ortynsky, left the Catholic church. Bitterly disappointed at not having been selected coadministrator of the eparchy, Dziubaj approached Archbishop Aleksander of the Russian Orthodox church and, on 20 August 1916, was consecrated a bishop with full power to create a new Orthodox diocese. Dziubaj eventually convinced ten Carpatho-Ruthenian parishes to join the diocese and, in time, the six Ukrainian national churches. Gradually, however, the Carpatho-Ruthenian parishes became disillusioned with Dziubaj's leadership and left the diocese. In an effort to retain the loyalty of the Ukrainian parishes, which were also becoming restless, Dziubaj appealed to Aleksander for more autonomy. This request was denied in 1919 and the Ukrainian parishes departed the diocese.[53]

The third phase in the evolution of Ukrainian Orthodoxy in America began when the six Ukrainian National parishes formed a separate Orthodox diocese under the nominal leadership of Metropolitan Germanos Shehediy, a Syrian Orthodox prelate whose principal function was to ordain priests and to participate in religious functions. The actual leadership of the diocese, however, remained in the hands of Ukrainians. Between 1920 and 1923, the diocese was administered by Rev. Mykola Kopachuk. Later, the administrative functions were inherited by a consistory which included Fr. Volodymyr Kaskiv, Rev. Khomitsky, and Fr. John Hundiak.[54]

The Ukrainian Autocephalous Orthodox Church of America

The fourth evolutionary phase in Ukrainian-American Orthodox history began in 1922 with the arrival in America of Deacon Pavlo Korsunovsky of the newly created Autocephalous Orthodox church in Ukraine. Meeting with the Ukrainian Orthodox leadership here, he convinced them to accept the new church and to petition Kievan Metropolitan Vasyl Lypkivsky for a Ukrainian bishop. The request was made and, on 13 February 1924, Bishop Ivan Theodorovich arrived in America. In June, Bishop Theodorovich was

formally installed as the first bishop of the Ukrainian Autocephalous Orthodox church of America,[55] inheriting a diocese which included 11 parishes,
8,580 members, and 14 priests.

Like Bohachevsky, Theodorovich came to America with impeccable
national credentials. Born in Volhynia in 1887, he had a distinguished
record as a chaplain in both the Ukrainian National and Galician armies
and was considered an able and energetic administrator who, as Orthodox
bishop of the diocese of Vynntsia and Podillia, had managed to expand
his jurisdiction from 18 to 247 parishes in a matter of two years.[56] Four
years after his arrival in America, the Ukrainian Autocephalous church had
increased to 34 parishes, 26,520 faithful, and 34 priests owing, in large
measure, to the disaffection of Catholics. Despite its rapid growth, however,
the newly established Orthodox church was faced with two major problems: its relationship with the mother church in Kiev and its lack of acceptance by the Orthodox world as a canonically legitimate body.[57]

The first issue was initially the most pressing, largely because of growing
Bolshevik influence in church affairs in Kiev, especially after Metropolitan
Lypkivsky was arrested in 1927. Beginning in 1927, the new church hierarchy in the UkrSSR began to admonish Theodorovich regarding the strongly
nationalistic posture of his diocese and the anti-Bolshevik articles that
appeared regularly in Dnipro, the Orthodox press organ. Theodorovich
was faced with a dilemma. Continued criticism of the Communists by the
church in America could adversely affect the delicate balance that then
existed between the church and the state in the UkrSSR. Concessions to the
Communists, however, could alienate the strongly nationalistic Ukrainian
Orthodox in America, the strongest supporters of the new church. Theodorovich decided to temper articles in Dnipro and to await further developments. Criticism of the Soviet Union was later resumed, however, and
again the mother church in Kiev demanded that Theodorovich cease and
desist. By this time, it was becoming increasingly uncomfortable for Theodorovich to continue ties with a mother church now completely under the
thumb of Soviet authorities. The Soviets soon accused the church hierarchy
in Ukraine of collaboration with the outlawed Union for the Liberation of
Ukraine and in December 1930 forced the dissolution of the church. In
1931, soon after learning that the Council of the Ukrainian Autocephalous
Church in Ukraine had proclaimed its self-dissolution, Theodorovich formally severed all ties with Ukraine.[58]

The question of canonicity was more problematic. The first All-Ukrainian
Orthodox Sobor convened in Kiev on 14 October 1921, with over 400
delegates (including 64 priests) in attendance. With no duly consecrated
Orthodox bishops present to take part in the elevation of new bishops, the
delegates elected to resurrect a mode of consecration not practiced in the

Christian church since the second century. Archpriest Vasyl Lypkivsky was consecrated Metropolitan of Kiev by other priests who held the Holy Gospel on his head while remaining in physical contact with all of the delegates. Lypkivsky then consecrated Archpriest Nestor Sharaivsky and the two of them elevated four more priests, including Theodorovich. Since the initial two elevations were not in accordance with traditional Orthodox canon law, the entire hierarchy of the Ukrainian Autocephalous Orthodox Church was not viewed as canonical by other Orthodox churches. The ecclesiastical legality of Theodorovich's episcopacy became an exceedingly pressing problem for the fledgling church when a second Ukrainian Orthodox diocese which had traditional apostolic orders was established in the United States in 1929. Despite his realization that to seek reconsecration was a tacit admission that the Autocephalous Orthodox Church was indeed "non-canonical," Theodorovich did attempt to obtain recognition of his status as a bishop on three separate occasions.

Theodorovich first approached the American Episcopal church in 1926 when the latter agreed to consider the possibility of establishing an ecclesiastical relationship. When the Episcopalians demanded that the Ukrainian Autocephalous church come under their jurisdiction entirely and that the English language be substituted for Ukrainian, all negotiations ceased.

A second attempt to obtain recognition was made in 1930, this time through Archbishop Athenagoras, the American representative of the Orthodox patriarch of Constantinople. Negotiations were suspended by the Ukrainians, however, once it was learned that a number of Orthodox lay leaders – primarily Volodymyr Kedrovsky in the United States and Vasyl Swystun in Canada – were violently opposed to even nominal leadership by "a foreigner."

A final attempt to obtain recognition was made in 1935 in conjunction with an effort to unite the two Ukrainian Orthodox churches in America. As we shall learn later, this effort also failed.[59]

The inability of the Ukrainian Autocephalous Orthodox church in America to be recognized as a traditional Orthodox church was the primary reason for its decline after 1930.[60] A number of leading clerics – most notably Fr. John Hundiak, editor of *Dnipro*, and Fr. Andrew Iwanishin, consistory secretary – left Theodorovich and joined the newly organized Ukrainian Orthodox diocese.[61] Their example was emulated by other Orthodox clergy along with their parishes. Even though Theodorovich gained five new parishes between 1928 and 1936, the combined strength of his church in 1939 was only 24 parishes, 18,720 members, and 22 priests.[62]

The Ukrainian Orthodox Church of America

While many Ukrainian Catholics were so alienated by Bohachevsky's administration of the exarchy that they were willing to join any Ukrainian Orthodox church, even one not recognized by the Orthodox world, other Catholics, especially the clergy, were wary of such a move. Faced with the choice of either remaining with Bohachevsky or joining Theodorovich – neither option to their liking – they decided on a third alternative: the establishment of a Ukrainian Orthodox diocese recognized by other Orthodox churches.

The fifth phase of Ukrainian Orthodox development in America began on 9 April 1929, when nine ex-Catholic priests and thirty-four lay representatives from twenty-five parishes met in Allentown, Pennsylvania, for the purpose of establishing a canonical Orthodox church in America. A consistory of three priests – Fathers Oleksa Ulitzsky, Peter Sereda, and Joseph Pelechowich – was elected with Ulitzsky as the chief administrator. Ulitzsky resigned the following day, however, and was replaced by Pelechowich, who, in turn, stepped down in favor of Fr. Joseph Zhuk.[63]

On 11 December 1930, the new Orthodox diocese, known as the Ukrainian Orthodox Church in America, was recognized by the patriarch of Constantinople and, on 15 July 1931, at a special council of the clergy held in New York City, the diocese was formally incorporated. Zhuk was designated bishop-elect,[64] and the patriarch was informed of the actions and presented with a petition requesting formal recognition of the church and the consecration of Zhuk.[65]

The patriarch of Constantinople delayed, however, and Zhuk, in an effort to obtain at least a modicum of status, permitted his consecration on 25 September 1932 by two Syrian Orthodox bishops, whose canonical status was also in question.[66] The new Orthodox church was now faced with a similar problem to that of the Autocephalous church.

Bishop Zhuk died on 23 February 1934, and the administration of the diocese passed to Father Mykola Pidhoretsky. Efforts were made during the next year to unite with the Autocephalous church and when such a union failed, the diocesan leadership decided to seek a successor to Zhuk in the person of an Orthodox priest. The search ended when Rev. Theodore Shpilka, then an Orthodox priest in Carpatho-Ukraine, agreed to accept the episcopacy. His nomination was approved by the patriarch of Constantinople on 13 October 1936, and, on 24 December 1936, he formally assumed the administrative duties of the diocese. On 28 February 1937, Shpilka, who came to be known as Bishop Bohdan, was consecrated by Archbishop Athenagoras and Bishop Kallistos of the Greek Archdiocese of America. The

Ukrainian Orthodox Church in America finally had a bishop consecrated according to traditional canons.[67]

Bishop Bohdan's diocese, the more dynamic of the two Ukrainian Orthodox groups in America in the 1930s, almost doubled in size by 1939, reaching a total of 43 parishes and 36 priests.[68] The combined Orthodox total for that same year was 67 parishes and 58 priests, a figure that compared favorably with the Ukrainian Catholic total of 105 parishes and 97 priests.[69]

Attempts at Orthodox Unity

Efforts to unite the two Ukrainian Orthodox dioceses in America began soon after Bishop Zhuk's death in 1934 when Zhuk's successors approached Theodorovich offering to unify the two churches provided Theodorovich could obtain canonical status. Negotiations began late in 1934, the "theses" (conditions) for union were signed by both parties on 6 March 1935, and Theodorovich again petitioned the patriarch of Constantinople for recognition through formal reconsecration.

Meanwhile, the Canadian branch of the Autocephalous church, opposed to the merger, inaugurated a bitter campaign under the leadership of Vasyl Swystun, claiming, among other things, that the union had not been previously discussed with the lay leadership. The Canadian church finally did approve the union but this time it was the Orthodox patriarch who did not act. In June 1935, the two parties were informed that the patriarch was unable to move on their request immediately because of illness. This response was interpreted as a polite refusal, and by the end of the year both churches reverted to their former status.[70]

Orthodox-Catholic Relations

Relations between Ukrainian Catholics and Ukrainian Orthodox in the United States became increasingly strained during the 1930s, a factor which only exacerbated the political division which already existed in the community.

Adding fuel to the fire was a series of expensive court battles for possession of church property. The dissident former Catholics claimed the property now belonged to the newly created Orthodox parishes, while Bohachevsky argued that it belonged to the Catholic exarchy. In most cases, the Orthodox claims were upheld.[71]

Both the Catholics and the Orthodox adopted the standard arguments for substantiating their claims to being the "true Christian church." In addition, however, both churches appealed to the nationalism of the Ukrainian-American community by also claiming to represent the "true faith of the Ukrainian people." The Orthodox argued that the Union of 1596 had been forced on the Ukrainian people by the Poles,[72] that the Papacy had always upheld the Roman Catholic Polish nation in its efforts to dominate its eastern frontiers,[73] and that Ukrainians could expect little from Pope Pius XI whose "favorite people – the Poles," he consistently upheld while a papal emissary in Warsaw in 1922.[74] The Catholics, in contrast, claimed that union with Rome was desired by most Ukrainians, that the Poles actually opposed it, and that it was later rejected by some Ukrainians because they believed the "lies" about the union circulated by the Russians.[75]

Most severely affected by the raging religious disputes were the youth. Separate youth organizations were formed and both churches demanded conversion to "the true faith" in the event of a religiously mixed marriage. While the adherence to this position varied from priest to priest, the younger Catholic clergy, especially the American-born, seemed most adamant. Orthodox priests appeared ready to bend – "at least he's Ukrainian" – while younger Catholic priests were more likely to sanction marriage to a Polish Catholic – "thank God he's Catholic" – than to a Ukrainian Orthodox.[76]

By 1938, the Orthodox, concerned more with national unity than with dogma, were urging rapproachement between the two Christian churches, especially during community commemorations. Commenting on the refusal of Catholic and Orthodox clergy to participate jointly in all such events, Theodore Swystun – who wrote a regular column in the official Orthodox periodical, *Dnipro* – condemned such behavior, arguing that "the only difference between the two churches is that Orthodox Catholics recognize only the primacy of Christ ... This is no reason for division among people of the same blood and the same family ... When 5 million Ukrainians belong to the Greek Catholic Church, they don't belong because they are enamored of Roman Catholicism but because the Greek Catholic Church has in large measure preserved the ancient Ukrainian Orthodox tradition."

> Both churches will remain among the Ukrainian people long after all of us are gone ... Wouldn't it be better if both churches were friendly competitors in the faithful service of God? ... Wouldn't it be better if one and the other church demonstrated solidarity to the world in the Christian struggle of the Ukrainian people to free themselves of Muscovite, Polish, Rumanian and Czech slavery? The Church cannot accomplish this by itself but a true Ukrainian church, a Church with a Ukrainian soul, can do much to bring

us sooner to that great moment about which we now talk and write so much but for which we do so little in an organized fashion.[77]

Despite many such appeals from Orthodox and Catholic laity alike, few Catholic priests were willing to risk Bohachevsky's ire and associate with their Orthodox counterparts until the wounds of the past had had an opportunity to heal.

The Growth of Ukrainian Protestantism in America

While Catholics and Orthodox feuded, Ukrainian Protestants in America – primarily Presbyterians and Baptists – continued to organize congregations within the community. In comparison to the Orthodox, however, progress was slow.

Rev. Basil Kusiw left the pastorship of the First Ukrainian Presbyterian Church in Newark in 1918 to conduct missionary work in Ukraine. His successor was Rev. John Kocan, who continued to maintain the Ukrainian character of the church by supporting the artistic development of both the Ukrainian choir and the Ukrainian drama troupe associated with the parish. Under Kocan's leadership, a Boy Scout troop and sports club were established for the youth along with an orchestra.

Late in 1925, Rev. Kusiw returned to resume his pastorship and to continue his proselytizing efforts among Ukrainian Americans. A year later, the church choir came under the directorship of George Kirichenko, a former member of the Ukrainian National Chorus in Kiev. Under his leadership the Ukrainian Presbyterian choir reached a new level of excellence, performing, on occasion, at Carnegie Hall and Radio City.[78]

By 1932, there were five Ukrainian Presbyterian parishes in America, all of which still retained their Ukrainian character.[79] In 1935, Rev. Kusiw again returned to missionary work in Western Ukraine and was succeeded by Rev. Alexander Kuman, who remained with the First Presbyterian Church until 1939.[80]

Ukrainian Baptists organized two more parishes in the United States before World War II, one in Detroit and one in Camden, New Jersey. The Detroit congregation had its beginnings in 1918 when Vasyl Boiko began his proselytizing activities in that city. It was firmly established by 1923 when Y. Zinkiv became the first pastor. The Camden congregation was organized by Vasyl Kolodey.[81]

In addition to the five Presbyterian and four Baptist congregations, Ukrainians were also active in other churches of varying Protestant convictions.[82] With the exception of the Newark Presbyterian church, Protestant involvement in the mainstream of Ukrainian-American ethnonational life remained minimal.

From Carpatho-Ruthenian to "Carpatho-Russian"

While Rome's promulgation of *Cum Data Fuerit* in 1929[83] caused hardly a ripple in the Ukrainian Catholic community in the United States – it merely legitimized what Bohachevsky had already accomplished two years earlier – the Carpatho-Ruthenian community reacted with shock and consternation. Even though the celibacy decree only applied to newly ordained Eastern-rite priests, the Carpatho-Ruthenian clergy (85 percent of whom were married) came to view the edict as a threat to their status in the Catholic community. The laity, however, was upset that the papal decree forced them to relinquish local control of church property. As priests began to openly question Rome's wisdom and as various parishes refused to turn over their real estate titles to Bishop Takach,[84] a strong and eventually vitriolic dissident movement emerged in the Carpatho-Ruthenian community led, as always, by the GCU.[85]

On 30 July 1930, GCU directors resolved to fight the celibacy decision as well as their bishop. Calling for the convocation of an all-Ruthenian congress, *Viestnik* inaugurated a long series of anti-Takach articles in 1931 – "On a Good Bishop" (15 May), "Celibacy Hurts Us" (6 June), "Bishop Takach Turning Faithful Sons against Their Rite" (25 June), and "Celibacy Now – What Later?" (25 June) – aimed at forcing the Ruthenian bishop to demur. When Takach remained steadfast in his support of Rome's ruling, *Viestnik* continued to press for a religious conclave and by 22 November was able to claim that 102 parishes were willing to participate.[86]

On 10 April 1932, the Committee for the Defense of the Eastern Rite (Komitet oborony vostochnoho obriada – KOVO) was founded in Johnstown, Pennsylvania, under the leadership of Rev. J. Hanulya (chairman) and A.M. Smor (secretary). Also present at the first organizational meeting were Gregory Zatkovich, Dr. P.I. Zeedick, Stephen Starunchak, and eight priests, three of whom – Revs. Orestes Chornock, Stephen Varzaly, and Constantine Auroroff – had already been suspended by Bishop Takach.

A KOVO-sponsored congress was held in Johnstown in June 1933 with some 1,500 delegates in attendance, and a new organization, the Religious National Congress of Carpatho-Russian Greek Catholic Churches, headed by Starunchak, came into being. In July, a KOVO convention was held in Pittsburgh with 311 lay delegates, 45 priests, and 60 *diaks* (cantors) in attendance. Twelve resolutions were presented by Starunchak and all were subsequently accepted:

1 Rome must adhere to the Uniate agreement signed at Uzhhorod.
2 The celibacy decree must be revoked and the attempted Latinization of the clergy must be stopped.
3 The bishop and his clerical advisors must be recalled immediately. If this is not done, the members of KOVO will refuse to obey his dictates.
4 Penalties inflicted upon those fighting celibacy must be rescinded.
5 Married seminarians must be ordained.
6 The new bishop must be an American citizen chosen by the American Carpatho-Ruthenian clergy.
7 The Pittsburgh Exarchate must be represented in the Sacred Congregation for the Oriental Rite.
8 Papal officials must use the term "Carpatho-Russian" rather than "Ruthenian" to designate the people of the Exarchate.
9 The exercise of local autonomy in such matters as salaries for priests and cantors must be approved. The Congress shall pick two priests, two cantors, and five laymen to compile these new Diocesan Statutes.
10 The articles of incorporation are to be changed to allow for the recording of church property in the name of the congregation. Neither the bishop nor the pastor are allowed to serve as trustees.
11 The parish is not obligated to pay the salary of priests who work against the interests of the Greek Catholic Union.
12 Papal authorities must comply with this communication within sixty days or KOVO will secede from the Catholic Church and organize an Independent Church.[87]

In the end, neither the Holy See nor Bishop Takach relented and, on 6 February 1936, the more recalcitrant of the dissidents gathered in Pittsburgh and established the American Carpatho-Russian Orthodox Greek Catholic Diocese under the leadership of Rev. Orestes Chornock who, along with five other priests, was subsequently excommunicated. On 18 September 1938, Chornock was consecrated a bishop by the Orthodox Holy Synod in Constantinople. By that time, the newly created Orthodox diocese had 40 parishes and approximately 50,000 members, most of whom were former Catholics.[88]

Related to the entire religiocultural conflict was the still murky issue of a Uhro-Rusyn or Carpatho-Ruthenian national identity. Whether the dissidents decided to adopt the Carpatho-Russian identity because they knew they would eventually become Orthodox is unknown. One thing is certain, however. During the heat of the battle over celibacy and parish autonomy, the specter of "Ukrainianization" was raised once again as one of the major enemies of the Carpatho-Ruthenian church. Warnings against the Ukrainian "threat" appeared in *Viestnik* in 1933.[89] In 1934 the GCU gazette published an article by A.M. Smor in which he wrote: "We will not tolerate that which the Ukrainian Roman circles work out for the UNIATE Greek Catholic Church – ONE UKRAINIAN national church. WE ARE NOT UKRAINIANS, and they want to Ukrainianize us from Rome, but if by means of the Church they want to destroy us nationally, we are raising our voice against this and will revolt."[90] The entire anti-Ukrainian argument was repeated in a 1934 GCU publication entitled *Nase Stanovice* (Our Stand), coauthored by Smor and Dr. Zeedick. Totally ignoring the fact that a similar fight over celibacy had been waged by Ukrainian Catholics in America in 1926, the authors declared that the Holy See promulgated *Cum Data Fuerit* at the insistence of the Ukrainians and that therefore the fight against Latinization is also a fight against Ukrainians.[91] Warranted or not, the Ukrainian ethnonational stream was once again the enemy of Carpatho-Ruthenians – some of whom came to call themselves "Carpatho-Russian."

Ukrainophobia among American Carpatho-Ruthenians was elicited by the GCU once again during the rise of Carpatho-Ukraine in 1939. Claiming that Msgr. Augustyn Voloshyn was a Nazi puppet, *Viestnik* printed unsubstantiated articles alleging atrocities against true Carpatho-Ruthenians, the creation of concentration camps, and attempts by the Ukrainians to establish a totalitarian reign of terror.[92]

Eventually, the Carpatho-Russian identity was accepted by many Ruthenians in America, Orthodox and Catholic alike, along with the traditional anti-Ukrainian antecedents. As late as 1954, *Viestnik* printed an article which, among other things, suggested that Ukrainians had "delivered" Carpatho-Ruthenians to the Communists and were still trying to amalgamate the Carpatho-Ruthenian Catholic church and to "Ukrainianize" it:

> The Ukrainians imagined that with one swing they will seize our bishop and the whole "Greek Catholic Union" as they delivered Carpathian Russia to the wicked Communists. They thought if it will be impossible to take us over through nationalism, they will be able to take us over under their jurisdiction religiously. To us, Carpatho-Russian people, as here, so in our native country under the green Carpathians, there can be no greater insult and offense than when someone calls us Ukrainians. We know not such people on the world's map.[93]

❧

Rome's decision to appoint two separate coadministrators, and later separate bishops, for the Carpatho-Ruthenians and Ukrainians in America helped seal the fate of the two ethnoculturally related peoples once and for all. Never again would Carpatho-Ruthenians come close to the Ukrainian ethnonational stream in America, but instead would develop along a different path, one that would eventually place most of them in the Russian ethnonational camp.

If Bishop Bohachevsky's principal goal was to establish a permanent Ukrainian Catholic presence in the United States, he achieved it. Even his detractors must admit that, taken as a whole, his episcopacy was a success. Bohachevsky restored order, provided episcopal discipline, built seminaries, schools, and churches, and accommodated the concerns of potentially inimical Catholic prelates by moving the Ukrainian Catholic church into greater conformity with Latin-rite practices. His supporters argued that Bohachevsky was a visionary who was preparing his people for life in the United States. They condemned his enemies as godless malcontents misleading the ignorant masses. Bohachevsky, they argued, was a martyr for the faith whose leadership would someday be vindicated in the eyes of the universal church.

Viewed from the perspective of Ukrainian nationalists relying on the church to reinforce the Ukrainian ethnonational identity, Bohachevsky's reviews were quite different. His approach, they argued, was brusque and imperial. He was insensitive to concerns of potential allies. He was oblivious to precedent and past practice in the United States. He appeased Latin-rite bishops at the expense of Ukrainian tradition. He was unaware that the compliant old country peasant had changed in the United States and was no longer willing blindly to obey dictates handed down by priests and bishops. Bohachevsky would never be vindicated, his enemies argued, because the price of his reforms – the loss of a large segment of the Catholic population to Orthodoxy, the rejection by many young people of Ukrainian Catholic ritual and tradition, and the alienation of many older priests and laity – was too high.

In the end, Bishop Bohachevsky must be judged from the perspective of his times. In this regard, he was little different from lay leaders who yearned for more order, more discipline, and less questioning from their followers, many of whom seemed predisposed to anarchy. Today, the Catholic church appears less authoritarian and we find it difficult to visualize "gathering around the episcopal throne" as Bohachevsky envisioned it. During the Bohachevsky era, however, the situation was quite different in the Roman Catholic church and for some it was a good thing. The tragedy lies in the fact that while at one time the Ukrainian Catholic church was a vehicle of Ukrainianization in America, during the 1930s it was viewed by many Ukrainian Americans as a source of denationalization.

Despite massive defections from Catholic ranks, the Ukrainian Autocephalous Orthodox church was not without its own peculiar problems.

Desperately striving to achieve acceptance within the Orthodox world in order to provide a more viable alternative to Catholicism for disenchanted clergy and laity alike, Bishop Theodorovich appeared willing to go to almost any length short of rejecting Ukrainianism to gain acceptance. He didn't succeed. Recognition was finally brought to the Ukrainian Orthodox by Bishop Shpilka, a move which established two Ukrainian dioceses in America, one canonically recognized, one not. In 1939, most ethnonationally conscious Ukrainians were members of one of three churches – Catholic, Autocephalous Ukrainian Orthodox, or Ukrainian Orthodox under Constantinople, imitating in the religious arena the tripartite division that existed in the political arena.

9 Ethnocultural Maintenance

While political and religious issues played a decisive role in the preservation of the Ukrainian community, cultural influences were also important. Complementing political and religious development were a variety of cultural endeavors initiated by enlightenment societies, women's organizations, choirs, dance groups, and various cultural committees that not only enriched the Ukrainian American but inspired him as well. It is to this comparatively happy chapter in Ukrainian-American history that we now turn our attention.

The Role of Enlightenment and Women's Societies

During and immediately after the First World War – when hopes for an independent Ukrainian nation-state were still high – the major emphasis in adult education shifted from general enlightenment to occupational preparation for a productive life in a free Ukraine. In Chicago, for example, Ivan Ivanovsky and members of the Ukrainian Circle of Self-Education[1] established the Ivan Franko College in 1919. Lectures on subjects such as bookkeeping, commercial law, mathematics, salesmanship, commercial correspondence, English, German and Ukrainian history, grammar, and literature were offered four nights a week. "This professional education," wrote Chicago's *Ukraina* in describing the college, "is necessary for those who want to start a business for themselves upon their return to their native land."[2] The Ivan Franko College folded within a year.

Another adult education enterprise was initiated in Chicago in 1920 when efforts were made to establish a "Ukrainian Machine Shop and Technical School" at the Central Stamping and Manufacturing Works, a firm purchased by Ukrainians earlier. To enroll, however, one had to buy at least one fifty-dollar share in the company. Courses advertised included machinist training and tool and die making. "Hurry," urged the advertisement in *Ukraina*, "acquire a trade so you can return to Ukraine as a productive citizen ... After all of the horrible havoc wrought by the world war and the invasions of various 'saviors,' our Ukraine needs thousands of professional people and tradesmen ... She also needs equipment and machinery for her reconstruction ... We will use the money from the shares to strengthen our company. Our company will build a factory in Ukraine in the near future."[3] This hopeful effort also never materialized.

The Circle of Self-Education, meanwhile, continued urging working-class Ukrainians to attend night classes to better their education. Special counseling sessions were announced and the Ukrainian laborer was urged to take advantage of them for "the good of Ukraine":

> Countrymen, the war is ended and now begins the reconstruction which is needed by Ukraine. All nations are preparing for this work but alas, we Ukrainians will add nothing to our Fatherland. Shall it not be a shame for us when other nations will occupy the higher positions all over the world and even in Ukraine? Will we not be ashamed of ourselves when we return to Europe without any profession or trade?[4]

Interest in adult education for the purpose of "helping Ukraine" faded quickly after the 1923 Council of Ambassadors' decision to award Galicia to Poland was announced and the full significance of Ukraine's partition hit home.[5] There would be no independent Ukraine; Ukrainians would have to try again to gain their freedom. It was not a reality which was faced easily, however. In the words of one Ukrainian pioneer: "We were not interested in America at that time but in the old country. For a long time after the war we didn't want to believe that there was no reason to return to our native land."[6]

Unable to accept the subjugation of Ukraine as a permanent state of affairs, Ukrainian Americans rededicated themselves to the liberation struggle and the preservation of their heritage, and began to reorganize. As "enlightenment" came to be associated with ideological indoctrination, those community members who were essentially nonpartisan in their political views were left to search for other avenues of expression and personal growth.

First to fill the need for a broader educational approach were Ukrainian women, who, inspired by the success of the American feminist movement[7] as well as the work of their Ukrainian sisters in Europe, started to play an increasingly vital role in community affairs beginning in the 1920s.[8]

The Ukrainian Women's Alliance of America

The second national women's organization to be created in the United States was the Ukrainian Women's Alliance of America, a fraternal insurance society. Established in Chicago in 1917, the new association, largely the result of the organizational efforts of Emily Strutynsky, was an outgrowth of resolutions passed at the 1915 All-Ukrainian Diet which urged the immediate formation of a Ukrainian-American women's organization on a national scale.

The alliance was born at a specially convened women's congress held in Chicago a few weeks after the successful nationwide "Ukrainian Day" in 1917. Having decided to form a fraternal benefit society exclusively for women, the eighty-six delegates also resolved to: (1) begin the immediate organization of local branches; (2) apply for a charter; (3) publish a journal.

Electing a pro-tem executive board headed by Stefanie Cymbalisty and Katherine Shabaya, they articulated the following objectives:

A To unite Ukrainian immigrant women in America for the purpose of: 1. Their enlightenment through a special women's journal. 2. Organizing schools for illiterate women. 3. Offering financial assistance in the event of injury, sickness, or death.
B To offer help, both moral and material, to orphans, widows, and all who are in need.
C To establish a fund to be called "Ukrainian Women's Aid" for the purpose of assisting Ukrainian women in Europe in their efforts to enlighten themselves.[9]

Adopting a decidedly progressive posture, the alliance began publishing its own journal, *Ranna Zoria* (Morning Star), in 1918. Calling all Ukrainian women to membership, the journal declared:

America – the land of education! And how have we taken advantage of this knowledge, these opportunities? Where is our enlightenment? Where shall we seek it?

Don't we have the same frightening number of illiterates as in the old country beyond the sea?

Ukrainian women!

The war will end and a few of us will return to our native land. We will not be greeted by our fathers who once sent us to the new land and if they do come to greet us they won't be the same. They will come before us tired and emaciated as the result of having been exposed to the terrible spilling of human blood, and they will lift their hands and eyes to us in hope of finding counsel and advice.

And what kind of advice will they receive from us when we ourselves are without enlightenment, when we are illiterate even though we have lived for such a long time in a land of enlightenment that offers so many opportunities?

Ukrainian women!

Doesn't all this speak to our conscience?

Doesn't this awaken in us a feeling of obligation toward a free Ukraine?

Doesn't this move us to work, to big work, to work on ourselves? ...

To work, Ukrainian women!

Let us learn with all of our strength, all of our energy; we will make up for what we have lost!

Let's read, listen and think! Let's familiarize ourselves with that which is ours and that which is foreign ...

Ukraine, independent, sovereign and free, is rising from her grave and is calling to us Ukrainian women:

To education!

To work!

To efforts for a better fate for the Ukrainian people![10]

Despite the great hopes expressed by its founders, the alliance – headquartered in the parish offices of St. Nicholas Church where Father Mykola Strutynsky was pastor – had a short history. It did organize classes for illiterates[11] and it did manage to publish a few more issues of *Ranna Zoria*. Within a few years, however, it followed the same road to oblivion as that of its prewar predecessor, the Sisterhood of St. Olga.[12]

The Ukrainian Women's Society of New York

An effort to organize Ukrainian women in New York City along less ambitious lines met with more success. On 4 December 1921, some thirty women meeting at the home of Mrs. Maria Skubova, who had just returned from a trip to Western Ukraine, decided to create a women's society that could assist the many war invalids in Ukraine. Headed by Skubova, the first executive of the new organization included Olena Krechkivsky, vice-president; Anna Kushnir, secretary; and Katherine Hupalov, treasurer. Calling themselves the Ukrainian Women's Society of New York, they quickly organized a benefit drama performance for 25 December and were able to begin their first full year of existence with approximately one hundred dollars in their treasury. By the end of 1922, the society had sponsored a total of ten separate functions – dramas, dances, balls, and cultural bazaars – and had sent $500 for relief purposes to Ukraine.

In 1923, the society decided to organize a Ukrainian Red Cross for service in Western Ukraine, but this decision was precluded by the ruling of the Council of Ambassadors. That same year, Mrs. Skubova resigned and was succeeded by Stefanie Abrahamovska, and the society sent another $330 to Europe for Ukrainian relief activities.

During 1924, the society became closely associated with the activities of the League of Ukrainian Women in Lviv and the Ukrainian Women's Committee to Aid Wounded Soldiers, an organization headquartered in Vienna. When Olha Bassarab, one of the founders of the latter organization, died in a Polish prison early in 1924, the society mobilized a protest meeting on 6 April in New York City condemning the Polish regime for the death of their Ukrainian sister. Later that month, society members voted to delegate a representative to the World Congress of the International League of Women for Peace and Liberty scheduled for Washington in May. Before the necessary arrangements could be made, however, a Dr. Nadia Surovtsova arrived from Europe as the Ukrainian women's representative. Pro-Soviet in her orientation, Dr. Surovtsova contacted the communist leadership in the United States, prompting the society to dissociate itself from both Dr. Surovtsova and the congress. Continuing to fulfill its initial objectives, the society sent an additional $750 to Ukrainians in Europe before the year ended.

In 1925, the society became one of the founding members of the newly formed Ukrainian National Women's League of America.[13]

The Ukrainian National Women's League of America (UNWLA)

In March 1925, the Ukrainian Women's Society of New York received a letter from the Society of Olha Kobylianska, a Ukrainian women's organization in Canada, indicating that a world congress of the International Council of Women was scheduled for Washington, DC, in May and that monies were needed to underwrite the costs of sending a Ukrainian female delegation from Europe. Responding to the letter – which was also received by a number of Ukrainian newspapers and private individuals – the society, in cooperation with other local Ukrainian women's organizations, called a women's rally on 5 April and helped establish a special congress committee to expedite the matter. Monies were raised and the society was able to forward $250 to the League of Ukrainian Women in Western Ukraine (Soiuz Ukrainok), the organization responsible for sending the delegation.

The Polish government, meanwhile, refused to issue passports to the Ukrainian delegation and, in a last-minute decision, the league in Lviv and other Ukrainian women's organizations in Europe agreed to designate Dr. Hanna Chikalenko-Keller – then living in Switzerland – as the official representative of Ukrainian women at the council congress. Upon learning that only one delegate from Europe would be arriving, the congress committee decided to designate two more women – Olena Lotocky of the society and Julia Jarema of the Ukrainian Democratic Club – to serve as representatives. Despite protests from the Polish delegation, all three women were duly recognized and seated by the council congress in Washington.

During her stay in the United States, Dr. Chikalenko-Keller urged Ukrainian-American women to create a national organization in America similar to Soiuz Ukrainok in Western Ukraine. At her suggestion, the ad hoc congress committee was transformed into a new organization, the Ukrainian National Women's League of America (Soiuz ukrainok ameryky) and the same executive – Julia Shustakevych, president; Olena Lotocky, secretary; and Katherine Shustak, treasurer – was retained. Within a few months, Shustakevych resigned to be succeeded by Julia Jarema. Before the year was out, the new organization (hereafter referred to as the UNWLA) included five separate, local Ukrainian women's organizations within its structure.

Efforts to expand the activities of the UNWLA beyond the confines of the New York and New Jersey area during the next four years proved difficult. Although other women's organizations existed in other American cities, few were willing to join the UNWLA. A turning point was reached in 1929 with the visit to America of Olena Kisilevsky, a Ukrainian member of the Polish senate. In her travels to various Ukrainian-American communities, Kisilevsky urged all women's organizations to join the UNWLA and to create a strong and unified front of Ukrainian women in the United States. By 1930, the UNWLA had eleven branches and though the gain was small, it represented a significant expansion away from the eastern seaboard states.

In 1931, a new executive board was elected, consisting of Olena Lotocky, president; Pauline Avramenko, vice-president; Katherine Kedrovsky, secretary; and Mary Lenchuk, treasurer. By the end of the year, the UNWLA had grown to seventeen branches.

Determined to accelerate their organization's somewhat sluggish growth, the new UNWLA executive called for a national congress of Ukrainian women in 1932 to discuss, among other things, the participation of Ukrainian women in the Chicago World's Fair. A nationwide membership campaign was launched in preparation for the congress and by May 1932, the UNWLA organizational network included forty-two branches.

A UNWLA convention, billed as "The First Congress of Ukrainian Women in America," was held on 29–30 May 1932 in New York City, with sixty-eight delegates in attendance. Adopting a new constitution for their organization, delegates passed resolutions pledging the UNWLA to further expansion, cooperation with other American women's organizations, fighting for women's rights, support of movements for the improvement of international relations, assistance for needy Ukrainians in America and abroad, support of progressive labor and social legislation, assistance for Ukrainian women seeking to become naturalized citizens, familiarizing Ukrainian-American youth and the general American public with Ukraine and her culture, and full support for the Ukrainian independence movement. Elected to the new executive were Olena Lotocky, president; Annette Kmetz and Anastasia Rybak, vice-presidents; Anastasia Wagner and Maria Bodnar, secretaries; and Stefanie Abrahamovska, treasurer.[14]

In May 1933, Mary Beck began to edit and publish *Zhinochyi Svit* (Women's World) as a UNWLA journal.[15] In the first issue, the editor wrote:

> The rebirth of our statehood requires hard work among all segments of our society.
>
> We will not reach our objective if we place the entire burden on the backs of fathers, husbands, and sons.
>
> Womanhood is no less important in the rebirth of a nation ... or in the situation in which the Ukrainian nation presently finds itself ... The Ukrainian nation has a right to ask Ukrainian women to take the same stand that women of other nationalities have taken in the reconstruction of the nation, or that is taken by women in nations that are already established.
>
> And that stand is serious, correct and important. It includes the ethno-national education of the younger generation and its preparation for creative national work in the future, the organization of our unorganized women into ethnonationally conscious, active, and productive cadres, and finally, the promulgation of the Ukrainian movement among international women's circles.
>
> That is the program adopted by Soiuz Ukrainok in the old country and that is the same program adopted by Soiuz Ukrainok in America.[16]

One of the first Ukrainian journals to include an English-language section for youth, *Zhinochyi Svit* adopted a clearly nationalistic posture publishing articles on the terrors in Soviet Ukraine,[17] the national martyrdom of Bilas and Danylyshyn,[18] and the UVO activities of Olha Bassarab.[19]

The second convention of the UNWLA was held on 26 May 1935, and a new executive headed by Anastasia Wagner was elected. One of the first projects undertaken by the new officers was the standardization of branch activity. Lesson plans for monthly branch seminars were printed along with the following guidelines for local activities:

January – Christmas caroling to raise funds for various causes in Ukraine; New Year's Day supper for all members and supporters; commemoration of Ukrainian Independence Day.

February – Birthday of Lesia Ukrainka to be commemorated in an appropriate fashion along with the death of Olha Bassarab. Similar commemorative services should be planned for George Washington and Abraham Lincoln.

March – Commemoration of Taras Shevchenko. Branches should cooperate with other Ukrainian organizations in this observance or organize their own.

April – Classes should be organized for the teaching of Ukrainian Easter egg decoration to young Ukrainian girls. A special class should be devoted to an explanation of Ukrainian Easter customs and traditions.

May – Every branch should organize a Mother's Day concert where the importance of Ukrainian motherhood is stressed along with the significance of raising children in the Ukrainian spirit. One meeting should also be devoted to the significance of Ivan Franko in the Ukrainian movement.

June – *Children's month* – During the month of June every mother should take her children to the doctor (to our doctor if there is one in the vicinity since he can communicate with you better). In those areas where no doctors are available, every effort should be made to contact the local health department for assistance ...

July and August – While no formal suggestions are offered for the summer months, branches are urged to enlarge their treasuries through the sponsorship of picnics and other affairs.

September – *School month* – Every member is obligated to find ways to guarantee a higher education – college or university – for the more talented boys and girls in the community. Every member should also make sure that there is a local Ukrainian ethnic school (Ridna Shkola) in existence and that the teacher is qualified.

October – *Book month* – The significance of books and other reading material should be emphasized during October. Every branch should take stock of its own library during this month and make an effort to improve it ...

November – This month should be devoted to the commemoration of the declaration of independence of the ZUNR (Listopadove Sviato) ... A meeting should be devoted to the life of Olha Kobyliansky, the well-known Ukrainian writer.

December – During this month each branch is to take stock of its previous year's activity through the annual reports of branch officers ... Preparations should be made for Christmas caroling activities and the New Year's Day supper.[20]

UNWLA conventions were held in 1937 and again in 1939, when Annette Kmetz was elected national president. By 1940, the UNWLA had sixty-one branches throughout the United States organized into three regional councils.[21]

The most significant educational accomplishments of the UNWLA during the first fifteen years of its existence occurred in the branches. While lectures and discussions varied in both frequency and caliber, active UNWLA members were exposed to them and thus were afforded an opportunity for further enlightenment. In addition, the national executive provided branches with mimeographed copies of lectures on infant care, female hygiene, the feminist movement, famous Ukrainian women, Ukrainian history, and cultural traditions.[22]

Another early UNWLA project was the preparation and dissemination of Ukrainian cultural exhibits. In keeping with resolutions passed at the first convention, the organization acquired several thousands of dollars worth of embroideries, rugs, village apparel, wood carvings, and paintings from the Ukrainian Peasant Art Co-op (Narodne mystetstvo coop) in Lviv. These items were originally displayed at the Ukrainian pavilion at the Chicago World's Fair in 1933 and were later made available to UNWLA branches participating in local folk fairs and cultural exhibitions.[23]

Finally, although the UNWLA maintained a politically and religiously neutral posture within the Ukrainian-American community, it was not indifferent to the political ramifications of the Ukrainian situation in Europe. Branches were constantly collecting monies for Ukrainian invalids, war orphans, educational institutions, political prisoners, victims of the Polish pacification and the Great Famine in the UkrSSR, as well as various catastrophes (floods, epidemics) that affected Ukrainians in Europe.[24] Nor was the organization reticent to bear witness to Polish persecution in Western Ukraine. When news of the Polish ban on Ukrainian organizations, including Soiuz Ukrainok, reached the United States, the UNWLA agreed to participate in a mass women's protest meeting which was held in New York City on 4 June 1938. The meeting adopted a resolution condemning "the Polish policy of extermination of Ukrainian, White Ruthenian, Lithuanian, Jewish, and other races" and urged "that in view of the consistent refusal of the American government to intercede with the Polish government on behalf of down-trodden Ukrainians in Poland," a grass-roots

American movement be organized to expose Polish minority policy for what it really was.[25]

The Ukrainian Red (Gold) Cross

The Ukrainian Red Cross – a national Ukrainian-American organization of nationalist women that changed its name to the Ukrainian Gold Cross in 1939 – came into being as the result of efforts to create a Red Cross affiliate within the local ODWU branch in New York City in 1931. The affiliate was an immediate success, and on 2 June 1933, a Nationalist women's congress was convened in New York City for the purpose of popularizing the idea and for creating similar auxiliaries within other ODWU branches. With assistance from the ODWU national executive, which appointed Anna Hladun as the Red Cross organizer, a total of twelve branches were in existence by 1935.

From its inception, the major purpose of the Red Cross was to assist ODWU with fund-raising functions such as concerts, plays, seminars, and door-to-door collections. Much of the money was later sent to pay legal fees for OUN members arrested in Western Ukraine.

At a conference of Red Cross branches on 27 September 1936, in New York City, a decision was reached to create an autonomous national executive for the organization. Elected to the new governing body were Anna Sereda, president; T. Diachuk, vice-president; Maria Bilyk, recording secretary; and Stefanie Halychyn, organizer. The conference also appointed Maria Demydchuk and Eugenia Ploschansky to edit a new women's page in *Natsionalist*, the official organ of ODWU. Under the leadership of the new executive, organizational activities were increased and by the end of 1938, there were thirty-three Red Cross branches in existence.

One of the most active periods for the Red Cross was the year 1938 when the organization joined with ODWU, MUN, and other Ukrainian organizations in a massive effort to assist Carpatho-Ukraine. By the beginning of 1939, the Red Cross had shipped 126 boxes, each weighing 500 pounds, of wearing apparel and foodstuffs to Carpatho-Ukraine.

In March 1939 – under pressure from an American Red Cross ruling that only nation-states already in existence could use the name "Red Cross" – the organization changed its name to the Ukrainian Gold Cross.[26]

The Ukrainian Women's Community

The third national Ukrainian women's organization, the Ukrainian Women's Community, was organized by the Defense of Ukraine organization.

With branches in New York, Rochester, Newark, and Detroit, the community assisted its parent organization in its various activities. Essentially socialist in political orientation, the community published a page of its own in the newspaper *Narodna Volya*.[27]

The Role of Cultural Enterprises

The rise and fall of the Ukrainian National Republic was a turning point in the cultural growth of the Ukrainian-American community for two major reasons: it enhanced national awareness and it led to the emigration of two of the most outstanding Ukrainian cultural activists of the postwar era, Alexander Koshetz and Vasyl Avramenko. Their extraordinary artistic talents elevated Ukrainian choral music and the Ukrainian dance to new heights of excellence in the United States and helped promote a better appreciation of "Ukrainianism" among Americans.

The postwar era was ethnoculturally notable for two other reasons as well: Ukrainian participation in the Chicago World's Fair and the erection of the Ukrainian Cultural Garden in Cleveland. Both landmark efforts enhanced pride in the Ukrainian ethnocultural heritage and generated a modicum of ethnonational unity in a community divided by political and religious differences.

The Ukrainian National Chorus and Its Legacy

"Ukrainian national songs," wrote Filaret Kolessa in *Sichovi Visti*, "have great significance because of their close tie with the life of the nation which they so faithfully reflect. They are the perfect mirror, so to speak, of the Ukrainian nation."[28]

Efforts to provide musical vehicles of ethnonational expression were made, as we have seen, by a number of individuals in the Ukrainian-American community before the war. Most such endeavors were relatively mediocre, but a few outstanding exceptions did exist, especially in those locales where competent choir directors could be found. Even these choirs began to disintegrate, however, once the differences that prevailed among religious and lay leaders began to affect all aspects of community life. Choir members who found themselves in the minority on a particular issue often left the group,[29] a phenomenon that led one Ukrainian periodical to plead:

> There can be various reasons for these misunderstandings but we must bear in mind that our native songs stand higher than our personal feelings. Everyone knows what great value music has ...
> Under the influence of music all work becomes lighter and more

interesting. People captivated by music become bolder and more daring of spirit ... Music and song make people more considerate of the suffering of their fellow man. Should we Ukrainians, members of an endowed musical nation, abandon those treasures which other peoples acquire with great difficulty? Are we really unfit and incompetent for the kind of group cooperation that is necessary in order to elevate the polyphonic art of singing to the high standards to which our nation is accustomed?[30]

Despite such appeals to ethnonational pride, ethnocultural cultivation remained relatively stagnant throughout the war. The Ukrainian-American community had other priorities to address and choral music was relegated to a position of secondary significance.

A new chapter in the history of Ukrainian-American choral music began in 1922 with the arrival in America of the Ukrainian National Chorus. Organized in Ukraine during the early days of independence, the choir had spent much of its time touring Europe. Under the directorship of Alexander Koshetz, the chorus received rave reviews wherever it performed.[31]

An American and Canadian tour was organized by impressario Max Rabinoff, and during the latter part of 1922 and for much of 1923, Koshetz and his singers toured the North American continent. Their reception by American music critics was without parallel. After their debut in New York City, one reviewer wrote: "The praise that preceded the chorus from all musical centers of Europe seemed excessive until one heard it, until one saw Alexander Koshetz with his extraordinary living hands mold the sound as a sculptor molds the pliant clay. Here was the noblest and austerest and most stringently moral thing in the world – perfection."[32] Other music critics were equally lavish in their praise. "There is nothing remotely approaching it in any choral singing to which the western world is accustomed," intoned the *Boston Evening Transcript;* "Koshetz sculpts in rhythms," exclaimed the *Pittsburgh Post;* "Marvelous precision of attack that defies description," rhapsodized the *Rochester Times Union;* "A choir of peerless ensemble," concluded the *Chicago Evening American.*[33] The phenomenal success of Koshetz and his choir popularized Ukrainian music in the United States and introduced, for the first time on the North American continent, the now popular Ukrainian Christmas classic, "Carol of the Bells."

Following the 1923 decision of the Council of Ambassadors, Koshetz and most of his choir members elected to remain in America. Koshetz himself settled in New York City and did not attempt another American tour until 1932 during the Washington Bicentennial. Reorganizing his chorus,

Koshetz toured a number of states, appearing jointly with Vasyl Avramenko and his Ukrainian dance troupe. Returning to New York, he directed various local musical festivals and devoted most of the remainder of his life to music composition and arrangement. By March 1935, twenty Ukrainian songs arranged by Koshetz had been translated into English and published by Witmark Educational Publications in New York City.

The Ukrainian National Chorus proved to be a vitally needed catalyst for Ukrainian choral music in America. It provided a new standard of excellence and, in the person of Michael Hayvoronsky, a composer, and such outstanding choral members as George Kirichenko, Leo Sorochinsky, and George Benetzky, all of whom later became choir directors in their own right, the chorus also provided the artistic leadership to maintain that standard.

By 1936, outstanding Ukrainian choirs had been organized in Scranton by Volodymyr Levytsky, in Newark by George Kirichenko, in Detroit by Dmytro Atamanec, in Cleveland by Leo Sorochinsky, in Boston by Father Joseph Zelechivsky, and in Chicago by George Benetzky.[34] In terms of recognition by the American musical public, however, it was Chicago that seemed to possess the greatest choral talent during this period. Competing in the choral competition associated with Chicagoland Music Festival, an annual affair sponsored by the *Chicago Daily Tribune* in Soldier's Field, the Chicago Ukrainian choir won first place four times – twice under the directorship of Leo Sorochinsky (1930 and 1931) and twice under the directorship of George Benetzky (1932 and 1934). Considering the fact that as many as thirty choruses from five different states competed, it was a notable musical accomplishment.

Another noteworthy development of this period was the organization of the Ukrainian Opera Company by Dimitry Chutro in Philadelphia in 1932. During the 1932–3 season, the company presented *Zaporozhets za Dunayem* (Cossack beyond the Danube) and Tchaikowsky's *Mazeppa*, both of which were favorably reviewed by *Svoboda*, *America*, the *New York Times*, and the *Buffalo Evening News*.

In addition to Koshetz, there were other composers who distinguished themselves during the 1930s. Paul Pecheniha-Uhlitzky's new compositions were broadcast on NBC from New York City on 10 October 1935. Michael Hayvoronsky, a popular composer in the community, specialized in folk and military songs. The talented Roman Prydatkevytch was also a concert violinist who consistently played to excellent reviews. Combining his musical skills with those of Olga Tkachuk, pianist, and Maria Hrebenetska, soprano, into a "Ukrainian Trio," Prydatkevytch toured the southeastern states performing on college campuses. Favorable reviews appeared in the

Durham Morning Herald (2 July 1931) and the *Greenville Daily Reflector* (3 July 1931).[35]

The popularity of Ukrainian folk music during this period attracted many young people and by the late 1930s, most Ukrainian choruses had a membership that was overwhelmingly American-born.[36] Maintaining the musical standards established in the 1920s and early 1930s proved to be difficult, however. By 1944, there were complaints that Ukrainian choral music in America was on the decline because professional sheet music was in short supply, Ukrainian composers in America were not properly rewarded for their efforts, there was no nationwide Ukrainian-American musical society that could coordinate and monitor Ukrainian musical endeavors in America, and there were fewer musical festivals to serve as performing incentives for choirs.

It was also during this period that Ukrainian music was being recorded by such American companies as Columbia and RCA Victor. Between 1923 and 1952, Columbia released over 430 separate Ukrainian recordings while Victor produced over 100. Fiddler Paul Humeniak, whose *Ukrainske Vesile* (Ukrainian Wedding) became a classic, and Wasyl Gula, conductor of the Trembita Orchestra, were leaders in their field. Both recorded for Columbia.[37]

The Avramenko Legacy

If Koshetz was the "father" of Ukrainian folk music in America, then Vasyl Avramenko, who emigrated to the United States in 1928,[38] can be considered the "father" of the Ukrainian folk dance. Believing, as he put it, that his singular mission in life was "to introduce the world to the Ukrainian dance," Avramenko approached his task with a zeal and determination that was challenging, inspiring, and, on occasion, exasperating.

In 1928, Ukrainian folk dancing in America was probably one of the least developed art forms in the cultural arena. In the words of one of Avramenko's students:

> Ukrainian folk dancing as I remember it from 1916 to 1929 was done in a very informal manner at the Ukrainian affairs I attended ...
>
> The Ukrainian dances would be done mostly to Kolomeyka tunes or occasionally to the Hopak tune that we all know. A big circle would form, with no partners, and whoever wanted could go in the middle and improvise in the center ...
>
> In between these dances we also did dances such as the Koro-

bushka, Karapyet (Russian two-step), Kohanochka and Polka Koketka, the last one being done many a time during a party as it was one of the more popular dances ... Ukrainian dance performances were mostly modeled on the Russian style being staged by ballet masters or "character dance teachers" and had no true Ukrainian feeling. The "prysyadka" was of course the big thing and even girls were allowed to do them by some dance teachers since the parents thought it cute.[39]

Settling in New York City, Avramenko, who lived almost exclusively on the donations of Ukrainian Americans, rented a hall and began to advertise his dance lessons in *Svoboda*. Despite his European background, he was able to relate to the younger generation and to organize large groups of dancers in a relatively short period of time. Describing his ability and mode of operation, one of his students later wrote:

I received my first impression of this man at a hall on the lower East side in New York City; I remember him as a dashing young man in a black kaftan coat teaching a group of youngsters very exciting dance steps which were quite like the solo ones we used to do in the free Hopak. But oh, what style he had! He seemed to give extra life and meaning to the steps. He seemed to be very strict in his teaching and yet he seemed to be able to capture both the dancers and audience in a sort of hypnotic spell.

Our parents immediately signed us up (my brother and I), mainly because at the end of the class Avramenko made an hour-and-a-half long speech about the patriotic duty of all parents to make their children like Ukrainian dancing. Avramenko had a gift of talk and we were able to hear him hundreds of times at various rallies, meetings and conferences. He hammered away at patriotism and the necessity of imparting the Ukrainian dance to the children as a means of getting freedom for Ukrainians.

My brother and I were in our late teens and we enjoyed the dance classes mostly because, like most Ukrainians, we liked to dance. However, we found ourselves held in by his very strict discipline: we were not allowed to chew gum; and the girls had to wear long-sleeved blouses. Avramenko was very quick to call the girls aside and scold them if their skirts were too wide or revealed too much thigh ... He wouldn't even allow the girls to wear fancy hair-dos, but wanted us to part our hair in Ukrainian style. He couldn't quite get us to fix our hair into braids, although some girls did.[40]

Capitalizing on his charisma and eloquence, Avramenko was soon visiting Ukrainian communities throughout the United States in an attempt to organize permanent local dance groups. Living with Ukrainian families who were honored to have him, Avramenko managed, between 1930 and 1936, to establish some fifty dance groups. In most major Ukrainian communities, permanent committees of prominent Ukrainian leaders were created to aid Avramenko financially and to interest parents and youth in his projects. "He was fanatical," writes Mary Ann Herman, "in his belief that only Ukrainian art and dance were good and above all else. He called rally upon rally and would speak endlessly. Such was his appeal that people would sit for hours, hypnotized, enthralled, and fascinated. He would then ask for donations and always received ample funds to carry on his large scale performances in major halls."

Although Avramenko preferred working with large groups of children, he focused his attention on the more gifted students. The latter served as assistant instructors and, after Avramenko departed, as instructors and leaders of the groups he left behind. "There came a time," concludes Herman, "when Ukrainians could all dance the same dance no matter where they went in America, for it was all pretty much standardized by Avramenko."[41]

Having trained thousands of dancers throughout the United States, Avramenko would occasionally organize a mammoth musical production in cooperation with local Ukrainian choirs. On 25 April 1931, Avramenko celebrated the tenth anniversary of his School of Ukrainian Folk Dance and Ballet (founded in Ukraine in 1921) at the Metropolitan Opera House with a folk orchestra, a choir of some 100 voices, and over 500 dancers. Describing the evening in the *New York Evening Post*, Henry Beckett wrote:

> Today we write with eagerness. We want to tell everybody about the unquestionably gorgeous and fascinating Ukrainian program under Vasile Avramenko on Saturday night in the old Metropolitan Opera House.
>
> On this occasion it is hard to follow newspaper custom and put the last thing first. On the second day after we are still excited over the kaleidoscopic ardors of the dance, the richness of the chorus, the congeniality of the audience and the fairly inspiring naturalness of what really amounted to a brilliant Ukrainian folk festival. And we refuse to turn from this event to the other without first going on record for unrestricted immigration from

the Ukraine. What this country needs is more Ukrainians! Through them Americans may learn to play.[42]

On 8 November 1932, Avramenko produced another Ukrainian extravaganza at the Civic Opera House in Chicago. Participating were an orchestra and the Boyan and Lysenko choirs – all under the direction of Leo Sorochinsky – and some 200 dancers.[43] The high point of Avramenko's early career, however, was reached on 20 April 1935. On that day the Avramenko dance group from the Baltimore area performed on the White House lawn for Mrs. Eleanor Roosevelt and other guests attending the annual White House Easter egg hunt. Enthusiastically received by the participants, Avramenko presented the president's wife with a set of exquisitely decorated Ukrainian Easter eggs as a remembrance of the momentous occasion.[44]

Not all of Avramenko's many enterprises were successful nor did he always enjoy the full support of the Ukrainian-American community. One grandiose project that never quite materialized was a "Ukrainian Hollywood," an idea Avramenko initiated in the mid-1930s. Establishing a film studio in New York City, the visionary dance master created a committee to raise funds for the production of *Natalka Poltavka*, a Ukrainian operetta, which was to become "the first Ukrainian sound film." Headed by M. Boychuk, the committee sent Vasyl Droboty, its vice-chairman, on a national fund-raising tour to America's Ukrainian communities.[45] A special appeal for help was made to Ukrainian-American youth. In a pamphlet entitled *Help Build a Ukrainian Hollywood*, the younger generation was asked:

> Have you at any time in your life been prompted by a desire to view a Ukrainian motion picture at a movie theater?
>
> Do you fully understand the gigantic significance such a production would bear to Ukrainians throughout the world?
>
> Were you ever stupified before your non-Ukrainian acquaintances with such a remark: "You say there are about a million Ukrainians in America; what have these people ever done to deserve notice or praise?"
>
> To be frank, did you not in many instances feel ashamed of your national identity because you were a member of an unknown, divided, and scoffed-at race?
>
> Did you not find a sad lack of Ukrainian educational, social or entertaining affairs for your American friends?[46]

After explaining the establishment of Avramenko's film studio, plans to produce *Natalka Poltavka,* and the significance of having something of which Ukrainian youth could be proud, the pamphlet concluded:

> But, to produce one film and relax is not the idea of those in and behind Avramenko's Studios. As mentioned above, the first film will be but a means to more important ends. An entire industry could and will be vested with life as something huge and representative of Ukrainian people. Such an industry will afford an opportunity for many of our people, both native and emigrant, to express their abilities in the numerous professions connected directly and indirectly with the industry.[47]

Despite growing skepticism toward the idea on the part of some Ukrainian newspapers,[48] Avramenko succeeded in raising the money not only for *Natalka Poltavka* but for film productions of *Zaporozhets za Dunayem,* another operetta; *Marusia,* a musical screenplay; and two documentaries – "The Tragedy of Carpatho-Ukraine" and "Forgotten Native Land" – as well. *Marusia,* based on the Ukrainian folk drama "Oy ne khody hryciu na vechernychiu," was probably the most successful of the films among American audiences. Koshetz arranged and directed the choral and vocal music, Andrei Kist directed the folk dances, and Leo Bulgakov was the director. The film was favorably reviewed by the *New York Daily News* (9 December 1938) and the *New York Daily Mirror* (13 December 1938).[49] Dreams of a Hollywood-style Ukrainian film industry in America, however, were never fulfilled.

Avramenko's many projects, almost all of which were financed by either donations or "loans" from the Ukrainian-American community, often brought him criticism from the Ukrainian press. *Svoboda* was especially wary of Avramenko, accusing him of producing "business" at the expense of the Ukrainian community.[50] Although many Ukrainians who loaned Avramenko money or goods were never repaid and often complained bitterly behind his back about how they were "taken," many of these same Ukrainians melted in confrontations with Avramenko and more often than not ended up "loaning" him even more.[51] In the words of one Ukrainian American:

> Avramenko was phenomenal. No one could deliver an oration on the Ukrainian cause or the Ukrainian soul more eloquently or more dramatically than Avramenko. He was a master. I saw him address initially hostile crowds, crowds that were prepared to tear him apart for not having delivered on past promises or for

not repaying past loans, and turn the people around. When
questioned concerning monies he would straighten up and, with
tears in his eyes, declare: "You are hurting me deeply. I am a
fighter for Ukraine, a land that I love and a land to which I plan
to return. Paderewski won Poland on his keyboards and I am
attempting to do the same. My keyboards are your beloved children, yes, your children that I love so deeply. They are the ones
who will bring us Ukraine. They are the ones we will someday
thank for restoring our native land with the Ukrainian dance.
They are the ones who will cherish their native heritage and ...
not put a *price* on its value." After a speech like that there wasn't
a dry eye in the house. More often than not, Avramenko would
get a standing ovation. He is the only one I know who could get
away with that kind of thing.[52]

As might be expected, the severest critics of a man of Avramenko's
obvious nationalistic value were the Communists. *The Hour* accused him
of being an Axis spy and the FBI opened an investigation during which
various secret informants alleged that Avramenko had "robbed a number
of people"[53] and was using his film company as a front for the Japanese
Intelligence Service to photograph "the entire United States–Mexico border
and also the International Bridge at Detroit, Michigan."[54] In their book
Sabotage! The Secret War against America, Sayers and Kahn alleged that
Avramenko had also photographed "American industrial cities, military
highways, bridges, airfields, rivers, railroads and factories."[55] As in all other
FBI investigations of the "Ukrainian conspiracy" against the United States,
none of the allegations were ever substantiated.

Ukrainian Participation in Two World Fairs

Plans to celebrate Chicago's one hundredth anniversary with a "Century
of Progress" Fair and exhibition were greeted by the city's Ukrainians as
a rare opportunity to better acquaint America with Ukraine and her people.
Early in 1932, a seventeen-member corporation – the Ukrainian American
World's Fair Exhibit Inc. – was founded with an executive board which
included Dr. Myroslaw Siemens, president; Stephen Kuropas, secretary;
Taras Shpikula, treasurer; and Jurij Nebor, financial secretary.[56] Addressing
itself to Ukrainians throughout the world, the corporation, with the full
support of *Svoboda, Narodna Volya, America,* and *Narodne Slovo,* made appeals
for money to construct the pavilion as well as for cultural artifacts to be
used in the pavilion displays.[57]

Early in 1933, Dr. Siemens and Michael Belegay, a member of the corporation, traveled to New York City to address a rally gathered to hear more about the progress of the corporation.[58] Later, *Svoboda* reported that following a meeting with representatives of the UNA, the Providence Association, and the UWA, a budget of $20,000 was approved for the project.

In March 1933, the architect's sketch of the proposed pavilion was published in the Ukrainian press,[59] and, on 12 April, a ground-breaking ceremony was held on the site.[60] The pavilion was officially opened on Sunday, 25 June 1933. Ceremonies included a six-block march to the pavilion by Ukrainian Americans in national costume and an afternoon concert featuring Benetzky's Chicago choir, Avramenko's dance group, and the ninety-five-piece Ukrainian orchestra of John Barabash.[61]

Culturally, the pavilion proved to be a high point in Ukrainian-American life. Divided into three sections – general, historical, and cultural[62] – it had exhibits donated by forty-eight individuals and societies,[63] including such European institutions as Ridna Shkola, the Ukrainian National Art Society, and the Ukrainian Technical-Agricultural Institute in Czechoslovakia.[64] The highlight of the cultural section – divided into folk and modern art – was the exhibition of the world-famous Ukrainian sculptor Alexander Archipenko. A restaurant and an open air theater were also part of the pavilion,[65] which attracted some 1.8 million visitors during its existence. Managing the entire effort on behalf of the corporation were Volodymyr Levytsky, pavilion director; Stefania Chyzhovych, technical assistant; Volodymyr Stepankiwsky, publicity; and Mary Beck, cultural assistant.[66]

The pavilion also served as a catalyst for Ukrainian organizational activities. A "Ukrainian Week" was promulgated beginning 14 August 1933, and thousands of Ukrainians traveled to Chicago to participate in the activities. During the week, congresses were held by Ukrainian youth, a conclave which led to the formation of the Ukrainian Youth League of North America (UYLNA); by Ukrainian professionals, which resulted in the establishment of the Ukrainian Professional Society of North America; and by Ukrainian women.[67]

The major shortcoming of the Ukrainian pavilion was financial, a problem that plagued the organizers from the beginning and prevented the pavilion from opening during the second year of the fair. The first problem was the $21,500 construction cost of the pavilion itself. By 31 October 1933, the day the fair closed for the season, only $16,792 had been raised to cover these costs. A second problem was the overhead involved in operating the pavilion, which at one point had sixty-three employees (forty-two in the restaurant alone) on the payroll. These costs, added to those encumbered by the restaurant band and the professional artists who appeared on weekends, proved to be higher than the receipts warranted. In the end, the corporation was forced into bankruptcy.

Despite serious financial problems, the Chicago effort has to be viewed as a tribute to the unceasing determination of Ukrainian Americans to establish ethnonational visibility in America. Taking into account the fact that the pavilion was the only national pavilion at the Chicago Fair not supported by foreign capital,[68] that its construction was financed almost exclusively by Ukrainian Americans during the height of the Depression, and that it served to bring Ukrainians together during a period of political and religious strife and led, among other things, to the formation of two new international organizations, the pavilion was a community success story.

A similar Ukrainian-American effort to participate in the New York World's Fair of 1939 was mobilized early in 1938. Organizational representatives from four eastern states were invited to New York City on 27 March and informed that in view of Soviet participation in the endeavor, the New York Fair committee could not permit a separate Ukrainian "national" pavilion but that either a "cultural" pavilion – costing approximately $100,000 – or a cultural exhibit in another pavilion – costing some $25,000 – was possible. After a long discussion, it was decided to begin a fund-raising campaign and to determine the extent of Ukrainian participation after the Ukrainian-American community had responded. A Ukrainian American Fair Association was organized headed by Dmytro Halychyn, president; Cyril Piddubcheshen and Anna Worobec, vice-presidents; Nicholas Muraszko, treasurer; Semen Demydchuk, secretary; and Volodymyr Riznyk and Stephen Shumeyko, assistant secretaries. Legal counsel was provided by Michael Piznak.

As a result of the massive financial push to raise funds for the Republic of Carpatho-Ukraine, an endeavor then taxing the entire community, the association's initiative faltered. Interest in the project was beginning to fade when, on 20 October 1938, an article written by Alexander Koshetz appeared in *Svoboda*. Arguing that millions of Americans would attend the fair and that a golden opportunity would be missed if Ukrainians did not at least make themselves known, Koshetz appealed to the ethnonational pride of the Ukrainian-American community, urging a renewed effort aimed at full participation.

Obtaining permission to participate from the New York Fair authorities, however, was not as simple a task as the association originally believed. The main obstacle was the Soviets, who argued that their pavilion was already representing Ukraine both nationally and culturally and that the Ukrainian-American community was not representative of Ukrainian sentiment. Responding to Soviet objections, New York Fair authorities agreed to permit the Ukrainian American Fair Association to organize a "Ukrainian-American Day" with the proviso that only cultural events would be planned and that the association would refrain from all "political" speeches and activities.

Thus, on Sunday, 18 June 1939, the Ukrainian-American community finally had its day at the New York World's Fair. As in Chicago, thousands of Ukrainians traveled to New York City to be present for the event, which was highlighted by the appearance of a 500-voice Ukrainian choir under the direction of Alexander Koshetz and the performance of some 500 dancers under the lead of A. Kist and M. Lavrenko, two of Avramenko's protégés. According to the *New York Herald Tribune*, approximately 50,000 Ukrainians were in attendance.[69]

The Ukrainian Cultural Gardens in Cleveland

Still another noteworthy endeavor was the erection of a Ukrainian cultural garden on public park land in Cleveland, Ohio. In 1916, the English community in Cleveland erected a statue to William Shakespeare in commemoration of the three hundredth anniversary of his death. Located on a large plot with trees common to the English countryside, the area came to be known as the English cultural garden. The English project was followed by similar endeavors by Jews (1926), Germans (1929), Italians (1930), Lithuanians (1933), Slovaks (1934), Poles (1935), Yugoslavs (Serbians, Croatians, and Slovenians; (1936), Czechs (1936), Ruthenians (1938), Hungarians (1939), Irish (1940), and Greeks (1940). Inspired by the earlier example of other nationalities, a number of Ukrainians in Cleveland – most notably Vasyl Volansky, Ivan Tarnawsky, Andrew Bilinsky, Jacob Volansky, Stephen Palivoda, and Omer Malisky – began to promote the idea of a Ukrainian cultural garden as early as 1934. By 1936, enough funds had been raised to commission a statue of Taras Shevchenko.[70]

The project was later taken over by the United Ukrainian Organizations of Cleveland and brought to successful completion. On 2 June 1940, the Ukrainian Cultural Garden, located in a three-acre site near other Cleveland ethnic gardens, was formally dedicated. At the time the garden included statues of Taras Shevchenko, Volodymyr the Great, and Ivan Franko – all rendered by Alexander Archipenko – and bronze plaques of Bohdan Khmelnytsky and Mykhailo Hrushevsky. All segments of the Ukrainian-American community participated in the dedication ceremonies. Bishop Theodorovich delivered the invocation, choral selections were presented by the combined Ukrainian Catholic Choir of Cleveland and the Detroit *Dumka* Choir of I. Atamanec, and speeches were delivered both by Nicholas Muraszko, president of the UNA, and by Miroslaw Sichynsky, president of the UWA.[71]

Cultural Life in the Community

Although they supported national projects of various kinds, the cultural life of Ukrainian Americans revolved around the local community. Most communities had at least one church, one choir, and one branch of a fraternal benefit society. Many communities also had a drama troupe, a dance ensemble, and an orchestra or band. There was a rich social calendar which usually included Ukrainian Independence Day (22 January), Shevchenko's birthday (9 March), and ZUNR Independence Day (1 November). In addition, there were lectures, concerts, plays, musicals, debates, and "veeche" or information nights. During the months of June, July, and August there were Sunday picnics. In larger communities, some organization sponsored a picnic every Sunday. During the months of December and January, there was Christmas caroling. All of that plus divine liturgy every Sunday and on holy days. There were many things to do and Ukrainian Americans participated as often as time and money would permit. For most Ukrainian Americans, their culture was a source of recreation as well as a way to build ethnonational cohesion.

If there was one bright spot, one oasis of apparent harmony among Ukrainian nationalists living in the United States after World War I, it was in the area of ethnocultural expression. Choirs and dance groups transcended political and religious differences while community-wide endeavors such as the establishment of a Ukrainian pavilion at the Chicago World's Fair in 1933 and the erection of cultural gardens in Cleveland in 1940 were eloquent testimony to the fact that ethnocultural growth had not ceased as a result of political and religious conflict and that in the cultural arena, at least, Ukrainians could work together.

10 From Generation to Generation

Having developed successfully a unique Ukrainian ethnonational identity in America, the Ukrainian-American community turned its attention to the problem of cross-generational transference. In the cultural arena, drama troupes, choirs, and dance ensembles proved to be the most popular vehicles for achieving this end, especially for passing on a Ukrainian culture to the American-born youth. The religious and political dimension of the preservation process was addressed by more formal institutions, including the ethnic heritage school, the day school, the youth organization, and the *Ukrainian Weekly*, a UNA English-language publication.

The Role of Heritage Schools

Ethnic heritage schools first emerged in the Ukrainian-American community in the 1890s. Once a particular community was firmly established, the next step was to find a full-time, salaried *diak-uchytel* (cantor-teacher) from the old country. If one was obtained, he had as one of his many duties (which included organizing and developing a choir, drama groups, and other cultural activities) the establishment of a local heritage school for the younger generation.

Heritage schools offered more than part-time, supplementary cultural classes initially conducted between five and seven in the evening in church halls or basements that often left a great deal to be desired in terms of a proper learning environment. Much depended on the *diak-uchytel*. If he was the kind of individual who could establish rapport with his pupils – not always an easy task for a European-trained teacher – the school was a success. If the *diak-uchytel* was not particularly skillful, the heritage school became what one critic of the Ukrainian-American education system called a "pedagogical absurdity." Before World War I, unfortunately, most heritage schools fell into the latter category.[1]

Attempts to upgrade the heritage school system began with the establishment in 1913 of the Ruthenian Greek Catholic Teachers' Association which by 1918 was using "Ukrainian" rather than "Ruthenian" as its ethnonational appellation. Under the leadership of Father Poniatyshyn who took a personal interest in its development – first as its director and later as the exarchial administrator – the association grew in influence and prestige. Poniatyshyn and his successors – Fr. V. Hryvnak (1916–18), Fr. O. Pavlyak (1918), and, after 1919, Theodosius Kaskiw – advocated teacher professionalization and community interest as important first steps in the process.[2]

Meeting for a combined religious retreat and convention in 1917, the association resolved to publish a monthly educational journal, and the following year *Ridna Shkola* (Native School) made its debut under the editorship of Dmytro Andreiko.[3] Calling attention to the fact that "yes, here was *still* another Ukrainian publication," and admitting that many Ukrainians would probably question its need, *Ridna Shkola* wrote:

> The Ukrainian immigration in America has been in existence for over 40 years. And yet, if we take a close look at American Ukrainians, we find that only a fraction live the American way – in a more cultured fashion. The majority live a life of the old country and there are not a few who live the life of immoral people.
>
> It is not surprising that our people in America aren't overly anxious to adopt a progressive and more cultured life; they are not those who will imitate the virtues of foreigners; on the contrary, they easily accept their vices, thus adding to our already numerous inborn natural vices foreign ones as well.[4]

Ridna Shkola also criticized "indifference to public schooling and home and community enlightenment by Ukrainian society," the low caliber of Ukrainian schools, the fact that many reading rooms and clubs had been neglected and "exist on paper only," the diminished role of fraternal insurance societies in the educational process, and the devotion of many organizations to politics. "They would rather 'politic than live,' " continued *Ridna Shkola*. "Can we leave such things be?" asked the editor. "No," was the obvious answer, "a hundred times no!"[5]

Committing itself to "the enlightenment of our people," *Ridna Shkola* was divided into three sections: (1) articles of a general pedagogical nature; (2) a children's section; (3) a professional section containing news of the association. During its brief existence – the last issue came out in April 1919[6] – *Ridna Shkola* published, among other things, a six-issue series of articles entitled "What Must Parents Do if They Want Their Children to Get the Most out of School"[7] as well as a Ukrainian version of the classic children's tale "Little Red Riding Hood."[8]

The association, meanwhile, continued its efforts to enhance the professionalism of Ukrainian teachers. The first national teacher's examination was held on 4 June 1918, under the general supervision of Father Poniatyshyn. Examination topics included Catechism and Bible history, the history of the Ukrainian Catholic church, liturgy, religious and popular music, church doctrine, church vernacular, the Ukrainian language, Ukrainian history, pedagogical techniques, and school hygiene.[9] That same year the association published *A Guide for Ukrainian Teachers in America* as well as a Ukrainian primer.[10] A second teacher's examination was held on 24 September.[11] By the end of the year, the association's membership had expanded to some fifty Ukrainian teachers.[12]

The question of community day schools was also reintroduced by the association in an editorial which appeared in *Ridna Shkola* in April 1918. Public schools have an important function to perform, *Ridna Shkola* declared, but "our children must have their *own* knowledge and their *own* education" or "they will leave us." "And who among us would permit such a thing? Would any one of us want his child to forget his native language, to leave the Church of his Fatherland or to deny his people? ... Such a child ... is of no value to anyone, not even his parents."[13]

By 1920, however, educational issues faded into the backwaters of Ukrainian-American life. The community was preoccupied first with the future of Ukraine, and later of Galicia, and all else was of secondary importance. It was not until the mid-1920s that the question of Ukrainian-American education reemerged as a crucial community concern.

Joseph Stetkewicz, a *diak-uchytel,* raised the problem of educating Ukrainian-American youth at the annual executive board meeting of the UUOA on 27 October 1926. Arguing that little professional progress had been made since the war, Stetkewicz proposed that the UUOA:

1 Establish a school commission charged with the task of creating a coordinated Ukrainian heritage school curriculum.
2 Request that every Ukrainian newspaper in America set aside a section for the full discussion of the school matter in order to familiarize the community with the severity of the problem and to establish a dialogue.
3 Prepare an educational position paper with appropriate resolutions and distribute it to all member organizations and their branches for reading and discussion at their meetings.
4 Replace all irrelevant texts with new material to be developed by the school commission.
5 Encourage the community to contribute to the school fund which would help cover immediate expenses as well as the eventual preparation and publication of textbooks.

6 Continue to encourage all *diak-uchytels* to pass their examination, receive their teaching certificates, and to attend summer classes to broaden their education background.

The UUOA executive board responded to Stetkewicz's proposal by establishing a commission under his leadership. Also appointed were Father Mykola Strutynsky and Volodymyr Kedrovsky.[14]

At the fourth UUOA Congress, held on 29 October 1927, Stetkewicz presented a paper entitled "The Reorganization of the Ukrainian School in America." Complaining that many Ukrainian ethnic schools were still being conducted in tight and damp quarters "where a good farmer would be afraid to store potatoes," and that many Ukrainian communities were still selecting *diak-uchytels* on the basis of "a powerful voice" (that is, on their musical talents) rather than their teaching credentials, Stetkewicz asked: "What have our schools given us after 30 years in existence? What has happened to the younger generation which our schools were supposed to educate?" Suggesting that only a complete reorganization of the Ukrainian heritage schools would meet current needs, Stetkewicz proposed that all Ukrainian schools, regardless of sponsorship, be united into one coordinated heritage school system. His plan was to have parents and interested organizational representatives form local councils that would later join forces to establish a national UUOA-affiliated education body to be known as Ridna Shkola. Convention delegates accepted the idea and passed the following resolutions regarding Ukrainian education:

1 The Ukrainian school must be free of all party affiliation and stand firmly on a purely national base. The purpose of the Ukrainian school is to educate Ukrainian children to be enlightened American citizens who are proud of their Ukrainian descent and culture and are willing to help the native land of their parents attain its independence.

2 Ridna Shkola in America will make every effort to see that all education is conducted by teachers who will be under the jurisdiction of the UUOA in all educational matters.

3 The school commission, to be known as the "Executive of the Ridna Shkola in America," will introduce the same curriculum, the same system-wide educational objectives, and the same textual materials.

4 Those teachers who lack the necessary proficiency must, within a period of two years, improve their educational background through self-enlightenment under school commission auspices and in special seminars established by Ridna Shkola.

5 The UUOA shall establish a special school fund which will accept membership dues as well as donations.

6 All schools associated with the UUOA shall be under the direct jurisdiction of Ridna Shkola in all matters related to education.

7 The Congress asks that all Ukrainian communities cooperate with Ridna Shkola in its efforts to coordinate the Ukrainian ethnic school system.

8 The Congress declares that all parents pay fifty cents a year dues to the School Fund regardless of the number of children attending school.

Elected to serve on the first national executive of Ridna Shkola were V. Kedrovsky, president; Joseph Stetkewicz, vice-president; Theodosius Kaskiw, treasurer; P. Kovalchuk, secretary; and V. Bilorusky, organizer.[15] An appeal for support from the Ukrainian-American community was published by the newly elected executive early in 1928 along with an approved list of history and geography texts, song books, and readers.[16]

Most Ukrainian teachers were willing to accept both the list of approved texts and the reforms proposed by the UUOA, but they resisted the idea of UUOA jurisdiction over their schools. Despite arguments that a national Ridna Shkola network was in their best interests, association teachers preferred to retain local control of their schools. This issue remained unresolved. With the exception of greater standardization of texts, most of the measures proposed by Stetkewicz were never realized.

Educational reform was again an issue at the sixth UUOA congress in 1933. Resolutions were passed to engage the professional services of American-born Ukrainian teachers and to create a nationwide system of school supervision.[17] These recommendations were also never implemented. In 1936, Stetkewicz wrote: "Heritage schools haven't changed much ... *Diaks* continue to teach there. Professional teachers are permitted to teach only if they are familiar with '*diakism*' ... Unfortunately, we have to admit that our school system in America is relatively primitive and for that reason does not produce the kind of result that it should."[18]

Another problem with which heritage schools had to contend was the reluctance of American-born youth to attend supplementary classes. "I know from personal experience," wrote Theodore Swystun in 1937, how difficult it is to motivate children "who are not interested in speaking Ukrainian or in doing their Ukrainian homework ... In our large cities our children have a nervous temperament. Often the father and mother both work and a major educational vehicle for such children is the street. And since so many of our people live in bad neighborhoods, their children are mischievous, ill-disciplined, and insolent." "Working with such children," concluded Swystun, "requires a teacher with nerves of steel and a willingness to sacrifice a great deal of personal time and much of his health as well."[19]

Finally, there was the cynicism of the older generation itself. "There are parents," complained Swystun, "who in the presence of their children disparage all that is Ukrainian. Such parents ridicule all of our meetings, all of our leaders, all of our organizations, all of our beautiful customs ... This influences the child."[20]

Despite the shortcomings of the schools, difficulties with the younger generation, and carping by parents, many American-born youth did attend Ukrainian heritage classes, which during the 1930s were usually held from 4:00 to 6:00 p.m., five days a week. Ukrainian reading, writing, and music were offered to the younger children and Ukrainian history, geography, and literature were added to the curriculum for youngsters between the ages of ten and fourteen. All received religious instruction, and in some schools folk dancing and embroidery were offered to a select few.[21] By 1939, there were eighty-six Ukrainian ethnic schools in America, most of which were organized by parents. Cantor-teachers taught in fifty-six of them; the Basilian Sisters taught in eighteen and the Sisters Servants of Mary Immaculate in the remaining twelve.[22]

Few youngsters attended Ukrainian school after the age of sixteen. Although the system never halted assimilation, it did provide the American-born generation with an appreciation of Ukrainian culture, a familiarity with Ukraine's national heroes, and a basic understanding of the Ukrainian language, both written and spoken.[23]

Another dimension of the educational response of Ukrainians in America during this period was their support of Ridna Shkola activities in Galicia. Financially strapped, the Ridna Shkola executive in Lviv dispatched Lev Yasinchuk to North America in 1928 and again in 1931/2 to collect monies for the support of Ukrainian schools in Europe. During his first visit, Yasinchuk collected a total of $20,000,[24] a sum that enabled his organization to finish the academic year in the black for the first time in years.[25] Yasinchuk's second visit (during which he was attacked by the Ukrainian Communists[26] and ignored by the UWA) was the occasion of a massive, nationwide cooperative effort among most other segments of the Ukrainian-American community.[27] At the annual sessions of the UUOA executive board in 1931, a resolution was passed to celebrate the fiftieth anniversary of Ridna Shkola throughout America in conjunction with Yasinchuk's visit.[28] *Svoboda* commented on similar observances in Western Ukraine and urged all Ukrainian-American communities to be certain to involve the youth in all local observances, especially when films brought over by Yasinchuk were being shown:

With these observances we will not only enliven our life but we will make it stronger, more idealistic and cultured. We will not only help the old country but we will also help ourselves, because this will be the best opportunity for the popularization and strengthening of our schools in America. That is why it is absolutely essential to bring our youth to these observances where Ridna Shkola in the old country will be discussed. Let that youth which is born here view those films which the delegate from the old country has brought with him and which represent life in Ridna Shkola. Let them see the success of the whole operation and let them become aware of the difficulties involved in educating our youth in the old country and in saving them from being a moral and national loss because of political circumstances which are against us.

As we know, Ridna Shkola is prepared to go all out in the years ahead to educate a strong, enlightened and energetic youth, fully aware of the fact that if they fail, all is lost.

We need the same kind of youth here in America. Without them, we will also die here, beyond the ocean.[29]

In contrast, *Visti*, the Ukrainian-American Communist daily, editorialized:

"Ridna Shkola! Ridna Shkola!" shout the Western Ukrainian patriots, bourgeoisie, and clerics and ask that we pour money into their pockets.

Ridna Shkola! Supporting it are the Ukrainian dollar patriots and the priests in America who pray to Christ that the naive will give money ... At a time when the laborers of Western Ukraine are struggling not only for their own *real* native school but for freedom from the clerical yoke as well, the Ukrainian bourgeoisie and priests stand on the side of the aristocratic order which is against the Ukrainian laboring class. This our Ukrainian laboring class should know and give our "native" bourgeois what they deserve.[30]

Accusing Yasinchuk of having brotherly ties with Poland and Pilsudski, the same periodical later condemned him for being "an agent provocateur."[31]

Despite strong Communist agitation against his visit in many of the Ukrainian communities he visited, and the fact that only $11,700 was collected, the tour was a morale boost for the Ukrainian-American community and helped focus attention on the overriding importance of a viable

educational program in the preservation and cross-generational transfer
of the Ukrainian heritage.[32]

The Role of Ukrainian Day Schools

The first attempt to establish a Ukrainian day school in the United States
was made by Fr. Pavlo Tymkevych, who tried to set up a dormitory-type
bursa in 1904. The project failed, however, because popular support for the
idea never materialized. The second serious attempt was initiated by
Bishop Soter Ortynsky in 1911. With the assistance of Basilian nuns
recruited in Europe by Metropolitan Sheptytsky, a Ukrainian-Catholic
orphanage was founded in Philadelphia in 1912. Within three years, the
institution housed 131 orphans. Later, summer camps were established in
Chesapeake, Maryland – on a parcel of land which the nuns finally paid
off in 1933[33] – and in Fox Chase, Pennsylvania. In 1939, there were eighty
orphans housed in the Philadelphia institution, eighteen of whom were
between the ages of fourteen months and six years.[34]

Parochial day schools were established in 1913 by Fr. Volodymyr Lotovych in Chester, Pennsylvania, and by Fr. Volodymyr Spolitakevych in
Wilkes-Barre.[35] Both schools, however, eventually folded.

The first permanent parochial day school was established by Bishop
Bohachevsky in Philadelphia in 1925. Originally known as "St. Joseph's,"
the school name was later changed to "St. Basil's" to avoid confusion with
the many local Latin-rite schools bearing the same name. No new day
schools were founded during the next eight years, largely as a result of the
religious controversy that raged around the person of the bishop.

By 1931, however, Bishop Bohachevsky had regained enough of his
popularity to initiate and maintain a day school organizational campaign,
which was perhaps his most significant contribution to the Ukrainian-
American community. Under Bohachevsky's leadership, accredited full-
time schools were founded in Pittsburgh (1933), New Kensington, Pennsylvania (1936), Chicago (1936), Hamtramck, Michigan (1936), Newark (1939),
and Watervliet, New York (1940). Four of the schools were located in
separate buildings and the remaining three were in rented quarters. In
addition to the standard elementary school curriculum offered by American schools, Ukrainian students also received instruction in the Catholic
faith as well as subjects common to most Ukrainian heritage schools. In
1939 the school enrollment in Ukrainian Catholic day schools ranged from
22 in Newark to 156 in Philadelphia.[36]

Organizing full-time elementary schools, especially for those Ukrainians
who desired a separate building, proved to be a difficult task even for larger
communities. The first decision to construct a separate school building in

Chicago, for example, was made by the church council as early as 1923.[37] The decision was reaffirmed in 1925[38] but by then the St. Nicholas church council was under attack for stalling on its original decision. "The problem," in the opinion of one *Sich* correspondent, "lies in the fact that we elect curators at annual meetings and among them are many illiterates who never went to school themselves and who are taking upon themselves certain decision-making powers for which they have no competence."[39] By 1926 *Sich* was able to report that the "school matter in Chicago was progressing very nicely" and that $12,000 had been collected for the school's construction.[40] The school did not open its doors, however, until ten years later and even then it required an extraordinary effort by the pastor to convince parents to take their children out of public or Latin-rite schools and to enroll them at St. Nicholas.[41]

The first accredited Ukrainian high school was St. Basil's Academy for Girls which was founded in Fox Chase, Pennsylvania, in 1931. In 1940, the academy had four teachers and fifty-two students and offered courses in Ukrainian language, literature, history, geography, and art, in addition to the standard American high school curriculum. Extracurricular offerings included Ukrainian embroidery and dancing. In 1939, the Sisters Servants of Mary Immaculate established St. Mary's Villa Academy, a high school for girls, adjoining their convent in Sloatsburg, New York.

A preparatory school for boys was opened in Stamford, Connecticut, in 1933. The curriculum stressed Greek and Latin and the Ukrainian rite in addition to Ukrainian and American subjects. A total of ninety-four students was enrolled in 1939, half of whom were in residence.[42]

The rationale promulgated by official exarchial publications usually addressed the need to create "our native school" in America.[43] Despite its nationalistic tinge, the concept was apparently well received by American-born Ukrainians, many of whom reacted with enthusiasm. In 1940, for example, Bohachevsky embarked on a campaign to raise funds for a Ukrainian college. Responding to Bohachevsky were a number of second-generation Ukrainians who, in a series of articles which appeared in *The Way*, the exarchial organ, expressed sentiments which were pan-Ukrainian in spirit. Calling on all Ukrainian youth – Catholic, Orthodox, and Protestant alike – Dietric Slobogin wrote:

> Whether you have or have not cooperated in Ukrainian-American activities in the past is not the issue right at the moment. You MUST do your part, large or small, in the current nationwide campaign for the establishment of a Ukrainian college. It is a necessity. We need an institution where our youth can acquire a higher education in their chosen field, together with an

advanced course in things Ukrainian; an institution where our
future Ukrainian youth leaders may receive their training.[44]

Defining the campaign as "our national must," Eva Piddubcheshen
declared:

> Today, we must not only provide leaders for our people in this
> country. We must also provide future leaders for the Ukrainians
> abroad. There our Ukrainian people have met with a sad fate.
> Their country has been overrun by brutal Soviets. Their leaders
> and their intelligentsia have either been put to death or exiled.
> Their schools have been closed or Sovietized. Our people read
> only Red Literature, for their own has been destroyed. The
> attempt to Sovietize the Ukrainians is in full force.
>
> The Ukrainian's only haven of protection is the United States
> of America. Here we can live. Here we can grow if we but have
> the desire to do so. Here we can educate our young people into
> leaders for the persecuted Ukrainians abroad.
>
> There shall come a time when the Soviet invasion will end.
> What then, if we are lacking our own leaders? And where shall
> these leaders be reared if not in our own college and university.
> The only country in which a college and university is possible
> is the United States of America. Thus, such an institution is our
> national MUST.[45]

Dr. Mamchur argued that Bishop Bohachevsky's primary educational goal
was to preserve Ukrainian Catholicism rather than to develop nationalism
among the youth. "The Ukrainianization program," wrote Mamchur, was
"only a medium for the achievement of the religious end."[46] That's true.
But it is also true that in providing for the future of the church, Bohachevsky
was preserving a nationalistic Ukrainian community's most significant base
of support.

The Role of Ukrainian Youth Organizations

With the demise of Sokol during the war and the transformation of Sich
into an increasingly middle-aged political organization in the 1920s, the
Ukrainian-American community was left with no viable national organization for its youth. The significance of this situation did not become apparent
until the 1930s when the generation born during and after the war was
nearing adulthood.[47] It was only then that Ukrainian communal leaders
realized that while heritage and day schools were adequate for youth

in their early teens, those who were older were drifting away.[48] Almost overnight, articles on the subject of "saving our youth" began appearing in various publications calling attention to a generational crisis facing the community. From the beginning, however, "our youth" did not necessarily mean Ukrainian youth as a whole. In most cases, appeals were addressed to parents associated with specific religious and political beliefs. In the 1930 almanac of the Providence Association, for example, one concerned Catholic wrote:

> The most important concern of our Ukrainian immigration is our youth.
> Our continuous fighting among ourselves has already cost us many people who have gone over to the schismatic and Protestant churches and by doing so they have rejected their Ukrainian nationality. They cut themselves and their children off from all contacts with us and are lost forever to the Ukrainian community. The same threat lies in the not too distant future for those who today parade under the banner of 100% Ukrainianism in all church matters ...
> The preservation of Ukrainianism in America was, is, and will continue to be the exclusive right of the Ukrainian Catholic Church and all organizations associated with it, namely, our organization – The Providence Association – and the church schools, choirs, national homes, etc. ...
> The Providence Association has a broad and challenging organizational field when it comes to youth born and educated in America. We must become more appealing to our youth who have a different life style and approach. The American-born cannot understand our talkative nature which makes mountains out of mole-hills and has little time for truly significant matters. They have been brought up in an American system which devotes time to matters in direct proportion to their significance.[49]

The article concluded with a condemnation of long Ukrainian meetings "which accomplish nothing" and which alienate any youth who may be present.[50]

A year later, the vice-president of Providence wrote:

> If we are honest with ourselves, we must realize that we are old and that the time to die is just around the corner. And let's ask ourselves if we really have anyone to whom we can leave that inheritance which we have developed in this new land. Will

anyone be left to attend our churches, our schools, our national
homes and the other institutions which now exist? ...
    Let us save our children, our blood, before it's too late. If we
don't wish to save them from assimilation then we have no right
to call ourselves their parents.[51]

After arguing that American-born youth "can't stand" most adult Ukrainian organizations, the author called for the formation of "separate and
autonomous youth associations."[52]
    The gravity of the youth problem was analyzed by Dr. Simenovych
shortly before his death in an editorial entitled "Why Your Youth Don't
Care." Outlining the nature of the problem and its causes the Ukrainian
pioneer wrote:

    Among our older organization involved with our political work
    we see very few young people.
        Our immigration is diminishing from day to day not because
    we are not receiving any more immigrants from Europe or
    because they are dying out, but because our immigrants are get-
    ting older. Tired by old age and hard work they are slowly
    leaving the field of national work and they are leaving behind
    people who are also old. The youth, however, our school youth,
    our university youth, and our professional youth, is not with us;
    they are not engaged in our political and patriotic work.
        In large measure we ourselves are to blame because we still
    believe that an older person, even without the slightest educa-
    tion, is wiser and more worthy of leadership than a younger
    person with a higher education.
        An older person has more dignity and experience, but a young
    person has more education and lives life with wider horizons.
    Let's bring in our youth, let's give them some of our work, let's
    give them an opportunity to develop themselves in our midst
    as Ukrainian patriots; only then will our task be easier and only
    then will we double our progress. If we do this we will help our
    cause now and we will keep our youth with us.[53]

    An awareness of the indifference of youth to Ukrainian life was not
confined to the older generation. It was also an issue of concern to younger
Ukrainian Americans, some of whom felt it was due to cultural conflict. In
an article which appeared in the Ukrainian Review, for example, Joan J.
Skuba wrote:

In order to solve any problem it is first necessary to understand what makes it a "problem." In this particular instance, it is not the mere fact that Ukrainian children have parents who were born abroad. No – rather it is created by social conditions and attitudes, so distinct and at variance with those of the Old World, that make "second generation" children cognizant and aware of a sense of difference. They see different home standards, discipline and numerous other conditions in their contact with American children that seem radically removed from their own surroundings.

Realizing this, what happens? They are embarrassed at being "a foreigner." They do not seem to "fit in" with the pattern of the New World. Hectic in their desire to become thoroughly American, they go to the extreme and imitate the worst that America has to offer in dress, manners, and customs. They too cut themselves off from all that is fine in their ancestral heritage and attach themselves to the low and degrading features of modern life in America.[54]

For Skuba, the solution was the adoption of "the happy medium of taking the best that tradition offers and moulding it with the best that America has to offer."[55]

Another solution was offered by Katherine Schutock in 1930. She suggested that the UNA create American scout troops as affiliates of local branches and charge them with the responsibility of "furthering also the manners, customs, traditions and language of our parents."[56] The idea was supported by Ivan Kashtaniuk, the UNA Supreme Secretary, who argued that the UNA should become involved with scouting because such a movement "is forbidden to our youth in our native land ... We are not suggesting the establishment of a separate scouting association ... That would be beyond our means" and "we don't need another immigrant organization for our youth. We merely wish to take advantage of the best organized and most popular youth movement for our purposes in the same way that this is being done by other immigrant groups and various American institutions."[57] Although some UNA branches and local parishes eventually established scout branches on a local level, the idea never materialized nationally.[58]

Efforts to organize a nationwide, apolitical, and nonsectarian Ukrainian youth organization, meanwhile, grew in popularity among Ukrainian youth disillusioned with the highly partisan and divided community model of their parents. Commenting on the phrase "Peace on Earth and

Good Will towards Men" in a Christmas issue of *Zhinochyi Svit* (Women's World), one young girl wrote:

> And as the echo of this expression resounds in our ears, we cannot help but sigh. If only the Ukrainian people would choose to adopt this golden rule and apply it to their lives! And as we continue to ponder, more questions arise in our minds. Will there ever come a time when peace will reign among the Ukrainians and they shall conduct themselves in a spirit of good will towards each other? Will there ever come a time when they finally realize that only one aim do they have even though they have chosen different methods of attaining it? Will there ever come a time when they will become broadminded enough to forgive and forget petty offenses and foolish quarrels which have differentiated them and brought about dissension and hostility in their midst?
>
> Yet as we voice these queries and lament the absence of harmony in our ranks a faint ray of hope creeps into our heart, seemingly dispelling our fears. Our youth! Our youth! Surely they will not succumb to the bigotry and intolerance which have embedded themselves so deeply in the souls of their fathers? Surely they will not stop to don those old-fashioned and outworn cloaks of their fathers' minds which have only served to disguise personal animosity and hatred? No! Our youth has been brought up in a new world, in a new environment, in a new age. And it is but logical that they should wish to garb their minds in rainment befitting this modern age ...
>
> So lead on, Ukrainian youth! May your unprejudiced minds and wholesome attitudes conduct you on the journey of your life ... May the spirit of your good will toward fellow Ukrainians fuse your ranks into a harmonious and effective organization, thus supplying the means to attain your aim![59]

In the end, despite wholesome desires on the part of many, and some notable efforts on the part of a few, Ukrainian youth did not "lead on." They were led by the older generation, which established youth organizations that were modified reflections of the partisanship which existed within the total Ukrainian-American community.

League of Ukrainian Clubs

One of the first Ukrainian-American institutions to seriously undertake the organization of its youth on a national scale in the 1930s was the Orthodox church. A "Young Ukraine" section was established in the journal *Dnipro* as early as 1930[60] and, in July 1931, a resolution was adopted by the Sobor (church council) advocating the creation of local youth clubs by Orthodox priests. An editorial in the *Ukrainian Herald* stated that the purpose of such clubs was to educate youth in a "religious and national spirit, to obligate them to preserve our Ukrainian traditions and to remember that they come from the Ukrainian people and have a duty to uphold their great strivings" and, finally, "to give youth an opportunity for group life, socials, meetings, enterprises, etc."[61]

With Rev. John Hundiak leading the way, the Orthodox youth movement initially stressed the need for establishing clubs that responded to the needs and desires of the younger generation. Hundiak permitted the "Young Ukraine" section to appear in the English language almost exclusively and, in response to charges that such permissiveness only served to denationalize Ukrainian youth, he wrote:

> Our critics tell us that we are wrong in not using the Ukrainian language in this department. They accuse us of having betrayed our people. They even suspect that we are trying to transform American-born youth into Irishmen. Why, our critics ask us, not use our dear Ukrainian language in this department? Yes, why not? There are some eight or ten periodicals in the United States but in none of them have we seen contributions in the Ukrainian language from American-born Ukrainians. Why don't they write Ukrainian? Ah! Let our young friends answer that question.[62]

By the end of 1931, a total of seven youth clubs had been established and in February 1932, "Young Ukraine" called for the creation of a national federation. The first convention was held in Carteret, New Jersey, on 2–4 July 1932, with twenty-six delegates representing eight local clubs in attendance, and the "League of Ukrainian Clubs" (LUC) was established. "Young Ukraine" was adopted as the official LUC organ and Father Hundiak was designated chaplain.[63]

In 1933 there were twenty LUC chapters in existence but only nine sent representatives to the annual convention. Theodore Swystun, an ODWU organizer, addressed the conclave and a resolution, introduced by Father Hundiak, was passed stressing the duty of each LUC member to fully support the activities of UVO in Western Ukraine.[64] The use of the English language in "Young Ukraine," meanwhile, had been restricted in 1932 and was prohibited entirely after 1933.[65]

LUC's ability to attract the younger generation started to decline soon after its second convention. Twelve member clubs were in existence in 1934 but only six sent representatives to the convention. A final convention was held in 1935 in an effort to revive the federation, but by the end of the year LUC ceased to exist as a national entity. The few active clubs that still remained joined the Young Ukrainian Nationalists (MUN) organized by ODWU in 1933.[66]

The Ukrainian Youth's League of North America (UYLNA)

The most sustained effort in response to the need for a national all-Ukrainian youth organization was initiated by Miss S. Czyzowich, a member of the Ukrainian Chicago World's Fair Committee. Calling together representatives from local youth organizations in the Chicago area, Czyzowich suggested that since a "Ukrainian Week" had been set aside at the fair for the month of August, a national Ukrainian youth congress ought to be convened at the same time. An organizational committee, headed by Anastasia Oleskiw, was established in April 1933, and the congress idea was soon being supported by a number of Ukrainian organizations. Especially enthusiastic was the UNA, which sent Stephen Shumeyko of the *Svoboda* staff to Chicago in May to assist in the preparations and to write progress reports for the UNA organ.

All went well until 20 June, when a group of Catholic youth representatives withdrew from the committee. According to Mamchur, the Catholic clergy – especially the Basilians at St. Nicholas – had become alarmed by the elaborate preparations for an essentially secular congress and had decided to call their own, separate Catholic youth convention for the same week. When efforts to reconcile the split failed,[67] the organizers decided to proceed with the congress without the formal representation of Catholic youth.[68]

On 16 August 1933, the first All-Ukrainian Youth Congress was convened in the North Hall of the Chicago Coliseum. Eighty-five delegates representing Ukrainian youth clubs in eleven states and four Canadian provinces were present for the historic meeting. Most of the first day's sessions were devoted to the reading of congratulatory telegrams and to addresses from prominent Ukrainian leaders.

Speaking on behalf of the UNA, Luka Myshuha stated that the congress was "our great hope and the first step toward a common understanding between our youth, the older generation, and the leaders of our people." Yaroslaw Chyz, representing the UWA, urged delegates to "speak frankly and open-mindedly," adding that he had not come to teach the delegates anything but to learn from them. Mr. Chandoha of the UNAA congratulated the assembled delegates for responding to "the call of their motherland." Other prominent Ukrainians who spoke to the delegates on behalf of the older generation were Olena Lotocky of the UNWLA, Mary Beck of *Zhinochyi Svit*, Theodore Swystun of ODWU, and Vasyl Avramenko.[69]

Stephen Shumeyko addressed the delegates on behalf of the organizers, stressing that the purpose of the congress was to establish an all-Ukrainian youth league which would

> take the initiative in the organization and leadership of American Ukrainian youth, ... disseminate among this youth a knowledge of Ukraine and the Ukrainian people in all of its manifold aspects, ... diffuse among the American people knowledge of Ukraine and Ukrainian aspirations, ... take an active part in all Ukrainian nationalistic manifestations, ... do all within its power to advance the Ukrainian cause.[70]

Only delegates were permitted to attend the second day's sessions and the congress was able to address its major task in a systematic way. Seven committees – organizational, cultural-educational, sports, art, student fund, propaganda, and resolutions – were created in the morning and asked to report in the afternoon. The delegates also voted in favor of Canadian inclusion, believing that any differences which existed between Ukrainian youth in the United States and Canada were minimal and closer ties would be beneficial to all Ukrainian youth. It was decided that the name of the new organization should be the Ukrainian Youth's League of North America. Four major aims were incorporated into the UYLNA constitution:

1 To foster all cultural interests of the members.
2 To promote athletic activities and sponsor annual events.
3 To further Ukrainian-American ideals and principles.
4 To organize into one single unit all Ukrainian youth organizations, irrespective of religious or political belief (excepting Communism).

Elected to head the new national organization were Stephen Shumeyko, president; Helen Hawryluk, vice-president; Anna Balko, secretary; Steven Danielson, treasurer; and Stephen Jarema, Stephania Kudrick, Anastasia Oleskiw, and William Skroba, district leaders.[71]

Under the leadership of Shumeyko – who, as editor of the UNA's widely read *Ukrainian Weekly*, was in a position to provide broad press coverage to UYLNA organizational activities – the fledgling organization was able to generate unprecedented support among Ukrainian-American youth. Shumeyko remained national president until the fourth annual convention in 1936. By that time the UYLNA attracted 360 registered delegates representing over fifty local Ukrainian youth organizations. The highlight of the 1936 conclave was the first Ukrainian-American Olympiad in which some 150 Ukrainian athletes participated. It attracted approximately 5,000 spectators.

During the first three years of its existence, the UYLNA maintained a comparatively benign posture regarding political issues of concern to the older generation. Convention addresses were neutral in both tone and substance, covering such topics as "Duties of Ukrainian American Students" (1934), "Ukrainian or American?" (1934), "Problems of Our Youth" (1935), "Sports and Our Youth" (1935), "The Question of Mixed Marriages" (1936), and "The Preservation of Our Ukrainian Heritage" (1936). Occasionally, a political question would find its way into the convention agenda but the address usually dealt with the dangers of Communism or with the participation of Ukrainian youth in the American political process, rather than with political factionalism so prevalent among Ukrainians.[72]

With the election of John Panchuk to the UYLNA presidency in 1936, however, the nonpartisan character of the organization began to change. Opposed to the ODWU brand of Ukrainian nationalism then beginning to dominate UNA thinking, Panchuk resisted continued UNA influence within the UYLNA, leaning instead towards positions advocated by the UWA and *Narodna Volya*.[73]

At the 1937 convention in Cleveland, Panchuk presented a paper, copies of which were printed in advance and allegedly distributed to the American press, entitled "Nationalism or Fascism." The major points were that: (1) ODWU's nationalism was fascistic and a menace to the Ukrainian-American youth movement; (2) *Svoboda* had been lax in its repudiation of fascist ideology. Panchuk was especially critical of UYLNA delegate Eugene Lachowitch for his articles in *Natsionalist* exemplifying Germany and Italy as models of spiritual and national unity. Rising to his own and ODWU's defense, Lachowitch engaged Panchuk in a bitter debate, citing other articles he had penned which rejected fascism, and argued that the roots of Ukrainian nationalist ideology could be found in Anglo-Saxon traditions and not in Germany and Italy. Later, after tempers cooled, the convention passed a resolution (147 to 3) making it clear that Panchuk's views were his alone and not those of the delegates. Panchuk himself voted in favor.[74] In a later reply to Panchuk which appeared in *Natsionalist*, MUN member Walter Bukata defended Lachowitch by arguing that nationalism was a means to an end, a way of *preparing* the Ukrainian people for revolution through a united effort. Germany and Italy are examples, he argued, of how much power defeated and demoralized nations could muster once their people were united. "No mass movement," observed Bukata, was ever characterized by democratic tolerance in the inception of its rise to power, only in the crystallizing of its demands ... Rebellion requires a unified front of the oppressed following a democratic review of various courses of action and the selection of the best approach ... To condemn a movement which reflects mass desires on the grounds that such a movement manifests spiritual and political unification and is therefore intolerant of criticism, is to refuse to a people their right to life on the trivial pretext that they should desire life only under conditions acceptable to a different group living under different conditions.

Condemning Panchuk for his suggestion that ODWU was un-American, Bukata concluded: "Assisting morally and materially the land of your fathers in its fight for freedom can never be interpreted as un-American. The method and form of the future government of the Ukrainian people in Ukraine has no bearing on our American ideals and existence." It is not enough to *want* Ukraine. "One must be willing to fight for it."[75]

The matter did not end there, however. John Romanition, elected UYLNA president in 1937 and again in 1938, attempted to maintain the organization's nonpartisan character but was soon perceived as a supporter of the so-called Scranton socialists.[76] By the time of the 1939 convention in Newark, Nationalist youth had mobilized their forces and were determined to change what they believed was a UYLNA drift to the left. They were especially incensed by an editorial entitled "Yellow Journalism" which appeared in the *Ukrainian Trend,* an official UYLNA publication. Written by Anne Zadorosne, daughter of a UWA activist, the commentary denounced those Ukrainian-American periodicals – presumably the *Ukrainian Weekly* and *Ukraine* – that had criticized *Narodna Volya,* the UWA organ. The convention turned into a tumultuous affair during which Zadorosne defended her criticism of the UNA and ODWU with excerpts from *Vistnyk ODVU* and *Svoboda,* while Stephen Shumeyko and Roman Lapica rebutted. During the height of the debate, Messrs. Granovsky, Lachowitch, and Sichynsky, who attended as guests, offered to present their views. Their offers were rejected by the delegates, who went on to defeat the incumbent officers with a slate headed by Michael Piznak, a New York City attorney, and Walter Bukata. Later, the following statement of principle was drafted.

Every American of Ukrainian descent has two equally fundamental duties to himself: 1) to support the democratic principles on which the United States was founded even to the point of sacrificing life itself; 2) to lend every support to the struggle of his 45,000,000 kinsmen in Europe for independence.

Other resolutions were passed, including one opposing "the foreign ideologies of communism, naziism and fascism" and another endorsing "those organizations here and abroad that support militant Ukrainian nationalism."[77] The resolution took pains to make clear that the UYLNA was not neglecting "organic nationalism," the educational process by which Nationalist ideology begins to permeate all aspects of Ukrainian life; it was merely emphasizing the priority of "militant nationalism," the maintenance of a constant state of revolt against foreign oppression among the Ukrainian people and the mobilization of all spiritual and material resources for the struggle.[78]

Zadorosne was determined to win her point, however. At the 1940 convention in New York City, she distributed a bulletin which declared:

> We, the American Ukrainians who have fought the pro-fascist
> ODWU and UNA group in the League ever since it raised its
> head, feel that the eighth annual convention of the Ukrainian
> Youth in the Hotel Pennsylvania must once and for all oust such
> undesirable elements from its midst and demonstrate the inherent
> Democratic structure of the League.

Citing extensively from *The Hour, The Fifth Column Is Here,* and the testimony of Emil Revyuk, Zadorosne argued that ODWU had placed its people into significant UYLNA posts at the 1939 convention and was planning to take total control of the league in 1940.[79] Following a rancorous fight, Attorney John Roberts, a UNA loyalist, defeated New York Assemblyman Stephen Jarema for the UYLNA presidency by a vote of 50 to 43; Helen Slobodian and Chester Manasterski edged out Zadorosne and Al Yaremko for the two vice-presidential slots, 48 to 45. A resolution was also passed condemning the publications cited by Zadorosne for their misrepresentation of Ukrainian Nationalism.[80] During the subsequent FBI investigation of ODWU, Zadorosne presented her bulletin for the FBI record, alleging that ODWU had engineered her coalition's defeat because she held pro-democratic views.[81]

The Ukrainian Catholic Youth League (UCYL)

Having withdrawn their support for the first Ukrainian Youth Congress at the eleventh hour, Catholic youth leaders began, in July 1933, to promote the convocation of a separate, all-Catholic youth congress during "Ukrainian Week" in Chicago. The organizing committee was aided in its endeavors by a letter to all diocesan pastors from the pastor of St. Nicholas parish in Chicago as well as by articles which appeared in *Sich*, *America*, and the *Canadian Farmer*.

Some one hundred persons attended the first Catholic youth congress, which officially opened with a divine liturgy at St. Nicholas Church in Chicago on 19 August 1933. Following the service, the delegates moved to St. Nicholas Hall to hear remarks by Brother Methodius, Rev. M. Kuzmak, and Rev. Basil Tremba.[82] They were followed with addresses by Stephanie Blidy ("The Meaning of Religion in the Life of Youth"), Walter Matakovsky ("Parents and Youth"), and Bohdan Katamay ("The Organization of the Ukrainian Catholic Youth League"). Later that day the Ukrainian Catholic Youth League (UCYL) was duly constituted and an executive board elected consisting of Bohdan Katamay, president; Vera Shpikula, first vice-president; William Ewaskiw, second vice-president; Helen Bahry, corresponding secretary; Stephanie Blidy, recording secretary; and Mary Dziavronyk, treasurer. An honorary executive consisting of Bishop Bohachevsky, Bishop Basil Ladyka of Canada, Rev. A. Truch, Brother Methodius, and Rev. Tremba was also approved to oversee UCYL's activities.[83]

In May 1934, the UCYL began publishing *Ukrainian Youth*, a monthly journal written in both English and Ukrainian. The first editor was Ukrainian-born UCYL president Bohdan Katamay, who outlined the Catholic periodical's goal in Ukrainian:

> In sending this journal to you we expect that it will become your good friend ... that it will increase your knowledge and understanding of people; that it will bring brother closer to brother, sister to sister, brother to sister, children to father and mother, and parents to children; that it will strengthen the golden threads which tie children to their parents, to their parents' friends and to that country from which their parents came; that it will help these children recognize why their parents are so poor, why the country from which they fled is in foreign hands and in slavery; that it will help these children understand that their parents suffer only as a result of goodness and sincerity and that their only flaw is that they did not strengthen their goodness to the point of being able to fight against the evils and depravity of the world ... that it will awaken in these children a sense of belongingness to the enslaved country of their parents and to its fate ... that it will educate knights for its Fatherland – Ukraine.[84]

The same issue contained another article – also in Ukrainian – by one "O.T." who reviewed the work that lay ahead for youth who were "sin-

cerely interested in working for the Ukrainian American community."
Observing that the crucial components of national life consisted of religion,
economics, politics (both foreign and domestic), education, sports, amuse-
ment, art, and communication, the author argued that only two components, religion and politics, had thus far been developed by Ukrainians.
"Unfortunately," the author observed, "these two components have
become intertwined" with only the Catholic church maintaining "the
purity of the religious component."

> Our politics here on American soil is highly developed, one can
> almost say overdeveloped, to the point that all other components
> are overshadowed. And again it is our misfortune that our politics
> here is nothing but a weak copy of our politics in the native land
> or among immigrants in Europe; and everyone knows that our
> situation here in America is entirely different and for that reason
> our politics here should be entirely different from politics in our
> native land ...
>
> Our foreign politics, that is, the cultivation of ties with other
> peoples, is only negative – that is, in international matters our
> only concern is with our enemies on our native soil – no one
> thinks about cultivating ties with other peoples. After all, we
> have many friends, even among Americans; our problem is that
> we don't know how to take advantage of this.

Pointing to similar weaknesses in other areas of organized community life,
the author urged Ukrainian youth to evaluate the shortcomings and to
push for a more balanced approach.[85]

Attempts to call another national UCYL convention in 1934 failed and it
was not until 13 and 14 July 1935 that the UCYL met again.

The second conclave was largely the work of Bohdan Katamay, who left
Chicago on an organizational tour to various eastern communities in an
effort to interest more youth in UCYL activities. The result of his endeavors,
according to *Ukrainian Youth,* was that "there were over 200 delegates
representing over 100 clubs from some 35 Ukrainian communities all over
the United States" in attendance at the convention.

Following a precedent established in 1933, the second UCYL convention
was officially opened with the celebration of a pontifical divine liturgy by
Bishop Bohachevsky in the exarchial cathedral in Philadelphia. Delegates
then proceeded to the Park Central Hotel where papers were read by
Father Basil Feddish ("Religion and Youth"), Stephen Mamchur ("The
Orientation of the Ukrainian American Student"), Michael Nahirny

("Youth and Sports"), and Eve Piddubcheshen ("Work Program of the Ukrainian Catholic Youth").[86] UYLNA president Stephen Shumeyko also addressed the delegates urging a merger of the two national Ukrainian youth organizations. That night a new executive board was elected.[87] In addition, three auditors were added to the executive along with Revs. Lev Sembratovich and Basil Feddish, who became members of the honorary executive.[88]

For Catholic youth in America the second UCYL convention was a turning point. In the first place, the new executive board was almost exclusively American-born, a factor that probably contributed to the almost total demise of the Ukrainian language in *Ukrainian Youth*.[89] Second, the new executive put to rest any further hope of a formal rapprochement with the UYLNA. The matter was fully discussed during the convention and finally referred to the new executive, which subsequently ruled that there was a "need" for a separate Ukrainian Catholic youth organization.[90] Finally, the UCYL, despite the monarchist leanings of its early leadership, was able to steer an ideological course during the next four years that was ostensibly apolitical.

In her remarks to the delegates before her election to the UCYL presidency, Eve Piddubcheshen emphasized the importance of belonging to organizations that were not only Ukrainian but Catholic as well. Stressing the contributions of the Ukrainian Catholic church – choirs, drama groups, heritage and day schools, and the orphanage – Piddubcheshen urged all Ukrainian youth to "carry on the work" by studying "our religion, learning the Ukrainian language" and "the history of Ukraine, its geography, manners, customs and traditions," as well as "its rich literature, music and all forms of art." America, Piddubcheshen contended, "is stretching her hands out for the cultural treasures of her citizens of foreign extraction." The time to begin taking advantage of this state of affairs is "now," she concluded.

> The program is both full and interesting. Let us begin at once. Let us show our parents what we can do. Let us prepare to take the reins of leadership from them and, benefitting from their mistakes, steer more carefully ourselves. Let us develop capable leaders and then respect them. Let us always remember that "united we stand and divided we fall" and then be prepared to lead or follow as the situation demands. When we learn this we will demonstrate to the world that we are a great people, that we are entitled to all the rights and respect that have thus far been refused us, that we are capable of governing ourselves and are ready for a free and independent Ukraine, and that we have no reason to wait

any longer for what is due us. We can and we will proceed to
do our part in the realization of our parents' dream – a free and
independent Ukraine.[91]

While Piddubcheshen emphasized the Ukrainian aspects of her Catholicism – especially in her dramatic rhetoric regarding her commitment to the
ideal of a free Ukrainian state – at least one clergyman found a different
set of priorities among the delegates. Commenting on the convention,
Father Chehansky wrote:

> There was but one thing in common that could possibly be accred-
> ited for this gathering; it was the devoted interest to Catholic
> tenets, enthusiasm, and culture. That, I can frankly state, was
> uppermost in the minds of the youth, though there was every
> indication that we are not overlooking the fact that we are all of
> a very cherished and dear Ukrainian ancestry.[92]

The issue of "being American" was also broached at the convention in
a paper presented by Stephen Mamchur, then a doctoral candidate at
Yale University. Contending that assimilation was "inevitable" Mamchur
argued that the "Ukrainian cultural carryover in America" was beneficial
but "of temporary duration." For Mamchur it was simply a "practicable
policy" for Ukrainian-American youth to cultivate and develop greater
contact with Americans. Condemning Ukrainian "isolationists" for rein-
forcing guilt feelings in Ukrainian youth for their lack of participation in
Ukrainian affairs, Mamchur cautioned the delegates against accepting any
of the political ideologies of the Ukrainian community:

> You should study this for yourself ... To put it concretely – without
> stating my view – do we want the armageddon of fascism? Do
> we want half-baked parliamentarian republicanism with capital-
> ists as the boys chuckling behind their grim visages? Do we want
> some nonentity as a monarch whose sole concern shall be to keep
> his crown? Do we want some semblance of socialism, or do we
> want undiluted socialism? All these – and other possibilities – are,
> implicitly or explicitly, in the programs of the parties which
> beckon our support.[93]

Despite Mamchur's somewhat uncomplimentary characterization of the
United Hetman Organization, the UCYL continued to include a number
of local "Junior Siege" clubs which enjoyed the support of UHO.

In 1936, the UCYL began to sponsor annual track and field meets for its members in conjunction with the annual convention. At the 1938 convention, membership in the UCYL was substantially increased when the Brotherhood of Ukrainian Catholics formally joined the league. In recognition of this expansion, the UCYL changed its name to the Ukrainian Catholic Youth League of North America. At the 1939 convention in Buffalo, the league included sixty clubs scattered throughout the continent.[94]

Junior Siege and Young Ukraine

Initially a youth organization in its own right, the Hetman Sich was faced with the same problem as other Ukrainian organizations in the early 1930s – an aging membership and no younger cadres in sight to take its place. In keeping with the tenor of the times, UHO began to establish "Junior Siege" branches in affiliation with its regular organizational structure.[95] This was followed with the publication of *Siege Youth* exclusively in the English language in 1931. The first issue contained the preamble to the Sich constitution as well as the usual appeal to Ukrainian youth to fulfill their "sacred duty to uphold the traditions of our Fatherland" and to be aware of "a sense of individual obligation to our country."[96]

The most successful aspect of the entire Junior Siege movement, however, appeared to be social. Paramilitary male youth companies were created in Detroit, Cleveland, and Chicago, and a number of "Red Cross" units were organized for the girls.[97] In the words of one young UHO member,

> Our maneuvers were great fun. The day would begin with an outdoor divine liturgy and at about 11:00 A.M. or so the maneuvers would begin. The girls participated as medical support personnel and if you saw one that was particularly attractive you'd kind of make sure you were "wounded" near her station. When the whole thing was over, the losers would buy a barrel of beer, the band would arrive, and we'd all dance until the early hours of the morning.[98]

By 1932, however, it was becoming clear to UHO leaders that the highly political and nationalistic approach to Junior Siege by some UHO members was alienating the youth. In an article entitled "The Organization of Ukrainian Youth," UHO member Bohdan Katamay criticized the initial organizers for their emphasis on politics and suggested that UHO support the establishment of "Young Ukraine" clubs of Catholic youth. "Young Ukraine," concluded Katamay, "will educate Ukrainian girls and boys into the best patriots and in that way will prepare the best membership for older organizations."[99] Reflecting the new UHO approach to American-born youth, Dr. B.I. Hayovich wrote:

> Helping the Ukrainian cause does not necessarily mean for every Ukrainian girl and boy to isolate themselves and to concentrate on the Ukrainian language so as to be able to read, write and speak fluently. This is not necessary and it will not help very much ...
>
> To be of greatest help to Ukrainians, every Ukrainian girl and boy should become good Americans. Upon first thought you might not see the connection but there is one and it is very great. America is in a position to help Ukrainians. There will come a time in the Ukrainian struggle ... when a good word from America, perhaps at a meeting of nations, might mean a great deal. But for America to say anything for Ukrainians, Americans must first know who and what Ukrainians are ...
>
> I would say then to every Ukrainian girl or boy: go forth, all of you, find your place in one of various fields of endeavor, go into it with ambition, work hard – establish a good reputation and then, whenever someone asks your descent, be proud and say "Ukrainian" and know enough about Ukrainian matters so that you can answer at least a few questions intelligently. And thus the time will soon come when you will not have to explain to others who the Ukrainians are. And when Ukrainians are accepted and known as well as the Germans, French, Swedish and other nationalities, then surely will today's Ukrainian youth have accomplished a great deal in helping the Ukrainian cause.[100]

Every effort was made to develop programs that appealed to the younger generation. In Chicago, for example, a boxing tournament was organized to raise funds for a school and a gymnasium,[101] and a "riding academy" was created to interest youth in what was described as a "Kozak art."[102] In Cleveland, track and field events were organized for UHO youth.[103]

Katamay, meanwhile, continued to press for the expansion of Young Ukraine activities and, with the help of Father Truch, Colonel Shapoval, and Dr. Tarnawsky, managed to establish an active "Young Ukraine" group in Chicago by the end of 1932.[104] It was within this group that the idea of forming a national Ukrainian youth league was initially supported and it was also this group which later led the move to form a separate Catholic league,[105] an action that enjoyed the whole-hearted backing of Katamay and the UHO organ *Sich*.[106]

UHO interest in the UCYL increased following Katamay's election to the presidency. *Ukrainian Youth* was initially printed by the Sich press and references to Sich activities would occasionally find their way into the journal.[107]

In Chicago, UHO actively supported Catholic youth organizations associated with the UCYL. One such organization was the Elk Social Athletic Club, which published the *U.Y.O.A.* (Ukrainian Youths of America) *Weekly* under UHO auspices.[108] The same publication was later taken over by the so-called UHO Journalist's Club.[109]

Never able to organize and maintain a separate and viable national youth organization during the 1930s, Ukrainian monarchists were content to lend their support to those Catholic youth activities that demonstrated potential for helping keep Ukrainian youth within the community fold.

Young Ukrainian Nationalists (MUN)

Efforts to establish an organization for Nationalist Ukrainian youth began in New York City in 1932 when the local ODWU branch created a separate division within the branch for American-born Ukrainian youth. Calling themselves Young Ukrainian Nationalists – Molodi ukrainski natsionalisty (MUN) in Ukrainian – the members of the youth section confined their organizational work to activities suited to their own particular interests and background. In the words of Pauline Myhal-Riznyk, one of the original members:

> Almost all of the New York MUN branch membership was American-born. Most of us didn't know Ukrainian well and for that reason our meetings were conducted in the English language ... Even though we maintained ties with the local ODWU branch, we were fully independent. We elected our own executive from among the youth, we developed our own work and activities program, and we prepared our own discussion evenings on a variety of subjects.[110]

Later, however, ODWU members introduced an ideological component into the fledgling organization with political courses designed to prepare MUN youth for "the struggle" then being waged against the Ukrainian Communists, who had also begun organizing Ukrainian youth on a massive scale.[111]

By the end of the year, the first MUN branch had successfully attracted about thirty members into its ranks. Pleased by what was considered a promising effort, the ODWU national executive dispatched Theodore Swystun, its chief organizer, to some fifty-five Ukrainian communities in an attempt to interest other ODWU branches in the project. By the end of 1934, new MUN branches were created in Brooklyn, Detroit, Hamtramck, Chicago, Wilmington, Baltimore, and Cleveland, as well as in Arnold and Ambridge, Pennsylvania, and Elmwood Park, Illinois. Replacing Swystun as ODWU's youth coordinator that same year was Stephen Droboty, who served in that position until 1936.

In 1935, *Vistnyk ODVU* began printing a MUN page in the English language. In a column entitled "American Ukraine," Droboty described MUN as "the youth section of the Organization for the Rebirth of Ukraine (ODWU), an organization which regards the interests of the Ukrainian people above everything else. It is an organization which supports the idea of the Ukrainian NATIONAL REVOLUTION which is being conducted by the Organization of Ukrainian Nationalists in Europe, morally and materially."[112] Before MUN, Droboty wrote in the next issue, there were a handful of Ukrainian youth clubs around the country most of which had a purely social orientation.

> For a while it appeared as if the "social mania" would overcome the Ukrainian youth in America, capture the little Ukrainian blood which this youth appeared to possess, and continue its unplanned road to chaos. However, a superior force was encountered enroute ... this force was Nationalism.
>
> The speed with which Nationalism has spread is not at all amazing because it preached something new, something unfamiliar, and above all it *preached the truth*. It advocated national consciousness. It clearly illustrated who we were, who we are, and what we had to do. It was not a nationalism copied or patterned after the nationalism of other countries. It was strictly Ukrainian Nationalism. It was a Nationalism born in Ukrainian minds and hearts.
>
> Nationalism is moving Ukrainian youth away from social clubs towards greater concern for political issues.[113]

Droboty observed that MUN organizers were aware that youth in America "were exceedingly democratic and fun-loving and that a strictly serious political organization was inconceivable," and so permitted branches to engage in a variety of activities "so long as the work of the branch lived up to the qualifications of the organization – *to regard the interests of the Ukrainian people above everything else.*"[114] That the Nationalist program initially appealed to the young is clearly demonstrated by the fact that some 25 percent of the 224 delegates to the Congress of Ukrainian Nationalists in 1935 were American-born.[115]

Youth activities organized by various MUN branches varied from city to city. Philadelphia, for example, had a basketball team,[116] as did Hamtramck.[117] The New York City branch had a military drill team,[118] a MUN theater group,[119] and offered flight lessons in the ODWU-sponsored aviation school.[120] Cleveland had a drama group that performed the original nationalist play *Bilas and Danylyshyn*[121] and participated in military drills. Chicago MUN branches gave birth to *The Trident,* an English-language journal[122] which was so successful it was later taken over by ODWU. MUN members were also urged to read Nationalistic literature and to discuss it at their meetings, form debating teams, establish Ukrainian libraries, join the UNA and UYLNA, sponsor essay contests, and correspond with Ukrainians in Europe.[123] Despite their relatively autonomous status, however, MUN branches were expected to support Nationalist ideals and to assist local ODWU branches in their efforts to overcome the "humiliation" of Ukraine's partition.[124] When individuals failed to measure up, they were sometimes expelled from the MUN branch by their fellow members.[125] During the administration of Pauline Myhal-Riznyk (1936–7), a year during which the number of branches more than doubled, the organization continued to exist without benefit of a formal national board of directors.

By 1937, MUN had some forty-eight branches and a decision was reached within ODWU to hold a national convention and to form an autonomous national executive for their rapidly expanding youth cadres. Meeting in New Haven, Connecticut, MUN delegates elected John Sawchyn the first national president.[126]

During Sawchyn's tenure, enthusiasm for the nationalist program reached a new high, leading some MUN members to conclude that their organization could well serve as a leadership source for the future Ukrainian liberation army.[127] Urging fellow members to take advantage of the training opportunities available in the Reserve Officers Training Corps (ROTC) and the Citizen's Military Training Camps (CMTC) – "Bunker Hill was an example of what trained officers can do even with untrained men" – one MUN member wrote: "We need leaders among our Ukrainian youth to organize and keep them together ... In military training we find leadership, discipline, courage, patriotism, altruism and excellent temperament. Each one of these characteristics would help make you an outstanding individual as well as a good citizen and a real Ukrainian."[128]

By the time Olga Zadoretsky completed her term as MUN president (1938–40), the American-born generation active in Ukrainian political and religious affairs was imitating the older generation in – as one MUN member wrote – the use of "ungentlemanly tactics to repudiate one another as a means to an end."[129] Lamenting the fact that the Ukrainian immigration – "the greatest hope of Ukrainians in Ukraine who are denied ... the right of self-determination" – was divided into a "multitude of cliques each in conflict with each other" the author concluded:

> Youth which at present is entering upon the Ukrainian political scene should take full cognizance of this and pledge, for the sake of those who are depending on us, to follow, in the course of their work, a system of principles, a code of ethics, when dealing with one another. Follow the example set for us by the English and French and other civilized peoples and keep our slate clean and wholesome until our common end is achieved.[130]

Unfortunately, such sentiments were not shared by others and MUN, an ODWU affiliate, began to decline in the wake of the anti-Nationalist slanders which became such an integral part of the Ukrainian-American political climate.

In 1940, Zadoretsky was succeeded by Roman Lapica. Declaring that "no other Ukrainian youth group in America ... is seriously working for the liberation of the Ukrainian people," Lapica launched a membership drive[131] to make up for losses sustained during the defamation campaign. The drive never got off the ground. The name of the organization was changed to Youth of ODWU and in the summer of 1941, Lapica informed his members:

> The President has declared an unlimited emergency exists in the United States ... We, the children of Ukrainian immigrants should be especially thankful at this time that we can be of service to our country. This does not mean we want war because we do not ... On the other hand we must support the government in every manner in its policy of giving aid to the embattled democracies fighting Nazi despotism. Meanwhile, let us continue to do what we can to drawn attention to the plight of the Ukrainian people who are even worse off under Soviet occupation than are the many nations conquered by the Nazis.[132]

With the outbreak of World War II, many members joined the armed forces and the organization went into hibernation. By 1942, only four Youth of ODWU branches were still active.

The Role of the Ukrainian Weekly

One of the few members of the older generation to appreciate the dilemma of the American-born was Luka Myshuha, editor of *Svoboda*. Explaining his views at the eighteenth UNA convention in 1933, Myshuha emphasized the affective dimension in attempts to reach the younger generation. We should always stress the joy, beauty, and excitement of Ukrainian history, culture, music, and language to our youth, he declared. But we should also be aware of the fact that every generation must develop its own Ukrainian identity. The education of our youth is composed of "elements found in the home of the Ukrainian immigrant, in Ukrainian community life, and in Ukrainian schools ... A young person who has been exposed to such an education is decidedly different from an immigrant. In addition to American life, he is familiar with the life from which [his] parents emerged." While biculturalism is an adequate alternative, argued Myshuha, it too has its drawbacks for the younger generation: "the life of their parents is not a model for them simply because their environment is different. It may be easier for them to break into American mainstream life than it was for their parents but it is still not as easy as it is for the children of American-born parents." The problem must be solved by the youth itself, concluded Myshuha, and to do that, they need a news forum that is written and edited exclusively by them.[133]

Myshuha's proposal was accepted by the UNA delegates and, on 6 October 1933, the first issue of the *Ukrainian Weekly* appeared with the following editorial:

> The *Ukrainian Weekly* is for the youth. The youth alone shall be its matter. Its voice alone shall be heeded here.
>   The Ukrainian National Association has undertaken to bear the extra cost of this publication in order to give our youth the opportunity of having an exclusive organ of their own, written in its own style and language, wherein it can meet, exchange its thoughts and ideas, come to a better understanding of each other and perhaps point out those paths of endeavor which shall lead to a newer and better life.[134]

Edited by Stephen Shumeyko, the *Ukrainian Weekly* became the most widely read youth publication in the Ukrainian-American community. Just as *Svoboda* had helped Ukrainianize the first generation, the *Ukrainian Weekly* devoted itself to the Ukrainianization of the second. We write about Ukraine, Shumeyko explained in 1933, because the *Weekly* "must serve as a guide to our American-Ukrainian youth by pointing out in its own inimitable language and style the road to the goal which is dear to all Ukrainians – a free and independent state of Ukraine."[135]

Much of what appeared in the *Weekly* during the 1930s concerned itself with such matters as the Great Famine and other acts of Soviet repression,[136] denationalization in partitioned Ukraine,[137] the OUN trials in Poland,[138] the dangers of pacifism and Polish-Ukrainian rapprochement in Galicia,[139] Romanian repression,[140] Hitler's designs on Ukraine,[141] Carpatho-Ukraine,[142] American misinformation regarding Ukrainian aspirations,[143] and Polish repression.[144] Domestic issues, however, were also considered.

Military training for Ukrainian youth was supported because "As the Ukrainian young men in Europe are *deprived* of the opportunity to learn the manipulations of modern war machines ... it remains for *us* here in the United States to produce the officers and instructors which the Ukrainian nation and its people need so badly! And which America can use too."[145]

Changing surnames was frowned upon because

> We of Ukrainian descent are especially duty-bound to retain our Ukrainian family names. Our parents are among the latest arrivals and naturally they did not have the time nor opportunity to make any outstanding contributions to American development. Such opportunities, however, are confronting us now ... And yet how will posterity judge our contributions to the development of this country if we lose our national identity by giving our Ukrainian names various Anglo-Saxon, Germanic and Scandinavian forms?[146]

No consensus was reached regarding the proper date for celebrating Ukrainian Christmas. Some youth argued that 25 December was acceptable "as long as all the traditions were maintained."[147] Others supported the traditional Julian calendar date (7 January) because a change could, among other things, make it easier for Ukrainians in Galicia to change and thereby give Poland "more power in her attempt to Polonize the Ukrainians."[148]

Nor were any conclusions reached regarding intermarriage. Some believed that from a nationalistic and family perspective, Ukrainians marrying non-Ukrainians was inadvisable.[149] Other youth were convinced that one had to be realistic. No policy, pro or con, was possible.[150]

Despite a decidedly nationalistic editorial policy, the *Weekly* did publish articles which were contrary to mainstream community sentiment. Especially popular (and controversial) was a column entitled "Potpourri" written by an insightful gadfly under the nom de plume "Burma Capelin." Complaining that second-generation organizations in 1936 were controlled by older immigrants, Capelin wrote:

> The attempt has been, in almost every instance, to inculcate Ukrainian culture or Ukrainian ideals – whatever the tinge may be, religious, nationalistic, socialistic or something else – into the second generation. While in itself this may be neither good nor

bad, it is a luxury, if you please, which the second generation cannot afford ... The immigrant organizations cannot reconcile themselves to the fact that the organizations, including the church, which have served the immigrant tolerably well are ill adjusted ("out of date") to the second generation as the horse and buggy is in our motorized urban life. The second generation simply cannot fit into the scheme of thinking, the way of behavior, and the organization of the first generation. By virtue of having been born in America, its fates and fortunes lie within American conditions ... Ukrainian youth organizations, if they are to achieve anything more viable than speech making or paper publicity, must recognize that it is American and not Ukrainian conditions to which primarily the second generation must adjust.

Older generation support of American-born youth should be unconditional, Capelin suggested.[151] Work in Ukrainian youth organizations, he continued, was based on "gross unreality, the reference being to making the second generation hostage, if you will, to either the 'cause abroad' or to a special brand of Ukrainianism as conceived by parties of the older generation." The first generation, Capelin observed, has not helped youth "to get jobs in American life" or "educated them on the values of contacts with Americans," or extended a helping hand "to scores of those who being 'at sea,' land in American social agencies, juvenile courts, etc."[152] The hope of older Ukrainians that youth will resist the "mania of Americanization" and help in some way in "fashioning the future Ukrainian state" rests on two fallacies: "One that by living in America and hoping to be Ukrainians they can be such and secondly, that they can be of significant help abroad." "The most healthy situation for the individual," concluded Capelin, "is a respect for Ukrainian ways and only a gradual absorption of American culture. In this sense it can be truly said that one cannot be either a good Ukrainian or a good American without being both."[153] Capelin's views, of course, generated a series of responses, mostly pro, which the *Weekly* published through the remainder of the year.[154]

Articles and editorials were also devoted to efforts by Russian-Americans to "capture" Ukrainian youth – "We cannot stand idly by and permit this Muscophilism to entice our American-Ukrainian youth away from their nationality,"[155] assimilation,[156] the defamation campaign,[157] and the American heritage.

It is interesting for us to observe how much pleasure our American-Ukrainians derive from taking part in the Fourth of July parades and manifestations ... For our parents are very much

aware of the fact that back in the old country they would not be
allowed to parade freely, carrying flags and dressed in Ukrainian
costumes ... But what about us, the younger generation, born and
raised here? Do we appreciate our American freedom and democracy? Does the Declaration of Independence mean as much to
us as to our parents?[158]

For the *Weekly*, the reluctance of the American-born to become involved
in Ukrainian affairs was due to immaturity, a lack of "clear, self-orienta-
tion," vagueness regarding their role in the community, a lack of experience,[159] and a debilitating emphasis on social activities.[160]

The single most important issue to which the *Weekly* devoted consistent
attention, however, was the problem of Ukrainian-American unity. As early
as 1933 Shumeyko wrote:

> Our youth has long been witness to the fact that the principal cause
> of the weakening and destructive divisions among the older genera-
> tion of American-Ukrainians has been the irreconcilable religious
> and political differences among many of our leaders ...
>
> We appeal ... to our youth to not pay any attention to these
> petty squabbles, selfish ambitions, religious and political intoler-
> ances of many of our older generation. Shun them as you would
> the plague ...
>
> Let us accept from the older generation only those elements
> which are good and honorable: tolerance, understanding and
> mutual self-respect; and ignore all of those which have been
> impregnable obstructions to our older generation's attempts to
> organize itself.[161]

"The Ukrainians have a disease," Shumeyko declared in 1934, "that may safely
be called great, not only because it is so widely prevalent but more so because
its results are so vast. It is costing Ukrainians their country and their freedom.
It is breeding discontent, fear and inertia ... I am referring to that cancerous
growth, 'discord.' "[162] Admitting to certain shortcomings on the part of the
younger generation in 1936, Shumeyko pointed to a "far more serious cancer
that threatens all organized American-Ukrainian youth life" – the "attempts
being made to segregate our youth into religious and partisan camps."[163]

The Aftermath

The older generation never succeeded in transforming the second generation into a political or military vehicle for the liberation of Ukraine. Ultimately, it was their "social mania" rather than political or religious

considerations that kept most of the American-born youth close to the Ukrainian hearth. This was especially true of the larger communities which had dance groups, choirs, various sports clubs, and a variety of social activities – dances, community picnics, parties, weddings – to attract the youth. And it really did not matter much which society or group sponsored a particular event. If it seemed like fun, the youth attended.[164]

For those who turned their back on the Ukrainian community completely, there were many reasons. One was the American milieu. Perceiving their American environment as essentially hostile to biculturalism, some younger Ukrainians preferred to make their way in society without the "stigma" of hyphenization.[165]

Another reason, no doubt, was the relative anonymity of Ukrainians. Since few Americans had ever heard of Ukraine, Ukrainian Americans were constantly forced to explain their ethnonational existence to their non-Ukrainian acquaintances. The more assertive individuals had no problem with this and even carried pamphlets and maps in their pockets to aid them in their explanations. In the words of some Ukrainians interviewed in Chicago in 1945:

> I don't have any trouble saying that I am Ukrainian. If a person doesn't know, I explain it to him ...[166]

> I usually explain to people what a Ukrainian is, but you can't do it to everybody. Some of them wouldn't understand anyway, no matter how much you talked to them. I just say I'm Ukrainian and that's the end of it.
>   Sometimes they say, "Is that the same as Russian?"
>   But I always say, "No, it's not the same as Russian; for Christ sake, it's Ukrainian!"
>   "What, Lithuanian?"
>   I'm telling you some people are too dumb to understand. They go to school – to high school and college – and if I asked them about their nationality, they wouldn't know.[167]

> The American people just didn't know where Ukraine was. I had to carry a pocket map around with me to show it to some of them. It took a man-sized war to put us on the map. Now everyone reads the newspapers about the Ukrainian armies and they see maps with "Ukraine" written on them. I have no trouble explaining my nationality any more.[168]

The less assertive, however, reconciled themselves to being called "Russian" rather than face the embarrassment of having to explain:

> I usually say I'm Russian. If you say you're Ukrainian, the guy
> tells you, "Jesus Christ, what's that?" and you have to go into a
> whole history of Ukraine and explain to the guy what you mean.
> It is easier to say you are Russian. Everybody has heard of that –
> especially now, during the war. You could say "Ruthenian," they
> seem to know that one, too. So few people have ever heard of
> the Ukrainians that it's embarrassing to say you are one.[169]

While the American "melting pot" milieu and the relative anonymity of
Ukrainians were significant contributing factors in the steady erosion of
youth interest in Ukrainian organizational life, an apparent major cause
was the nature and the structure of the Ukrainian-American community
itself. Ironically, it was the older Ukrainian generation which, despite
its efforts to the contrary, alienated many young people and kept them
estranged from organized Ukrainian life.

The Ukrainian-American community was founded, developed, and
maintained by foreign-born Ukrainians. After World War I, the primary
focus of most of their activities was on Ukraine proper. Demonstrations
were organized to protest conditions *in* Ukraine. English-language books
were published and participation in American folk fairs and their cultural
activities was encouraged to acquaint America *about* Ukraine. It became, in
a sense, the "duty" of every Ukrainian to become involved in the Ukrainian
freedom crusade.

The emphasis on "duty" and "obligation" was reflected by the youth
organizations which were established and controlled by the older generation. Although appeals to the self-interest of youth were made occasionally – usually in terms of the cultural benefits one derived from being
Ukrainian – the major purpose of these organizations was the perpetuation
of the European-oriented ideals of the older generation. What the latter
seemed unwilling or unable to appreciate was that American-born Ukrainians were often confused when "helping Ukraine" appeared to be in conflict
with American international interests. During most of the 1930s, for example, American interests dictated the support of the Soviet Union, Poland,
Czechoslovakia, and Romania, nations which were then occupying Ukrainian territory. The mental conflict for the American-born in such instances
was very real and often led to a weakening of ties with Ukrainians.[170]

But the most negative feature of Ukrainian life for the American-born
was the division that existed within the community along religious and
political lines. If the future of the Ukrainian-American community
depended, in part, on intermarriage and the preservation of Ukrainian
families, then religious and political dissonance severely restricted the
availability of "suitable" Ukrainian partners. The attitudes of the Orthodox
and the Catholics in this regard have already been mentioned. The same

phenomenon seems to have existed among Ukrainian youth concerning political loyalties. For example, in 1945, John Zadrozny interviewed two young people in Chicago and elicited the following responses:

> You know those Ukrainians on Western Avenue – those right-wingers, those fascists – they want the good old days back again. They want the rich land-owning class to come back into power in Ukraine. Everybody knows that they want a reactionary government back in power ...
>
> I went to the Ukrainian Civic Center to a "shindig" they had there once. I felt as if I was invading the camp of the enemy – no kidding. I hate 'em. After the dance, I took one of those fascist dames home from there, and as we were passing this building, I asked her as if I didn't know,
>
> "By the way, what is this place?"
>
> And she said, "Oh, that's the People's Auditorium; that's where the Bolsheviks hang out."
>
> Boy, I'm telling you, if she had known who she was being walked home by, I'm sure she would have died.[171]

> I wouldn't be caught dead in that Bolshevik house. Those pro-Russian people – I don't know if you can call them people; *hudoba* (cattle) is a better word.[172]

In the end, the bitter political and religious struggles which characterized the 1920s and 1930s took their toll. The youth, especially those whose Ukrainian sentiment was marginal to begin with, became "American." Other youth, disenchanted with the constant infighting among Ukrainians, became organizationally inactive.[173]

The older generation was also affected. As a result of the Dies Committee investigation and its aftermath, many ODWU and UHO members left their organizations during the early 1940s and never returned to active Ukrainian community work. Others simply burned out. In the words of one pioneer: "Things were very quiet in the early 1940s. The political and religious battles had been fought – bitterly – and in the end, no one had won. Our youth wanted no part of our fights. Our community was quiet alright – no more political battles – no more religious battles – we were dying."[174]

❧

None of the organizations established as vehicles of cross-generational maintenance accomplished as much as their founders and supporters would have liked.

Despite outstanding individual efforts by sensitive and knowledgeable educators such as Stetkewicz, Kaskiw, and Andreiko, who urged that the Ukrainian heritage school system be professionally constituted, and despite the endeavors of such professional organizations as Ridna Shkola to upgrade the level of teaching in these schools, most of them remained relatively primitive enterprises. Ukrainian children, nevertheless, attended these schools in fairly large numbers, mainly because their parents insisted on it.

Ukrainian day schools generally reflected the Catholicism-over-nationalism posture of Bishop Bohachevsky and the American-born clergy. Still, without seminaries and day schools, there might not have been any priests and lay leaders. Without priests and lay leaders, there would be no Ukrainian church. Without a Ukrainian church, there would be no Ukrainian-American community. Regardless of perceived shortcomings in other areas, Bishop Bohachevsky's strong commitment to Ukrainian Catholic education was a long-term benefit to the Ukrainian-American community.

Although Ukrainian parents could induce their children to attend heritage and day schools up to about age sixteen, other institutions had to be developed to retain older and more independent youth within the communal fold. Realizing that the older organizations were unappealing, Ukrainian communal leaders began to call for organizations which the youth itself created and managed. Unfortunately this never happened. Most of the earlier youth associations were organized along lines which reflected the partisanship of the older generation both politically and religiously. Thus, there were Orthodox, Catholic, Communist, Hetman, and Nationalist youth organizations established for the purpose of maintaining a particular type of belief and behavior rather than something called Ukrainianism.

The most sustained effort to establish a truly representative, nonpartisan youth organization came about with the creation of the Ukrainian Youth League of North America. The UYLNA failed to become representative of all Ukrainian youth when Catholic youth, largely under the influence of their clergy, withdrew from the organizing committee and proceeded to form their own league. Thus, although individual Catholic youth belonged to the UYLNA, no Catholic club as such was an official member of the league.

The Ukrainian community in America could not afford the luxury of different youth organizations for every partisan position held by the older generation. In the end, the factionalism that existed among Ukrainians, the ever-present need to explain to Americans what a Ukrainian was, the melting pot climate which prevailed in the United States during the 1930s, and the negativism towards Ukrainians generated by the defamation campaign combined to produce an anomic attitude among not only the American-born, but Ukrainian-born as well. By the early 1940s, after two decades of almost ceaseless controversy and strife, the Ukrainian-American community was exhausted and relatively inactive. Some Ukrainian Americans even believed the community was dying.

11 Epilogue

The Ukrainian-American community, of course, did not fade out of existence as some pre-war sages had predicted. On the contrary, the community survived the war years and after the arrival of the third mass immigration in the 1950s, it was able to regain much of its former vigor and vitality.

Displaced Persons

When World War II came to an end, Ukraine was in ruins. "No single European country," wrote journalist Edgar Snow in 1945, "suffered deeper wounds to its cities, its industries, its farmlands, and its humanity."

During the course of the conflict, some 6.8 million Ukrainians perished. This included 3.9 civilians (including 800,000 Jews), 1.3 military dead, and slave laborers. The war also destroyed over 700 Ukrainian cities and towns and some 28,000 villages. "The whole titanic struggle which some are so apt to dismiss as 'the Russian glory' was first of all a Ukrainian war," concluded correspondent Snow after a tour of the war-ravaged Ukrainian countryside.[1]

By the end of September 1945, the Western Allies and the Soviets claimed to have some 14 million displaced persons under their care, of which 7.2 million were Soviet citizens.[2] They included *Ostarbeiter* (forced laborers), POWs, military collaborators, non-returners, and those ultimately repatriated. Most (52.6%) of the non-returners were Ukrainian.[3]

Hundreds of thousands of Ukrainians were in Germany voluntarily, the result of an often agonizing decision to leave everything behind – home, career, friends, and relatives – and to move out with the retreating Germans rather than to remain in Ukraine and wait for the reimposition of Soviet rule. Most Ukrainians and other Eastern European nationals living in Western Europe in 1945 were placed in displaced persons (DP) camps administered by the United Nations Relief and Rehabilitation Administration

(UNRRA). Few had any inkling that their fate had been decided by the Allies earlier in the year.

On 11 February 1945, the United States, Great Britain, France, and the USSR signed a repatriation agreement at Yalta guaranteeing the return of all displaced Allied nationals on a reciprocal basis. Significantly, the agreement defined Soviet nationals as all those refugees who had lived within the borders of the USSR prior to 1 September 1939. This excluded, obviously, all those Ukrainian refugees who had resided in the pre-war, Polish-governed regions of Galicia and Volhynia.

At Yalta, the Soviets had insisted that the repatriation agreement obligated signatory nations to return all nationals without exception, by force if necessary, as soon after the war ended as possible. Great Britain adopted a policy of mandatory repatriation as early as August 1944, prompting Admiral William Leahy, President Roosevelt's chief of staff, to urge the president to follow suit. Behind America's acquiescence at Yalta was the fear (reinforced by Soviet threats) that Moscow would refuse to repatriate American POWs found in Germany internment camps in Poland, Hungary, and eastern Germany.

The Soviets took the position that all Soviet citizens who found themselves in Germany and Austria at the end of the war were anxious to return home except those who had collaborated with the Nazis. This view was shared by the *New York Times* – which argued on 24 January 1945 that most refugees who did not wish to return were "collaborationists who have no claim on the sympathies of Russia's western allies – and the UNRRA director for the American occupation zone in Germany who made the assertion that "anti-repatriation groups are not the product of democratic processes but are rather the remnants of pre-war regimes that reflect Nazi and fascist concepts."[4]

Concerned that they would be forced to care for millions of refugees during the upcoming winter, the U.S. military command in Germany commandeered every available means of transportation in order to move Soviet nationals into the Russian zones of occupation before the autumn ended. It was an incredibly efficient operation. By 19 November 1945, western commands had repatriated 2,037,000 people.

For American soldiers, forced repatriation was a dirty business. Refugees were often dragged kicking and screaming to trucks and railroad cars. Others, preferring death to repatriation, hanged themselves, rammed their heads through windows to sever their necks, and bit each other's jugular veins. Appalled by such incidents, General Dwight D. Eisenhower ordered a ban on the use of force on 4 September. On 6 September, United States authorities attempted to move 600 Ukrainians and others from Mannheim to a DP center in Stuttgart. Believing they were headed for the Soviet zone

of occupation, the refugees rioted, prompting Congresswoman Clare Booth
Luce to later query the War and State departments regarding the Yalta
Agreement and "our common understanding here of the kind of freedom
for which our soldiers fought." On 20 December, the State-War-Navy
Coordinating Committee exempted Soviet civilians from mandatory repatriation.[5] Although the end of forced repatriation was a welcome relief for
most Ukrainians still languishing in DP camps, their future was still in
doubt. It would remain in doubt for the next three years.

The Birth of the United Ukrainian American Relief Committee (UUARC)

It was at the second convention of the Ukrainian Congress Committee of
America (UCCA) in 1944 that the post–World War II future of Ukrainians
in Europe was first discussed by the Ukrainian-American community. "In
view of the fact that Ukraine is one of the major victims of the war,"
declared one of the convention resolutions, "it is absolutely essential that
the UCCA organize a purely humanitarian and apolitical Ukrainian relief
committee for war victims and refugees."

At the first UCCA executive board meeting held in New York City on 16
March, a commission consisting of *Svoboda* editor Luka Myshuha, Longin
Cehelsky, and Olena Shtogryn was created to explore the Ukrainian refugee problem in depth. In April, all three commission members traveled to
Washington, DC, where they met with representatives of the American
Red Cross and UNRRA, an organization founded by 44 nations in 1943 for
the purpose of reuniting families, caring for displaced persons, assisting in
the repatriation process, and aiding liberated peoples to rebuild their lives
and nations.

At the next UCCA executive board meeting, commission members
reported that although UNRRA had the best-developed network for assisting refugees, it only cooperated with organizations which were accredited
members of the Council of American Voluntary Agencies for Foreign Services and were recognized by the president's Relief Board. Since UNRRA
aided refugees without regard for national or religious affiliation, moreover, it could not guarantee assistance earmarked exclusively for Ukrainians even when donors specifically requested such consideration.
Furthermore, UCCA commission members reported, all food, clothing,
and monies sent overseas by American voluntary agencies required prior
approval by the State Department.

A final problem identified by commission members was the resistance of
the Soviet government to any assistance for Soviet citizens that was not
under direct Soviet control. The American Red Cross, it was learned, had
already sent some $20 million to the Soviet Union, designating much of it

for Ukraine. Since the Soviets would not allow anyone from the United States to monitor how and where war relief funds were used, there was no way to determine if the donated funds actually had benefited the Ukrainian people. All funds to the USSR had to be channeled through Russian War Relief, an organization which dutifully forwarded all of its monies directly to Moscow for distribution within the USSR.

Given the nature of the existing war relief system, the UCCA commission concluded that only an accredited Ukrainian organization created by Ukrainians for Ukrainians could guarantee that donations collected from Ukrainian Americans would be spent the way donors expected.

On 20 June 1944, the UCCA established the Ukrainian American Relief Committee (URC) as an independent organization. Headed by Dr. Walter Gallan, the executive board included Dr. Neonilya Pelechowicz-Hayvoron-sky, vice-chair; Dr. Paul Dubas, secretary; and Evhen Rohach, treasurer. Completing the board were Roman Slobodian, UNA treasurer; Wasyl Sha-batura, UNAA president; Anastasia Wagner and Ivanna Bencal, controllers; Andrew Melnyk, Anna Nastiuk, Eve Piddubcheshen, Maria Staleva, Platon Stasiuk, Irene Tarnawsky, and Semen Uhorchak, members.

While the URC was being formed in New York, a second Ukrainian relief committee was established in Michigan under the chairmanship of John Panchuk. Officially called Ukrainian War Relief, the executive of the new committee decided to join forces with the URC when it was learned that all of its work would have to be coordinated with Russian War Relief. A unity conference was held in October, a merger was agreed upon, and the URC conference was renamed the United Ukrainian American Relief Committee (UUARC). John Panchuk became the first vice-chairman of the newly constituted organization.

Ukrainian Communists in America, meanwhile, voiced their opposition to Ukrainian-American relief efforts organized by the nationalist camp. Arguing that since the Soviet government was already taking care of Ukrainian needs in Europe, *Ukrainski Schodenni Visti*, the Ukrainian-American Communist periodical, accused the UUARC of "racketeerism." At the same time, members of Russian War Relief complained to the White House that Ukrainians in America were planning to raise funds to assist Nazi war criminals and collaborators who had fled with the Germans to escape Soviet justice.

The Growth of UUARC

Approaching the President's War Relief Board for permission to raise funds for Ukrainian relief efforts in Western Europe, the UUARC executive was informed in November 1944 that no permission was required since there were many overseas relief organizations which would gladly accept Ukrainian funds. With the help of the board, the UUARC eventually established ties with the Unitarian Service Committee, UNRRA, and CARE, a non-profit organization created to send food and clothing parcels to the needy overseas.

Still seeking formal recognition as an independent entity, the UUARC was accepted as a full member of the Council of American Voluntary Agencies for Foreign Services on 7 March 1945. Recognition enabled the UUARC to expand its ties to other relief organizations including the Catholic Welfare Conference, the American Friends Committee, the International Students' Fund, the International Immigration Service, and the Swedish Red Cross. In response to a second request for government accreditation, the President's War Relief Board recognized the UUARC on 22 September. Once accreditation was assured, the UUARC began to broaden its organizational base by establishing branches in Detroit, New York City, Minneapolis, Rochester, Buffalo, Baltimore, Chicago, Syracuse, Olyphant, and other cities throughout the United States. Fund raising was intensified with the help of the Ukrainian-American press and by the end of 1945 some $100,000 had been raised for the purchase of food, medicines, and other supplies needed by Ukrainian refugees. An additional $200,000 worth of wearing apparel was also collected by UUARC and sent to Europe.[6]

The single most distressing problem facing the Ukrainian-American community during this period was the issue of forced repatriation. Learning of the tragedy from refugee letters sent to relatives and friends in America as well as from correspondence with Ukrainian-American soldiers stationed in Germany and Austria (many of the letters were subsequently published in *Svoboda, America, Narodna Volya,* and the *Ukrainian Weekly*), the UCCA published a 31-page brochure entitled *Plight of Ukrainian DPs.* Emphasizing that Ukrainian refusal to return to the USSR was prompted by fears of Soviet repression – "they well know that on account of their patriotic Ukrainian sentiments and their anti-totalitarian and pro–free Ukraine actions, they face imprisonment, banishment to Siberian wastelands or execution" – the brochure appealed to "all Americans of good conscience" to intercede on behalf of the Ukrainian refugees.[7] Letters were sent to the White House, the State Department, and various United States Congressmen.[8] The official United States reply was always the same: "You may be assured that insofar as it is within the power of the United States Government, no persons of Russian origin who are not Soviet citizens are being repatriated to the Soviet Union."[9]

The UUARC was not satisfied with the American response. In a letter addressed to various government officials, UUARC president John Panchuk wrote:

In the ordinary course of events, the resettlement of all displaced persons into the country of their origin would not go unquestioned. President Roosevelt and Marshall Stalin anticipated the repatriation of war torn populations and made it a subject of agreement providing for mutual repatriation of Americans found in the Soviet zone of occupation and of Soviet citizens found in the American zone.

As subsequent events proved, however, the vast majority of Ukrainians, whose melancholy destiny was the subject of barter at Yalta without their knowledge and consent, did not welcome the "agreement" for their repatriation into the Soviet Union. When one recalls that Russia's claim to them rests upon military occupation of their homeland, forceful annexation, confiscation of their lands and property, and ruthless subjugation, their determined unwillingness to comply with repatriation is understandable.

To avoid future miscarriages of justice, Panchuk argued, Ukrainians should be recognized as a separate ethnic group, "segregated from all other nationals of like status, and placed in exclusively Ukrainian camps."[10] The US War Department replied that it was the policy of the United States government "to deal with Ukrainian displaced persons according to their national status as Soviet citizens, Polish citizens, Czechoslovak citizens, nationals of other countries of which they may be citizens, or as stateless persons. In view of this policy, it has not been considered appropriate to segregate all Ukrainian stateless and displaced persons and to place them in exclusive Ukrainian camps." With respect to forced repatriation, the War Department concluded, "Ukrainian displaced persons are not being repatriated to their countries of origin unless they so desire." The only exceptions, the department noted, were "Ukrainians covered by the United States–USSR Yalta Agreement who were both citizens of and actually within the Soviet Union on September 1, 1939," those Ukrainians who were "captured in German uniforms," those "who were members of the Soviet Armed Forces on or before 22 June 1941 and were not subsequently discharged therefrom," and "those who on the basis of reasonable evidence have been found to be collaborators with the enemy, having voluntarily rendered aid and comfort to the enemy."[11]

Still hoping to undermine the Ukrainian relief effort, America's Ukrainian Communists continued to condemn the UUARC and its activities. On 21 November 1945, the Ukrainian American Fraternal Union (ORDEN), a communist front organization, sent a letter to the State Department requesting clarification of the official American position regarding relief activities among Ukrainian Americans in the nationalist camp. On 25 June 1946, the Ukrainian American League, Inc., another Communist-front organization, sent a letter to the State Department protesting all efforts to assist Ukrainian "war criminals," "quislings," and "collaborators posing as displaced persons and refugees."[12]

From Relief to Resettlement

On 28 July 1945, the Central Ukrainian Relief Bureau was established in London with the cooperation of the UUARC and the Ukrainian Canadian Relief Fund. The following summer UUARC president Walter Gallan traveled to Europe, where he met with representatives of Ukrainian relief organizations in England, France, Belgium, Italy, and Switzerland. In Paris, Gallan participated in the purchase of a building that became the center of a coordinated Ukrainian relief effort for displaced persons camps. Gallan returned to the United States to lobby American authorities for the necessary approval. While in America, Gallan was appointed executive director of the UUARC. John Panchuk became the new president.

Permission to visit displaced persons camps in Germany and Austria was granted early in 1947 and Gallan returned to Europe, where he learned that repatriation remained a major concern among Ukrainian refugees. Ukrainians were still not recognized as a separate ethnic group by some authorities, and many UNRRA officials, committed as they were to repatriation, were screening Ukrainian refugees with an eye jaundiced by the Soviets. Ukrainian fears were allayed somewhat when UNRRA was dissolved and replaced by another UN-sponsored agency, the International Refugee Organization (IRO), which pledged to honor the wishes of displaced persons who refused to return to their homelands for political or religious reasons. From that moment on, the primary focus of the UUARC shifted from relief to resettlement.

UUARC credibility in the United States, meanwhile, was further enhanced on 16 September 1947, when it was accredited by the Advisory Committee on Voluntary Foreign Aid, a federal board established in 1946 to "guide the public and agencies seeking the support of the public in the appropriate and productive use of voluntary contributions for foreign aid."

When IRO began its work in Europe, there were approximately one and a quarter million refugees still remaining in displaced persons camps in Germany, Austria, and Italy. Some 210,000 were refugees from Ukraine. Working closely with other Ukrainian refugee organizations in Europe, UUARC representatives succeeded in finding homes for many of them in England, France, Belgium, various countries in South America, Australia, and New Zealand.

Resettlement in the United States, however, was still not a realistic option because of immigration quotas established in 1929 which discriminated against Ukrainians in two ways: first because quotas were lower for all immigrants from Eastern and Southern Europe, and second, because only nations in existence after World War I were assigned official quotas. Since Ukraine was not a recognized nation-state, Ukrainians who immigrated to the United States were forced to do so within the relatively low quotas assigned to Poland, Czechoslovakia, Romania, and the Soviet Union.

The immigration door opened slightly in December 1945 when President Harry Truman issued a directive granting preference to refugees within the specified quotas who had a U.S. sponsor willing to sign an affidavit pledging assistance to the new immigrant after his arrival in the United States. Some 42,000 displaced persons were admitted in 1946 as a result of the directive, including a small group of Ukrainians. The president's action was significant because it broadened the criteria for displaced person status beyond the accepted norms. For the first time, the designation "displaced person" included not only victims of Nazi oppression (forced laborers, concentration camp inmates, and others), but victims of Communist oppression as well.

Truman's directive was not well received by the American public. Mail to the White House ran 7 to 1 against admission of displaced persons and executives of the American Legion and the Veterans of Foreign Wars made public statements opposing resettlement in America. The president persevered, however. In his 1947 State of the Union message to Congress, Truman urged America's legislative branch "to turn its attention to this world problem in an effort to find ways whereby we can fulfill our responsibilities to those thousands of homeless and suffering refugees of all faiths."[13]

The Displaced Persons Act

It was obvious to all concerned ethnic leaders, but especially to Jewish Americans, that if displaced persons were ever to find a haven in the United States, American public opinion would have to change. Resisting pressure from the Zionists, who were supporting Jewish refugee resettlement in Israel exclusively, the American Jewish Committee joined forces with other like-minded Jewish groups, convened a meeting of distinguished Americans (mostly non-Jews), and, on 20 December 1946, established the Citizens Committee on Displaced Persons (CCDP). Headed by Earl Harrison, formerly United States commissioner of immigration, the CCDP became one of the largest and best-run lobbying operations in the nation. By May 1948, some 600 radio stations had used its materials and millions of Americans had viewed the film *Passport to Nowhere* on the plight of DPs, which RKO distributed nationally. Within a relatively short time, the CCDP was able to turn public opinion around, prompting one authority to comment that "almost all editorials on the displaced person problem appearing in the press of the nation were inspired if not written by the CCDP." Exaggerated or not, the claim was a reflection of the important role the AJC and CCDP played in preparing the groundwork for congressional action. Although its primary concern was quite understandably the approximately 100,000 Jewish DPs then in Europe, the AJC was astute enough to realize that the CCDP could never succeed unless it worked on behalf of all DPs. Pushing for an American "fair share" quota of 400,000 DPs, the CCDP later welcomed the support of many ethnic leaders in its lobbying efforts.[14]

Not all Jews were so favorably disposed toward non-Jewish DPs, especially Balts, Ukrainians, and Poles who some Jews claimed had collaborated with the Nazis. Ira Hirschmann, UNRRA Director-General Fiorello LaGuardia's personal emissary, toured the DP camps and reported that the "hard core" of the non-Jewish DPs "has proved to be a criminal and fascist group, many of whom left their homes voluntarily to work for Hitler." Chaplain Judah Nadich, General Eisenhower's first Jewish chaplain, wrote that Ukrainians and *Volksdeutsche* "were Nazis to the very core of their being." Koppel S. Pinson, the American Jewish Joint Distribution Committee's educational director for DPs in Germany and Austria, wrote that "a large group of Poles, Ukrainians, Russians and Balts" now residing as DPs "are some of the bloodiest henchmen of the SS and the Gestapo." Another savage attack came from Abraham G. Duker, a Zionist and a member of the American legal team at the Nuremberg war crimes trials, who argued that many Estonians, Latvians, and Lithuanians, in conjunction with Ukrainians and Croatians, were especially egregious collaborationists."[15] Criticizing the CCDP for its efforts, Duker later claimed that "Balts, Ukrainians, White Russians and other nationalities ... were placed by the Nazis in the same categories as the racial Germans."[16]

Soon after the Eightieth Congress convened in 1947, a number of bills were introduced to ease immigration restrictions, including one by Congressman Emanuel Cellar (D., NY) which would have made available the immigration quota of any European nationality that was unused by 30 September of fiscal years 1947 and 1948. The Cellar Bill was never reported out of committee.

On 1 April, a bill was introduced by Congressman William G. Stratton (R., IL) authorizing the admission of 100,000 displaced persons a year for a period of four years. As defined in the Stratton bill, a displaced person was anyone living in Germany, Austria, or Italy who: (1) was out of his country of former residence as a result of events subsequent to the outbreak of World War II and (2) was unable or unwilling to return to the country of his nationality of former residence because of persecution or his fear of persecution on account of race, religion, or political opinions. Despite almost unanimously favorable press reaction to the bill, opposition was still voiced by American Legion and VFW executives who argued that admission would only exacerbate the shortage of housing and lead to unemployment among veterans. Other opponents of the bill labeled displaced persons as degenerates, criminals, and subversives who would never adjust to American life. Urging a return to the national origins system of the 1920s, they proposed resettlement in Africa and Alaska. Still other opponents argued that many of the refugees were Communist agents anxious to come to America in order to subvert the American way of life. The Stratton bill was also defeated in committee.

On 7 July, President Truman sent a message to Congress reemphasizing the need for legislation permitting displaced persons to enter the United States. These people, he argued, were hardy and resourceful or they would not have survived. They are opposed to totalitarianism and "because of their burning faith in the principles of freedom and democracy," they have suffered privation and hardship. Many of the displaced persons already have "strong roots in this country – by kinship, religion or national origin." A source of America's strength, the president concluded, "was the varied national origins, races and religious beliefs of the American people."

During the fall congressional recess, a House Foreign Affairs subcommittee traveled to Europe to gain, according to the committee chairman, "a grasp of the problem of displaced persons through direct observation." Visiting over 150 displaced persons camps in the American, British, and French zones of Germany and Austria, subcommittee members met with various IRO representatives, governmental officials, military command authorities, voluntary agency directors, and other interested parties. In their report, subcommittee members rejected forced repatriation of persons "who have a legitimate fear of political or religious persecution in their homelands" as morally unacceptable and urged all nations "capable of receiving these displaced persons into their economies and national life" to do so.

A senate judiciary subcommittee visited displaced persons camps early in 1948 and the result was S.2242, a controversial bill which adopted the IRO definition of a displaced person but restricted it to persons who entered the American, French, or British zones of occupation between 1 September 1939 and 22 December 1945. Preference was to be given to people with agricultural skills – some 50 percent of those admitted were to be in this category – and persons with skills needed in their resettlement locale; also people from Estonia, Latvia, Lithuania, and east of the Curzon Line in Poland. Only 100,000 refugees were to be admitted under the bill's provisions.

On the House side, Congressman Frank Fellows (R., ME) introduced a bill on 7 April 1948, which defined displaced persons as persons who were in the camps on 21 April 1947, and authorized the issuance of visas in proportion to the total number of displaced persons in each nationality group. Preference was given to people with professional and technical skills as well as to agricultural workers and persons with blood relatives in the United States. The bill provided for the admission of 200,000 displaced persons. The original bill never came out of committee but on 29 April, Congressman Fellows introduced a similar bill which passed the House on 11 June by a vote of 289 to 91.

After much acrimonious debate, an amendment to increase the number of displaced persons to 200,000 was accepted by the Senate and S.2242 was passed by a vote of 63 to 13 on 2 June. Senate and House conferees met, compromised over their differences, and passed the legislation on to the president. The final version of the bill permitted a total of 205,000 refugees to enter the United States over a two-year period. Although unhappy with many provisions of the legislation, President Truman signed the Displaced Persons Act on 25 June 1948, expressing his hope that future amendments would rectify the defects. At the time, there were approximately 835,000 displaced persons still living in Europe, of whom an estimated 138,622 were Ukrainians.

The United States Displaced Persons Commission was created in August and from its inception it became apparent that two years was not enough time to organize a resettlement program, create an effective administrative apparatus, develop rules, regulations, and procedures, and physically transport 205,000 persons to the United States. In its first semiannual report to the president and Congress, the commission made twelve specific legislative recommendations, including expanding the program to authorize 400,000 visas over a four-year period, establishing a revolving fund for loans to voluntary agencies in order to meet reception and transportation expenses of displaced persons from ports of entry to their destinations, and, most significantly for Ukrainians, changing the eligibility date for displaced persons to have been in Germany, Austria, and Italy from 22 December 1945 to 21 April 1947, a provision which removed discriminatory restrictions against worthy refugees who fled Iron Curtain countries subsequent to 1945.

On 13 January 1949, Congressman Cellar introduced a bill which embodied many of the commission recommendations including a provision to extend the life of the commission to 30 June 1953. The bill died in committee, but Congressman Cellar introduced a similar bill (HR 4557) on 9 May and, after more heated debate during which opponents argued that screening procedures were inadequate, the bill passed the House on 3 June.

Senate debate over HR 4567 lasted for months. In the interim, the displaced persons program was investigated by several congressional committees, including the subcommittee on Relations with International Organizations of the Senate Committee on Expenditures in the Executive Department. Reporting in 1949, the subcommittee recommended nine basic changes in the law which closely followed commission recommendations. Also significant was the special subcommittee report of the House Committee on the Judiciary entitled "Displaced Persons in Europe and their Resettlement in the United States" submitted on 20 January 1950. The subcommittee, supported by staff experts, visited various displaced persons camps, stressing personal contact, unscheduled visits, hearings with a free exchange of questions and answers, and briefings by military and civilian personnel. Investigating charges of widespread fraud and falsification and forging of documents by prospective DPs, the subcommittee reported: "The number of screening agencies, screening sessions, interrogations and checks that a displaced person must pass before reaching the United States is so extensive that the chance of a fraudulent statement or a forged document to 'slip through' is practically nil." At the time, every applicant under the Displaced Persons Act was checked by:

a The Federal Bureau of Investigation.
b The Counter-Intelligence Corps of the United States Army, which required twenty-one separate investigative steps before a report was submitted to the commission.
c The Central Intelligence Agency.
d The Provost-Marshall General of the United States Army in Germany.
e The fingerprint record center in Heidelberg, Germany.
f The Berlin Document Center.
g The Immigration and Naturalization Service of the Department of Justice through stationing of immigration inspectors overseas in the DP resettlement centers as well as at ports of entry.
h Consular officers especially assigned for this program.
i A special investigation in connection with displaced persons whose country of origin had been overrun by Communists.

The Senate passed HR 4567 on 5 April and on 16 June 1950, the bill was signed into law by President Truman. Amendments to the 1948 Displaced Persons Act extended the life of the DP Commission to 30 June 1951 and

included a change in the eligibility deadline from 22 December 1945 to
1 January 1949; expansion of the admission quota to 341,000 persons;
elimination of an agricultural workers' quota; a requirement that DP sponsors be U.S. citizens; a provision for commission loans to accredited public
and private agencies involved with resettlement. Legislation enacted in
1951 extended the life of the commission to 31 December 1951.[17] Subsequent
legislation permitted the Commission to terminate its activities on 31
August 1952.[18] By the time the last displaced persons ship arrived on 21
July 1952, some 395,000 new immigrants had been admitted to the United
States under provisions of the Displaced Persons Act.[19]

The Resettlement Process

In addition to the various federal agencies with which the Displaced Persons Commission cooperated during its four-year history, it established a
close working relationship with various American voluntary agencies and
the thirty-six state DP commissions created by local governors and state
legislatures. In both of the latter instances, the Ukrainian presence was
evident.

During the initial months of its existence, the commission limited its
accreditation to those agencies that had resettlement experience and were
registered by the Advisory Committee on Voluntary Foreign Aid. On 21
October 1948, the commission recognized nine agencies of which only one,
the UUARC, was a purely ethnic American organization. By the end of the
program, ten more organizations were accredited, five of which were
ethnic. All registrants worked under the supervision of a special U.S. agency
established for the purpose of assuring reliability and were required to file
fiscal and program reports and to place their overseas operations under
the directorship of a U.S. citizen.[20]

Of all the state commissions, that of Michigan enjoyed the greatest local
support. State employees were assigned to assist in its operations and
donations were received from such organizations as the Community Chest
of Metropolitan Detroit.[21] The Michigan commission was headed for a time
by John Panchuk, who remained UUARC president until 1951, when he
was succeeded by Luka Myshuha.[22]

The Displaced Persons Act, as well as the extraordinary relationship
which the UUARC enjoyed within the DP Commission framework, permitted the UUARC to create an organizational network that resulted in the
resettlement in the United States of almost 33,000 Ukrainians by 30 June
1952.[23] Five important activities were involved in the process.

The first order of business was to find thousands of qualified Ukrainian-
American sponsors willing to sign housing and employment assurances

for most of the Ukrainian displaced persons which the UUARC sponsored. With the help of the Ukrainian-American press, which consistently emphasized the moral and national obligation of Ukrainian Americans to help their needy brethren overseas, as well as through various meetings, speeches, and rallies throughout the United States, the UUARC succeeded in finding sponsors in all of the states where Ukrainian communities existed.

A second priority was the expansion of the UUARC's European apparatus in order to process assurances overseas, prepare prospective immigrants for life in America (among other things, the UUARC sponsored English-language classes and provided copies of Ukrainian-American newspapers), and coordinate travel arrangements to the United States. Anticipating eventual congressional passage of some type of displaced persons legislation, the UUARC established its main office in Munich, Germany, on 1 December 1947, under the directorship of Roman Smook, a lawyer from Chicago. Branches were created in other cities, including Frankfurt, Stuttgart, Bremen, and Salzburg, Austria. The UUARC operation in Europe eventually included fifty-eight full-time employees and an additional thirty volunteers from IRO. Smook returned to the United States after two years and was succeeded by Michael Rodyk who, with the exception of a one-year period during which Dr. Myroslav Kalba was director, remained at that post until 1953. By the end of 1950, when Dr. Gallan visited Europe for a third time, some 200,000 displaced Ukrainians had been processed through the Munich office.

A third important aspect of the resettlement process was the creation of a UUARC organizational apparatus in the United States to greet Ukrainian displaced persons at their port of entry, attend to all necessary immigration formalities, provide temporary room and board, and assist the new immigrants to their final destinations. Reception centers were established in New York City, New Orleans, and Boston, where, on 30 October 1948, the first boatload of IRO-sponsored refugees arrived. Included were some 200 Ukrainians. The first boat with UUARC-sponsored displaced persons arrived in Boston on 17 January 1949.

A fourth UUARC priority was the creation of inland resettlement centers where new immigrants could receive temporary room and board until their sponsors could attend to their needs. UUARC centers were created in seventy centers (located mostly in UNA, UWA, and UNAA fraternal halls and Catholic and Orthodox parish halls) in Philadelphia, Detroit, Cleveland, Rochester, Chicago, Pittsburgh, Hartford, Scranton, Minneapolis, Milwaukee, Baltimore, and other smaller towns throughout the United States. In every one of the larger cities there were Ukrainian Americans who sponsored fifty or more families (many of whom were not even related to the sponsor) and were willing to take time off from their own jobs to find housing and employment for all of them.

Despite the UUARC's best efforts, however, there were still a number of displaced persons in Europe for whom no Ukrainian-American sponsors could be found in the time allotted. Hoping to provide American farmers with Ukrainian agricultural workers, UUARC representatives traveled to various states and were able to obtain commitments from DP commissions in North Dakota, Oklahoma, Indiana, Illinois, and Michigan. The most enthusiastic response came from Maryland, where on 8 March 1949, the governor signed a blanket assurance for some 200 Ukrainian families (771 individuals), all of whom were expected to arrive in time for the spring or summer seasons. Owing to travel delays and other problems, the UUARC was never able fully to honor its contract with Maryland farmers, many of whom refused to accept displaced persons who came after the fall harvest. Among those who did arrive on time, moreover, there were many who either had no agricultural skills or who were too weak to take on the hard physical labor required of them. Although the majority did complete the one year of work for which they were contracted, some Ukrainians fled to the cities at the first opportunity. Given all these problems, the UUARC was forced to curtail its Maryland project and to work only with those farmers who had good experiences with Ukrainians and were willing to sponsor more.

The UUARC was not the only Ukrainian-American organization to become involved in the resettlement process. The Ukrainian Catholic church in America also played a major role.

Soon after Bishop Buchko was appointed apostolic visitor to Ukrainian refugees in Western Europe in 1942, Pope Pius XII appointed Ambrose Senyshyn, a Basilian monk, as Bishop Bohachevsky's new auxiliary. In 1946, a Ukrainian Catholic Committee for Refugees was established in Stamford, Connecticut, under the direction of Bishop Senyshyn. In August of the same year, the committee, which worked closely with the National Catholic Welfare Council (NCWC), dispatched Fr. John Stock as its representative in Europe, where he remained for the next six years. In 1952, Bishop Senyshyn reported that some 175 priests (many of whom were married), approximately 300 orphans, and over 45,000 other displaced persons had been resettled in the United States through the efforts of his committee.

The Church World Service (CWS) of the National Council of Churches of Christ in America also played a significant role in the resettlement process, bringing the total number of Ukrainians who arrived in the United States as a result of the Displaced Persons Act to approximately 70,000 or 15 percent of all displaced persons who came to America.[24]

The Refugee Relief Act

Although the number of refugees had been substantially reduced, over-population in Europe was still a problem. At the initiative of the U.S. government, an international conference was called to address the issue in December 1951. On 24 March 1952, President Truman sent a special message to Congress recommending the admission of 100,000 additional persons a year for three years from the Netherlands, Germany, Italy, and Greece. Included in the president's recommendation were refugees from Communism.[25] Legislation was subsequently introduced and on 31 July 1953, the Refugee Relief Act was signed into law, permitting an additional 210,000 persons to immigrate to the United States. Of this number, 35,000 was allocated for refugees still living in Western Europe.

Appealing once again to the Ukrainian-American community, the UUARC managed to collect the necessary assurances and to resettle an additional 5,000 Ukrainians from Germany as well as a few from France and Belgium. At about the same time, the UUARC succeeded in bringing over 774 Ukrainians who had completed their work contracts in Tunisia and were still eligible to resettle under the provisions of the Displaced Persons Act of 1948.[26]

Thus ended the last mass Ukrainian immigration to America. Given the comparatively stable economic conditions that prevailed in the United States during the 1950s and 1960s, most post–World War II Ukrainian immigrants prospered in their adopted homeland. Their impact on Ukrainian-American community life has been substantial and while too little time has passed to provide a dispassionate historical analysis, it is possible to review some of the major religious, political, cultural, and educational developments which have occurred during the past forty years.

The Last Forty Years

Thus ended the last Ukrainian mass immigration to the United States. Of the three Ukrainian immigrant groups to arrive on American shores, the third was perhaps the most fortunate. Ukrainian immigrants who reached the United States after 1950 came to a community that was fully established. They came at a time when Ukrainian churches, fraternal societies, cultural clubs, and women's and youth organizations were all in place. The identity battles and turf wars had all been fought. The Ukrainian community in America had survived. Unlike the first immigration, the third immigration was welcomed to the United States by their own people, in their own language. Unlike the second immigration, the third immigration came at a time when the United States assisted refugees, jobs were plentiful,

Communism was in disrepute, and the climate for ethnonational preservation and development, especially during the 1970s, was never better.

With the exception of the Ukrainian Communists, every segment of
the Ukrainian-American community benefitted from the influx of new
immigrants from Ukraine.

By 1978, the Ukrainian National Association had 89,000 members and the
Ukrainian Workingman's Association (now called the Ukrainian Fraternal
Association) had 24,000 members. The Providence Association and the
Ukrainian National Aid Association reached membership highs of 18,900
and 8,802 respectively.

In 1958, Ukrainian Catholic exarchies were elevated to eparchy status
by the Vatican, and Bishop (later Metropolitan) Bohachevsky's major
administrative emphasis was on the establishment of liturgical norms.
Adherence to Byzantine-Slavonic traditions was stressed in all areas, from
the design of church interiors (which were now to include a heretofore
ignored iconostasis, the screen of icons which separates the altar from the
congregation) to a variety of ecclesiastical directives. In 1978, the Ukrainian
Catholic church reached a membership of 265,000.

Bishop (later Metropolitan) Theodorovich was canonically consecrated
in 1949 opening the door for a number of Orthodox, formerly associated
with Bishop Bohdan's diocese, to eventually join the Ukrainian Orthodox
Church of the USA. By 1966, Bishop Theodorovich's diocese numbered over
87,000 members. Bishop Bohdan's diocese included some 30,000 members.

In 1967, there were some 50,000 Ukrainian Protestants in the United
States. Most belonged to one of two federations: the Ukrainian Evangelical
Baptist Convention headed by the Rev. Olexa Harbuziuk and the Ukrainian
Evangelical Alliance headed by Rev. Volodymyr Borowsky.[27]

Although there was relative peace in the religious arena for many years,
this was not the case in the political realm. With the fading of both the
monarchists and the Communists, the Nationalists began fighting among
themselves, leading to a return of ideological strife.

The full story of the last forty years and the third immigration, however,
has yet to be told. At another time. In another book.

Notes

Preface

1 S. Dillon Ripley, "Foreword," *A Nation of Nations*, ed. Peter C. Marzio (New York: Harper and Row, 1976), p. xiii.
2 Ibid. For a different perspective, see Stephen Steinberg, *The Ethnic Myth: Race, Ethnicity and Class in America* (New York: Atheneum, 1981).
3 Joshua A. Fishman, "Childhood Indoctrination for Minority Group Membership," *Minorities in a Changing World*, ed. Milton L. Barron (New York: Alfred A. Knopf, 1967), pp. 178–9.
4 Robert E. Park and Herbert A. Miller, *Old World Traits Transplanted* (New York: Harper and Brothers, 1912), p. 25.
5 Amitai Etzioni, *Modern Organizations*, Foundations of Modern Sociology Series (Englewood Cliffs: Prentice-Hall, 1964), p. 3.
6 See Myron B. Kuropas, *Ukrainians in America* (Minneapolis: Lerner Publications, 1972); Vasyl Markus, "Ukrainians in the United States," *Ukraine: A Concise Encyclopedia*, vol. 2, ed. Volodymyr Kubijovic (Toronto: University of Toronto Press, 1971), pp. 1100–51; Paul Robert Magocsi, "Ukrainians," *Harvard Encyclopedia of American Ethnic Groups* (Cambridge: Harvard University Press, 1980), pp. 997–1009.
7 Milton M. Gordon, *Assimilation in American Life: The Role of Race, Religion and National Origins* (New York: Oxford University Press, 1964), p. 32. Also see Abraham Rosman and Paula G. Rubel, *The Tapestry of Culture* (Glenview: Scott Foresman & Co., 1981), p. 6.
8 Norman Sheffe, ed., *Many Cultures, Many Heritages* (Toronto: McGraw-Hill Ryerson Limited, 1975), pp. vii–viii.
9 See William Petersen, "Concepts of Ethnicity," *Harvard Encyclopedia of American Ethnic Groups*, ed. Stephen Thernstrom (Cambridge: Harvard University Press, 1980), pp. 234–42.
10 James Stuart Olson, *The Ethnic Dimension in American History*, vol. II (New York: St. Martin's Press, 1979), p. xv.
11 James Banks et al., *Curriculum Guidelines for Multiethnic Study* (Arlington: National Council for the Social Studies, 1976), pp. 9–10.

12 Hans Kohn, *Nationalism: Its Meaning and History*, An Anvil Original (Princeton: D. Van Nostrand Co., 1955), p. 9.

13 Louis Snyder, *The Meaning of Nationalism* (New Brunswick: Rutgers University Press, 1954), p. 11.

14 Boyd C. Schafer, *Nationalism: Myth and Reality* (New York: Harcourt Brace and World, 1955), p. 7.

15 Paul Robert Magocsi, *The Shaping of a National Identity: Subcarpathian Rus, 1848–1948* (Cambridge: Harvard University Press, 1978), p. 2.

16 Kohn, pp. 29–30. For a detailed analysis of the genesis of nationalism in Eastern Europe, see Peter F. Sugar, "External and Domestic Roots of East European Nationalism," *Nationalism in Eastern Europe*, ed. Peter F. Sugar and Ivo J. Lederer (Seattle: University of Washington Press, 1969), pp. 3–54.

Chapter 1

1 J.B. Rudnyckyj, "The Name Ukraîna," *Ukraine: A Concise Encyclopedia*, vol. 1 (Toronto: University of Toronto Press, 1963), pp. 5–7. Historically the terms "Ukraine" and "Ukrainian" were associated with the frontier territories of the Cossacks and the unique society and culture that emerged there. In the nineteenth century, activists of the nascent national movement, eager to stress continuity with the Cossack past, advocated the use of "Ukraine" and "Ukrainian" in place of the traditional designations Rus' and Ruthenian. By the mid twentieth century the terms "Ukraine" and "Ukrainian" were in general use in all areas of what is today referred to as "Ukraine."

2 See Nicholas Chubaty, "The Ukrainian and Russian Conceptions of the History of Eastern Europe," *Proceedings of the Shevchenko Scientific Society*, 1 (1951), pp. 1–25; Natalia Polonska-Vasylenko, *Two Conceptions of the History of Ukraine and Russia*, ed. Wolodymyr Mykula (London: The Association of Ukrainians in Great Britain, 1968), pp. 67–73; M. Tikhomirov, *The Towns of Ancient Rus'* (Moscow: Foreign Languages Publishing House, 1959), p. 463. Both Ukrainian and Russian historians have claimed Kiev as part of the historiography of their respective nations. Tsarist Russian historians proclaimed Kiev "the mother of all Russian cities," declared Moscow to be Kiev's sociopolitical successor, and categorically denied the existence of a separate ethnic identity for the Ukranian people. Ukrainian historians, most notably Michael Hrushevsky, have argued that the many spiritual, political, social, and cultural differences which existed between Kiev and Moscow precluded the inclusion of early Kiev in Russian history. Significantly, Soviet Russian historians have modified the prerevolutionary Russian historical posture. Soon after the 1917 revolution, M.N. Pokrovsky, the "official" Soviet historian, accepted Hrushevsky's interpretation and assigned the entire Kievan-Rus' period to Ukrainian history. After his death, however, Pokrovsky's school was declared "anti-Marxist" and "anti-Leninist." The current Russian posi-

tion is that Kievan Rus' "left its imprint on the history of three fraternal peoples – the Russians, the Ukrainians and the Belorussians."

3 N. Chubaty, "The Medieval History of Ukraine: The Princely Era," *Ukraine: A Concise Encyclopedia,* 1:581–600; George Vernadsky, *Kievan Russia* (New Haven: Yale University Press, 1948).

4 I.L. Rudnytsky, "Transcarpathia (Carpatho-Ukraine)," *Ukraine: A Concise Encyclopedia,* 1:710–14. Also see Walter C. Warzeski, "Religion and National Consciousness in the History of the Rusins" (PhD dissertation, University of Pittsburgh, 1964). The region referred to as Carpatho-Ukraine has been and continues to be identified in a variety of ways. The region has been called "Subcarpathian Rus'," "Subcarpathia," "Trans-carpathia," "Subcarpathian Ruthenia," "Ruthenia," "Carpatho-Rus'," "Carpatho-Russia," and "Uhro-Rus'." All the various names refer to the Carpathian Mountains, which traverse the area. Differences are related to ethnonational preference.

5 Michael A. Hrushevsky, *A History of Ukraine,* ed. O.J. Fredriksen (New Haven: Yale University Press, 1941), pp. 92–112. Also see: D.S. Mirsky, *Russia: A Social History* (London: The Crossett Press, 1931), pp. 121–3; Orest Subtelny, *Ukraine: A History* (Toronto: University of Toronto Press, 1988), pp. 19–68.

6 John Meyendorff, *The Orthodox Church: Its Past and Present Role in the World Today* (New York: Pantheon Books, 1962); Oscar Halecki, *From Florence to Brest, 1493–1956* (Rome: Sacrum Polonia Millenium, 1958); Subtelny, pp. 92–102.

7 Donald Attwater, *The Christian Church of the East: Churches in Communion with Rome,* vol. I (Milwaukee: Bruce Publishing Co., 1961); Hrushevsky, pp. 210–11; Samuel Koenig, "The Ukrainians in Eastern Galicia: A Study of Their Culture and Institutions" (PhD dissertation, Yale University, 1935), pp. 121–3; Subtelny, pp. 92–102.

8 Hrushevsky, pp. 144–346; Dmytro Doroshenko, *History of Ukraine,* trans. Hanna Chikalenko-Keller (Edmonton: Alberta Institute Press, 1939), pp. 134–330; George Vernadsky, *Bohdan, Hetman of Ukraine* (New Haven: Yale University Press, 1941), pp. 101–5; Clarence A. Manning, *The Story of Ukraine* (New York: Philosophical Library, 1947), pp. 27–8; Subtelny, pp. 105–98.

9 Meyendorff, pp. 111–13; Isidore Nahayewsky, *History of Ukraine* (Philadelphia: "America" Publishing House of Providence Association of Ukrainian Catholics in America, 1962), pp. 185–206.

10 E. Borschak, "Ukraine in the Russian Empire in the Nineteenth and Early Twentieth Centuries (1880–1917)," *Ukraine: A Concise Encyclopedia,* 1:667–89; C.H. Andrusyshen and Walter Kirkconnell, eds., *The Ukrainian Poets, 1189–1962* (Toronto: University of Toronto Press, 1962); *Taras Shevchenko: The Poet of Ukraine* (Jersey City: The Ukrainian National Association, 1945); Subtelny, pp. 202–78.

11 For a concise and informed discussion of this process, see Ivan L. Rudnytsky, "The Ukrainians in Galicia under Austrian Rule," *Nationbuilding*

and the Politics of Nationalism: Essays on Austrian Galicia, ed. Andrei S. Markovits and Frank E. Sysyn (Cambridge: Harvard Ukrainian Research Institute, 1982), pp. 23–67.

12 Nahayewsky, pp. 198–206; Hrushevsky, pp. 487–8; Andruyshen and Kirk-connell, pp. 261–92; N. Hlobenko, "Literature: The Period of Realism," *Ukraine: A Concise Encyclopedia*, 1:1019–30.

13 E. Vytanovych, "Galicia, 1772–1849," *Ukraine: A Concise Encyclopedia*, 1:698–707; *Istoriia Naukovoho Tovarystva Im. Shevchenka* (History of the Shevchenko Scientific Society), ed. Volodymyr Kubijovyc (Munich: Shevchenko Scientific Society, 1949).

14 Cited in Bohdan Krawciw, "100 Richchia Materi Prosvity" (On the 100th Anniversary of Mother Prosvita), *Almanac of the Ukrainian National Association for 1968* (Jersey City: Svoboda Press, 1968), pp. 176–7.

15 Ibid., pp. 177–8.

16 Another Ukrainian gymnastic organization, Sokol, patterned after the Czech organization of the same name, was founded in 1894. Most Sokol activities were concentrated in the large urban areas of Ukraine.

17 "Sich as a Factor in Ukrainian History," *Hei Tam Na Hori Sich Ide* (Hey on the Hill, Sich Is Coming), ed. Peter Trylowsky (Edmonton: Publishing Committee of the Sich Jubilee Book, 1965), pp. 413–16 and passim.

18 Gregory Luzhnytsky, "Ukrainian Cultural Activities in Lviv, 1858–1918," *Lviv: A Symposium on Its 700th Anniversary* (New York: Shevchenko Scientific Society, 1962), pp. 169–82.

19 John Zadrozny, "The Development of a Nationality Movement" (PhD dissertation, University of Chicago, 1953), p. 341; also see Subtelny, pp. 279–335.

20 Zadrozny, pp. 342–3.

21 Ibid., p. 342.

22 Koenig, pp. 105–6.

23 In reality, there are four major "histories" of Carpatho-Ukraine – the Carpatho-Ruthenian, the Hungarian, the Russian, and the Ukrainian – each of which is written from the national perspective of its authors. For an excellent review of these four interpretations, see Magocsi, *The Shaping of a National Identity*, pp. 105–29.

24 The dates of these migrations, which occurred in waves, are controversial. Ukrainian authorities argue that the initial settlement of the Slavs occurred at about the same time as that of the Magyars. Hungarian sources claim that there was no Ruthenian colony before the sixteenth and seventeenth centuries. See Oscar Jaszi, "The Problem of Sub-Carpathian Ruthenia," *Czechoslovakia*, ed. Robert J. Kerner (Los Angeles: University of California Press, 1949), pp. 195–6.

25 I.L. Rudnytsky, "Transcarpathia (Carpatho-Ukraine)," *Ukraine: A Concise Encyclopedia*, 1:710–14.

26 Hrushevsky, pp. 427–33.

27 C.A. Macartney, *Hungary and Her Successors: The Treaty of Trianon and Its Consequences, 1919–1937* (London: University of Oxford Press, 1937), p.

106: "In every case," writes Macartney, "the country of origin appears to have been some part of the enormous Ukrainian linguistic area and the various local dialects, of which there are great numbers, appear in every case to be at bottom variants, strongly and diversely corrupted by local elements – Polish, Slovak or Magyar – and by Russian and Old Slavonic terms of the Ukrainian language. In this sense, it is correct to classify Ruthenes as Ukrainians."

28 Warzeski, p. 11.

29 Ibid., pp. 35–6.

30 Macartney, p. 202.

31 "The sovereign stag," wrote one Hungarian in describing Ruthenian life as late as 1901, "should not be disturbed in its family entertainments ... What is a Ruthenian compared to it? ... only a peasant ... Wild deer and boar were allowed to destroy corn, oats, potatoes, and clover planted by the Ruthenians – sometimes an entire year's harvest – in order to provide sport for the aristocracy ... (cited in Jaszi, pp. 196–7).

32 Warzeski, pp. 94–6.

33 Macartney, p. 209. Also see Warzeski, pp. 78, 95. With the exception of a relatively brief period under Austrian administration, the Magyarophile posture of the Ruthenian clergy remained an important determinant of Carpatho-Ukrainian ethnic consciousness until the beginning of World War I.

34 Warzeski, pp. 63–6.

35 Ibid., pp. 94–108.

36 Magocsi, *The Shaping of a National Identity*, pp. 47–50. Also see Augustin Stefan, "Contacts between Carpatho-Ukraine and Lviv," *Lviv: A Symposium*, pp. 272–5.

37 Magocsi, *The Shaping of a National Identity*, p. 45.

38 Warzeski, pp. 91–109.

39 Stephen C. Gulovich, "The Rusin Exarchate in the United States," *The Eastern Churches Quarterly*, 6, no. 8 (January–March 1945), p. 463.

40 Warzeski, p. 91.

41 Ibid., pp. 109–10.

42 George Barany, "Hungary: From Aristocratic to Proletarian Nationalism," *Nationalism in Eastern Europe*, pp. 274–9.

43 Rudnytsky, "Transcarpathia," pp. 712–13.

44 Henry Baerlin, *Over the Hills of Ruthenia* (London: Leonard Parsons Ltd., 1923), p. 19. The Magyarization efforts of these schools are mentioned again on pages 99, 101, and 194.

45 Nahayewsky, p. 212.

46 Rudnytsky, "Transcarpathia," p. 713.

47 Mona Harrington, "Loyalties: Dual and Divided," *Harvard Encyclopedia of American Ethnic Groups*, p. 677.

48 I.L. Rudnytsky, "Bukovina," *Ukraine: A Concise Encyclopedia*, 1:707–10.

49 Andrusyshen and Kirkconnell, pp. 181–93.

50 Hrushevsky, pp. 500–1.

51 Rudnytsky, "Bukovina," p. 710.
52 For an overview of this period of Ukrainian history, see Subtelny, pp. 201–335.
53 For an overview of this period, see Subtelny, pp. 330–79.
54 For an overview of this period, see Subtelny, pp. 453–80.

Chapter 2

1 Yaroslav Chyz, "The Ukrainian Immigration in the United States," *Calendar of the Ukrainian Workingmen's Association for 1940* (Scranton: Narodna Volya Press, 1939), pp. 97–100.
2 *Dziennik Chicagoski*, 12 December 1962.
3 *Illinois Central Magazine*, September 1914, pp. 9–16.
4 D. Mirsky, *Russia: A Social History*, ed. C.G. Seligman (London: The Cressett Press, 1931), p. 133.
5 During the first year of its existence, Honcharenko's newspaper operated under three different mastheads: *The Alaska Herald* (1 March 1868 through 15 April 1868), *The Free Press and Alaska Herald* (2 May through 30 May), *The Alaska Herald-Svoboda* (1 June 1868 through 15 February 1869).
6 Yaroslav Chyz, "Andrii Ahapii Honcharenko – Andrew Ahapius Honcharenko," *Calendar of Svoboda for 1957* (Jersey City: The Ukrainian National Association, 1957), pp. 73–80. See also Wasyl Luckiw and Theodore Luckiw, *Ahapius Honcharenko, "Alaska Man"* (Toronto: Slavic Library, 1963).
7 *Alaska Herald*, 1 March 1868; see also *Alaska Herald-Svoboda*, 15 September 1868.
8 *Alaska Herald*, 15 March 1868.
9 Ibid., 1 April 1868.
10 Ibid., 1 March through 15 March 1868.
11 Ibid., 1 April through 15 April 1868.
12 Ibid., 1 March 1868.
13 Ibid., 1 August 1868.
14 *Free Press and Alaska Herald*, 2 May 1868.
15 Ibid., 23 May 1868.
16 Ibid., 9 May 1868.
17 Ibid., 2 May 1868.
18 Ibid., 30 May 1868.
19 Wasyl Halich, *Ukrainians in the United States* (Chicago: University of Chicago Press, 1937), pp. 68–9. For a detailed account of these events, see Michael Ewanchuk, *Hawaiian Ordeal: Ukrainian Contract Workers, 1897–1910* (Winnipeg: Michael Ewanchuk, publisher, 1986), pp. 76–85.
20 Halich, pp. 12 and 22. According to Fr. Nestor Dmytriw, who arrived in the United States in 1895, the Ukrainian immigration really began around 1868, "possibly ten years sooner," with the mass exodus commencing in 1875 (see *Svoboda*, 24 May 1904).

21 Orest Kyrylenko, *Ukraintsi Amerytsi* (Ukrainians in America) (Vienna: Association for the Liberation of Ukraine, 1916), pp. 1–7.

22 Koenig, "Ukrainians in Eastern Galicia," p. 72.

23 It is significant that by the time of the arrival of the first Ukrainian priest in 1884, there were upwards of a half-million Poles in the United States. The Poles already had their own priests as well as a variety of organizations, including the Polish National Alliance (founded 1880), a strongly nationalistic organization dedicated to the resurrection of an independent Poland. According to the 1900 census, of all the foreign-born Poles in this country, 40 percent were from Congress Poland (under the Romanoffs), 39 percent were from Prussian (later German) Poland, and only 15 percent were from Austrian Poland. See Victor R. Greene, *The Slavic Community on Strike: Immigrant Labor in Pennsylvania* (Notre Dame: University of Notre Dame Press, 1968), p. 16.

24 Iuliian Bachynskyi, *Ukrains'ka Imigratsiia v Z'iednanykh Derzhavakh Ameryky* (The Ukrainian Immigration in the United States of America) (Lviv: Iuliian Bachynskyi and Alexander Harasevych Publishers, 1914, printed by the Shevchenko Scientific Society), p. 88. Iuliian Bachynskyi, a member of the Ukrainian Radical party in Galicia, came to the United States early in 1905 to begin his monumental research on the Ukrainian immigration. He remained on this continent until December 1906 when he returned to Lviv to complete his work. His 492-page treatise, based on firsthand observations as well as a variety of documents, is a classic primary sociohistorical work for students of Ukrainian immigration history written from the point of view of a Ukrainian socialist. For a critique of Bachynskyi and his work, see Lubomyr Vynar, *Iuliian Bachyns'kyi: Vydatnyi Doslidnyk Ukrains'koi Emigratsii* (Iuliian Bachynskyi: Renowned Researcher of the Ukrainian Immigration), Historical Studies Series, no. 8 (Munich and New York: Ukrainian Historical Society, 1971).

25 Koenig, p. 56.

26 Oscar Handlin, *The Uprooted* (New York: Grosset and Dunlap Publishers, 1951), p. 186.

27 See Vladimir J. Kaye, *Early Ukrainian Settlements in Canada, 1895–1900*, published for the Ukrainian Canadian Research Foundation (Toronto: University of Toronto Press, 1964).

28 According to Maldwyn Allen Jones, "In Galicia alone, it was reported, two of the leading steamship companies employed no fewer than five thousand agents in a 'great hunt for immigrants' " *American Immigration* ([Chicago: University of Chicago Press, 1960], p. 182).

29 Bachynskyi, pp. 1–5; Emily Greene Balch, *Our Slavic Fellow Citizens* (New York: Charities Publication Committee, 1910), pp. 13–32; Halich, pp. 12–18; Koenig, pp. 254–6; Warzeski, "Religion and National Consciousness in the History of the Rusins," pp. 119–22.

30 Balch, p. 433.

31 Bachynskyi, p. 5.

32 Balch, p. 139.
33 Koenig, p. 105.
34 Balch, p. 46.
35 Ibid., p. 56.
36 Koenig, p. 531.
37 Balch, p. 141. Of all the Slavic groups to immigrate to the United States during this period, the Ukrainians had the highest rate of illiteracy, which, although high, was still lower than that of the southern Italians, Portuguese, and Syrians.
38 Koenig, p. 532.
39 Jerome Davis, *The Russians and Ruthenians in America: Bolsheviks or Brothers?* (New York: George H. Doran, 1922), p. 69.
40 Halich, p. 12.
41 Bachynskyi, pp. 89–91.
42 Halich, pp. 150–3.
43 *Svoboda*, founded in 1893 and now the daily organ of the Ukrainian National Association, is the oldest continuously published Ukrainian newspaper in the world.
44 Bachynskyi, pp. 103–14.
45 Ivan Ardan, "The Ruthenians in America," *Charities* 13 (1901–5), pp. 246ff.
46 Bachynskyi, pp. 139–40.
47 The largest Jewish population in all of Europe at one time was located in Ukraine. In the 1930s, 11 percent of the total population in eastern Galicia was Jewish, concentrated for the most part in urban areas. On the average, 36 percent of the urban population in eastern Galicia during this period was Jewish. In eastern Ukraine, the Jews lived in what came to be called the "Jewish Pale of Settlement," an area proscribed by Catherine II as the only locality in which Jews of the Russian Empire were permitted to settle. Over a million Jews lived in this region, which included, in addition to Ukraine, those sections of Poland and the Baltic countries under Russian rule. See Koenig, pp. 38–9; Francis Butwin, *The Jews in America* (Minneapolis: Lerner Publications, 1969), pp. 48–52; Moses Rischin, *The Promised City: New York's Jews, 1870–1914* (Cambridge: Harvard University Press, 1962), pp. 20–32.
48 Even beggars were not destitute, especially if they had musical talent, as many of them did. Blind lyre players who wandered from town to town singing for the local denizens were often the richest men in their villages (Koenig, p. 239).
49 Ibid., pp. 234–44.
50 Ibid., pp. 240–2.
51 Dennis Holod, "Spomyny Staroho Imigranta · Memoirs of an Old Immigrant" as recorded by Emil Revyuk, *Jubilee Book of the Ukrainian National Association*, ed. Luka Myshuha (Jersey City: Svoboda Press, 1936), p. 255.
52 Damian Merena, "Pro Pershykh Lemkiv v Amerytsi – First Lemko Immigrants," *Golden Jubilee Almanac of the Ukrainian National Association*, ed.

Luka Myshuha (Jersey City: The Ukrainian National Association, 1944), p. 250.

53 Malcolm C. Jensen, *America in Time* (Boston: Houghton-Mifflin, 1977), pp. 103–6. See also Matthew Josephson, *The Robber Barons* (New York: Harcourt Brace, 1934); Upton Sinclair, *The Jungle* (New York: Signet Classics, 1905).

54 Cited in Josephson, p. 362.

55 Ibid., p. 363. See also Jane Addams, *Twenty Years at Hull House* (New York: Signet Classics, 1910).

56 Jensen, pp. 103–28.

57 Bachynskyi, p. 135.

58 Greene, pp. 1–6.

59 Paul Beers, *The Pennsylvania Sampler* (Harrisburg: The Stockpole Co., 1970). Cited in Michael Novak, *The Guns of Lattimer* (New York: Basic Books, 1978), p. 9.

60 Sidney Lens, *Radicalism in America* (New York: Thomas Y. Crowell, 1969), p. 139.

61 Novak, p. 13.

62 Lens, pp. 139–44.

63 Novak, p. 15.

64 See Dmytro Kapitula, "Shcho Znachylo Kolys' Buty Imigrantom – What It Once Meant to Be an Immigrant," *Jubilee Book of the Ukrainian National Association*, pp. 265–6; Merena, p. 251.

65 Ruthenians, of course, were not the only Slavic group given to occasional drunkenness. Poles and other peasant nationalities followed similar patterns. Rev. Peter Roberts, for example, condemned the "baccanalian Polish orgies" that he observed at weddings and christenings, while another commentator called Sunday in mining towns "Sodom and Gomorrah revived" (see Greene, p. 48).

66 Bachynskyi, pp. 232–47.

67 See Balch, p. 143.

68 Bachynskyi, pp. 195–220.

69 Greene, p. 45.

70 Ibid., p. 55.

71 Bachynskyi, p. 188.

72 Ibid., p. 227.

73 Ibid.

74 Ibid.

75 Ibid., pp. 188–9.

76 Greene, p. 57.

77 Bachynskyi, pp. 190–4.

78 Cited in Novak, p. 5.

79 Ibid., p. 18.

80 Bachynskyi, p. 143.

81 Ibid., pp. 114–21.

82 Halich, pp. 31–2.
83 Ibid., pp. 32–5.
84 Interview with Dr. Semen Kochy, 13 February 1969. See also *Ukrainian Life*, 28 October 1961.
85 Grace Abbott, *The Immigrant and the Community* (New York: The Century Co., 1917), pp. 55–6.
86 Bachynskyi, p. 205.
87 Ibid., pp. 153–6.
88 Ibid., p. 226. See also *Svoboda*, 14 November 1894.
89 Abbott, pp. 71–2.
90 Ibid., pp. 73–80.
91 Bachynskyi, pp. 165–70.
92 The Protestant movement in Ukraine began during the 1840s, soon after the arrival of German Baptist missionaries in the German colonies, the first of which were established in eastern Ukraine during the time of Catherine II. Critical of the seeming indifference of the Orthodox clergy to the spiritual needs of the masses, the Baptists advanced a program of moral uplift that appealed to Ukrainian peasants and convinced them to convert to the Baptist faith.

   In its initial phases, the Ukrainian Protestant movement contributed little to the development of Ukrainian ethnonational consciousness. Believing that there was little difference between Ukrainians and Russians, the German missionaires published religious works in the Russian language. By late in the first decade of the 1900s, however, a Ukrainian presence began to emerge within the Protestant movement under the influence of such indigenous religious leaders as Ivan Onyshchenko, Mykhailo Ratushnyi, Iukhym Tsymbal, Tryfon Khlystun, and Fedir Ihnativ (H. Domashovets, *Narys Istorii Ukrains'koi Ievanhel's'ko-Baptysts'koi Tserkvy* [Historical Sketch of the Ukrainian Evangelical-Baptist Church] [Toronto: Harmony Printing Ltd., 1967], pp. 142–67). See also Michael Hrushevsky, *Z Istorii Relihiinoi Dumky na Ukraini* (On the History of Religious Thought in Ukraine) (Lviv: Shevchenko Scientific Society, 1925), p. 82ff.
93 Halich, pp. 53–6; Bachynskyi, pp. 175–6; *Ukrainian Weekly*, 20 June 1936.
94 Bachynskyi, pp. 175–84.
95 Halich, pp. 46–9.
96 Ibid., pp. 52–3.
97 Stephen W. Mamchur, "Nationalism, Religion and the Problem of Assimilation among Ukrainians in the United States" (PhD dissertation, Yale University, 1942), pp. 24–8.
98 In Shenandoah, both Poles and Lithuanians participated in the establishment of St. Casimir Roman Catholic Church in 1874. It was not until 1891, after losing a legal suit for title to the church, that the Shenandoah Lithuanians established their own, separate parish (Greene, p. 36).
99 Ibid., p. 36.
100 Isidore Sochocky, "The Ukrainian Catholic Church of the Byzantine Sla-

vonic Rite in the U.S.A.," *Ukrainian Catholic Metropolitan See, Byzantine Rite, U.S.A.* (Philadelphia: America Press, 1958), p. 250.

101 Mykhailo Pavlyk, "Rusyny v Amerytsi" (Ruthenians in America), *Tovarish*, 10 July 1888, as condensed in *Kalendar of the Ukrainian National Association for 1920* (Jersey City: Svoboda Press, 1919), p. 52.

102 Cited in Sochocky, p. 251.

103 Ivan Wolansky, "Pam'iati Pershoho Ukrains'koho Katolyts'koho Sviashchennyka v Amerytsi" (Memoirs of the First Ukrainian Catholic Priest in America), *Jubilee Almanac of the Ukrainian Greek Catholic Church in the United States, 1884–1934* (Philadelphia: America Press, 1934), p. 12. This twelve-page edited article contains excerpts from the personal memoirs of Father Wolansky. See also Count Lelyva, "Polozhennia Rusyniv v Spoluchenykh Derzhavakh Pivnochnoi Ameryky" (The Situation among Ruthenians in the United States of North America), *First Ruthenian-American Kalendar* (Mt. Carmel: Svoboda Press, 1897), pp. 51–4.

104 Wolansky, p. 13.

105 Pavlyk, pp. 52–3; Lelyva, pp. 52–5.

106 See Alexander Lushnycky, "The United Greek Church," *Almanac of the "Providence" Association of Ukrainian Catholics in America, 1984–1985* (Philadelphia: America Publishing, 1984), pp. 17–26.

107 Lelyva, pp. 54–5; Bachynskyi, p. 268.

108 Bachynskyi, p. 257. The parish name was later changed to St. Michael the Archangel and a new church edifice was built in 1908 (see Alexander Lushnycky, "Ukrainians in Pennsylvania," *Ukrainians in Pennsylvania*, ed. Alexander Lushnycky [Philadelphia: Ukrainian Bicentennial Committee, 1976], pp. 18–19). St. Michael the Archangel Church remained standing until 1980, when it was destroyed by fire.

109 Bachynskyi, p. 168.

110 Halich, p. 98.

111 Bachynskyi, p. 287. Lushnycky, "Ukrainians in Pennsylvania," pp. 17–21; Ronald Peter Popivchak, "History of the Ukrainian Catholic Church," *Ukrainians in Pennsylvania*, pp. 59–60; Osyp Krawczeniuk, *The Ukrainian Church in America: Its Beginnings* (Detroit: Ukrainian Millennium Committee of Detroit, 1988), pp. 4–12.

112 Bachynskyi, pp. 311–13; Krawczeniuk, pp. 12–13; Lushnycky, pp. 20–2.

113 Volodymyr Simenovych, "Z Moho Zhyttia" (From My Life), *Kalendar of the Ukrainian National Association for 1931* (Jersey City: Svoboda Press, 1931), pp. 69–70.

114 Bachynskyi, p. 443.

115 Ibid., p. 360.

116 Ibid., p. 375.

117 Simenovych, p. 71.

118 Bachynskyi, pp. 338–9.

119 Greene, p. 87.

120 Ibid., pp. 106–7.

121 Ibid., p. 109.

122 Simenovych, p. 70.

123 Bachynskyi, p. 287.

124 One group of Ruthenians maintains that Fr. Nicholas Zubricky, who arrived in 1887, was the first Uhro-Rusyn priest (see Warzeski, p. 128).

125 Bachynskyi, pp. 187–8. According to Alexander Lushnycky, a scholar who has studied Shenandoah's Ruthenian community extensively, Father Wolansky had begun to weary of his assignment and its many pressures. He welcomed the recall and may have even requested it (interview with Alexander Lushnycky, 13 July 1981).

126 Koenig, p. 271.

127 D. Mirsky, *Russia: A Social History*, ed. C.G. Seligman (London: The Cressett Press, 1931), p. 80.

128 Koenig, p. 268.

129 Attwater, pp. 27–9.

130 Ibid., p. 23.

131 Ibid., p. 24.

132 Cited in Koenig, p. 271.

133 Pope Pius XII, "The Encyclical on the Ruthenians," *The Eastern Churches Quarterly*, April–June 1961, pp. 209–306.

134 Koenig, p. 272.

135 Handlin, pp. 126–36; see also Jones, pp. 225–6.

136 Polish condemnation of both Lithuanians and Ukrainians for their efforts in organizing separate parishes reached its zenith at the 1895 convention of the Unia Polska w Ameryce (Polish Union in America) in Buffalo when Polish marchers carried signs through the Polish section of the city proclaiming that "He who advocates the division of Poland, Rus' and Lithuania is a traitor to his country and offends God" (Bachynskyi, p. 414).

137 Bachynskyi, pp. 287–9.

138 Ibid., pp. 257–8. See also *Jubilee Almanac of the Ukrainian Greek Catholic Church, 1884–1934*, p. 41; *Silver Jubilee Almanac of the Byzantine-Slavonic Rite Catholic Diocese of Pittsburgh, 1924–1949*.

139 Bachynskyi, p. 445.

140 Ibid., pp. 339–41.

141 Ibid., p. 341; Simenovych, p. 72.

142 Bachynskyi, pp. 341–2. Cf. Simon Demydchuk, "Pochatky Ukrains'koi Immigratsii v Amerytsi Na Osnovi Spomyniv O. Konstantyna Andrukhovycha" (The Beginnings of the Ukrainian Immigration on the Basis of the Memoirs of Rev. Constantine Andruchowicz), *Kalendar of the Providence Association for 1932* (Philadelphia: Providence Association of Ukrainian Catholics in the United States, 1932), pp. 81–7.

143 Bachynskyi, pp. 289–91.

144 Keith Paul Dyrud, "The Rusin Question in Eastern Europe and America, 1890–World War I" (PhD dissertation, University of Minnesota, 1976), pp. 192–3.

145 Ibid., p. 235.

146 Mamchur, pp. 36–45.

147 Bachynskyi, pp. 292–4.

148 Ibid., pp. 292–300.

149 In Latin theology, the *Filioque* holds that the Holy Spirit proceeds from the Father and the Son. Eastern theologians hold that the Holy Spirit is consubstantial with the Father and the Son and has its own existence and function in the inner life of God and the economy of salvation. It is the task of the Holy Spirit to bring about the unity of the human race in the Body of Christ (Meyendorff, *The Orthodox Church*, pp. 196–7).

150 Koenig, p. 268.

151 Paul Robert Magocsi, "Russians," *Harvard Encyclopedia of American Ethnic Groups*, pp. 886–7; Nancy Eubank, *The Russians in America* (Minneapolis: Lerner Publications, 1973), pp. 26–7.

152 Cited in Dyrud, p. 146.

153 Alex Simirenko, *Pilgrims, Colonists, and Frontiersmen: An Ethnic Community in Transition* (New York: Free Press, 1964), pp. 40–53. Also see: review of Mervin R. O'Connell's *John Ireland and the American Catholic Church* in the *National Catholic Reporter*, 16 June 1989; Paul Robert Magocsi, *Our People: Carpatho-Rusyns and Their Descendants in North America* (Toronto: Multicultural Historical Society of Ontario, 1984), pp. 26–7.

154 Cited in Simirenko, p. 44.

155 See ibid., p. 42.

156 Bachynskyi, p. 259.

157 Dyrud, p. 149.

158 Bachynskyi, p. 259.

159 Paul Yuzyk, "The Expansion of the Russian Orthodox Church among the Ukrainians of North American to 1918," paper presented in St. Paul, Minnesota on 14 November 1981, at a seminar sponsored by the Immigration History Research Center. See also *The Ukrainian Weekly*, 20 December 1981, and Paul Yuzyk, *The Ukrainian Greek Orthodox Church of Canada, 1918–1951* (Ottawa: University of Ottawa Press, 1981), pp. 42–3.

160 Dyrud, pp. 149–50.

161 See *The Fraternal Sales Training Program*, vol. 1 (Chicago: Fraternal Field Managers Association, 1969), pp. 1–4.

162 *Viestnik* and *Svoboda* were the fourth and fifth consecutive newspapers published by Ruthenians in the United States. The first was *Ameryka*, published by Father Wolansky, the second was *Ruske Slovo* (Ruthenian Word) published by Father Andruchowicz, the third was *Novyi Svit* (New World) published by Father Hrushka. The first three went out of existence (Bachynskyi, p. 445).

163 Bachynskyi, 310–16.

164 Warzeski, pp. 134–5.

165 Mamchur, pp. 61–4.

166 Ibid.

167 Ibid., pp. 32–6.

168 *Viestnik*, 25 June 1894.

169 Ibid., 21 February 1895.
170 Ibid., 11 July 1901.
171 Ibid., 8 October 1901.
172 Dyrud, pp. 232–5.
173 Mamchur, p. 36.
174 *Viestnik*, 17 July 1902.
175 Dyrud, pp. 237–8. See also *Washington Post* and *New York Times*, 26 July 1903.
176 Slovakia became a part of the kingdom of Hungary in 906 and initially enjoyed full cultural autonomy. In 1844, however, Budapest instituted an intensive Magyarization campaign aimed at full cultural and political assimilation of its minorities. Hungarian concern with the activities of Slovak Americans, many of whom either returned to their homeland or were planning a return, was merely a reflection of Hungarian national policy.
177 *New York Times*, 27 July 1903.
178 Dyrud, pp. 238–65.
179 *Viestnik*, 11 October 1906.
180 Ibid., 4 April 1907.
181 Ibid., 16 July 1903.
182 Ibid., 5 May, 13 October, 3 November, 1 December, and 22 December 1904.
183 Ibid., 25 January 1906.
184 Ibid., 8 March 1906.
185 See ibid., 12 November 1908.
186 *Svoboda*, 13 February 1902.
187 Mamchur, pp. 64–5; also see Walter Paska, *Sources of Particular Law for the Ukrainian Catholic Church in the United States* (Washington: Ukrainian Catholic Archeparchy of Philadelphia, 1975), p. 36.
188 Bachynskyi, pp. 301–2.
189 See *Svoboda*, 3 April 1902.
190 Ibid.
191 See ibid., 3 April through 5 June 1902.
192 Mamchur, p. 34.
193 Dyrud, pp. 258–9.
194 Ibid., p. 264–7.
195 Mamchur, p. 34.
196 Dyrud, p. 269.
197 *Svoboda*, 4 July 1907.
198 Sochocky, pp. 258–9.
199 Lev I. Sembratovych, "Iak Pryshlo do Imenuvannia Nashoho Pershoho Iepyskopa v Amerytsi" (How It Came to Nominating Our First Bishop in America), *Jubilee Almanac of the Ukrainian Greek Catholic Church in the United States, 1884–1934* (Philadelphia: America Press, 1934), p. 104.
200 Ibid., pp. 103–7; Sochocky, pp. 260–1.
201 See *Viestnik*, 5 November 1907.

202 Sochocky, pp. 262–3; Mamchur, p. 40; Warzeski, p. 143.

203 Mamchur, pp. 40–1.

204 A number of Ukrainian churches built or purchased after 1900 stipulated that the property could only belong to a Ukrainian bishop or a church council. At the first organizational meeting of the St. Nicholas parish in Chicago, for example, the following statement was recorded: "It was further decided by the trustees to adopt the corporate name of said St. Nicholas Ruthenian Catholic Church with this provision, however, that all the property of the said church that may be hereafter acquired be held in the name of its incorporated name but under no circumstances shall said church or its priests or pastors be ever under the jurisdiction of a bishop or bishops except of the same faith and rite." See Meeting of 31 January 1905, *Minutes of the St. Nicholas Board of Trustees*, vol. 1.

205 Mamchur, p. 41.

206 According to the memoirs of Sheptytsky's secretary, the metropolitan was reluctant to ask Rome for permission to visit the United States lest his request be denied. In 1910, however, the opportunity to attend the Eucharistic Congress in Montreal, Canada, presented itself. Once in Canada, it was not difficult to remain a little longer and to visit the faithful in both the United States and Canada. See Y.H. (probably Y. Hrodsky), "Vidvidyny Ameryky Mytr. A. Sheptyts'kym v 1910 Rotsi" (Metropolitan A. Sheptytski's Visit to America in 1910), *Kalendar of the Providence Association for 1927* (Philadelphia: America Press, 1927), p. 104.

207 Sochocky, pp. 264–72; see also Mykola Baranetskyi, "Zhytt'owyi Shlakh Iepyskopa Kyr Sotera Ortyns'koho" (The Life Style of Bishop Soter Ortynsky), *Kalendar of the Providence Association for 1956* (Philadelphia: America Press, 1956), pp. 59–68; Y. Chaplynskyi, "Diialnist'i Zasluhy Pershoho Ukrains'koho Katolyts'koho Iepyskopa v Zluchenykh Derzhavakh Bl. p. Vladyky Sotera Ortyns'koho" (The Activity and Accomplishments of the First Ukrainian Catholic Bishop in the United States, the Late Bishop Soter Ortynsky), *Jubilee Almanac of the Ukrainian Greek Catholic Church in America, 1884–1934*, pp. 108–9.

208 Sochocky, p. 267; see also Warzeski, p. 151.

209 Gulovich, "The Rusin Exarchate in the United States," p. 478; Dyrud, p. 192.

210 Warzeski, pp. 147–51.

211 *Viestnik*, 13 June 1907.

212 Warzeski, pp. 147–51.

213 *Viestnik*, 18 July 1907.

214 Warzeski, pp. 147–51.

215 See Athanasius Pekar, "Historical Background of the Carpatho-Ruthenians in America," *Ukrainskyi Istoryk*, XIII, nos 1–4 (1976), pp. 87–102; and XIV, nos 1–2 (1977), pp. 70–84.

216 *Viestnik*, 23 April 1908.

217 Ibid., 30 July 1908.

218 Ibid., 26 November 1908.

219 Ibid., 12 November 1908.
220 Ibid., 18 March 1909.
221 Ibid., 15 July 1909.
222 Ibid., 1 September 1910.
223 Ibid., 15 December 1910.
224 Ibid., 3 March, 17 November, 1 December 1910.
225 Ibid., 10 March, 16 June, 17 November 1910.
226 Warzeski, pp. 147–51.
227 Bachynskyi, pp. 424–5; Sochocky, pp. 270–1; Mamchur, pp. 46–7.
228 See Anatol Hornysky, "Ukrains'ka Baptysts'ka Tserkva v Shikago" (The Ukrainian Baptist Church in Chicago), *The Evangelical Kalendar "Good Friend" for 1956* (Toronto: Christian Printers, 1956), pp. 59–65.
229 Domashovetz, pp. 360–79.
230 Cited in Kenneth D. Miller, *Peasant Pioneers: An Interpretation of the Slavic Peoples in the United States* (New York: Council of Women for Home Missions and Missionary Education Movement, 1925), p. 161.
231 Ibid., pp. 159–61. See also *Golden Jubilee Book of the First Ukrainian Presbyterian Church* (Irvington: Jubilee Committee, 1959); "Spomyny O. Petra Poniatshyna Na Osnovi Rozmovy Spysav D-r Semen Demedchuk" (Memoirs of the Rev. Peter Poniatyshyn on the Basis of an Interview with Dr. Semen Demydchuk), *Kalendar of the Providence Association for 1932* (Philadelphia: America Press, 1931), p. 110.

Chapter 3

1 See Handlin, *The Uprooted*, p. 188.
2 Bachynskyi, *Ukrains'ka Imigratsiia v Z'iedynanykh Derzhavakh Ameryky*, p. 436.
3 *Svoboda*, 19 February 1899.
4 Ibid., 7 January 1904.
5 Ibid., 11 January 1906.
6 Ibid., 3 March 1900.
7 Mykola Muraszko, "Konventsii U.N. Soiuzu" (Conventions of the U.N. Association), *Jubilee Book of the Ukrainian National Association*, ed. Luka Myshuha (Jersey City: Svoboda Press, 1936), p. 220. See also *Svoboda*, 19 January 1915.
8 Antin Dragan, *The Ukrainian National Association: Its Past and Present, 1894–1964* (Jersey City: Svoboda Press, 1964), p. 26. See also Bachynskyi, pp. 313–14.
9 Cited in Dragan, pp. 15–17.
10 *Svoboda*, 1 March 1894; cited in Dragan, p. 27.
11 Dragan, p. 27.
12 Ibid., p. 163.
13 Bachynskyi, p. 330.
14 Ibid., p. 292.
15 Ibid., p. 434.

16 Ibid., pp. 292–3.
17 Balch, Our Slavic Fellow Citizens, pp. 419–24.
18 *Svoboda*, 21 November 1894.
19 Ibid., 20 April 1894.
20 Ibid., 27 April 1894.
21 Ibid., 22 March 1900 and subsequent issues.
22 Ibid., 6 June 1894.
23 Luka Myshuha, "Iak Formuvavsia Svitohliad Ukrains'koho Imigranta v
    Amerytsi" (The Development of the Ukrainian-American Outlook),
    1936 Jubilee Book of the Ukrainian National Association, p. 106.
24 See *Svoboda,* 17 October through 21 November 1895.
25 Ibid., 6 July 1896.
26 Ibid., 7 December 1899.
27 Ibid., 1 December 1893; see also ibid., 23 November 1899.
28 Ibid., 15 December 1893.
29 Ibid., 23 March 1894.
30 Ibid., 30 March 1894.
31 Ibid., 1 March 1894.
32 Ibid., 29 January 1903; cited in Myshuha, p. 112.
33 Myshuha, p. 107.
34 Ibid., p. 105.
35 See Stephen Makar, "American Boy," *Svoboda,* 7 and 14 December 1899.
36 See *Svoboda,* 22 August through 27 December 1900.
37 Ibid., 2 March 1896; cited in Myshuha, p. 68.
38 Robert E. Park, *The Immigrant Press and Its Control* (New York: Harper &
    Brothers, 1922), p. 41.
39 *Svoboda,* 20 April 1894; cited in Dragan, pp. 29–30.
40 *Svoboda,* 25 July 1895.
41 Ibid., 10 April 1895.
42 Ibid., 4 February 1897.
43 Ibid., 25 February 1897.
44 Ibid., 23 March 1894.
45 Ibid., 3 October 1894.
46 Ibid., 10 October 1894.
47 Ibid., 13 June 1894.
48 Ibid., 15 February 1894.
49 Ibid., 7 December 1899.
50 Ibid., 1 March 1894.
51 Ibid., 5 January 1901.
52 See Myshuha, pp. 71–2.
53 *Svoboda,* 6 August 1896.
54 Ibid., 26 July 1906.
55 Myshuha, pp. 52–3.
56 *Svoboda,* 15 October 1893.
57 Ibid., 6 June 1894. "Shche ne vmerla Ukraina" later became the Ukrainian
    national anthem.

58 *Svoboda,* 28 August through 9 October 1902.
59 Ibid., 3 March 1910. Cited in Emil Revyuk, "Rozvii Politychnoho Svitohliadu Ukrains'koho Imigranta" (The Development of the Ukrainian-American Outlook), *Jubilee Book of the Ukrainian National Association,* p. 308.
60 *Svoboda,* 31 March 1910.
61 Ibid., 7 April 1910.
62 Ibid., 22 August 1912.
63 Ibid., 3 April 1895.
64 Ibid., 29 April 1897.
65 Ibid., 20 December 1900.
66 Ibid., 27 March 1902.
67 Dragan, p. 54.
68 Bohdan Krawciw, "Kalendari i Almanakhy Ukrains'koho Narodnoho Soiuzu i Svobody" (Kalendars and Almanacs of the Ukrainian National Association and *Svoboda*), *Ukrainian Fortress in America: Jubilee Almanac on the Occasion of the 75th Anniversary of the Ukrainian National Association* (Jersey City: Svoboda Press, 1969), pp. 120–3.
69 "Shanuimo Ridnu Movu" (Let's Respect the Native Language), *Kalendar of the Ruskyi Narodnyi Soiuz for 1911* (Jersey City: Svoboda Press, 1911), pp. 147–9.
70 In describing the unanimous approval for the change from Ruthenian to Ukrainian at the UNA convention in Buffalo, *Svoboda* proudly wrote: "After all, Ukrainians are now in fashion" (*Svoboda,* 19 January 1915).
71 "Ukrainski Narodni Zapovidy" (Ukrainian National Commandments), *Kalendar of the Ukrainian National Association for 1915* (Jersey City: Svoboda Press, 1915), p. 150.
72 Bachynskyi, pp. 357–60.
73 "Nasha Slava" (Our Glory), *Kalendar for the American Ruthenians for 1908* (New York: Svoboda Press, 1908), pp. 149–50.
74 Bachynskyi, p. 360.
75 Ibid., pp. 361–2.
76 "Nasha Slava," p. 149.
77 Bachynskyi, pp. 362–70.
78 Joseph Stetkewicz, "Ukrains'ke Shkil'nytsvo v Amerytsi" (Ukrainian Schools in America), *1936 Jubilee Book of the Ukrainian National Association,* p. 335.
79 Bachynskyi, p. 370; Stetkewicz, pp. 336–7.
80 Myshuha, pp. 136–42; Dragan, pp. 136–42.
81 "Amerykanski Ukrainky na Hromadski Pratsi" (American-Ukrainian Women in Community Work), *Jubilee Almanac of the Ukrainian Women's Society of New York, 1921–1931* (New York: Ukrainian Women's Society of New York, 1931), pp. 77–8; see also Yaroslav Chyz, "Ukrainian Women and Their Organizations," *Jubilee Book of the Ukrainian Women's League of America, 1925–1940* (New York: Ukrainian National Women's League of America, 1940), p. 236.

82 *Svoboda*, 19 November 1908.
83 "Amerykanski Ukrainky na Hromadski Pratsi" (American-Ukrainian Women in Community Work), pp. 80–1.
84 Interview with Ivan Muzyka (6 February 1969); see also Bachynskyi, p. 375.
85 Bachynskyi, pp. 375–6; Theodosius Kaskiw, "Ridna Pisnia – Ridnyi Teatr" (Ukrainian Song and Theater in America), *Jubilee Book of the Ukrainian National Association*, pp. 421–2.
86 Kaskiw, p. 422.
87 Bachynskyi, pp. 376–8; Kaskiw, pp. 422–4.
88 Bachynskyi, pp. 378–9.
89 Ibid., p. 379; Kaskiw, pp. 426–8.
90 Bachynskyi, pp. 380–1; Kaskiw, pp. 420–1 and 426.
91 Emil Revyuk, "Nashi Literaturni i Mystets'ki Nadbannia v Amerytsi" (Ukrainian Literary and Art Achievements in America), *Jubilee Book of the Ukrainian National Association*, p. 350.
92 Bachynskyi, pp. 381–3.
93 Ibid., pp. 383–4.
94 Ibid., pp. 159–61.
95 Ibid., pp. 228–9.
96 Ibid., p. 229.
97 Volodymyr Lotovych, "Ukrainske Shkilnytstvo v Amerytsi" (Ukrainian Schools in America), *Souvenir Book, Dedication of the First Ukrainian Catholic High School* (Stamford: America Press, 1933), p. 10. Father Lotovych mentions that both a Sunday school and an evening school were organized by Father Honcharenko in Hayward, California. Technically, then, Honcharenko's school was the first school organized by a Ukrainian in the United States. Because it probably catered to both Ukrainian and Russian children, however, it cannot be considered an exclusively Ukrainian school.
98 Simenovych, "Z Moho Zhyttia," p. 71.
99 Bachynskyi, p. 385; Stetkewicz, p. 326; Lev Yasinchuk, "Ukrains'ke Shkil'nytstvo Poza Ridnymy Zemliamy" (Ukrainian Schools beyond the Native Land), *Ukrainians in the Free World, Jubilee Book of the Ukrainian National Association, 1894–1954* (Jersey City: Svoboda Press, 1954), p. 164; Natalie Ann Czuba, *History of the Ukrainian Catholic Parochial Schools in the United States: A Thesis* (Chicago: Basilian Press, 1956), p. 21.
100 Bachynskyi, p. 386.
101 *Svoboda*, 1 March 1894; cited in Stetkewicz, p. 325.
102 See *Svoboda*, 20 April 1894.
103 Ibid., 27 April and 25 July 1894.
104 Ibid., 5 December 1894; cited in Stetkewicz, p. 326.
105 Bachynskyi, pp. 385–6.
106 Stetkewicz, pp. 331–2.
107 See *Svoboda*, 28 July 1904.
108 Bachynskyi, p. 398; Stetkewicz, p. 331. Stetkewicz maintained that

Tymkevych's *bursa* managed to survive until 1907, when the building was sold.

109 Bachynskyi, p. 386.
110 Interview with Dmytro Atamanec (5 and 6 March 1969).
111 *Svoboda*, 7 October 1897.
112 Stetkewicz, pp. 328–9.
113 "Our Schools," *Svoboda*, 21 September 1905.
114 Ibid.
115 Bachynskyi, p. 387.
116 Nestor Dmytriw, "Duzhe Vazhna Sprava" (A Very Important Matter), *Svoboda*, 20 August 1903; cited in Stetkewicz, p. 329.
117 *Svoboda*, 13 July 1905; see also Stetkewicz, p. 332.
118 Stetkewicz, pp. 333–4.
119 Ibid., p. 334; see also: *Svoboda*, 13 August 1908.
120 Stetkewicz, pp. 336–7.
121 *Svoboda*, 16 December 1909; cited in Stetkewicz, p. 337.
122 *Ridna Shkola*, vol. I, no. 1–2 (January–February 1918), pp. 47–8. By 1918, the teachers association had adopted "Ukrainian" rather than "Ruthenian" as its ethnonational appellation. For the early contributions of the Sisters of St. Basil, see Bohdan P. Procko, *Ukrainian Catholics in America: A History* (Washington: University Press of America, 1982) p. 27.
123 *Svoboda*, 4 July 1894.
124 Ibid., 5 August through 9 September 1897.
125 Myshuha, pp. 165–6.
126 Greene, *The Slavic Community on Strike*, pp. 138–41.
127 See *Svoboda*, 21 October 1897. For a description of this American tragedy, see Michael Novak, *The Guns of Lattimer* (New York: Basic Books, 1978).
128 Myshuha, p. 168.
129 Ibid., p. 167.
130 *Svoboda*, 3 October 1900.
131 See, for example, ibid., 23 April 1896 and 14 May 1897.
132 Myshuha, p. 167.
133 Ibid., pp. 111–12.
134 Theodore Swystun, "Tovarystvo Ukrainsko-Amerykans'kykh Horozhan u Filiadel'fii" (The Ukrainian-American Citizen's Association of Philadelphia), *Sixty Years of the Ukrainian Community in Philadelphia* (Philadelphia: The Ukrainian-American Citizen's Association, 1944), pp. 28–34.
135 Bachynskyi, pp. 404–10.
136 Cited in Myshuha, pp. 111–12.
137 See "Socialism and the Question of the Worker," *Svoboda*, 31 July 1902.
138 *Svoboda*, 10 October 1894.
139 Ibid., 31 October 1900.
140 Bachynskyi, p. 302.
141 *Svoboda*, 27 June 1894.
142 Ibid., 14 November 1894.
143 Ibid., 10 April 1895.

144 Ibid., 18 October 1900; see also Dragan, pp. 43–4.
145 Ibid., 28 February 1901; see also Myshuha, p. 124.
146 Ibid., 26 February 1903.
147 Ibid.
148 Ibid., 7 July 1904.
149 Ibid., 19 December 1908.
150 Ibid., 27 May 1909.
151 Ibid., 14 September 1914.
152 Dragan, p. 45; see also *Svoboda,* 12 June 1902.
153 *Svoboda,* 19 December 1912.
154 Peter Poniatyshyn, "Ukrains'ka Tserkva i U.N. Soiuz" (The Ukrainian Church and the U.N.A.), *Jubilee Book of the Ukrainian National Association,* p. 288.
155 Bachynskyi, p. 320.
156 Poniatyshyn, p. 291.
157 Dragan, p. 58.
158 N. Nalyvaiko, "Osnovni Viddily U.R. Soiuzu" (Charter Branches of the U.W. Association), *Jubilee Book of the Ukrainian Workingman's Association, 1910–1960* (Scranton: Narodna Volya Press, 1960), pp. 137–40; "Iak Povstav Ukrainskyi Robitnychyi Soiuz" (How the Ukrainian Workingman's Association Came into Being), based on V.N. Verhana's interview with Vasyl Gnus, *Jubilee Book of the Ukrainian Workingman's Association,* p. 65.
159 Teodor Mynyk, "Ukrains'kyi Robitnychyi Soiuz, 1910–1960" (The Ukrainian Workingman's Association, 1910–1960), ibid., p. 37.
160 Matthew Stachiw, "Nova Ukraina v Amerytsi" (New Ukraine in America), ibid., p. 95.
161 Dragan, pp. 80 and 163.
162 *Svoboda,* 13 October 1910; cited in Dragan, p. 58.
163 Sochocky, "The Ukrainian Catholic Church of the Byzantine Slavonic Rite in the U.S.A.," p. 269.
164 Nalyvaiko, p. 140.
165 Dragan, pp. 59–60 and 163.
166 Bachynskyi, p. 332.
167 *Svoboda,* 12 March 1914.
168 Mykhailo Lozynskyi, "The Need for Ideology," *Svoboda,* 26 May 1904.
169 Bachynskyi, p. 434.
170 M. Nastasivsky [Mykhailo Tkach], *Ukrains'ka Imigratsiia v Spoluchenykh Derzhavakh* (The Ukrainian Immigration in the United States) (New York: Union of Ukrainian Toilers Organizations, 1934), pp. 78–9.
171 Lens, *Radicalism in America,* p. 210.
172 Nastasivsky, pp. 75–6; Stachiw, p. 93.
173 Nastasivsky, pp. 81–9. Also see Leon Tolopko, *Working Ukrainians in the U.S.A.,* book 1 (1890–1924) (New York: Ukrainian American League, 1986), pp. 93–7.
174 Bachynsky, pp. 438–40.
175 Ibid., pp. 476–81.

176 *Svoboda*, 12 March 1914.
177 *Viestnik*, 17 July 1895.
178 Ibid., 31 July 1894.
179 Ibid., 4 April 1895.
180 Ibid.
181 Ibid., 20 June 1907.
182 Ibid., 1 August 1901.
183 Ibid., 1 October 1896.
184 Ibid., 17 April 1902, 18 October 1906.
185 Ibid., 13 August 1903.
186 Ibid., 2 July 1896.
187 Bachynskyi, p. 416.
188 In order to lower its publishing costs, *Viestnik* later asked its readers to decide between the two scripts and to vote their preference (*Viestnik*, 17 July 1907).
189 Bachynskyi, p. 416.
190 Gulovich, "The Rusin Exarchate in the United States," pp. 474–6.
191 *Viestnik*, 6 February 1894.
192 Ibid., 24 July 1894.
193 See ibid., 13 February, 13 September, 20 September, 27 December 1894.
194 Ibid., 30 May 1895.
195 Ibid., 26 October 1896.
196 Ibid., 31 January 1901.
197 Ibid., 16 May 1901.
198 Ibid., 11 July 1901.
199 Ibid., 30 March, 3 April, 1902.
200 Ibid., 13 March, 10 April, 17 April 1902.
201 Gulovich, p. 475.
202 *Viestnik*, 17 March 1908.
203 Ibid., 17 March 1908.
204 Ibid., 28 October 1908.
205 Ibid., 3 December 1908.
206 Ibid., 8 September, 6 October 1910.
207 Ibid., 7 March, 29 March, and 26 March 1912.
208 Ibid., 2 March 1911.
209 Ibid., 6 May 1909.
210 Ibid., 15 July 1906.
211 Ibid., 16 June 1910.
212 Ibid., 17 November 1910.
213 Ibid.
214 Ibid., 1 December 1910.
215 Ibid., 15 June 1911.
216 Ibid., 27 March 1913.
217 Ibid., 21 May 1908.
218 Ibid., 24 September 1908.
219 Ibid., 29 April 1909.
220 Ibid., 26 August 1909.

221 Ibid., 3 March 1910.
222 Ibid., 18 January 1912.
223 Cited in Bachynskyi, p. 424.
224 *Viestnik*, 24 December 1914.
225 Yuzyk, "The Expansion of the Russian Orthodox Church among Ukrainians of North America to 1918," p. 14.
226 Dyrud, p. 149.
227 Ibid., pp. 149–50.
228 The Chicago church was designed by world-famous architect Louis Sullivan, whose original plan was patterned after the onion-domed churches in Russia. Significantly, the church council rejected the first design because it wasn't "Russian." The final edifice, completed in 1903, is a highly stylized version of church architecture common in Carpatho-Ukraine (Theodore Turak, "A Celt among the Slavs: Louis Sullivan's Holy Trinity Church," *The Prairie School Review*, fourth quarter, 1972, p. 7).
229 Dyrud, p. 154.
230 Yuzyk, "The Expansion of the Russian Orthodox Church among Ukrainians of North America to 1918," p. 4.
231 Dyrud, pp. 191–2.
232 Bachynskyi, pp. 447–50; see also *Svoboda*, 21 January 1897. Upon his return to Ukraine, Hrushka worked for a short time in a Russian Orthodox parish in Volhynia. Later he returned to the Greek Catholic faith, served penance in a Basilian monastery, and eventually became a Greek Catholic pastor in Galicia, where he remained until his death in 1913.
233 According to Dyrud, more than twice as many Ruthenian congregations converted to Orthodoxy after 1907, the year Bishop Ortynsky arrived in the United States, than before. Most were Subcarpathians (Dyrud, p. 92).
234 Bachynskyi, pp. 330, 425–30, and 451–3; Dyrud, pp. 133, 154–5, 191–2.
235 Dyrud, pp. 150–1.
236 Ibid., p. 167.
237 Cited in ibid., p. 167.
238 Cited in ibid., p. 168.
239 Bachynskyi, pp. 425–30 and 451–2.
240 Cited in Dyrud, p. 135.
241 See Bachynskyi, pp. 425 and 451–2. See also *Russko Amerikanskii Spravochnik* (Russian American Register) (New York: Russian American Publishing Co., 1920), pp. 212–14.
242 Dyrud, pp. 174–6.
243 Cited in ibid., p. 175.
244 Ibid., p. 174.

Chapter 4

1 For a detailed historical analysis of the rise and fall of the Ukrainian National Republic see Arthur E. Adams, *Bolsheviks in Ukraine: The Second*

Campaign, 1918–1919 (New Haven: Yale University Press, 1963); W.E. Allen, *The Ukraine: A History* (Cambridge: Cambridge University Press, 1940); William Henry Chamberlin, *The Ukraine: A Submerged Nation* (New York: Macmillan Co., 1944); Solomon I. Goldelman, *Jewish National Autonomy in Ukraine, 1917–1920* (Chicago: Ukrainian Research and Information Institute, 1968); Taras Hunczak, ed., *The Ukraine, 1917–1921: A Study in Revolution* (Cambridge: Harvard Ukrainian Research Institute, 1977); Clarence Manning, *Twentieth Century Ukraine* (New York: Bookman Associates, 1951); Arnold Margolin, *From a Political Diary: Russia, the Ukraine, and America, 1905–1945* (New York: Columbia University Press, 1946); Michael Palij, *The Anarchism of Nestor Makhno, 1918–1921: An Aspect of the Ukrainian Revolution* (Seattle: University of Washington Press, 1976); John S. Reshetar, *The Ukrainian Revolution, 1917–1920* (Princeton: Princeton University Press, 1952); *Ukrainians and Jews: A Symposium* (New York: The Ukrainian Congress Committee of America, Inc., 1966). For an analysis of the origins of the Ukrainian Autocephalous church see Bohdan Bociurkiw, "Soviet Church Policy in the Ukraine, 1919–1939" (PhD dissertation, University of Chicago, 1961), pp. 61–106. For an analysis of Simon Petliura's relationship with Ukrainian Jews, see Taras Hunczak, "Symon Petliura and the Jews: A Reappraisal," Ukrainian Historical Association, Series: Ukrainian Jewish Studies (#7), Toronto, 1985; Subtelny, pp. 339–79.

2 Arnold Margolin, *From a Political Diary,* pp. 38–40; Subtelny, pp. 372–4.

3 See Paul R. Magocsi, "The Ruthenian Decision to Unite with Czechoslovakia," *Slavic Review,* 34, no. 2 (June 1975), pp. 364–81.

4 Margolin, pp. 39–40; Reshetar, pp. 271–88. Also see A. Bilinsky, "The Law: Western Ukrainian Territories between the Two World Wars, Galicia and the Northwestern Territories" and I.M. Novosivsky, "The Law: Western Ukrainian Territories between the Two World Wars, Bukovina and Bessarabia" in *Ukraine: A Concise Encyclopedia,* vol. 2 (Toronto: University of Toronto Press, 1971), pp. 70–4; Louis Gerson, *Woodrow Wilson and the Rebirth of Poland, 1914–1920: A Study in the Influence on American Policy by Groups of Foreign Origin* (New Haven: Yale University Press, 1953), pp. 48–71; Elena Lukasz, "The Ukraine at the Paris Peace Conference, 1919" (MA thesis, University of Chicago, 1962); Francis Pridham, *Close of a Dynasty* (London: Allan Wingate, 1956); Peter G. Stercho, *Diplomacy of Double Morality: Europe's Crossroads in Carpatho-Ukraine, 1919–1939* (New York: Carpathian Research Center, 1971); Konrad Syrod, *Poland: Between Anvil and Hammer* (London: Hale Publishers, 1968), pp. 101–9.

5 *Svoboda,* 6 August 1914.

6 Ibid., 20 August 1914; cited in Dragan, *The Ukrainian National Association,* p. 70.

7 *Svoboda,* 1 September 1914.

8 Cited in Dragan, pp. 70–1.

9 Steffen was a Swedish university professor who had become interested in the Ukrainian question through the effort of Emil Revyuk, then a

student in Sweden and an occasional contributor of articles on Ukraine to the Swedish press (see Gustaf F. Steffen, *Russia, Poland and the Ukraine* [Jersey City: The Ukrainian National Council, 1915], pp. 7–24).

10 Stepankovsky was a Ukrainian living in England (see Vladimir Stepankovsky, *The Russian Plot to Seize Galicia (Austrian Ruthenia)* [Jersey City: The Ukrainian National Council, 1915], p. 3).

11 See *The Russians in Galicia,* ed. Bedwin Sands (Jersey City: The Ukrainian National Council, 1916), pp. 7–22.

12 *Svoboda,* 4 September 1915.

13 Revyuk, "Rozvii Politychnoho Svitohliadu Ukrains'koho Imigranta," p. 317.

14 Volodymyr Lototsky, "Iak Osvobodyvsia Myroslav Sichyns'kyi" (How Miroslav Sichynsky Freed Himself), *Kalendar of the Ukrainian National Association for 1916* (Jersey City: Svoboda Press, 1915), pp. 36–43.

15 Edwin Bjorkman et al., *Ukraine's Claim to Freedom: An Appeal for Justice on Behalf of Thirty-Five Millions* (New York: The Ukrainian National Association and the Ruthenian National Union, 1915), p. 120.

16 Stakhiv, "Nova Ukraina v Amerytsi," pp. 96–9; Revyuk, pp. 315–16; Dragan, p. 73; Nastasivsky, *Ukrains'ka Imigratsiia v Spoluchenykh Derzhavakh,* p. 121; Simon Demydchuk, *Pivstorichchia Hromadians'koi Pratsi D-ra Semena Demydchuka, 1905–1955* (The Half-Century of Community Work of Dr. Simon Demydchuk) (New York: Carpathian Star Publishing Co., 1956), pp. 28–30.

17 *Svoboda,* 2 January 1915.

18 Ibid., 3 January 1915.

19 Ibid., 19 January 1915.

20 Ibid., 28 January 1915.

21 Ibid., 6 May 1915.

22 Ibid., 27 May 1915.

23 Ibid., 12 August 1915.

24 Ibid., 24 April 1915.

25 Ibid., 12 August 1915.

26 Bishop Ortynsky and the Providence Association were invited to the congress but politely refused to participate (see *Svoboda,* 9 September 1915).

27 All organizations were invited to send delegates and no prohibition was made against sending priests. Those groups that could not afford to send representatives were urged to designate proxy delegates who were already planning to attend as representatives of other organizations or who lived near New York. In addition to the delegates, the congress included approximately 600 guests (Stachiw, p. 102).

28 The executive committee included Ivan Ardan, Ivan Artymovych, Michael Baydyuk, Zhygmont Bachynskyi, Ivan Boradaikevych, Ievhen Vasylenko, Lev Vesolovsky, Stephen Hladkiwyj, Natalie Hrynevetsky, Stepan Hrynevetsky, Peter Zadoretsky, Dmytro Kapitula, Volodymyr Lototsky, Volodymyr Malyevych, Vasyl Momryk, Emil Revyuk, Miroslaw

Sichynsky, Joseph Stetkewicz, Iurii Khyliak, Iliya Chornij, and Semen
Yadlovsky. The original name of the new organization was the All-
Ukrainian Committee. This was changed in December (see *Svoboda*, 9
December 1915).

29 "T." (author unknown), "Ukrains'ko Amerykans'ka Politychna Aktsiia u
Rokakh 1914–1920" (A Chronicle of Political Activities of Ukrainian
Americans, 1914–1920), *Golden Jubilee Almanac of the Ukrainian National
Association*, p. 115.

30 James D. Bratush, *A Historical Documentary of the Ukrainian Community of
Rochester, New York*, trans. Anastasia Smerychynska (Rochester: Christopher Press, 1973), p. 52.

31 *Svoboda*, 27 January 1916.

32 Ibid., 29 January 1916.

33 Ibid., 29 February 1916.

34 Ibid.

35 Ibid., 14 January 1917; see also Revyuk, "Rozvii Politychnoho Svitohliadu
Ukrains'koho Imigranta," pp. 317–18, and Dragan, p. 73.

36 Nastasivsky, pp. 85–9.

37 An extraordinarily capable individual, Bilyk began working on behalf of
his people while still an undergraduate at the University of Chicago.
Joining the Ukrainian Education Club, a socialist society established by
Simenovych, Dr. Stepan Hrynevetsky, and Emily Strutynsky (wife of
Father Strutynsky and sister of Sichynsky, Bilyk taught English to newly
arrived Ukrainian immigrants. Urged to continue his education by
Simenovych and Hrynevetsky, he graduated from Rush Medical College
where Simenovych was a professor of gynecology. He established a
medical practice in New York and remained active in the community
until his untimely death shortly after World War I. Interview with Philip
Wasylowsky, 26 September 1968; Toma Lapychak, "D-r Kyrylo Bilyk"
(Dr. Cyril Bilyk), *Medical Almanac* (Chicago: American Ukrainian Medical
Society, Chicago Branch, 1958), p. 51.

38 Stachiw, pp. 102–7; Dragan, p. 74; Miroslaw Sichynsky, "Editorial Experiences" (manuscript), cited in Park, *The Immigrant Press and Its Control*,
pp. 334–46.

39 *Ukraina*, 19 May 1917; see also *Ukraina*, 2 January 1919.

40 *Svoboda*, 30 January 1917.

41 Ibid., 8 March 1917.

42 *Svoboda* was sued by Sichynsky and Ceglinsky for "libel and calumny."
On 16 April 1921, the UNA gazette printed a long retraction in Ukrainian
and English admitting "all those untrue accusations and malicious
reproofs were aimed to defame and dishonor Mr. Sichynsky and Mr.
Ceglinsky and to ruin their work." Accusations, however, went both
ways. Federation members consistently attacked the alliance and its
supporters for their pro-Austrian sentiments and, according to Dr.
Demydchuk, probably corresponded with the United States Justice
Department regarding this matter. Soon after the United States entered

the war, Demydchuk was interned as a political prisoner at Fort Ogle-
thorpe, Georgia, where he remained until 15 May 1919 (*Svoboda,* 16 April
1919; Demydchuk, p. 31).

43 Stakhiv, p. 103; Nastasivsky, p. 126; Bratush, pp. 55–7.

44 Nastasivsky, pp. 184–5; Warzeski, "Religion and National Consciousness
in the History of the Rusins," p. 184; Gerson, *The Hyphenate in Recent
American Politics and Diplomacy* (Lawrence: University of Kansas Press,
1964), p. 97.

45 Bratush, pp. 57–9.

46 Miroslaw Sichynsky, *Narodna Sprava v Amerytsi* (The National Matter in
America) (New York: The Federation of Ukrainians in the United States,
1919), pp. 4–5.

47 *Ukrainska Hazeta,* 16 August 1919; cited in Nastasivsky, p. 187.

48 Nastasivsky, pp. 187–8. For a history of the Ukrainian National Aid Associ-
ation (UNAA) see Leonid Poltava, *Istoria Ukrayinskoyi Narodnoyi Pomochi*
(History of the Ukrainian National Aid Association of USA and Canada)
(Pittsburgh: Ukrainian National Aid Association, 1976).

49 Sochocky, "The Ukrainian Catholic Church of the Byzantine Slavonic
Rite in the U.S.A.," pp. 272–3.

50 *Svoboda,* 1 November 1916.

51 See "Ukrainska Rada v Amerytsi" (The Ukrainian Council in America),
The Kalendar of the Ukrainian National Association for 1919 (Jersey City:
Svoboda Press, 1918), pp. 38–44; see also *Svoboda,* 14 January 1916.

52 Born in Jersey City, New Jersey, on 30 March 1877, James Alphonsus
Hamill served as a United States representative from 1907 to 1921. Upon
retiring from Congress he worked for a time as Corporation Counsel for
Jersey City. A strong supporter of the Ukrainian freedom movement,
Hamill was also a linguist who spoke Greek, Latin, Russian, German, and
French. In 1931, he was made a Chevalier of the French Legion of Honor
for his work in French literature. He died in Jersey City on 15 December
1941 (*New York Times,* 16 December 1941).

53 Peter Poniatyshyn, "Ukrains'ka Sprava v Amerytsi Pid Chas Pershoi
Svitovoi Viiny" (The Ukrainian Situation in America during the First
World War), *Jubilee Almanac of Svoboda, 1893–1953* (Jersey City: The Ukrainian National Association, 1953), pp. 65–71; see also *Svoboda,* 1 February
1917.

54 A photostatic copy of the resolution can be found in *Shisdesiat Lit Organizatsiinoho Zhyttia Ukrainstsiv u Filadelfii* (Sixty Years of the Ukrainian
Community in Philadelphia), p. 67; see also *Svoboda,* 21 April 1917.

55 *Svoboda,* 22 September 1917.

56 Ukrainians, anxious to receive as much press coverage as possible from
the proclamation, made sure the term "Ukrainian" was used in all press
releases. See article in *Philadelphia Inquirer,* 15 April 1917, cited in *Shisdesiat
Lit Organizatsiinoho Zhyttia u Filadelfii,* p. 66.

57 *Svoboda,* 10 April 1917.

58 Ibid., 28 April 1917.

59 Ibid., 11 May 1917.
60 Ibid., 19 May 1917.
61 Ibid., 28 June 1917.
62 Ibid., 20 November 1917.
63 Ibid., 27 November 1917.
64 Ibid., 13 December 1917.
65 Ibid., 22 January 1918.
66 Ibid., 31 January 1918.
67 Ibid., 29 January 1918.
68 Poniatyshyn, "Ukrains'ka Sprava v Amerytsi Pid Chas Pershoi Svitovoi Viiny," pp. 72–3.
69 *Svoboda*, 26 November 1918; Dragan, p. 76.
70 Ibid., 7 December 1918.
71 Ibid., 22 January 1919.
72 Ibid., 23 January 1919.
73 Julian Batchinsky (Iuliian Bachynskyi), *The Jewish Pogroms in Ukraine and the Ukrainian Peoples Republic* (Washington: Friends of Ukraine, 1919).
74 Julian Batchinsky, *Memorandum to the Government of the United States on the Recognition of the Ukrainian People's Republic* (Washington: Friends of Ukraine, 1920).
75 Stachiw, pp. 107–9.
76 *Svoboda*, 3 June 1920.
77 Ibid., 10 July 1920.
78 Poniatyshyn, "Ukrainska tserkva i U.N. Soiuz," pp. 295–7.
79 *Svoboda* 13 July 1920.
80 Ibid., 12 July 1919.
81 Ibid., 29 July 1919.
82 Ibid., 20 January 1920.
83 Ibid., 2 August 1919.
84 Ibid., 25 June 1919.
85 Ibid., 20 January 1919.
86 Ibid., 10 June 1919.
87 Ibid., 2 September 1919.
88 Ibid., 20 September 1919.
89 Ibid., 20 January 1920.
90 Ibid.
91 Poniatyshyn, "Ukrains'ka Sprava v Amerytsi Pid Chas Pershoi Svitovoi Viiny," p. 74.
92 *Svoboda*, 14 May 1920.
93 Ibid., 17 August 1920.
94 Gerson, *The Hyphenate in Recent American Diplomacy and Politics*, p. 107.
95 Of all ethnic groups in America, the Poles gained the most during Wilson's administration. According to Louis Gerson, the re-creation of the Polish state might not have occurred except for the interest which President Wilson and some of his associates had previously shown in the

effective cultivation of the Polish-American vote. As Paderewski acknowledged in his last speech to the Polish parliament on 22 May 1919, "Without the powerful support of President Wilson whose heart had been won to our cause by our best friend, Colonel House, Poland would undoubtedly still be an internal question of Germany and Russia ..." (ibid., p. 78).

96 Ibid., p. 107. "In electing a Republican president," writes Gerson, "German-Americans voted for Germany, Irish-Americans voted against Britain and for Ireland, Italian-Americans voted against Yugoslavia, Greek-Americans voted for the inclusion of Northern Epirus in the Kingdom of Greece, Lithuanian-Americans voted against Poland, Arab-Americans voted against Britain and France, and Chinese-Americans voted against Japan."

97 Poniatyshyn, "Ukrains'ka Sprava v Amerytsi Pid Chas Pershoi Svitovoi Viiny," pp. 74–6.

98 Svoboda, 21 April 1921.

99 Ibid., 5 August 1921.

100 Ibid., 23 January 1921 through 12 March 1923.

101 Poniatyshyn, "Ukrains'ka Sprava Pid Chas Pershoi Svitovoi Viiny," p. 74.

102 Robitnyk, 21 July 1919.

103 Ibid., 21 December 1919.

104 Svoboda, 27 July 1920.

105 Ibid., 3 January 1922.

106 Ibid., 4 February 1922.

107 Ibid., 19 January 1922.

108 Ibid., 16 March 1923.

109 Ibid., 13 January 1922.

110 Ibid., 16 March 1923.

111 Ibid., 21 March 1923.

112 Paul R. Magocsi, "The Political Activity of Rusyn-American Immigrants in 1918," Eastern European Quarterly, X, no. 3 (1976), p. 351.

113 Ibid., p. 352.

114 Ibid., p. 353.

115 Ibid., pp. 352–5.

116 Cited in ibid., p. 354.

117 Cited in ibid., p. 355.

118 Ibid., pp. 354–5; see also Viestnik, 29 August and 5 September 1918.

119 Magosci, "The Political Activity of Rusyn-American Immigrants in 1918," p. 364; see also Viestnik, 14 November and 21 November 1918.

120 Gerson, pp. 79–80.

121 Masaryk later claimed he had discussed the future of "Subcarpathian Ruthenia" with Ukrainian leaders in Kiev in 1917 and they were not opposed to a union with Czechoslovakia. Given the political situation in Kiev at the time – the Rada was still seeking autonomy within a federated Russia and even unification with Galicia and Bukovina seemed unrealis-

tic – the statement rings true. What Masaryk fails to mention, however, is the strong efforts of Ukrainian leaders in Lviv to include Carpatho-Ukraine in their republic (Warzeski, pp. 182–3).

122 Ibid.
123 Magocsi, "The Political Activity of Rusyn-American Immigrants in 1918," pp. 355–64; Warzeski, pp. 183–5.
124 Stercho, *Diplomacy of Double Morality*, p. 10.
125 Magocsi, "The Political Activity of Rusyn-American Immigrants in 1918," pp. 358–9; Warzeski, pp. 187–9.
126 Warzeski, pp. 189–95.

Chapter 5

1 For a detailed historical analysis of Soviet Ukraine see Yaroslaw Bilinsky, *The Second Soviet Republic: The Ukraine after World War II* (New Brunswick: Rutgers University Press, 1964); Jurij Borys, *The Sovietization of Ukraine, 1917–1923: The Communist Doctrine and Practice of National Self-Determination* (Edmonton: Canadian Institute of Ukrainian Studies, 1980); Basil Dmytryshyn, *Moscow and the Ukraine, 1918–1953: A Study of Bolshevik Nationality Policy* (New York: Bookman Associates, 1956); Bohdan Krawchenko, ed., *Ukraine after Shelest* (Edmonton: Canadian Institute of Ukrainian Studies, 1938); George S.N. Luckyj, *Literary Politics in the Soviet Ukraine* (New York: Columbia University Press, 1956); James E. Mace, *Communism and the Dilemmas of National Liberation: National Communism in Soviet Ukraine, 1918–1933* (Cambridge: Harvard Ukrainian Research Institute, 1983). Clarence Manning, *Ukraine under the Soviets* (New York: Bookman Associates, 1953); Richard Pipes, *The Formation of the Soviet Union: Communism and Nationalism, 1917–1923*, rev. ed. (Cambridge: Harvard University Press, 1964); Robert S. Sullivant, *Soviet Politics and the Ukraine, 1917–1957* (New York: Columbia University Press, 1962).
2 Robert Conquest, *The Harvest of Sorrow: Soviet Collectivization and the Terror-Famine* (New York: Oxford University Press, 1986) p. 329; *Investigation of the Ukrainian Famine: Report to Congress, Commission on the Ukraine Famine* (Washington, DC; United States Government Printing Office, 1988), pp. vi–vii. For more details regarding the Great Ukrainian Famine of 1932/3 see: William Henry Chamberlin, *The Ukraine: A Submerged Nation* (New York: The Macmillan Company, 1944); Conquest, *The Great Terror: Stalin's Purges of the Thirties* (New York: Collier Books, 1968); Vasyl Hryshko, *Experience with Russia* (New York: Ukrainian Congress Committee, 1956); Hryhory Kostiuk, *Stalinist Rule in the Ukraine: A Study of the Decade of Mass Terror* (New York: Praeger Publishers, 1960); Anton Antonov-Ovseyenko, *The Time of Stalin: Portrait of Terror* (New York: Harper & Row, 1981); S.O. Pidhainy et al., *The Black Deeds of the Kremlin: A White Book*, vol. 2 (Detroit: Dobrus, 1955). Also see *London Daily Telegraph*, 9 September 1933; *Forthnightly Review*, 1 May 1933; *New York Herald Tribune*, 21 August 1933; *Jewish Daily Forward*, 27 December 1933; *Christian Science*

Monitor, 29 May 1934; *Chicago American*, 4 March 1935. An excellent overview of the Great Famine can be found in the *Ukrainian Weekly* special
issue of 20 March 1983 and in a special commemorative publication of
the Ukrainian National Association entitled *The Great Famine in Ukraine:
The Unknown Holocaust*, also published in 1983. See also Miron Dolot,
Execution by Hunger: The Hidden Holocaust (New York: Norton, 1985).

3 Theodore Draper, *The Roots of American Communism* (New York: Viking
  Press, 1957), pp. 11–35.

4 Eugene Lyons, *The Red Decade: The Stalinist Penetration of America* (Indianapolis: Bobbs-Merrill Company, 1941), pp. 31–2.

5 Benjamin Gitlow, *I Confess: The Truth about American Communism* (New
  York: E.P. Dutton, 1940), pp. 21–7. An active member of the Communist
  Party of America all through the 1920s, Gitlow was purged in 1929.

6 "Resolution of the Russian-Ukrainian Mass Meeting," *Russkaia Pochta*, 16
  June 1917.

7 Nastasivsky, *Ukrains'ka Imigratsiia v Spoluchenykh Derzhavakh*, pp. 89–92.

8 Ibid., pp. 95–107.

9 Ibid., pp. 107–44.

10 *Robitnyk*, 20 February 1918; cited in Nastasivsky, p. 144.

11 Ibid., 5 March 1918; cited ibid., p. 145.

12 Ibid., 27 April 1918; cited ibid., p. 146–7.

13 Ibid., 16 May 1918; cited ibid., p. 151.

14 Nastasivsky, pp. 14–51; Tolopko, 103–21.

15 Sydney Lens, *Radicalism in America* (New York: Thomas Y. Crowell Company, 1969), p. 271.

16 Ibid., pp. 271–3.

17 Draper, pp. 92–6.

18 Nastasivsky, pp. 154–62.

19 *Robitnyk* 17 January 1919.

20 Ibid., 10 February 1919.

21 Ibid., 24 February 1919.

22 Ibid., 3 March 1919.

23 Ibid., 7 March 1919.

24 Ibid., 24 March 1919.

25 Ibid., 28 July 1919.

26 Ibid., 21 July 1918.

27 Ibid., 18 July 1919.

28 Ibid., 4 April 1919.

29 Anthony Cave Brown and Charles B. MacDonald, *On a Field of Red: The
   Communist International and the Coming of World War II* (New York: G.P.
   Putnam's & Sons, 1981), pp. 86–7.

30 Ibid., pp. 85–9.

31 Lyons, pp. 20–33.

32 Ibid., p. 33; Lens, pp. 276–7.

33 Draper, pp. 176–206; Gitlow, pp. 33–57.

34 Gitlow, p. 57.

35 *Robitnyk*, 20 June 1919; see also Natasivsky, pp. 174–5.

36 *Robitnyk*, 25 September 1919.

37 Ibid., 11 September 1919. The new editors were M. Durda, M. Andriychuk, and V. Shopinsky.

38 Ibid., 7 October 1919.

39 Ibid., 30 October 1919.

40 Ibid., 25 November 1919.

41 Ibid., 25 September 1919.

42 Cited in Park, *The Immigrant Press and Its Control*, pp. 235–6.

43 Tolopko, pp. 136–7. Elected to the Executive Committee were F. Savitsky, V. Savchyn, V. Sapovych, S. Valchuk, O. Sarvan, P. Kerkera, I. Fiyalko, I. Bodak, A. Senyk, I. Ilkiv, L. Ploshchansky, A. Radvenetska, J. Shevchuk, M. Vitenko, A. Bilska, E. Osadchuk, D. Moisa, A. Kushlyak, V. Sabatiuk, N. Tomiuk, I. Popov, I. Hutsulyak, A. Sodoma, F. Osadchuk, S. Lukeniuk, and I. Dyus. Controllers included O. Moss, P. Makhmit, I. Nakonechny, and V. Skulsky. The editorial board consisted of V. Shopinsky, M. Durdela, M. Andriychuk, M. Tarnovsky, N. Kysil, and Ye. Kruk.

44 Brown and MacDonald, pp. 142–6; Draper, p. 202.

45 Draper, pp. 197–209; Lens, pp. 276–7.

46 *Svoboda*, 9 September 1920.

47 Nastasivsky, pp. 225–8.

48 Ibid., pp. 179–82; Stachiw, "Nova Ukraina v Amerytsi," pp. 110–15; Yaroslav Chyz, "The Ukrainian Immigrants in the United States"; Reshetar, *The Ukrainian Revolution*, pp. 324–5; interview with Stephen Kuropas, 2 August 1970.

49 Draper, pp. 210–25; Lyons, pp. 22–3.

50 Draper, pp. 267–81.

51 Ibid., pp. 327–42.

52 Ibid., pp. 353–8; see also R.M. Whitney, *Reds in America* (New York: Beckwith Press, 1924), p. 12.

53 Ibid., pp. 376–90; Whitney, pp. 231–5.

54 *Visti*, 2 January 1921.

55 Ibid., 7 January 1921.

56 Nastasivsky, pp. 229–38; Leon Tolopko, "Sorok Rokhiv na Shliakhu Postupu" (Forty Years on the Road of Progress), *Visti*, 14 April 1966.

57 Tolopko, "Sorok Rokhiv na Shliakhu Postupu," pp. 5–6; Nastasivsky pp. 238–9; see also M. Kniazevych, "Soiuz Ukrains'kykh Robitnykiv" (United Ukrainian Toilers Organization), *Narodnyi Kalendar na rik 1939* (People's Calendar for the Year 1939) (New York: Ukrainian Section of the International Worker's Order, 1939), pp. 228–9.

58 John Kolasky, *The Shattered Illusion: The History of Ukrainian Pro-Communist Organizations in Canada* (Toronto: Peter Martin Associates Limited, 1979), p. 10.

59 Ibid., pp. 25–6.

60 Lyons, p. 47.

61 Tolopko, "Sorok Rokhiv na Shliakhu Postupu," pp. 6–7.

62 Brown and MacDonald, pp. 332–3.
63 Richard W. Leopold, *The Growth of American Foreign Policy: A History* (New York: Alfred A. Knopf, 1962), pp. 516–18.
64 "Establishment of Diplomatic Relations with the Union of Soviet Socialist Republics," p. 6. Complete text in FBI files on UHO, section I.
65 *Ukrainian Weekly,* 23 November 1933.
66 Leopold, pp. 516–18.
67 Brown and MacDonald, p. 335.
68 Lens, p. 297.
69 Arthur M. Schlesinger, Jr., *The Age of Roosevelt: The Politics of Upheaval,* vol. 3 (Boston: Houghton-Mifflin Company, 1960), pp. 181–2. See also Earl Browder, "The American Communist Party in the Thirties," *As We Saw the Thirties,* ed. Rita James Simon (Urbana: University of Illinois Press, 1967), pp. 218–19.
70 Schlesinger, pp. 183–5.
71 Cited in Paul Hollander, *Political Pilgrims: Travels of Western Intellectuals to the Soviet Union, China, and Cuba, 1928–1978* (New York: Oxford University Press, 1981), p. 124.
72 Ibid., p. 103n.
73 Cited in ibid., p. 127.
74 Cited in ibid., pp. 144–5.
75 Ibid., pp. 102–76.
76 Cited in ibid., p. 106.
77 Ibid., p. 170.
78 Cited in ibid., p. 164.
79 Joseph E. Davies, *Mission to Moscow* (New York: Simon and Schuster, 1941), pp. 191–2.
80 Ibid., pp. 272–80.
81 Ibid., p. 262.
82 Tolstoy, *Stalin's Secret War,* p. 340.
83 Ibid., pp. 339–41. Also see George F. Kennan, *Memoirs, 1925–1950* (Boston: Little, Brown, 1967), pp. 84–5.
84 Lyons, pp. 116–23.
85 Eugene Lyons, *Assignment in Utopia* (New York: Harcourt Brace & Company, 1937), pp. 572–80. The entire news manipulation episode is recounted in a chapter entitled "The Press Corps Conceals a Famine." Also see chapter entitled "Concealing Stalin's Famine" in Whitman Bassow, *The Moscow Correspondents: Reporting on Russia from the Revolution to Glasnost* (New York: William Morrow and Company, 1988), pp. 63–91.
86 Lyons, *The Red Decade,* pp. 117–19.
87 Cited in Hollander, p. 120.
88 Ibid.
89 Cited in ibid., p. 162.
90 Lyons, *Assignment in Utopia,* pp. 577–8.
91 Lens, p. 297.
92 Frederick L. Schuman, "Liberalism and Communism Reconsidered,"

Southern Review, Autumn 1936, pp. 326–8; cited in Frank A. Warren, III, *Liberals and Communism: The "Red Decade" Revisited* (Bloomington: Indiana University Press, 1966), p. 109.

93 James J. Martin, *American Liberalism and World Politics, 1931–1941: Liberalism's Press and Spokesman on the Road back to War between Mukden and Pearl Harbor*, vol. 1 (New York: The Devin-Adair Company, 1964), p. 634.

94 Warren, p. 105.

95 Louis Fischer, "The First True Democracy," *Soviet Russia Today*, May 1937; cited in Warren, p. 105.

96 *New Republic*, 1 June 1938; cited in Warren, p. 149.

97 "The Dies Committee Mess," *New Republic*, 31 August 1938; cited in Martin, p. 638.

98 Lyons, *The Red Decade*, pp. 170–3; J. Edgar Hoover, *Masters of Deceit: The Story of Communism in America and How to Fight It* (New York: Henry Holt & Co., 1958), p. 70.

99 Lyons, *The Red Decade*, pp. 365–73; Hoover, p. 71.

100 Lyons, *The Red Decade*, pp. 342–51.

101 Browder, pp. 240–1.

102 Lens, p. 317.

103 Lyons, *The Red Decade*, p. 197.

104 T. Richynskyi, "Pochatky i Rozvytok Ukrains'koi Sektsii Mizhnarodnoho Robitnychoho Ordenu" (The Genesis and Development of the Ukrainian Section of the International Workers' Order), *Narodnyi Kalendar na rik 1939*, pp. 37–41.

105 See photostatic copy of letter from "Friends of the Abraham Lincoln Brigade," *Narodnyi Kalendar na rik 1939*, p. 113.

106 M.T. "Ukrains'ki Biitsi v Espanii" (Ukrainian Fighters in Spain), *Narodnyi Kalendar na rik 1939*, pp. 115–16.

107 Tolopko, "Sorok Rokhiv na Shliakhu Postupu," pp. 6–7; Richynskyi, pp. 40–1; Leon Tolopko, "Na Shliakhu Nevpynnoi Borot'by" (In the Continual Struggle), *Visti*, 29 January 1970.

108 See Michael Hanusiak, "50 Glorious Years Dedicated to Progress, Peace, and Friendship," *Visti*, 29 January 1970.

109 *Visti*, 25 March 1934.

110 *Narodna Volya*, 23 January 1936.

111 *Mizhnarodnyi Robitnychyi Orden i Ieho Ukrains'ka Sektsia v Svitli Faktiv i Tsyfriv* (The International Workers' Order and Its Ukrainian Section in Facts and Figures) (New York: Robitnyk Publishing Co., 1937), pp. 17–18.

112 *Visti*, 14 May 1937.

113 Ibid., 11 September 1938.

114 Ibid.

115 Kolasky, p. 25.

116 Ibid., pp. 20–5.

117 See Eric Hofer, *The True Believer: Thoughts on the Nature of Mass Movements*

(New York: Mentor Books, 1951), p. 76; see also Vivian Gornick, *The Romance of American Communism* (New York: Basic Books, 1977).

118 Kolasky, pp. 20–1.

119 Nastasivsky, "Zackidna Ukraina," pp. 23–8; *Narodnyi Kalendar na rik 1939*, pp. 23–8.

120 See "Karpatska Rus – Karpatska Ukraina" (Carpatho-Rus – Carpatho-Ukraine), *Narodnyi Kalendar na rik 1939*, p. 227.

121 "Shcho Take Suverennist" (What Is Sovereignty), *Narodnyi Kalendar na rik 1939*, p. 106.

122 Tolopko, "Sorok Rokhiv na Shliakhu Postupu," p. 7; Kniazevych, pp. 229–30.

123 Harvey Klehr, *The Heyday of American Communism: The Depression Decade* (New York: Basic Books, 1984), pp. 378–85.

124 Ibid., p. 382.

125 Lyons, *The Red Decade*, pp. 355–64.

126 Hoover, p. 72.

127 *Visti*, March 1941; cited in the *Ukrainian Weekly*, 28 November 1942.

128 Lyons, *The Red Decade*, p. 374.

129 Hoover, pp. 70–3.

130 Lyons, *The Red Decade*, pp. 377–81.

131 See ibid., p. 321.

Chapter 6

1 Alexander J. Motyl, *The Turn to the Right: The Ideological Origins and Development of Ukrainian Nationalism, 1919–1929* (Boulder: East European Monographs, 1980), pp. 23–39; Viacheslav Lypynskyi, *Lysty Do Brativ Khliborobiv* (Letters to Brother Agrarians), 2d printing (New York: Bulava Publishing Co., 1954), pp. 5–39, and "Kommunikat" (Communiqué), *Zbirnyk Khliborobs'koi Ukrainy* (An Anthology of Agrarian Ukraine) (Prague: Brotherhood of Ukrainian Classocratic Monarchists-Hetmanates, 1931), pp. 13–34; John A. Armstrong, *Ukrainian Nationalism*, 2nd ed. (New York: Columbia University Press, 1963), p. 28.

2 Petro Zadoretsky, "Korotkyi Narys Istorii Sichovoi Orhanizatsii u Z.D.A." (A Short Outline History of the Sich Organization in the USA), *Hei Tam Na Hori, Sich Ide*, pp. 349–56.

3 *Sichovi Visti*, 13 July 1918.

4 Ibid., 15 August 1918.

5 Zadoretsky, p. 356.

6 Memorandum for the Chief of Staff from the War Department Office of Brigadier General Lytle, 13 July 1918. Photostatic copy in Zadoretsky, p. 360.

7 Memorandum for Colonel Conrad from the Military Intelligence Division of the War Department, 11 September 1918. Photostatic copy in Zadoretsky, p. 361.

8 Zadoretsky, pp. 356–63; Simenovych, "Z Moho Zhyttia" p. 72.

9 Zadoretsky, p. 363; Stephen Musiychuk, "Prychyny Opadku Sichovoi Orhanizatsii u Z.D.A." (Reasons behind the Decline of the Sich Organization in the USA), *Hei Tam Na Hori, Sich Ide*, pp. 373–4.

10 Zadoretsky, p. 363.

11 Ibid., p. 364.

12 *Sichovi Visti*, 11 January 1920.

13 *Ukraina*, 3 April 1920.

14 Zadoretsky, p. 369; interview with Philip Wasylowsky, 6 August 1970.

15 *Sichovi Visti*, 14 April 1921.

16 Ibid., 16 May 1921.

17 Ibid., 15 March 1922.

18 "Stepan Hrynevetsky," *Medical Almanac*, pp. 42–6; also see Osyp Nazaruk, "Po Rokakh Pratsi v Amerytsi" (After Years of Work in America), *Sich*, 15 March 1926.

19 *Sichovi Visti*, 15 March 1922.

20 Ibid., 15 June 1922.

21 Nazaruk, "Po Rokakh Pratsi v Amerytsi"; see also Stepan Hrynevetsky, "Shcho Musyt' Buty (What Must Be), *Sich*, 15 March 1926.

22 *Sichovi Visti*, 20 March 1924.

23 Ibid., 25 January 1924.

24 Ibid., 25 May 1924.

25 Musiychuk, pp. 375–6; interview with Philip Wasylowsky, 6 August 1970.

26 *Sichovi Visti*, 10 June 1924.

27 *Sich*, 15 August 1924.

28 Nazaruk, "Po Rokakh Pratsi v Amerytsi."

29 *Sich*, 5 December 1924; Musiychuk, p. 376; interview with Philip Waslowsky, 6 August 1970. Both Musiychuk and Wasylowsky maintained that the monarchist oath of allegiance came as a complete surprise to all present. "The solemnity of the occasion," stated Wasylowsky, "prevented us from openly protesting the move at that moment."

30 *Sich*, 1 December 1926.

31 Zadoretsky, p. 371; Musiychuk; interviews with Philip Wasylowsky, 26 September and 20 November 1968.

32 *Sich*, 15 March 1926.

33 Ibid., 1 June 1926.

34 Ibid., 15 January 1928.

35 Ibid., 1 July 1928.

36 Ibid., 1 January 1928.

37 Ibid., 1 February 1928.

38 Ibid., 1 January 1932.

39 Ibid., 20 October 1926.

40 Ibid., 1 October 1929.

41 Ibid., 15 July 1930; interview with Nicholas Olek, 8 August 1970.

42 *Sich*, 1 March 1930.

43 Ibid., 1 January 1930.

44 Interview with Nicholas Olek, 8 August 1970.
45 *Sich*, 1 September 1931.
46 Ibid., 15 March 1930.
47 Ibid., 15 January and 1 February 1930.
48 Ibid., 15 August 1930.
49 See *Za Ukrainu* (For the Ukraine: The Tour of His Highness Hetmanych Danylo Skoropadsky through the United States of America and Canada) (Chicago: United Hetman Organizations, 1938), pp. 54–7.
50 *Sich*, 21 April 1934; *Nash Styakh*, 15 September 1934; interview with Nicholas Olek, 8 August 1970.
51 *Sich*, 31 March 1934.
52 Ibid., 2 June 1934.
53 Ibid., 15 December 1929.
54 Ibid., 15 October 1930.
55 Interview with Philip Wasylowsky, 6 August 1970.
56 *Sich*, 1 December 1930.
57 See *Za Ukrainu*, pp. 33–6.
58 Interviews with Philip Wasylowsky, 26 September and 20 November 1968; interview with Stephen Kuropas, 2 August 1970.
59 Volodymyr Duzey, "A Few Words about Democracy and Foreign and Ukrainian Fascism," *Sich*, 17 December 1932.
60 Schlesinger, *The Age of Roosevelt*, pp. 17–28.
61 Ibid., pp. 72–84. See also Richard O'Connor, *The German Americans: An Informal History* (Boston; Little, Brown and Co., 1968), pp. 435–48.
62 O'Connor, pp. 445–50.
63 Interview with Nicholas Olek, 8 August 1970. It was at about this time that Olek decided to leave UHO.
64 *Za Ukrainu*, pp. 33–128.
65 Department of Justice memo for the director of the Federal Bureau of Investigation (11 February 1936), File #61-9183-1 UHO, Section I.
66 FBI memo (10 April 1936), File #61-9183-3, UHO, Section I.
67 August R. Ogden, *The Dies Committee: A Study of the Special House Committee for Investigation of Un-American Activities, 1938–1943* (Washington: Murray and Heister Publishers, 1944), pp. 43–6.
68 Ibid., p. 64.
69 Ibid., p. 153.
70 Ibid., pp. 111–13.
71 U.S. Congress, House of Representatives, *Investigation of Un-American Propaganda Activities in the United States: Hearings before a Special Committee on Un-American Activities*, 76th Cong., 1st ss., 1939, 9: pp. 5250–61.
72 Ibid., p. 5269.
73 Ibid., p. 5270.
74 Ibid., p. 5271.
75 Ibid., p. 5315.
76 Ibid., pp. 5307–14.
77 Ibid., p. 5322.

78 *Chicago Daily News*, 28 September 1939.

79 Ogden, p. 113.

80 *Congressional Record*, 14 June 1940.

81 Ibid., 1 July 1940.

82 Ibid., 4 October 1940.

83 Ibid., 21 October 1940.

84 FBI memo (13 June 1940), File #61-9183-6X, UHO, Section I.

85 FBI memo (2 August 1940), File #61-9183-8, UHO, Section I.

86 Ibid.

87 Cited in FBI memo to Mr. Clegg from J.F. Pryor (23 August 1940), UHO, Section I.

88 *Visti*, 25 February 1941.

89 FBI memo (3 March 1941), File #61-9183-18X, UHO, Section I. The memo is dated 3 March but refers to a 22 March issue of *The Hour*. Because it was received on 10 April, the memo probably should have been dated 3 April 1941.

90 FBI memo (2 August 1940), File #61-9183-8, UHO, Section I.

91 FBI memo for Mr. Clegg from J.F. Pryor.

92 FBI memo (1 May 1941), File #61-9183-20X1, UHO, Section I.

93 FBI memo for Mr. M.C. Lawrence, Chief Special Defense Unit, from John Edgar Hoover, Director (1 October 1941), UHO, Section 2.

94 Interview with Stephen Kuropas, 21 December 1982. Kuropas remained a close personal friend of Alexander Shapoval, who moved to a farm in Three Rivers, Michigan, following the UHO debacle. Kuropas also had a farm in the area and the two of them would often meet to reminisce about "old times."

95 FBI memo (5 September 1942), File #61-9183-65, UHO, Section 4.

96 *The Hour*, 9 November 1942.

97 FBI memo (31 May 1943), File #61-9183-85, UHO, Section 4.

98 *Narodna Volya*, 25 September 1941.

99 FBI memo (7 April 1943), File #61-9183-78, UHO, Section 4.

100 FBI memo (28 February 1944), File #61-9183-101, UHO Section 4.

101 Department of Justice memo to the Director of the FBI (9 November 1943), File #61-9183-95, UHO, Section 4.

102 Michael Sayers and Albert E. Kahn, *Sabotage! The Secret War against America* (New York: Harper and Brothers, 1942), p. 83.

103 *Reader's Digest*, October 1942, p. 159.

104 Michael Sayers and Albert E. Kahn, *The Great Conspiracy: The Secret War against Soviet Russia* (San Francisco: Proletarian Publishers, 1946), p. 89.

105 Ibid., p. 396.

106 Lyons, *The Red Decade*, pp. 250–4; Brown and MacDonald, *On a Field of Red*, p. 133.

107 *Communist Passport Frauds: A Staff Study Prepared for the Subcommittee to Investigate the Administration of the Internal Security Act and Other Internal Security Laws of the Committee on the Judiciary, United States Senate* (Washington, DC: United States Government Printing Office, 11 July 1958),

pp. 64–7. Also see Albert E. Kahn, *The Matusow Affair: Memoir of a National Scandal* (Mt. Kisco, NY: Moyer Bell Limited, 1987).

Chapter 7

1 Motyl, pp. 62–76; also see Mykhailo Sosnovskyi, *Dmytro Dontsov: politychnyi portret* (Dmytro Donzov: A Political Portrait) (New York: Trident International, Inc., 1974); Subtelny, pp. 441–3.

2 Stercho, pp. 128–37 and 357–80; Manning, pp. 129–30; Barany, pp. 259–309; Magocsi, *The Shaping of a National Identity: Subcarpathian Rus, 1848–1948*, pp. 234–49; A. Stefan, "Ukraine between the Two World Wars: Transcarpathia (Carpatho-Ukraine)," *Ukraine: A Concise Encyclopedia* 1:850–6; Julian Revay, "The March of Liberation of Carpatho-Ukraine," *The Ukrainian Quarterly*, Summer 1954; Vasyl Markus, "Carpatho-Ukraine under Hungarian Occupation (1939–1944)," *The Ukrainian Quarterly*, Summer 1954; John A. Armstrong, *Ukrainian Nationalism* (New York: Columbia University Press, 1963), pp. 110–14; Subtelny, pp. 446–51.

3 Stephan Fischer-Galati, "Roumanian Nationalism," *Nationalism in Eastern Europe*, pp. 373–95; Joseph Roucek, *Contemporary Roumania and Her Problems: A Study in Modern Nationalism* (Stanford: Stanford University Press, 1932); T. Halip and A. Zhukovsky, "Ukraine between the Two Wars: Bukovina and Bessarabia," *Ukraine: A Concise Encyclopedia*, 1:856–9; *Roumania Ten Years After*, A Report of the American Committee on the Rights of Religious Minorities (Boston: Beacon Press, 1928), pp. 94–110.

4 Stephen Horak, *Poland and Her Minorities, 1919–1939* (New York: Vantage Press, 1961), pp. 62–71; Konrad Syrod, *Poland: Between Anvil and Hammer* (London: Robert Hale Publishers, 1968), pp. 114–19; Richard M. Watt, *Bitter Glory: Poland and Its Fate, 1918–1939* (New York: Simon and Schuster, 1979), pp. 188–209; Peter Brock, "Polish Nationalism," *Nationalism in Eastern Europe*, pp. 360–4; S. Andreski, "Poland," *European Fascism*, ed. S.J. Wolff (London: Weidenfeld and Nicholson, 1968), pp. 167–81; S. Vytvytsky and S. Baran, "Ukraine between the Two World Wars: Western Ukraine under Poland," *Ukraine: A Concise Encyclopedia*, 1:833–50; Subtelny, 425–46.

5 Horak, pp. 143–6; I. Herasymovych, V. Kubijovyc, M. Terletsky, and O. Terletsky, "Education in Western Ukraine in 1919–44 and Abroad: Ukrainian Lands under Poland," *Ukraine: A Concise Encyclopedia*, 2:374–8.

6 Stephen M. Mamchur, "Nationalism, Religion and the Problem of Assimilation among Ukrainians in the United States" (PhD dissertation, Yale University, 1942), p. 90.

7 W. Lencyk, "History of Ukrainian Churches: The Ukrainian Catholic Church since 1800," *Ukraine: A Concise Encyclopedia*, 2:191.

8 Vytvytsky and Baran, p. 847.

9 I. Korowytsky, "History of Ukrainian Churches: The Orthodox Church in Poland, 1919–1939," *Ukraine: A Concise Encyclopedia*, 2:178–9. Most of the Ukrainian Orthodox churches were located in Volhynia, a Ukrainian

province that had been under Russian jurisdiction until World War I. See George Fedoriw, *History of the Church in Ukraine,* trans. Petro Krawchuk (Toronto: no publisher, 1983), pp. 226–32.

10 Vytvytsky and Baran, pp. 838–40.

11 Herasymovych et al., pp. 372–9.

12 I. Vytanovych, "The Ukrainian Economy: The Cooperative Movement in Western Ukraine, 1920–1944," *Ukraine: A Concise Encyclopedia,* 2:982–7.

13 Some Ukrainian historians date the founding of UVO from the final conference of the Council (Rada) of Sichovi Striltsi held in Prague in July 1920 (Petro Mirchuk, *Narys Istorii Orhanizatsii Ukrains'kykh Natsionalistiv, 1920–1939* [Outline History of the Organization of Ukrainian Nationalists, 1920–1939], ed. Stephen Lenkavsky [Munich: Ukrainian Publishers, 1968], pp. 15–18).

14 V. Martynets, *Ukrains'ke Pidpillia vid UVO do OUN: Spohady i Materialy do Peredistorii ta Istorii Ukrains'koho Orhanizovanoho Natsionalizmu* (The Ukrainian Underground from UVO to OUN: Memoirs and Materials Concerning the Prehistory and History of Organized Ukrainian Nationalism) (Winnipeg: The Ukrainian National Federation, 1949), pp. 19–40.

15 One of the first UVO martyrs was Olha Bassarab, a female UVO courier, who was tortured to death in a Polish prison in 1924 (Mirchuk, pp. 26–34; Vytvytsky and Baran, pp. 836–42).

16 Dontsov's principal works during and after the war included *Istoriia Rozvytku Ukrainskoi Derzhavnoi Idei* (1917) (A History of the Development of the Ukrainian National Idea); *Ukrainska Derzhavna Dumka i Evropa* (1919) (Ukrainian National Thought and Europe), *Pidstavy Nashoi Polityky* (1921) (The Foundation of Our Politics); *Natsionalizm* (1926) (Nationalism); *Polityka Pryntsypiialna i Oportunistychna* (1928) (The Politics of Principles and the Politics of Opportunism). Motyl, pp. 62–76; Jurij Boyko, *Osnovy Ukrayinskoho Natsionalizmu* (Foundations of Ukrainian Nationalism) (Abroad: no publisher, 1951).

17 V. Martynec, "Ukrains'ka Natsionalistychna Presa" (The Ukrainian Nationalistic Press," *OUN, 1929–1954,* pp. 148–53; Mirchuk, pp. 54–70; Jurij Artiushenko, *Po Torach Bortsia Pravdy i Voli* (To Be for Truth and Freedom) (Chicago: Ukrainian Printers, 1957), pp. 36–47; "Dontsov, Dmytro," *Entsyklopediia Ukrainoznavstva,* p. 570; Armstrong, p. 21.

18 Martynets, pp. 148–53; Mirchuk, pp. 54–70; Artushenko, pp. 36–47.

19 Zenovii Knysh, *Pry Dsherelakh Ukrainskoho Orhanizovanoho Natsionalizmu* (Among the Sources of Organized Ukrainian Nationalism) (Toronto: Surma Publishers, 1970), pp. 30–1.

20 Mykola Sciborsky, "Shliakh Natsionalizmu" (Nationalism's Path), *Derzhavna Natsiia,* November 1927, cited in ibid., p. 32.

21 Martynets, pp. 178–329.

22 Armstrong, pp. 21–2.

23 Martynets, pp. 329–43.

24 See Yaroslav Bilinsky, *The Second Soviet Republic: The Ukraine after World War II* (New Brunswick: Rutgers University Press, 1964), pp. 342–3.

25 *By-Laws of the Organization of Ukrainian Nationalists* (Paragraphs 15 and 16). For the complete text see Knysh, pp. 152–72.

26 Knysh, p. 119.

27 Zenovii Knysh, "Boiovi Dii OUN na ZYZ u Pershomu Desiatylitti ii Isnuvannia" (The Revolutionary Activities of OUN in Western Ukraine during the First Decade of Its Existence), *OUN, 1929–1954*, p. 9.

28 Bilinsky, p. 120; Mirchuk, p. 126.

29 Motyl, pp. 153–61.

30 Ibid., pp. 162–73. Ernest Nolte, *The Three Faces of Fascism* (New York: New American Library, 1963), pp. 285, 570–4. Hans Kohn, *Political Ideologies of the Twentieth Century* (New York: Harper Torchbooks, 1949), pp. 149–53.

31 Motyl, pp. 161–73.

32 Like Ukrainian Nationalism, Zionism emerged as a messianic liberation movement aimed at the redemption of the Jewish nation through the establishment of a Jewish state. Zionists condemned Jews who were willing to assimilate in order to survive – "to live," declared Max Nordeau, "whether it be as a slave, or a dog ... without a future, without purpose, without hope" – and zealously tried to convince world Jewry that only a Jewish state could save the Jewish nation. While most Zionists were committed to socialism and the democratic process, there were revisionist Zionists who believed in direct action and, if necessary, military suppression of opposition. In time, the revisionists formed the New Zionist Organization and began to advocate certain internal measures to eliminate class struggle, and to favor totalitarian control for more effective action. See Yigal Allon, "What Is Zionism?" *Zionism: A Basic Reader*, ed. Mordecai S. Chertoff (New York: Herzl Press, 1975), p. 75; Simon Dubnow, "The Jewish Nationality, Now and in the Future," *Nationalism and History: Essays on Old and New Judaism by Simon Dubnow*, ed. Koppel S. Pinson (Philadelphia: The Jewish Publication Society of America, 1958), pp. 170–2; also see Baron, p. 231.

33 Motyl, p. 158–61.

34 *Dilo*, 4 April 1929; cited in Mirchuk, p. 109.

35 Koenig, p. 115.

36 Hugh Seton-Watson, *Eastern Europe between the Wars, 1918–1941*, 3rd ed. rev. (New York: Harper and Row, 1962), p. 335.

37 For a detailed Ukrainian account of the pacification, see *Na Vichnu Han'bu* (For Eternal Shame) (Prague: Provid of the Organization of Ukrainian Nationalists, 1931).

38 *New York Times*, 19 October 1930; cited in Horak, p. 163.

39 *Manchester Guardian*, 14 October 1930; cited in Horak, p. 163. See also lengthy accounts in the *New York Herald Tribune*, 15 October 1930 and the *Philadelphia Inquirer*, 10 October 1930.

40 Horak, p. 162.

41 In addition to the "Ten Commandments of the Ukrainian Nationalist," which every OUN member had to memorize, the OUN educational program included "Twelve Characteristics of the Ukrainian Nationalist"

and "Forty-four Rules of Life," which had to be learned. Characteristics included being "every-ready" to "sacrifice one's life" for the revolution in addition to being "honest ... loyal ... active ... brave ... reliable ... persistent ... prudent ... punctual ... healthy ... careful." Among the rules of life were such directives as "Accept life as a heroic task"; "Your greatest love is the Ukrainian Nation and your brothers are all the members of the Ukrainian national community"; "Be conscious of the fact that you share the responsibility for the fate of the entire Nation"; "Live with risk, danger, and constant struggle"; "Don't be dependent upon anyone. Accept only that which you have earned through your own worth and work"; "Whatever you do, do in conscience, as if this effort was to be eternal and the last and greatest testament to the meaning of your life." For the complete text, see Mirchuk, pp. 127–9.

42 A distinction was made within OUN between those who served in Western Ukraine – the *krai* – and those who, like most members of the Provid, served elsewhere (Armstrong, pp. 22–3; Bilinsky, pp. 119–20).

43 According to two OUN members active in Western Ukraine during this period, the hard-core membership, those who had taken the oath of allegiance and who were involved with OUN affairs on an almost daily basis, never numbered more than 500. According to Subtelny, the total membership of OUN on the eve of the Second World War is estimated to be approximately 20,000. (Interview with Teofil Bak-Boychuk and Jurij Daczyszyn, 13 August 1971; Subtelny, p. 444)

44 Two OUN members, Vasyl Bilas and Dmytro Danylyshyn, were captured in the fall of 1932 after a successful "expropriation" raid on a Polish postal truck near Lviv. Following a widely publicized trial, the two were sentenced to death. As they were being led to the scaffold, Ukrainian church bells throughout Western Ukraine began to ring in tribute to their heroic defiance. Fearing a mass uprising of Ukrainians in the future, the Poles commuted all OUN death sentences to life imprisonment (Mirchuk, pp. 305–22; interview with Teofil Bak-Boychuk and Jurij Daczyszyn, 13 August 1971).

45 Knysh, "Boiovi Dii OUN na ZYZ u Pershomu Desyatylitti ii Isnuvannia," p. 94.

46 The assassin, Mykola Lenyk, a freshman at the University of Lviv, missed his mark, killing a consulate secretary instead (Bohdan S. Budurowycz, *Polish-Soviet Relations, 1932–1939* [New York: Columbia University Press, 1963], p. 34).

47 Mirchuk, pp. 373–86; Subtelny, pp. 444–5.

48 Martynec, p. 245.

49 P.K. Boiyarsky, "Ukrains'kyi Natsionalistychnyi Rukh i Suspil'no-Hromads'kyi Sektor" (The Ukrainian Nationalistic Movement and the Social-Community Sector), *OUN, 1929–1959*, pp. 350–7.

50 Vytvytsky and Baran, pp. 842–7.

51 Analyzing collaboration and resistance in Hitler's Europe between 1939

and 1945, Werner Rings developed a nine-point scale that ranges from unconditional collaboration ("I join forces with the occupying powers because I endorse its principles and ideals") and neutral collaboration ("I accept that life must go on") at one end, to offensive resistance ("I fight to the death") and resistance enchained ("I resist even in prison") at the other end. Rings places tactical collaboration ("I agree to collaborate despite my hostility") fourth on the collaboration continuum. Included among reasons for tactical collaboration in the Rings paradigm are national liberation and prevention of mass murder of innocent people (Werner Rings, *Life with the Enemy: Collaboration and Resistance in Hitler's Europe, 1939–1945*, transl. J. Maxwell Brownjohn [Garden City: Doubleday and Co., 1982]).

52 Allan Bullock, *Hitler: A Study in Tyranny* (New York: Harper and Row, 1962), p. 411.

53 Ihor Kamenetsky, *Hitler's Occupation of Ukraine, 1941–1944: A Study in Totalitarian Imperialism* (Milwaukee: Marquette University Press, 1956), p. 7.

54 Ibid., pp. 1–27.

55 Armstrong, pp. 33–9.

56 The exact reasons for the split remain obscure because of the varying interpretations offered by the two sides. Differences seemed to be the result of personal rather than ideological considerations and centered around the *krai* contention that the Provid had been too subordinate to the Germans and that it lacked the necessary will and vigor to lead the Ukrainian Nationalist movement. When Melnyk refused to dismiss some of the Provid members and to replace them with younger leaders, the *krai* contingent met in Cracow and designated Bandera as the chief of the new, "revolutionary" Provid. In March 1941, OUN(B) formalized the split by rejecting the Rome OUN Congress and convening a "second OUN Congress" in Cracow. In keeping with its emphasis on action, OUN(B) subsequently organized two Ukrainian battalions for the German Wehrmacht – Nachtigall, which wore German uniforms and Ukrainian insignia, and Roland, which had Ukrainian uniforms patterned after the 1918 Galician army model. Both units participated in Hitler's subsequent invasion of the USSR (Armstrong, pp. 53–74).

57 Ibid., pp. 53–74.

58 Alexander Dallin, *German Rule in Russia, 1941–1944* (London: Macmillan & Co., 1957), pp. 126–7.

59 Ibid., pp. 112–19.

60 V. Kubijovyc, V. Holubnychy, and H.M., "Ukraine during World War II," *Ukraine: A Concise Encyclopedia*, 1:877–8.

61 Armstrong, pp. 76–81.

62 Dallin, p. 120.

63 Kamenetsky, p. 26.

64 Dallin, pp. 127–8.

65 Kamenetsky, p. 56.
66 Bohdan Wytwycky, *The Other Holocaust* (Washington: The Novak Report, 1980), p. 52.
67 Kubijovyc et al., p. 881.
68 Kamenetsky, pp. 44–5.
69 Kubijovyc et al., p. 881.
70 This policy was outlined by the German Economic Armament Staff in a 2 December 1941 report that proposed to reduce inland traffic by "the elimination of superfluous eaters (Jews and Kievan Ukrainians)" and "the drastic reduction of rations ... in Ukrainian cities." One source suggests that a million people may have died in Ukraine as a result of this policy (Wytwycky, pp. 62–3).
71 A Soviet Ukrainian study concluded that there were 160 separate Nazi concentration camps in Ukraine, clustered near Rivne in Volhynia, near Kharkiv, and in the Donetsk region. One of the largest was the camp at Ianiv. Administered by Gustav Wilhaus – a sadist who amused his family by having two-to-four-year-old children thrown in the air for target practice – Ianiv saw some 200,000 inmates die during the course of its existence (ibid., pp. 58–9).
72 Kubijovyc et al., p. 883.
73 Armstrong, pp. 124–5.
74 Wytwycky, p. 64.
75 Kubijovyc et al., p. 884.
76 According to the chief of staff of its military intelligence service, the French underground had no more than 45,000 "true resistance fighters" in the whole of France prior to the June 1944 Allied invasion of Europe (Rings, pp. 210–12).
77 Armstrong, pp. 130–65; Kamenetsky, pp. 67–82.
78 Kubijovyc et al., p. 892; V. Holubnychy, "Ukraine since World War II, 1945–62," *Ukraine: A Concise Encyclopedia,* 1:896.
79 Poniatysyhn, "Ukrains'ka Sprava v Amerytsi Pid Chas Pershoi Svitovoi Viiny," p. 74.
80 Luka Myshuha, "Ob'iednannia Ukrainskykh Orhanizatsii v Amerytsi" (The United Ukrainian Organizations in America), *Golden Jubilee Almanac of the Ukrainian National Association,* pp. 129–32.
81 Ibid., pp. 132–3; see also *Svoboda,* 28 October, 30 October, 1 November, 1922.
82 By this time, fund raising in the Ukrainian-American community had been elevated to the level of an art. The most effective money-raising vehicle was Christmas caroling, an activity in which most Ukrainian organizations engaged and which required every Ukrainian household to set aside a certain amount of money for the many caroling groups that would visit them during the Christmas season. In addition, money collections for various Ukrainian causes were an integral part of almost every Ukrainian gathering, such as a concert, commemorative festival, and the many religious and national manifestations in which Ukrainians

participated during any one calendar year. By 1924, the UUOA had raised $15,697.72 of which $13,046.80 was sent to Europe (*Svoboda*, 2 September 1924).

83 Myshuha, "Obiednania Ukrains'kykh Organizatsii v Amerytsi," p. 133.

84 See *Svoboda*, 28 May 1926.

85 Antin Dragan, "Svoboda v Mynulomu i Suchasnomu" (*Svoboda* in the Past and Present), *Jubilee Almanac of Svoboda, 1893–1953*, p. 37.

86 Chyz, "The Ukrainian Immigrants in the United States," p. 112.

87 Dragan, "Svoboda v Mynulomy i Suchasnomu," p. 35.

88 There were approximately 2,500 disabled veterans of the Ukrainian army living in Western Ukraine in 1931. Of this number, the Ukrainian Invalids' Help Association, a voluntary organization, was able to directly assist the 502 who were most in need of financial support. Between 1923 and 1931, the UUOA and other Ukrainian-American organizations and individuals contributed a total of $58,748.54 to this organization (*Ukrains'ka Emigratsiia Ukrains'kym Invalidam* [The Ukrainian Emigration for the Ukrainian Invalids] [Lviv: The Ukrainian Invalids' Help Association, 1931], pp. 5–7; see also Chyz, p. 117).

89 By the end of 1924, there were 981 Ukrainian-American members of the Prosvita Society in Lviv of which 118 were associated with the UUOA. Other organizations which supported Prosvita in 1924 were Sich Bazaar and the Association of Ukrainian National Organizations, both in New York City. That year, the UUOA contributed $580, the Sich Bazaar (243 members) donated $546, and the Association (147 members) contributed $385 (*Amerykanskyi Prosvitianyn* [American Enlightenment] [Lviv: Prosvita Society, 1925], pp. 14, 36–7).

90 Myshuha, "Ob'iednannia Ukrains'kykh Orhanizatsii v Amerytsi," p. 136.

91 Ibid., p. 135.

92 The activities of the UYLNA and other Ukrainian youth organizations are discussed more fully in chapter 9.

93 See D. Snowyd, *Spirit of Ukraine: Ukrainian Contributions to World's Culture* (New York: The United Ukrainian Organizations of the United States, 1935), pp. 3–6.

94 Myshuha, "Ob'iednannia Ukrains'kykh Orhanizatsii v Amerytsi," p. 135.

95 Chyz, p. 116.

96 *Philadelphia Inquirer*, 1 December 1930; *Philadelphia Record*, 9 December 1930; cited in *Shistdesiat Lit Organizatsiinoho Zhittia Ukraintsiv u Filadelfii*, pp. 84–7.

97 Myshuha, "Ob'iednannia Ukrains'kykh Orhanizatsii v Amerytsi," p. 135.

98 See the *Boston Globe*, 13 November 1933; *New York Herald-Tribune*, 19 November 1933; *Chicago Daily Tribune*, 18 December 1933; *Bridgeport Post*, 27 November 1933; *Detroit Free Press*, 5 November 1933; cited in Chyz, p. 116.

99 *Chicago Daily Tribune*, 18 December 1933. Also see *Famine in Ukraine* (New York: United Ukrainian Organizations of the United States, 1934).

100 Dragan, *The Ukrainian National Association*, pp. 109–10.

101 *Ukrainian Weekly,* 5 November 1938.
102 Volodymyr Riznyk, "Pochatky ODWU u Rozbudovi ii Merezhi: Nashi Uspikhy i Trudnoshchi" (The Beginnings of ODWU and the Development of Its Affiliates: Our Successes and Problems), *Samostiina Ukraina,* October–November 1968, pp. 6–7.
103 Alexander Granovsky Private Papers, Immigration History Research Center (IHRC), the University of Minnesota, box 65; copies of the original Articles of Incorporation and the Certificate of Change of Name were placed in FBI files on 11 October 1941 (ODWU, section IV).
104 Zadoretsky, "Korotkyi Narys Istorii Sichovoi Orhanizatsii u z.d.a.," p. 371; interview with Philip Wasylowsky, 20 November 1968.
105 *Sich,* 1 June 1929.
106 See Armstrong, p. 35.
107 "Korotkyi narys istorii ODVU v Z.S.A." (A Short Outline History of ODWU in the USA), *Samostiina Ukraina,* p. 11; interview with Stephen Kuropas, 2 August 1970. Senyk-Hribiwsky traveled under a Lithuanian passport, hence the nom de guerre "Grabauskas."
108 The original English translation for ODWU was the Association for Ukrainian Regeneration. The name was officially changed to the Organization for the Rebirth of Ukraine on 6 December 1935 (see FBI files, ODWU, Section IV and Granovsky Papers, Box 65).
109 *Natsionalist,* 1 June 1936.
110 V. Riznyk, pp. 7–8.
111 Pauline Riznyk, "25 Richchia Diial'nosty Ukrains'koho Zolotoho Khresta" (25 Years of Activity of the Ukrainian Gold Cross), *Twenty-Fifth Jubilee Convention of the Ukrainian Gold Cross* (Detroit: Ukrainian Gold Cross, 1956), p. 7.
112 Pauline Riznyk and Oleh Domaratskyi, "MUN u Nedavno-Mynulomu i Suchasnomu" (MUN in the Past and Present), *Jubilee Almanac of MUN, 1933–1958* (New York: MUN, 1958), pp. 9–10.
113 V. Riznyk, p. 8.
114 Volodymyr Dushnyck, "Do Istorii Ukrains'koi Natsionalistychnoi Presy v Amerytsi" (To the History of the Ukrainian Nationalist Press in America), *Samostiina Ukraina,* October/November 1968, p. 3.
115 "Korotkyi narsy istorii ODVU v Z.S.A.," pp. 12–14; *Natsionalist,* 5 September 1935.
116 For the complete text of the resolutions passed at the congress see *Samostiina Ukraina,* October/November 1968, pp. 16–18.
117 *Svoboda,* 4 September 1935.
118 Dushnyck, pp. 3–4.
119 Born in Ukraine in 1887, Granovsky immigrated to the United States in 1913. After serving with the United States Army in France, he enrolled at the Colorado State School of Agriculture. On graduation he taught in Colorado high schools until 1922, when he enrolled at the University of Wisconsin. He received his PhD in 1925 and remained at the university as an assistant professor of economic entomology until 1930, when he

became an associate professor of entomology at the University of Minnesota. A widely published and renowned scholar, Granovsky brought prestige to the ODWU presidency, a post he held until 1961 (FBI files on Alexander Granovsky, File #62-86250-2).

120 *Natsionalist,* 15 July 1936.
121 Interview with Stephen Kuropas, 2 August 1970.
122 V. Riznyk, p. 8.
123 Interview with Ivan Popovich, 28 August 1971.
124 *Vistnyk ODVU,* October 1934.
125 *Natsionalist,* 5 July 1935.
126 Ibid., 1 December 1937.
127 Interview with Stephen Kuropas, 2 August 1970.
128 Eugene Lachowitch, "Natsionalistychnyi Providnyky" (Nationalist Leaders), *Vistnyk ODVU,* December 1932.
129 Ievhen Skotsko, "Ne Budmo Rabamy Na Chuzhyni" (Let's Not Be Serfs in the Diaspora), *Vistnyk ODVU,* January 1933.
130 *Vistnyk ODVU,* March 1934.
131 Ibid., 1 April 1935.
132 Ibid., 20 May 1935.
133 Ibid., September 1933.
134 ODWU Membership Pledge, Granovsky Papers, IHRC, Box 65.
135 *Vistnyk ODVU,* October 1934.
136 Ibid., June 1934.
137 Ibid., October 1934.
138 Ibid., January 1933.
139 *Natsionalist,* 15 February 1936.
140 Ibid., 1 November 1935.
141 Ibid., 1 January 1936.
142 Ibid., 15 August 1936.
143 *Vistnyk ODVU,* April–May 1934 and July 1934.
144 The prolific Lachowitch wrote comparative articles on the socialists, Communists, monarchists, UNDO, and the Nationalists during much of 1936 (see *Natsionalist,* 15 March–15 August 1936).
145 *Vistnyk ODVU,* April–May 1934.
146 Ibid., 1 April 1935.
147 *Natsionalist,* 15 May 1936.
148 *Vistnyk ODVU,* July 1934.
149 *Obizhnyk ODVU,* 4 October 1933, Granovsky Papers, IHRC, Box 65.
150 *Vistnyk ODVU,* January 1933.
151 Ibid., March 1934.
152 *Natsionalist,* 1 April 1936.
153 *Vistnyk ODVU,* March 1934.
154 Even though the Nazi party was in ascendancy in 1934, Hitler had not as yet consolidated his control over the party and the German people. Hindenburg was still president of Germany and Hitler's chief party rival, Ernest Roehm, had not been eliminated. As chancellor, Hitler's major

domestic objective was the eradication of unemployment. This was partially accomplished between 1933 and 1937 when the number of jobless fell from 6 to 1 million. Hitler's two goals in the foreign policy arena were the removal of the shackles of the Versailles Treaty and rearmament without the risk of war. Significantly, the Nazis were anxious to gain world approval for the "New Germany" and welcomed visitors from other countries, especially Great Britain and the United States. Lloyd George visited in 1936 and publicly praised Hitler as a "great man." During the 1936 Olympics, writes Shirer, visitors from England and America "were greatly impressed by what they saw: apparently a happy, healthy, friendly people united with Hitler – a far different picture, they said, than they had got from reading newspaper dispatches from Berlin." Persecution of Jews, while clearly evident for those who wished to look below the surface, was carefully hidden from foreign eyes (Shirer, *The Rise and Fall of the Third Reich* I:218–55).

155 *Vistnyk ODVU*, April–May 1934.
156 *Natsionalist*, 1 January 1936.
157 Ibid.
158 *Natsionalist*, 15 August 1936.
159 Ibid., 1 October 1936.
160 Ibid.
161 Ibid., 15 November 1936.
162 Chyz had replaced Nicholas Ceglinsky – who had had a falling out with Sichynsky earlier – soon after the latter became UWA president. An incredible survivor, Ceglinsky returned to *Narodna Volya* when Sichynsky himself was dumped in 1941 and Chyz and Levytsky were forced out. Levytsky then became editor of *Hromadsky Holos* (FBI memo [16 May 1942], File #61-10850, UNA, section 1). Attached to this particular memo is a long overview of Ukrainian-American organizational life obviously written from a socialist perspective. Given the erudite language, the overview was probably prepared by Jaroslav Chyz. Also see *Forum*, Spring 1982, pp. 23–4.
163 *Vistnyk ODVU*, June 1934.
164 *Natsionalist*, 15 June 1936.
165 *Narodna Volya*, 4 January 1936.
166 Ibid., 16 January 1936.
167 Ibid., 31 March 1936.
168 Ibid., 25 January 1936.
169 Ibid., 16 April 1936.
170 *Visti*, 3 January 1935.
171 *Natsionalist*, 1 October 1937.
172 Ibid., 15 February 1938; see also *Narodna Volya*, 15 January 1938.
173 See *Natsionalist*, 15 November 1937.
174 Ibid., 1 November 1937.
175 Ibid., 13 July 1938.
176 Ibid., 17 August 1938.

177 Ibid., 15 May 1938.

178 The socialists disputed Konovalets's popularity. "Not even 100% Nationalists grieve for Konovalets," wrote *Narodna Volya*. "He was a fixation of the Provid ... Many Nationalists paid more attention to Hitler than to Konovalets" (*Narodna Volya*, 23 June 1938).

179 *Natsionalist*, 7 September 1938; interview with Volodymyr Riznyk, 28 August 1971.

180 *Natsionalist*, 7 September 1938.

181 Ibid., 14 September 1938.

182 Ibid., 7 September 1938.

183 *Visti*, 11 September 1938.

184 *Narodna Volya*, 20 May 1939.

185 Petro Stercho, "Dopomoha ODVU Karpats'kyi Ukraini" (ODWU's Support of Carpatho-Ukraine), *Samostiina Ukraina*, October/November 1968, pp. 31–3; see also *Svoboda*, 7 September 1938.

186 *Natsionalist*, 7 September 1938.

187 Stercho, "Dopomoha ODVU Karpats'kyi Ukraini."

188 Michael C. Lapica, "The Rise of Carpatho-Ukraine," *The Trident*, January–February 1939.

189 Stercho, "Dopomoha ODVU Karpats'kyi Ukraini," pp. 33–7.

190 *Natsionalist*, 11 January 1939.

191 Ibid., 25 January 1939.

192 Ibid., 22 February 1939.

193 Ibid., 11 January 1939.

194 Ibid., 15 February 1939.

195 Ibid., 22 February 1939.

196 Ibid., 5 April 1939.

197 Ibid., 3 May 1939.

198 Ibid., 19 April 1939.

199 Ibid.

200 Ibid., 31 May 1939.

201 *Narodna Volya*, 10 June 1939.

202 Ibid., 15 and 17 June 1939.

203 *Natsionalist*, 14 June 1939.

204 *Ukrainian Weekly*, 1 July 1939.

205 *Narodna Volya*, 2 September 1939.

206 Warzeski, "Religion and National Consciousness in the History of the Rusins," p. 233. See also Michael Roman, "With Unclean and Bloody Hands," *Viestnik*, 9 September 1954.

207 *Time*, 23 January 1939.

208 *American Observer*, 31 May 1939.

209 *Look*, 14 March 1939.

210 *Natsionalist*, 31 May 1939.

211 *Ukrainian Weekly*, 10 December 1938.

212 V.S. Dushnyck, "What Ukraine Wants," *The Trident*, January–February 1939.

213 "The Ninth ODWU Convention," *The Trident*, July–August 1939.

214 *Ukraine,* 12 July 1939.

215 Stachiw purposely substituted "Nazionalist" for "Nationalist" in most of his English-language articles and justified it on the basis of a 1935 publication by Mykola Sciborsky entitled "Natsiokratiia" – which Stachiw chose to spell "Nazicratia." Written, in part, as a response to Lypynskyi's concept of "kliasokratiia" (classocracy), the title of Sciborsy's monograph should have been spelled correctly if the reviewer were concerned with accuracy (Paul Stachiw, "Those Who Live in Glass Houses ... ," *Narodna Volya,* 27 July 1939).

216 V.S. Dushnyck, "Ukraine and the Balance of Power," *The Trident,* June 1939.

217 V.S. Dushnyck, "No Peace without Ukraine," *The Trident,* September 1939.

218 V.S. Dushnyck, "Finland and Ukraine," *The Trident,* December 1939.

219 U.S. Congress, House of Representatives, *Investigation of Un-American Propaganda Activities in the United States,* pp. 5259–60.

220 Ibid., pp. 5262–70.

221 Ibid., p. 5271.

222 Ibid., p. 5301.

223 Ibid., p. 5303.

224 Ibid., pp. 5306–7.

225 Ibid., p. 5309.

226 Ibid., pp. 5307–14.

227 Ibid., p. 5317–5318.

228 Ibid., pp. 5315–16.

229 Ibid., p. 5316.

230 Ibid., p. 5320.

231 Ibid., p. 5317.

232 Ibid., p. 5319.

233 Ibid., p. 5321.

234 Ibid., p. 5318.

235 Ibid., p. 5321.

236 Ibid., p. 5288.

237 Ibid., p. 5293.

238 Ibid., pp. 5297–5305.

239 Ibid., p. 5305.

240 Ibid., pp. 5305–11.

241 Ibid., pp. 5263, 5285, 5294.

242 Ibid., pp. 5297, 5319.

243 Ibid., p. 5280.

244 Ibid., p. 5322.

245 *Chicago Daily News,* 28 September 1939.

246 "Dies Demands Reds and Bund List Members: Aroused over Account of Ukrainian Activity," *Chicago Daily Tribune,* 29 September 1939.

247 Revyuk had more than one reason to testify as he did. First of all, he had been a socialist for most of his adult life and though he worked within

the nationalist framework of the UNA and the UUOA, he was probably inclined to socialism in 1939. More significant, however, was Revyuk's dislike of OUN, ODWU, and Dr. Myshuha. Approached by Colonel Konovalets during the OUN leader's visit to America in 1929, Revyuk refused to cooperate in the organization of ODWU, arguing that the United States had too many Ukrainian organizations already and that the UUOA filled the need for a strong anti-Bolshevik front. When Konovalets went ahead without him, Revyuk attempted to stifle ODWU's development. He was convinced that his later demotion from editor in chief of *Svoboda* to associate editor was the result of his earlier opposition to Konovalets. Revyuk also believed that Luka Myshuha, his successor at *Svoboda*, had helped engineer his ouster (FBI memo [15 March 1943], File #100-1309, Luka Myshuha).

248 No mention was made, for example, of the many favorable references to the United States found on the pages of the ODWU press. Nor were the far more numerous citations renouncing fascism, Nazism, and Hitler ever entered into the record. Instead, only carefully extracted quotations that appeared to cast ODWU in a bad light were submitted and even then the context and circumstances were omitted.

Matthews, for example, consistently added the phrases "in Berlin" or "in Germany" whenever Revyuk spoke about the Provid. In reality, very few Provid members lived in Berlin. Konovalets himself lived in Geneva, where he moved in 1930 after the Polish press began to associate OUN with Germany. Other Provid members lived in Paris, Brussels, and Prague. OUN representatives also lived in Rome and Vienna. Letter from Ie. Konovalets to K. Lissiuk (26 April 1930), FBI file, ODWU, section III.

249 In a book published in 1940, Congressman Dies wrote that he asked himself ten questions in attempting to determine if a particular group had Nazi tendencies:

1 Does the organization through its leaders and literature laud the achievement of Adolf Hitler?
2 Does the organization use the swastika as its emblem? ...
3 Is the Nazi salute used at the gatherings of the organization or when its members greet each other? ...
4 Does the organization use German consular or diplomatic officers as speakers for its gatherings? ...
5 Does the organization circulate or reprint official Nazi propaganda emanating from the propaganda ministry in Germany?
6 Does the organization have fraternal or cooperative relations with Nazi-minded groups? ...
7 Has the organization gone on record against Nazism as unequivocally as it has against communism?
8 Does the organization have uniformed "storm troopers" or advocate the formation and use of private military groups for dealing with its chosen enemies?

9 Does the organization advocate and disseminate racial hatred?

10 Does the organization follow the "line" of the Nazis in promulgating an anti-democratic and pro-totalitarian system of government? ... Do they teach the doctrine of "fuehrership" or a "strong man" in national affairs?

(Martin Dies, *The Trojan Horse in America* [New York: Dodd & Mead Co., 1940], pp. 22–4)

250 Ogden, *The Dies Committee*, p. 177.

251 *Ukraine*, 11 October 1939.

252 Ibid., 29 November 1939.

253 Like Revyuk, Kedrovsky was an editor of *Svoboda* when he was approached by Konovalets to help organize ODWU in 1929. He refused and together with Revyuk attempted to stifle ODWU within his sphere of influence. Later, he lost his position with *Svoboda*, was defeated in a reelection bid for UUOA financial secretary, and was forced to resign from a post he held with the consistory of the Ukrainian Autocephalous Orthodox church—only to be replaced by Theodore Swystun, an ODWU activist. Kedrovsky blamed all his humiliations on Konovalets, OUN, Myshuha, and ODWU (FBI memo [12 December 1941], File #100-249, ODWU, Section IV).

254 Once an associate of Konovalets in both the Sichovi Striltsi and UVO, Chyz became disenchanted with OUN leaders while still in Europe. Immigrating to America, he joined the staff of *Narodna Volya* and became an activist in the socialist camp. Testifying before the Dies Committee, Chyz declared that the Nationalists had worked on behalf of the Nazis during the dismemberment of Czechoslovakia. He also alleged that ODWU was engaged in terrorist activities, giving as one of his examples the physical attack on Hrivnak in Passaic in 1934 (FBI memo [15 March 1943] File #100-309, Luka Myshuha).

255 *Minneapolis Times*, 11 January 1940; see also *Ukraine*, 26 January 1940.

256 Interview with Stephen Kuropas, 2 August 1970.

257 *Narodna Volya*, 4 November 1939.

258 *Ukraine*, 29 November 1939.

259 Ibid., 13 December 1939.

260 Ibid., 9 February 1940.

261 Ibid., 23 February 1940.

262 Ibid., 26 April 1940.

263 Also elected to the national executive were Gregory Herman, Maria Malievych, Dmytro Halychyn, Roman Slobodian, and Luka Myshuha of the UNA; F. Volodymyr Lotovych, Theodore Chemerys, Ivan Borysevych, and Volodymyr Lototsky from Providence; Miroslaw Sichynsky, Volodymyr Levytsky, Theodore Mynyk, Peter Duchak, and Yaroslav Chyz of the UWA; and Michael Markiv, Ivan Soroka, and Matthew Chandoha from the UNAA (*The Story of the Ukrainian Congress Committee of America* [New York: The Ukrainian Congress Committee of America, 1951], p. 11).

264 Organizations with representatives on the UCCA advisory board included the Ukrainian National Women's League of America, the Ukrainian Youth League of North America, the Ukrainian Catholic Youth League, the Organization for the Defense of Lemkivshchyna, the Women's League, Chornomorska Sich, the Association of Former Soldiers (Striletska Hromada), the United Ukrainian Organizations, the Organization of Ukrainian Professionals, ODWU, UHO, MUN, and the Ukrainian Gold Cross (ibid., p. 10).

265 Ibid., pp. 10–11.

266 *Ukraine*, 24 May 1940.

267 Ibid., p. 12.

268 A few months after the Ukrainian congress in Washington, former Dies Committee investigator John C. Metcalfe telephoned the FBI to inform them that the UCCA "is a Nazi outfit" (FBI memo to E.A. Tamm from K.R. McIntire [9 September 1940], File #102-8-X5, ODWU, Section I).

269 Cited in Summarized Translation of Pamphlet Distributed at the XXth UNA Convention (FBI files, UNA, Section II; also in FBI files, ODWU, Section VI).

270 *Ukraine*, 30 August 1940.

271 Ibid., 6 and 13 September 1940.

272 Ibid., 13 September 1940.

273 Ibid., 15 October 1940.

274 *The Hour*, 27 July 1940.

275 Ibid., 10 August 1940.

276 While in the United States, he described the Nationalists as "the flower of the Ukrainian nation" (see *Ukraine*, 16 August 1940).

277 *PM*, 29 September 1940; cited in *Ukraine*, 1 October 1940.

278 See *Ukraine*, 1 December 1940.

279 *The Hour*, 19 December 1940.

280 *Ukraine*, 13 September 1940.

281 See *Svoboda*, 1 and 3 February 1941.

282 FBI memo (15 March 1943), File #100-9002-37, Luka Myshuha.

283 *The Hour*, 8 February 1941.

284 Ibid., 15 April 1941.

285 Ibid., 1 November 1941.

286 *Time*, 30 June 1941.

287 *The Hour*, 1 November 1941.

288 "Our Stand," *Ukrainian Weekly*, 28 July 1941.

289 See Lyons, *The Red Decade*, pp. 344–5.

290 Louis Adamic, *Two Way Passage* (New York: Harper & Bros., 1941), p. 132.

291 FBI memo (15 March 1943), File #100-9002-37, Luka Myshuha.

292 Adamic, *Two Way Passage*, pp. 132–3.

293 Ibid., pp. 123–6.

294 Ibid., p. 126.

295 "Mr. Adamic and Ukrainian Americans," *Ukrainian Weekly*, 20 October 1941.

296 Sayers and Kahn, *Sabotage!* p. 85.

297 Ibid., pp. 93–4.
298 Ibid., p. 82.
299 Ibid., p. 86.
300 Ibid., pp. 87–90.
301 The envelope, which was from a John V. Sweet, had postmarks and
     stamps that were difficult to recognize. Nevertheless, the caption read:
     "This envelope contained certain documents which were sent from Axis
     territory in Asia to Luke Myshuha's *Svoboda* offices in Jersey City, N.J.
     Myshuha's offices served as a clearing house for confidential directives
     from Berlin, Rome, and Tokyo."
302 Sayers and Kahn, *Sabotage!* p. 95.
303 See photostatic copy of the letter, dated 20 May 1943, in Dragan, *The
     Ukrainian National Association*, p. 115.
304 See Sayers and Kahn, *Sabotage! The Secret War against America*, rev. ed.
     (New York: Metro Publications, 1944).
305 A year after *Sabotage!* was published in the United States, a similar
     "exposé" entitled *This Is Our Land* appeared in Canada. Written by
     Raymond Arthur Davies, the book condemned the Canadian UHO and
     the Ukrainian National Federation (ODWU's counterpart in Canada)
     as "fascist organizations" engaged in "fifth column" activities. Citing
     from the Dies Committee report, *Sabotage!* and *The Hour*, Davies
     attempted to demonstrate the existence of an international conspiracy
     against the Allied war effort. The Ukrainian Canadian Committee, a coali-
     tion similar to the UCCA, was also taken to task for its "anti-Soviet, anti-
     Polish, and anti-Czechoslovak agitation" (see Raymond Arthur Davies,
     This Is Our Land: Ukrainian Canadians against Hitler (Toronto: Progress
     Books, 1943).
306 See cover of the 1944 edition of *Sabotage!*
307 *The Hour*, 5 September 1942.
308 "What's Behind the Smear Campaign," *Ukrainian Weekly*, 3 October
     1942.
309 "The Effrontery of It," *Ukrainian Weekly*, 28 November 1942.
310 FBI memo to E.A. Tamm from K.R. McIntire (7 December 1939), File #102-
     8-X1, ODWU, Section I.
311 FBI memo to Special Agent in Charge, Newark, New Jersey, from John
     Edgar Hoover (9 January 1941), File #100-9002-1, Luka Myshuha.
312 FBI memo to Special Agent in Charge, New York, from John Edgar
     Hoover (16 May 1942), File #61-10497-2, UNA, Section I.
313 FBI file on Gregory Herman, beginning 8 November 1940, File #100-4653
     and ending 11 January 1946, File #100-4653-32.
314 Granovsky's file (#62-86250) does not begin until 25 February 1948. The
     first five pages have been culled.
315 Department of Justice memo to J. Edgar Hoover from Matthew J.
     McGuire, Asst. to the Attorney General (4 April 1941), File #102-8-X23,
     ODWU, Section I. The complete text of the Voorhis Act was attached.

316 Letter to K. Lissiuk from the High Command of the Ukrainian Military Organization (13 November 1929). Draft of Constitution attached. FBI File #102-8-1X1, ODWU, Section III.

317 Letter to Frank J. Wilson, Chief, Secret Service Division from J. Edgar Hoover (10 April 1941), FBI File #61-10497-32, UNA, Section I.

318 Letter to Visa Division from Lemuel B. Schofield, Special Assistant to the Attorney General, FBI File #61-10497-33, UNA, Section I.

319 FBI memo (6 December 1941), File #100-5936, ODWU, Section IX.

320 FBI memo (11 October 1940), File #61-9183-10, UHO, Section I.

321 FBI memo (15 December 1941), File #61-10497, UNA, Section III.

322 FBI memo (19 May 1941), File #61-9183-21, UHO, Section I.

323 FBI memo (1 October 1941), File 361-10497, ODWU, Section III.

324 FBI memo (6 October 1942), File #61-10497-121, UNA, Section V.

325 FBI memo (7 April 1943), File 365-1389DB, UHO, Section IV.

326 FBI memo (12 December 1941), File #100-259, ODWU, Section IX.

327 The UNA executive would have happily fired Revyuk were it not for their fear of the negative publicity the move would inspire (interview with Stephen Kuropas, 8 August 1982).

328 FBI memo (15 March 1943), File #100-9002-37, Luka Myshuha.

329 Memo to Lawrence M.C. Smith, Chief, Special Defense Unit, from J. Edgar Hoover (20 November 1941), File #102-8-62, ODWU, Section X.

330 FBI memo (12 December 1941), File #100-259, ODWU, Section IX.

331 FBI memo (7 November 1941), File #102-8-21, ODWU, Section VI.

332 FBI memo (12 January 1942), File #100-1309, Luka Myshuha.

333 FBI memo (15 March 1943), File #100-9002-37, Luka Myshuha.

334 Ibid.

335 FBI memo (24 November 1943) File #61-10497-71, UNA, Section VI. Also see memorandum for James R. Sharp from Asher William Schwartz (10 October 1943).

336 FBI memo (22 May 1944), File #61-10497-176, UNA, Section VI.

337 See *Svoboda* 21 August 1941.

338 Stephen Kuropas, "Vidznachynnia 30 Chervnia i Ameryka" (Commemoration of June 30 and America), *Samostiina Ukraina*, July–August 1981.

339 FBI file (28 November 1941), File #102-8-38, ODWU, Section VII.

340 Ibid.

341 Copy of Report Presented to the Department of Justice under Public Law 870 (1 January 1942), Granovsky Papers, IHRC, Box 69.

342 Interview with Stephen Kuropas, 8 August 1982.

343 Summarized translation of pamphlet distributed at the twentieth UNA convention, FBI files, UNA, Section II.

344 Dragan, *U Dzerkali Koventsii UNS* (The Conventions of the UNA) (Jersey City: Svoboda Press, 1982), p. 51. Interview with Stephen Kuropas, 8 August 1982.

345 FBI memo (15 March 1943), File #100-9002-37, Luka Myshuha. Interview with Stephen Kuropas, 8 August 1982.

346 Interview with Stephen Kuropas, 8 August 1982.

347 The group included Prof. Nicholas Chubaty, John Panchuk, Wasyl Dovhan, John Evanchuk, Marcel Wagner, Wasyl Onyskiw, Nicholas Dutkevych, and Roman Smook (*The Story of the Ukrainian Congress Committee*, p. 14).

348 Ibid., p. 19.

349 Also elected to the executive were: John Panchuk, Walter Gallan, Wasyl Shabatura, and Olena Shtogryn, vice-presidents; Stephen Kurlak, recording secretary; Bohdan Katamay, financial secretary; Dmytro Halychyn, treasurer; Rev. V. Bilinsky, V. Fedash, W. Dovhan, Rev. V. Bilon, Rev. H. Pytiuk, N. Chubaty, L. Cehelsky, C. Olesnicky, O. Zaporozhets, A. Malanchuk, Rev. A. Kist, A. Granovsky, and M. Chemny, advisors; G. Zepko, C. Khomiak, L. Myshuha, J. Evanchuk, M. Demydchuk, and N. Dutkevych, auditors (ibid., pp. 13–21).

350 Ibid., pp. 18–19.

Chapter 8

1 It is interesting to note that Rome decided on Ukrainian-Ruthenian coadministration of the exarchy not when relations between the two groups were at their lowest but, rather, when ties—as evidenced by the later decision of a great number of Ruthenians to unite with Galicia and Bukovina—seemed to be improving.

2 Since a number of Ukrainian Catholic parishes were without priests, another ploy of Bishop Aleksander of the Russian Orthodox church was to "appoint" Orthodox priests to these parishes. Most of them were rejected by the parishioners, but in one case, the Ukrainian Catholic church in Butler, Pennsylvania, the majority decided for Orthodoxy and refused to oust the priest. The ownership of the church finally had to be settled in a civil court which ruled in favor of the Catholic minority. See Peter Poniatyshyn, "Iz Chasiv Administratsii Eparkhii" (From the Times of Eparchical Administration), *Jubilee Almanac of the Ukrainian Greek Catholic Church in America*, p. 112.

3 Poniatyshyn's relationship with the Hungarians was greatly aided by the fact that Father Victor Kovalitsky, the pastor of the Hungarian church in Perth Amboy, spoke both Ukrainian and Hungarian fluently (ibid., pp. 111–14).

4 Procko, pp. 49–52.

5 After an eight-year hiatus, the Holy See appointed a successor to Ortynsky only four months after the arrival in America of Bishop Theodorovich of the Ukrainian Autocephalous Orthodox church. The first Ukrainian Orthodox church in America was founded in Chicago in 1915 and by 1924 was growing at a rate that was disquieting to the Ukrainian Catholic leadership.

6 Sochocky, p. 275; Warzewski, pp. 246–8.

7 The son of a priest, Bohachevsky served for a time as a village pastor and

later, after receiving a doctorate in theology from the University of Innsbruck, as pastor of the Cathedral Church in Peremyshl, professor of theology in the Peremyshl seminary, and finally, vicar-general of the diocese. During the war years he had been an army chaplain and had organized relief work during the Ukrainian-Polish war. For his latter efforts he was jailed for a brief period in the Polish prison of Dbie, near Cracow. See Sochocky, pp. 276–7.

8 Cited in ibid., pp. 276–7.

9 Procko, pp. 53–9; Paska, pp. 76–82; Danilo Bohachevsky, *Vladyka Konstantyn Bohachevskyi, Pershyi Mytropolyt Ukrainskoi Katolytskoi Tserkvy v ZSA* (Bishop Constantine Bohachevsky, First Metropolitan of the Ukrainian Catholic Church in the USA) (Philadelphia: America Publishers, 1980), pp. 34–40.

10 Mamchur, pp. 71–2.

11 See complete text of *Cum Episcopo* in Warzewski, pp. 289–92.

12 Mamchur, p. 71; Bohachevsky, pp. 35–41.

13 Sochocky, p. 7.

14 *Svoboda,* 24 December 1926.

15 *Sich,* 15 December 1926.

16 *America,* 23 December 1926. By this time, Dr. Osyp Nazaruk, who had left *Sich,* was the editor of *America.*

17 Ukrainian-American lay leaders argued that since many of the ethnonational leaders in Galicia had been sons of priests – then the most educationally advanced stratum of Ukrainian society – celibacy would deprive the Ukrainian people of an invaluable reservoir of national leadership (Mamchur, p. 89).

18 *Svoboda,* 31 December 1926; Paska, pp. 82–6; Procko, pp. 58–9.

19 *Svoboda,* 3 January 1927.

20 Sochocky, p. 281; Procko, p. 59; Bohachevsky, p. 38.

21 *Svoboda,* 16 February 1927.

22 Ibid., 25 February 1927; Bohachevsky, pp. 36–9.

23 Sochocky, p. 281.

24 *Svoboda,* 25 May 1927. For the text of Father Strutynsky's retraction see *Katolytsky Provid,* 1 December 1927.

25 *Svoboda,* 24 June 1927.

26 Sochocky, p. 281.

27 Bohachevsky, pp. 38–9.

28 Mamchur, p. 72.

29 *Katolytsky Provid,* 1 September 1927.

30 Ambrose Senyshyn, "Ukrainian Catholics in the United States," *Eastern Churches Quarterly,* October–December 1946, pp. 415–52; also see the *Double Jubilee Book of the Sisters Servants of Mary Immaculate, Immaculate Conception Province* (Sloatsburg, NY, 1985).

31 Mamchur, p. 216.

32 Sochocky, p. 278.

33 Mamchur, pp. 215–17.

34 Interview with Stephen Kuropas, 16 August 1970.

35 Mamchur, p. 211.

36 The younger generation was especially alienated by the length of the divine liturgy, the difficulties encountered when they tried to confess their sins to a European-born priest in the English language, missing school to attend a Julian calendar religious observance, the amount of kneeling and standing required during the divine liturgy, the separation of sexes during religious services, as well as such hygienic matters as receiving communion from the same spoon as everyone else and the passing around of the gospel book for everyone to kiss (ibid., p. 212).

37 *Svoboda*, 11 January 1927.

38 Mamchur, pp. 212–14.

39 Ibid., p. 48.

40 Bohachevsky, pp. 39–40.

41 Letter to the author from Rev. John Terlecky, 8 March 1989.

42 Paska, pp. 76–80.

43 Ibid., pp. 82–4.

44 Cited in Bohachevsky, pp. 39–40.

45 Procko, p. 61.

46 Cited in ibid., p. 63.

47 *America*, 29 August 1933; cited in Procko, p. 63.

48 Procko, pp. 64–83.

49 See St. Nicholas Church Council Minutes for 25 January 1914, 1 June 1914, and 7 February 1915.

50 The exact reasons for the exodus are rather obscure and appear to be more personal than national. It is known that the new St. Nicholas Church was then under construction and that there was some dissatisfaction with the amount of time this was taking. It is also fairly well established that the parish was in financial difficulty, and that Father Strutynsky, a dynamic and powerful man, was rather authoritarian and cavalier in his administration of the parish. Finally, there seems to be a general consensus that the precipitating cause for the exodus was the fact that during an especially heated debate over church affairs with members of the church council, Father Strutynsky grabbed a wooden cross and struck one of his more vociferous opponents on the head. See St. Nicholas Church Council Minutes for 1913 and 1914; interview with Father (later Bishop) Hundiak, 26 February 1969; "Do Istorii Ukrains'koho Pravoslavnoho Rukhu v Chikago, Ill." (On the History of the Ukrainian Orthodox Movement in Chicago, Ill.), *Dnipro*, May 1946, pp. 5–6.

51 At this time Dr. Hrynevetsky was still a radical socialist and, therefore, probably a nonbeliever as well. His decision to support the Ukrainian National church was most likely due to his conviction at the time that the masses should be given a greater voice in those decision-making processes which directly affected their lives. Hrynevetsky was later converted to Catholicism, largely through the efforts of Revs. Steciuk and Tarnawsky of St. Nicholas. After his conversion, Hrynevetsky became a

devout Catholic and, as Supreme Otaman of the Hetman Sich, played a crucial role in influencing the organization to support Bishop Bohachevsky. Interview with Dmytro Atamanec, 6 March 1969.

52 Mamchur, p. 101. Also see John Hundiak, "The National, Independent Church and the Origin of the Ukrainian Orthodox Church," *Ukrainians and Their Church*, ed. Rev. Peter Bilon (Johnstown, Pa: The Western Pa. Regional Branch of the UOL, 1953), p. 23.

53 Mamchur, pp. 101–2.

54 Ibid., pp. 102–3.

55 Ibid., pp. 103–4; Hundiak, p. 23.

56 Yuzyk, *The Ukrainian Greek Orthodox Church of Canada, 1918–1951*, pp. 119–20.

57 Mamchur, p. 124.

58 Ibid., pp., 109–11. In 1927 the Bolshevik government had forced Metropolitan Lypkivsky to resign and during the next two years various leaders of the original church were imprisoned, exiled, arrested, or simply shot. In 1929, the church was ordered dissolved and, in 1930, an essentially new Autocephalous church was established totally under Soviet control.

59 Mamchur, pp. 112–16.

60 Ibid., p. 130.

61 *Dnipro*, press organ of the Autocephalous church, carried a series of articles and letters – signed by priests and faithful – condemning the two priests for their exodus. Especially harsh were references to Hundiak who was accused of having socialist leanings (*Dnipro*, 15 August 1931).

62 Mamchur, p. 124.

63 Ibid, p. 127.

64 Father Zhuk, who had a doctorate in theology, was very popular with his fellow Ukrainian Catholic priests in America. After Ortynsky's death, a petition was circulated and forwarded to Rome requesting Zhuk's appointment as Ortynsky's successor. According to Father Hundiak, Bohachevsky was threatened by Zhuk's popularity, and at one point attempted to have him recalled to Ukraine. As one of the "New York 26" who refused to retract, Zhuk was excommunicated. (See Mamchur, p. 127; interview with Father Hundiak, 26 February 1969.)

65 Mamchur, p. 105.

66 Ibid., p. 129. It is difficult to determine why Zhuk acted as he did. Some believe it was because of his ambition. Others have argued that after having waited for over a year he came to believe that the patriarch would never agree to his consecration and, in an effort to gain status in the Ukrainian community, he agreed to the move.

67 Mamchur, pp. 128–31.

68 Ibid., p. 106. No figures are available for the exact number of former Catholics belonging to the two Orthodox dioceses. A conservative estimate is 70 percent.

69 Ibid.

70 Ibid., p. 118.
71 Halich, *Ukrainians in the United States*, p. 103. See also *Dnipro*, 1 October 1934.
72 Francis Donahue, "The Ukrainian Orthodox Church: Past, Present and Future," *The Trident*, April 1941, pp. 7–8. See also *Dnipro*, 1 March 1937.
73 Hundiak, p. 24.
74 *Ukrainians and Their Church*, p. 8. Also see *Dnipro*, 1 October 1938.
75 Basil Tremba, *Inside Story of the Ukrainian Church* (Woonsocket, RI: St. Michael's Ukrainian Catholic Church, n.d.). Father Tremba, the author of the cited reference, was pastor of a parish in Woonsocket which later voted to join the Ukrainian Autocephalous Orthodox church. See *Dnipro*, 1 October 1934.
76 Interview with Stephen Kuropas, 16 August 1970; interview with Nicholas Olek, 12 February 1972. See also *Dnipro*, 1 September 1937.
77 Theodore Swystun, "Iakos to bude" (Somehow It Will Be), *Dnipro*, 15 February 1938.
78 *Golden Jubilee Book of the First Ukrainian Presbyterian Church*, p. 6.
79 Halich, p. 110.
80 *Golden Jubilee Book of the First Ukrainian Presbyterian Church*, pp. 6–7.
81 Domashovets, "Narys Istorii Ukrains'koi Ievanhe's'koho-Baptyts'koi Tserkvy," pp. 379–81.
82 Halich, p. 106.
83 For the complete text of the decree, see Warzewski, pp. 343–9.
84 For an account of the long and often bitter struggle that developed over church ownership and that was finally resolved in American courts, see Warzewski, pp. 269–83.
85 According to Warzewski, the GCU had suffered a number of serious financial reversals during this period and became involved in the church conflict as a means of diverting its membership's attention from its own shortcomings (Warzewski, pp. 216–62).
86 Ibid., pp. 261–5.
87 Ibid., pp. 284–7.
88 Ibid., pp. 254–78 and 311. Also see "An Appreciation: On the Occasion of the 30th Anniversary of the Consecration to the Espiscopacy of Metropolitan Orestes Chornock, 1938–1968," St. Michael's Church, Binghamton, New York (10 November 1968).
89 *Viestnik*, 4 April 1933; cited in Warzewski, p. 311.
90 A.M. Smor, "Against the Ukrainianizational Rome," *Viestnik*, 12 April 1934; cited in Warzewski, p. 311.
91 Warzewski, pp. 289–90.
92 Ibid., pp. 232–34. Significantly, the major source for the alleged atrocities was a book written by Dr. Hubert Ripka, the Czech editor of *Prague-Moscow* and a Sovietophile. See H. Ripka, *Munich: Before and After* (London: The Macmillan Company, 1939), pp. 261–3.
93 *Viestnik*, 9 September 1954; cited in Warzewski, p. 312.

Chapter 9

1 The Ukrainian Circle of Self-Education was organized in 1916 by Kyrylo Bilyk while he was still a university student in Chicago. Originally established to teach English to new immigrants, the circle expanded its curriculum as more and more professionals and students – then in Chicago to pursue their higher education – volunteered their services on a part-time basis. Lectures were presented by Dr. Simenovych, Dr. Hrynevetsky, and university students such as Roman Smook (later a lawyer), Semen Kochy (later a dentist), and H.G. Skehar (later a dentist). The circle grew, in time, to a membership of some eighty people of various ages. A library of approximately 200 books was created for members. At first the circle was associated with the Defense of Ukraine organization; later it came under the leadership of the Ukrainian Communists. It was absorbed by the Sich in 1926.

2 *Ukraina*, 14 August 1919.

3 Ibid., 14 August 1920.

4 Ibid., 21 August 1920.

5 Adult education among Ukrainians did not disappear entirely, however. The Sich organization, as we have seen, played a significant role in this area of endeavor in the 1920s. When its influence began to decline, other organizations emerged to fill the void. In Chicago, for example, the Ukrainian American Social Club was established in the early 1930s. According to Dmytro Atamanec, many wives had begun to complain to him that their husands were drinking and playing cards in various taverns once they were no longer in Sich, adding that they never knew where they were. Atamanec and several others organized the club and, in time, rented a storefront for the exclusive use of its members. A bar was installed and members drank and played cards there, recalls Atamanec, but "we had formal meetings at least twice a month where lectures by Dr. Hrynevetsky and others were offered on various educational topics ... and the wives knew where their husbands were" (Interview with Dmytro Atamanec, 6 February 1969).

6 Ibid.

7 The amendment granting suffrage to American women was ratified by the thirty-sixth state in 1920.

8 Chyz, "Ukrainian Women and Their Organizations," p. 231.

9 Other members of the executive were Katherine Kociubynsky, executive secretary; Maria Pidhaya, Katherine Kushchak, Katherine Bunda, secretaries; Maria Koroloyshyn, Anna Muzyka, Olha Korinovsky, treasurers; Eugenia Tsishetsky, Sofia Banach, Anastasia Yazlovetsky, Emily Strutynsky, Barbara Kurey, Eudokia Budhyk, organizers (ibid., p. 236; see also *Ranna Zoria*, January–February 1918).

10 "Poklyk" (A Call), *Ranna Zoria*, March–April 1918, pp. 60–2.

11 Ibid., p. 64.

12 Chyz, "Ukrainian Women and Their Organizations," p. 236.

13 "Desiat Lit Pratsi Ukrains'koi Zhinochoi Hromady v N'u Yorku" (Ten Years of Work of the Ukrainian Women's Society of New York), *Jubilee Almanac of the Ukrainian Women's Society of New York, 1921–1931*, pp. 5–24.

14 Stefanie Abrahamovska, "P'iatnadtsiat' Lit Pratsi Soiuz Ukrainok Ameryky, Chastyna Persha, 1925–1934" (Fifteen Years of Work of the League of Ukrainian Women of America, Part I, 1925–1934), *Jubilee Book of Soiuz Ukrainok, 1925–1940*, pp. 7–43; Chyz, "Ukrainian Women and Their Organizations," p. 238; Helen Lototsky, "Soiuz Ukrainok Ameryky" (The League of Ukrainian Women of America), *Zhinochyi Svit*, June–July 1933.

15 While it supported the UNWLA program initially and claimed, for a time, to be the "organ of the Ukrainian Women's League of America," *Zhinochyi Svit* was never formally recognized by the UNWLA as its official journal.

16 *Zhinochyi Svit*, May 1933.

17 Ibid., October–November 1933.

18 Ibid., January–February 1934.

19 Ibid.

20 Annette Kmetz, "P'iatnadtsiat' Lit Pratsi Soiuzu Ukrainok Ameryky, 1934–1940, Chastyna Druha" (Fifteen Years of Work of the League of Ukrainian Women of America, 1934–1940, Part II), *Jubilee Book of Soiuz Ukrainok, 1925–1940*, pp. 46–52.

21 Chyz, "Ukrainian Women and Their Organizations," pp. 239–44. One branch, no. 62, was located in Prudentopolis, Brazil.

22 Ibid., p. 240.

23 Ibid., pp. 241–2; see also Paraska Bencal, "P'iatnadtsiat' Lit Pratsi Soiuzu Ukrainok Ameryky, 1925–1940, Chastyna Tretia" (Fifteen Years of Work of the League of Ukrainian Women of America, 1925–1940, Part III), *Jubilee Book of Soiuz Ukrainok, 1925–1940*, pp. 94–9.

24 Chyz, "Ukrainian Women and Their Organizations," pp. 244–5. For a review of the amounts of monies raised by individual UNWLA branches, see *Jubilee Book of Soiuz Ukrainok*, pp. 111–91.

25 For the complete text of the resolution, see Kmetz, pp. 69–71.

26 Pauline Riznyk, "25 Richchia Diial'nosty Ukrains'koho Zolotoho Khresta," pp. 7–13.

27 Chyz, "Ukrainian Women and Their Organizations," p. 246.

28 Filaret Kolessa, "Ukrains'ki Narodni Pisni i Znachennia Dlia Narodu" (Ukrainian National Songs and Their Significance for the People), *Sichovi Visti*, November 1922.

29 Michael Hayvoronsky, "Nasha Muzyka v Amerytsi" (Ukrainian Music in America), *Jubilee Book of the Ukrainian National Association*, p. 432.

30 *Ukraina*, 9 August 1917.

31 It would be hard to imagine anything better," stated Vienna's *Der Morgen*, 16 September 1919; "The concert was altogether a remarkable and delicious performance, one that will make English choirs hang their heads with envy," declared London's *Daily Herald*, 4 February 1920; "A human pipe organ," exclaimed *Vossische Zeitung*, 29 May 1920; "We no longer

witness ordinary singers obeying their conductor; these are priests and priestesses of a deep religion reverently bent before a Demiurge, who projects and transmits his own flame with eloquent and dominating gestures, by turns impressive, tragic, wrathful, or imploring. He plays, so to say, on a magnificent instrument, whose forty hearts and forty brains are connected in a telepathic and mysterious correspondence with his heart and brain" wrote Georges Pierfitte in Toulouse's *La Depeche*. These quotations were cited in a program published by Max Rabinoff entitled *The Ukrainian National Chorus*. It was distributed at Orchestra Hall in Chicago on 30 October 1922. Copy in possession of the author.

32 Cited in Halich, *Ukrainians in the United States*, p. 145.

33 Cited in Chyz, "The Ukrainian Immigrants in the United States," p. 119.

34 Kaskiw, "Ridna Pisnia – Ridnyi Teatr," pp. 424–5; Halich, pp. 133–5.

35 In 1933, Benetzky's choir took second place (Halich, pp. 136–45; also see *Ukraina*, 29 August 1930; *Sich*, 1 September 1931; and Mykola Novak, *Na Storozhi Ukrayine* [On Guard for Ukraine] [Los Angeles: published by author, 1979], p. 159).

36 An example of youth involvement in Ukrainian choral activity was the all-male Ukrainian Cossack Chorus of Chicago. Founded in 1933, the ensemble presented seventeen performances in Chicago and three in Detroit during its first year of existence (*U.O.Y.A. Weekly*, 8 July and 19 August 1934).

37 Stepan Marusevych, "Molod' i Ukrains'ka Muzyka" (Youth and Ukrainian Music), *Golden Jubilee Almanac of the Ukrainian National Association*, pp. 197–201. Also see *Ethnic Recordings in America: A Neglected Heritage* (Washington: Library of Congress, 1982), pp. 23, 161–2, and 209–10.

38 Born in Ukraine, Avramenko organized his first dance ensemble in Western Ukraine in 1921. Emigrating to Canada, he established dance groups in Toronto in 1926 and Winnipeg in 1927. He traveled throughout the country in an effort to gain popular support for his efforts. In 1928, he immigrated to the United States, where he established his permanent residence and began to organize dance schools and other cultural enterprises throughout the country.

39 Mary Ann Herman, "Vasyl Avramenko as I Knew Him," *Trident Quarterly*, Summer 1962, pp. 36–7.

40 Ibid., p. 37. Another of Avramenko's concerns during this period was with the authenticity of Ukrainian costumes. "Before Avramenko's arrival in the United States," writes Herman, "the Ukrainians wore a hodgepodge costume; Polish scalloped bodices, vulgarly embroidered aprons – it was a far cry from the original Ukrainian costumes worn in Europe. It was Avramenko who insisted that everyone in his classes discard these costumes and wear instead what he called a true Ukrainian costume."

41 Ibid., pp. 38–9; interview with Stephen Kuropas, 7 February 1972.

42 Henry Beckett, "Avramenko's Gorgeous Ukrainian Festival," *New York Evening Post*, 27 April 1931; cited in Vasile Avramenko, *Ukrainian*

National Music and Dances (Winnipeg: National Publishers Ltd., 1947), p. 67.

43 *Sich,* 15 November 1932.
44 *Promin,* April 1936, pp. 12–13.
45 Ibid., pp. 15–16.
46 Basil A. Stephens, "Help Build a Ukrainian Hollywood," reprinted in *Promin,* April 1936, p. 12.
47 Ibid., p. 14.
48 *Svoboda,* for example, refused to print Avramenko's original advertisements on the grounds that they were misleading (*Promin,* April 1936, pp. 9–10, 16).
49 Avramenko, pp. 9–10. Also see Mykola Novak, pp. 157–8.
50 Dr. Simenovych chided *Svoboda* for its accusations, writing: "Those who know our way of life in America know that no one ever has nor ever will make money off of the Ukrainians" (see Simenovych, "Chy Vy Znaiete" [Do You Know], *Ukraina,* 19 September 1930).
51 Interview with Stephen Kuropas, 7 February 1972.
52 Interview with Nicholas Olek, 14 February 1972.
53 FBI memo (7 October 1941), File #100-4233, ODWU, Section IV.
54 FBI memo (17 November 1941), File #100-9002-14, Luka Myshuha.
55 Sayers and Kahn, *Sabotage! The Secret War against America,* p. 91.
56 Stepan Kuropas, "Shykago" (Chicago), *Jubilee Book of the Ukrainian National Association,* p. 545.
57 Ibid.
58 *Svoboda,* 13 February 1933.
59 [L]uka [M]yshuha, "Ukrains'ka Uchast' u Dvokh Svitovykh Vystavakh" (Ukrainian Participation in Two World Fairs), *Golden Jubilee Almanac of the Ukrainian National Association,* pp. 215–16.
60 *Sich,* 22 April 1933.
61 Ibid., 24 June 1933.
62 Myshuha, "Ukrains'ka Uchast' u Dvokh Svitovykh Vystavakh," p. 216.
63 Halich, p. 142.
64 Kuropas, "Shykago," p. 545.
65 Halich, p. 142.
66 Kuropas, "Shykago," p. 545; interview with Stephen Kuropas, 7 February 1972.
67 Myshuha, "Ukrains'ka Uchast' u Dvokh Svitovykh Vystavakh," pp. 217–18.
68 Volodymyr Levytsky, "Uchast' Ukraintsiv u Shikagovs'kyi Vystavi" (Ukrainian Participation in the Chicago Fair), *Kalendar of the Ukrainian Workingman's Association for 1935* (Scranton: Narodna Volya Press, 1934), pp. 129–35.
69 Myshuha, "Ukrains'ka Uchast' u Dvokh Svitovykh Vystavakh," pp. 219–22.
70 [O]mer E. Malisky, "Ukrains'kyi Kulturnyi Horod v Amerytsi" (The Ukrainian Cultural Garden in America), *Golden Jubilee Almanac of the*

Ukrainian National Association, pp. 241–5; Mykola Busko and Omer Malisky, "Kleveland" (Cleveland), *Jubilee Book of the Ukrainian National Association,* p. 661.

71 The leadership of the umbrella organization included Omer Malisky, president; Ivan Tarnawsky and Maria Oleksik, vice-presidents; Gregory Stepanek, financial secretary; Ivan Spodar, recording secretary; and Dmytro Szmagala, treasurer.

Chapter 10

1 See chapter 3.
2 Theodosius Kaskiw, "Ukrains'ka Shkola v Zluchenykh Derzhavakh" (The Ukrainian School in the United States), *Souvenir Book of the Solemn Celebration of the Ukrainian Catholic College* (Philadelphia: America Press, 1940), p. 38.
3 *Ridna Shkola,* January–February 1918, p. 48.
4 Ibid., p. 3.
5 Ibid., pp. 3–5.
6 Stetkewicz, "Ukrains'ke Shkil'nytstvo v Amerytsi," p. 342.
7 *Ridna Shkola,* May through October 1918.
8 Ibid., January–February 1918.
9 Ibid., June 1918.
10 Ibid., August 1918.
11 Ibid., October 1918.
12 Ibid., August 1918.
13 Ibid., April 1918.
14 Stetkewicz, pp. 338–9.
15 Ibid., pp. 339–40.
16 *Svoboda,* 12 January 1928.
17 Stetkewicz, pp. 341–2.
18 Ibid., p. 342.
19 Theodore Swystun, "Iakos' to bude" (Somehow It Will Be), *Dnipro,* 15 September 1937.
20 Ibid.
21 An important aspect of the entire educational process was the children's "concerts" which were organized by the more talented *diak-uchytels* and which provided an opportunity for children to sing, recite poetry, dance, and take part in dramatic skits. The quality of the concerts usually determined the enrollment of the school. In Chicago, for example, Dmytro Atamanec, a *diak-uchytel* who took charge of the school in 1922, was able to boost his enrollment from 40 students in 1922 to 520 students in 1924 largely as a result of parental enthusiasm for the cultural presentation of his students (interview with Dmytro Atamanec, 6 February 1969).
22 Mamchur, "Nationalism, Religion and the Problem of Assimilation among Ukrainians in the United States," p. 168.
23 Ibid., pp. 222–4.

24 Lev Yasinchuk, *Dlia Ridnoho Kraiu* (For the Native Land) (Lviv: Shevchenko Scientific Society, 1933), pp. 6–7.

25 Yasinchuk, "Starokraiovym Okom Na Ukrains'ku Emigratsiiu v Amerytsi" (How the Old Country Views the Ukrainian Immigration in America), *Jubilee Book of the Ukrainian National Association,* p. 373.

26 See *Visti,* 21 October and 2 December 1931.

27 Yasinchuk, *Dlia Ridnoho Kraiu,* pp. 9–23; see also *Svoboda,* 22 October 1931; *Narodne Slovo,* 15 October 1931; *Sich,* 15 May 1932.

28 Yasinchuk, *Dlia Ridnoho Kraiu,* pp. 21–2.

29 *Svoboda,* 22 October 1931.

30 *Visti,* 21 October 1931.

31 Ibid., 2 December 1931.

32 Manifestations honoring Ridna Shkola and Yasinchuk were held in Pennsylvania (Easton, Wilkes-Barre, Hannover, Shamokin, Chester, Carnegie, MeKees Rock, Philadelphia, Pittsburgh), New York (Buffalo, Lancaster, Niagara Falls, Jamaica, LI, New York City, Syracuse, Troy), New Jersey (Newark, Elizabeth, Passaic, Bayonne, Jersey City), Ohio (Toledo, Cleveland, Akron, Youngstown), Connecticut (New Haven, New Britain), Rhode Island (Providence, Woonsocket), New Hampshire (Manchester), Maryland (Baltimore), Massachusetts (Boston), Delaware (Wilmington), Missouri (St. Louis), Michigan (Hamtramck, Detroit), Illinois (Chicago), and Minnesota (Minneapolis–St. Paul). Yasinchuk, *Dlia Ridnoho Kraiu,* pp. 16–88.

33 "Dvadtsiat Piat' Lit Mynaie!" (Twenty-Five Years Have Passed!), *Jubilee Kalendar of the Orphanage, 1911–1936* (Philadelphia: Orphanage Printing Press 1936), pp. 36–9.

34 Mamchur, p. 166.

35 Lotovych, "Ukrainske Shkil'nytstvo v Amerytsi," p. 12.

36 Czuba, *History of the Ukrainian Catholic Parochial Schools in the United States,* pp. 25–7, 66; Mamchur, p. 167.

37 See St. Nicholas Church Council Minutes, 1 June 1923.

38 Ibid., 15 November 1925.

39 O. Prestai, "Chomu My Nemaiemo Shkoly" (Why We don't Have a School), *Sich,* 21 February 1925.

40 "Nasha Shkola v Shikago" (Our School in Chicago), *Sich,* 1 January 1926.

41 Czuba, pp. 36–7.

42 Mamchur, pp. 170–2; Procko, p. 69.

43 Mamchur, pp. 217–19.

44 Dietric Slobogin, "Huge Ukrainian College Campaign," cited in *Souvenir Book of the Solemn Celebration of the Ukrainian Catholic College,* p. 20.

45 Eve Piddubcheshen, "Our National Must," cited in ibid., p. 21.

46 Mamchur, p. 217.

47 According to Dmytro Atamanec, a *diak-uchytel* who emigrated to the United States in 1913, the inability of single young men to return to Ukraine during and after the war led to a decision to marry and to settle in America permanently. The inevitable result was a baby boom a few years

later followed by peak ethnic school enrollments all through the mid- and late 1920s (interview with Dmytro Atamanec, 6 February 1969).

48 One of the first organizations to respond to the challenge was the UNA. Realizing that many Ukrainian youth did not read the Ukrainian press, the UNA began to publish an English-language quarterly entitled the *Ukrainian Juvenile Magazine* which contained articles of historical significance as well as news of Ukrainian sports stars and local youth organizations (see the *Ukrainian Juvenile Magazine,* December 1927).

49 Diadko Naum (pseud.), "Orhanizuimo Nashu Molod'!" (Let's Organize Our Youth), *Kalendar of the Providence Association for 1930* (Philadelphia: The Providence Association, 1930), p. 42.

50 Ibid., pp. 42–4.

51 Theodosius Kaskiw, "Orhanizuimo Nashu Molod' v Amerytsi" (Let's Organize Our Youth in America), *Kalendar of the Providence Association for 1931* (Philadelphia: The Providence Association, 1931), pp. 40–1.

52 Ibid., p. 42.

53 Volodymyr Simenovych, "Chomu Vashi Molodi Nedbaiut" (Why Your Youth Don't Care), *Ukraina,* 4 December 1931.

54 Joan J. Skuba, "Good Americans: The Problem of Ukrainian Youth," *The Ukrainian Review,* May 1931, p. 10. An English language nonsectarian, nonpartisan monthly publication, the *Ukrainian Review* first came out on 15 March 1931. It had a threefold purpose: (1) to inform Americans about Ukraine and Ukrainians; (2) to educate second-generation Ukrainians about Ukraine; (3) to provide a vehicle of expression for facts about Ukraine.

55 Skoba, "Good Americans: The Problem of Ukrainian Youth."

56 See "Letters from Our Readers," *Ukrainian Juvenile Magazine,* January 1930, p. 14.

57 Ivan Kashtaniuk, "Ukrains'kyi Plast i Ukrains'kyi Narodnyi Soiuz v Amerytsi" (Ukrainian Scouts and the Ukrainian National Association in America), *Kalendar of the Ukrainian National Association for 1932* (Jersey City: The Ukrainian National Association, 1932), p. 32.

58 Interview with Stephen Kuropas, 16 February 1972.

59 "The Spirit of Good Will," *Zhinochyi Svit,* December 1933, p. 20.

60 Mamchur, p. 248.

61 *Ukrainian Herald,* July–August 1931; cited in Mamchur, p. 304.

62 Ibid., February 1932, cited in Mamchur, p. 305.

63 By this time Hundiak had cut his ties with the Ukrainian Autocephalous Orthodox church (July 1931) and had joined forces with Bishop Bohdan.

64 Mamchur, pp. 303–4.

65 Ibid., p. 252.

66 Ibid., pp. 303–4; *Ukraine,* 23 August 1939.

67 There seems to be little doubt that one of the major reasons behind the Catholic youth exodus was the great interest in the congress demonstrated by the UNA, an organization that was anathema to the Ukrainian Catholic hierarchy because of *Svoboda's* strong support of the dissidents

during the church controversy of 1926–7. There were also political over-
tones. *Svoboda's* editor supported the Nationalists while Bohdan Katamay, one of the leaders of the Catholic youth contingent, was associated
with the UHO. According to Anastasia Volker (née Oleskiw), the Basilian
Fathers at St. Nicholas were opposed to any youth organizations that
had Orthodox youth involved (Interview with Anastasia Volker, 28 July
1973).

68 Mary Kozyra and Theodore Luciw, "Minutes of the First Ukrainian
   Youth's Congress," *Zhinochyi Svit*, August–September 1933, p. 31; Jennie
   H. Kohut, "The ULYNA Story," *the Ukrainian Trend*, Autumn 1957, p. 6;
   Mamchur, p. 176.

69 Kozyra and Luciw, pp. 30–2.

70 Kohut, p. 7.

71 Kozyra and Luciw, "Minutes of the First Ukrainian Youth's Congress,"
   Zhinochyi Svit, October–November 1933, pp. 30–2; Kohut, pp. 6–8.

72 (L)uka (M)yshuha, "Liha Ukrains'koi Molodi Pivnichnoi Ameryky" (The
   Ukrainian Youth's League of North America), *Golden Jubilee Almanac of
   the Ukrainian National Association*, pp. 169–72. See also *Ukrainian Weekly*,
   26 August 1939.

73 Kohut, pp. 8–12; interview with John Evanchuk, 2 September 1972.
   Evanchuk, a UNA activist, was elected UYLNA financial secretary at
   the 1936 convention.

74 *Natsionalist*, 15 September 1937; *Ukrainian Weekly*, 11 September 1937.

75 *Natsionalist*, 15 October and 1 November 1937.

76 See *Ukraine*, 23 August 1939.

77 Ibid., 6 and 20 September 1939.

78 Ibid., 6 September 1939.

79 The complete text of Miss Zadorosne's bulletin is part of an FBI memo
   (10 November 1941), File #102-8-22, ODWU, Section VI.

80 *Ukraine*, 13 September 1940.

81 FBI memo (10 November 1941). Miss Zadorosne also informed the FBI
   that Stephen Mostowy of the Ukrainian Committee to Combat Naziism
   was a "hoboish sort of adventurer" and probably "pro-Communist."

82 Reverend Tremba, whose remarks were entitled "How to Regain the Lost
   Ukrainian Youth for the Ukrainian Cause," had initially agreed to present the same address at the All-Ukrainian Youth Congress which gave
   birth to the UYLNA. See "Minutes" in *Zhinochyi Svit*, August–September
   1933.

83 "Organization and Work of the Ukrainian Catholic Youth League," *Ukrainian Youth*, May 1934.

84 Bohdan Katamay, "Z Viroy'u v Molod" (With Faith in Our Youth), *Ukrainian Youth*, May 1934.

85 T.O., "Poli Pratsi Dlia Nashoi Molodi" (A Field of Work for Our Youth),
   Ukrainian Youth, May 1934.

86 Mary Check, Rose Lishak, Anna Masliak, Mary Kalborn, "Second Con-

gress of the Ukrainian Catholic Youth League," *Ukrainian Youth*, November 1935.

87 The executive board consisted of Eve Piddubcheshen, president; Paul Hysa, first vice-president; Mary Kalborn, recording secretary; Rose Lishak, corresponding secretary; Joseph Romanetz, financial secretary; and Mary Lishak, treasurer. A second vice-president was later appointed by the new executive board. See Check et al., pp. 11–14.

88 The auditors were Mary Check, Irene Tarnawsky, and Walter Synenko (ibid.).

89 During the first two years of its existence, the UCYL published six issues of *Ukrainian Youth* in both Ukrainian and English. Beginning in 1935, the only Ukrainian articles which appeared in the UCYL journal were short reprints from other Ukrainian periodicals.

90 Check et al., p. 13. The "need" for a separate Catholic youth league was stressed by the clergy in subsequent issues of *Ukrainian Youth* and was postulated on the grounds that the Catholic faith was the true national faith of the Ukrainian people.

91 Eve Piddubscheshen, "Work Program of the Ukrainian Catholic Youth," *Ukrainian Youth*, November 1935.

92 Stephen Chehansky, "Our Catholic Spirit," *Ukrainian Youth*, November 1935.

93 Stephen W. Mamchur, "Orientation of the Ukrainian American Student," *Ukrainian Youth*, October 1935.

94 John Kiselicia, "The Ukrainian Catholic Youth League of North America," *Yearbook, Sixth Annual Convention of the Ukrainian Catholic Youth League of North America* (Buffalo: The Ukrainian Catholic Youth League of North America, 1939), p. 15.

95 *Sich*, 15 July 1931.

96 *Siege Youth*, March 1931.

97 *Sich*, 5 November 1932.

98 Interview with Nicholas Olek, 7 July 1972.

99 Bohdan Katamay, "Orhanizatsiia Ukrains'koi Molodi" (The Organization of Ukrainian Youth), *Sich*, 5 November 1932.

100 B.I. Hayovich, "How Can Ukrainian Youth Help the Ukrainian Cause?" *Sich*, 26 November 1932.

101 *Sich*, 15 March 1932.

102 Ibid., 17 December 1932.

103 Ibid., 24 June 1933.

104 Ibid., 19 November 1932.

105 Interview with Helen Olek-Scott, 7 July 1972.

106 See "The Ukrainian Catholic Youth Convention," *Sich*, 12 August 1933.

107 See Nicholas, "The Ukrainian Aeronautical Movement," *Ukrainian Youth*, July–August 1934.

108 See *U.Y.O.A. Weekly*, 8 July 1934.

109 See ibid., 17 March 1935.

110 Riznyk and Domaratsky, "MUN u Nedavno Mynulomu i Suchasnomu,"
    p. 9.
111 Ibid., p. 10. See also Oleh Riznyk, "The History of MUN," *The Senior MUN
    Manual: A Guide to Action for the Ukrainian National Youth Federation of
    America* (Chicago: MUN Enterprises, 1961) pp. 6–9.
112 By the later 1930s, Droboty had become disillusioned with MUN and
    ODWU, joined the opposition, and become editor of *Ukrainian Life*, a
    UWA publication.
113 *Vistnyk ODVU*, 1 March 1935.
114 Ibid., 15 March 1935.
115 *Natsionalist*, 15 October 1935.
116 *Vistnyk ODVU*, 20 April 1935.
117 The Hamtramck team had future Hollywood star John Hodiak as one of
    its members. See photo in *Vistnyk ODVU*, August, September, October
    1934.
118 Ibid., 1 April 1935.
119 *Natsionalist*, 15 November 1935.
120 *Vistnyk ODVU*, August, September, October 1934.
121 Ibid., 1 April 1935.
122 *Natsionalist*, 15 November 1935.
123 *Vistnyk ODVU*, July 1934.
124 Ibid., 15 March 1935.
125 Ibid., 1 March 1935.
126 Riznyk and Domaratsky, pp. 10–19; interview with John Sawchyn, 21
    October 1982.
127 Military training for the youth, of course, was advocated during the 1930s
    by many Ukrainian-Americans, including the UHO. One of the strong-
    est supporters was Walter Gallan of the Ukrainian Legion in Philadelphia.
    Among the 5 million Ukrainians in Austria during World War I, he wrote,
    there was only one officer with General Staff training and one division
    commander. Pacifism was deep-rooted among Ukrainians. If the Ukrai-
    nian nation was to have adequate military personnel in the future, argued
    Gallan, the Ukrainian-American community had to become "militarily
    minded" through literature, excursions to military establishments, the
    enrollment of youth in military schools and colleges, and the formation of
    local military science and Red Cross study groups. A survey, urged Gallan,
    should be made to determine who in the community had military
    knowledge and experience and their names should be sent to the Ukrai-
    nian Legion. Gallan reasoned that the 1 million Ukrainians in the United
    States and Canada could produce some 1,500 officers and 20,000 men in
    the future. See Walter Gallan, "Do We Need Military Training?" *Ukrai-
    nian Weekly*, 9 October and 11 November 1933.
128 John Chmelyk, "Military Training and Our Ukrainian Youth," *Natsiona-
    list*, 1 November 1937.
129 See "Youth and Ethics," *Natsionalist*, 15 January 1938.
130 Ibid.

131 *Ukraine,* 2 August 1940.

132 *Youth of ODWU,* Circular #6 (5 June 1941), Granovsky Papers, Box 66.

133 Myshuha, "Iak Formuvavsia Svitohliad Ukrains'koho Imigranta v Amerytsi," pp. 144–6.

134 Cited in ibid., p. 146.

135 *Ukrainian Weekly,* 9 December 1933.

136 Ibid., 24 November 1933.

137 Ibid., 1 December 1933.

138 Ibid., 20 June and 29 November 1935.

139 Ibid., 4 April 1936 and 6 March 1937.

140 Ibid., 12 March and 8 October 1938.

141 Ibid., 18 June and 6 August 1938.

142 Ibid., 8 October and 10 December 1938; 18 and 25 March 1939.

143 Ibid., 10 December 1938.

144 Ibid., 7 May, 5, 19, and 26 November 1938; 21 January and 14 November
1939.

145 Dmitri Horbaychuk, "Militarism and the Ukrainian Young Man," *Ukrainian Weekly,* 15 March 1935.

146 "Changing One's Name," *Ukrainian Weekly,* 11 January 1936.

147 *Ukrainian Weekly,* 21 February 1936.

148 Ibid., 14 March 1936.

149 Ibid., 18 July 1936.

150 Ibid., 1 August 1936.

151 Ibid., 12 September 1936.

152 Ibid., 3 October 1936.

153 Ibid., 19 September 1936.

154 See ibid., 19 and 26 September, 24 October, and 7 November 1936.

155 Ibid., 15 February and 5 December 1936.

156 Ibid., 13 July 1937.

157 Ibid., 1 July 1939.

158 "Cherishing Our American Ideals," *Ukrainian Weekly,* 12 July 1936.

159 "Reviewing Ourselves," *Ukrainian Weekly,* 29 July 1935.

160 "For More Harmony and Progress," *Ukrainian Weekly,* 4 January 1936.

161 "Discard Intolerance," *Ukrainian Weekly,* 20 October 1933.

162 "The Ukrainian Disease," *Ukrainian Weekly,* 23 February 1934.

163 "For More Harmony and Progress."

164 Interview with John Sawchyn, 23 October 1982. "Chicago," according to
Sawchyn, "had two or three dance groups, choirs, baseball teams, basketball teams, drama groups and other kinds of activities for the youth.
In addition, there was hardly a weekend during which some function –
a picnic, dance, wedding, party, or play – wasn't scheduled. In those days
there were more group activities than now. It was fun to be Ukrainian."

165 Mamchur, p. 224. Interviews with John Sawchyn, Helen Olek, Nicholas
Olek, Pauline Riznyk, Anastasia Volker.

166 Cited in Zadrozny, "The Differences of Opinion among Ukrainians in
Chicago in Regard to the Soviet Union: A Study of Opinions, Attitudes,

and Beliefs of a National Minority in the United States" (unpublished
MA thesis, University of Chicago, 1946), p. 76.

167 Ibid.

168 Ibid. The Ukrainian armies referred to were the First and Second Ukrainian Fronts, the major Soviet divisions used against the Germans in the
Second World War.

169 Ibid., pp. 78–9.

170 See Mamchur, "Nationalism, Religion, and the Problem of Assimilation
among Ukrainians in the United States," p. 225.

171 Zadrozny, "The Differences of Opinion among Ukrainians in Chicago in
Regard to the Soviet Union," p. 68.

172 Ibid.

173 Interview with Nicholas Olek, 7 February 1972.

174 Interview with Dmytro Atamanec, 6 March 1969.

Chapter 11

1 Bohdan Krawchenko, *Social Change and National Consciousness in Twentieth
Century Ukraine* (New York; St. Martin's Press, 1985); also see *Forum*,
Spring 1985, and the *Saturday Evening Post*, 27 January 1945.

2 Mark R. Elliott, *Pawns of Yalta: Soviet Refugees and America's Role in Their
Repatriation* (Urbana: University of Illinois Press, 1982), pp. 30–44. Also
see Nikolai Tolstoy, *Victims of Yalta* (London: Hodder and Stoughton,
1977), pp. 77–99.

3 Mark R. Elliott, "Soviet Military Collaborators during World War II,"
Ukraine during World War II: History and Aftermath, ed. Yury Boshyk
(Edmonton: Canadian Institute of Ukrainian Studies, 1986), pp. 89–98.

4 "UNRAA's Chief of Displaced Person's Operations Urges Reparations,"
Press Release, 24 March 1947. John Panchuk Papers, Immigration History Research Center (IHRC), University of Minnesota, *Reparation News,*
14 June 1947; Elliott, *Pawns of Yalta,* pp. 30–44 and 156–7; Tolstoy, 77–99.

5 Elliott, *Pawns of Yalta,* pp. 80–97 and 172.

6 Ostap Tarnavsky, *Brat-Bratovi: Knyha Pro ZUADK* (Brother's Helping
Hand: History of UUARC) (Philadelphia: United Ukrainian American
Relief Committee, 1971), pp. 7–83.

7 See *Plight of Ukrainian DPs* (New York: Ukrainian Congress Committee,
1945).

8 See archives of John Panchuk and the United Ukrainian American Relief
Committee, Immigration History Research Center (IHRC), University
of Minnesota, Minneapolis, Minnesota.

9 Letter to Charles Wolch, United American Organizations (Philadelphia)
from Marshall M. Vance, Assistant to the Adviser on Refugees and
Displaced Persons, Department of State (30 November 1945). UUARC
Papers, Box 193, IHRC.

10 Letter from John Panchuk, UUARC President, to the U.S. Secretary of
War (28 January 1946). Panchuk Papers, IHRC.

11 Letter to John Panchuk from Edward F. Witsell, Adjutant General, U.S. War Department (20 February 1946). Panchuk Papers, IHRC.

12 See Yuri Boshyk and Boris Balan, *Political Refugees and "Displaced Persons": A Selected Bibliography and Guide to Research with Special Reference to the Ukrainians* (Edmonton: The Canadian Institute of Ukrainian Studies, 1982), pp. 100–2.

13 Tarnavsky, p. 44, 83–100, 184. Also see *The DP Story: The Final Report of the United States Displaced Persons Commission* (Washington: U.S. Government Printing Office, 1952), pp. 6–11.

14 Leonard Dinnerstein, *America and the Survivors of the Holocaust* (New York: Columbia University Press, 1982) pp. 117–36.

15 Ibid., pp. 21–3.

16 Abraham G. Duker, "Admitting Pogromists and Excluding Their Victims," *The Reconstructionist*, 1 October 1948.

17 *The DP Story*, pp. 11–41 and 100.

18 Ibid., p. 120.

19 Ibid., p. 242.

20 Ibid., pp. 269–70.

21 Ibid., p. 298.

22 Tarnavsky, p. 116.

23 *The DP Story*, p. 292. In his history of the UUARC, Tarnavsky claims that more than 35,000 displaced persons were resettled in the United States by the UUARC while Gallan claims 40,000. See Tarnavsky, pp. 140 and 188.

24 Tarnavsky, pp. 91–143. Also see Bohdan F. Procko, *Ukrainian Catholics in America: A History*, pp. 72–4.

25 *The DP Story*, p. 351.

26 Tarnavsky, pp. 161–70.

27 Paul Robert Magocsi, "Ukrainians," *Harvard Encyclopedia of American Ethnic Groups*, ed. Stephen Thernstrom (Cambridge: Harvard University Press, 1980), pp. 997–1002.

Bibliography

Memoirs and Firsthand Accounts

Fortunately for the student of Ukrainian-American history, the activities of Ukrainian-American immigrants have not gone unrecorded. While the records are not as complete as one would like, memoirs and other firsthand accounts have been written by immigrants, their offspring, and participant observers from Europe. Their recordings can be found in kalendars (almanacs), jubilee books, newspapers, and other periodicals, and in two major books – one by Iuliian Bachynskyi, published in Ukraine in 1914, and the other by M. Nastasivsky, the nom de plume of Michael Tkach, published in the United States in 1934. The latter two observers, the first a socialist, the other a Communist, have perspectives which are leftist in sociopolitical orientation. Toward the other end of the political spectrum, we have the observations of Luka Myshuha and Rev. Peter Poniatyshyn, both of whom were prolific writers and major contributors to the 1936 Jubilee Book of the Ukrainian National Association, the first major attempt of the Ukrainian community to systematically record and interpret its American experience.

Abrahamovska, Stefanie. "P'iatnadtsiat' Lit Pratsi Soiuzu Ukrainok Ameryky, Chastyna Persha, 1925–1934" (Fifteen Years of Work of the League of Ukrainian Women of America, 1925–1934, Part I). In *Jubilee Book of the Ukrainian Women's League of America, 1925–1940*, pp. 7–43. New York: Ukrainian National Women's League of America, 1940.

Bachynskyi, Iuliian. *Ukrains'ka Imigratsiia v Z'iednanykh Derzhavakh Ameryky* (The Ukrainian Immigration in the United States of America). Lviv: Iuliian Bachynskyi and Alexander Harasevych Publishers, 1914.

Bencal, Paraska. "P'iatnadtsiat' Lit Pratsi Soiuzu Ukrainok Ameryky, 1925–1940, Chastyna Tretia" (Fifteen Years of Work of the League of Ukrainian Women of America, 1925–1940, Part III). In *Jubilee Book of the Ukrainian Women's League of America, 1925–1940*, pp. 94–9. New York: Ukrainian National Women's League of America, 1940.

Busko, Mykola; Malisky, Omer. "Klivlend" (Cleveland). In *Jubilee Book of the*

Ukrainian National Association, ed. Luka Myshuha, p. 6. Jersey City: Svoboda Press, 1936.

Check, Mary; Lishak, Rose; Masliak, Anna; Kalborn, Mary. "Second Congress of the Ukrainian Catholic Youth League." *Ukrainian Youth*, November 1935, pp. 10–14.

Demydchuk, Simon. *Pivstorichchia Hromadians'koi Pratsi D-ra Semena Demydchuka 1904–1955* (The Half-Century of Community Work of Dr. Simon Demydchuk). New York: Carpathian Star Publishing Co., 1956.

– "Pochatky Ukrains'koi Immigratsii v Amerytsi Na Osnovi Spomyniv O. Konstantyna Andrukhovycha" (The Beginnings of the Ukrainian Immigration on the Basis of the Memoirs of Fr. Constantine Andruchovych). In *Kalendar of the Providence Association for 1932*, pp. 81–7. Philadelphia: Providence Association of Ukrainian Catholics in the United States, 1932.

Dmytriw, Nestor. "Z Pochatkiv Nashoho Zhittia v Amerytsi" (The Beginnings of Our Life in America). In *Golden Jubilee Almanac of the Ukrainian National Association, 1894–1944*, pp. 246–9. Jersey City: Ukrainian National Association, 1944.

Dushnyck, Volodymyr. "Do Istorii Ukrains'koi Natsionalistychnoi Presy v Amerytsi" (On the History of the Ukrainian Nationalist Press in America). *Samostiyna Ukrayina*, October–November 1968, pp. 2–6.

Herman, Mary Ann. "Vasyl Avramenko as I Knew Him." *The Trident Quarterly*, Summer 1962, pp. 36–42.

Holod, Dennis. "Spomyny Staroho Imigranta" (Memoirs of an Old Immigrant). As recorded by Omelian Revyuk. ed. Luka Myshuha, In *Jubilee Book of the Ukrainian National Association*, pp. 255–9. Jersey City: Svoboda Press, 1936.

Hrodsky, Y. "Vidvidyny Ameryky Mytr. A. Sheptyts'kym v 1910 Rotsi" (Metropolitan A. Sheptytsky's Visit to America in 1910). In *Kalendar of the Providence Association for 1927*. Philadelphia: America Press, 1927.

"Iak Povstav Ukrains'kyi Robitnychyi Soiuz" (How the Ukrainian Workingmen's Association Came into Being). Based on V.N. Verhana's Interview with Vasyl Gnus. In *Jubilee Book of the Ukrainian Workingmen's Association, 1910–1960*, pp. 62–70. Scranton: Narodna Volya Press, 1960.

Kapitula, Dmytro. "Shcho Znachylo Kolys' Buty Imigrantom" (What It Once Meant to Be an Immigrant). In *Jubilee Book of the Ukrainian National Association*, ed. Luka Myshuha, pp. 260–9. Jersey City: Svoboda Press, 1936.

Kaskiw, Theodosius. "Ukrains'ka Shkola v Zluchenykh Derzhavakh" (The Ukrainian School in the United States). In *Souvenir Book of the Solemn Celebration of the Ukrainian Catholic College*. Philadelphia: America Press, 1940.

Kmetz, Annette. "P'iatnadtsiat' Lit Pratsi Soiuzu Ukrainok Ameryky, 1934–1940, Chastyna Druha" (Fifteen Years of Work of the League of Ukrainian Women of America, 1925–1940, Part II). In *Jubilee Book of the Ukrainian Women's League of America, 1925–1940*. New York: Ukrainian National Women's League of America, 1940.

Kohut, Jennie H. "The UYLNA Story." *The Ukrainian Trend*, Autumn 1957.

Kuropas, Stephen. "Chikago" (Chicago). In *Jubilee Book of the Ukrainian National Association*, ed. Luka Myshuha, p. 545. Jersey City: Svoboda Press, 1936.

- *Spohady z Ukrainy i 60 Rokiv v Amerytsi* (Memoirs from Ukraine and 60 Years in America). Chicago: published by author, 1988.
Lotocky, Olena. "Soiuz Ukrainok Ameryky" (The League of Ukrainian Women of America). *Zhinochyi Svit*, June–July 1933.
Malisky, Omer E. "Ukrains'kyi Kulturnyi Horod v Amerytsi" (The Ukrainian Cultural Garden in America). In *Golden Jubilee Almanac of the Ukrainian National Association, 1894–1944*, pp. 241–5. Jersey City: The Ukrainian National Association, 1944.
Merena, Damian. "Pro Pershykh Lemkiv v Amerytsi" (First Lemko Immigrants). In *Golden Jubilee Almanac of the Ukrainian National Association*, pp. 250–2. Jersey City: The Ukrainian National Association, 1944.
Musiychuk, Stephen. "Prychyny Upadku Sichovoi Orhanizatsii u Z.D.A." (Reasons behind the Decline of the Sich Organization in the USA). In *Hei Tam Na Hori, Sich Ide* (Hey on the Hill, Sich Is Coming), pp. 373–8. Edmonton: Trident Press, 1965.
Myshuha, Luka. "Iak Formuvavsia Svitohliad Ukrains'koho Imigranta v Amerytsi" (The Development of the Ukrainian-American Outlook). In *Jubilee Book of the Ukrainian National Association*, pp. 6–176. Jersey City: Svoboda Press, 1936.
- "Ob'iednannia Ukrains'kykh Orhanizatsii v Amerytsi" (The United Ukrainian Organizations in America). In *Golden Jubilee Almanac of the Ukrainian National Association, 1894–1944*, pp. 129–37. Jersey City: The Ukrainian National Association, 1944.
Nastasivsky, M. [Mykhailo Tkach]. *Ukrains'ka Imigratsiia v Spoluchenykh Derzhavakh* (The Ukrainian Immigration in the United States). New York: Union of Ukrainian Toiler Organizations, 1934.
Nazaruk, Osyp. "Po Rokakh Pratsi v Amerytsi" (After Years of Work in America). *Sichovi Visty*, 15 March 1926.
Novak, Mykola P. *Na Storozhi Ukrainy* (On Guard for Ukraine). Los Angeles: published by author, 1979.
Pavlyk, Michael. "Rusyny v Amerytsi" (Ruthenians in America). *Tovarish*, 10 July 1888. As condensed in the *Kalendar of the Ukrainian National Association for 1920*. Jersey City: Svoboda Press, 1919.
Poniatsyshyn, Peter. "Iz Chasiv Administratsii Eparkhii" (From the Times of the Eparchial Administration). In *Jubilee Almanac of the Ukrainian Catholic Church in America, 1884–1934*, pp. 110–14. Philadelphia: America Press, 1934.
- "Spomyny O. Petra Poniatyshyna Na Osnovi Rozmovy Spysav D-r Semen Demedchuk" (Memoirs of Rev. Peter Poniatyshyn on the Basis of an Interview with Dr. Semen Demydchuk). In *Kalendar of the Providence Association for 1932*. Philadelphia: America Press, 1931.
- "Ukrayinska Tserkva i U.N. Soyuz" (The Ukrainian Church and the UNA). In *Jubilee Book of the Ukrainian National Association*, ed. Luka Myshuha, pp. 287–99. Jersey City: Svoboda Press, 1936.
- "Ukrayinska Sprava v Amerytsi Pid Chas Pershoyi Svitovoyi Viyny" (The Ukrainian Situation in America during the First World War). In *Jubilee Almanac of Svoboda, 1839–1953*, pp. 65–76. Jersey City: The Ukrainian Association, 1953.
Riznyk, Pauline; Domaratsky, Oleh. "MUN u Nedavno Mynulomu i Suchas-

nomu" (MUN in the Past and Present). In *Jubilee Almanac of MUN, 1933–1958*. New York: MUN, 1958.

Riznyk, Volodymyr. "Pochatky ODWU u Rozbudovi II Merezhi: Nashi Uspikhy i Trudnoshchi" (The Beginnings of ODWU and the Development of Its Affiliates: Our Successes and Problems). In *Samostiyna Ukrayina*, October–November 1968, pp. 6–10.

Sichynsky, Miroslaw. *Narodna Sprava v Amerytsi* (The National Matter in America). New York: The Federation of Ukrainians in the United States, 1919.

Simenovych, Volodymyr. "Z Moho Zhyttia" (From My Life). In *Kalendar of the Ukrainian National Association for 1931*. Jersey City: Svoboda Press, 1931.

Stetkewicz, Joseph. "Ukrains'ke Shkil'nytstvo v Amerytsi" (Ukrainian Schools in America). In *Jubilee Book of the Ukrainian National Association*, ed. Luka Myshuha, pp. 35–42. Jersey City: Svoboda Press, 1936.

Wolansky, Ivan. "Pam'iati Pershoho Ukrains'koho Katolyts'koho Sviashchenyka v Amerytsi" (Memoirs of the First Ukrainian Catholic Priest in America). In *Jubilee Almanac of the Ukrainian Greek Catholic Church in America, 1884–1934*, pp. 12–13. Philadelphia: America Press, 1934.

Zadoretsky, Peter. "Korotkyi Narys Istorii Sichovoi Orhanizatsii u Z.D.A." (A Short History of the Sich Organization in the USA). In *Hei Tam Na Hori, Sich Ide* (Hey on the Hill, Sich Is Coming). Edmonton: Trident Press, 1965.

Interviews

Interviews were conducted by the author with individuals who had been active in Ukrainian-American community affairs prior to World War II. In conducting these interviews, no special set of questions was used. Respondents were usually asked a number of fairly general questions to determine both their familiarity with the past and their ability to accurately recall it. Specific questions were then asked about individuals, events, relationships, and other information not found in other sources. Lengthy interviews were conducted with Dmytro Atamanec, Philip Wasylowsky, and Semen Kochy, all of whom arrived in the United States before the advent of Ukrainian independence.

Atamanec, Dmytro. Interviewed 5 and 6 March 1969. Dmytro Atamanec came to the United States in 1911. He was active in the Hetman Organization, where he came to know Dr. Stephen Hrynevetsky, Dr. Osyp Nazaruk, and Dr. Volodymyr Simenovych intimately.

Evanchuk, John. Interviewed 2 September 1972. Born in Canada, John Evanchuk came to the United States as a young man and became active in such organizations as the Ukrainian National Association and the Ukrainian Youth League of North America where he held national posts.

Hundiak, John. Interviewed 26 February 1969. Father (later Bishop Mark) Hundiak came to the United States as a young man in 1913 and became active in the Ukrainian socialist movement. Later he became a Catholic priest and an assistant pastor at St. Nicholas Church in Chicago. Finding the Catholic church too confining, Father Hundiak became an Orthodox priest and rose to become chancellor to Bishop John Theodorovich. Still later, Father Hundiak had a falling out with Bishop Theodorovich and joined the newly created Orthodox church of Bishop Bohdan, rising, in time, to become his chancellor. Father Hundiak became an Orthodox activist, organizing, among other things, the first national organization for Orthodox youth.

Kochy, Semen. Interviewed 13 February 1969. Dr. Kochy has published historical accounts of early life in America's Ukrainian communities.

Kuropas, Stephen. Interviewed 2 and 16 August 1970, 7 and 16 February 1972, and 12 July 1985. Active in the Ukrainian Veteran's Organization in Galicia and Czechoslovakia after World War I, Stephen Kuropas came to the United States in 1927. One of the first organizers of ODWU in America, Kuropas was intimately associated with the entire Nationalist movement in this country and helped engineer the ODWU takeover of the UNA in 1936. A member of the national boards of both the UNA and ODWU since the early 1930s, Kuropas also has written about the Ukrainian immigration, publishing his memoirs in 1988.

Muzyka, Wasyl. Interviewed 6 February 1969. Wasyl Muzyka came to America in 1904 at the age of ten. He had been active in the socialist party, the Hetman Organization, and the Ukrainian National Association.

Olek, Nicholas. Interviewed 14 February and 7 July 1972. Born in Cleveland, Ohio, Nicholas Olek was an active member of the Hetman Youth Corps in the 1930s. He left the organization in 1938, believing that its leadership was too closely allied with German-American fascists.

Olek-Scott (née Bahry), *Helen.* Interviewed 7 July 1972. Born in the United States, Helen Olek was active in the initial efforts to establish the Ukrainian Youth League of North America and later joined the Catholic youth exodus which resulted in the formation of the Ukrainian Catholic Youth League.

Popovych, Ivan. Interviewed 28 August 1971. Arriving in the United States as a young man, Ivan Popovych was active in the Nationalist movement in the 1930s.

Riznyk, Volodymyr. Interviewed 28 August 1971. Volodymyr Riznyk was secretary of ODWU from its inception until his election as president in 1961.

Sawchyn, John. Interviewed 23 October 1982. Born in Ukraine, John Sawchyn came to the United States in 1921 at the age of eleven. He joined MUN in 1934 and became the first national president of the organization in 1936. He remained a MUN member until his induction into the United States Army in 1942.

Volker (née Oleskiw), *Anastasia.* Interviewed 28 July 1973. Like Helen Olek-Scott, Anastasia Volker was an early organizer of the Ukrainian Youth League of North America, being elected to the national executive board of the organiza-tion at the first convention. Of Orthodox background, Anastasia Volker was active in the UYLNA all through the 1930s.

Wasylowsky, Philip. Interviewed 26 September and 20 November 1968, and 6 August 1970. By far the most valuable resource respondent for this study, Mr. Wasylowsky came to this country before World War I. After the war, he was active in the Hetman Organization, where he rose to the rank of "sotnik." When Hrynevetsky left the organization, Wasylowsky joined ODWU.

Newspapers and Periodicals

Newspapers and periodicals were another valuable source of information, especially *Svoboda*, a faithful recorder of the Ukrainian-American scene since 1893, and various organizational publications. Also helpful in this regard was the Chicago Foreign Press Survey, a WPA project that provided additional excerpts from Ukrainian periodicals published in Chicago during the period under study. American periodicals, especially those cited only once or twice, are not listed in this bibliography since they were not studied as extensively as the Ukrainian press.

The Alaska Herald, 1 March through 15 April 1868. Published in San Francisco, California.

The Alaska Herald-Svoboda, 1 June 1868 through 15 February 1869. Published in San Francisco, California.

Amerykanskiy Russkiy Viestnik, 25 June 1894 through 17 December 1914.

The Free Press and Alaska Herald, 2 May through 30 May 1868. Published in San Francisco, California.

The Hour, 27 July 1940 through 5 September 1942.

Narodna Volya, 23 June 1938 through 25 September 1941. Published biweekly in Scranton.

Nash Styakh, December 1933 through July 1936. Published weekly in Chicago, Illinois.

Nationalist, 20 June 1935 through 5 July 1939. Published biweekly in New York City.

News from Ukraine, January 1980 through December 1984. Published monthly in Kiev, Ukraine.

Ranna Zorya, January–February 1918. Published monthly in Chicago, Illinois.

Rassviet, 19 December 1933 through 25 February 1935. Published daily in Chicago, Illinois.

Ridna Shkola, January 1918 through April 1918. Published monthly in Jersey City, New Jersey.

Robitnyk, 20 February 1918 through 23 December 1919. Published weekly in Cleveland, Ohio.

Samostynyist, 15 March 1936 through 17 January 1937. Published weekly in New York City.

Sich, 15 August 1924 through 2 June 1934. Published biweekly in Chicago, Illinois.

Sichovy Visti, 13 July 1918 through 10 June 1924. Published biweekly in Chicago, Illinois.

Svoboda, 1893 through 1939. Published biweekly, weekly, and daily, primarily in Jersey City, New Jersey.

The Trident, 1937 through 1941. Published monthly in Chicago and New York City.

Ukraine, 12 July 1939 through 15 January 1941. Published biweekly in New York City.

Ukrainian Weekly, 6 October 1933 through 7 July 1985. Published weekly in Jersey City, New Jersey.

Ukrayina, 1917 through 1920 and 1930 through 1931. Published weekly in Chicago, Illinois.

Ukrayinskiy Shchodenni Visty, 2 January 1921 through 11 September 1938. Published daily in New York City.

Vistnyk ODWU, October 1932 through 20 May 1935. Published monthly and biweekly in New York City.

Zhinochyi Svit, May 1933 through January/February 1934.

Documents and Reports

Archives of the United Ukrainian American Relief Committee (UUARC), Immigration History Research Center (IHRC), University of Minnesota.

By-laws of the Organization of Ukrainian Nationalists (OUN). Manuscript; copy in possession of author.

Communist Political Subversion, Part 2 (Annex), Nov. 12–14, 28; Dec. 3–8, 11, 13, 14, 1956. Washington: U.S. Government Printing Office.

The DP Story: The Final Report of the United States Displaced Persons Commission. Washington: U.S. Government Printing Office, 1952.

FBI Files, Luka Myshuha, 9 January 1941 through 30 August 1945.

FBI Files, Organization for the Rebirth of Ukraine (ODWU), 7 December 1939 through 22 May 1944.

FBI Files, United Hetman Organization (UHO), 11 February 1936 through 9 October 1944.

FBI Files, Ukrainian National Association (UNA), 5 April 1942 through 23 November 1945.

Alexander Granovsky Private Papers, Immigration History Research Center (IHRC), University of Minnesota.

Kersten Committee 1954 *Reports.* House Select Committee to Investigate Communist Aggression and the Forced Incorporation of the Baltic States into the USSR. U.S. Senate Document No. 122.

Kluckhorn, Frank L., ed. *Soviet Total War.* Vols. 1 and 2. Committee on Un-American Activities, House of Representatives, 1956.

Kozyra, Mary; Luciw, Theodore. "Minutes of the First Ukrainian Youth's Congress." *Zhinochyi Svit,* August–September 1933, and October–November 1933.

Minutes of the Meetings of the St. Nicholas Board of Trustees, Chicago, Illinois, 1905–1933. Translated manuscript in possession of author.

John Panchuk Private Papers, Immigration History Research Center (IHRC), University of Minnesota.

Pope Pius XII. "The Encyclical on the Ruthenians." *The Eastern Churches Quarterly,* April–June, 1961

Ukrainian National Chorus. Program published by Max Rabinoff. Copy in possession of author.

U.S. Congress. House of Representatives. Investigation of the Un-American

Propaganda Activities in the United States: Hearings before a Special Committee on Un-American Activities. 76th Cong., 1st Sess., 1939, Vol. 9.

Manuscripts

A number of unpublished manuscripts, dissertations, and theses were also consulted during the course of this research. The dissertations of Samuel Koenig, describing conditions in Western Ukraine prior to and during the emigration, Stephen Mamchur, on Ukrainian-American religious history, and Walter Warzeski, focusing on the Carpatho-Ruthenian experience in America, were especially helpful.

Bociurkiw, Bohdan R. "Soviet Church Policy in the Ukraine, 1919–1939." Unpublished PhD dissertation, University of Chicago, 1961.

Dyrud, Keith Paul. "The Rusin Question in Eastern Europe and America, 1890–World War I." Unpublished PhD dissertation, University of Minnesota, August 1976.

Koenig, Samuel. "The Ukrainians in Eastern Galicia: A Study of Their Culture and Institutions." Unpublished PhD dissertation, Yale University, 1935.

Krasnow, H.R. Scrapbooks. Vol. 1, Russian Section, the Chicago Foreign Press Survey, Chicago Public Library. (Microfilms)

Letwin, Shirley Robin. "The Soviet Nationality Program and Its Implications for World Unity." Unpublished MA thesis, University of Chicago, 1944.

Lukash, Elena. "The Ukraine at the Paris Peace Conference, 1919." Unpublished MA thesis, University of Chicago, 1962.

Mamchur, Stephen W. "Nationalism, Religion, and the Problem of Assimilation among Ukrainians in the United States." Unpublished PhD dissertation, Yale University, 1942.

Markus, Daria. "Education of Ethnic Leadership: A Case Study of the Ukrainian Ethnic Group in the United States, 1970–1974." Unpublished PhD dissertation, Loyola University (Chicago), 1976.

Raley, Deane D. "The Influence of Nationalism on the Communist Design." Unpublished MA thesis, University of Chicago, 1960.

Warzeski, Walter C. "Religion and National Consciousness in the History of the Rusins." Unpublished PhD dissertation, University of Pittsburgh, 1964.

Yuzyk, Paul. "The Expansion of the Russian Orthodox Church among the Ukrainians of North America." Paper presented in St. Paul, Minnesota, on 14 November 1981 at a seminar sponsored by the Immigration History Research Center.

Zadrozny, John. "The Development of a Nationality Movement." Unpublished PhD dissertation, University of Chicago, 1953.

– "The Differences of Opinion among Ukrainians in Chicago in Regard to the Soviet Ukraine: A Study of Opinions, Attitudes, and Beliefs of a National Minority in the United States." Unpublished MA thesis, University of Chicago, 1946.

Articles

For purposes of easy identification, articles have been divided into the major subject areas of significance to this study.

Ukrainian Immigration History

"Amerykans'ki-Ukrainky na Hromads'kyi Pratsi" (American Ukrainian Women in Community Work). In *Jubilee Almanac of the Ukrainian Women's Society of New York, 1921–1931*, pp. 77–8. New York: Ukrainian Women's Society of New York, 1931.

Ardan, Ivan. "The Ruthenians in America." *Charities*, 13 (1901–5), pp. 246ff.

Baranetskyi, Mykola. "Zhytt'owyi Shlakh Iepyskopa Kyr Sotera Ortyns'koho" (The Life Path of Bishop Soter Ortynsky). In *Kalendar of the Providence Association for 1956*, pp. 59–68. Philadelphia: America Press, 1956.

Beckett, Henry. "Avramenko's Gorgeous Ukrainian Festival." *New York Evening Post*, 27 April 1931.

Chaplynski, Y. "Diialnist' i Zasluhy Pershoho Ukrains'koho Katolyts'koho Iepyskopa v Zluchenykh Derzhavakh, Bl. p. Vladyky Sotera Ortyns'koho" (The Activity and Accomplishments of the First Ukrainian Catholic Bishop in the United States, the Late Bishop Soter Ortynsky). In *Jubilee Almanac of the Ukrainian Greek Catholic Church in America, 1884–1934*, pp. 108–9. Philadelphia: America Press, 1934.

Chehansky, Stephen. "Our Catholic Spirit." *Ukrainian Youth*, November 1935, pp. 1–4.

Chyz, Yaroslav. "Andrii Ahapii Honcharenko" (Andrew Agapius Honcharenko). In *Kalendar of Svoboda for 1957*, pp. 73–80. Jersey City: The Ukrainian National Association, 1957.

– "The Ukrainian Immigrants in the United States." In *Kalendar of the Ukrainian Workingmen's Association for 1940*, pp. 97–128. Scranton: Narodna Volya Press, 1939.

– "Ukrainian Women and Their Organizations." In *Jubilee Book of the Ukrainian Women's League of America, 1925–1940*. New York: Ukrainian National Women's League of America, 1940.

"Desiat' Lit Pratsi Ukrains'koi Zhinochoi Hromady v Niu Iorku" (Ten Years of Work of the Ukrainian Women's Society of New York). In *Jubilee Almanac of the Ukrainian Women's Society of New York, 1921–1931*, pp. 5–24. New York: Ukrainian Women's Society of New York, 1931.

Dmytriw, Nestor. "Duzhe Vashna Sprava" (A Very Important Matter). *Svoboda*, 20 August 1903.

"Do Istorii Ukrayins'koho Pravoslavnoho Rukhu v Shikago" (On the History of the Ukrainian Orthodox Movement in Chicago). *Dnipro*, May 1946, pp. 4–12.

Dragan, Antin. "Svoboda v Mynulomu i Suchasnomu" (Svoboda in the Past and Present). In *Jubilee Almanac of Svoboda, 1893–1953*. Jersey City: Svoboda Press, 1953.

Dubas, Pavlo. "Vazhni Podii v Orhanizatsiinomu Zhytti Ukraintsiv v Filiadelfii" (Highlights of the Organizational Life of Ukrainians in Philadelphia). In *Sixty Years of the Ukrainian Community in Philadelphia*. Philadelphia: The Ukrainian American Citizen's Association, 1944.

"Dvadtsiat' P'iat' Lit Mynaie" (Twenty-Five Years Have Passed). In *Jubilee Kalendar of the Orphanage, 1911–1936*, pp. 36–9. Philadelphia: Orphanage Printing Press, 1936.

"Friends of the Lincoln Brigade." In *Narodnyi Kalendar na rik 1939*, pp. 112–14. New York: Ukrainian Section of the International Worker's Order, 1939.

Gulovich, Stephen C. "The Rusin Exarchate in the United States." *The Eastern Churches Quarterly*, 6, no. 8 (October–December 1946), pp. 459–86.

Hanusiak, Michael. "50 Glorious Years Dedicated to Progress, Peace and Friendship." *Ukrayinski Visti*, 29 January 1970.

Hayovich, B.I. "How Can Ukrainian Youth Help the Ukrainian Cause?" *Sich*, 26 November 1932.

Hayvoronsky, Michael. "Nasha Muzyka v Amerytsi" (Ukrainian Music in America). In *Jubilee Book of the Ukrainian National Association*, ed. Luka Myshuha, pp. 431–8. Jersey City: Svoboda Press, 1936.

Hornysky, Anatol. "Ukrains'ka Baptysts'ka Tserkva v Shikago" (The Ukrainian Baptist Church in Chicago). In *The Evangelical Kalendar, "Good Friend" for 1956*, pp. 59–65. Toronto: Christian Printers, 1956.

Hrynevetsky, Stephen. "Shcho Musyt' Buty" (What Must Be). *Sichovi Visty*, 15 March 1926.

Kashtaniuk, Ivan. "Ukrains'kyi Plast i Ukrains'kyi Narodnyi Soiuz v Amerytsi" (Ukrainian Scouts and the Ukrainian National Association in America). In *Kalendar of the Ukrainian National Association for 1932*, pp. 30–2. Jersey City: The Ukrainian National Association, 1932.

Kaskiw, Theodosius. "Orhanizuimo Nashu Molod' v Amerytsi" (Let's Organize Our Youth in America). In *Kalendar of the Providence Association for 1931*, pp. 39–41. Philadelphia: The Providence Association, 1931.

– "Ridna Pisnia – Ridnyi Teatr" (Ukrainian Song and Theater in America). In *Jubilee Book of the Ukrainian National Association*, ed. Luka Myshuha, pp. 420–30. Jersey City: Svoboda Press, 1936.

Katamay, Bohdan. "Orhanizatsiia Ukrains'koi Molodi" (The Organization of Ukrainian Youth). *Sich*, 5 November 1932.

– "Z Viroyu v Molod" (With Faith in Youth). *Ukrainian Youth*, May 1934, pp. 1–3.

Kiselicia, John. "The Ukrainian Catholic Youth of North America." In *Yearbook, Sixth Annual Convention of the Ukrainian Catholic Youth League of North America*, pp. 2–20. Buffalo: The Ukrainian Catholic Youth League of North America, 1939.

Kniazevych, M. "Soiuz Ukrains'kykh Robitnykiv" (United Ukrainian Toilers Organization). In *Narodnyi Kalendar na rik 1939*, pp. 225–32. New York: Ukrainian Section of the International Workers' Order, 1939.

"Korotkyi Narys Istorii ODWU v. Z.S.A." (A Short Outline History of ODWU in the USA). *Samostiina Ukraina*, October–November 1968, pp. 10–30.

Krawciw, Bohdan. "Kalendari i Almanakhy Ukrains'koho Narodnoho Soiuzu i

Svobody" (Kalendars and Almanacs of the Ukrainian National Association
and Svoboda). In *Ukrainian Fortress in America: Jubilee Almanac on the Occasion
of the 75th Anniversary of the Ukrainian National Association,* pp. 120–40. Jersey
City: Svoboda Press, 1969.

Kuropas, Myron B. "Ukrainian Chicago: The Making of a Nationality Group in
America." In *Ethnic Chicago,* ed. Peter d'A Joes and Melvin G. Holli, pp. 140–79.
Grand Rapids: William B. Eerdmans Publishing Company, 1981.

Kuropas, Stephen. "Vidznachennia 30 Chervnia i Ameryka" (Commemoration
of June 30 and America). *Samostiyna Ukrayina,* July–August 1981.

Kyrylenko, Orest. "Ukraintsi v Amerytsi (Ukrainians in America)." Vienna: Association for the Liberation of Ukraine, 1916.

Lachowitch, Eugene. "Natsionalistychnyi Providnyky" (Nationalist Leaders),
Vistnyk ODVU, December 1932

Lapychak, Toma. "D-r Kyrylo Bilyk" (Dr. Cyril Bilyk). In *Medical Almanac,* p. 51.
Chicago: American Ukrainian Medical Society, Chicago Branch, 1958.

– "D-r Stephan Hrynevetsky" (Dr. Stephen Hrynevetsky). In *Medical Almanac,*
pp. 42–6. Chicago: American Ukrainian Medical Society, 1968.

Lelyva, Count. "Polozhennia Rusyniv v Spoluchenykh Derzhavakh Pivnichnoi
Ameryky" (The Situation among Ruthenians in the United States of North
America). In *First Ruthenian-American Kalendar,* pp. 51–6. Mt. Carmel: Svoboda
Press, 1897.

Levytsky, Volodymyr. "Uchast' Ukraintsiv u Shikagovs'kyi Vystavi" (Ukrainian
Participation in the Chicago Fair). In *Kalendar of the Ukrainian Workingmen's
Association for 1935,* pp. 129–35. Scranton: Narodna Volya Press, 1934.

Lotovych, Volodymyr. "Za Khrystyians'kyi Natsionalizm" (For Christian Nationalism). In *Jubilee Almanac of the Ukrainian Greek Catholic Church in the United
States, 1884–1934,* pp. 118–20. Philadelphia: America Press, 1934.

– "Ukrains'ke Shkil'nytstvo v Amerytsi" (Ukrainian Schools in America). In
Souvenir Book, Dedication of the First Ukrainian Catholic High School, pp. 10–12.
Stamford: America Press, 1933.

Magocsi, Paul Robert. "Ukrainians." In *Harvard Encyclopedia of American Ethnic
Groups,* ed. Stephen Thernstrom, pp. 997–1009. Cambridge: Harvard University Press, 1980.

Makar, Stephen. "American Boy." *Svoboda,* 7 and 14 December 1899.

– "Iakyi Maie Buty Pip" (What Should a Priest Be Like). *Svoboda,* 10 October
1901.

Mamchur, Stephen W. "Orientation of the Ukrainian American Student." *Ukrainian Youth,* October 1935, pp. 5–14.

Markus, V. "In the United States." In *Ukrainians Abroad,* pp. 10–60. Offprint from
Ukraine: A Concise Encyclopedia, vol. 2. Toronto: University of Toronto Press, 1971.

Marusevich, Stephen. "Molod' i Ukrains'ka Muzyka" (Youth and Ukrainian
Music). In *Golden Jubilee Almanac of the Ukrainian National Association,
1894–1944,* pp. 197–201. Jersey City: Ukrainian National Association, 1944.

M.T. "Ukrains'ki Biitsi v Espanii" (Ukrainian Fighters in Spain). In *Narodni
Kalendar na rik 1939,* pp. 115–16. New York: Ukrainian Section of the International Worker's Order, 1939.

Muraszko, Nicholas. "Konventsii U.N. Soiuzu" (Conventions of the UN Association). In *Jubilee Book of the Ukrainian National Association*, ed. Luka Myshuha,
pp. 209–30. Jersey City: Svoboda Press, 1944.

Mynyk, Theodore. "Ukrains'kyi Robitnychyi Soiuz, 1910–1960" (The Ukrainian
Workingmen's Association, 1910–1960). In *Jubilee Book of the Ukrainian Workingmen's Association, 1910–1960*, pp. 34–58. Scranton: Narodna Volya Press,
1960.

Myshuha, Luka. "Liha Ukrains'koi Molodi Pivnichnoi Ameryky" (The Ukrainian
Youth League of North America). In *Golden Jubilee Almanac of the Ukrainian
National Association, 1894–1944*, pp. 169–76. Jersey City: The Ukrainian National
Association, 1944.

– "Ukrains'ka Uchast' u Dvokh Svitovykh Vystavakh" (Ukrainian Participation
in Two World Fairs). In *Golden Jubilee Almanac of the Ukrainian National Association, 1894–1944*, pp. 215–23. Jersey City: The Ukrainian National Association,
1944.

Nalyvayko, N. "Osnovi Viddily U.R. Soiuzu" (Charter Branches of the U.W.
Association). In *Jubilee Book of the Ukrainian Workingmen's Association, 1910–
1950*, pp. 137–40. Scranton: Narodna Volya Press, 1960.

"Nasha Slava" (Our Glory). In *Kalendar for the American Rusins for 1908*, pp. 149–54.
New York: Svoboda Press, 1908.

Naum, Dyadko (pseud.). "Orhanizuimo Nashu Molod'" (Let's Organize Our
Youth). In *Kalendar of the Providence Association for 1930*, pp. 42–4. Philadelphia:
The Providence Association, 1930.

Nicholas. "The Ukrainian Aeronautical Movement." *Ukrainian Youth*, July–
August 1934, p. 17.

"Ninth ODWU Convention." *The Trident*, July–August 1939, pp. 58–9.

"Organization and Work of the Ukrainian Catholic Youth League." *Ukrainian
Youth*, May 1934, pp. 15–19.

O.T. "Pole Pratsi Dlia Nashoi Molodi" (A Field of Work for Our Youth). *Ukrainian
Youth*, May 1934, pp. 6–7.

Piddubcheshen, Eve. "Our National Must." In *Souvenir Book of the Solemn Celebration of the Ukrainian Catholic College*, pp. 20–4. Philadelphia: America Press, 1940.

– "Work Program of Ukrainian Catholic Youth." *Ukrainian Youth*, November
1935, pp. 6–9.

"Poklyk" (A Call). *Ranna Zorya*, March–April 1918, pp. 60–2.

Prestai, O. "Chomu My Nemaiemo Shkoly" (Why We Don't Have a School). *Sich*,
21 February 1925.

Revyuk, Emil. "Nashi Literaturni i Mystets'ki Nadbannia v Amerytsi" (Ukrainian
Literary and Art Achievements in America). In *Jubilee Book of the Ukrainian
National Association*, ed. Luka Myshuha, pp. 343–59. Jersey City: Svoboda Press,
1936.

– "Rozvii Politychnoho Svitohliadu Ukrains'koho Imigranta" (The Development
of a Ukrainian American Outlook). In *Jubilee Book of the Ukrainian National
Association*, ed. Luka Myshuha, pp. 300–23. Jersey City: Svoboda Press, 1936.

Richynskyi, T. "Pochatky i Rozvytok Ukrains'koi Sektsii Mizhnarodnoho Robitnychoho Ordenu" (The Genesis and Development of the Ukrainian Section

of the International Worker's Order). In *Narodnyi Kalendar na rik 1939*, pp. 37–43. New York: Ukrainian Section of the International Worker's Order, 1939.

Riznyk, Oleh. "The History of MUN." In *The Senior MUN Manual: A Guide to Action for the Ukrainian National Youth Federation of America*, pp. 5–12. Chicago: MUN Enterprises, 1961.

Riznyk, Pauline. "25 Richchia Diial'nosty Ukrains'koho Zolotoho Khresta" (25 Years of Activity of the Ukrainian Gold Cross). In *Twenty-Fifth Jubilee Convention of the Ukrainian Gold Cross*. Detroit: Ukrainian Gold Cross, 1956.

Riznyk, Pauline, and Domaratsky, Oleh. "MYN u Nedavno-mynulomu i Suchas-nomu" (MUN in the Past and Present), *Jubilee Almanac of MUN, 1933–1958* (New York: MUN, 1958).

Riznyk, Volodymyr. "Pochatky ODWU u Rozbudovi ii Merezhi: Nashi Uspikhy i Trudnoshchi" (The Beginnings of ODWU and the Development of Its Affiliates: Our Successes and Problems). *Samostiina Ukraina*, October–November 1968, pp. 6–7.

Sembratovych, Lev I. "Iak Pryshlo do Imenuvannia Nashoho Pershoho Iepyskopa v Amerytsi" (How It Came to Nominating Our First Bishop in America). In *Jubilee Almanac of the Ukrainian Greek Catholic Church in the United States, 1884–1934*, pp. 103–7. Philadelphia: America Press, 1934.

Senyshyn, Ambrose. "Ukrainian Catholics in the United States." *Eastern Churches Quarterly*, October–December 1946, pp. 439–57.

"Shanuimo Ridnu Movu" (Let's Respect the Native Language). In *Kalendar of the Ruskiy Narodni Soyuz for 1911*, pp. 147–51. Jersey City: Svoboda Press, 1911.

Simenovych, Volodymyr. "Chomu Vashi Molodi Nedbaiut' " (Why Your Youth Don't Care). *Ukrayina*, 4 December 1931.

– "Chy Vy Znaiete" (Do You Know). *Ukrayina*, 19 September 1930.

Skotsko, Eugene, "Ne Budmo Rabamy na Chuzyni" (Let's Not Be Serfs in the Diaspora). *Vistynk ODVU*, December 1932.

Skuba, Joan J. "Good Americans: The Problems of Ukrainian Youth." *The Ukrainian Review*, May 1931, pp. 10–13.

Slobogin, Dietric. "Huge Ukrainian College Campaign." In *Souvenir Book of the Solemn Celebration of the Ukrainian Catholic College*, p. 20. Philadelphia: America Press, 1940.

Sochocky, Isidore. "The Ukrainian Catholic Church of the Byzantine Slavonic Rite in the U.S.A." Condensed and freely translated by Constantine Berder. In *Ukrainian Catholic Metropolitan See, Byzantine Rite, U.S.A.*, pp. 249–86. Philadelphia: America Press, 1958.

"Socialism and the Question of the Workers." *Svoboda*, 31 July 1902.

"The Spirit of Good Will." *Zhinochyi Svit*, December 1933, p. 20.

Stachiw, Matthew. "Nova Ukraina v Amerytsi" (New Ukraine in America). In *Jubilee Book of the Ukrainian Workingmen's Association, 1910–1960*, pp. 73–115. Scranton: Narodna Volya Press, 1960.

Stevens, Basil A. "Help Build a Ukrainian Hollywood." *Promin*, April 1936, p. 12.

Swystun, Theodore. "Tovarystvo Ukrains'ko-Amerykans'kykh Horozhan u Filia-del'fii" (The Ukrainian-American Citizen's Association of Philadelphia). In *Sixty Years of the Ukrainian Community in Philadelphia*, pp. 28–34. Philadelphia:

The Ukrainian-American Citizen's Association, 1944.

"T." (author unknown). "Ukrains'ko Amerykans'ka Politychna Aktsiia u Rokakh 1914–1920" (A Chronicle of Political Activities of Ukrainian Americans, 1914–1920). In *Golden Jubilee Almanac of the Ukrainian National Association, 1894–1944*, pp. 112–27. Jersey City: The Ukrainian National Association, 1944.

Tolopko, Leon. "Na Shliakhu Nevpynnoi Borot'by" (In the Unfinished Struggle). *Ukrayinski Visti,* 29 January 1970, Part II, pp. 3–6.

– "Sorok Rokhiv Na Shliakhu Postupu" (Forty Years on the Road of Progress). *Ukrayinski Visti,* 14 April 1966, pp. 5–7.

Turak, Theodore. "A Celt among Slavs: Louis Sullivan's Holy Trinity Church." *The Prairie School Review,* Fourth Quarter, 1972.

"Ukrainians in America." *Literary Digest,* 15 November 1919, p. 40.

"Ukrains'ka Rada v Amerytsi" (The Ukrainian Council in America). In *Kalendar of the Ukrainian National Association for 1919*, pp. 38–44. Jersey City: Svoboda Press, 1918.

"Ukrains'ki Narodni Zapovidi" (Ukrainian National Commandments). In *Kalendar of the Ukrainian National Association for 1915*, pp. 150–1. Jersey City: Svoboda Press, 1915.

Wowchok, Stephanie, "Seventy Years of Dedication," *Jubilee Almanac of the Providence Association, 1912–1928.* Philadelphia: Providence Ukrainian Catholic Association, 1982.

Yasinchuk, Lev. "Starokraiovym Okom Na Ukrains'ku Emigratsiiu v Amerytsi" (How the Old Country Views the Ukrainian Immigration in America). In *Jubilee Book of the Ukrainian National Association,* ed. Luka Myshuha, pp. 365–79. Jersey City: Svoboda Press, 1936.

– "Ukrains'ke Shkil'nytstvo Poza Ridnymy Zemliamy" (Ukrainian Schools beyond the Native Land). In *Ukrainians in the Free World, Jubilee Book of the Ukrainian National Association, 1849–1954*, pp. 164–70. Jersey City: Svoboda Press, 1954.

Ukrainian National History

Andrusiak, Mykola. "Lviv: From Its Beginnings to 1772." In *Lviv: A Symposium on Its 700th Anniversary,* pp. 108–23. New York: Shevchenko Scientific Society, 1962.

Baran, S. "Ukraine between the Two World Wars: Ukrainian Political Refugees." In *Ukraine: A Concise Encyclopedia,* vol. 1 (1963), pp. 859–70.

Biletsky, L.; Herasymovych, I. "Education and Schools: The Period of Ukrainian Statehood." In *Ukraine: A Concise Encyclopedia,* vol. 2 (1971), pp. 341–3.

Bilinsky, A. "The Law: Western Ukrainian Territories between Two World Wars: Galicia and the Northwestern Territories." In *Ukraine: A Concise Encyclopedia,* vol. 2 (1971), pp. 70–3.

Borschak, E. "Ukraine in the Russian Empire in the Nineteenth and Early Twentieth Centuries (1880–1917)." In *Ukraine: A Concise Encyclopedia,* vol. 1 (1963), pp. 667–89.

Boiyarsky, P.K. "Ukrains'kyi Natsionalistychnyi Rukh i Suspil'no-Hromads'kyi Sektor" (The Ukrainian Nationalistic Movement and the Social-Community Sector). In *OUN, 1929–1954*, pp. 350–7. Paris: The Organization of Ukrainian Nationalists, 1955.

Chubaty, N. "The Medieval History of the Ukraine: A Princely Era." In *Ukraine: A Concise Encyclopedia*, vol. 1 (1963), pp. 581–612.

– "The Ukrainian and Russian Conceptions of the History of Eastern Europe." *Proceedings of the Shevchenko Scientific Society*, 1 (1951), pp. 10–25.

Donahue, Francis. "The Ukrainian Orthodox Church: Past, Present and Future." *The Trident*, April 1941, pp. 3–12.

"Dontsov, Dmytro." *Entsyklopediia Ukrainoznavstva* (The Ukrainian Encyclopedia), p. 570. Munich: Shevchenko Scientific Society, 1949.

Doroshenko, V.; Krawciw, B.; Zlenko, P. "Book Publishing and the Press: The Years of Ukrainian Statehood, 1917–20." In *Ukraine: A Concise Encyclopedia*, vol. 2 (1971), pp. 457–8.

Dushnyck, V.S. "Finland and Ukraine." *The Trident*, December 1939, pp. 3–7.

– "No Peace without Ukraine." *The Trident*, September 1939, pp. 1–5.

– "Ukraine and the Balance of Power." *The Trident*, June 1939, pp. 1–5.

– "What Ukraine Wants." *The Trident*, January–February 1939, pp. 1–6.

Halip. T.; Zhukovsky, A. "Ukraine between the Two World Wars: Bukovina and Bessarabia." In *Ukraine: A Concise Encyclopedia*, vol. 1 (1963), pp. 856–9.

Haras, M.; Simovych, T.; Terletsky, O. "Education in Western Ukraine in 1919–44 and Abroad: Ukrainian Lands under Rumania." In *Ukraine: A Concise Encyclopedia*, vol. 2 (1971), pp. 383–4.

Herasymovych, I.; Kubijovc, V.; Terletsky, M.; Terletsky, O. "Education in Western Ukraine in 1919–44 and Abroad: Ukrainian Lands under Poland." In *Ukraine: A Concise Encyclopedia*, vol. 2 (1971), pp. 371–81.

Herasymovych, I.; Terletsky, O. "Shkil'nytstvo v Halychyni v Druhyi Pol. XIXst. i Na Poch. XXst" (Education in Galicia in the Latter Half of the 19th Century and the Beginning of the 20th Century). In *Entsyklopediia-Ukrainoznavstva*, pp. 927–30. Munich: Shevchenko Scientific Society, 1949.

Hlobenko, N. "Literature: The Period of Realism." In *Ukraine: A Concise Encyclopedia*, vol. 1 (1963), pp. 1019–30.

Horbatsch, O. "The Armed Forces: Ukrainians in Foreign Armies during World War II." In *Ukraine: A Concise Encyclopedia*, vol. 2 (1971), pp. 1086–9.

Hundiak, John. "The National Independent Church and the Origin of the Ukrainian Orthodox Church." In *Ukrainians and Their Church*, ed. Peter Bilon. pp. 23–6. Johnston: The Western Pennsylvania Regional Branch of the UOL, 1953.

"Karpatska Rus – Karpatska Ukraina" (Carpatho-Rus – Carpatho-Ukraine). In *Narodni Kalendar na rik 1939*, p. 227. New York: Ukrainian Section of the International Worker's Order, 1939.

Knysh, Zenovij. "Boiovi Dii OUN na ZYZ u Pershomu Desiatylitti ii Isnuvannia" (The Revolutionary Activities of OUN in Western Ukraine during the First Decade of Its Existence). In *OUN, 1929–1954*, pp. 90–110. Paris: The Organization of Ukrainian Nationalists, 1955.

Kolessa, Philaret. "Ukrains'ki Narodni Pisni i Znachennia Dlia Narodu" (Ukrainian National Songs and Their Significance for the People). *Sichovy Visti*, November 1922.

Korduba, M. "The Renascence of Ukraine: Bukovina." In *Ukraine: A Concise Encyclopedia*, vol. 1 (1963), p. 787.

Korowytsky; I. "History of the Ukrainian Churches: The Orthodox Church in Poland, 1919–39." In *Ukraine: A Concise Encyclopedia*, vol. 2 (1971), pp. 178–82.

Krawciw, Bohdan. "100 Richchia Materi Prosvity" (On the 100th Anniversary of Mother Prosvita). In *Almanac of the Ukrainian National Association for 1968*, pp. 176–83. Jersey City: Svoboda Press, 1968.

Krawciw, B.; Ohloblyn, A. "Scholarship in Central and Eastern Lands after 1917." In *Ukraine: A Concise Encyclopedia*, vol. 2 (1971), pp. 252–66.

Krupnytsky, B. "The Rebirth of the State: Ukraine under the Rule of the Hetmans." In *Ukraine: A Concise Encyclopedia*, vol. 1 (1963), pp. 634–65.

Kuzela, Z. "Tribal Division and Ethnographic Groups." In *Ukraine: A Concise Encyclopedia*, vol. 1 (1963), pp. 280–5.

Lapica, Michael C. "The Rise of Carpatho-Ukraine." *The Trident*, January–February 1939, pp. 12–15.

Lencyk, W. "History of the Ukrainian Churches: The Ukrainian Catholic Church since 1800." In *Ukraine: A Concise Encyclopedia*, vol. 2 (1971), pp. 182–95.

Lewin, Kurt I. "Andreas Count Sheptytsky, Archbishop of Lviv, Metropolitan of Halych, and the Jewish Community during the Second World War." *The Annals of the Ukrainian Academy of Sciences in the U.S.*, vol. VII, nos. 1 and 2 (1959), pp. 1565–1667.

Lototsky, Volodymyr. "Iak Osvobodyvsia Myroslav Sichyns'kyi" (How Miroslaw Sichynsky Freed Himself). In *Kalendar of the Ukrainian National Association for 1916*, pp. 36–43. Jersey City: Svoboda Press, 1915.

Lushnycky, Alexander, "The United Greek Church," *Almanac of the "Providence" Association of Ukrainian Catholics in America, 1984–1985*, pp. 17–26. Philadelphia: "America" Publishing, 1984.

Luzhnytsky, Gregory. "Ukrainian Cultural Activities in Lviv, 1848–1918." In *Lviv: A Symposium on Its 700th Anniversary*, pp. 168–80. New York: Shevchenko Scientific Society, 1962.

Markus, V. "The Armed Forces: Ukrainian Military Formations in 1938–43." In *Ukraine: A Concise Encyclopedia*, vol. 2 (1971), pp. 1085–6.

– "Carpatho-Ukraine under Hungarian Occupation (1939–1944)." *The Ukrainian Quarterly*, Summer 1954, pp. 252–5.

Martynec, V. "Ukrains'ka Natsionalistychna Presa" (The Ukrainian Nationalistic Press). In *OUN, 1929–1954*, pp. 240–56. Paris: The Organization of Ukrainian Nationalists, 1955.

Nastasivsky, M [Michael Tkach]. "Zakhidna Ukraina" (Western Ukraine). In *Narodnyi Kalendar na rik 1939*, pp. 23–8. New York: Ukrainian Section of the International Workers Order, 1939.

Novosivsky, I.M. "The Law: Western Ukrainian Territories between the Two World Wars, Bukovina and Bessarabia." In *Ukraine: A Concise Encyclopedia*, vol. 2 (1971), pp. 73–4.

Possony, Stefan. "Anti-Semitism in the Russian Area." *Plural Societies,* vol. 5, no. 4 (Winter 1974).

Pritsak, Omeljan; Reshetar, John S. "The Ukraine and the Dialetics of Nation Building." *Slavic Review* 22, no. 2 (June 1963), pp. 243–4.

Prochazka, Theodore. "Some Aspects of Carpatho-Ukrainian History in Post-Munich Czechoslovakia." In *Czechoslovakia Past and Present,* ed. Miloslaw Rechiegh, Jr. The Hague: Mouton Press, 1968.

Revay, Julian. "The March to Liberation of Carpatho-Ukraine." *The Ukrainian Quarterly,* Summer 1954, pp. 227–34.

Rosocha, Stephen. "Karpatska Sich" (Carpathian Sich). In *Istoriia Ukrains'koho Viis'ka* (A History of the Ukrainian Armed Forces), 2d rev. ed., pp. 593–4. Winnipeg: Ivan Tyktor Publisher, 1953.

Rudnyckyj, J.B. "The Names for the Ukrainian Territory and People Used by Other Peoples." In *Ukraine: A Concise Encyclopedia,* vol. 1 (1963), pp. 10–12.

Rudnytsky, Ivan L. "The Role of Ukraine in Modern History." *Slavic Review* 22, no. 2 (June 1963).

– "The Western Ukrainian Lands under Austria and Hungary, 1772–1918: Bukovina." In *Ukraine: A Concise Encyclopedia,* vol. 1 (1963), pp. 707–10.

– "The Western Ukrainian Lands under Austria and Hungary, 1772–1918: Transcarpathia (Carpatho-Ukraine)." In *Ukraine: A Concise Encyclopedia,* vol. 1 (1963), pp. 710–14.

Shulhyn, A. "The Renascence of Ukraine: The Ukrainian State, 1917–20: The Period of the Central *Rada* (Council)." In *Ukraine: A Concise Encyclopedia,* vol. 1 (1963), pp. 725–46.

Shypynsky, Vasyl. "Ukrains'kyi Natsionalizm na Bukovyni" (Ukrainian Nationalism in Bukovina.) In *OUN, 1929–1954,* pp. 216–22. Paris: Organization of Ukrainian Nationalists, 1955.

"Sich as a Factor in Ukrainian History." In *Hei Tam Na Hori Sich Ide* (Hey on the Hill, Sich Is Coming), pp. 413–16. Edmonton: Trident Press, 1965.

Stefan, Augustine. "Contacts between Carpatho-Ukraine and Lviv." In *Lviv: A Symposium on the Occasion of Its 700th Anniversary,* pp. 272–5. New York: Shevchenko Scientific Society, 1962.

– "Education and Schools: Transcarpathia, 1918–39." In *Ukraine: A Concise Encyclopedia,* vol. 2 (1971), pp. 381–3.

– "The Renascence of Ukraine: Transcarpathia, 1918–19." In *Ukraine: A Concise Encyclopedia,* vol. 1 (1963), pp. 787–9.

– "Ukraine between the Two World Wars: Transcarpathia (Carpatho-Ukraine)." In *Ukraine: A Concise Encyclopedia,* vol. 1 (1963), pp. 850–6.

Stercho, Peter. "Dopomoha ODWU Karpats'kyi Ukraini" (ODWU's Support of Carpatho-Ukraine). In *Samostyna Ukraina,* October–November 1968, pp. 33–7.

Vytanovich, E. "The Western Ukrainian Lands under Austria and Hungary, 1772–1918: Galicia, 1772–1849." In *Ukraine: A Concise Encyclopedia,* vol. 1 (1963), pp. 698–707.

Vytanovich, I. "The Ukrainian Economy: The Cooperative Movement in Western Ukraine, Prior to 1918; 1920–44." In *Ukraine: A Concise Encyclopedia,* vol. 2 (1971), pp. 982–7.

Vytvytsky, S.; Baran, S. "Ukraine between the Two World Wars: Western Ukraine under Poland." In *Ukraine: A Concise Encyclopedia,* vol. 1 (1963), pp. 833–50.

Zhyvotko, A.; Krawciw, B. "The Press." In *Ukraine: A Concise Encyclopedia,* vol. 2 (1971), pp. 476–518.

European History

Andreski, S. "Poland." In *European Fascism,* ed. S.J. Woolf. London: Weidenfeld and Nicholson, 1968.

Armstrong, John A. "Collaborationism in World War II: The Integral Nationalist Variant in Eastern Europe." *Journal of Modern History,* September 1968, pp. 396–410.

Barany, George. "Hungary: From Aristocratic to Proletarian Nationalism." In *Nationalism in Eastern Europe,* ed. Peter F. Sugar and Ivo J. Lederer, pp. 259–309. Seattle: University of Washington Press, 1969.

Barbu, Z. "Rumania." In *European Fascism,* ed. by S.J. Woolf, pp. 146–66. London: Weidenfeld and Nicholson, 1968.

Brock, Peter. "Polish Nationalism." In *Nationalism in Eastern Europe,* ed. Peter F. Sugar and Ivo J. Lederer, pp. 317–72. Seattle: University of Washington Press, 1969.

Carr, Edward Hallett. "The Climax of Nationalism." In *The Dynamics of Nationalism,* ed. Louis L. Snyder, pp. 357–9. New York: D. Van Nostrand & Co., 1964.

Sugar, Peter F. "External and Domestic Roots of Eastern European Nationalism." In *Nationalism in Eastern Europe,* ed. Peter F. Sugar and Ivo J. Lederer, pp. 3–54. Seattle: University of Washington Press, 1969.

Zacek, Joseph. "Nationalism in Czechoslovakia." In *Nationalism in Eastern Europe,* ed. Peter F. Sugar and Ivo J. Lederer, pp. 166–206. Seattle: University of Washington Press, 1969.

Books and Pamphlets

For purposes of easy identification, books have been divided into the major subjects of significance to this study.

Ukrainian Immigration History

Adamic, Louis. *Two-Way Passage.* New York: Harper & Bros., 1941.

Amerykans'kyi Prosvitianyn (American Enlightenment). Lviv: Prosvita Society, 1925.

An Appreciation: On the Occasion of the 30th Anniversary of the Consecration to the Episcopacy of Metropolitan Orestes Chornock, 1938–1968. St. Michael's Church, Binghamton, New York, 1968.

Avramenko, Vasile. *Ukrainian National Dances, Music and Song.* Winnipeg: National Publishers Ltd., 1947.

Balch, Emily Greene. *Our Slavic Fellow Citizens.* New York: Charities Publication Committee, 1910.

Basarab, Stephen, et al. *Ukrainians in Maryland.* Baltimore: Ukrainian Education Association of Maryland, Inc., 1977.

Batchinsky, Julian. *The Jewish Pogroms in Ukraine and the Ukrainian People's Republic.* Washington: Friends of Ukraine, 1919.

– *Memorandum to the Government of the United States on the Recognition of the Ukrainian People's Republic.* Washington: Friends of Ukraine, 1920.

Bohachevsky, Danilo, *Vladyka Konstantyn Bohachevs'kyi, Pershyi Mytropolyt Ukrains'koi Katolyts'koi Tserkvy v ZSA* (Bishop Constantine Bohachevsky, First Metropolitan of the Ukrainian Catholic Church in the USA). Philadelphia: America Press, 1980.

Bratush, James D. *A Historical Documentary of the Ukrainian Community of Rochester, New York.* Translated by Anastasia Smerchynska. Rochester: Christopher Press, 1973.

Czuba, Natalie Ann. *History of the Ukrainian Catholic Parochial Schools in the United States: A Thesis.* Chicago: Basilian Press, 1956.

Davies, Raymond Arthur. *This Is Our Land: Ukrainian Canadians against Hitler.* Toronto: Progress Books, 1943.

Davis, Jerome. *The Russian Immigrant.* New York: Macmillan Co., 1922.

– *The Russians and Ruthenians in America: Bolsheviks or Brothers?* New York: George H. Doran, 1922.

Domashovets, H. *Narys Istorii Ukrains'koi Ievanhel's'ko-Baptysts'koi Tserkvy* (Historical Sketch of the Ukrainian Evangelical-Baptist Church). Toronto: Harmony Printing Ltd., 1967.

Double Jubilee Book of the Sisters Servants of Mary Immaculate, Immaculate Conception Province. Sloatsburg, NY, 1985.

Dragan, Antin. *The Ukrainian National Association: Its Past and Present.* Jersey City: Svoboda Press, 1964.

Golden Jubilee Book of the First Ukrainian Presbyterian Church. Irvington: Jubilee Committee, 1959.

Greene, Victor R. *The Slavic Community on Strike: Immigrant Labor in Pennsylvania.* Notre Dame: University of Notre Dame Press, 1968.

Halich, Wasyl. *Ukrainians in the United States.* Chicago: University of Chicago Press, 1937.

Hanusiak, Michael. *Lest We Forget.* New York: Ukrainian American League, 1976.

Kaye, Vladimir J. *Early Ukrainian Settlements in Canada, 1895–1900.* Published for the Ukrainian Canadian Research Foundation. Toronto: University of Toronto Press, 1964.

Kolasky, John. *The Shattered Illusion: The History of Ukrainian Pro-Communist Organizations in Canada.* Toronto: Peter Martin Associates Limited, 1979.

Kuropas, Myron. *To Preserve a Heritage: The Story of the Ukrainian Immigration in the United States.* New York: The Ukrainian Museum, 1984.

– *Ukrainians in America.* Minneapolis: Lerner Publications, 1972.

Luciw, Wasyl; Luciw, Theodore. *Ahapius Honcharenko, "Alaska Man."* Toronto: Slavia Library, 1963.

Lushnycky, Alexander, ed. *Ukrainians in Pennsylvania.* Philadelphia: Ukrainian Bicentennial Committee, 1976.

Magocsi, Paul Robert. *Our People: Carpatho-Rusyns and Their Descendants in North America.* Toronto: Multicultural History Society of Ontario, 1984.

Miller, Kenneth D. *Peasant Pioneers: An Interpretation of the Slavic Peoples in the*

United States. New York: Council for Women for Home Missions and Missionary Education Movement of the United States and Canada, 1925.

Poltava, Leonid. *Istoria Ukrayinskoyi Narodnoyi Pomochi v Amerytsi i Kanadi* (History of the Ukrainian National Aid Association of USA and Canada). Pittsburgh: Ukrainian National Aid Association, 1976.

Procko, Bohdan F. *Ukrainian Catholics in America: A History.* Washington: University Press of America, 1982.

Russko-Amerykanskii Spravochnik (Russian-American Register). New York: N.S. Tertiakoff & Co., 1920.

Sayers, Michael; Kahn, Albert E. *Sabotage! The Secret War against America.* New York: Harper & Brothers, 1942.

– *Sabotage! The Secret War against America.* Rev. ed. New York: Metro Publications, 1944.

Shlepakov, A.M. *Ukrains'ka Trudova Emigratsiia u SSHA i Kanadi* (The Ukrainian Social Emigration in the USA and Canada). Kiev: The Ukrainian Academy of Sciences, 1960.

Silver Jubilee Almanac of the Byzantine-Slavonic Rite, Catholic Diocese of Pittsburgh, 1924–1949.

Simirenko, Alex. *Pilgrims, Colonists and Frontiersmen: An Ethnic Community in Transition.* New York: Free Press, 1964.

Stefaniuk, Myroslava; Dohrs, Fred E. *Ukrainians of Detroit.* Detroit: Center for Urban Studies, Wayne State University, 1979.

The Story of the Ukrainian Congress Committee. New York: The Ukrainian Congress Committee, 1951.

Tarnavsky, Ostap. *Brat-Bratovi: Knyha Pro ZUADK* (Brother's Helping Hand: History of the UUARC). Philadelphia: United Ukrainian American Relief Committee, 1971.

Tolopko, Leon. *Working Ukrainians in the U.S.A.* New York: Ukrainian American League, 1986.

Tremba, Basil. *Inside Story of the Ukrainian Church.* Woonsocket, RI: St. Michael's Ukrainian Catholic Church, n.d.

Ukrains'ka Emigratsiia Ukrains'kym Invalidam (The Ukrainian Emigration for the Ukrainian Invalids). Lviv: The Ukrainian Invalids Help Association, 1931.

Vynar, Lubomyr. *Iuliian Bachyns'kyi: Vydatnyi Doslidnyk Ukrains'koi Emigratsii* (Iuliian Bachynskyi: Renowned Researcher of the Ukrainian Immigration). Historical Studies Series, No. 8. Munich–New York: Ukrainian Historical Society, 1971.

Yuzyk, Paul. *The Ukrainian Greek Orthodox Church of Canada, 1918–1951.* Ottawa: University of Ottawa Press, 1981.

Zeedick, P.J.; Smor, A.M. *Nase Stanovisce* (Our Stand). Homestead, Penn.: Greek Catholic Union Press, 1934.

Ukrainian National History

Adams, Arthur E. *Bolsheviks in the Ukraine: The Second Campaign, 1918–1919.* New Haven: Yale University Press, 1963.

Allen, W.E. *The Ukraine: A History.* Cambridge: Cambridge University Press, 1940.

Andrusyshen, C.H.; Kirkconnell, Watson, trans. *The Poetical Works of Taras Shevchenko.* Published for the Ukrainian Canadian Committee. Toronto: University of Toronto Press, 1964.

– *The Ukrainian Poets, 1819–1962.* Published for the Ukrainian Canadian Committee. Toronto: University of Toronto Press, 1963.

Armstrong, John A. *Ukrainian Nationalism.* 2d ed. New York: Columbia University Press, 1963.

Artiushenko, Jurij. *Po Torach Bortsia Pravdy i Volyi* (To Be for Truth and Freedom). Chicago: Ukrainian Printers, 1957.

Bilinsky, Yaroslaw. *The Second Soviet Republic: The Ukraine after World War II.* New Brunswick: Rutgers University Press, 1964.

Bjorkman, Edwin, et al. *Ukraine's Claim to Freedom: An Appeal for Justice on Behalf of Thirty-Five Millions.* New York: The Ukrainian National Association and the Ruthenian National Union, 1915.

Chamberlin, William Henry. *The Ukraine: A Submerged Nation.* New York: Macmillan Co., 1944.

Dmytryshyn, Basil. *Moscow and the Ukraine, 1918–1953: A Study of Russian Bolshevik Nationality Policy.* New York: Bookman Associates, 1956.

Doroshenko, Dmytro. *History of Ukraine.* Edmonton, Alta.: Institute Press, 1939.

Dushnyck, Walter. *The Ukrainian Rite Catholic Church at the Ecumenical Council, 1962–1965.* New York: Shevchenko Scientific Society, 1967.

Fedoriw, George. *History of the Church in Ukraine.* Translated by Petro Krawchuk. Toronto: no publisher, 1983.

Goldelman, Solomon I. *Jewish National Autonomy in Ukraine, 1917–1920.* Chicago: Ukrainian Research and Information Institute, 1968.

Hrushevsky, Michael A. *A History of Ukraine,* ed. O.J. Fredriksen. Published for the Ukrainian National Association. New Haven: Yale University Press, 1941.

– *Z Istorii Relihiinoi Dumky Na Ukraini* (On the History of Religious Thought in Ukraine). Lviv: Shevchenko Scientific Society, 1925.

Hryshko, Vasyl. *Experience with Russia.* New York: The Ukrainian Congress Committee, 1956.

Istoriia Naukovoho Tovarystva Im. Shevchenka (History of the Shevchenko Scientific Society). Munich: Shevchenko Scientific Society, 1949.

Kamenetsky, Ihor. *Hitler's Occupation of Ukraine, 1941–1944: A Study in Totalitarian Imperialism.* Milwaukee: Marquette University Press, 1956.

– *Secret Nazi Plans for Eastern Europe: A Study of Lebensraum Policies.* New York: Bookman Associates, 1961.

Knysh, Zenovy. *Pry Dzherelakh Ukrains'koho Orhanizovanoho Natsionalizmu* (Among the Sources of Organized Ukrainian Nationalism). Toronto: Surma Publishers, 1970.

Kostiuk, Hryhory. *Stalinist Rule in the Ukraine: A Study of the Decade of Mass Terror.* New York: Praeger Publishers, 1960.

Koutaisoff, Alexander. *Ukraina.* Copenhagen: Jensen & Ronager, 1918.

Krawchenko, Bohdan. *Social Change and National Consciousness in Twentieth Century Ukraine.* New York: St. Martin's Press, 1985.

Luckyj, George S.N. *Literary Politics in the Soviet Ukraine.* New York: Columbia University Press, 1956.

Lypynskyi, Viacheslav. *Lysty Do Brativ Khliborobiv* (Letters to Brother Agrarians). 2d printing. New York: Bulava Publishing Co., 1954.

– *Zbirnyk Khliborobs'koi Ukrainy* (An Anthology of Agrarian Ukraine). Prague: Brotherhood of Ukrainian Classocratic Monarchists-Hetmanates, 1931.

Magocsi, Paul Robert. *The Shaping of a National Identity: Sub-Carpathian Rus, 1848–1948.* Cambridge: Harvard University Press, 1978.

Manning, Clarence A. *Ivan Mazeppa, Hetman of Ukraine.* New York: Bookman Associates, 1957.

– *The Story of Ukraine.* New York: Philosophical Library, 1947.

– *Taras Shevchenko: The Poet of Ukraine.* Jersey City: The Ukrainian National Association, 1945.

– *Twentieth Century Ukraine.* New York: Bookman Associates, 1951.

– *Ukrainian Literature.* Jersey City: The Ukrainian National Association, 1944.

– *Ukraine under the Soviets.* New York: Bookman Associates, 1953.

Margolin, Arnold. *From a Political Diary: Russia, the Ukraine and America, 1905–1945.* New York: Columbia University Press, 1946.

– *Ukraine and the Policy of the Entente.* Translated by V.P. Sokoloff. Berlin: S. Effron Izdatel'stvo, 1921.

Martynets, V. *Ukrains'ke Pidpillia vid UVO do OUN: Spohady i Materiialy do Peredistorii ta Istorii Ukrains'koho Orhanizovanoho Natsionalizmu* (The Ukrainian Underground from UVO to OUN: Memoirs and Materials Concerning the Prehistory and History of Organized Ukrainian Nationalism). Winnipeg: The Ukrainian National Federation, 1949.

Mijakovsky, Volodymyr; Shevelov, George Y., eds. *Taras Shevchenko, 1814–1861: A Symposium.* The Hague: Mouton & Co., 1962.

Mirchuk, Peter. *Narys Istorii Orhanizatsii Ukrains'kykh Natsionalistiv, 1920–1939* (Outline History of the Organization of Ukrainian Nationalists, 1920–1939), ed. Stephen Lenkavsky. Munich: Ukrainian Publishers, 1968.

Motyl, Alexander. *The Turn to the Right: The Ideological Origins and Development of Ukrainian Nationalism, 1919–1929.* Boulder: East European Monographs, 1980.

Na Vichnu Han'bu (For Eternal Shame). Prague: Provid of the Organization of Ukrainian Nationalists, 1931.

Pidhainy, S.O., et al. *The Black Deeds of the Kremlin: A White Book.* Vol. 2. Detroit: DOBRUS, 1955.

Polonska-Vasylenko, Natalia. *Two Conceptions of the History of Ukraine and Russia.* London: The Association of Ukrainians in Great Britain, 1968.

Pospishil, Victor J. *Ex Occidente Lex (From the West – the Law): The Eastern Catholic Churches under the Tutelage of the Holy See of Rome.* Carteret, NJ: St. Mary's Religious Action Fund, 1979.

Reshetar, John S. *The Ukrainian Revolution, 1917–1920: A Study in Nationalism.* Princeton: Princeton University Press, 1952.

The Russians in Galicia, ed. Bedwin Sands. Jersey City: The Ukrainian National Council, 1916.

Snowyd, D. *Spirit of Ukraine: Ukrainian Contributions to World's Culture*. New York: The United Ukrainian Organizations of the United States, 1935.

Sosnowsky, Michael. *Dmytro Dontsov: Politychnyi Portret* (Dmytro Donzow: A Political Portrait). New York: Trident International Inc., 1974.

Spirit of Flame: A Collection of the Works of Lesya Ukrainka. New York: Bookman Associates, 1950.

Stachiw, M.; Sztendera, J. *Western Ukraine at the Turning Point of Europe's History, 1918–1923*. New York: Shevchenko Scientific Society, 1969.

Steffen, Gustaf F. *Russia, Poland and the Ukraine*. Jersey City: The Ukrainian National Council, 1915.

Stepankovsky, Vladimir. *The Russian Plot to Seize Galicia (Austrian Ruthenia)*. Jersey City: The Ukrainian National Council, 1915.

Stercho, Peter G. *Diplomacy of Double Morality: Europe's Crossroads in Carpatho-Ukraine*. New York: Carpathian Research Center, 1971.

– *Karpato-Ukrains'ka Derzhava* (The Carpatho-Ukrainian State). Toronto: Shevchenko Scientific Society, 1965.

Subtelny, Orest. *Ukraine: A History*. Toronto: University of Toronto Press, 1988.

Sullivant, Robert S. *Soviet Politics and the Ukraine, 1917–1957*. New York: Columbia University Press, 1962.

Sydoruk, John P. *Ideology of the Cyrillo-Methodians and Its Origins*. Slavistica No. 19. Winnipeg: The Ukrainian Free Academy of Sciences, 1954.

Tikhomirov, M. *The Towns of Ancient Rus'*. Moscow: Foreign Languages Publishing House, 1959.

Tysovskyj, Oleksander. *Zhittia v Plasti* (Life in Plast). 2d rev. ed. Toronto: Young Life Publishers, 1961.

Ukrainians and Jews: A Symposium. New York: Ukrainian Congress Committee, 1966.

Vernadsky, George. *Bohdan, Hetman of Ukraine*. New Haven: Yale University Press, 1941.

– *Kievan Russia*. New Haven: Yale University Press, 1948.

Wlasowsky, Ivan. *Outline History of the Ukrainian Orthodox Church*, vol. 1. New York: Ukrainian Orthodox Church of the USA, 1956.

Yasinchuk, Lev. *Dlia Ridnoho Kraiu* (For the Native Land). Lviv: Shevchenko Scientific Society, 1933.

European History

Antonov-Ovseyenko, Anton. *The Time of Stalin: A Portrait of Terror*. New York: Harper and Row, 1981.

Attwater, Donald. *The Christian Churches of the East: Churches in Communion with Rome*, vol. 1. Milwaukee: Bruce Publishing Co., 1961.

Baerlin, Henry. *Over the Hills of Ruthenia*. London: Leonard Parsons Ltd., 1923.

Baring, Maurice. *Landmarks in Russian Literature*. University Paperbacks. New York: Barnes and Noble, 1960.

Braddick, Henderson B. *Germany, Czechoslovakia and the "Grand Alliance" in the*

May Crisis, 1938, vol. 6, Monograph Series in World Affairs. Denver: University of Denver Press, 1969.

Brown, Anthony Cave; MacDonald, Charles B. *On a Field of Red: The Communist International and the Coming of World War.* New York: G.P. Putnam's Sons, 1981.

Budorowycz, Bohdan S. *Polish-Soviet Relations, 1932–1939.* New York: Columbia University Press, 1963.

Bullock, Allan. *Hitler: A Study in Tyranny.* New York: Harper and Row, 1962.

Butler, Ralph. *The New Eastern Europe.* New York: Longmans, Green & Co., 1919.

Chamberlin, William Henry. *The Russian Revolution,* vol. 1. New York: Grosset & Dunlap, 1965.

Cherniavsky, Michael. *Tsar and People: A Historical Study of Russian National and Social Myths.* New Haven: Yale University Press, 1961.

Clark, Charles Upson. *United Roumania.* New York: Dodd Mead & Co., 1932.

Clarkson, Jesse. *A History of Russia.* New York: Random House, 1961.

Conquest, Robert. *Soviet Nationalities Policy in Practice.* New York: Praeger Publishers, 1967.

– *The Great Terror: Stalin's Purge of the Thirties.* New York: Collier Books, 1968.

– *The Harvest of Sorrow: Soviet Collectivization and the Terror-Famine.* New York: Oxford University Press, 1986.

Crocker, George N. *Roosevelt's Road to Russia.* Chicago: Henry Regnery Company, 1959.

Dallin, Alexander. *German Rule in Russia, 1941–1944.* London: Macmillan & Co., 1957.

de Colonna, Betram. *Czecho-Slovakia Within.* London: Thornton Butterworth Ltd., 1938.

Diehl, Charles. *Byzantium: Greatness and Decline.* New Brunswick: Rutgers University Press, 1957.

Dmytryshyn, Basil. *USSR: A Concise History.* New York: Charles Scribners Sons, 1965.

Fainsod, Merle. *How Russia Is Ruled.* Rev. ed. Cambridge: Harvard University Press, 1963.

Fedotov, George P. *The Russian Religious Mind: Kievan Christianity – The Tenth to the Thirteenth Centuries.* New York: Harper & Brothers, 1960.

Gentz, Friedrich; Possony, Stefan. *Three Revolutions.* Chicago: Henry Regnery Co., 1959.

Glaser, Kurt. *Czecho-Slovakia: A Critical History.* Caldwell, Idaho: The Claxton Printers, 1961.

Halecki, Oscar. *From Florence to Brest, 1493–1596.* Rome: Sacrum Poloniae Millenium, 1958.

Hanak, Walter. *The Subcarpathian-Ruthenian Question, 1918–1945.* Munhall, Penn.: The Bishop Tkach Carpatho-Russian Historical Society, 1962.

Horak, Stephen. *Poland and Her National Minorities, 1919–1939.* New York: Vantage Press, 1961.

Johnson, Hewlett. *Soviet Russia since the War.* New York: Boni & Gaer, 1947.

Kann, Robert A. *The Multinational Empire: Nationalism and National Reform in the*

Habsburg Monarchy, 1848–1918, vol. 1. New York: Columbia University Press, 1950.

Kluckhorn, Frank L. *The Naked Rise of Communism*. Derby: Monarch Books Inc., 1962.

Kohn, Hans. *Basic History of Modern Russia*. An Anvil Original. New York: D. Van Nostrand Company, 1957.

– *Pan-Slavism: Its History and Ideology*. 2d rev. ed. New York: Vintage Russian Library, 1953.

Lencyk, Wasyl. *The Eastern Catholic Church and Czar Nicholas I*. Rome: Centro di Studi Universitari Ucraini a Roma, 1966.

Macartney, C.A. *Hungary and Her Successors: The Treaty of Trianon and Its Consequences, 1919–1937*. London: University of Oxford Press, 1937.

Machray, Robert. *The Poland of Pilsudski*. London: George Allen and Unwin Ltd., 1936.

Maurus, Michael; Paxton, Robert O. *Vichy France and the Jews*. New York: Basic Books, 1981.

Meyendorff, John. *The Orthodox Church: Its Past and Its Role in the World Today*. New York: Pantheon Books, 1962.

Miller, Russel. *Resistance*. New York: Time-Life Books, 1979.

Mirsky, D. *Russia: A Social History*, ed. C.G. Seligman. London: The Cressett Press, 1931.

Nisbet, Robert. *Roosevelt and Stalin: The Failed Courtship*. Washington: Regnery Gateway, 1988.

Palmer, R.R. *A History of the Modern World*. 2d ed. rev. in collaboration with Joel Colton. New York: Alfred A. Knopf, 1962.

Pipes, Richard. *The Formation of the Soviet Union: Communism and Nationalism, 1917–1923*. Rev. ed. Cambridge: Harvard University Press, 1964.

Pridham, Francis. *Close of a Dynasty*. London: Allan Wingate, 1956.

Rings, Werner. *Life with the Enemy: Collaboration and Resistance in Hitler's Europe, 1939–1945*. Translated by J. Maxwell Brownjohn. Garden City: Doubleday & Co., 1982.

Ripka, H. *Munich: Before and After*. London: Macmillan Co., 1939.

Rostow, Walter W. *The Dynamics of Soviet Society*. A Mentor Book. New York: New American Library, 1954.

Roucek, Joseph. *Contemporary Roumania and Her Problems: A Study in Modern Nationalism*. Stanford: Stanford University Press, 1932.

Roumania Ten Years After, a Report of the American Committee on the Rights of Religious Minorities. Boston: Beacon Press, 1928.

Seton-Watson, Hugh. *Eastern Europe between the Wars, 1918–1941*. 3d ed. rev. New York: Harper & Row, 1962.

Shachtman, Tom. *The Phony War, 1939–1940*. New York: Harper and Row, 1982.

Shirer, William L. *The Rise and Fall of the Third Reich*. Garden City: International Collectors Library, 1959.

Syrod, Konrad. *Poland: Between Anvil and Hammer*. London: Robert Hale Publishers, 1968.

Tolstoy Nikolai. *Victims of Yalta*. London: Hodder and Stoughton, 1977.

Vernadsky, George. *A History of Russia.* 4th ed. New Haven: Yale University Press, 1954.

Watt, Richard M. *Bitter Glory: Poland and Its Fate, 1918–1939.* New York: Simon and Schuster, 1979.

Wytwycky, Bohdan. *The Other Holocaust.* Washington: The Novak Report, 1980.

Zeman, Z.A.B. *The Break-up of the Hapsburg Empire: A Study in National and Social Revolution.* London: Oxford University Press, 1961.

American History

Abbott, Grace. *The Immigrant and the Community.* New York: The Century Co., 1917.

Davies, Joseph E. *Mission to Moscow.* New York: Simon & Schuster, 1941.

Dies, Martin. *The Trojan Horse in America.* New York: Dodd & Mead Co., 1940.

Dinnerstein, Leonard. *America and the Survivors of the Holocaust.* New York: Columbia University Press, 1982.

Draper, Theodore. *The Roots of American Communism.* New York: Viking Press, 1957.

Elliot, Mark R. *Pawns of Yalta: Soviet Refugees and America's Role in Their Repatriation.* Urbana: University of Illinois Press, 1982.

Ethnic Recordings in America: A Neglected Heritage. Washington, DC: Library of Congress, 1982.

Gerson, Louis L. *The Hyphenate in Recent American Politics and Diplomacy.* Lawrence: University of Kansas Press, 1964.

– *Woodrow Wilson and the Rebirth of Poland, 1914–1920: A Study in the Influence on American Policy by Groups of Foreign Origin.* New Haven: Yale University Press, 1953.

Gitlow, Benjamin. *I Confess: The Truth about American Communism.* New York: E.P. Dutton, 1940.

Gordon, Milton M. *Assimilation in American Life: The Role of Race, Religion, and National Origins.* New York: Oxford University Press, 1964.

Gornick, Vivian. *The Romance of American Communism.* New York: Basic Books, 1977.

Handlin, Oscar. *The Uprooted.* New York: Grosset & Dunlap, 1951.

Higham, Charles. *American Swastika.* New York: Doubleday & Co., 1985.

Hollander, Paul. *Political Pilgrims: Travels of Western Intellectuals to the Soviet Union, China and Cuba, 1928–1978.* New York: Oxford University Press, 1981.

Hoover, Edgar J. *Masters of Deceit: The Story of Communism in America and How to Fight It.* New York: Henry Holt & Co., 1958.

Jensen, Malcolm C. *America in Time.* Boston: Houghton-Mifflin, 1977.

Jones, Maldwyn Allen. *American Immigration.* Chicago: University of Chicago Press, 1960.

Josephson, Matthew. *The Robber Barons.* New York: Harcourt-Brace, 1934.

Klehr, Harvey. *The Heyday of American Communism: The Depression Decade.* New York: Basic Books, 1984.

Leopold, Richard W. *The Growth of American Foreign Policy: A History.* New York: Alfred A. Knopf, 1962.

Lyons, Eugene. *Assignment in Utopia.* New York: Harcourt Brace & Company, 1937.

– *The Red Decade: The Stalinist Penetration of America.* Indianapolis: Bobbs-Merrill, 1941.

Martin, James J. *American Liberalism and World Politics, 1931–1941: Liberalism's Press and Spokesmen on the Road Back to War between Mukden and Pearl Harbor,* vol. 1. New York: The Devin-Adair Company, 1964.

Marzio, Peter C., ed. *A Nation of Nations.* New York: Harper and Row, 1976.

Novak, Michael. *The Guns of Lattimer.* New York: Basic Books, 1978.

– *The Rise of the Unmeltable Ethnic: Politics and Culture in the Seventies.* New York: Macmillan, 1971.

Ogden, August R. *The Dies Committee: A Study of the Special House Committee for Investigation of Un-American Activities, 1938–1943.* Washington, DC: Murray and Heister Publishers, 1944.

Olson, James Stuart. *The Ethnic Dimension in American History,* vol. 2. New York: St. Martin's Press, 1979.

Park, Robert E. *The Immigrant Press and Its Control.* New York: Harper & Brothers, 1922.

Sayers, Albert E.; Kahn, Michael. *The Great Conspiracy: The Secret War against Soviet Russia.* San Francisco: Proletarian Publishers, 1946.

Schlesinger, Arthur M., Jr. *The Age of Roosevelt: The Politics of Upheaval,* vol. 3. Boston: Houghton-Mifflin Company, 1960.

Sinclair, Upton. *The Jungle.* New York: Signet Classics, 1905.

Steinberg, Stephen, *The Ethnic Myth: Race, Ethnicity and Class in America.* New York: Antheneum, 1981.

Warren, Frank A. III. *Liberals and Communism: The "Red Decade" Revisited.* Bloomington: Indiana University Press, 1966.

Whitney, R.M. *Reds in America.* New York: Beckwith Press, 1924.

Nationalism

Barghoorn, Frederick C. *Soviet Russian Nationalism.* New York: Oxford University Press, 1956.

Baron, Salo Wittmayer. *Modern Nationalism and Religion.* New York: Meredian Books, Inc., 1960.

Kohn, Hans. *The Age of Nationalism: The First Era of Global History.* New York: Harper & Bros., 1962.

– *Nationalism: Its Meaning and History.* An Anvil Original. Princeton: D. Van Nostrand Co., 1955.

Pinson, Koppel S. *Nationalism and History: Essays on Old and New Judaism by Simon Dubnow.* Philadelphia: The Jewish Publication Society of America, 1958.

Shafer, Boyd C. *Nationalism: Interpreters and Interpretations.* 2d ed. A Publication of the American Historical Association's Service Center for Teachers of History. New York: Macmillan, 1963.

– *Nationalism: Myth and Reality*. New York: Harcourt Brace and World, 1955.
Snyder, Louis. *The Meaning of Nationalism*. New Brunswick: Rutgers University
    Press, 1954.

Index